SEARCHING FOR A NEW PARADIGM

A Cultural Anthropology Reader

First Edition

Edited by Marcia Mikulak, Ph.D
University of North Dakota

Bassim Hamadeh, CEO and Publisher
Michael Simpson, Vice President of Acquisitions
Jamie Giganti, Managing Editor
Jess Busch, Graphic Design Supervisor
Becky Smith, Acquisitions Editor
Monika Dziamka, Project Editor
Natalie Lakosil, Licensing Manager
Mandy Licata, Interior Designer

First published in the United States of America in 2014 by Cognella, Inc.

Cover image: Copyright © Bradford Hansen-Smith

Printed in the United States of America

ISBN: 978-1-60927-398-9 (pbk)/ 978-1-60927-399-6 (br)

www.cognella.com   800-200-3908

Contents

Chapter 7: Truth as Culturally Constructed Realities

Chapter 8: Childhood and Social Hierarchy—Social and Cultural Constructions of Power

Chapter 9: Violence and Society and Violence and Culture

Introduction

Anthropology has long been viewed within the social sciences as the most comprehensive discipline engaged in the study of humankind. Historically, American anthropology has consisted of four fields: Archaeology, Cultural or Ethnography Anthropology, Biological Anthropology (Human Origins), and Linguistic Anthropology. In the past few decades Forensic Anthropology and Medical Anthropology, Human Ecology, and Environmental Anthropology have become commonly viewed as additional sub-specialties within the discipline.

The comprehensive nature of anthropology lies in the study of what it means to be human. The discipline has been dedicated to exploring the archaeological pre-history of human tracings across the globe, and probing living cultures (including our own through ethnology and cultural anthropology), for deeper understandings of how humans construct social lives that in some measure reflect the cacophony of everyday experiences socially, institutionally, and perceptually. Dedicated biological anthropologists have probed the origins of our evolutionary trajectory through time by intimately observing our human primate ancestors, and now our genetic legacies throughout our evolutionary history. By studying metaphors, myths, tropes, and human perceptual worlds expressed as linguistic communication systems, linguistic anthropologists have discovered encoded meanings embedded in the vast array of languages constructed by humans across cultures.

Each subfield has produced a prodigious wealth of theoretical understandings and methodological tools that define the human experience from very different perspectives. Quantitative and qualitative methods are used to gather both subjective and objective data and our theoretical paradigms often reside at opposite epistemological spectra. Questions about the authenticity of qualitative data analysis and the nature of objectivity, reflexivity, and constructed realities have promoted heated debates about the validity of postmodern theoretical paradigms in cultural anthropology when compared to the rising tide of powerful genetic data viewed as authentically bias free and scientifically pure.

This edited volume is an attempt to bring together recent articles discussing such polemics currently found within the discipline of anthropology about what constitutes an authentic reality of the human experience. The readings in this book provide students with a variety of perspectives about our biological and evolutionary origins, our culturally constructed notions of self and others, and the increasing knowledge that perceived realities represented by our theoretical models may not accurately reflect actual truths as we have come to know them.

It is my hope that this collection of readings will support classroom discussions about how we build our various perspectives, methods, and models within the discipline of anthropology. As a professor of cultural anthropology, I feel an increasing urgency to understand the world and our human interactions within it as both cultural and biological beings within a paradigm that embraces the interfaces between them. Beyond this, my students seek new understandings of their relationships to the environments in which they live, and to the worlds that they inhabit; they seek to understand global communities as complexes formed and made real by human actors who create a competing array of world views, yet who inhabit the same environment whose resources continue to be strained beyond sustainability. While discussions arise in both lower- and upper-division courses in anthropology classrooms about human origins, primatology, diversity, ethnicity, gender, language, political economies, human ecology, human and environmental rights, and more, our teaching and research tends to continue to present each topic as a separate area of study. The value of narrowing a field of study is undeniable in that such a perspective provides for thorough explorations in research and in teaching. Yet it is rare that the complexity of our discipline provides an exploration of how we as anthropologists turn our inquisitive lens upon ourselves and ask how we know what we think we know, and how what we think we know adds up in terms of a macro view of the state of humans in a global perspective today. Such an investigation could prove to be both insightful and perhaps invigorating for the discipline as a whole.

My hope is that this book will be used as both a textbook for a course that asks such questions and that it serves as a reader that provides professors and students the opportunity to produce open dialogues on the tensions existing within the discipline itself. Finally, it is my hope that the book encourages students to see themselves as social actors who carry within themselves the biases inherent in their cultures and that as social actors, they are agents for change who can deconstruct and reconstruct themselves and their worlds from more holistic paradigms based on the foundations of their promise as stewards of change.

The book is organized into nine sections around the following topics. Each section has the following articles addressing the topic headings under which they fall:

- Chapter 1: The Nature of Meaning
  a. "Cultures of Science: Translation and Knowledge." Mike Crang, 1998
  b. "Making Wanga: Reality Constructions and the Magical Manipulation of Power." Karen McCarthy Brown, 2003
  c. "The Belief Machine." Richard Robbins, 1985

- Chapter 2: The Nature of Culture
  a. "Science as a Cultural Process." Sidney Greenfield, 2010
  b. "Debunking 'Man the Hunter.'" Robert Sussman and Donna Hart, 2008
  c. "A Pound of Biology and a Pinch of Culture or a Pinch of Biology and a Pound of Culture? The Necessity of Integrating Biology and Culture in Reproductive Studies." Susan Sperling and Yewoubdar Beyene, 1997

- Chapter 3: The Hierarchy of Nations
  a. "The Story—How Things Got to Be This Way." Sharif M. Abdullah, 2009
  b. "The Social Construction of the State: State-Building and State-Destroying as Social Action." Franke Wilmer, 2002

- Chapter 4: The Geographical Exploration of the World
  a. "The Ideal of Civilization: Its Origins, Meanings, and Implications." Brett Bowden, 2009
  b. "Development and Its Discontents." Philip McMichael and Karuna Morarji, 2010

- Chapter 5: Progress and Development and the Rise of Poverty and Inequality
  a. "Explaining Poverty, Social Exclusion, and Inequality: Toward a Structural Approach." Gerry Mooney, 2008
  b. "Toward a Healthier Planet: The Creation of a Democratic Ecosocialist World System." Hans Baer and Merrill Singer, 2010
  c. "Opal Waters, Rising Seas: How Sociocultural Inequality Reduces Resilience to Climate Change Among Indigenous Australians." Donna Green, 2008

- Chapter 6: What Is Kinship? Everyday Foundations for Politics
  a. "Kinship, Gender, and the New Reproductive Technologies: The Beginning of the End?" Linda Stone, 2005
  b. "Feminists or 'Postfeminists'?: Young Women's Attitudes Toward Feminism and Gender Relations." Pamela Aronson, 2003

- Chapter 7: Truth as Culturally Constructed Realities
  a. "Is Postmodernism Just Modernism in Drag?" Michael Eric Dyson, 2004
  b. "People as Symbol Makers and Users: Language and the Creation of Social Reality." Kent L Sandstrom, Daniel D. Martin, and Gary Alan Fine, 2006
  c. "Learning Privilege: Lessons of Power and Identity in Affluent Schooling." Adam Howard, 2008

- Chapter 8: Childhood and Social Hierarchy—Social and Cultural Constructions of Power
  a. "Childhood." Marcia Mikulak, 2007
  b. "Social Constructions of Childhoods: Historical Framework." Marcia Mikulak, 2003
  c. "Curricular History and Social Control: The Creation of Ideological Hegemony in Education." Michael Apple, 2004

- Chapter 9: Violence and Society and Violence and Culture
    a. "The Texas–Mexico Border Wall and Ndé Memory." Margo Tamez, 2012
    b. "An Illustrative Supergenocide—The Holocaust." David Hamburg, 2010
    c. "The Sociology and Anthropology of Genocide." Adam Jones, 2011

Chapter 1 <u>The Nature of Meaning</u> explores how we acquire what we know and how knowledge is based on constructed meanings. Is our knowledge a truthful account of what we experience in the concrete world of everyday interactions with others and our environment? How do we construct the historical knowledge of ourselves and others?

Mike Crang's article "Cultures of Science: Translation and Knowledge" explores the cultures of science, the nature of objective and subjective knowledge and the impact such knowledge has on Western European cultures, and the culture of science itself. Crang asks who the observer actually is, and what the position of the observer is within the epistemological order embedded in the cultures of science, environment, politics, and power.

Karen McCarthy Brown's article "Making Wanga: Reality Constructions and the Magical Manipulation of Power" explores the power relations of "race," place, and power, drawing on the 1997 case of Abner Louima, a Haitian immigrant who was brutally raped and beaten by New York City police. "Making Wanga" enters the world of Mama Lola, a Vodou Priestess and healer living in New York City who eventually worked with Abner Louima. Exploring Mama Lola's epistemological world of spiritual healing provides the non-Haitian reader with many slippery slopes upon which one's foothold on reality is challenged. Indeed, most of the immigrant Haitian community in New York City protested the crimes perpetrated against Abner Louima and indirectly supported Mama Lola's perceptions. The denial of the practice of Vodou by those within the immigrant community and by Mama Lola herself added to the complexity of the constructions that defined the Abner Louima case and the New York City policemen who so viciously abused him. McCarthy Brown's article asks that we contemplate the relations of power within normative society (the New York City Police Department) as well as the constructed assumptions and performances of identity by the Haitian immigrant community.

"The Belief Machine" by SUNY anthropologist Richard Robbins explores the problem of perception. Why, he asks, do humans who essentially have the same biological make-up differ so widely in their perceptions of what the world is really like? In this article, Robbins explores various knowledge fields (anthropology, philosophy, sociology, history, and psychology), bringing them together to understand how cultures and their institutions profoundly influence how we come to know and what we come to accept as truth. "The Belief Machine" is a thought experiment that allows students to explore how they biologically and perceptually construct the ways in which they learn how to view and experience the world.

Chapter 2 <u>The Nature of Culture</u> explores the nature of "culture" and attempts to identify what this overly appropriated term may mean from a variety of disciplines.

In "Science as a Cultural Process," Sidney Greenfield argues that radical divisions between Christianity, Evangelical Protestantism, Umbanda, Candomblé, and other African religious traditions perhaps do not exist and argues that religious constructions of faith, health, and healing exist through a continuum within a religious marketplace. In Brazil, where he researched the practice of spiritual surgery, religion is not necessarily a process based on belief in a specific deity/God, but rather is a type of commodity that is negotiated and bargained for based on the stringent needs foisted upon those living in extreme economic poverty. Once again the world views of both practitioners and patients explored reveal that alternative views of reality exist and are based on the symbolic nature of cultures. Greenfield argues that the doing of science is a cultural process that is linked to the cultures from which we are imbedded.

"Debunking 'Man the Hunter'" by Robert Sussman and Donna Hart asks why humans are the way they are; after all, birds fly and snakes slither. Why do we walk upright and why do we cultivate and create elaborate communication systems unique to humans? The long evolutionary journey from primate to human is explored, including the states involved in developing and constructing humans as residing on the top of the evolutionary heap. Sussman and Hart, like the previous authors in this collection, ask that we view our superior attitudes through the lens of both history and the driving ambitions of the discipline of paleontology. Sussman and Hart ask that we keep a flexible attitude about our ancestors and current status as humans. According to recent evidence, brain size and superior capacities may not have resulted in modern humans.

Lori Hager's *Women in Human Evolution*, the book from which "A Pound of Biology and a Pinch of Culture or a Pinch of Biology and a Pound of Culture? The Necessity of Integrating Biology and Culture in Reproductive Studies" by Susan Sperling and Yewoubdar Beyene originates, is the first of its kind to explore the role of women paleontologists and archaeologists, a field in which men have traditionally been dominant. This article questions many of the assumed paradigms put forth by male researchers regarding human development and evolutionary history. The authors argue that reductionist approaches and assumptions about evolutionary biology ignore the role of culture in shaping the body and its functions, while cultural anthropologists often deny the importance of bodily phenomena.

Chapter 3 The Hierarchy of Nations argues that nations as well as cultures are created from constructed notions of self, others, and collectives. Relations of power are embedded in local and national hierarchies based on the unique geographical and environmental locations within which they are embedded.

"The Story—How Things Got to Be This Way" by Sharif M. Abdullah explores through the use of metaphor and tropes how we got to where we are today in relation to our world views, and where are we going in terms of cultural and environmental sustainability. Essentially, Sharif Abdullah explores the differences between the practice of exclusivity and inclusivity. By using stories based on examples of sustainability, we are prodded to consider how we might change the ways in which we view humans' relationship to our planet. Three criteria are offered as tools for changing the world and our place in it, such that we achieve a kind of sustainability stasis: 1. the criterion of enoughness; 2. the criterion of exchangeability; and 3. the criterion of common benefit. In short, we are asked to reconsider our place within the spectrum of all life that shares a limited home with limited resources.

"The Social Construction of the State: State-Building and State-Destroying as Social Action" by Franke Wilmer examines the constructions of ethnic identity. Through the use of individual interviews with Yugoslavian citizens, documentary evidence, and historical archives, Wilmer unravels the complexities involved in the construction of ethnic identities and questions if such identities are inevitable. We are led to contemplate the linkages between ethnicity, identity, sovereignty, violence, and peace.

Chapter 4 <u>The Geographical Exploration of the World</u> argues that notions of development and progress are embedded in Western European epistemologies steeped in dichotomous perceptions of the known world. Such views continue to constitute the paradigms that drive global politics and economies.

In "The Ideal of Civilization: Its Origins, Meanings, and Implications," Brett Bowden argues that the idea of civilization comes with abundant baggage that dichotomizes peoples, cultures, and histories, rendering them either civilized or savage. Through an exploration of wars, conflicts, and conquests usually undertaken and propagated in the name of progress, development, and civilization, Bowden argues that commonalities are more common than differences in terms of humankind. Is an authentic dialogue based on intercivilizational communication possible? What would the basis for such a dialogue be and where might it begin?

"Development and Its Discontents" by Philip McMichael and Karuna Morarji asks if globalization can bypass the market imperative. By examining the realities of the lives of those who represent the disempowered among us living in poverty and inequality, this article explores the theories that currently explain development, revealing limiting assumptions about development, its inevitability, and consequences.

Chapter 5 <u>Progress and Development and the Rise of Poverty and Inequality</u> explores the historical processes that generate social inequality, poverty, racism, and sexism. This chapter grows out of the previous chapter's articles that critique Western European dichotomous epistemologies.

"Explaining Poverty, Social Exclusion, and Inequality: Toward a Structural Approach" by Gerry Mooney extends the discussion offered by Philip McMichael and Karuna Morarji. This reading introduces notions of poverty and inequality from a structural perspective and explores various structural models that might provide some solutions to addressing inequalities. Mooney provides an overview of a Marxist analysis of poverty and inequality and makes an argument for an in-depth analysis of the wealthy, arguing that understanding inequality can be understood in relation to wealth rather than separate from it.

"Toward a Healthier Planet: The Creation of a Democratic Ecosocialist World System" by Hans Baer and Merrill Singer offers a refreshing and badly needed overview and analysis of the relationship between climate change, environmental devastation, and human health. The authors coin a new paradigm that they call ecosyndemics, a new understanding about the relationship between environmental change and disease. The authors call for changes within the global world systems of economics, health, education, marketplaces, and human ecology, arguing that it is essential to our survival to mitigate our impact on our planet's climate and ecosystems if we are to survive.

Donna Green's "Opal Waters, Rising Seas: How Sociocultural Inequality Reduces Resilience to Climate Change Among Indigenous Australians" argues that historically adaptive indigenous peoples are often presented as extremely vulnerable to the ravages of climate change, particularly in light of government mismanagement and neglect of native peoples' rights and perspectives. Dr. Green examines how traditional knowledge and local-level adaptation strategies for managing rising sea levels among the Torres Straits Islanders in Australia and Papua New Guinea are successfully implemented. This article points out the urgency of government funding that will support and allow us to learn from new strategies for adaptation developed by Indigenous peoples' science.

Chapter 6 What Is Kinship? Everyday Foundations for Politics offers two articles on contemporary gender politics in terms of reproduction and contemporary feminist perceptions of gender relations. How will kinship be structured in the near future and what will constitute family as new reproductive technologies continue to push the boundaries of human reproduction and fertility? How do young women view the feminist movement in its first and second waves, and what does the third wave of contemporary feminism look like today?

"Kinship, Gender, and the New Reproductive Technologies: The Beginning of the End?" by Linda Stone provides us with a discussion of the New Reproductive Technologies (NRTs) present within today's high-tech reproductive marketplace. Issues of determining the father of a baby; knowing the sex of an unborn child; and the use of artificial insemination, in vitro fertilization, embryo adoption, and cloning are but a few of the NRTs discussed. What are the implications for kinship, gender determination, legal parental rights and obligations, and how will families and communities be redefined by our increased ability to control and define the nature of our reproduction?

"Feminists or 'Postfeminists'?: Young Women's Attitudes Toward Feminism and Gender Relations" by Pamela Aronson argues that despite prior research on postfeminist perspectives by concurrent generations, there is currently an appreciation of recent changes to women's status within contemporary society. This article explores young women's attitudes toward feminism based on social class, economic status, ethnicity, and identity. How this changing gender perspective and social landscape will affect the current generation of young women is discussed.

Chapter 7 Truth as Culturally Constructed Realities provides a series of articles that discuss the ongoing polemics produced by postmodernism, social constructionism, and truth in terms of objectivity and reality in everyday life. Individual identities, social hierarchies, gendered selves, social and economic classes, and ethnic boundaries are explored as constructed identities within both individual and social contexts.

"Is Postmodernism Just Modernism in Drag?" by Michael Eric Dyson argues for an understanding of the impermanence of identity. Self and knowledge of the self is a constructed reality generated by social actors who are both products of their cultural inheritance and revolutionaries against the weight of historical norms. Linked to the exploration of the fluidity of identity are notions of "race" and ethnicity, gendered selves, and sexual identities. Since all these categories of identity are what also construct cultures, notions of place and home are also identified as both historical and impermanent. Dyson pushes us to the edge of our own cherished notions of self as a cohesive entity in our everyday lives.

"People as Symbol Makers and Users: Language and the Creation of Social Reality," co-authored by Kent L. Sandstrom, Daniel D. Martin, and Gary Alan Fine, offers readers an interactionist perspective on the social constructions of reality. This article provides the reader with the perspective that reality is constructed phenomena that are neither fixed nor completely accurate. Through the daily experience of living, social actors create, negotiate, and change realities such that what is experienced as an external concrete world can ultimately be understood as a complex of interactions capable of producing startling new phenomena.

"Learning Privilege: Lessons of Power and Identity in Affluent Schooling" by Adam Howard explores the lessons that students born into privilege who attend affluent educational institutions learn about themselves and the world at large. Based on ethnographic research, this article provides the reader with an explanation of the concept of privilege while demonstrating how the cultural and social institutions that educate privileged youth reify their social position and individual identities as the privileged. The values that support economic inequality are exposed, and understood as tools used to pass on notions of superiority. Finally, the article articulates how such identities are constructed in daily practice.

Chapter 8 <u>Childhood and Social Hierarchy—Social and Cultural Constructions of Power</u> investigates the polemics of childhood and the construction of Western European notions of who the child is as a social and a biological being. Children represent a special population in the Western world; they are viewed as innocent, in need of protection, and seen as vulnerable to corruption and pollution. The child is viewed as unformed and incapable of participation in the public world of the adult that includes the marketplace where economies are produced. Yet in many parts of the world, children are incorporated into the adult world as they learn to walk, carry objects, talk, and participate in the daily life of their communities. Their participation in the everyday life of adults is welcomed and valued. What are the cultural, social, and institutional differences between such constructions of childhood? To answer this question the articles presented here explore the relations of power inherent in notions of adulthood and childhood unique to Western European societies.

"Childhood, " written by me, explicates how children have been historically constructed since the industrial revolution in Western European cultures. Notions of the innocence, purity, and fragility of childhood are linked to the processes that evolved out of the industrial modes of production intimately linked to the political economy of the Western world. In this article, childhood is understood to not be a cultural universal. Childhoods exist and are constructed based on cultural variations that frequently include children in all the daily life events of adults. This article asks that the reader deconstruct their understanding of the child. Who are children, what are they capable of knowing and doing, and where do they belong in society?

"Social Constructions of Childhoods: Historical Framework," also written by me, compares and contrasts post-industrial Western European conceptions of childhood as a time of innocence and separateness with the constructionist view, which describes children as active and viable social agents. These two opposing theoretical notions of childhood are problematized and applied to the current polemics of childhood in Brazilian society today through the life experience and voices of street and working youth.

"Curricular History and Social Control: The Creation of Ideological Hegemony in Education" by Michael Apple examines the hegemony of educational practices in contemporary society. Apple provides an historical account of the development of specific curricula that have been successfully applied with the intention of creating a form of social control of the imagination. Cultural values are embedded in educational curricula and as such play a vital role in the perpetuation of social hierarchies and world views. Apple explores the role that the social sciences have had on the function and form of our educational curricula and their social outcomes.

Chapter 9 <u>Violence and Society and Violence and Culture</u> concludes the readings in this collection by exploring the structural causes of violence that produce holocausts and genocides within nation-states. The articles share a common theme: crimes against humanity have recognizable structural patterns that can be identified and stopped, and stopping them requires the consensus of the global community and local citizen actors who are committed to engaged participation with the construction of new paradigms that respect the viability of all life while recognizing the need to limit greed, privilege, and hoarding by individuals and nation-states.

"The Texas–Mexico Border Wall and Ndé Memory," written by Margo Tamez, presents recent research on the border between Mexico and the United States, where the US deports nearly 400,000 people and imprisons approximately 2.3 million individuals per year. In this article, the authors challenge the notion that borders and prisons create safety and security for communities regardless of which side of the border they inhabit. This article argues that walls, borders, and prisons increase inequality, destabilize families and kinship systems, and generate misery and heartbreak for millions.

"An Illustrative Supergenocide—The Holocaust" by David Hamburg studies the issues of genocide and crimes against humanity from three perspectives: principle steps, early detection, and effective action. Hamburg uses illustrative cases from records of genocides to identify the patterns and processes that produce the horrors of mass killings by governments and to illustrate how these patterns can be identified and stopped if the international community has the will to become involved. In addition Hamburg argues that societies can build strong systems for the detection of genocide since the signs of their violence appear long before the actual perpetration of mass killings. Hamburg's research is very interdisciplinary and links policy with research findings, challenging us as citizens of nations-states and as global actors to get informed and become involved in the protection of human rights.

"The Sociology and Anthropology of Genocide" by Adam Jones explores an interdisciplinary approach to understanding crimes against humanity by analyzing the discourses about genocide in psychology, anthropology, sociology, and political science. Each discipline explores the areas of race, gender, ethnicity, and nationalism (frequently informed by a nation's experts in the sciences and technologies) as culprits leading to acts of genocide. Jones argues for international cohesion in terms of prompt and exacting actions by global actors in the prevention of global acts of genocide.

Chapter One

The Nature of Meaning

Cultures of Science

Translation and Knowledge

By Mike Crang

- The culture of the scientific community
- Relationships of objective and subjective knowledge
- Relativism, universal and situated knowledge

By way of a conclusion, I want to ask *how* we can claim to know things about cultures. This may sound odd after a whole book suggesting different ways of interpreting different forms and practices. However, we have not asked how we might assess whether they are truthful accounts of the world—what is called their *epistemology*. In cultural geography this often raises the ideas of relativism, reflexivity and self-reflexivity. On the first count, *relativism* is often part of the background of cultural study—though not always, and rarely without reservations. Many would regard it as unethical, and often counter-productive, to study a different culture with a view to saying how it is worse than our own or to take our own culture as normal. This does not mean we can never criticise but that we need to be careful that it is not just our prejudices shaping such a criticism. For instance, peoples who live by hunting and gathering may have developed very elaborate cultures—with as many rules and quirks as our own; they may have very sophisticated local knowledges, though they may not have as much technological knowledge. Why call these cultures primitive? A trite example from the developed world would be to attempt to evaluate the culture of a jazz fan with a blues fan—a careful comparison might reveal interesting differences, but saying which is better is likely to prove impossible. This is not to say cultural geographers can never judge. It might be better to say they should be careful never to prejudge.

Equally, geographers do not speak in a silent world, they are one voice among many. Cultural geographers may interpret the transnational links of music say (see Chapters 6 and 10), but this phenomenon has already been interpreted by media (specialist, print, TV), by artists, by listeners, by DJs and by the music industry. There are already multiple interpretations attached to this cultural form before geographers add theirs—people are *reflexive* agents. That is, they already learn from and interpret the world about them as part of normal life. We need some care, then, not only over how we judge different cultures but also about whether we believe our forms of understanding are better than other people's. In short we must be careful not only how we judge between different cultures but also different accounts of the same culture. There are no easy answers, and total relativism would suggest we had nothing worth saying, nothing to contribute—which is about as extreme as saying we always know best. Instead this chapter will briefly look at different approaches to how we assess versions of the world—and suggest how different standards rest upon different assumptions and foundations. The first section will briefly outline some 'traditional' scientific beliefs about what is true. Leading out of this is a critique of the idea that being 'outside' provides better knowledge. I shall suggest that being outside of culture is impossible and what is usually meant is being inside 'scientific culture'. I shall then suggest that the way most cultural geography deals with these problems is to see all knowledge as both partial and situated. This leads to the third idea mentioned above—*self-reflexivity*. This idea is very simple but has profound consequences. At its most basic it suggests that if we cannot get outside culture, if we are always embedded in various value systems just as much as those we study, then we should be scrupulous in examining our presuppositions. Our accounts should acknowledge where we are speaking from as affecting what we say.

Objectivity and Knowledge

In Western societies, knowledge has often been structured around binary oppositions—rational against emotional, cultural against natural. A consequence is seeing objective against subjective where the former is privileged. Thus 'objectivity' tends to be valued in knowledge and we find 'that "symbolic" opposes to "real" as fanciful to sober, figurative to literal, obscure to plain, aesthetic to practical, mystical to mundane, and decorative to substantial' (Geertz, quoted in Baker 1993). The question this then raises is how there can possibly be a 'neutral' or objective knowledge about cultures where cultural differences tend to deny an impartial viewing position. The topic of cultural geography is often so 'subjective', about feelings emotions and meanings, that objectivity seems problematic. Some strategies for dealing with this have been covered through the course of this book. For instance, a focus on the material culture of the landscape works to look at how beliefs or meanings are embedded in and expressed through material artefacts (Chapter 2). This is also reflected in the approaches that look to read the landscape in their varied ways—seeing how, for instance, paintings or gardens reflect the cultural beliefs, assumptions of 'lenses' through which the world is viewed (Chapters 3 and

4). Such a concentration on cultural forms thus responds to arguments about 'intangibility' and thus an assumed 'unknowability' of culture.

Other approaches instead embrace and celebrate the idea that human culture is indeed subjective and mysterious in some respects. For instance we have seen the fear that total planning, removing all human foibles from the built environment, is a potentially alienating policy (Chapter 7). Such an approach might also be used to suggest the importance of going beyond 'cultural' objects and seeing how they are inserted in society and daily life. Thus the German Marxist critic Theodor Adorno was working on the consumption of radio programming shortly after the Second World War. The director of the project told him that in order to be scientific, he had to produce some way of measuring, of quantifying, changes in programming and audience reception. Adorno was horrified:

> When I was confronted by the demand to 'measure culture', I reflected that culture might be precisely that condition that excludes a mentality capable of measuring it.
> (Cited in Porter 1995: 43)

Adorno (1993) famously criticised the politics of this sort of research. For Adorno, and other thinkers such as Max Horkheimer and Herbert Marcuse of the Frankfurt School, this represented a creeping danger of reducing all life to numbers, that might then form the basis of 'objective' judgements and management. The trend they saw was the development of ever more refined ways of calculating and 'objectively' knowing society that allowed ever more systems of management—both private and public bureaucracies—to dominate people's lives. The result seemed to be that people became objects of knowledge rather than subjects—the power of rationalisations returned to haunt and dominate those in whose service they were meant to be used.

Scientific knowledge in this view is not 'found', truth is not revealed; on the contrary it is constructed. Science, the arts, local belief systems all work to create different knowledges about the world. Saying which one is valid is thus a political issue—it is about empowering the group who sees the world in that way and disabling the arguments of other groups. Differences between different world views may thus be inevitable, as indeed may be the risks of silencing or marginalising groups, but the criteria over which these choices are made are by no means foreordained. The 'objectivity' of science is partial—giving one account of the world—and works to exclude or marginalise other accounts; it is not in that sense neutral. It does not reveal a natural order. If it did there would hardly need to be so many rules governing the conduct of science, nor would studies show that in operation these are generally compromised and often contradictory. An emphasis on the practice of science is important to remind us that we should see people engaged in creating knowledge in different ways. Adorno (1993) highlights that the supposed unification of science through method 'has more to do with administering the world than understanding it. But the bureaucratic imposition of uniform standards and measures has been indispensable for the metamorphosis of local skills into generally valid scientific knowledge' (Porter 1995: 21).

Objective knowledge thus created claims to be universal and untainted by local influences. This claim is extremely important in politically marginalising other forms of knowledge. It can also be enormously effective in regulating social life—something that is not entirely bad in a highly interdependent complex world. This is not an attempt at Luddism, rejecting all scientific knowledge for claiming a spurious objectivity. This kind of knowledge is often invaluable, but a cultural geographer needs to be aware of what such claims to objectivity may imply. Indeed arguing science constructs truths, makes knowledge and is a creative process is not a criticism. It does not make that knowledge wrong or valueless—it is not an attack on science. Instead it is trying to say that we need to rethink how we categorise knowledge, why it is that some knowledge comes to be called universal and others are confined to local belief systems.

Outside Cultures: Claims to Universal Truth

One of the tendencies in studying cultures is to equate objectivity with detachment—a separation between observer and observed (see Chapter 7). This is problematic, especially if cultural geography is very often trying to see how people make sense of the world in their own terms by understanding the insider's viewpoint. In one sense we could say that the approaches to iconography (Chapter 3) are caught in precisely this problem—in that they tend to suggest the academic is outside, looking in and saying what is going on from afar, rather than necessarily relating to the actual experiences of people involved in the culture. In part this is inevitable with historical material—even firsthand accounts allow only a vicarious access to the community; all we have are artefacts of varying sorts. However, sometimes this distance means the observer views a culture as a unified whole—'they', the people studied, are suggested to be similar to each other in contrast to the difference from the researcher. In part this is often true, but there is a balance to be kept in mind. Tuan (1992: 33) argues that people in general try to deal with the messiness of cultures, with the complex patterns of individual characters and beliefs, either by submerging themselves into the group or by attending mostly to commonalities and aspects that suggest order rather than chaos. He concludes that '[a]cademics, who tend to be individualists, favour the second approach: more than other people they seek to escape the world's messiness by withdrawing into a crystalline realm of ideas'. We should be careful, then, of whether 'cultural areas', or indeed holistic, local cultures are not more in the mind of the observer than those of the people they study. Indeed Chapters 5 and 10 suggest we need to be careful indeed about the implications of holistic areas—as to whom they cut out and the implications of boundaries.

The idea of detachment poses some practical problems. A study of subcultures, of (say) gangs or football hooligans, will often be interesting only if it looks at how the people themselves understand what they are doing—how it makes sense to them. But uncritical 'cheerleading' is also unlikely help. The cultural geographer is often in the perilous position of standing between—or, better, shuttling between—different worlds or world-views. The cultural geographer can never stand outside culture. Standing outside the beliefs of those being studied does not mean having no beliefs—instead it means being in your own culture.

Many interesting studies have relied on precisely how looking at different cultures reveals the taken-for-granted assumptions of the researcher's own. But neither culture is neutral or objective. There is no Archimedean vantage point from which the cultural geographer can see it as it 'really is'. Street graffiti expressing how gangs see a geography of the city, or academic books saying how geographers see the gangs' territorial patterns are both cultural forms. Neither is neutral or outside. One may circulate more widely around the globe than the other, one may have hugely different effects—no one would deny that, and indeed why one account is adopted or spread instead of another can make the basis of important studies—but both are 'fabrications', ways in which humans have given meaning to their world.

Philosophers, such as Jean-François Lyotard and Ludwig Wittgenstein, have argued that we should thus see the world comprised of various *language games*—that is, ways of describing things and accounting for events that are structured to be internally coherent, and which are acceptable in terms of specific communities. However, these interpretations may well be incommensurable between communities—that is, they may be unintelligible to a different audience, who use different assumptions and rules to decide what is a valid account. These arguments have opened up a huge debate in the social sciences: often described as *postmodern*, they are (to follow Lyotard's definition) hostile to *meta-narratives*. That is, these lines of thought cast doubt on overarching explanations that claim to speak for all people; that claim to be universal and not 'particular'; that claim not to be bounded in a language game unlike the cultures they comment upon. One way in which this debate has developed is to see science not as a finder of universal laws but as a culture in itself.

Cultures of 'Outsideness': Science and the Academy

Much of the emphasis in geography on detachment, or the separation of the observer from the observed as a prerequisite of 'objectivity', can be traced back to the history of the discipline. The idea of a privileged observer as producing truthful knowledge bears the marks of the model of geographical exploration. The relative position of a traveller, moving through territory underpins ideas about an 'outside' view and provides a historical precedent of how knowledge is created in geography. Such travel has the tendency to reduce people encountered to a series of objects people met in the context of exploration, that is, in relationship to an explorer's journey, not to the context of the rest of their lives or their own ideas of their identity or geography. This then forms a way of looking at the world that turns people into 'objects'. It may well be that this legacy has fed into the way geographers have looked at outside and inside knowledge about cultures.

Cultural geographers have examined the culture of travel, as a way in which geographical knowledge is produced (see Chapter 5). Some researchers have looked at popular travel but, more interestingly for ideas about science, the links of academic knowledge and travel have begun to be explored. Looking at the practices of travellers, researchers have found not so much a detachment but an active repression of evidence of contact. Thus writing in the passive voice to describe people and landscapes (e.g. 'the river was crossed') denies any sense of agency—and, given that many explorers had large numbers of local people as porters, represses the copresence of explorer and people. Likewise talking of peoples in a generic term serves to make them silent objects of study not groups of people with whom the researcher interacted (famously the anthropologist Evans Pritchard referred to 'the Nuer', never individuals whom he met). Amid all this the ethnic divisions and relations of power and wealth that enabled the explorer to travel tend to be downplayed. Exploration was rarely disinterested; newspapers funded missions to generate sensational stories; colonial powers sought new markets or resources; and military planners promoted the idea of geographical training as useful to empire. In addition the embodied nature of the explorer, their gendered position tends to be omitted. It is clear from 'adventure stories' that the heroic explorer on the frontier of civilisation and knowledge was set up as a romantic ideal for boys to aspire to—travel 'alone' in foreign lands was set up in the image of a particular sort of masculine identity. In short, it has been argued that the impression of a detached, objective knowledge is more a textual, rhetorical one—an appearance created through conventions of how accounts were written up—rather than an accurate model of how knowledge was created.

So much for the history of exploration, but does this impact on other scientific modes of looking at the world? One lesson is to study the practices of 'knowing' rather than just the accounts of what is known. We cannot say knowledge is ever fully detached from the locales where it is created. It circulates through academic institutions and learned societies designed to allow the exchange of knowledge—it does not float free but relies on these knowledge-producing networks. Transmission does not mean researchers are detached, rather that others are learning the tacit knowledge and assumptions necessary to understand the new research. Even in the most rigorous science, based in laboratories working on DNA or physics, we can suggest that the idea of mechanistic objectivity, where knowledge is based completely on explicit rules, is never fully attainable. Even in the physical sciences the importance of tacit knowledge is now widely recognised. Thus let us think of something as 'objective' as sheer strain in soil. Currently one of my colleagues has one of only seven machines in the country capable of performing a particular test on soil samples. Obviously then transmitting and developing the ideas derived from experiments will mean transmitting practical skills to others about how the machinery works:

> Experimental success is reflected in the instruments and methods as well as factual assumptions of other laboratories. Day-to-day science is as much about the transmission of skills and practices as about the establishment of theoretical doctrines
>
> (Porter 1995: 12)

If that applies to experimental science it applies as much to assessing knowledge about cultures. We may well have then to look at the moral economy of science as a culture—a culture that rewards and values diligence and that relies on trust in respecting others' ideas. It is in that sense a culture about knowledge, where the value of ideas tends to be defined by other researchers. That is, ideas are not held up in isolation but are assessed by a community of fellow experts. The ideas, be they about soil or culture, are then judged according to the norms of that community—using tacit knowledge, practical experience and so forth to assess the worth of any contribution.

Situated Knowledge

Cultural geographies are embedded in a series of relationships. There is, first, the relationship with the people studied but, second, there is the position within the academy. So many would argue that there is no kernel of absolute truth for all time—we cannot bracket out 'impurities'. It is not the case that social factors (our backgrounds, the context of research) can either be factored out, or that they devalue our knowledge; instead such tacit or practical factors are vital in creating knowledge. They cannot then be simply removed as though they contaminate or corrupt the work. Scientific knowledge should not be seen as being contaminated or 'biased' by social factors; rather science should be seen as a social process.

The logic of this is to say that cultural geography should not be in the business of creating absolute truths—as though they were true for all people—because there is no position where such detached, disembedded and a social knowledge could be created or circulated. Knowledge, academic or popular, is about cultural systems of belief and validation—and cultural geography does not escape that. So how can we see ways forward? One way is to say this highlights a need to think about whom and how we are studying. Anthropologists have recently remarked that in the study of the cultures of the globe, modern Western society is often absent, as though it did not have a culture(s). We need then to think that cultural geography is not just a matter of studying exotic other peoples, but thinking about how we define them as 'exotic', what is thus going on in our own taken-for-granted worlds.

The situatedness of knowledge in and between the cultures of researcher and researched highlights the importance of thinking about why we carry certain assumptions and connecting our biographies to what we study. This is generally said to be about *self-reflexivity* and is marked in the very least by using the first person—saying what you and others did rather than hiding it in a passive voice. Going further it is generally marked by an attention to tacit assumptions made by the researcher (often requiring a fairly hard, long self-analysis) or made about the researcher. It is thus very much attuned to the social process of creating knowledge. Of course there is a problem in all this that such careful self-reflection, such thinking about the research process, may downplay the original aim of the research. These works are also generally marked by an attention to writing. That is, they do not see writing as passively transmitting information but as playing an active part in constructing an idea of the world for the readers. The idea of texts as transparently reflecting reality is as much a rhetorical strategy as any other style of writing. The common academic voice of the impersonal narrator distances us from what is recounted making it appear self-evident, repressing the activity that went into producing the account, whom it allows to speak and whom it may silence.

Current work suggests we need to examine this process, to look at the way writing creates particular effects. This concern for the process of shaping and transmitting knowledge suggests that one way of thinking of cultural geography is as 'a translation', a making of connections between different ways of seeing the world. Rather than seeing our position between different interpretive frames—those of our own culture, academia, and the culture we study—as constituting a problem, we can think of it as the most exciting and exhilarating place of all. In a world of increasingly rapid change and flows, such points of contact are becoming all the more common between groups and cultures. Cultural geography may thus be one of the best avenues through which to address these changing definitions of who is an insider and an outsider, who knows what about whom and how we adapt to new ways of being in the world.

Summary

This chapter has not sought to bring the studies in previous chapters to a conclusion. It does not resolve the differences between them or sum them up into a grand pattern. Instead it tries to leave a few questions that lead on to issues of greater depth. It is concerned with the practice and process of academic knowledge. It has tried to point out how we see academic accounts producing truthful knowledge. It has asked how we set up criteria to judge this, and has made an argument that we need to be sensitive to cultural difference in such judgements. This is especially important given both the cultural topic of study and the legacy of colonial geography; claims to objective, absolute knowledge have been closely linked to real exploitation and colonisation (see also Chapter 5). I have thus argued we need to be aware of our own position in producing knowledge, seeing it as a process of actively making academic knowledge rather than finding already-existing truths. The model then for the cultural geographer may be that of a translator or intermediary rather than an arbiter of what is right and wrong. It will be clear that the different approaches in different chapters react to these issues in different ways, answering the challenges or disputing them according to their own lights. It is my hope that as you approach these different topics in more detail in later years these questions of how we can claim to know things, and the implications of this will continue to develop.

Further Reading

Barnes, T. (1996) *Logics of Dislocation: Models, Metaphors and Meanings of Economic Space* (esp. chs 4 and 5). Guilford Press, New York.

Bryant, R. (1996) 'Romancing Colonial Forestry: The Discourse of Forestry as Progress in British Burma', *The Geographical Journal* 162(2): 169–78.

Clifford, J. and Marcus, G. (eds) (1986) *Writing Culture: The Poetics and Politics of Ethnography*. University of California Press, Berkeley.

Porter, T. (1995) *Trust in Numbers: The Pursuit of Objectivity in Public Life*. Princeton University Press, Princeton, NJ.

Bondi, L. and Domosh, M. (1992) 'Other Figures in Other Places: On Feminism, Postmodernism and Geography', *Society and Space* 10: 199–213.

Duncan, J. and Ley, D. (eds) (1992) *Place/Culture/Representation*. Routledge, London.

Riffenburgh, B. (1993) *The Myth of the Explorer*. Oxford University Press, Oxford.

Making Wanga

Reality Constructions and the Magical Manipulation of Power

By Karen McCarthy Brown

In August 1997, Abner Louima, a thirty-two-year-old Haitian immigrant living in Brooklyn and working as a security guard, got in trouble with the New York City police. The encounter sparked what is now an infamous case of police brutality. Analyzing mainstream media coverage of the incident and comparing it to the coverage of another case of police violence in New York reveal an elaborate dance of secrecy and transparency, a contredanse if you will, in which secrecy demands transparency and transparency provokes new forms of secrecy, in spite of itself and at times in the name of justice. So it goes. When raw power and the most fundamental kinds of racism are involved, as they are in the Louima case, both victims and perpetrators are at times compelled to hide the factual truth and to keep secrets while simultaneously making claims on some of the most rudimentary of institutions created to enhance transparency, the news media and the judicial courts.

The night Louima was arrested, Phantoms, his favorite band, was playing at the Club Rendez-Vous in Brooklyn. Around four o'clock in the morning, the almost entirely Haitian crowd spilled out onto the street. As I later heard the story, two women started exchanging ritual insults about each other's clothing. Bystanders playfully urged them on; the shouting increased, and someone called the police. A Haitian friend who was there assured me that, before the police arrived, no one in the crowd had crossed the line between play and violence. The police cars nevertheless arrived with lights flashing and sirens screaming. Officers yelling and brandishing nightsticks pushed their way into the crowd. Before Abner Louima knew what was happening, he was face down on the ground with his hands cuffed behind his back.

Then, according to witnesses, he was thrown roughly into the back of a police car. By Louima's account, the four policemen involved in the arrest stopped twice to beat him en route to the Seventieth Precinct stationhouse; they used fists, clubs, and even a police radio. Once there, Officer Justin A. Volpe rammed the wooden handle of what appeared to be a toilet plunger into Abner Louima's rectum, yanked it out, and, rudely pushing it at his mouth, told him, "Now you are going to taste your own shit." [1] Louima was then placed in a holding cell, where he sat bleeding for a long time, perhaps hours, before being taken to a hospital. Louima's rectum was perforated and his bladder torn. His injuries required two months in the hospital and three surgeries, including an initial colostomy later reversed. He is now in better health than his doctors had predicted.

Eventually, it was revealed that Officer Volpe had mistaken Louima for someone else in the crowd who had taken a punch at him. At the time of Volpe's trial, David Barstow reported in the *New York Times* (21 May 1999) that, when a nurse at the hospital where Louima was originally taken referred to him as the man who had beaten up a police officer, Louima replied: "Lady, do you think I'm stupid? I'm a black man. Do you think I would beat a police officer in New York City?" From the beginning, the press was suspicious of Abner Louima's accounts of what happened to him. The jury in the initial trial also did not appear to trust him. They dismissed all charges related to the beatings administered on the way to the police station, events for which Louima himself was the only prosecution witness. At times, Abner Louima was treated as if he were the one accused of a crime.

Mama Lola Reconfigures Louima's Reality

In 1997, shortly after he was released from the hospital, Abner Louima was introduced to Mama Lola, a respected Haitian Vodou priestess and healer living in Brooklyn. She is also my teacher in the arts of Vodou and my friend. These days Louima occasionally visits Mama Lola at her home, and that is how I have come to know him. When Mama Lola first mentioned him to me, she said simply, "He a very quiet, respectable man." Then she mused on what had happened to him: "Maybe they think he some bum in the street. ... Like he don't have no family ... no one to help him." If that is what the police thought, they were mistaken because a significant proportion of the Haitian immigrant community in New York City, along with many non-Haitians, stepped forward to protest what had been done to him.

In April 1999, I interviewed Lola about Louima's situation. It was a strange conversation. At the time, Lola was caught between powerfully conflicting desires. She wanted to discuss Louima with me because we were working on a book on healing and she considered Louima one of her most interesting and important cases, yet the trial of his attackers was just about to begin, and she did not want to say anything that might compromise that process.

Mama Lola chose to deal with her ambivalence by telling me and my tape recorder substantially different stories. With the tape rolling, she spoke with all the caution of a public figure facing the press, yet, at the same time, she signaled further, secret meanings to me. For example, she would occasionally pull down her right eyelid with a finger to signal that I should not take something she said too seriously, or, if I asked a sensitive question, she would silently draw her thumb and forefinger across her lips as if closing a zipper. Once she shut off the tape recorder and whispered to me, even though no one was in the room except the two of us. I have repeated here only the taped version of the interview. For the purposes of this essay, the contorted progress of the conversation and its modes of secrecy production are far more important than any of the particular topics discussed.

When I asked Mama Lola if she were "doing some work" for Louima, a tactful reference to Vodou healing practices, she replied:

MAMA LOLA (ML): Oh, we pray. We do prayer! I always pray for him a lot. ...

KAREN BROWN (KB): Right.

ML: I ... uh ... do something ... but I don't think he know if I do it or not. ... I go downstairs to my altar, I pray to the spirits, and do some work with coconut. I use coconut water for clarity. I take the coconut water, and I put some good luck powder. I take lots of *veven* leaves ... High John the Conqueror root too. ... I add olive oil, and I make a lamp for him ... for three days.

KB: So, the lamp has to burn for three days, huh?

ML: Yes. After three days, I put the coconut [shell, with ingredients,] in the sea to sail it away. ... I go to Coney Island to do that.

KB: Why did you have to take it to the sea?

ML: To wash all the bad thing people ... [saying] about him. You know, to clear him ... to clear him ... in front of everybody.

KB: Don't you also take it to the sea because you can get closer to the spirits there?

ML: Yes, my ancestors, that's right. His ancestors too. ... The pigeon was after that. I do it in my house ... in the basement. I talk to the pigeon, and I put Abner' name inside the pigeon mouth, and I let it fly away.

KB: You talked to the pigeon first, like you told it what needs to happen?

ML: Exactly. Exactly. Then I sent it away.

KB: But when you're with Louima, you just pray?

ML: He don't ask me, don't pay me to do nothing. ...

KB: He's afraid if somebody thought he was doing Vodou, it would hurt his case?

ML: Oh, that's the truth! They will think maybe he come to me to do something. ...

KB: Something evil?

ML: Exactly, yup!

KB: Is his name on your altar now? [I knew that she did that for her clients.]

ML: No, I don't put his name on the altar. I don't want nobody to come in to my altar to see his name there.

KB: But otherwise you would have put it there?

ML: Yes.

KB: Did you put anything else of his on the altar?

ML: His name. I put it um ... um ... behind the statue, but nobody don't see it.

KB: Lola, it's so sad. ... You're helping him ... and you have to be so secretive. ...

ML: You know, people take everything in the wrong way. And they just blah, blah, blah, blah, blah the mouth. ... So, in this world, you have to be careful.

Mama Lola set out to change Louima's "luck" through the manufacture of two types of *wanga,* "charms," drawn from her repertoire of ritual healing practices, one based on a coconut and the other on a pigeon (see Brown 1995). Her intention was to bring about a situation in which Abner Louima and the things that motivated him would be more transparent to those who were judging him every day in the media and on the streets. In order for her to do this, it was necessary to keep some things secret.

Secrecy and Discretion in the Lives of the Haitian Immigrants

If he did "serve the spirits," the most common expression for what outsiders call *practicing Vodou,* Louima would have denied it when asked about it by journalists pursuing the police brutality case. Thanks to the advice of his community, practically every time Louima was in front of television cameras he was accompanied by a Protestant minister said to be his uncle. This was a politically astute move if not an absolutely honest one. For Haitians, conversion to Protestantism automatically entails a total rejection of the Vodou spirits. So, while the minister's presence communicated many things, chief among them was that Abner Louima is not into Vodou.

Furthermore, even if Louima were not the central character in a major news story, he probably would ask Lola to keep any spiritual work that she did for him secret. Healing work almost always deals with personal problems, so it follows that the most respected healers are those who know how to be discrete. For political, social, and religious reasons, secrecy is an important virtue in the lives of Haitians living in Haiti, a crowded country with scarce resources. In somewhat different ways, secrecy is important in the diaspora communities as well. In general, poor immigrants from Haiti dislike giving out information about themselves. Officially, there are around 250,000 Haitians living in New York City itself, a significant underestimation since many Haitians living in the city are undocumented and resist being counted. Yet even those who have their papers try to avoid bureaucratic accountability. They sometimes have the telephone bill in one name and the mortgage in another, and, when questioned by people they do not know, they frequently give misleading information about age, family, and work history. This practice reflects a deep lack of trust in bureaucracy of any kind, but it is also influenced by everyday social relations. Since so much of what it can mean to be a Haitian (poverty, illiteracy, blackness, Vodou) is liable to provoke prejudicial treatment in New York City, immigrants keep their heads down, and they school their children in secretiveness as a survival strategy in urban America. This old pattern is currently shifting. What happened to Abner Louima and the community response that it evoked have contributed to a new assertiveness among Haitians, a new willingness to take a public stand on issues that affect their lives.

The Haitian Community Acts Against Police Brutality

Historically, Haitians in the United States have avoided political activity. This attitude began to change when Jean-Bertrand Aristide, a populist candidate for president of Haiti, won the election in 1990. Much of his campaign was financed by expatriates. Aristide's victory galvanized the diaspora community, increasing their pride and making them bolder participants in U.S. as well as Haitian politics. Even though the United States was complicit in the 1991 coup, afterward Aristide set up his government in exile in Washington, D.C. Then the Haitian political presence in New York City took on a new character as angry crowds demonstrated on more than one occasion. The demonstration for Louima in 1997 was in this assertive mode, but it also marked a new stage in the growing involvement of Haitians in local politics. Many protest signs blamed Mayor Rudolph Giuliani for what happened to Abner Louima. When Louima was first interviewed by the police, he claimed that, while attacking him, Office Volpe bragged: "It's not Dinkins time anymore. This is Giuliani time now." David Dinkins preceded Giuliani in the mayor's office; he is an African American. Louima later retracted this testimony. Apparently, a Haitian community leader told him to use the mayor's name so that the incident would get the attention of the media and not be quickly forgotten, as other cases of police brutality against Haitians have been.

The crowd that marched from Grand Army Plaza in Brooklyn to City Hall in Manhattan to protest the brutalization of Abner Louima at the hands of the New York City Police Department (NYPD) made up one of the largest Haitian demonstrations ever held in New York City. There were many reasons for the size of this August 1997 event. Al Sharpton, a well-known African American minister and activist, stepped in to help organize the march for Louima, while at the same time a half dozen other Caribbean communities in New York chose to stand in solidarity with Haitians on the issue of police violence. Yet I doubt that any circumstance was more responsible for the protest's size and energy than the basic affront to human worth and dignity that the Louima case represented. Haitians were simply fed up. This time the New York City police had gone too far.

Mustering early at the Manhattan end of the Brooklyn Bridge, the police were out in force on the day of the demonstration, and they were nervous. Hours before the protest was scheduled to begin, more than one hundred officers, men and women, gathered in lower Manhattan. A dozen police cars were parked in formation at the end of the bridge, a roadblock ready to be deployed if things got out of hand. Helmets, shields, and batons were in evidence everywhere. Metal gates cordoned off areas for the police along the edges of the demonstration route.

As soon as the crowd appeared over the crest of the Brooklyn Bridge, it was clear that the Haitian demonstrators and the NYPD had quite different scenarios in mind. This was not a crowd bent on violence. Colorfully dressed, carrying a wide variety of protest signs, accompanied by energetic dancers and drummers, singing songs and shouting slogans, the protesters articulated a virtual directory of strategies for handling fear and outrage. In order to contain the awful power of the Louima event and turn it toward something more constructive, the Haitian community was calling on every meaning-making system they had access to, traditional or newly acquired.

Some of the protest rhetoric focused on psychological explanations; "Justin A. Volpe is a sexual sadist," one sign shouted. Other protesters turned to the authority of the Christian religion, terrain that Haitian Americans share with most other Americans.[2] A huge placard, dense with earnest long-hand script, argued for the connection of this terrible event to the Second Coming of the Messiah. Also, rhetorics of justice and human rights were peppered throughout the signs carried by the protesters. Marking it a truly Haitian event were two people in costume, both possessed by Vodou spirits. One had Papa Gede, the spirit of sex, death, and humor, and another had the peasant farmer Azaka, a character valued for his plain speech and blunt truth telling. The first was dressed in black, his face covered in white powder. The second wore the embroidered blue denim outfit that in Vodou temples has become emblematic of Haitians from the countryside.

Many homemade placards castigated the current political climate in the city, a problem for which they laid the blame squarely at Mayor Rudy Giuliani's feet. Because of his "get tough on crime" policies, many people, not only Haitians, hold the mayor responsible for a general increase in racial discrimination in New York City and specifically for an increase in police harassment of blacks and Hispanics. The mayor was depicted on one sign with his head in a toilet bowl. Other signs showed Giuliani, not Louima, as the one whose pants got pulled down. This was not a crowd that was going to gloss over the details of the attack on Louima or turn away from its shaming aspects. At short intervals along the route of the march, a theater group reenacted the brutalization of Abner Louima, albeit in a somewhat abstract way.

Several Haitian marchers had drawn caricatures of the offending police officers on their placards, while other demonstrators, many others, carried toilet plungers that they used in creative ways to comment on the frightening events in the Seventieth Precinct. A couple of men in the crowd fixed the rubber cup of the plunger to the top of their heads. Other Haitian men communicated more directly and attached it to their crotches. Three men carried a coffin with a toilet plunger handle emerging from its lid, positioned like the erection of a corpse, a further signal of the presence of the randy Vodou death spirit, Gede. Dozens of people in the crowd painted their plunger handles red, and sign after sign depicted toilet plungers with blood dripping from the stem.

Late in the afternoon, the crowd gathered near City Hall to listen to speeches about police violence. On the stage were the Reverend Al Sharpton and several leaders of the Haitian community, including the Reverend Philius H. Nicolas, Louima's putative uncle and pastor of the Evangelical Crusade Church in Flatbush, Brooklyn. When one of the speakers made an especially powerful point, a sea of toilet plungers bobbed enthusiastically over the heads of the crowd. A marcher told me it was impossible to buy a toilet plunger in Brooklyn that day. He reported that all the hardware stores were sold out before the march began. The *New*

York Times, which otherwise covered the demonstration in detail, made no mention of toilet plungers.

I remember thinking at the time that there was something very wangalike about the way in which the Haitian protesters used the toilet plungers. One of the most important things that this demonstration accomplished was changing the emotional valence of an instrument of torture. Prior to the march, the toilet plunger was a sign of shame and pain, but, on that hot August day, Haitians took what they feared most, brought it out into the light of public scrutiny, and turned it into an instrument of resistance. What initially appeared to be mere play with the plungers was actually what Vodou practitioners call *working the wanga.* It is true that, as a rule, the making of Vodou charms is a private matter, yet, in some circumstances, it is the public exposure of such a secret thing that gives it real clout. For example, I once heard a story of a Port-au-Prince shop owner who was trying to ruin the business of a competitor by telling false stories about her. A trail of yellow powder across the doorway of the gossip not only served as a serious warning but also moved that person's offense into the realm of the larger community's responsibility.

Black Magic and the Making of Wanga

Issues of secrecy, especially the malevolent kind, are overdetermined in relation to things Haitian, a culture that, in the United States, is often portrayed as virtually synonymous with black magic. Haitians have absorbed the colonial language about magic. These days they refer to both "white magic" and "black magic" in their traditional African-based religion, Vodou.[3] In spite of this superficial rhetoric, Haitian Vodou actually tends to avoid the good/evil dichotomy. Vodou priests and priestesses make wanga in order to help clients with love, health, money, and, not infrequently, legal problems, and giving such help is often morally complex. Helping one person may mean limiting or controlling another. Those who specialize in the Vodou arts of healing are as likely as not to refer to all dimensions of these healing practices as *maji*, "magic." Because such practices are deeply rooted in their culture, it is understandable that the larger Haitian community turned to a kind of maji to deal with the trauma of the Louima incident.

Wanga, such as Mama Lola made for Abner Louima, are simultaneously representations of troubled relationships and the means for solving the problems they represent. The High John the Conqueror root in Lola's coconut wanga, for example, points both to the fact that Louima is under attack and to the resources that he has to fight that battle. The coconut "water," a clear sweet liquid, prefigures the power of the ancestors and spirits to improve the vision of those having trouble seeing Abner Louima clearly and to sweeten their attitudes toward him. Ideally, the person with the problem should "work the *wanga*," that is, maintain a prescribed regimen of ritual practices such as praying and lighting candles before the wanga, but I have seen Lola take over this responsibility for clients other than Louima when they could not conveniently keep a wanga in their own home.

This was the case, for example, with a wanga that Lola made for a woman whose husband was unfaithful. Out of an article of the husband's clothing, Lola made a soft and pliable little doll, complete with male genitalia. Then, using heavy wire and a padlock, she bound the doll into a small wooden chair. For months, it was Mama Lola who kept an oil lamp burning next to the bound figure of the woman's husband. Here also, the wanga describes both the problem and the solution. Lola predicted that, sooner or later, the wandering husband would "bow his head" before his wife just as Santa Clara bowed her head in the image of the saint that, as a finishing touch, Lola placed on the wall directly in front of the male doll.

Bringing an imagined change into reality is what working a wanga is all about. The making of wanga and related diaspora practices are venerable, old traditions. I will never forget the emotional impact of an eighteenth-century wanga that I saw in the Port-au-Prince ethnographic museum on one of my first trips to Haiti. It was composed from an old pitted glass bottle, bound with a short section of old slave chains. Wanga can be traced to ritual practices found throughout West and Central Africa. Among other sources, Haitian Vodou wanga have roots in Dahomean *bocio* (Blier 1995) and Kongo *minkisi* (MacGaffey 1993).

In all cases, the practices associated with wanga are used to manipulate power by changing human relationships. When looked at in this way, the power of the wanga is largely discursive power; it is the power to rewrite the existential narrative at issue. The wanga that Mama Lola made for Abner Louima are not, therefore, all that different from newspaper accounts of Abner Louima's experience with the police or from arguments made by defense and prosecuting attorneys in the courtrooms where the crimes committed against Louima were adjudicated. All, including Mama Lola's wanga, are competing narratives empowered by their various abilities to convince key audiences (including spiritual ones) of their points of view and, therefore, shift problematic situations. This process is complex because each new narrative is unavoidably launched into a sea of old ideologies, automatic associations, and rigid interpretations. Some people have to work against this situation; others profit from it. While some masters of narrative must anticipate and guard against possible points of *meconnaissance* (perhaps by keeping certain things secret), others work at making a narrative say things indirectly, things that otherwise would be unspeakable in this particular place and time. The discussion now turns to what I will call *word wanga* and, thus, to the many ways in which the person and the experience of Abner Louima are reconfigured in the press and in the courtroom. Following the path of the African wanga has led to the magical practices of largely white, bureaucratic institutions in the United States.

The Media Construction: Abner Louima and Amadou Diallo

On 4 February 1999, eighteen months after Louima's encounter with the officers of the Seventieth Precinct, Amadou Diallo, a West African immigrant who worked as a sidewalk merchant in New York City, was fired on fortyone times at close range, late at night, while standing in the entryway to his Bronx apartment. He was unarmed. All shots fired came from four NYPD officers, members of an elite anticrime unit that traveled in plain clothes. According to a *New York Times* (12 February 1999) editorial, the macho slogan of this unit is, "We own the night." Nineteen bullets entered the body of Diallo, and he died shortly thereafter.

Approximately two months after Amadou Diallo's death, in a guest editorial in the *New York Times* (19 April 1999) titled "For Most Brutality Isn't the Issue," New York City police commissioner Howard Safir called the shooting of Diallo "a tragedy" that "only the judicial system can produce answers for. ..." He added that, even though he does hear complaints about the police, "the complaints ... are not of officers being brutal, but of officers being brusque." He concluded with the announcement of a police "civility campaign." "We are giving officers tips on how to be more polite," Safir wrote. He made no mention of Abner Louima. Nevertheless, the two cases were immediately linked by the media and by the general public.

The Louima and Diallo cases both involved police violence against recent immigrants to the United States; both victims were black. Given these similarities, it was initially puzzling that the two cases received significantly different treatment from the public and from the media. The Diallo case was in the news continuously starting from the day he was killed. There were dozens of events protesting the shooting: a memorial; demonstrations before and after the memorial; vigils; religious services; and concerts. These events attracted people from across New York's social, racial, and ethnic spectrum. There were several demonstrations for Abner Louima, one of them sizable, yet Haitian immigrants made up the great majority at all events. Also, by contrast with Diallo, Abner Louima disappeared from the newspapers and the evening television news rather quickly. His case actually got more coverage later, during the second trial, for obstruction of justice. By then, the offense against Louima had become so involved with other incidents of police violence, including Diallo's death, that jury verdicts often seemed to be responding more to the larger context of police brutality in New York City than to the specific events that the jury members were asked to judge.

A U.S. film crew followed Diallo's mother at the height of her grief back to Africa, to Guinea, where she took her son's body for a traditional funeral and burial. Long segments of the Africa footage were broadcast on the evening news on several U.S. channels. Since her first visit, occasioned by her son's death, Kadiatou Diallo has become something of a public figure in the United States, speaking out repeatedly against police violence and for gun control. There was an "interfaith prayer and community healing" service for Diallo, a Muslim, at the Brooklyn Academy of Music, and, according to David M. Haiszenhorn, in a *New York Times* article of 15 March 1999 titled "Mayor Expresses Regret over Police Shooting of Immigrant," at the service Mayor Giuliani referred to Diallo's death as the "loss of an innocent person." He also called the event "a terrible rending tragedy." I do not recall anyone in the media characterizing Louima as an "innocent" person. However, a story on the *New York Times* website on 8 June 1999 reported that one of the attorneys defending the police officers did refer to him as "a 'professional victim' looking for big money damages from the city." Furthermore, neither the names of Louima's parents, nor those of his children, nor that of the place where he was born in Haiti was ever mentioned in the newspapers I read. On the contrary, parts of Louima's identity—his Haitianness in general and especially his religion—had to be muted and handled with discretion. In spite of the fact that the great majority of people in Haiti serve the Vodou spirits in one way or another, any possible Vodou connection to Abner Louima had to be thoroughly hidden so that, in a context of prejudice, he could remain a credible witness against his attackers.

Mayor Giuliani and Police Commissioner Safir honored Diallo by going to his memorial service, held at the impressive Islamic Cultural Center of New York on East Ninety-Sixth Street in Manhattan. That event and the one at the Brooklyn Academy of Music became occasions on which multicultural and religiously pluralistic New York City was put on display, but Abner Louima's case represented nothing about the city that the larger public wanted to honor.

The cases of Abner Louima and Amadou Diallo differed in other ways. Diallo came from Africa, and, in death, he conveniently went back there, sounding an end note for the whole affair, while Louima survived the sadistic sexual attack against him and so must continue to be dealt with, like all the other impoverished people from his country who will not stop knocking at the backdoor of the United States. Furthermore, Louima filed a personal damage suit against the city of New York.

Deeper and more trenchant reasons for the different media treatment given Louima and Diallo have to do with the hypersexualized black body. Viewing blacks in this way is a frequent and historically deep habit of mind among Euro-Americans. Reason might never have been crowned in the aftermath of the French Revolution if Africans (and a few others) had not long been designated to carry the burden of sexuality with all its inherent irrationality and potential for untidiness and loss of control. Partly because Louima was already in place to carry the burden, Diallo escaped evoking this image. His sexuality simply got erased by the media. In fact, it was never an issue. Diallo's body under attack was configured as a clean, fully clothed body. At times, it was represented by an anonymous two-dimensional outline of a human body crosshatched by nineteen bullet trajectories. The more common visual icon of the violence unleashed against Diallo, however, was a photograph of the empty, bullet-pocked entryway to his Bronx building. Diallo's body, doubly contained (both safely buried and on the other side of the ocean), is gone from this picture, and, thus, Amadou Diallo could be reconfigured as deemed necessary by journalists and politicians alike. Via this process, Diallo approached the type of pure victim that motivates politics on both the Left and the Right in America.

Partly because of the comparison with the murdered Diallo, Louima, who is alive, has not been allowed to be an innocent victim. What is more, his body under attack was highly problematic; it had trousers pulled down around the ankles. In newspapers, and on the television news, the most common visual icon of the violence against Louima was, like Diallo's vestibule, empty of a human presence. In this case, however, the iconic photograph showed, not a neutral, public space, but instead an empty precinct bathroom. This scene-of-the-crime photograph functioned as a highly suggestive erasure, daring the reader to imagine what happened there. The hypersexual, penetrable, and penetrating black (read colonized) body, made excitingly vulnerable and accessible through extremes of social power and physical control, is positioned at the center of Abner Louima's story of torture, as it was at the center of slavery.

In another, related dimension of media word magic, homosexuality can be detected as a partially submerged theme in the narrative of Louima's torture. A *Washington Post* (28 May

1999) article repeatedly refers to Louima as having been *sodomized,* a word whose common usage neatly erases the violence from the incident and accentuates the fact that it occurred between two men. During the two years following Louima's torture by the police, the verb *to sodomize* appeared in several articles, yet, more recently, members of the press (including more than one writing for New York's *Haitian Times*)[4] have almost unanimously fallen into this extended, half-conscious fantasy that Abner Louima is gay. *To sodomize* is now, across the board, the verb of choice in the frequent articles on police brutality that mention Louima's case. In such word wanga, some degree of unconsciousness (a form of keeping secrets from oneself) on the part of the writer is essential. Were the language more transparent to its meaning, its foolishness and lack of integrity would also be more apparent.

A more straightforward charge of homosexuality was at issue in the first trial of Abner Louima's attackers. In his opening statements, Marvyn Kornberg, Justin Volpe's attorney, suggested that Louima might have sustained his injuries prior to arrest, from consensual gay sex in the bathroom of the Club Rendez-Vous. In the weeks of testimony following the opening of the trial, this stunningly irrational argument did not make it back into the courtroom. Never mind. The damage had been done. Kornberg's underlying point, coyly signaled to the jury, was that, if Louima had sex with men, then what happened to him, grotesque as it was, was in some way his own fault. Robert Volpe, Justin Volpe's father, spun his own tale about how Louima shared the blame with his son.[5]

Abner Louima's moral stature was attacked in other ways as well. For example, he was called a liar because of discrepancies between his description of the attack when he was first interviewed in the hospital and his current version of it. According to Joseph P. Fried, writing in an article published on the *New York Times* website on 17 May 1999, one issue was his comment about it being "Giuliani time," while another concerned his body posture at the time of the attack. Was he crouched down and bending over, as he now says, or was he pinned down on the floor, as he said when first questioned? It is not difficult to see how Louima might have initially hedged his story, feeling his manhood to be at stake in these postural differences. Either way, such goings-on do not produce good victims. Sexual tension lies just below the surface in practically everything written about Louima's story, and it is fed by secrecy, silence, and erasure. The biggest erasure was what I kept expecting to see in print but never did: "Justin Volpe raped Abner Louima."

Reconfigurations from the Judge's Bench and the Jury Box

The May–June 1999 trial led to acquittals for all officers involved on charges related to the immediate circumstances of Abner Louima's arrest and to the beatings that he had received on the way to the police station. This is significant because these are the dimensions of the crime against Louima that connect with patterns of police violence widely experienced in the Haitian immigrant community and other such communities. The Louima case, like Diallo's, involved racial profiling (suspecting people of color for no reason other than their color) and street justice (precipitous and unjustified use of force by police on the streets). When these dimensions of the Louima case are taken away, the whole affair shrinks to a weird event that happened in a precinct bathroom, a one-time thing to be dealt with and quickly forgotten. In the first trial, Justin Volpe, who did the deed, got thirty years, and Charles Schwarz, who was convicted of assisting him, received the same sentence. Even though neither Volpe nor Schwarz pleaded insanity, in the process of the jury sorting out the evidence and deciding whose claims were credible and whose were not, these out-of-control police officers, who routinely operated in an ethos that supported such things as racial profiling and street justice, were transformed into rogue cops at worst and psychologically troubled individuals at best. The systemic corruption of the NYPD was what motivated Louima to resist and what brought out Haitian (and other) protesters in large numbers, yet it was never a real issue in the courtroom.

In February 2000, Amadou Diallo's attackers were on trial for murder. By this time, the Diallo case had become *the* police brutality case, the lightning rod for a city's fear and suspicion of its police force. Around the same time, three of the four former police officers who attacked Louima went on trial again, this time for conspiracy to impede a police investigation. In the trial of the men who shot Diallo, it was word wangas, the way in which the event was reconfigured—what evidence was admissible, what not, and how the defense and prosecution shaped their cases—that determined the outcome. During the trial, the defense repeatedly discredited witnesses not present for the entire event by claiming that they did not have the context to interpret what they saw and heard. There were, however, no witnesses who were present the entire time except the officers themselves. The case against the men who shot Amadou Diallo thus came to rest entirely on the state of mind of the four defendants. It all came down to whether the officers believed that Diallo had a gun and continued to believe that he had a gun for the entire time it took them to fire forty-one bullets. It was no surprise that all four testified in the affirmative on that point. The acquittal of the four undercover officers provoked frustration and anger among Caribbean immigrants, but no real surprise. Many of them have emigrated from countries controlled by their armies. These immigrants have also had firsthand experience with the NYPD. They know that members of the NYPD are rarely held responsible for using excessive force. After the acquittal, groups of young men stood a silent and angry vigil in Diallo's Bronx neighborhood, holding up their black wallets. It was a black wallet that Diallo had in his hand, not a gun.

A leaflet, written in Haitian Creole and circulated in Brooklyn shortly after the Diallo verdicts, announced a protest demonstration. These were the words used to encourage people to come: "Pote Tanbou! Pote Plonje Twalet!" (Bring drums! Bring toilet plungers!). The tie between the Louima and the Diallo cases lives on among the people. I am convinced that it was the offense caused by the acquittals in the Diallo case that ricocheted into the second Louima trial courtroom, producing unexpected guilty verdicts there. Three officers involved in the Louima arrest, Charles Schwarz, Thomas Bruder, and Thomas Wiese, were indicted on charges of conspiracy to obstruct justice. Volpe confessed and plea bargained halfway through the first trial, so he was out of the picture by the time of the second trial, even though he had done more than any of the other officers to impede the internal police investigation. For example, Volpe never came clean about who was in the bathroom with him when he assaulted Louima. In the second round of verdicts, Charles Schwarz got another fifteen years and eight months, and Thomas Bruder and Thomas Wiese each ended up with a sentence of five years in jail. Thus, Louima's attackers received what were probably well-deserved sentences, but, in the trade-off, Diallo's killers, part of a larger structural source of police brutality (an undercover police unit that claimed to "own the night"), sidestepped accountability. As the Haitian proverb says: "Konplo pi fò passe wanga" (Conspiracies are stronger than magic).

Racism in the Shadow of the Fetish

It seems that, whenever Haitians are in the news, a reference to Vodou cannot be far behind. In a 20 June 2000 *Village Voice* article titled "Police Brutality and Voodoo Justice," Peter Noel, a black journalist whose byline appears frequently in the *Voice*, wrote that "the father of Justin Volpe, the white cop who was accused of sodomizing Louima, ... told friends he was warned by Haitian spiritual healers that Louima is a wicked voodoo high priest bent on deadly revenge." In the same article, Noel also reported that a cop improbably named Ridgway de Szigethy, who spends his time investigating occult organizations, told Noel that, for his son's protection during the first trial, Robert Volpe carried "a little purple crystal ... and a little vial of holy water." By looking down his nose at crystals and holy water as well as Vodou wanga, Peter Noel exhibited a democratic disdain for all things religious, but, as a result, he missed the depth and significance of the racism in Robert Volpe's attempt to condemn Abner Louima through references to the African-based religion of his homeland. This is an old ploy and one with a long, continuous history. This maneuver is, in fact, a cornerstone in the historic and current structure of European and American racism. A look at the history of the term *fetish,* a word that is in most cases interchangeable with *wanga,* will give a glimpse into the depth and complexity of the racist tropes peppered throughout the coverage of Louima's encounter with the officers of New York's Seventieth Precinct.

More than four hundred years ago, Europeans chose the term *fetish* to stand for powerful material objects used in traditional African religious settings. Chief among these objects were charms related to what would later become Vodou wanga. Not long after, the term *fetishism* or *fetish religion* began to be routinely applied to all aspects of all indigenous African religions. To this day, the Vodun (Fon spirits or deities found in the Republic of Benin, formerly Dahomey) are called *fetiches* and their priests *feticheurs,* another instance of a colonized people swallowing colonial rhetoric. Diviners throughout Benin are routinely called *charlatans,* yet another remnant of the French presence in the former Dahomey.

According to William Pietz, who has written an important series of articles on the history of the concept of fetishism, "the fetish, as an idea and a problem, and as a novel object not proper to any prior discrete society, originated in the cross-cultural spaces of the coast of West Africa during the sixteenth and seventeenth centuries" (Pietz 1985: 5). Fetish theory, Pietz says, "was fully established in European intellectual discourse by 1800" (1987: 23). The term *fetish* subsequently became an unusually influential one in a wide range of intellectual, political, and economic interactions between Europe and Africa. For a remarkably long period of time, fetish theory has provided the most pervasive and broadly influential rationale for racism, colonialism, and general Western cultural chauvinism.

Newton and Locke, figures of the seventeenth and early eighteenth centuries, both had in their libraries copies of the book that introduced "fetish religion" to the European world, Wilem Bosman's 1702 *A New and Accurate Account of the Coast of Guinea* (Pietz 1988). According to the theory of fetishism, "consecrated at the end of the eighteenth century by no less than G. W. F. Hegel in *The Philosophy of History*, Africans were incapable of abstract and generalizing thought; instead their ideas and actions were governed by impulse," and, as a consequence, it was commonly assumed that "anything upon which an African's eye happened to fall might be taken up by him and made into a 'fetish,' absurdly endowed with imaginary powers" (MacGaffey 1993: 32). In the nineteenth century, the concept of fetishism became theoretically indispensable to three of the founders of social science: Comte, Marx, and Freud. It is my purpose here to demonstrate that this intellectual arrangement has, from the beginning, been devastating for black people and that, at the beginning of the twenty-first century, the fetish trope still covertly and overtly shapes the images that Euro-Americans hold of Africans and African Americans in cosmopolitan New York City.

A "theoretically suggestive" term (Pietz 1985), the word *fetish* provided the rubric under which all Africa came to play the Other to Enlightenment rationalism. Most important was the role that the European idea of the fetish played in crystallizing the notion that so-called primitive thinking was characterized by a false theory of causality, a mistaken belief that material objects could be manipulated in such a way as to change the conditions of a person's life (Pietz 1988). When the presumed immorality of the feticheur was added to this mix, the fetish became the perfect foil for making the (illogical) connection so crucial to the Enlightenment, the connection between reason and righteousness. When seen from this perspective, it appears that the humble, antiaesthetic fetish was nothing less than a midwife to the Enlightenment.

Two things are, thus, important to remember from this short history of the fetish/wanga: First is the act of almost unbelievable meconnaissance that led Europeans to characterize all African religions, each one different from the other and each a rich moral universe, as nothing but instrumental magic carried out by bumbling sacerdotes paradoxically characterized as both childlike and evil. Second is the equally inappropriate characterization of African religion as bad science, that is, as primitive thinking or mistaken reasoning.

The European indictment of the African fetish was not merely a matter of slander. The configuration of African religion as fetishism had very tangible political and religious effects. This was the story in Haiti from the beginning of the eighteenth century until long after the end of European domination. In the early eighteenth century, Haitian slaves found making the benign protective charms called *gad-kò*, "body guards," which may consist of nothing more than herbal mixtures put under the skin or small cloth bags pinned inside clothing, were tortured brutally as sorcerers who gained power by deception. Even after the Haitian slave revolution (1791–1804), what Anna Wexler calls *the long shadow of the fetish* did not lift. In

1835, Boyer, then president of Haiti, promulgated a penal code that outlined hideous punishments for all religious practitioners who trafficked in such things as wangas. As late as 1935, Haitian president Vincent launched a campaign against traditional priests for suggesting that they could change people's lives through "occult methods" (Wexler, in press; Hurbon 1987).

It is sobering to realize how important maneuvers such as the misrecognition of African religion and its equation with bad science are to the representation of the African-based religion practiced in Haiti and by Haitians in diaspora today. A microexample: The *New York Times* currently refuses to spell *voodoo* with a capital *V* (spelling it *Vodou* as Haitians prefer is beyond question) even though it capitalizes the names of other religions, including those of other African-based Caribbean religions.[6] This commitment to a deeply compromised form of the term keeps it handy for use in put-down phrases such as *voodoo economics*.[7]

A more complex and weighty example is to be found in the language of Stephen Worth, a lawyer from the Patrolmen's Benevolent Association. On the same day that jury selection was completed for the Louima case, 3 May 1999, the official coroner's report on Diallo was finally released—three long months after the shooting. An earlier autopsy, requested by lawyers engaged by the Diallo family, concluded that the police continued to shoot after Amadou Diallo was already down and immobilized. The coroner's report confused this issue by initially making no judgments about which shots came first or how fast they were fired.[8] Kevin Flynn, writing in the *New York Times* (4 May 1999), reported that Stephen Worth, attorney for one of the men charged with second-degree murder in the death of Amadou Diallo and at the same time attorney for one of the officers accused of beating Louima, celebrated the second coroner's report, crowing that it "puts the lie to the Dream Team's voodoo autopsy and shows it for the pseudoscience that it is." Thus, Worth called on one of the oldest and most enduring "voodoo" tropes, its equation with bad science, and in so doing managed simultaneously to compromise the authority of scientific evidence in the Diallo case and, in his other case, to cast doubt on the credibility and morality of both the lawyers and the main witness, Abner Louima. Worth sent a potent racist message that demeaned the lawyers working for Louima and the Diallo family (initially Johnnie L. Cochran's infamous Dream Team served as counsel for both) by making an invisible reference to the O. J. Simpson murder case while simultaneously linking the lawyers to a religion whose name is synonymous with *black magic* and, as a result, with Haiti, Abner Louima's country.

Conclusion

Our language and the habits of our bodies and minds carry our history. Such habits as racial prejudice, sexual fundamentalism, and even habitual disdain for all things Haitian are prominent in the U.S. habitus. (Evidence of the latter prejudice is apparent in the similarity, and significant difference, between the treatment of the Diallo case and that of the more recent shooting death of the Haitian Patrick Dorismond.)[9] This prejudice against Haitians began when blacks and mulattoes in Haiti had the temerity to win their freedom from slavery and their dignity by fighting for them and did so during a period when the United States and many European countries were still holding slaves. Habits of the heart and mind, such as the historically rooted prejudice against Haitians, exercise a downward pull on transparent civic values such as those represented by a free press, trial by jury, and police accountability. In the events surrounding Abner Louima, the strategies of transparency set in place actually spawned elaborate strategies of secrecy, and vice versa.

In theory, secrecy and transparency are opposing power dynamics, yet, in the Abner Louima case, they appear to have worked together, evoking one another in a paradoxical dance of increasing complexity. Major players in this drama convinced of the importance of their ultimate goals (or at least equipped with those goals as rationalizing devices) competed for the control of institutions of transparency, such as the press, the judicial system, and police review processes. In the name of keeping peace, Police Commissioner Howard Safir painted a ridiculously mild, even insulting picture of the problems between police and civilians in New York City. In the name of providing their clients with the best defense possible, Kornberg and Worth, Police Benevolent Association lawyers, mounted their defense in the press through innuendo, secrecy, and erasure. In the name of covering the news, the media repeated what Kornberg and Worth said and eventually turned from Louima in order to focus on Amadou Diallo's death. In the name of revealing all the dirty secrets, Peter Noel reported that Robert Volpe, Justin's father, carries a bottle of holy water and used it to make crosses on his own forehead in order to protect against Louima's Vodou powers.

The way in which race interacted with these complex impulses was especially visible in the repeated connection of the Louima and Diallo cases, a linkage that remained in the minds of Haitians and other immigrants. The dense, racially charged images that public personalities and journalists called up so effortlessly in commentary on the cases are representations constructed "in the shadow of the fetish." Like the charms that Mama Lola made to help Louima, they are wanga.

Like wanga, these representations of Louima—spoken out but also present in the silences within the words of police, lawyers, and journalists— characterized complex and troubled relational situations with the intention of influencing them. The police commissioner, the press, and lawyers involved in the Louima case deployed their own word wanga. The Haitian community, in turn, responded to the affront to Louima, and to decades of mistreatment at the hands of New York City officials, by putting their universe of explanations on display, including their much-maligned religion, Vodou. More to the point, they put their fear-charged, blood-soaked toilet plunger wanga, an externalization of their most intimate and most horrific relational nightmares, on public display. They literally thrust their plungers in the face of the NYPD. This process of exposing wanga power in public worked to some extent like sprinkling yellow powder across the threshold of a troublemaker. It brought Abner Louima's experience to public attention. It threw down the gauntlet in a challenge to the city government to do something about patterns of police brutality while simultaneously tempering the fear of the Haitian community and increasing its political capital. It also contributed to a lengthy legal process that finally got jail sentences for the four men directly involved in the arrest and brutalization of Abner Louima.

In the year 2000, a focus on wanga and wanga-like constructions does a surprisingly good job of revealing the everyday workings of power on all levels of society in New York, an ethnically diverse city with a heritage of racism. One of the most interesting aspects of this comparison is the similarity between the workings of Mama Lola's wanga and the workings of what I have called the *word wanga* of politicians, journalists, and lawyers. All are narrative reconfigurations, and all are constructed in order to control key narratives. It is ironic that the homely African wanga, the very objects used by Europeans at the dawn of the Enlightenment to draw absolute boundaries between themselves and primitive others, should reveal themselves as close cousins of Euro-American "magical" maneuvers.

In the Louima case, the Haitian community won the battle only to lose the war. The police conspiracy of silence and especially Volpe's withholding of crucial testimony, the evidentiary rulings of the courts, the unconscious racism and homophobia of the press, the ancient racist tropes buried deeply in the speech of just about everybody who got near to the case, proved more powerful than what either Mama Lola or the Dream Team could do to bring justice, not only to Abner Louima, but also to the larger Haitian community that experiences continuous police harassment. Institutionalized patterns of abuse, including what could be called *racial profiling* and *street justice*, were identified in a 1994 Mollen Commission report on corruption in the NYPD, but nothing was done to address these problems at that time, and nothing has yet been done to address them. While convictions in the Diallo case could at least have raised these issues of institutionalized racism, the convictions of the four men who brutalized Louima were not seen as relevant to such concerns.

Brian Stevens, writing in the *Haitian Times* (19–25 July 2000), acknowledged that Volpe and his new lawyer had already been to court seeking to cut Volpe's sentence in half. So far, such efforts have not succeeded. Abner Louima turned down more than one offer to settle his civil suit because those offers involved no promises for reforms in New York police practices. In the summer of 2001, Louima finally accepted an offer of $7.125 million from the city and $1.625 million from the Patrolmen's Benevolent Association (PBA). While the PBA payment involved no admission of guilt, it was the first time that a police union anywhere in the country had been forced to pay in a police-violence incident. Yet Louima still got no official promises for police reform. He had to settle for informal promises that had more to do with public relations than with a commitment to changing oppressive police practices.

On 28 February 2002, a federal appeals court threw out the obstruction-of-justice convictions of Schwarz, Bruder, and Wiese because of a technicality. Also, Schwarz's conviction for aiding Volpe in the attack on Louima was set aside because of another technicality, a conflict of interest on the part of his attorney, Stephen Worth. From the moment Schwarz was freed on $1 million bail, the district attorney made it clear that he would be indicted and tried again on these charges.

During the 1999 trials of the cases concerning Louima and Diallo, a large percentage of New Yorkers were deeply concerned about police violence. Then, it was a high-priority issue, but the atmosphere had changed drastically by the time Schwarz's convictions were set aside. Jeffrey Toobin, writing for the *New Yorker*, described the *Times* coverage of Schwarz's return to the Staten Island home of his mother as "a dewy portrait." Toobin also noted that the three leading New York tabloids—the *News*, *Newsday*, and the *Post*—were also Schwarz boosters. "Free," trumpeted the *News*, while *Newsday* and *Post* cried out, "He's Home," and, "He's Out." It was the events of 11 September 2001 that caused this dramatic change. Because of the attack on the World Trade Center, every police officer, including Charles Schwarz, automatically became a hero, a person larger than life, someone no true patriot would consider criticizing. Thus, in July 2002, Schwarz's third trial ended in a single perjury conviction with a possible five-year sentence, while the jury was unable to reach verdicts on any of the charges that concerned Schwarz's participation in torturing Louima. There may well be another trial; whether justice will be served remains to be seen.

After the attack on the World Trade Center, the United States plunged with astonishing speed into a period of feverish patriotism. The words *At War* appeared in the *Times* 12 September 2001 headline. What transparency there had been in the U.S. media and in the criminal court system is rapidly being crowded out by yet another word wanga, the War on Terror. On a daily basis, irrational acts of war are being simultaneously revealed and concealed, justified and obscured, in the U.S. media and, at times, in its courts of law.

Notes

1   It was later revealed that the instrument that Volpe used to torture Abner Louima was actually the broken-off handle of a broomstick. The toilet plunger, nevertheless, continued to be mentioned in newspapers, and its image became the icon of the protest movement that developed out of this case of police brutality.

2   Most of those who serve the Vodou spirits also consider themselves to be good Catholics.

3   The most basic difference between *white magic* and *black magic*, as the terms are used in Haitian Vodou, is that the first is practiced for the good of the family or a larger community and that the second is about the pursuit of selfish and/or individualistic goals.

4   The *Haitian Times*, an English-language newspaper, started by former *New York Times* reporter Gary-Pierre Pierre, routinely refers to the "sodomizing" of Abner Louima.

5   In an article appearing on the *New York Times* website on 2 June 1999, David Barstow reported that Robert Volpe claimed that his son's trial was a "modern day lynching." Barstow quoted the senior Volpe as saying: "This was not an unprovoked situation. ... There was no innocence on the street that night." Barstow continued: "He said his son took Louima to the bathroom that night because he wanted to hit him, to continue the fight. After assaulting him with the stick, Officer Volpe, his father said, yelled, 'Look what you made me do' at Louima."

6   The oddness of this practice was apparent in a 10 January 2000 *New York Times* article, "Catholics Battle Brazilian Faith in 'Black Rome,' " in which the following sentence appeared: "Like Santeria in the Spanish-speaking Caribbean or voodoo in Haiti, Candomble merges the identities of African deities and Roman Catholic saints. ..." An

example of the usefulness of the generic *voodoo* comes from the 15 June 2000 edition of the *New York Review of Books*, which carried a full back-page ad for Robert Park's book *Voodoo Science: The Road from Foolishness and Fraud*, published by Oxford University Press. A "blurb" from Richard Dawkins promises that "Park does more than debunk, he crucifies. And the result is huge fun … . Not only will you enjoy reading it. You'll never again waste time or your money on astrologers, 'quantum healers,' homeopaths, spoon benders, perpetual motion merchants or alien abduction fantasists."

7   The low-budget film *Voodoo* released in the 1990s is a textbook example of the first part of the operation by which Europeans positioned Africans in relation to themselves, the one whereby all Africa-related religion becomes fetishism. Oddly enough, there are no black characters in this film, and an atmosphere of fear and dread is created entirely with drumming and quick glimpses of dolls, lighted candles, bits of rafia, and knotted pieces of rope—all the materials of wanga making. That is the only way in which anything connected to Vodou appears in the film that bears its name.

8   A fuller report from the Coroner's Office issued at a later date agreed with the first autopsy report that Diallo was fired on after he had been knocked down by police bullets.

9   According to Roosevelt Joseph, writing for the *Haitian Times* (22–28 March 2000), Dorismond, a twenty-six-year-old security guard, was shot to death by a member of NYPD's Gang Investigation Division. Dorismond, the son of a popular Haitian musician, had just left a midtown cocktail lounge when he was approached by an undercover policeman participating in a marijuana sweep. It was a "buy-and-bust" operation. The plainclothes officer asked Dorismond if he had drugs to sell. Dorismond said no, but the assumptions behind the approach angered him. There was a struggle, and the undercover agent's gun went off. Patrick Dorismond died from a single shot. He had no gun. Neither Police Commissioner Safir nor Mayor Giuliani went to his funeral. Quite the contrary, they went on the attack instead. Giuliani commented that Dorismond was "no altar boy" and instructed Safir to release his criminal record. Dorismond had two juvenile indictments for disorderly conduct. He did not go to jail for either. Both were resolved through plea bargaining.

References

Blier, Suzanne Preston. 1995. *African Vodun: Art, Psychology, and Power.* Chicago: University of Chicago Press.

Brown, Karen McCarthy. 1995. "Serving the Spirits: The Ritual Economy of Haitian Vodou." In *Sacred Arts of Haitian Vodou,* ed. Donald J. Cosentino, 205–23. Los Angeles: UCLA Fowler Museum of Cultural History.

Hurbon, Laennec. 1987. *Le barbare imaginaire.* New ed. Port-au-Prince: Henri Deschamps.

MacGaffey, Wyatt. 1993. *The Eyes of Understanding: Kongo Minkisi.* In *Astonishment and Power: Kongo Minkisi and the Art of Renee Stout,* 21–103. Washington, D.C.: National Museum of African Art, Smithsonian Institution.

Pietz, William. 1985. "The Problem of the Fetish I." *Res: Anthropology and Aesthetics* 9 : 5–17.

———. 1987. "The Problem of the Fetish II: The Origin of the Fetish." *Res: Anthropology and Aesthetics* 13 : 23–45.

———. 1988. "The Problem of the Fetish IIIa: Bosman's Guinea and the Enlightenment Theory of Fetishism." *Res: Anthropology and Aesthetics* 16: 105–23.

Toobin, Jeffrey. 2002. "The Driver: Did the Prosecutors in the Louima Case Have the Right Man All Along?" *New Yorker,* 10 June, 34–39.

Wexler, Anna. 2001. "Fictional Oungan: In the Long Shadow of the Fetish." *Research in African Literature* 32 (1): 83-97.

The Belief Machine

Chapters 1 and 2

By Richard Robbins

Chapter One: Introduction

He lay back, closing his eyes and breathing coolly through his nose. Then he said in somewhat oracular fashion: "Haven't you noticed Charlock that most things in life happen just outside one's range of vision? One has to see them out of the corner of one's eye. And any one thing could be the effect of any number of others? I mean there seem to be always a dozen perfectly appropriate explanations to every phenomenon. That is what makes our reasoning minds so unsatisfactory; and yet, they are all we've got, this shabby piece of equipment." He would doubtless have had more to say, but sleep gained on him steadily and in a while his mouth fell open and he began to snore. I slipped off the light and closed the door softly.

—Lawrence Durrell, *The Alexandria Quartet*

There is a problem central to the study of man that goes something like this: why is it that beings, virtually identical in physical makeup and equipped with the same perceptual and cognitive tools, have such different conceptions of what the world is really like? Why do some of these beings think the world is alive with spirits, while others look out on the same world and see only inert matter? Why are some people convinced that one group of human beings is innately superior to another, or that the future can be predicted by the proper study of the stars, while others are equally sure such notions are nonsense? Why do some people believe illness is caused by witchcraft or sorcery, while others claim illness is brought on by unseen micro-organisms? Why do some people believe objects or persons have mystical and magical properties, while others scoff at such ideas? And equally baffling, why do people tenaciously hold to their beliefs even when faced with experiences that contradict them?

The problem is not new. It is a puzzle that men and women in all epochs encountered whenever they met with new peoples and beliefs. Generally they had a ready solution to the dilemma: "We are right, they are mistaken." But why are so many people certain the universe they construe can be sustained, while that of others is so obviously in error? Even we, of course, feel that our beliefs about the world are the "correct" ones. As Barry Barnes puts it:

> ... there is an *obvious* rightness about our own world view. It seems, in some way, to mirror reality so straightforwardly that it must be a consequence of direct apprehension rather than effort and imagination. Conversely, alternative beliefs possess an obvious wrongness. The more natural our own perspective becomes, the more puzzling become the strange propositions of ancestors, aliens and eccentrics. How did such mistaken ideas come to be held? However have they remained uncorrected for so long? (Barnes 1974:2)

There is a tendency for us to think that what we know, what we perceive, is solely a function of two things: our cognitive tools—our senses—and the physical reality that provides the stimuli for the senses. What we fail to realize, what we find difficult to admit as human beings is that what we know is as much a function of our cultural and social setting as it is of our senses or the physical world outside us. As anthropologists have argued, human beings are active creators of their worlds, not simply passive receptors of experience. This book, then, is an attempt to provide a framework to understand how people construct the reality they inhabit, why there are so many different ways of interpreting experience, and why people are so certain their interpretations are correct.

To accomplish my purpose I need to make two sets of connections. First, I want to connect work that has been done in various fields of knowledge—anthropology, philosophy, sociology, history and psychology—to help understand how our social settings and patterns of relationships come to influence what we think and believe. The material in the book is not new; rather it is a compilation of the findings of philosophers, anthropologists, sociologists, historians and psychologists that bear on the cultural construction of reality.[1] Second, I want to try to make connections between a number of social and cultural phenomenon, especially between social forms, ideas, rituals, magic, science and technology. To help make these connections I propose to construct a belief machine. This belief machine is, of course, a totally imaginary device and will bear no resemblance to those "thinking machines" being built by specialists in artificial intelligence. Instead the belief machine is intended solely as a conceptual device for understanding the worlds that humans create and occupy.

A belief machine of the kind I have in mind must be capable of generating the sorts of beliefs we know people to hold, and convincing the user of the machine that the beliefs it generates are true renditions of reality. In its most basic sense, *the machine must convert experience into meaning.*

I am going to assume that for a machine to transform experience into meaning it must be capable of performing four separate operations. First, the machine must organize the input into workable units or modules by structuring experience into some manageable form. Second, the machine must be able to portray what it has organized; it must render to the user of the machine the meaning it generates. Third, the machine must have some type of feedback mechanism to correct for outputs that were unacceptable to the user. Finally, the machine must have a built in capability to select the unit or module through which the experience is structured.

I want to demonstrate that it is possible to imagine a device that is able to generate a variety of beliefs, give those beliefs the taken-for-grantedness quality that beliefs seem to have, protect the beliefs from being falsified, and commit the user of the machine to one particular point of view rather than another. Moreover, I am going to try to build this machine solely from social and cultural components and in such a way that it can function without reference to any external reality. The point is that, if such a device can be constructed, even in our imagination, and it is capable of generating all the beliefs we know people to hold, then we must seriously consider the idea that our view of the world is very much constrained by limits set by our social and cultural setting. We might begin by thinking of the belief machine like this:

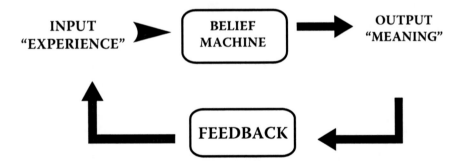

The building of the belief machine will proceed as follows. In the remainder of this chapter I want to examine more closely the two notions of "experience" and "meaning." In the next Chapter I want to identify the major components of the belief machine. I will be particularly concerned with the role of metaphor in belief, and how metaphors serve as organizing principles of thought. In Chapter Three I will examine the role of ritual, humor and magic in belief. Ritual, I will argue, plays the role of rendering to the user of the machine the meaning it generates. Moreover, through humor and magic, the meaning is rendered in such a way as to mask the fact that metaphor is not a perfect portrayal of experience. In Chapter Four I will turn to the feedback mechanisms that serve to reduce doubt and engender certainty when a belief has been called into question. Then in Chapter Five I will deal with the social and cultural factors that determine how the belief machine chooses among alternative meanings or convinces the user that the correct meaning has been chosen. Chapters Six and Seven will be reserved for examining some of the consequences of accepting the implications of the belief machine if it is to be constructed in the way I propose.

However before we begin constructing a belief machine, it is necessary to examine more critically the two most important aspects of the machine, the notions of experience and meaning.

The Three Paradoxes of Experience

How is the input of our belief machine to be received? What does the input consist of? Sir Ernest Gombrich supplies a provocative answer. When you look at an object, he says, you get a welter of dancing light points stimulating the sensitive rods and cones that fire the messages into the brain. What we see is a stable world. It takes an effort of the imagination and a fairly complex apparatus to realize the tremendous gulf that exists between the two (Gombrich 1959:45).

The actual world, as he puts it, "is a chaos of swirling impressions that never repeat themselves" (Gombrich 1959:45). Gombrich is dramatizing what we might call the three paradoxes of experience. The first paradox is that we receive far more experience through the senses than we are capable of assimilating. When you "look" out on the world your visual apparatus is flooded with stimuli. The tiny bones of the inner ear are constantly picking up what we call sounds, and our tactile senses are deluged with stimuli from the environment. Clearly, since we cannot possibly comprehend at any moment all the stimuli acting on us, we must be selective in the experience we attend to at any given moment.

The second paradox has even greater import. Since the set of stimuli we receive at any given moment is totally unique and unlike any other have received or will receive, then it follows that no experience we have is ever like any other experience. As Greek philosopher Heraclitus aptly put it, you cannot step twice into the same river. All experience is new experience. Yet we believe that some experience is the same, that we are the same people, or that our surroundings are the same.

The third paradox has to do with the fact that all of our experience is localized in or on our bodies. The things we "see" are simply sensations on the rods and cones of the eye; what we "hear" are vibrations of the bones of the inner ear; what we "feel" are pressures on the nerves on our skin. Yet the objects we see, the sounds we hear and the things we touch and feel seem to be "out there" away from and outside our bodies. It requires a certain act of faith to jump from the fact that our bodies feel, hear or see something to the fact that that objects or sounds are located away from us.

These paradoxes are plainly troublesome. A universe where everything changed at every instant and appeared as a chaotic flux and which seemed localized in our bodies, is intolerable for an organism that depends for survival on order, continuity and a belief in external reality. Stability, order and pattern must somehow be brought into the world; we must believe some things remain the same, that what we experience bears some relationship to what we have previously experienced, and that there is a world beyond the localized sensations we feel. And, of course, we are able to do this; the question is how?

One way to answer this question is to assume that when we have a new experience (and every experience is new), we make sense of it by consciously or unconsciously relating it to some prior experience we have had. In this regard the process of converting experience into meaning is essentially a process of interpreting the new according to the known.

Imagine discovering a new word, one whose meaning is unknown to you. The obvious thing to do is consult a dictionary. But a dictionary is useless in a world where everything is new. You would go to look up the meaning of the new word and discover all the words used to describe it were also new, and their meaning unknown. To discover the meaning of a new word, you must first know the meaning of at least some of the words used to describe it. You must first know something to know anything else. All knowing must proceed like this; a matter of interpreting the new according to the known.

Gombrich illustrates this nicely with an example from art. Figure 2 is a print from a sixteenth century woodcut of locusts.

56. ANONYMOUS: *Locust.* 1556. Woodcut

Figure 2

According to the artist, the drawing was "the exact counterfeit" of insects which swarmed into Europe. As any entomologist will tell you however, it is unlikely there was ever a prancing insect like the one in the drawing. Instead, the artist was influenced by previous drawings of locusts and the fact the archaic German word for locust is "heupferd" (hayhorse).

Or compare the rhinoceros in Figure 3 with the one in Figure 4. The animal in figure four was, according to the artist, "designed from the life"; that is done with a live model. It was more likely that the artist was influenced by past representations of a rhinoceros, such as the one in figure five by Durer, and by descriptions which likened the skin of a rhinoceros to armor.

59. DÜRER: *Rhinoceros.* 1515. Woodcut

60. HEATH: *Rhinoceros of Africa.* 1789. Engraving

Figure 3

Figure 4

The familiar, as Gombrich says,

> will always remain the likely starting point for the rendering of the unfamiliar: an existing representation will always exert its spell over the artist even while he strives to record the truth (Gombrich 1959:72).

Like the artist, all persons bring the past to bear on the present. We take the known and we use it to comprehend the new. Put another way, what we already know must play a role in what we see. In his book, *Patterns of Discovery: An Inquiry into the Conceptual Foundations of Science,* Norwood Hanson writes,

> Significance, relevance—these notions depend on what we already know. Objects, events, pictures, are not intrinsically significant or relevant. If seeing were just an optical-chemical process, then nothing we saw would ever be relevant to what we know, and nothing known could have significance for what we see. Visual life would be unintelligible; intellectual life would lack a visual aspect. Man would be a blind computer harnessed to a brainless photoplate (Hanson 1958:26).

It would seem, then that the first step in converting experience to meaning, taking the "chaos of swirling impressions" and from them constructing a meaningful world, is to seek relations between separate objects and events; the machine must seek similarities among unique experiences, and classify them together and make it seem each new experience is like some previous experience. This process is, of course, a relatively primitive one. All living organisms can make discriminations between objects, states or experiences and react to them accordingly. If you take an egg from a gulls nest, and place it a short distance away, the gull will not only roll the egg back to the nest, but also all roughly egg-shaped rocks in the same area. It perceives similarities among different objects.

There is another way of looking at how we translate our experience into a sense of an external world. There are two ways, says Michael Polanyi, that we are aware of things: one he calls "focal awareness", and the other he calls "subsidiary awareness." Imagine hammering a nail. Your direct experience consists of the pressure of the handle on the palm of your hand and the image striking the retina. Yet the head of the hammer and the head of the nail are "out there" at the spot where we bring the two together. For Polanyi our focal awareness is of the head of the hammer and the head of the nail. Our subsidiary awareness, however, is of the pressure on our palms and the image on the retina, or the flexing and extending of the muscles in our arm.

Or imagine holding a probe or stick; imagine you experience the outside world only through the probe. The feeling in your palm is the subsidiary through which you are aware of the chair touched by the probe. Yet you think you "feel" the chair at the end of the probe! Close your eyes and with a pen or pencil tap on a chair or table; you hear the tapping external to yourself, and feel the table *at the end* of the probe. *But the sensory experience is all localized in your body.*

Polanyi calls the relationship of the subsidiary to the focal point a "from-to" relationship. We go *from* the subsidiaries *to* the focal point. In essence, our focal awareness of the world is based on the subsidiaries we bring to it. We can destroy this relationship, and our focal awareness, by switching our attention to the subsidiaries through which we are aware of something. Close your eyes and strike the table or chair again with a pencil or pen, but this time focus your attention on the feeling of the pencil on your fingers or hand. When that feeling becomes the focal point, the table or chair "disappear", so to speak. Try to hit a nail with a hammer while focusing on the feeling of the hammer in your hand and the muscles contracting and expanding in your arm. You'll probably miss.

Polanyi says all our knowing is "from-to" knowing; we are aware of things—objects, persons, ideas, or rules—through subsidiaries such as sensory stimuli on our bodies or memories of past experiences that we bring with us to the act of knowing.

Thus, says Polanyi,

> The subsidiaries of from-to knowing bear on a focal target, and whatever a thing bears on may be called its meaning (Polanyi and Prosch 1975:35).

The artist who drew the rhinoceros "from the life" brought with him to the creative act, not only his perception of the animal, but also past representations he had seen, past descriptions he had heard, and probably a whole host of other subsidiaries, all merging into his drawing as a focal object. Our experiences can only be comprehensible through the subsidiaries that we bring to bear on those experiences.

We can represent from-to knowing in the following diagram:

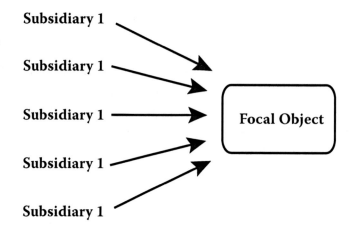

Polanyi's idea of from-to knowing has interesting consequences for the belief machine. First, since there must be many subsidiaries that we bring to bear on a focal object or experience, the machine must work a phenomenal transformation by fusing the subsidiaries into a focal object. Take a stereo-viewer. The focal image we see through it is a single three-dimensional picture, but the subsidiaries are two separate, two-dimensional pictures. The stereo-viewer has performed a phenomenal transformations; there is a new sense perception not contained in the two separate two-dimensional pictures.

> In this manner the meaning we see in nature has a new sensory quality not possessed by the sense perceptions from which it was tacitly created (Polanyi and Prosch 1975:35).

In addition, the subsidiaries that we bring to our knowledge of a focal object or experience are unspecifiable. This does not mean we cannot be focally aware of subsidiaries. However, it does mean that when we switch our awareness to the subsidiaries, as we did when we tapped the table with the probe, the original focal object disappears. We must, says Polanyi,

> distinguish between two types of unspecifiability of subsidiaries. One type is due to the difficulty of tracing the subsidiaries—a condition that is widespread but not universal: the other type is due to a sense deprivation which is logically necessary and in principle absolute (Polanyi and Prosch 1975:39).

To illustrate what Polanyi is saying, imagine your encounters with new words, that is words you don't know the meaning of. Take the word "rhadamanthine." If you don't know its meaning, it is itself a focal object. Now contrast your perception of "rhadamanthine" with familiar words. Take any word on this page, such as "illustrate." This word is itself a subsidiary you bring to bear on its meaning. Your familiar use of a word, your subsidiary use of it, renders it bodiless, says Polanyi; it becomes transparent. And it must, for if all words were focal objects, like "rhadamanthine," they would be unable to bear on and give meaning to the things they represent.

In sum, the paradoxes of experience must be overcome by some mechanism that allows us to select from our sensory intake a portion of the stimuli we receive, must make it seem that some experiences are like others, and must encapsulate the subsidiaries we bring to bear on focal objects. But if we need a mechanism to overcome the paradoxes of experience, what do we get when they are overcome?

Man, it seems, is distinguished by the ability to take experience and encode it into highly complex forms, and transfer these forms from one experience to another. These forms contain systems of relations that create a "connectedness" in the world. These forms encapsulate meaning. When something is meaningless, on the other hand, it lacks coherence or sense. Objects and events in a meaningless universe are isolated from each other, and enter no relationship with other objects or events. Objects or events in such a world are like a string of nonsense syllables none of which relates to any other. Meaning is the experience of connectedness. Things are seen as bearing some relation to each other and to other things. The relationship between things can be of different types; things or events may be similar to each other, may be physically bound together, may co-occur, have an affinity for each other, or call forth each other. Regardless, when things relate to other things we can say they are meaningful. Objects and events in a world with meaning are linked together in systems of relations. In a totally meaningful universe all things would be related to all other things.

We have, then, some general idea of what is required as a first step for a machine to convert experience into meaning, to take an input of essentially chaotic, bodily centered and non-repeating experience and convert it into an output in which things are connected or related to other things. The problem now is to find some organizing principle capable of working such a transformation.

Note

1. There are already some excellent works that try to make accessible to the general reader work on social construction of reality. One of the first is Emile Durkheim's classic work *The Elementary Forms of Religious Life*. Of the more recent works, especially noteworthy are the works of Peter Berger and Thomas Luckmann (1967), Barry Barnes (1974), David Bloor (1976), and Michael Kearney (1984).

Chapter Two: The Construction of the World

… we have come to think of our social and cultural world as a series of sign systems, comparable to languages. What we live among and relate to are not physical objects and events; they are objects and events with meaning; not just complicated wooden constructions but chairs and tables; not just physical gestures but acts of courtesy or hostility. If we are able to understand our social and cultural world we must think not of independent objects but of symbolic structures, systems of relations which by enabling objects and actions to have meaning, create a human universe (Culler 1977:100).

The Notion of Metaphor

Many terms have been used to label the subsidiaries, the "known," that we bring to each new experience to give it meaning: "schemata," "themata," "paradigm," "world vision," "world view," "model," "framework," and "theory" are just some of these labels. But, in the most rudimentary sense, all these things—schemata, theories, world visions, and the rest—are metaphors; like metaphors, we transfer theories and schemata, world visions and world views, paradigms and themata to experiential phenomena as our way of understanding the phenomena. When we say with the poets that "love is like a rose," the rose, as metaphor, is a concrete known through which we comprehend the notion of love. The rose is a paradigm, a theory. And in comparing love to a rose, not only does the abstract notion of love come into focus, but the rose itself becomes more clearly defined, in the same way that a theory changes each time it is applied to some new phenomenon (Black 1962).

Every theory, world view or paradigm contains assumptions about the way things or events relate to each other, and each is used to interpret and give meaning to the new. They all, in one way or another, encapsulate the subsidiaries we bring to bear on focal objects. All these things are, like metaphor, a way of moving from the known to the unknown,

> … a way of cognition in which the identifying qualities of one thing are transferred in an instantaneous, almost unconscious flash of insight to some other thing that is, by remoteness or complexity, unknown to us (Nisbet 1969:4).

Metaphors filter our experience. Suppose, Max Black says,

> I look at the night sky through a piece of heavily smoked glass on which certain lines have been left clear. Then I shall see only the stars that can be made to lie on the lines previously prepared upon the screen, and the stars I see will be seen as organized by the screen's structure. We can think of a metaphor as such a screen and the system of "associated commonplaces" of the focal world as the network of lines upon the screen. We can say that the principal subject is "seen through" the metaphorical expression—or, if we prefer, that the principal subject is "projected upon" the field of the subsidiary object (Black 1962:41).

Metaphors create meaning by embedding each experience into a system of relations that are like systems of relations we already know. By comparing love to a rose, the system of relations into which we place a rose (flower, fragrance, color, beauty) is the system of relations through which we comprehend love; or a system of relations through which we understand the movement of the planets, becomes the system of relations through which we understand the relationships of the parts of the atom to each other. But why use the metaphor as the basic component of the belief machine? Why not use another concept: world view, theory, model, or even culture? There are two reasons. First, others have already equated such things as theories, models or schemata with the concept of metaphor (see Barnes 1974:49). As early as 1940, Stephen Pepper was referring to "world hypothesis" as "root metaphors," and Mary Hesse (1963) has claimed that all theories are metaphors. But more importantly, the idea of metaphor more clearly calls attention to the central feature of the belief machine. Given that each experience we have must always be mediated by some previous experience, then it follows that there can never be a perfect fit between the new and the known. Metaphors are always different from the objects, events, or people they are brought to bear on. Love is not a rose. A person is not a fox. Time is not a river. No theory, model or paradigm can be the phenomena it is designed to comprehend. They can only be approximations of those phenomena. That is why our reasoning minds are so unsatisfactory. I choose the metaphor in part, then, because it better conveys this central feature of the belief machine.

Metaphor, then, will be the basic component of the belief machine. We will assume the metaphoric process is the central idea behind such notions as "theory," "schemata," "model," and "world view," and that it is the essential part of the process by which the belief machine converts experience to meaning. We are asking the metaphor to carry a heavy load. Generally metaphor is thought of mainly as verbal decoration, a vivid way of saying things. In the belief machine, however, we are assuming metaphor to be the basic component for converting experience to meaning.

For the remainder of this chapter I want to illustrate the power and elegance of metaphor as the fundamental component of the belief machine. I will first examine where our metaphors come from and the variety of things that can be used as a metaphor. Second, I want to demonstrate that metaphors have the power to make highly abstract ideas, such as "love," "time" and "space," concrete and understandable. Third, I want to show that metaphors are economical and efficient. Only a few metaphors are necessary to comprehend an enormous range of phenomena. Fourth, I will illustrate how metaphors guide our experience, and persuade us that the world is as the metaphor represents it. Five, I will show how metaphor gives us a feeling of power and control, and, finally, I will illustrate how metaphor has the power to "carry us away," to evoke powerful emotions.

The major point I want to make is that all of our thinking is metaphoric; I want to demonstrate that if we were to build a belief machine to convert experience into meaning, the machine could work on what we might call a metaphoric principle that holds that we need make no distinction between what is metaphoric and what is literal, and that, therefore, the machine can generate meaning without explicit reference to the structure of external reality. If we are to hold that beliefs can be explained solely on the basis of social and cultural factors, then demonstrating how metaphors function as the prime converters of experience into meaning is crucial.

The Availability of Metaphors

The things we use as metaphor are generally the things we know best. The human body is a good example. As a child matures, its body is the first thing it comes to know, and so it uses this known experience to comprehend each new experience. The infant learns about its mouth, genitals, hands, eyes, and what they do. The infant uses its instinctive grasping reflex to classify things into those that are graspable and those that are not. The innate sucking motion of the mouth can be used to order the universe into things that are suckable and things that are not. The body and its actions become a template, a coding device, a model of reality. Even as adults, of course, we speak of the "head" of state, the ruling "body," "hands" of justice, a "right-hand" man, or a "left-handed" compliment. We speak of the "foot" of the mountain, or the "shoulder" of the road. We can get something off our "chest," or get to the "heart" of things. Someone can be a "finger" man, or have a "nose" for news. The body, as a system of relations, is used as a device for assigning meaning to other things—people, actions or physical objects.

Virtually anything is capable of being used as a metaphor; in other words, anything we know can help us understand something new. Certain things, such as the automobile, the game of cricket, or the computer, are unique to certain cultures or times. Other things, such as the body, are probably used in all societies.

Some people claim that there are innate metaphors, forms for understanding we are born with. The archetype of Carl Jung is one example of an innate metaphor. The archetypes are contained in what Jung called the collective unconscious; all men are genetically programmed with certain basic experiences, and these are expressed in literature, art, and myth.

Up-down, light-dark, blood, water and the wheel are archetypal metaphors, according to Phillip Wheelright (1962:110). Rodney Needham says "percussion," like the beating of drums, has intrinsic meaning, perhaps because of analogy with the beating of the heart (Needham 1967). Robert Hertz (1960), in a classic essay, showed how common meanings attach to the left hand and the right hand in virtually all societies; the right hand tends to be associated with goodness, light, cleanliness and maleness, and the left with evil, darkness, dirt and femaleness.

Are certain things used as metaphor by all persons? The body is, as we've seen, an almost universally used metaphor. Stephen Pepper (1942:120) suggests that the body is the most appealing metaphor that has ever been suggested, and that to take the body, its shape, its actions, its expressions, and emotions is the most natural thing in the world.

The Dogon of the Sudan organize their entire village and buildings within as if they were human bodies. The village, for example, is supposed to extend from north to south as if it were a man lying on his back. The head of the village is the council house; to the east and west are houses for menstruating women that represent the hands of the village; the large family houses in the center represent the chest and belly of the village, while the communal alters at the south of the village represent its feet. In the middle of the village are stones on which certain fruits are crushed; these stones represent the female sexual parts.

> Beside them should be set the foundation alter, which is its male sex organ; but out of respect for women this alter is erected outside the walls (Griaule 1965:96–97).

The Dogon portray a granary as a woman lying on her back with her arms and legs raised to support the roof (the sky). The two legs that are on the north side and the door to the granary, that is at the sixth step, represent the female sexual parts (Griaule 1965:39).

Many of our traditional structures are conceptualized as a human body. The European Gothic cathedral was laid out in the shape of a human body, to represent Christ, with the nave as the body and the alter as the heart.

Herbert Spencer's late nineteenth century description of society as a body is one of the more elaborate examples of the use of the human body as metaphor; like the body, society exhibits augmentation of mass; it grows. Like the body, societies increase in structure as they increase in size.

> Further, in social organisms, as in individual organisms, differentiations cease only with that completion of the type which marks maturity and decay (Spencer 1961: 140).

Societies, like organisms, Spencer says, not only grow, divide and die, but, as with living things, exhibit a division of labor.

> As living organisms have different parts, so it is with the parts into which society divides. A dominant class arising does not simply become like the rest, but assumes control over the rest; and when this class separates into the more and less dominant, these, again, begin to discharge distinct parts of the entire control (Spencer 1961:140).

And, as different parts of an organism relate to and depend on other parts, so it is in society; if the lungs stop working, the heart stops. If the stomach fails, the rest of the body will soon die. If the eyes fail, the organism will soon stop functioning.

> And when, in a society, we see the workers in iron stop if the miners do not supply materials; that makers of clothes cannot carry on their business in the absence of those who spin and weave textile fabrics; that the manufacturing community will cease to act unless food-producing and food distributing agencies are acting; that the controlling powers, governments, bureaux, judicial officers, police, must fail to keep order when the necessities of life are not supplied to them by the parts kept in order; we are obliged to say that this mutual dependence of parts is similarly rigorous (Spencer 1961:141).

After the human body, the most common source of metaphor is the world of nature. It is easy to transfer systems of relations we know to exist in the natural world to some other system of relations we seek to understand.

Totemism, the identification of a social group with a plant, animal, or other feature of the natural world, is an almost universal use of metaphor. A clan is said to be associated with "crows," or the "white cockatoo," "bears" or the "moon." Totemic societies, those which name social groups after objects or beings in nature, are called by anthropologists segmentary societies. Each group with a totemic designation is structurally identical; each performs the same activities, produces the same goods and food, and has similar norms. Unlike societies where group differences are created by intrinsic features of the groups, such as castes, groups in segmentary societies have no intrinsic characteristic to differentiate it from other groups.

Claude Levi-Strauss says that if groups in segmentary societies are to interact with each other they need to be able to think of themselves as distinct entities. Since there is no structural feature to differentiate them, such as the objects they make, or activities they perform, they draw on nature, and transfer the differences they perceive in nature to differences they wish to create in society. Naming one group "the bears" and another "the lynx," effects a metaphorical transfer, and the relationship between the groups is thought to be the same as exists between the species in nature; the bear clan is to the lynx clan, as the bear is to the lynx.

But, according to Levi-Strauss, there is more. The animals used to differentiate groups are not randomly chosen; rather, they are selected because certain traits or behaviors of the animal resemble certain features of the group or characterize relationships between certain groups. When contact with Europeans resulted in individuals of mixed Ojibwa and European parentage, the Ojibwa grouped them into their own clan, the Pig clan, since the pig was an animal introduced by Europeans. The natives of the Torres Straits believed there existed a psychological and physical affinity between men and their totems, and believed men have an obligation to pursue the appropriate behavior. The Cassowary, Snake, Shark and Hammer-head shark clans were supposed to love fighting, while the Shovel-nosed Skate and Sucker-fish clans were peace loving. Members of the Dog clan were unpredictable, since dogs were supposed to be unpredictable. Members of the Cassowary clan were thought to have long legs and run fast, and members of the Crocodile clan were thought to be strong and ruthless (Levi-Strauss 1966:115–116).

In our culture, as James Fernandez notes, we are surrounded by machines, yet still draw from nature for metaphors. As he puts it:

> Since children in 20th-century urban America and Europe spend so much of their time identifying with machinery—themselves assuming the dynamics and making the power sounds as they push car and truck or plane around—it may be hard to convince a reader from such a culture of the importance of these animal metaphors and the primordial nature of the horse play. Since we are surrounded not by animals but by machinery, we may have forgotten man's close relation for millennia to animals, with which he has identified and from which he has learned. But the sense of this powerful source of identity and learning survives. We have only to think of how we surround our infants with stuffed animals and tell them animal stories; how we give them animal nicknames (tiger, kitten, little bear); how in rough-and-tumble with young children we play at eating them up or carrying them piggyback. The primordial metaphors are still there. We are still in some part being taught by the animals through identification with them (Fernandez 1974:121–122).

Sports teams in America often use nature metaphors. Football teams, like clans in segmentary societies, are structurally identical—they have the same number of players, require people to play similar roles, and have identical norms and goals. And, like clans, they sometimes draw from the animal kingdom to identify themselves. Consequently we have "tigers," "lions," "bears," "wolverines," "wildcats" and "mustangs." There is an attempt to transfer, not only the name, but also certain characteristics of the species; tigers are fierce, bears strong, and so on. We would be hard-pressed in America to find football teams with nicknames of "rabbits," "sheep," or "kittens."

As some societies have taken from the world of animals to organize experience, industrial societies take from the world of machines. The clock was probably one of the first machines to be widely used as metaphor in the Western world. The French philosopher Descartes, speculating about the relationship between God, man and the universe, suggested looking at the universe as a watch whose face was visible, but whose internal mechanisms were hidden. The most we could then say about the mechanism would be conjectural, since the watch might be constructed a number of ways. In this analogy, the scientist is like a skilled watchmaker who is given a watch, but cannot see its internal mechanism. He knows the general principles that govern his subject, but he is uncertain about precisely how it works. Consequently, we can "never get inside nature's clock to see if nature's mechanisms are what we think them to be" (Laudens 1966:77).

The clock was a wonderful spur to the imagination. Through some literary inventiveness it even became a euphemism for sexual intercourse. In Laurence Sterne's eighteenth century comic novel, The Life and Opinions of Tristram Shandy, the narrator could identify the day he was conceived because his father, a man of "punctilious regularity," always wound the family clock on the same day of the month he

> brought some other little family concernments to the same period, in order, as he would often say to my Uncle Toby, to get them out of the way at the same time, and be no more plagued and pestered with them the rest of the month (Sterne 1967 [1759-67]:39).

Because of the popularity of the novel, "winding the clock" became, in the latter half of the eighteenth century, a popular metaphor for sexual intercourse.

The development of the steam engine provided a rich store of metaphors. "Letting off steam," "safety valve," "working under pressure" are present-day survivals of the steam engine as a source of meaning. Later, with the advent of electrical power, we became "charged up" at "electrifying" events. Today with computers and the popularity of information theory it is common to use such terms as "input," "output" and "feedback." So once we know one system of relations, whether it be the human body, the world of nature or the world of machines, we can use it as a tool to understand other systems of relations.

It is evident that different cultures and epochs use the metaphors available to them; but are there a limited number of metaphors or types of metaphors that each culture has available to it? Lucien Goldmann, for example, says there are a limited number of "world visions," but we have not yet cataloged them (Goldmann 1964:20). And Gerald Holton (1972:29) asserts that there are a limited number of what he calls themata, and that while the range of experience and theory have multiplied, the themata used to comprehend this experience—metaphors of constancy and change, materialism, and mechanism, for example—have changed very little.

Since Parmenides and Heraclitus, the members of the thematic dyad of constancy and change have vied for loyalty, and so have, ever since Pythagoras and Thales the efficacy of mathematics versus the efficacy of materialistic or mechanistic models. The (usually acknowledged) presuppositions pervading the work of scientists have long included also the thematic couples of experience and symbolic formalism, complexity and simplicity, reductionism and holism, discontinuity and the continuum, hierarchical structure and unity, the uses of mechanisms versus teleological or anthropomorphic modes of approach. These, together with others. … —a total of fewer than fifty couples or triads—seem historically to have sufficed for negotiating the great variety of discoveries. Both nature and our pool of imaginative tools are characterized by a remarkable parsimony at the fundamental level, joined by fruitfulness and flexibility in actual practice.

According to Stephen Pepper, there have been in the history of ideas a limited number of what he calls "root metaphors" such as "mysticism," "animism," "formism," "mechanism," "contextualism" and "organicism." Formism, for example, uses as its "primitive root metaphor" the work of the artisan or workman making different objects on the same plan, the shoemaker using the same pattern to make shoes, or the potter using the same form to make his pots. Each thing that exists be it plant, tree, or person, develops according to some innate plan or form, and objects and events. In a world dominated by formism, objects and events are related to each other by their similarity to each other; all red things have some connection to each other, or all round things are somehow connected. Animism uses the human body as its primitive root metaphor, and things relate to each other as parts of the body relate to each other. Mechanism uses the machine as its basic metaphor, and things and events relate to each other as the parts of a machine relate to each other. According to Pepper, each culture draws its distinctive style from the root metaphor or metaphors it uses.

Metaphors and the Transition from the Abstract to the Concrete

Metaphors are capable of giving meaning to highly abstract notions such as love, time and space. Robert Solomon, in his book Love: Emotion, Myth and Metaphor, describes some of the metaphors we use to give meaning to the idea of "love." There is the economic metaphor of love as fair exchange; love is an economic partnership in which each partner gives something in exchange for something; love is a tradeoff of interests and concerns, particularly approval: "I make you feel good about yourself and in return you make me feel good about myself" (Solomon 1981:17).

Or love can be something you "work at":

> Love, according to the work model, gets evaluated above all on its industriousness, its seriousness, its success in the face of the most difficult obstacles. Devotees of the work model not infrequently choose the most inept or inappropriate partners,

rather like buying a run-down-shack—for the challenge. They will look with disdain at people who are merely happy together (something like buying a house from a tract builder). They will look with admiration and awe at a couple who have survived a dozen years of fights and emotional disfigurements because "they made it work" (Solomon 1981:19).

Then there is the dramatic model where love is theatre and melodrama. Or there is the communication metaphor where love is understood as "getting through to each other," or a matter of self-expression. And we can use a medical model for love; a lack of love, as some psychologists contend, may cause sickness, or love itself, as some feminists argue, can be a pathological condition, or a "search for self-annihilation." Not surprisingly, says Solomon, many of today's books on love are written by doctors and psychiatrists (Solomon 1981:25–26).

Time is another highly abstract notion difficult to conceptualize. Yet we can make it meaningful by associating it with a familiar area of experience. For example, since we can look at love as an economic commodity, why not do the same with time? Time is money; "You're wasting my time," "This gadget will save you hours," "I don't have the time to give you," "That flat tire cost me an hour," "You need to budget your time," "Is that worth your while?," "He's living on borrowed time;"

Time in our culture is a valuable commodity. It is a limited resource we use to accomplish our goals. Because of the way that the concept of work has developed in modern Western culture, where work is typically associated with the time it takes and time is precisely quantified, it has become customary to pay people by the hour, week, or year. In our culture TIME IS MONEY in many ways: telephone message units, hourly wages, hotel room rates, yearly budgets, interests on loans, and paying your debt to society by "serving time." These practices are relatively new in the history of the human race, and by no means do they exist in all cultures. They have arisen in modern industrialized societies and structure our basic activities in a very profound way (Lakoff and Johnson 1980:8).

Time can also be represented as straight line, or as a cyclical movement of heavenly bodies. Edmund Leach maintains that some societies represent time as an oscillation between polar opposites such as night and day, winter and summer, drought and flood, life and death. These metaphors of oscillation imply a third element, the thing that oscillates. For example, in some societies time is represented by a soul which moves from one world to another and back again. To the Greeks the soul was thought of as a material substance (much the same as we view a clock as a material representation of time), and time was represented as the oscillation of the soul between life and death. Since the Greeks believed the soul was concentrated in the male semen, time was therefore associated with sexual intercourse:

[When] the Greeks conceived the oscillations of time by analogy with the oscillations of the soul, they were using a concrete metaphor. Basically it is the metaphor of sexual coitus, of the ebb and flow of sexual essence between sky and earth (with the rain as semen), between this world and the underworld (with marrow-fat and vegetable seeds as semen), between man and woman. In short, it is the sexual act itself which provides the primary image of time. In the act of copulation the male imparts a bit of his life-giving soul to the female; in giving birth she yields it forth again. Coitus is here seen as a kind of dying for the male; giving birth as a kind of dying for the female. Odd though this symbolism may appear, it is entirely in accord with the findings of psychoanalysts who have approached the matter from quite a different point of view (Leach 1979:224).

Or, finally, take our conception of space. Here we have another highly abstract notion which can only be comprehended by something other than itself. In a wonderful book, Physics as Metaphor, Roger Jones examines the metaphors we use to understand such concepts as space. We see it as a void to be filled by concrete objects; it is like an empty room where we put discrete but separate objects such as tables, chairs or pictures. This is not, however, the only way to conceptualize space. In the Aristotelian universe of medieval times, space was not an empty void; it was full of essence which connected all things to each other.

It is difficult for us to conceive of space as other than an empty void to which the laws of perspective can be applied, and this has led us to believe that there is something objective or absolute about our spatial notions. But the preeminence of our own view is not so difficult to challenge if we look at the art forms, belief patterns, and languages of societies remote from ours in time, place or experience. For example, to the mind of medieval people, space did not have the cold, empty, geometric character that it has for us. We experience ourselves as an isolated, disconnected entity in a vast, empty void. But medieval people felt more a part of their surrounding environment. They felt a kind of extra-sensory, but conscious connection to the plants and animals around them, to the heavenly objects, to the very elements and minerals of the earth itself. We tend to dismiss such experiences as primitive or misguided (Jones 1982:59).

Yet we misinterpret the medieval experience. A man born under Mercury who feels an affinity for the planet and the substance mercury on earth does not feel these things as forces acting at a distance. They are part of him, and contained within him. As Owen Barfield said, "the man of the Middle Ages was rather less like an island, rather more like an embryo, than we are" (quoted from Jones 1982:60).

Jones also asks the question of why we think of space as an empty void full of discrete, but isolated objects. He suggests it a consequence of our social experience. Our metaphor for space embodies our own experiences of separation, distinction, differentiation and identity. Our social experience leads us to emphasize distance, because we cannot distinguish and identify things that overlap. A fundamental physical law, for us, is that two things cannot occupy the same place at the same time. This is the essence of our spatial metaphor. But, says Jones, it is not "space" itself that suggests this idea; it is our social experience that gives meaning to this idea of space:

The laws of perspective and of geometry for us are a codified summary of our normal experience of alienation, unique identity, and unrelatedness. It has all been abstracted, externalized, and synthesized into the cold, empty void we call space. But it is all our own doing and the result of idolizing our creation. Yet we continue to believe that space is simply there independent of us, and so it always was and always will remain (Jones 1982:61).

The Economy of Metaphor

Economy is a basic requirement of the central component of a belief machine. Since each experience we have is unique, each metaphor must be capable of assimilating and organizing a vast number of experiences. If we were not able to use one metaphor to understand others, we would need a unique vocabulary for every metaphor, and either a vast vocabulary of elementary terms, or an incredible elaboration of composite terms (Goodman 1976:80). But the metaphor, as Nelson Goodman points out, is wonderfully economical. Since we are able to transfer metaphors from one domain to another—animals to groups, economic activities to emotions, biological activities to time—we can cope with a limited vocabulary and a limited stock of metaphors. It is theoretically possible that with deep knowledge of only one system of relations, one set of metaphors, we would be able to cope with an infinite range of experience. Most of the Bible is probably comprehensible to a person whose sole store of metaphors is taken from herding sheep.

Common things such as houses or shelters are capable of organizing all kinds of experience. We think of houses as utilitarian objects, when, in fact, they are rich sources of meaning. The houses of the Atoni of Indonesia are literally models of their cosmos. The "right-side" and "left-side" of an Atoni house corresponds to a division of the world into male and female. The door to the house is always oriented to the south, a direction the Atoni call ne'u (right); a porch-like section is attached to this side of the house and is associated with men. It is here the men eat and receive visitors.

The left side of the house is associated with women and women's activities. The naming of houseparts, such as roof spars and houseposts, follow the same right-left division. The left (women) is always subordinate to the right (men). The roof is associated with the ancestors because of its height. In sum, the Atoni house is a metaphorical encapsulation of the entire Atoni universe. The house, is a kind of mechanical model of the cosmos as conceived by the Atoni. Their notions of social and political order are encapsulated in their homes; the Atoni dwell in their cosmos.

However the references extend beyond the social order: space, time, man and animals, man and plants, man and the supernatural are conceived to be ordered by principles related to those expressed in the house (Cunningham 1972:134).

Americans, like the Atoni, use living quarters as vehicles of understanding. The house is a metaphor for the family. We speak of creating a family as "making a home together"; a wife was a "homemaker" or "housewife," while the term "homewrecker" is used for a person who threatens the sanctity of the family.

The classic "two-story" American house consisted of systems of relations used to give meaning to social relations in the family. The "den"—an interesting animal metaphor—is associated with the male of the family, while the kitchen is female. Consequently the relationship between husband and wife is like the relationship between the den and the kitchen. Like the Atoni, Americans set aside a section of the house for entertaining, and in doing this conceptualize a division between relations within the family, and external relations.

In cross-section, the classic American house—to the extent we can talk of a typical house—seems a representation of the Christian cosmos. The two main floors are divided into public and private functions, and devoted to the activities of everyday living—eating, sleeping, or socializing. The basement, since it is "underground," "dark" and "crypt-like" is where we place the fires of the furnace, family bar and other recreational, items of pleasure and perhaps sin. The attic, the summit of the house, is where we, like the like the Atoni, store old objects and family heirlooms—things of the ancestors.

It may be argued, of course, that these patterns of use reflect utilitarian concerns; we store valuable objects in the attic because it is dry, and basements are convenient places to put furnaces because they need to be supplied with oil or coal. Nevertheless, like the Atoni house, the American house is a source of order and pattern. It is a source of metaphor, and, consequently, of meaning.

The Dinka of the Sudan provide us with one of the best examples of how a single metaphorical domain can be used to encapsulate a vast range of experience. The Dinka are cattle herders, and most of their lives center on their animals. Every Dinka cow or bull is described by a composite name which indicates the color, sex, and stage of maturation of the animal, and these terms are used to describe all sorts of experience. Lienhardt says the Dinka would be lost without cattle terms to describe all sorts of visual experience. Their very perception of color, he says, is inextricably linked to their recognition of color-configurations in their cattle. Without their cattle-color vocabulary, says Lienhardt, the Dinka would have no way of describing visual experience in terms of color, light and darkness (Leinhardt 1961:12–13). The color white is taken from the term used to describe the white of cattle; a spotted pattern, such as of a leopard, is called after the spotted cow.

The Dinka also use their cattle as a means of comprehending people. Boys take the color names of oxen when they reach manhood and are called by these ox-names by intimate friends and agemates. It would be like us calling our friends by the colors of our favorite automobiles.

A man's metaphorical ox-name in not expected to refer directly to anything in his personal appearance, though in some cases, especially in the ox-names given to Europeans, a distinctive feature of the appearance may be seized upon for inclusion in the total association of perceptions of the ox-name. In songs the same man may be given several metaphorical ox-names, perhaps derived from oxen of colours and configurations which he has never owned. The object is praise to him. A Dinka's self-esteem and standing in the community are intimately bound up with cattle in this way (Lienhardt 1961:16).

Cattle are also used to comprehend the structure of Dinka society; the system of relations making up the body of the animal are used to give meaning to the relations among men:

Perhaps the clearest example of the way in which cattle represent not only human beings but human relationships may be seen in the division of the sacrificial meat when a beast is killed. "The people are put together as a bull is put together" said a Dinka chief on one occasion. It will be seen from the plan of the division [Figure 6] when it has been sacrificed, most

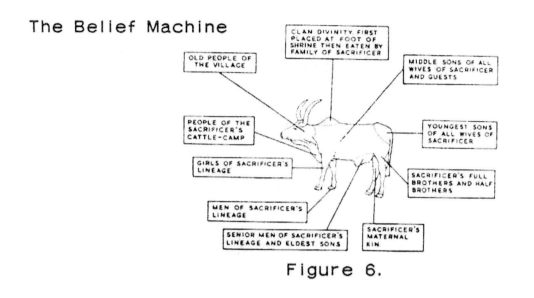

The Belief Machine

CLAN DIVINITY, FIRST PLACED AT FOOT OF SHRINE THEN EATEN BY FAMILY OF SACRIFICER

OLD PEOPLE OF THE VILLAGE

MIDDLE SONS OF ALL WIVES OF SACRIFICER AND GUESTS

PEOPLE OF THE SACRIFICER'S CATTLE-CAMP

YOUNGEST SONS OF ALL WIVES OF SACRIFICER

GIRLS OF SACRIFICER'S LINEAGE

SACRIFICER'S FULL BROTHERS AND HALF BROTHERS

MEN OF SACRIFICER'S LINEAGE

SENIOR MEN OF SACRIFICER'S LINEAGE AND ELDEST SONS

SACRIFICER'S MATERNAL KIN

Figure 6.

of it is divided according to the division of groups within a kinship system, leaving some over for the community in general, distinguished according to sex and age (Lienhardt 1961:23).

Cattle are also used to express legal transactions between people, and as a standard of value. All important transactions and acquisitions are expressed in terms of cattle (Lienhardt 1961:24).

We see, then, the economy of metaphor. It takes knowledge of few systems of relations contained in a metaphor for the belief machine to be able to assign meaning to the infinite diversity of our experiences.

Metaphors Direct Meaning in Certain Directions

Metaphors also determine how we view phenomena; they define the context of our experience. The use of one metaphor instead of another leads you to certain conclusions about an experience that another metaphor might not. Compare the view of the world from the perspective of an animate universe with that of a mechanistic universe. In medieval times the world was thought of differently; it was alive, it was not a machine. Consequently the meaning assigned to objects was different. Chemistry in the fourteenth century, for example, as Ludwik Fleck tells us, operated in a world very different from our mechanistic universe. In the medieval world metals were thought of as suns and moons, kings and queens, red bridegrooms and lily brides. Gold was the God Apollo, silver was Diana chasing Apollo through celestial groves. Quicksilver was mercury, Iron the ruddy-eyed Mars. Lead was Saturn, tin the Diabolus Metallorum (Fleck 1978 [1935]:125).

Contrast these metaphors of metals with our mechanistic systems of relations. Instead of the personalized things of the medieval world, metals are structures composed of tiny, inert molecules linked in characteristic ways to each other. Contrast also the seventeenth century view of the human skeleton with a nineteenth century version (Figure 7). The seventeenth century skeleton was alive, showing emotions of contemplation and grief. The nineteenth century skeleton is a mechanical structure like the superstructure of a building or a machine. Thus each age has its dominant metaphors to give a distinctive meaning to the universe it constructs.

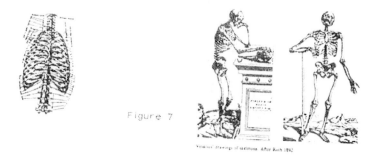

Figure 7

Versalius' drawings of skeletons. After Roth 1992

Using Stephen Pepper's idea of root metaphor, compare a formistic universe with a mechanistic universe. For example, the statement "smoking causes cancer" makes sense in a mechanistic universe where the body is treated like a machine, and a substance (e.g. tars and nicotine) can have a direct effect on the "parts" of the machine. It makes little sense, however, in a formistic universe which seeks similarities among things that relate to each other, for what is the similarity between a cigarette and cancer? In a formistic world an illness is more likely to be caused by something similar to the illness or the symptoms of the illness. In a formistic universe coming into contact with something yellow might cause jaundice, and something red (or associated with red) might cause fever.

The connections we create in a mechanistic universe can be highly complex and involved. The association of smoking and cancer, for example, is a complicated example of co-occurrence involving a complex mechanistic scheme of cellular disruption and breakdown. But relations of similarities can be equally involved.

The Dinka organize themselves into clans, each of which is named after some plant or animal that is considered the clan divinity or guardian. Members of one of these clans, the Pajieng, were referred to as "shit" because of an elaborate system of association by similarity. The black cobra is one divinity of the Pajieng clan. It is a deadly snake and the Dinka regard its bite as inevitably fatal. Consequently, the Dinka associate the snake with night-witches who use blood and venom to kill their victims. The black cobra is associated with witches also because as the snake sheds and leaves its skin only to appear again and claim new victims, the witch is thought also to be able to renew itself and return to cause further injury. One of the signs of witchcraft is human excrement left at night in a homestead. To excrete in a homestead is a singularly unpleasant act among the Dinka, and is thought to be the kind of thing that witches do. Hence the association excrement=witches=black cobra, and the idea that excrement may be the divinity of a clan associated with the black cobra.

The metaphors we use define the limits of the possible and the impossible. Metaphors not only associate things in systems of relations, but they also define the nature of the association. To say "smoking causes cancer" in a society dominated by formistic metaphors makes no sense, while the idea of eating a red berry to cure fever is equally nonsensical in a mechanistic world. In each case the nature of the system of relations will not allow that type of connectedness.

In America today, sports events are gigantic public spectacles and rituals; 100,000,000 people watch a Super Bowl or World Series. And sports have contributed to the meaning we assign to experience by supplying a rich supply of metaphors. And since these things are contests, our lives become contests. American business has made football a private metaphorical preserve. Businessman speak of "team effort," admire people who can "take the ball and run with it," and not "fumble" their opportunities. Vince Lombardi, the famous American football coach and cult hero, made films for businessman drawing analogies between success in football and success in business sales and management. One football fan referred to cancer as a "15 yard penalty," and a minister, giving the eulogy at the funeral of a famous baseball player, gave meaning to his death by saying "he was rounding third and coming home."

The important thing in all this is that the metaphor we select determines the way we think of things. Take our idea of "argument" for example. We use expressions such as "His point was right on target," "Your claims are indefensible," "He attacked my argument," "I had to defend my position," "He shot down my argument" or "I think I won the argument." Argument, in effect, is seen as akin to war. We don't simply talk about argument in terms of war, we actually win and lose arguments (Lakoff and Johnson 1980:4). What would happen if, instead of metaphors of war, we used metaphors of dance to comprehend argument. Instead of two protagonists in a win or lose situation, we have two partners trying to coordinate their movements to arrive at a mutual accommodation?

Let's combine the world of sport with the medieval universe to illustrate further how metaphor guides our perception of things . Take a baseball player and an astrologer. Each has an encounter with a member of the opposite sex. The shortstop might say; "I met a girl, I thought she'd play ball, and that I'd not only get to first base, but score; but I struck out." The astrologer, on the other hand, describing the same event, would put it differently: "I met a girls, I thought we'd be Leo and Cancer, that we'd be in conjunction, and she would be the sun to my moon, but our stars were crossed." The differences between the two descriptions of the same event involve more than a simple difference in language. The use of different metaphors assigns a different meaning to the event. The shortstop, using a metaphor common to American youth, sees the experience as an encounter, a contest to be won or lost, and a way of demonstrating proficiency. The astrologer, on the other hand, sees the meeting as a fated, predetermined event; it does not involve winning or losing but rather the discovery of pre-existent compatibilities.

The metaphor we use to assign meaning to experience highlights certain features of a phenomenon, and obscures or even ignores others. This is what Spencer did when he used the living organism as a metaphor for society. The use of the organistic metaphor focused attention on certain features of society: the interrelation of parts, the division of labor, the hierarchy of control, the phenomena of growth and decline. However the use of the organistic metaphor suppressed other features of society: the positive function of conflict, or the advantages of institutional autonomy. Instead of comparing society to a living organism, we could, as other sociologists have done, compare society to theater, to a play in which people play "roles" and "present selves." The dramaturgical metaphor shifts our attention from society as a whole to the individual "actors." Or, like Rousseau, imagine the relations among people as "social contracts," as, perhaps, in a business organization, where the fixed and rigid relations among people implied by Spencer's metaphor are replaced by individually negotiated "pacts" and "agreements." As you can see, there is a great difference assuming that each person is a cell in a living organism rather than of an actor or actress in a cosmic play.

Metaphors have the Power to Evoke Strong Feelings

Metaphors give a feeling of power and control. If we have a thorough understanding of one system of relations—say baseball, business, or nature—we can use it to comprehend a system of relations we only begin to grasp, and, as a result, we get a feeling of security, well-being and power. Simply by naming features of a new experience, we fix and control that experience. In every instance of the use of known metaphor to interpret a new experience there is a transition from helplessness to power. Where something was puzzling, it suddenly becomes clear (Schon 1963:60).

This flash of creative insight provided by metaphor is illustrated nicely by Friedrich August von Kekule's discovery of the chemical structure of benzene. One afternoon in 1865, after puzzling over the nature of benzene, he fell asleep in front of his fire. Soon, he said,

> the atoms were gamboling before my eyes. This time the smaller groups kept modestly in the background. My mental eye, rendered more acute by repeated visions of this kind, could now distinguish larger structures, of manifold conformation; long rows, sometimes more closely fitted together; all twining and twisting in snakelike motion. But look! What was that? One of the snakes had seized hold of its own tail, and the form whirled mockingly before my eyes. As if by a flash of lightning I awoke. … (quoted in Koestler 1964:118).

This vision suggested to Kekule that the molecules of certain organic compounds were not open strings, but closed chains or rings—like a snake swallowing its tail.

But the metaphor does even more than give us a sense of power; it can take us places we had no idea we were going. When we create a metaphor, says Israel Scheffler, we often surprise ourselves at the meanings which emerge; the maker of the metaphor does not have the special key to its meaning or use. Instead the use of metaphor is an invitation to find new meanings. In using a metaphor, the scientist, such as von Kekule, forges relationships that may lead us to rethink old concepts in new ways; we begin to think of the mind as an electronic computer or black holes as vacuum cleaners.

Whether the task is to incorporate the novel or reorganize the familiar, metaphor serves often as a probe for connections that may improve our understanding or spark theoretical advance (Scheffler 1979:129–130).

Transferring a system of relations from one domain to another gives us a sense of well-being in another way. If something we know well is used to understand something we do not know well, the new phenomena will already have some of the familiarity of the known metaphor. John Ziman speaks of this in regard to the use of models in science. When we take a model or metaphor from one domain, and apply it to another, it brings with it a certain pre-existing understanding. The Rutherford-Bohr picture of the atom as a system of electrons orbiting a nucleolus owes its strength not only to classical physics, but also to our familiarity of such a system in astronomy. Our metaphors contain a good deal of intuitive and experiential understanding.

> It would be difficult, even now, to give a precise logical definition of Darwin's model of interspecific competition as the motive force of organic evolution. This model derived its explanatory power from the fact that its audience was familiar with industrial and social competition, of which many characteristic features could be grasped and compared with biological phenomena without formal demonstration or proof ... (Ziman 1978:23–24).

The fact that our metaphors contain elements of personal experience explains why metaphors have, as Michael Polanyi says, "the capacity to carry us away."

Let me illustrate with an event which occurred in the Southern United States a couple of years ago. The account is taken from the *New York Times*;

> Years of racial animosity in the Florida panhandle city have erupted into violence in recent weeks on the issue of whether athletic teams at the local high school will be called 'Rebels' or 'Raiders'. The controversy over the name, simmering for several years in and out of court, caused a riot as Escambia County High School February 5. Subsequently, crosses were burned in the yards of school board members, a shot was fired through the window of a black member and the homes of a human relations board member and a state legislator were burned by arsonists ... . Four students were hit by gunfire in the school riot, 26 others were injured and $5,000 damage was done to the school during four hours of fighting, rock throwing, and smashing windows, trophy cases, and other school property ... . Some three-quarters of the school's 2,523 students were involved ... . The school riot occurred as the result of a school election the day before on whether to change the nickname of the athletic teams from the Raiders back to their old name, the Rebels. The nickname Rebels, chosen by the students when the school was built in 1958, and used thereafter, first became the focus of racial trouble in 1973 when black students, attending the school under a court ordered desegregation plan since 1969, protested that the name, along with the Confederate flag, flown at games and other school functions, was a direct insult to blacks. Several fights and protests resulted from the controversy, and on July 24, 1973, a United States District Court permanently enjoined the use of the name, the flag and related symbols on the grounds they were 'racially irritating'. Students subsequently chose the name Raiders as their nickname. However the school board and a group of white students appealed the court order and on January 25, 1975, the

United States Court of Appeals overturned the injunction and returned the matter to the school board to make its own decision in the matter.

Of course there is more than a name involved in this dispute. The metaphor "Rebel" contains all sorts of subsidiary meanings for both sides in the dispute. To one group it carries the meanings "pride," "manhood," "honor," "whiteness." To others, however, the nickname fused notions of "oppression," "slavery," "white supremacy," and "shame." The subsidiaries packed into the term include personal ones; each black in Escambia County High School could bring some personal experience to bear on the term, as each of us does when we draw from a familiar metaphor. As a result, metaphor embodies us in itself, moves us deeply as we surrender ourselves to it. Each metaphor we use carries a host of subsidiaries we bring to bear on an object of experience, and some of these subsidiaries are personal, and, as Michael Polanyi points out, unspecifiable.

The Defects of Metaphor

There is, I think, a compelling case to be made that the metaphoric process is at the heart of the way we create meaning. This does not mean that what we "see" is determined by metaphor, but that the meaning of what we see is determined by the system of relations in which we imbed what we see. We may all see an apple fall off a tree (although this statement is already full of metaphoric assumptions), but the meaning we give to that experience is very different if, like the ancient Greeks, we see the apple as an animate object seeking it rightful place in the world, instead of seeing the apple as an inanimate object affected by an external force called gravity.

Nevertheless, while it may be compelling to see the metaphor as the major component of our belief machine, the metaphor is, in many ways, an unsatisfactory device to organize experience. Like any classificatory process, the use of metaphor is selective, it loses information by channeling our understanding in some directions and away from others. If John is a "wolf," he is not a "tiger" or "pussycat"; to the extent argument is war it is not a dance; and to the extent an encounter with the opposite sex is a game, it is not a seeking of compatibilities. Our metaphors allow us to see some things, and leave us blind to others. The "point of view" is an intrinsic part of every act of knowing.

In addition, metaphors are absurd. A man is not a fox, a family is not a house, a football is not a bomb, and the human brain is not a computer. Meaning generated by the metaphor process is always imperfect. Since the known is never the same as the new, since no metaphor, no system of relations, can ever be exactly like the experience it seeks to understand, the meanings generated by the belief machine must always be potentially ambiguous, anomalous, or puzzling. There must be always the potential for conflict and doubt.

Nor is there any way of reducing the potential for ambiguity and anomaly in belief by checking a metaphor against reality, since, for a metaphoric view of belief, there can be no valid distinction between the metaphoric and the literal. There is no way of getting outside a metaphorical representation of reality, so to speak, in order to see things "as they are." In this sense a metaphor is not simply a tool to help us understand things, or a rhetorical device to enliven our language. The metaphor is the very stuff from which meaning is created. To the extent that our metaphors are ambiguous, vague or anomalous, so, too, are the meanings created by the metaphors. The difference between the literal and the metaphorical, as Barry Barnes (1974:53–54) points out, is simply a matter of social convention, and of what is institutionalized and what is not. This has an important implication for our idea of "truth," as Donald Schon realizes:

> Contemporary philosophy would like to say that a statement is true if and only if it asserts what is the case. But this assumes a univocal, literal relationship between the statement and some state of affairs; that is a single literal meaning theory for all statements as well as words. But a metaphor cannot be "true" in this way. All metaphors are in one sense false, in fact absurd. ... In the sense in which we believe the statement is not absurd, it may be believable. But in this sense it is also far from univocal. Metaphors are subject, with equal appropriateness, to an indefinite number of interpretations. ... In short, if there are no literal statements, there is no literal truth (Schon 1963:50).

From the perspective of a metaphorical view of knowledge, truth is not something objective and absolute. Instead truth is a function of our conceptual system, of our point of view, and of the metaphors through which we construe experience. In fact the idea of absolute truth in a world given meaning by metaphor is a dangerous one. George Lakoff and Mark Johnson in their book, Metaphors We Live By, vividly describe the consequences of the idea that we can discover some absolute, objective truth:

> We believe that the idea that there is an absolute objective truth not only mistaken but socially and politically dangerous. ... truth is always relative to a conceptual system that is defined in large part by metaphor. Most of our metaphors have evolved in our culture over a long period, but many are imposed upon us by people in power—political leaders, religious leaders, business leaders, advertisers, the media, etc. In a culture where the myth of objectivism is very much alive and truth is always absolute truth, the people who get to impose their metaphors on the culture get to define what we consider to be true—absolutely and objectively true (Lakoff and Johnson 1980:159–160).

The idea that the major process through which we create meaning is inherently flawed raises the question of why is it that sometimes people are aware of these flaws and other times not. How are the ambiguities inherent in any system of beliefs masked; how does the belief machine create certainty and alleviate doubt?

Put another way, while we might not accept all the meanings generated by the belief machine, we at least accept some. But if the ones we accept are as potentially absurd as the ones we reject, how are we able to maintain them? How is it that we come to accept one meaning as literal truth, and reject others as false and nonsensical? And what happens when a meaning that we have accepted as truth suddenly is called into doubt? How does the machine deal with that?

To sum up, at this point let us assume that our belief machine looks something like this:

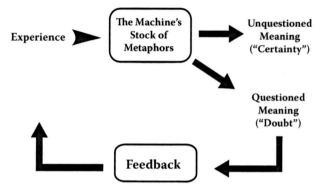

Experience flows into the machine, is assigned a metaphor that creates meaning. The meaning may be unquestioned (creating certainty), or it may be questioned (doubt), in which case it is fed back into the machine through a feedback device. The goal of the machine is to produce certainty and alleviate doubt.

If one accepts a metaphorical view of knowledge (and it is difficult to comprehend what another conception would be), then one must accept the fact that there are problems with a belief machine constructed of metaphors. Yet a belief machine must convince its user that the meaning it generates is an accurate rendition of experience. It must give reality the taken-for-grantedness quality that it must have.

There are two questions, then, that will set the agenda for the next two chapters: first, if we assume that every meaning generated by the belief machine is, in essence, absurd, how can certainty be created? Second, what happens when there is doubt, and why does it arise?

Chapter Two

The Nature of Culture

Science as a Cultural Process

By Sidney Greenfield

I n his classic study *The Structure of Scientific Revolutions*, the late Thomas Kuhn (1970:3–4) asks how someone ignorant of the history of science would examine electrical or chemical (or other) phenomena if inclined to do so. "What must the world be like," he queries in his closing argument, "in order that man may know it?"

To anthropologists, the answer is found in symbolism. That is, it calls for the formulation of a mental picture, expressible in words that order representations of what the world is like. Alternative images are possible. The specifics of any one image selected serve as the building blocks on which an understanding of the chemical, electrical, or other phenomena can be developed. Since people other than scientists are curious about the world around them, they too must develop a mental picture or symbolic model that will enable them to explore, analyze, and eventually gain an understanding of the events they experience and the phenomena they encounter. Science, as we have become increasingly aware, is a cultural process. Acknowledging this enables us to treat the doing of science as comparable to, and illustrative of, our understanding of other forms of cultural practice. Furthermore, it enables us to separate persons seeking to understand the world into two categories: 1) scientists and scholars; 2) at least some of those they study (Greenfield and Droogers 2003:32).

To satisfy their curiosity about aspects of the world they encounter, actors in both categories develop models that, when elaborated and tested over time, form a basis for understanding. Occasionally, the scientist, more specifically the social scientist, and the people studied find

Sidney Greenfield, "Science as a Cultural Process," *Spirits With Scalpels: The Cultural Biology of Religious Healing in Brazil*, pp. 163–166. Copyright © 2010 by Left Coast Press. Reprinted with permission.

themselves interested in the same events or phenomena. The images, models, and theories of the scientist may or may not overlap or be congruent with those of the people studied.

The simplest answer to Kuhn's "what must the world be like" question is to be found in metaphor (see D'Andrade 1995; Quinn 1991; Fernandez 1991, 1986; Quinn and Holland 1987). By likening the world to something already known, the curious person (scientist or lay-person) may use what knowledge he or she has about the known to think about the unknown and formulate questions about it. The answers to the questions provide further insights and understandings that may be explored in detail.

> Kuhn reminds us that effective research scarcely begins before a scientific commu-
> nity thinks it has acquired firm answers to questions like the following: What are the
> fundamental entities of which the universe is composed? How do these interact with
> each other and with the senses? What questions may legitimately be asked about the
> entities and what techniques employed in seeking solutions? (1970:4–5)

Kuhn acknowledges that far from being absolute, the answers are arbitrary. They derive from the particular image of what the world is like adopted by members of a scientific community.

Kuhn then does something that shows keen anthropological insight. He moves from his initial discussion of an isolated individual asking about natural phenomena to a scientific community. Such a community is a social group formed around a shared image of what the world is like and how one studies it. The consensus its members hold enables them to ask similar questions, the answers to which expand their collective understanding of their field or subject of interest.

Once a paradigm, defined as "an accepted model or pattern," is agreed upon, the individual members do "puzzle solving," posing questions, the hypothesized answers to which can be tested (Kuhn 1970:23). This process requires agreement by members of a scientific community as to the terms, referred to as concepts, that enable them to relate observed events or data to the conceptual categories of their paradigm.

Taken cumulatively, the answers to the many questions asked and puzzles solved fill in the blanks or unknowns in the paradigm or model. This in turn expands the scientific community's knowledge of what the world is like and hence its ability to explain the phenomena of interest to it.

Before proceeding, two points in Kuhn's presentation are worth emphasizing. First, the questions asked by scientists and scholars are not about some absolute reality but rather are derived from, and are the products of, the specific model or paradigm around which a consensus has developed. Independent of a shared mental picture, concepts, and the hypotheses they are used to formulate, have neither meaning nor relevance.

Secondly, techniques used to solve the puzzles and methods employed by members of a scientific community to test and validate theories are based on and derived from the images of their shared paradigm or model. In Kuhn's words: "The existence of the paradigm sets the problem to be solved; often the paradigm theory is implicated directly in the design of the apparatus able to solve the problem" (Kuhn 1970:27).

Not all puzzles can be solved. Occasionally scientists encounter anomalies that cannot be explained in terms of their agreed-on paradigm, such as those posed by the Spiritist surgeries and other controversial therapies reported here. If the anomalies are of a sufficient magnitude, they may bring the utility of the paradigm itself into question. With the consensus shattered, members of the scientific community may propose an alternative image as to what the world is like that ideally will incorporate previous knowledge while making it possible to account for the anomalies.

In the natural sciences, where a single paradigm had tended to dominate studies of particular subject matters or disciplines, the proposal of a new imagery to deal with anomalies in any one invariably led to conflict between members of the scientific community. This process of paradigm replacement is the "scientific revolution" referred to in Kuhn's title.

The paradigm that informed the medical sciences and provided our commonsense standards of "reality" with respect to healing was based on the Cartesian mind/body opposition. It led us and our medical professionals to treat the body as *if* it were a machine. Based on this mechanical imagery, a doctor might be likened to a mechanic who repairs or replaces parts of, or introduces materials into, human bodies in an effort to get them to retain or return to optimal operating efficiency. Once the imagery was accepted as the paradigm for treating the sick, it was possible for researchers to zero in on specific problems—solving puzzles in Kuhn's terms. The thousands of hypotheses, experiments, theories, and research trials analyzed statistically and reported regularly in the scientific literature and the popular press exemplify how scientists have tried to solve puzzles. Some seemed not to be solvable, meaning that certain forms of suffering—whether or not classified as illnesses—continued to afflict patients, while some treatments that led to cures could not be explained in terms of the paradigm. The anomalies, corroborating Kuhn's view of paradigm shifts, led individuals to search for other imageries, or ways to modify the prevailing one, that might explain the anomalies, thus resulting in the modification or transformation of the predominant framework. The direction this change took emphasized process, transformation, and interrelatedness and not the stasis of the mechanical model.

By the end of the nineteenth century, the absolutes of space, time, object, and determinism were apparently securely enthroned in an unmysterious, mechanically determined world, basically simple in structure at the atomic level and, statistically at least, unchanging in form—for even geological and biological transformations operated under fixed laws (Peacocke 1979:54).

In the early years of the twentieth century, as McFague summarized it, "there was a movement toward a model more aptly described as organic, for there occurred a profound realization of the deep relations between space, time, and matter, which relativized them all. ... [R]elationships and relativity as well as processes and openness, characterize reality as it is understood at present in all branches of science" (1987:10).

Chance and necessity replace determinism in this new picture. Individuals always exist within structures of relationship. Process, change, transformation, and openness replace stasis. Interdependence, novelty, and even mystery are part of the new understanding of reality (McFague 1987:10). In this imagery, one does not "enter into relations" with others, as McFague informs us, "but finds oneself in such relationships as the most basic given of existence" (1987:11). In the mechanistic model, entities are separated dualistically and hierarchically, while in the organic, or "mutualistic" one, all entities are considered to be subjects as well as objects. A key element is their communication with each other and the interaction it makes possible. This thinking is at the forefront of anthropology and the newly expanding fields of medicine such as immunology, endocrinology, neurology, and psychoneuroimmunology. Researchers have questioned the Cartesian mind/body dualism and are replacing it with a framework of interrelatedness and information flow to integrate the biophysiological, mental, and emotional dimensions of being human into the understanding of illness and its treatment.

Debunking "Man the Hunter"

By Robert W. Sussman and Donna Hart

W hy are we the way we are? What makes us think and act the way we do? Birds fly and snakes slither because they must. What are we impelled to do? Well, humans walk upright, they verbalize language, and they manipulate their environment to suit their needs. But did we start out with those legacies or did they come slowly over time? Yes, most birds fly, but the ancestors of birds were probably terrestrial dinosaurs. Snakes slither, but the skeletal remnants of hind legs are found in primitive snakes. Considering these strange and drastic developments over time in other animals, we might well question in what state of nature we humans may have started out. To look generally at our past and specifically at our position in the food chain—predator or prey?—we need to study our roots; we need to get down to the very beginnings of the first steps on the human path.

The evolution of our species—*Homo sapiens*—is a story told in fits and starts, through new fossil discoveries and breaking headline news. *Missing Link Found* is often the lead in any media report about new findings in our hominid line. The "missing link" has not yet been found and is—in scientific terms—a quite inappropriate term. *Missing Common Ancestor of Chimps and Humans Found* would be the correct (but not nearly as generally exciting) headline that would stun the world of paleontology. That would be *the* find! The one sought by every researcher who spends years raising research money through grant-writing and then years more painstakingly grubbing in out-of-the-way locations for fossils—the elusive creature at mile-marker zero of our evolutionary highway whose progeny took two different forks in the road. One road led to modern chimpanzees and one led to modern humans. In no way did "we" (modern humans) pass through a stage in which we were chimpanzees. The chimps are as modern in their approach to life in the trees of tropical Africa as we are in our two-legged wandering all over the earth.

The question that drives paleo-detectives to distraction is *when* did that fork in the road appear?

First, a cautionary disclaimer. As has been the case with every volume published that contains theories of where, when, and what constituted our beginnings, this chapter may be overridden by a new discovery of a fossil hominid that changes the whole story line once again. One irrefutable statement, though, is that our hominid lineage begins much farther back in geologic time than science estimated a decade ago. Even in the 1990s, 4-million-year-old petrified remains were considered close to the seminal divergence from a common ancestor with chimps. Now, six-to-seven-million-year-old fossils have been discovered in the African nations of Chad and Kenya. Newly discovered finds appear to be hominid species that lived sometime after the chimpanzee and the human lines diverged from a common ancestor because they show evidence of upright walking, or bipedalism—which is a trait of humans but not of chimpanzees.

It is only fair to state that the oldest known hominid fossils have their detractors. The major controversy revolves around whether the fossil remains do indeed indicate bipedality, which is the initial and singular characteristic most indicative of hominid lineage. Pelvis, knee, and leg bones will answer this question quite nicely, but what if those are not among the retrieved remnants of long-deceased kin? Well, if cranial (skull) bones are found, one of the indicators of bipedality is the placement of the foramen magnum, the large hole at the base of the skull through which the spinal cord attaches to the brain. Picture how the back and head of a quadrupedal animal—like a horse for example—is oriented; the spine is on a horizontal plane so the foramen magnum, the entryway to the brain, is positioned high up on the back of the skull. Now visualize a bipedal animal whose spine is on a vertical plane; the foramen magnum is located as far down on the base of the skull as possible. Currently, it is the sense of the anthropology community that the fossils we will discuss here imply *obligate* bipedal hominids; in other words, they had upright bodies and hips that made bipedal striding the most comfortable form of locomotion and this necessitated the placement of the foramen magnum at the bottom of the skull.

Will the First Hominid Please Stand Up?

Asking for the identity of the first hominid should be an easy entreaty, right? We just mentioned that upright walking was the litmus test of human ancestors. But, even the technical categorization of a hominid has now become more enigmatic than a few years past. Taxonomists—the scientists who immerse themselves in Latin nomenclature to classify species and devise the relationships of all living creatures one to another—have added another layer of stupefaction. First, all monkeys, apes, and humans are primates—that's a given. The latest taxonomic blueprints, however, group orangutans, gorillas, chimpanzees (that is, all the so-called great apes), and humans in the same taxonomic family—designated by the Latin term *Hominidae* (commonly anglicized to "hominid"). Gorillas, chimps, and humans are subsequently grouped together within the same *sub*family level. Why? Because, currently, based on DNA similarities, it is only at the descending level of our genus—*Homo*—that taxonomists can separate our genetic building blocks from our ape relatives.

Despite total acceptance of this powerful DNA evidence, we realize that the new blueprint, combining humans and apes into one taxonomic family, exponentially increases the bewildering jungle of taxonomy. So, for the sake of ease in reference to our subject matter and to avoid potential esoterica as much as possible, we will continue throughout this book to employ a more conventional approach and distinguish as *hominids* only those species that diverged from the human-ape stem some 7–10 million years ago and were bipedal. The alternative is repeatedly to identify forerunners to modern humans by their individual Latin names (*Australopithecus, Paranthropus, Kenyanthropus, Ardipithecus, Orrorin,* and *Sahelanthropus*), a decision that would cause this book to be much longer than intended.

Some of those Latin monikers may sound familiar and some are so new they are just entering the most recent editions of college textbooks on hominid evolution. We'll start with *Sahelanthropus tchadensis* (not a name that exactly ripples off the tongue, but a celebrity nonetheless) because it is the oldest fossil hominid so far discovered. What makes it a paleontologist's dream—and nightmare simultaneously—is that its existence stretches our human history back to between 6 and 7 million years, while at the same time refuting a slew of theories concerning the location and habitat of hominid origins.

Nicknamed *Toumai*, or "hope of life" in the local Goran language of the Djurab Desert, the fossil was unearthed in the African nation of Chad. *Sahelanthropus* is represented by a cranium, a jaw fragment, and several teeth. It was found in 2001 by a team of French and Tchadian paleoanthropolgists led by Michel Brunet of the University of Poitiers and his colleague Djimdoumalbaye Ahounta. The landlocked equatorial nation of Chad is bounded on the north by Libya, on the south by the Central African Republic, on the east by Sudan, and on the west by Niger, Nigeria, and Cameroon. As is apparent from the geographic description, Chad's location is smack in the center of Africa. The discovery of *Toumai* was a bit like finding medieval Christian artifacts in the middle of Australia. Fascinating, but how can you reconcile it with traditional theories? And traditional theory had it that Central Africa is a peculiar place to find hominid fossils because it is the "wrong" side of the Rift Valley.

The Great Rift Valley, which stretches from Mozambique in the south up through Ethiopia in the north, is a monstrous gash in the East African landscape. If you are peacefully driving north from Nairobi, Kenya, to Lake Nakuru National Park, at one point you will see an innocuous 12-by-12 inch sign that reads, "Beware the Escarpment." Before you have time to think what that decorous command may imply, you are hurtling over the edge of the Great Rift Valley on a switchback road that seems to angle downward at 45 degrees. Below you lies the valley, stretching endlessly and shimmering in the dry heat. Until the excavations in Chad, all of the earliest hominid fossils have been found on the east side of the Rift Valley (Ethiopia, Kenya, and Tanzania to be specific). One neat, and now retired, theory stated that when chimps and hominids evolved from their common ancestor, the chimp line stayed in the trees of the forested region to the west of the Rift Valley and the hominids began—successfully and bipedally—to colonize the drier savannas of the east. This ceased to be a viable theory when hominid fossils started popping up in places on the west side of the Rift, like Chad.

The Great Rift Valley of East Africa is shaded. To date, only two early hominid fossils have been found west of the Rift Valley. (C. Rudloff)*

As often happens behind closed doors, when the startling fossil description of *Toumai* was published in *Nature* in July 2002, pundits tended to remark something on the order of "It'd be better if they had covered it back up!"—echoing the frustration of fitting this new piece into the paleo puzzle. And who is to say that fossils are not to be found in other unexamined areas of interest to anthropologists. For instance, Malawi in southeastern Africa, said to lie in a

*The images in this reading appear as they do in the original source.

"hominid corridor" between the fossil-rich eastern and southern regions of the continent, has been tossed out as a fresh, new location to investigate for ancient hominid bones.

The second oldest of the hominid finds (represented by the thigh bone, teeth, and lower jaw of an individual estimated to have lived 6 million years ago) startled the world of anthropology likewise. French researchers Brigette Senut and Martin Pickford discovered *Orrorin tugenensis* (called "Millennium Man" because of the relic's unveiling at the dawn of the new age) in the Tugen Hills, Baringo region of Kenya. Senut and Pickford had only a short interval to revel in finding the 6-million year-old fossil and publishing their findings before the more ancient *Toumai* from Chad was stealing the show.

As we work our way forward over the millions of years from the beginning of smallish bipedal beings to the present, another character in the geologic drama walked on stage. We next encounter *Ardithpithecus ramidus* ("ardi" meaning ground and "ramid" translating as root in the local Afar language), unearthed in Ethiopia in 1993 by Tim White and Alemayehu Asfaw. This was the first of the excavated hominid remains in excess of 4 million years of age. Bones and teeth of 17 individuals, while highly fragmentary, have been dated at 4.4–5.8 million years ago and a new find of the same species, measured at 5.2–5.8 million years, confirms the great age of this hominid.

Having briefly glanced at these three hominids who we know lived approximately 6 million years or more prior to the present, let's continue meandering through the various life-forms that preceded our own species. Meave Leakey of the famous Leakey clan of paleoanthropologists *par excellence*—we'll talk about her husband's, father-in-law's, and mother-in-law's stunning discoveries a little later—found *Kenyanthropus platyops* (this translates as "flat-faced Kenyan man") in the area of Lake Turkana where the Great Rift Valley exits northern Kenya. The emphatically vertical plane of this fossil face motivated Leakey to suggest *K. platyops* as a direct ancestor to modern humans. (Jutting jaws are considered a trademark of those hominids less likely to be in the direct human ancestry; flat faces are more "human-like.") *K. platyops* represents a 3.5-million-year-old skull from what Leakey claims may be an entirely new branch of the early human tree.[1]

All the extinct hominid species we have described so far preceded the legendary "Lucy" (a.k.a. *Australopithecus afarensis*) found in Ethiopia by Donald Johanson in 1974. Lucy is a hominid fossil with personality. Her discovery was celebrated in the field with a rollicking party that boomed pop music through the desert night. She was named after the Beatles' song "Lucy in the Sky with Diamonds," and Johanson and his colleagues truly rock 'n' rolled the world of science when they presented the nearly complete post-cranial (below the skull) skeleton of a young female hominid who lived 3.2 million years ago. Lucy is thought to have stood upright at 3 and one-half feet (males of her species may have been as much as a foot taller). She was bipedal but had long feet with an exceptionally powerful big toe that was divergent like our modern human thumbs and could be used to grasp and climb trees. She may have exploited the forest fringes, using those grasping toes to evade predators by shinnying up a tree.

Two relatives of Lucy left their footprints in newly fallen ash at another spot in East Africa called Laetoli (these immortalized footfalls constitute another Leakey family find—Mary, the family matriarch, this time). A pair of australopithecines, possibly male and female from the difference in how their respective weights imprinted the ash, were walking side by side over 3 million years ago. Their footprints give a tantalizingly personal nature to australopithecines as individuals. Where were these two going? Were they a mated pair? What might they have been leaving or going toward on their journey?

A "robust" relative of Lucy (*Paranthropus boisei*) had been discovered at Olduvai Gorge in Tanzania by the incomparable first-generation husband and-wife team of fossil-hunting Leakeys—Louis and Mary—in the 1960s. The "robust" appellation doesn't refer to any gigantic stature of the prehistoric hominid but to the incredibly large jaws and huge molars possessed by this particular branch of the family tree, making them capable of grinding hard, fibrous plant material. Another robust species of early hominid was found by Richard Leakey (son of Louis and Mary), who is not only a world-renowned paleoanthropologist but a giant in the field of wildlife conservation and the Kenyan political scene. The younger Leakey commenced a dig at Lake Turkana, Kenya, and disinterred the famous "Black Skull." This mineral-stained cranium is the most extreme example of the robust branches on the family tree found so far. Although no teeth accompanied the Black Skull, it's estimated that the molars for this individual were four to five times the size of a modern human's teeth.

The elder Leakeys also discovered the earliest member of our own genus, *Homo habilis* (baptized "handy man," although a penchant for dreary labor hardly seems the case for any of the Olduvai residents). Evidence in the form of simple stone tools at the gorge left clues of this early human who lived about 2.3 million years ago.

During our whirlwind tour of early hominids we must not forget the very first of the African hominid fossils to be discovered—the one that *should* have thrown the world of anthropology into a tailspin in 1924 but didn't. Raymond Dart, a young anatomy professor at the University of Witwatersrand in Johannesburg, South Africa, had issued a standing request to the fore-man at a limestone quarry called Taung (the Setswana word for "place of the lion") to bring him anything that might be a fossil. When Dart gleefully utilized his wife's knitting needles to chip the breccia (cemented limestone, sand, and bone) off a putative fossil, the brain and face of a young (but obviously not human) toddler appeared—the "Taung child" (*Australopithecus africanus*)—and the modern era of paleoanthropology began. Until Dart's breakthrough, the human lineage was assumed to have been European or Asian in origin. None other than Charles Darwin had suggested that the African residence of gorillas and chimpanzees might be the key to human evolution, but great skepticism greeted all who thought of African human origins during the racist colonial nineteenth and early twentieth centuries.

This might be a good time to mention that there has always been a lot at stake in concepts of human ancestors—more than objective science, more than impartial pursuit of truth. Especially in the late 1800s and early years of the twentieth century, we—humans and our ancestors—had to be on the top of the species heap. We had to be the smartest species. We had to be special and powerful and above other animals. And very importantly, humans had to be ranked in a hierarchy of races with European humans at the apex. With the development of the theory of evolution through natural selection, Darwin put humans in their place with the rest of the animal kingdom, subject to the same laws of nature. However, in so doing,

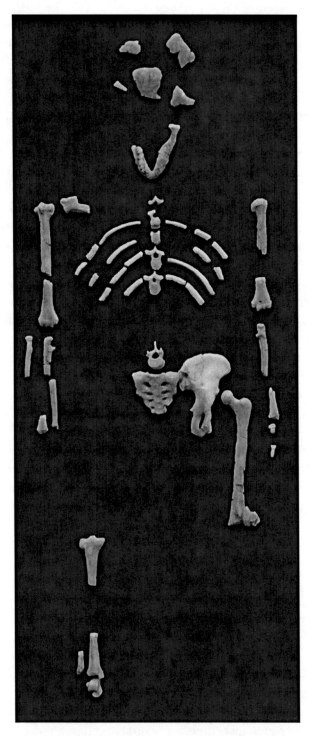

The fossil skeleton of Lucy, a young female hominid, from 3.2 million years ago.

even Darwin visualized a spiritual and intellectual gap between humans and their closest living relatives, the apes. As he stated: "There can be no doubt that the difference between the mind of the lowest man and that of the highest animal is immense."[2] What separated the biology and behavior of all humans from other animals was the presence of a large brain. Late nineteenth-century theorists took the amount of gray matter residing in our modern brains as the truly "human" aspect and looked for early human fossils that fit the big-brained expectations.

Slipping forward past the tangled morass of inchoate relatives, our evolutionary tale gets a little clearer with what may be an immediate predecessor of modern humans, *Homo erectus*. In 1891 this early representative of our genus, initially known as Java Man, was stumbled upon by a Dutch physician named Eugene Dubois who was stationed in Indonesia on military duty. He thought the island of Java was a logical place to look for fossils since Asia at that time was hypothesized to be a possible site of origin for the human species. Later in the 1920s more *H. erectus* fossils were found in a cave outside of Beijing, China.

Java Man was an acceptable human ancestor to the late Victorian fossil hunters—certainly more than anything from Africa—but nothing would be as satisfying as a European origin for humanity. The English scientific establishment found what it desired in "Piltdown Man." In 1912 an amateur fossil hunter discovered pieces of a cranium and jaw in England. The greatest men in British science put the puzzle pieces together and marveled over the extremely large brain case combined with a primitive jaw. This was hard to explain, but explain it they did in a burst of chauvinistic pride. Their explanation? Encephalization (increase in brain size) was the forerunner for all other hominid features in ancient Europeans.

As with all scientific shrines built on ideology alone, this one had a spurious foundation. About 40 years later, it was revealed that Piltdown Man was an utter hoax. If practical jokes were awarded the Nobel Prize, than surely Piltdown's perpetrator deserves the honor. The best minds in the field of anthropology did not recognize that the wonderfully brainy fossil was an amalgamation of a modern orangutan jaw and a modern human skull, both stained to look ancient.

A Messy Bush

You may at this point have a surreal feeling of drowning in names, places, and millions of years ... of sinking down, down, down into a bottomless pool of *anthropus*—this and *pithecus*—that ... and, omigosh, we've still got millions of years to go! You have every right to suffer the headache of how untidily complex our family tree is growing; you are not alone—the experts are often just as confounded by the constantly fluctuating nature of this branch of science.

Ian Tattersall of the American Museum of Natural History has been a prestigious fixture in the analysis of paleoanthropological finds for several decades. So when Tattersall suggests the need for a mental paradigm shift concerning our hominid past, people tend to listen. There has been a tendency to portray the human ancestral line in a neat linear diagram—one early hominid with primitive features slowly evolving into a more human-like successor and so on and so on.

Tattersall, instead, sees our hominid past as that of a messy bush—branches and twigs sprouting in all directions. That is, he sees in the fossil record a great diversity of hominid species, many of them living at the same time, if not in the same place. The human "family bush" contains many dead ends—extinctions—mostly because of environmental changes. In fact, extinctions are the rule rather than the exception, with the result that there is only one hominid—modern humans—alive today.

Another eminent authority, Bernard Wood of George Washington University, postulates that the ancient fossils being found now in Chad and other places are just the tip of the metaphorical iceberg. He thinks that fossil ape-like creatures were diverse and prolific—and that there will be evidence of wide proliferation of numerous ape-like creatures, including the common ancestor of humans and chimps, in a bewildering array that cannot be imagined today.[3]

And on the messy bush occurs one branch that managed to survive as the only still-living hominid—anatomically modern humans. As Tattersall eloquently states: "In pondering our history as human beings we should never forget that we are simply the sole surviving twig on this ramifying bush, rather than the products of a slow, steady, and single-minded process of perfection."[4] Where did all the other branches on the messy hominid bush go? Smallish, bipedal primates came and went for possibly 7–10 million years. Some were successful—consider the 1-million-year-plus reign of *H. erectus*—but nothing in our history points to a starring role for one branch over another. A fascinating question that science ponders endlessly is why so much diversity existed in our past and yet now only one hominid species inhabits the earth.

Wanderlust

One last example of how important it is to keep a flexible attitude toward our ancestors involves our eventual exit from Africa. Previous to 2002 it was accepted as fact that no hominid emigrated from Africa until we arrive at the relatively large-brained direct predecessor to humans, *Homo erectus*. As mentioned earlier, *H. erectus* fossils have been found in China and Indonesia for over a century. The large leap in cranial capacity between *H. habilis* (the first known member of our genus) and *H. erectus* is substantial: a jump from under 700 to over 1,000 cubic centimeters (cc) of brain mass. The length of the leg bones and, therefore, of walking stride between the short-limbed *H. habilis* and the long-legged *H. erectus* is also significant.

In an example of the exciting and unpredictable twists and turns in the world of paleoanthropology, *habilis*-like fossils were recently uncovered in the Republic of Georgia, overturning the theory that hominids stayed put in Africa, the continent of origin, until *H. erectus'* long strides and larger brain carried him/her out sometime after 1.75 million years ago.[5]

At some point the size of the brain must have reached a critical mass that enabled more and more manipulation of the environment through complex communication and tool making. At such a point it seems feasible that early humans would begin their colonization of the world. Nevertheless, the pioneers who traveled thousands of miles to decidedly different biomes may have been small, short-legged hominids with cranial capacities of 680 cc. Hardly the imagined progenitor of our human wanderlust.

Man the Hunter?

The question "Why is man man?" has been posed since literal biblical origins gave way to scientific inquiries. "Because man evolved as a meat eater" is one answer to the question. Robert Ardrey stated in one of his series of immensely popular books of the 1970s, *The Hunting Hypothesis*:

> If among all the members of our primate family the human being is unique, even in our noblest aspirations, it is because we alone through untold millions of years were continuously dependent on killing to survive.[6]

There are several misconceptions included in this proposal of human hunting singularity. First, we are not the only primate that hunts for living prey. Hunting is a common feeding strategy throughout the primate order. Baboons are adept at capturing infant antelope; chimpanzees, especially, excel in hunting and eating monkeys. Even different methods and approaches toward hunting have been observed in different chimpanzee populations. At Jane Goodall's field site, Gombe Reserve in Tanzania, the male chimps hunt as lions do—the more individuals involved the greater the success rate, but no coordinated team effort is manifested. In the Tai Forest of Côte d'Ivoire the chimps hunt like wolves, each individual playing a key role in a team effort.[7]

Whether hunting could have been the main food-procurement venture for early hominids is also subject to anatomical constraints. We need to look carefully at teeth and digestive systems, the critical parts of human anatomy that lend themselves to answers about early hominid dependence on hunted meat. Intestines do not fossilize, but teeth make up a good portion of the fossil remains of australopithecines and their dentition is not that of a carnivore.

So, where did the Man the Hunter idea come from? When did the certitude that humans were too busy *killing* to *be killed* arise? Who were the proponents of the myth of fierce and dangerous hominids? When you consider the reality, what a public-relations coup!—a fangless, clawless, smallish bipedal primate gets a reputation for being Godzilla wielding an antelope jawbone!

In some sense the Taung child is the key to the Man the Hunter theme. Taung child was the first fossil in a series of australopithecine finds. It is somewhat ironic that Raymond Dart's painstaking reclamation of this fossil—probably the young victim of a predator—was so instrumental in creating a trend toward "killer-ape" status for human ancestors.

To view the inception of Man the Hunter's forceful accession and acceptance, we need to go back and fill in the people who inhabited the rather small and esoteric world of

Raymond Dart with his discovery, the Taung child, the first of many early hominid fossils to be found in Africa. Dart initially described this fossil in 1924. (F. Herholdt)

paleoanthropology in the 1920s. As emphasized earlier, Africa was not then the important arena for fossil humans. The English had their Piltdown Man, reassuring the white European experts that large brains came before flat faces. The Neanderthal finds in Europe were augmented by Java Man and Peking Man from the Far East. What did it matter if an obscure anatomy professor in South Africa had found a skull and fossilized brain that didn't look like a chimp but whose brain was way, way too small to be considered human?

In the atmosphere of the day it is no wonder that the Piltdown Man, with its ape-like jaw and large cranium, was immediately accepted as the earliest hominid ancestor, while the small-skulled, ape-like australopithecine discovered by Raymond Dart was considered a pathological specimen or a mere ape. While Piltdown supporters were busy explaining the intellectual endowments of our large-brained ancestors, Dart was convinced his small-brained creature was the first ape-man, and he developed a theoretical picture of the behavior of this transitional form. At first Dart believed that australopithecines were scavengers barely eking out an existence in the harsh savanna environment; a primate that did not live to kill large animals but scavenged small animals in order to live.

Few cared what Dart believed, however, because few took his ape-man seriously. In fact it was not until a quarter of a century later, with the unearthing of many more australopith-ecines and the discovery in 1953 that Piltdown was a fraud, that students of human evolution realized our earliest ancestors were more ape-like than they were modern-human-like. This led to a great interest in using primates to understand human evolution and the evolutionary basis of human nature.[8] With these discoveries began a long list of theories attempting to re-create the behavior and often the basic morality of the earliest hominids.

By 1950 Dart had developed a wholly new and different view from his former scavenger model. His ponderings about strange depressions in the crania of fossil australopithecines eventually flowered into a full-blown theory about killers who murdered their own kind. Given the game animals with which australopithecine fossils were associated and the dents and holes in the skulls of the australopithecines themselves, Dart became convinced that the mammals had been killed, butchered, and eaten by the ape-men, and that these early homi-nids had even been killing one another.

Dart once believed that the australopithecines had been forced to scratch out a meager existence on the savanna once they abandoned the trees of the African forest. But Dart now saw that hunting, and a carnivorous lust for blood, actively drew man-apes out of the forest and were together a main force in human evolution. He stated more than once that "the ancestors of *Australopithecus* left their fellows in the trees of Central Africa through a spirit of adventure and the more attractive fleshy food that lay in the vast savannas of the southern plains."[9] Dart was himself influenced by a University of London professor, Carveth Read, who suggested in 1925 that human ancestors were similar to wolves; they hunted in packs and lived off the meat of large game. Read suggested that the name *Lycopithecus* (literally, "wolf-ape") would be descriptive of early hominids.

The discovery of baboon skulls mysteriously bashed in on the left side of the skull inspired Dart to conclude that only the australopithecine ancestor of humans could have killed with such precision. Since no stone weapons or tools were found in the South African sites, Dart postulated that the unusually high frequency of thigh bones and jawbones from antelopes must have been the weapons of choice. His "osteodontokeratic" culture—that early man had used the bones, teeth, and horns of his prey to kill even more prey—provided the means by which these killer apes accomplished their bloody work.

In 1953 Dart published a paper entitled "The Predatory Transition from Ape to Man." In it he hypothesized that the dentition and geography of australopithecines precluded any type of diet other than heavy reliance on meat. And not only did they eat meat but they armed themselves with weapons to hunt large prey. None of the well-known journals would accept the article, so readership within the scientific community was sparse. Robert Ardrey, a successful playwright, visited Dart in South Africa and was convinced that this theory would revolutionize the science of anthropology. Ardrey spent 5 years between 1955 and 1960 researching and writing *African Genesis*—a popular account of our beginnings as killer apes.[10] The book was a best-seller and had tremendous influence both on the general public and the scientific community.

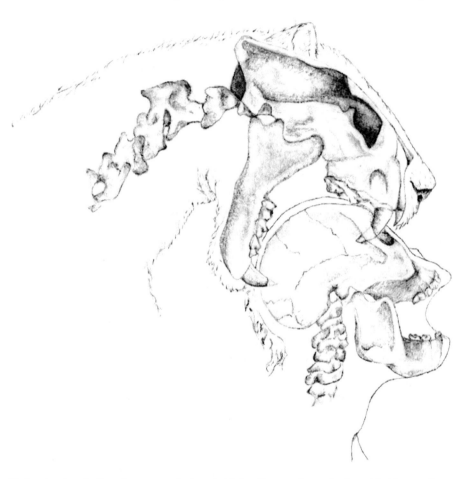

Holes in the skulls of some early hominid fossils match perfectly with big cat fangs. (C. Rudloff, redrawn from Cavallo 1991)

By the mid-1970s Dart's claim that a hominid with a brain no larger than our ape cousins expertly fashioned weapons and went on the hunt because it was easier than scavenging was fully accepted. But, Dart's *evidence* for Man the Hunter was not good, and his particular vision of the human hunter/killer hypothesis did not stand up to rigorous scrutiny. C. K. Brain, a South African specialist in how fossils are formed by natural forces, was skeptical of the baboon-killing theory from the first. Upon examination of the evidence, Brain noted that the bones associated with the man-apes were exactly like fragments left by leopards and hyenas.[11] He saw the holes in the baboon skulls and the similar indentations in *A. africanus* as oddly similar to the tooth patterns of living African carnivores. He set about measuring the distance between the lower canines of African big cats and found that the space between the lower fangs of leopards fit precisely into the fossil skull holes.

Round holes that match perfectly with fangs of leopards. It seems that the australopithecines were likely the hunted and not the hunters. Fossil bones of early hominid origin were found with baboon remains in South African cave excavations at Swartkrans, Kromdraii, and Sterkfontein, places that have become famous for their australopithecine remains.[12] Brain hypothesized that baboons and early hominids slept in caves, providing an excellent opportunity for leopards to kill them and drag the carcasses farther into the caves for feeding.[13] The Mt. Suswa lava caves in Kenya provide a current analogy to the paleontological record in South Africa and lend significant credibility to the hypotheses. Mt. Suswa is a favorite sleeping site for baboons, and leopards in the area subsist almost entirely on these primates.[14]

Man the Dancer!

The next widely accepted version of the recurring Man the Hunter theme was presented in the late 1960s by Sherwood Washburn (the father of American field primatology) and his colleagues. They claimed that many of the features that define *men* as hunters (more about why the other 50% of the species was not defined will be discussed later in this book) again separated the earliest humans from their primate relatives.

> To assert the biological unity of mankind is to affirm the importance of the hunting way of life. It is to claim that, however much conditions and customs may have varied locally, the main selection pressures that forged the species were the same. The biology, psychology, and customs that separate us from the apes—these we owe to the hunters of time past. And, for those who would understand the origin and nature of human behavior there is no choice but to try to understand "Man the Hunter."[15]

Like Dart, Washburn related human hunting to human morality, both of which had their biological basis in our evolutionary past. What he termed the "carnivorous psychology" of the australopithecines resulted in a human species that takes pleasure not just in the chasing, hunting, and killing of other animals, but in dark depredations on fellow humans. The public spectacles of torture and suffering in "most" cultures are for the *enjoyment* of all humans. This interpretation led him to the conclusion that only careful *un*training of our natural drives can lay a veneer of compassion for others on top of naturally human "carnivorous curiosity and aggression."[16]

Using the nineteenth-century anthropological concept of cultural survivals, "Man the Dancer" explains early hominid behavior just as well as does "Man the Hunter." (C. Rudloff)

Again, much like Dart before him, Washburn did not amass a large amount of evidence to support his theory and seemed to have recognized that evidence to the contrary existed.[17] Rather, he relied upon a nineteenth century anthropological concept of cultural "survivals."[18] These are behaviors that are no longer useful in society but that persist as leftover survival mechanisms from a time when they *were* adaptive. Washburn saw a connection between the ease with which modern sports (including hunting) are learned and the pleasures they confer, and the survival mechanisms of a bygone age. Because successful ancestral humans were those who hunted best, their genetic legacy is an easy and pleasurable acquisition of huntinglike behaviors.[19]

Using a similar logic, we have developed an alternative (sarcastic, yes—but no less feasible) theory to challenge Man the Hunter. We call our theory "Man the Dancer." After all, men *and* women love to dance, it is a behavior found in all cultures, and it has less obvious function in most cultures than does hunting.

Although it takes two to tango, a variety of social systems could develop from various types of dance: square dancing, line dancing, riverdance, or the funky chicken. The footsteps at Laetoli might not represent two individuals going out for a hunt but the Afarensis shuffle, one of the earliest dances. In the movie *2001: A Space Odyssey*, it was wrong to depict the first tool as a weapon. It could easily have been a drumstick, and the first battle may not have involved killing at all but a battle of the bands. Other things such as face-to-face sex, cooperation, language and singing, and bipedalism (it's difficult to dance on all fours), even moving out of the trees and onto the ground might all be better explained by our propensity to dance than by our desire to hunt. Although we are being facetious with our Man the Dancer hypothesis, the evidence for dancing is certainly as good and no more preposterous than that for hunting.

We Were Not "Cat Food"!

Between 1961 and 1976, the playwright Robert Ardrey popularized the then-current version of the Man the Hunter myth with a number of best-sellers. Ardrey believed that it was the competitive spirit, as acted out in warfare, that made humans what they are today: "the mentality of the single Germanic tribe under Hitler differed in no way from that of early man or late baboon." Because of a lack of a competitive territorial instinct, gorillas—Ardrey believed—had lost the will to live and with it the drive for sex. He argued that gorillas defend no territory and copulate rarely. And their story "will end, one day, not with a bang but with a whimper."[20]

African Genesis may well have been the starting point for the public popularity of Man the Hunter, but the prominence brought to paleoanthropology by the patriarch of the Leakey family was the strong suit that clinched the public's acceptance. The great Dr. Louis S. B. Leakey, a larger-than-life personality, was the premier paleoanthropologist of the mid-twentieth century and the personification of the fossil-hunting field scientist. His dynamic personality and exciting ideas took the quest for human origins to the heights of media coverage, catching the public's imagination. Inquiring minds finally *did* want to know about our origins! Along with his wife, Mary, who accomplished much of the actual discovery and reconstruction of the fossils, the Leakeys became worldwide celebrities. From their home base at the Kenya Museum of Natural History, they made Olduvai Gorge in Tanzania synonymous with human origins. Leakey also gave the world an eventual look at our closest relatives through his support for Jane Goodall's research on chimpanzees, Dian Fossey's work on mountain gorillas, and Birute Galdikas' study of orangutans. He was particularly thrilled when Goodall identified hunting and meat-eating in chimpanzees.

And Leakey's endorsement of Man the Hunter gave it the academic credentials that Ardrey's popular books lacked. In a famous defense of Man the Hunter as fearless and bellicose, Leakey stated that we were *not* "cat food," and the ramification was a change in perception of human origins for the entire Western world.[21]

The designation of early humans as Man the Hunter rapidly attained axiomatic status. Our ancestry as fearless hunters and remorseless killers of our own and other species has been the generally accepted perception now for nearly 50 years. And not just the layperson, but academics as well, fall easily into using this paradigm. Here's a common example from an evolutionary psychologist, Charles Crawford of Simon Fraser University in Burnaby, British Columbia. Crawford lamented in an article about human evolutionary adaptations gone awry in modern times: "I used to hunt saber-toothed tigers all the time, thousands of years ago. Now I sit in front of a computer and don't get exercise."[22]

We think it's time to put this particular myth to rest. Tweaking Charles Crawford's theme, our hominid ancestors probably got plenty of exercise from desperately trying to *avoid* saber-toothed cats, not from blatantly suicidal attempts to hunt them. Instead of Man the Hunter, we contend that Man the Hunted is a more accurate snapshot. For smallish bipedal primates, we envision a whole host of predators were licking their chops with anticipation.

A Pound of Biology and a Pinch of Culture or a Pinch of Biology and a Pound of Culture?

The Necessity of Integrating Biology and Culture in Reproductive Studies

By Susan Sperling and Yewoubdar Beyene

N owhere is the polarization within anthropology between biological and cultural schools more distinct than in the study of human reproduction. Recipes for major reproductive events vary, not only in relative proportions ("to a pound of biology add a pinch of culture"), but in the ingredients themselves ("leave out biology altogether.") Reductionist approaches in evolutionary biology ignore the power of culture to shape the body and its functions, while cultural theorists too often deny the relevance and variety of bodily phenomena. But the ovary and its functions are shaped by evolution, culture, and the ecologies in which individuals develop, offering insights into the exquisite intertwining of biology and cultural practice.

Since the mid-1970s a particular postulation of biological ultimate causality, sociobiology, has dominated many studies of human evolution; these have been widely disseminated in scholarly and popular discourses (Hamilton 1964; Hrdy 1981; Kitcher 1985; Sperling 1991; Trivers 1972; Wilson 1975). Sociobiologists view behavior and biology through the lens of kin selection, asking questions about how observed structures and behaviors increase the fitness of individuals and their close relatives, maximizing their chances of contributing genes to future generations. The roots of sociobiology lie in nineteenth- and early-twentieth- century arguments about whether natural selection operates at the group or individual level. Evolutionists like Darwin, Haldane, and Wynne-Edwards believed that traits may be selected for because they are advantageous for populations (Darwin 1859; Haldane 1932; Wynne-Edwards 1962), while sociobiologists contend that selection occurs only at the level of the individual. They have made two key assertions: that all-important social behaviors are genetically controlled, and that natural selection of the genome is caused by a set of specific adaptive mechanisms (kin selection) that produce behaviors which maximize an organism's ability to contribute the greatest number of genes to the next generation.

Hamilton's theory of kin selection (1964) is based on the concept that the fitness of an organism has two components: fitness gained through the replication of its own genetic material by reproduction, and "inclusive fitness" gained from the replication of copies of its own genes carried in others as a result of its actions. According to this theory, when an organism behaves "altruistically" toward related individuals, it is also benefiting itself, by increasing the fitness of relatives and therefore their likelihood of contributing shared genes to future generations. Thus genes are viewed as being selected for because they contribute to their own perpetuation, regardless of the organism of which they are a part. This paradigm has often led sociobiologists to speculate about the ultimate cause (reproductive advantage) of human reproductive characteristics from mate choice and marriage patterns to menopause.

Sociobiology has influenced both academic and popular discourses about human evolution over the last decades (Kitcher 1985; Sperling 1991). The reasons for this are varied and include its appeal to certain political perspectives and the continuing public curiosity about animal and human behavior. Most recently this perspective has informed a new popular literature of "evolutionary psychology" in articles in popular magazines like *Time* and *Psychology Today*, and in books like *The Moral Animal* by science writer Robert Wright (Furlow and Thornhill 1996; Wright 1994).

The epistemological issues raised by sociobiology's reductionist assertions of ultimate causality have been widely debated in a number of critiques (Fausto-Sterling 1985; Kitcher 1985; Oyama 1985; Sperling 1991). Sociobiology's popular literature posits that complex behaviors have simple genetic roots. But the association of biology with the invariant is a mistake: complex traits arise in a variety of ways, not just through natural selection of particular genotypes. Other things shape behavior besides genes and shape it in important ways for the organism in question. In many species only females show parenting behaviors, whereas males are always aggressive or indifferent towards infants (Oyama 1985). But this difference is not determined only by genes or hormones; parental caretaking is a developmental behavioral response in females, who are always present at the time of birth. Males develop some of the same caretaking patterns, such as posturing for nursing, when exposed to newborn young (Oyama 1985). From an evolutionary point of view, new behaviors may develop and persist in a population either because of changes in the average genotype by natural selection or by enduring changes in the environment in which the average genotype develops. Gould and Vrba (1982) illuminate problems with this limiting adaptationist model, limning the ways that characteristics may represent historically contingent processes rather than natural selection.

As biologist Susan Oyama (1985) points out, an ant larva may develop into a worker or a queen, depending on nutrition, temperature, and other variables, just as a male rodent may exhibit nurturant behaviors when exposed to certain stimuli. Control does not flow only from the gene outward. To understand the much more complex developmental sequences involved in the acquisition of human reproductive characteristics and behavior requires developmental studies in different cultural, ecological, and historical settings (Ellison 1990; Konner and Shostak 1986; Konner and Worthman 1980; Lee 1972, 1979).

There is much more to understanding the development of reproductive characteristics than retrospectively hypothesizing their adaptive functions, although clearly adaptation is one factor among many to be considered. This does not imply that natural selection is a minor force: a significantly maladaptive trait (one which consistently reduces reproductive fitness) is unlikely to persist over time in populations, unless balanced by some other strong reproductive advantage. Nor should the fundamental role played by evolution in determining reproductive structures and behaviors be underestimated. However, evolution and ultimate causality cannot help us understand the complexity and variation within our own and other species in many reproductive events, which are reflective of changing proximate environmental and ecological factors, and cultural realities.

In comparison to evolutionary studies of reproduction, focused studies of human reproduction by cultural anthropologists are relatively new. Cultural studies have viewed reproductive practices as the cultural regulation of the body through marriage patterns, birthing and child-rearing patterns, the cultural meanings and management of reproduction. Up to the 1960s traditional scholarship in this area focused on culturally variable beliefs, norms and values surrounding reproductive behavior (Ford 1964; Mead 1928). As more women took part in the field, studies of the structural and cultural dynamics that affect women as recipients or consumers of health care became important (Jordan 1983; Kay 1982; MacCormack 1982; Browner and Sargent 1990.) Since the 1970s the analysis of reproduction has been greatly enriched by the encounter between feminism and anthropology, in which women's reproductive experiences are analyzed as sources of power and subordination (Ginsberg and Rapp 1991.) These studies have had a major impact on current popular discourse about pregnancy, birth, and motherhood.

Studies of the medicalization of women's reproductive experiences in western culture have expanded into studies of the increasing role of reproductive technologies in every aspect of women's lives. These draw attention to the political economy of reproductive health, noting powerful economic circumstances that affect access to prenatal and postnatal care, among other disenfranchisements (Boone 1988; Johnson and Snow 1982; Lazarus 1988, 1990; E.Martin 1987; McClain 1985; Poland 1988; Rapp 1988,1991).

This approach provides a valuable contribution to the understanding of constraints on women's autonomy in health matters, but has left biological issues out of the equation. Cultural anthropological studies of childbirth or reproductive health have focused solely on political, cultural and social factors, avoiding biology and ignoring ecological variables such as climate, nutrition, disease and other environmental factors known to affect reproduction. The body is universalized in cultural studies and its systematic interactions within the social and physical environment are ignored.

Such studies have understood the body itself as a cultural construct without reference to its physiological responses. This perspective has been particularly acute since the 1980s, when many cultural anthropologists rejected the possibility of empiricism and explanation in favor of interpretation (Townsend and McElroy 1992). The exclusion of the body's role reflects in part a reaction to the reductionism of much current evolutionary biology; there has been an understandable distrust on the part of many cultural anthropologists of the "biologizing" of human behavior by neo-social Darwinists. But this is throwing out the baby with the bathwater: the variability and plasticity of human biology are always germane to reproductive studies.

Human reproductive phenomena always take place within a cultural context in which their meanings are culturally constructed. Given our unique propensity for employing the body's rich potential as a symbolic medium, it is not surprising that a great variety of meanings are derived and expressed through important reproductive life-cycle events (Beyene 1989). For example, symbolic elaborations of menstruation, childbirth and menopause are an important component of human social organization (Beyene 1989; Lock 1993; Brown and Kerns 1985; Skultans 1988). But the body and its physiological mechanisms as they interact with cultural practices have been left out by most cultural theorists, as well as most evolutionists. Notable exceptions to this are the important studies of the San of southern Africa (despite some reductionist spinoffs which have erroneously represented the San as the "universal" food-forager and "type specimen" for the hominid past) which provide insight into the interlocking nature of biology, culture and ecology (Bentley 1985; Konner and Shostak 1986; Konner and Worthman 1980) and among Efe women of Zaire (Ellison *et al.* 1986; Ellison 1990). These studies show some of the variation in reproductive experiences among populations of our species and that few aspects of women's reproduction are universal or unified experiences.

The biology of reproduction is always mediated through widely ranging fertility experiences. This has relevance to Western biomedicine, in which reproduction is understood as a series of universal biological events common to all humans regardless of the cultural and ecological context. This biomedical model relies on a set of endemic Western beliefs based on recent Western cultural reproductive patterns. Where high fertility and prolonged lactation are the norm, menstrual cycling may be relatively uncommon and its loss unremarkable to the physical and social body (Beyene 1989; Anderson 1983; M.C.Martin *et al.* 1993). By contrast in the West, phenomena such as premenstrual syndrome and menopausal symptoms (i.e., hot flashes) are a major focus in women's health care. The limited ethnocentric view of Western biomedicine has important ramifications for clinical practice in a pluralistic society in which not all women share the same reproductive history. As Western biomedicine is exported to the rest of the world through "well-meaning" development projects, this issue is particularly acute.

A potential strength of medical anthropology in studying reproductive health is that it is situated to bridge these gaps in data and theory, working as it does in all three of these realms (biology, culture and biomedicine). Broader insights may be gained by studying the life course as continually subject to changing social and ecological environments, and the way in which these interact with human biology.

Nonhuman Primates

Biological anthropologists have viewed certain human reproductive characteristics as crucial to the hominid transition and as unique adaptations in our species (Fedigan 1986; Hrdy 1983; Isaac 1978; Lovejoy 1981; Washburn and Lancaster 1968; Zihlman and Tanner 1978). When human reproductive biology is viewed within the larger context of primate evolution, major physiological reproductive changes are not impressive between our species and other higher primates, particularly those most closely related to us. Rather what we see is the plasticity of the primate reproductive system within differing ecological and social contexts (Bernstein 1976; Fedigan 1982; Smuts 1987).

There is interspecific variation among nonhuman primates in the timing and expression of major female reproductive events. These include menarche, the onset of sexual receptivity and proceptivity, the existence or lack of sexual swelling around the perineum of the female, the existence or lack of birth seasonality in a group, conception, pregnancy, lactation, and menopause (Koyama *et al.* 1992; Jurke 1996; Torii *et al.* 1996; Michael and Zumpe 1993; Helvacioglu *et al.* 1994). The physiological template upon which these variations play is the primate menstrual cycle, a complex set of neuroendocrine events producing mid-cycle ovulation, whether or not copulation has occurred, and the shedding of the uterine endometrium at approximately 25–35 day intervals, in the absence of conception (Timiras 1974). The menstrual cycle is unique to the primates; other female placental mammals have a variety of systems controlling ovulation (rabbits, for instance, are reflex ovulators, releasing ova when copulation occurs). Although the selective advantages of the menstrual cycle, as compared to other reproductive systems in female mammals, are not readily apparent, we can be sure that it worked well enough to be sustained by numerous species over 65 or so million years of primate evolution.

In *Primate Paradigms* (1982) Fedigan reviews much of the data available from the first twenty years of post-World War II field and laboratory studies on primate reproductive behavior. Numerous studies have confirmed the relative independence of primate sexual behavior from strictly hormonal control (Beach 1965; Nadler 1994; Nigi *et al.* 1990). Primate reproductive behavior is subject to socioenvironmental factors, displaying a wide variety of patterns that defy neat phylogenetic analysis. For instance, there are significant differences between the sexual behavior of both subspecies of chimpanzees, gorillas and orangutans that do not relate to their respective evolutionary relationships to our species. Hormonal and behavioral states appear closely correlated in gorilla reproductive behavior, somewhat less so in chimps, and least of all in orangutans (Rowell 1972; Nadler 1975).

The primate menstrual cycle is one part of an enormously varied and complex set of developmental, physiological and behavioral characteristics responsible for primate reproductive patterns. Male endocrine physiology, including fluctuations in testicular size in response to social and ecological variables (Enomoto *et al.* 1995; Michael and Zumpe 1993) must also be considered an important factor in the reproductive behavior of primate groups, although it rarely has been (Fedigan 1982; Rowell 1972).

Human females share the basic physiology of the menstrual cycle with nonhuman primates, with fluctuations of estrogen and progesterone producing mid-cycle ovulation. But what of the cessation of hormonal cycling at menopause? Although until recently many evolutionary anthropologists viewed menopause as a uniquely human phenomenon, it is now clear that menopause is probably quite widely distributed among the approximately 200 members of the primate order, given that females survive long enough to reach old age. Captive data show that female nonhuman primates of a number of species undergo irregular and lengthened menstrual cycles, lower estrogen levels and cessation of reproductive viability as they age (Walker 1995; Takahata *et al.* 1995; Koyama *et al.* 1992). The pattern of vaginal bleeding and alterations in serum hormone profiles of macaques in the third decade of their lives are similar to those described in perimenopausal and postmenopausal women (Hogden *et al.* 1977). Aged captive chimpanzees cease ovulation completely (Gould *et al.* 1981; Graham *et al.* 1979; Small 1984). Recent improvements in data collection on the hormonal status of free-ranging primates will make it easier to determine how common menopause is in a variety of species given that animals survive to old age (Stavisky *et al.* 1995; Shideler *et al.* 1995). Thus the differences in important reproductive characteristics emerge as relative rather than absolute between our species and other primates, calling into question evolutionary postulates of "uniquely human" reproductive "adaptations" such as "the loss of estrus" (see Power and Aiello this volume).

Social factors may also influence ovarian function in nonhuman primates. Altmann *et al.* (1987) found that in a population of baboons *(Papio cynocephalus cynocephalus)* daughters of high-ranking females underwent puberty as much as a year earlier than those of low-ranking mothers, and conceived their first infants earlier as a result.

Primatologists have noted an inverse relationship between group size and female fertility, positing food competition and access as causative factors (Altmann and Altmann 1987). Differences in demographics between populations of the same species are often striking in primates and may frequently relate to chance events affecting small groups, for instance a series of births altering significantly the sex ratio of a small group will change social behavior in important ways (Altmann and Altmann 1987).

Upon the basic template of the primate menstrual cycle great variation is played out in reproductive life-history patterns. At the extremes, adult female mouse lemurs *(Microcebus murinus)* are reproductively viable at about one year and produce up to two litters of two or three offspring each year. At the other extreme, the gorilla *(Gorilla gorilla gorilla)* female produces a single offspring every four to five years, and does not breed until about ten years old (Harvey *et al.* 1987). Such differences have probably evolved partly as adaptations for exploiting different ecological niches. Other factors in the evolutionary histories of species must be considered. As Gould and Vrba point out (1982) some characteristics of organisms are "exaptations" (or traits "coming along for the ride"). Such traits are not selected for, but are secondary results that occur when other structures or behaviors are selected for. It is possible, for instance, that monthly shedding of the uterine endometrium is an exaptation; not particularly adaptive, but rather a consequence of features of the menstrual cycle under selective pressure.

Some important elements of reproductive life history in primates appear to be roughly correlated with body size: sexual maturity, gestation length, lactation interval, and life-span are longer in larger primate species (Harvey *et al.* 1987). In addition, a significant relationship exists between some important reproductive life-history events and brain size among primates and other mammals (Sacher 1982). Ultimately, maturation of the nervous system may be an important factor because the brain is an energetically expensive organism. Life-history studies across several nonprimate phyla suggest that animals who have relatively slow prenatal development, or produce relatively large young, are also those that wean and mature relatively late in life (Sacher 1982).

In terms of the timing of major reproductive life-cycle events, gorillas and chimpanzees, genetically the most closely related primates to our own species, share many similarities with humans. This is not surprising since we have an approximately 98 percent chromosomal likeness with the African apes, and fossil and genetic evidence strongly suggest a time of divergence from a common ancestor of only 5 to 7 million years ago (Cronin 1986). Free-ranging chimpanzees experience menarche between age 10–11.5 and first birth typically two years thereafter (Eaton *et al.* 1994). The duration of lactation per birth is 3–4 years with frequent nursing. A completed family size of five off spring is typical. This suggests a pattern very similar to that of some human foragers (Eaton *et al.* 1994).

Modern Humans

Although as primates we share basic reproductive patterns with other members of the order, human reproductive experiences are profoundly culturally influenced. Over the last several decades a number of important studies have looked at the relationships between cultural and ecological parameters (menarche, menstruation, menopause, age at marriage, subsistence patterns, lactation patterns, nutrition, energy output, disease) and reproductive physiology (Beyene 1989; Martin 1993; Campbell and Wood 1994; Ellison 1990, 1994; Ellison *et al.* 1986; Knodel 1983; Konner and Worthman 1980; Howell 1987; Newman 1985; Wood 1989). Moreover, reproductive patterns have altered historically in our own and other cultures. A few centuries ago the reproductive patterns of many individuals in Western societies resembled those of certain nonindustrial societies (Short 1994). Although change occurs in all societies, the change in reproductive patterns with the introduction of postindustrial technologies and their consequences has been dramatic; its impact on women's bodies cannot be overestimated.

For example, cross-cultural studies reveal that the prolonged, frequent and continuous pattern of menstrual cycles of women in contemporary post-industrial Western societies are anomalous. In nonindustrialized societies, female life cycles have typically been characterized by late menarche, frequent pregnancies, and prolonged lactation that suppresses menstrual cycles (Anderson 1983; Harrell 1981). This has implications for theory and practice by calling into question, for example, the use of exogenous hormones patterned after this unusual situation (Anderson 1983; Short 1994).

When put in cross-cultural perspective, the unusual nature of the long gap between menarche and social adulthood which characterizes the contemporary West is evident. In the US the median age for the onset of menarche is 12.8 years, while the median age at marriage is

20.8 years. In many non-industrialized societies, the median age at menarche is much later, around 17 years, and often closely coincides with social adulthood and marriage (Eveleth 1986). The average age of menarche in many of the world's societies as late as 1940 was typical of that found among living foragers, such as the San and Efe (in 1940 the age of menarche in rural China was 17.1 years and 16 years in the nineteenth-century West). In most cultures, the onset of menarche is considered to be the chief index of readiness for marriage, which typically follows soon thereafter. First birth is on the average two years following menarche, with three to four years of lactation creating an ovulation interval. With this pattern of hiatus in ovulation of three to four years following birth, combined with "late" menarche and "early" onset of menopause (relative to the west), the average family size of surviving off spring seems to be about five children in many populations (Howell 1987; Konner and Worthman 1980; Wood *et al.* 1985, 1990; Worthman *et al.* 1993). The total number of menstrual cycles most women in such societies have experienced in a lifetime amounts to approximately 4 years (or 48 cycles).

By contrast, average family size in much of the postindustrial west is 2.5 children. Breast-feeding may not occur at all or occur only on a limited basis (Short 1994). There is evidence that relatively high nutritional availability induces ovulation shortly after the birth of an infant and delays the onset of menopause, which occurs typically in a woman's early fifties (Short 1994). Many women in these settings thus experience approximately thirty-five years of ovulatory cycles, a pattern seemingly unheralded in nonindustrial human or nonhuman primate reproduction. The hormonal milieu of modern Western women over the life cycle is thus dramatically different from that of most female primates.

As with the experience of menstruation, the timing of menopause also varies between and within populations. The average age for onset of menopause for Western industrialized women is 51 years, while it is between 42 and 43 years for many women from nonindustrialized societies (Gosden 1985; Gray 1976; Leidy 1991; Treloan 1974; WHO 1981). Cross-cultural studies indicate that in some cases menopause is unmarked either biologically or socially (Beyene 1989), in contrast to the postindustrial western pattern.

Not only physiological manifestations but also cultural meanings of menopause differ between and within societies (Lock 1993). In contrast to Western biomedical assumptions about women's experience of menopause, studies by anthropologists have noted that the onset of menopause may bring greater social freedom, enhanced sexual pleasure and greater status for women in many cultures. This may be particularly true where fertility is high and access to reliable birth control is limited for much of the woman's adult life (Beyene 1989; Brown 1982; Skultans 1988).

Such studies illustrate some of the proximate mechanisms affecting menopausal experience such as life-style changes (Lau and Cooper 1993), parity (Murphy *et al.* 1994), and nutrition (Beall 1987), which have been hypothesized to affect bone loss and fracture rate in pre- and postmenopausal women. While the precise biological mechanisms involved in these relationships are not always clear, progress continues to be made in this area (Beall 1987; Gosden 1985; Murphy *et al.* 1994). Reproductive events cannot be separated from the ongoing life course, and therefore there is a need for life-history approaches in considering the timing and experience of menopause and bone loss leading to osteoporosis. Taking a life-span approach involves considering a woman's history within the context of cultural, social, and environmental experiences. Chronically elevated estradiol levels may exacerbate the physical transitions of menopause. For example the Maya, whose exposure to estradiol throughout reproductive life is much lower than women in postindustrial settings, have an absence of hot flashes and other menopausal symptoms common in the West (Beyene 1989 and M.C.Martin *et al.* 1993).

Theoretical models and clinical practices in Western biomedicine have not encompassed this variation in experience. The historically recent reproductive patterns of Western women exemplify the extreme plasticity of the body in response to changing cultural practices, and are a distinct departure from many previous patterns as current western cultural practices have profoundly affected the timing of the reproductive clock. With few exceptions, biomedicine has largely ignored these historical changes in reproduction: the focus is an ovary that exists in a constantly stimulated hormonal environment, cycling for 35 years or more, and producing both eggs and ovarian hormones. It has universalized this pattern in the belief that it characterizes all women regardless of fertility history and cultural practices.

We see the clinical implication of this model dramatically expressed in the current treatment of menopause and the etiology of osteoporosis and cardiovascular illness as "estrogen-deficiency disease." At the same time, recent research suggests that some reproductive carcinomas result from a surplus of gonadal steroids over the life span, viewing the reduction in age of reproductive maturity as a risk factor for breast and perhaps prostate cancers (Eaton *et al.* 1994; Short 1994). Altered physical activity, fertility patterns, and breast-feeding practices related to changed workloads and new technologies also increase the risk of reproductive cancer (Bernstein *et al.* 1994), as do diet, including reduced fiber and increased fat intake (Adlecrentz 1990; Rische *et al.* 1994). Changes in lifetime exposure to gonadal steroids foster these health risks: gonadal activity has increased not only in lifetime duration but also in level of hormonal output in women (Ellison *et al.* 1993).

Biomedical interventions as currently conceived may reset an already disrupted clock, perpetuating the unusual pattern of constant ovarian cycling found in the postindustrial West (Voda 1993; Short 1994). Yet there are no easy solutions to the issue of exogenous hormone use given the state of current research and clinical models, nor can we, or should we, turn the clock back to past reproductive patterns which have no viability in the context of world-wide cultural change. But hormonal regimes that attempt to mimic an anomalous constantly cycling pattern should be questioned as the means to address postmenopausal osteoporosis and cardiovascular risk.

Studying human reproduction within the context of the extreme plasticity of primate bodies and behaviors leads away from reductionist postulations of ultimate causality: that reproductive experience is either "culturally constructed" or "biologically invariable." Anthropologists must study the highly contingent processes that are responsible for individual and group variation over the life-span. When genes or cultural norms are reified as "ultimate causes" the complexity of biocultural interactions in human reproduction is obscured. Anthropologists can resituate the ovary within a body that is itself situated in evolutionary biological, cultural, ecological, and political economic realms.

Bibliography

Adlecrentz, H. (1990) "Western Diet and Western Diseases: Some Hormonal and Biochemical Associations," *Scandinavian Journal of Clinical and Laboratory Investigation,* Suppl. 50:3–23.

Altmann, J., Altmann, S.A., and Hausfater, G. (1987) "Determinants of Reproductive Success in Savannah Baboons *(Papio cynocephalus)*" in T.H.Clutton-Brock (ed.) *Reproductive Success,* Chicago: University of Chicago Press.

Anderson, P. (1983) "The Reproductive Role of the Human Breast," *Current Anthropology* 24 (1):24–45.

Beach, F. (ed.) (1965) *Sex and Behavior,* New York: Wiley.

Beall, C.M. (1987) "Nutrition and Variation in Biological Aging," in F.E.Johnston (ed.) *Nutritional Anthropology,* New York: Liss.

Bentley, G.R. (1985) "Hunter-Gatherer Energetics and Fertility: A Reassessment of the ! Kung San," *Human Ecology* 13 (1):79–109.

Bernstein, I.S. (1976) "Dominance, Aggression, and Reproduction in Primate Societies," *Journal of Theoretical Biology* 60:459–472.

Bernstein, L., Henderson, B.E., Hamisch, R., Sullivan-Halley, J., and Ross, R.K. (1994) "Physical Exercise and Reduced Risk of Breast Cancer in Young Women," *Journal of the National Cancer Institute* 86:1403–1408.

Betzig, L.L., Borgerhoff Mulder, M., and Turke, P.W. (eds.) (1988) *Human Reproductive Behaviour,* Cambridge: Cambridge University Press.

Beyene, Y. (1989) *From Menarche to Menopause: Reproductive Lives of Peasant Women in Two Cultures,* Albany, NY: SUNY Press.

Biberoglu, K.O., Yildez, A., and Kandermir, O. (1993) "Bone Mineral Density in Turkish Postmenopausal Women," *International Gynecology & Obstetrics* 41:153–157.

Boone, M. (1988) "Social Support for Pregnancy and Childbearing among Disadvantaged Blacks in an American Inner City," in K.Michaelson (ed.) *Childbirth in America: Anthropological Perspectives,* South Hadley, MA: Bergin and Garvey.

Brown, J.K. (1982) "Cross-Cultural Perspective on Middle-Aged Women," *Current Anthropology* 23:143–156.

— and Kerns,V. (1985) *In Her Prime: A New View of Middle-Aged Women,* South Hadley, MA: Bergin and Garvey.

Browner, C.H. and Sargent, C.F. (1990) "Anthropology and Studies of Human Reproduction," in T.M.Johnson and C.F.Sargent (eds.) *Medical Anthropology: Contemporary Theory and Method,* New York: Praeger, pp. 215–229.

Campbell, B. (ed.) (1972) *Sexual Selection and the Descent of Man 1871–1971,* Chicago: Aldine.

Campbell, K.L. and Wood, J.W. (1994) *Human Reproductive Ecology: Interactions of Environment, Fertility, and Behavior,* Annals of the New York Academy of Sciences: 709.

Crews, D.E. (1993) "Biological Anthropology and Human Aging—Some Current Directions in Aging Research," *Annual Review of Anthropology* 22:395–423.

Cronin, J.E. (1986) "Molecular Insights into the Nature and Timing of Ancient Speciation Events: Correlates with Paleoclimate and Paleogeography," *South African Journal of Science* 82:83–85.

Cronk, L. (1991) "Human Behavioral Ecology," *Annual Review of Anthropology 1991* 20: 25–53.

Dahl, J.F. (1991) "Monitoring the Ovarian Cycles of *Pan troglodytes* and *Pan paniscus*—a Comparative Approach," *American Journal of Primatology* 24 (3–4):195–209.

Darwin, C. (1859) *On the Origin of Species by Means of Natural Selection*, London: John Murray.

Delvoye, R, Demacy, M., and Deloyne-Desnoeck, J. (1977) "The Influence of the Frequency of Nursing and of Previous Lactation Experience on Serum Prolactin in Lactating Mothers," *Journal of Biosocial Science* 9:447–451.

DeVore, I. (ed.) (1965) *Primate Behavior: Field Studies of Monkeys and Apes*, New York: Holt, Rinehart and Winston.

Dittus, W. (1975) "Population Dynamics of the Toque Monkey, *Macacca sinica*" in R.H.Tuttle (ed.) *Socioecology and Psychology of Primates*, The Hague: Mouton.

Draper, P. (1989) "African Marriage Systems: Perspectives from Evolutionary Ecology," *Ethology and Sociobiology* 10:145–169.

Dunbar, R.H. (1987) "Demography and Reproduction," in B.Smuts, D.Cheney, R. Seyfarth, R.Wrangham, and T.Struhsaker (eds.) *Primate Societies*, Chicago: University of Chicago Press.

Eaton, S.B, Pike, M.C., Short, R.V., Lee, N.C., and Trussell, J. (eds.) (1994) "Women's Reproductive Cancers in Evolutionary Context," *Quarterly Review of Biology* 69:353–367.

Ellison, P.T. (1990) "Human Ovarian Function and Reproductive Ecology: New Hypotheses," *American Anthropologist*, 92:933–952.

— (1994) "Breastfeeding and Fertility," in K.A.Deltwyler and P.Stuart-Macadam (eds.) *Breastfeeding: A Biocultural Perspective*, New York: Aldine.

—, Parter-Brick, C, Lipson, S.F., and O'Rourke, M.T. (1993) "The Ecological Context of Human Reproduction," *Human Reproduction* 8:2240–2258.

—, Peacock, N.R., and Lager, C. (1986) "Salivary Progesterone and Luteal Function in Two Low-Fertility Populations of Northeast Zaire," *Human Biology* 58:473–483.

Enomoto, T., Matsubayashi, K., Nagato, Y., and Nakano, M. (1995) "Seasonal changes in Spermatogenic Cell Degeneration in the Semeniferous Epithelium of Adult Japanese Macaques *(Macaca fuscata fuscata)*," *Primates*, vol. 36 (3):411–422.

Eveleth, P. (1986) "Timing of Menarche: Secular Trends and Population Differences," in J.B.Lancaster and B.Hamburg (eds.) *School-Age Pregnancy and Parenthood: Biosocial Dimensions*, Hawthorne NY: Aldine de Gruyder.

Fausto-Sterling, A. (1985) *Myths of Gender: Biological Theories about Women and Men*, New York: Basic Books.

Fedigan, L.M. (1982) *Primate Paradigms: Sex Roles and Social Bonds*, Montreal: Eden Press.

(1986) "The Changing Role of Women in Models of Human Evolution," *Annual Review of Anthropology* 15:25–66.

Ford, C.S. (1964) *A Comparative Study of Human Reproduction*, New Haven, CT: Human Relations Area Files.

Ford, K. and Huffman, S. (1980) "Nutrition, Infant Feeding and Post-Partum Amenorrhea in Rural Bangladash," *Journal of Biosocial Science* 20:461–469.

Furlow, F. and Thornhill, R. (1996) "The Orgasm Wars," *Psychology Today* (Jan.), pp. 42–46.

Ginsburg, F. and Rapp, R. (1991) "The Politics of Reproduction," *Annual Review of Anthropology* 20:311–343.

Goldman, N., Westhoff, C.F, and Paul, L.E. (1987) "Variations in Natural Fertility: The Effect of Lactation and Other Determinants," *Population Study* 41:127–146.

Gosden, R.G. (1985) *Biology of Menopause: the Causes and Consequences of Ovarian Aging,* New York: Academic Press.

Gould, K.G., Flint, M. and Graham, C. (1981) "Chimpanzee Reproductive Senescence: A Possible Model for Evolution of Menopause," *Maturitas* 3:157–166.

Gould, S.J. and Vrba, E. (1982) "Exaptation: A Missing Term in the Science of Form," *Paleobiology* 8:4–15.

Graham, C. (1981) "Menstrual Cycle Physiology of the Great Apes," in C.E.Graham (ed.) *Reproductive Biology of the Great Apes: Comparative and Biomedical Perspectives,* New York: Academic Press.

—, King, O.R., and Steiner, R.A. (1979) "Reproductive Senescence in Female Nonhuman Primates," in D.Bowden (ed.) *Aging in Nonhuman Primates,* New York: Van Nostrand Reinhold.

Gray, R.H. (1976) "The Menopause: Epidemiological and Demographic Considerations," in R.J.Beard (ed.) *The Menopause,* Baltimore: University Park Press.

Haldane, J.B.S. (1932) *The Causes of Evolution,* London: Longmans, Green.

Hamilton, W.D. (1964) "The Genetical Evolution of Social Behavior, I and II," *Journal of Theoretical Biology* 7:1–52.

Haraway, D. (1989) *Primate Visions: Gender, Race, and Nature in the World of Modern Science,* New York: Routledge.

Harrell, B. (1981) "Lactation and Menstruation in Cultural Perspective," *American Anthropologist* 83:796–823.

Harvey, Paul H., Martin, R.D., and Clutton-Brock, T.H. (1987) "Life Histories in Comparative Perspective," in B.Smuts, D.Cheney, R.Seyfarth, R.Wrangham and T.Struhsaker (eds.) *Primate Societies,*Chicago: University of Chicago Press.

Heistermann, M., Finke, M., and Hodges, J.K. (1995) "Assessment of Female Reproductive Status in Captive-Housed Hanuman Langurs *(Presbytis entellus)* by Measurement of Urinary and Fecal Steroid excretion Patterns," *American Journal of Primatology* 37 (4):275–284.

Helvacioglu, A., Aksel, S., Yeoman, R.R., and Williams, L.E. (1994) "Age-Related Hormonal Differences in Cycling Squirrel Monkeys *(Samiri boliviensis boliviensis),*" *American Journal of Primatology* 32 (3):207–213.

Hogden, G.D., Goodman, A.K., O'Conner, A., and Johnson, D.K. (1977) "Menopause in Rhesus Monkeys: Models for Study in the Human Climacteric," *American Journal of Obstetrics and Gynecology* 127:581–584.

Howell, N. (1987) *Demography of the Dobe !Kung,* New York: Academic Press.

Hrdy, S.B. (1981) "'Nepotists' and 'Altruists': The Behavior of Old Females among Macaques and Langur Monkeys," in P.Amoss and S.Harrell (eds.) *Other Ways of Growing Old,* Stanford: Stanford University Press.

— (1983) "Heat Lost," *Science 83* (October): pp. 73–78.

— (1987) "Patterning of Sexual Activity," in B.Smuts, D.Cheney, R.Seyfarth, R. Wrangham and T.Struhsaker (eds.) *Primate Societies,* Chicago: University of Chicago Press.

Isaac, G.L. (1978) "The Food-Sharing Behavior of Protohuman Hominids," *Scientific American* 238 (4):90–106.

Johnson, S.M. and Snow, L.F. (1982) "Assessment of Reproductive Knowledge in an Inner-City Clinic," *Social Science and Medicine* 16:1657–1662.

Jordan, B. (1983) *Birth in Four Cultures: A Cross-Cultural Study of Childbirth in Yucatan, Holland, Sweden, and the U.S.,* Shelborne VT: Eden Press.

Jurke, M.H. (1996) "Behavioral and Hormonal Aspects of Reproduction in Captive Goeldis Monkeys *(Callimico goeldii)* in a Comparative Evolutionary Context," *Primates* 37 (Jan.) 1:109–116.

Kaufman, F.R, Xu, Y.K, Ng, W.G, Silva, P.D., Lobo, R.A, and Donnell, G.N. (1989) "Gonadal Function and Ovarian Galactose Metabolism in Classic Galactosemia," *Acta Endocrinologica* 120:129–133.

Kay, M. (ed.) (1982) *Anthropology and Human Birth,* Phila.: F.A. Davis.

Kitcher, P. (1985) *Vaulting Ambition: Sociobiology and the Quest for Human Nature,* Cambridge, MA: MIT Press.

Knodel, J. (1983) "Natural Fertility: Age Patterns, Levels and Trends," in R.A. Bultatao and R.D.Lee (eds.) *Determinants of Fertility in Developing Countries,* New York: Academic Press.

Konner, M. and Shostak, M. (1986) "Timing and Management of Birth among the ! Kung: Biocultural Interaction in Reproductive Adaptation," *Cultural Anthropology* 2 (1):11–28.

Konner, M. and Worthman, C. (1980) "Nursing Frequency, Gonadal Function and Birth Spacing among !Kung Hunter-Gatherers," *Science* 207:788–791.

Koyama, N., Takahata, Y., and Huffman, M.A. (1992) "Reproductive Parameters of Female Japanese Macaques: Thirty Years of Data from the Arashiyama Troops, Japan," *Primates* 33 (Jan.) 1:33–47.

Lau, E.M.C. and Cooper, C. (1993) "Epidemiology and Prevention of Osteoporosis in Urbanized Asian Populations," *Osteoporosis International,* supp. 1:23–26.

Lazarus, E.S. (1988) "Poor Women, Poor Outcome: Social Class and Reproductive Health," in K.Michaelson (ed.) *Childbirth in America: Anthropological Perspectives,* South Hadley MA: Bergin and Garvey.

— (1990) "Falling Through the Cracks: Contributions and Barriers to Care in Prenatal Clinics," *Medical Anthropology Quarterly* 12:269–87.

Lee, R.B. (1972) "Population Growth and the Beginnings of Sedentary Life among the! Kung Bushmen," in B.Spooner (ed.) *Population Growth: Anthropological Implications.* Cambridge, MA: MIT Press, pp. 329–342.

— (1979) *The !Kung San: Men, Women and Work in a Foraging Society,* Cambridge: Cambridge University Press.

— and DeVore, I. (eds) (1968) *Man the Hunter,* Chicago: Aldine.

— and Lancaster, J. (1965) "The Annual Reproductive Cycle in Monkeys and Apes," in I.DeVore (ed.) *Primate Behavior: Field Studies of Monkeys and Apes,* New York: Holt, Rinehart and Winston.

Leidy, L. (1991) "The Timing of Menopause in Biological and Sociocultural Context: A Lifespan Approach," PhD thesis, Albany: State University of New York.

Lock, M. (1993) *Encounters with Aging: Mythologies of Menopause in Japan and North America,* Berkeley: University of California Press.

Lovejoy, C.O. (1981) "The Origin of Man," *Science* 211 (4480):341–350.

McClain, C.S. (1985) "Why Women Choose Trial of Labor or Repeat Caesarean Section," *Journal of Family Practice* 21 (3):210–216.

MacCormack, C.P. (1982) *Ethnography of Fertility and Birth,* New York: Academic Press.

MacMahan, B. and Worcester, J. (1966) "Age at Menopause: United States 1960–1962," *National Center of Health Statistics,* Series 11 (19).

Martin, E. (1987) *The Woman in the Body,* Boston: Beacon.

Martin, M.C., Block, J.E., Sanchez, S.D., Arnaud, C.D., and Beyene, Y. (1993) "Menopause Without Symptoms: The Endocrinology of Menopause among Rural Mayan Indians," *American Journal of Obstetrics and Gynecology* 100:1837–1845.

Mayer, P.J. (1982) "Evolutionary Advantages of the Menopause," *Human Ecology* 10: 477–493.

Mead, M. (1928) *Coming of Age in Samoa,* New York: William Morrow.

Michael, R.P and Zumpe, D. (1993) "A Review of Factors Influencing the Sexual and Aggressive Behavior of Macaques," *American Journal of Primatology* 30 (3): 213–241.

Murphy, S., Khaw, K.T., May, H., and Compston, J.E. (1994) "Parity and Bone Mineral Density in Middle-Aged Women," *Osteoporosis Journal* 4 (3):162–166.

Nadler, R.D. (1975) "Laboratory Research on Sexual Behavior of the Great Apes," in C.E.Graham (ed.) *Reproductive Biology of the Great Apes,* New York: Academic Press.

— (1994) "Walter Heape and the Issue of Estrus in Primates," *American Journal of Primatology* 33 (2):38–87.

Newman, F.L. (ed.) (1985) *Women's Medicine: A Cross-Cultural Study of Indigenous Fertility Regulation,* New Brunswick: Rutgers University Press.

Nigi, H., Hayama, S.I., and Torii, R. (1990) "Copulatory Behavior Unaccompanied by Ovulation in the Japanese Monkey *(Macaca fuscata),*" *Primates* 31 (Apr.) 2:243–250.

Oyama, S. (1985) *The Ontogeny of Information: Developmental Systems and Evolution,* Cambridge: Cambridge University Press.

Poland, M. (1988) "Adequate Prenatal Care and Reproductive Outcome," in K. Michaelson (ed.) *Childbirth in America,* South Hadley, MA: Bergin and Garvey.

Rapp, R. (1988) "Chromosomes and Communication: The Discourse of Genetic Counseling," *Medical Anthropology Quarterly* 2 (2):143–157.

— (1991) "Constructing Amniocentesis: Maternal and Medical Discourses," in F.Ginsberg and A.Tsing (eds.) *Uncertain Terms: Negotiating Gender in American Culture,* Boston: Beacon Press.

Riley, M.W. (1979) *Aging from Birth to Death: Interdisciplinary Perspectives,* Boulder, CO: Westview.

Rische, H.A., Jain, M., and Marrett, Z.D. (1994) "Dietary Fat Intake and Risk of Epithelial Ovarian Cancer," *Journal of the National Cancer Institute* 86:1409–1415.

Rowell, T. (1972) *The Social Behaviour of Monkeys,* Middlesex, England: Penguin Books.

Sacher, G.A. (1982) 'The Role of Brain Maturation in the Evolution of the Primates," in E.Armstrong and D.Falk (eds.) *Primate Brain Evolution,* New York: Plenum Press.

Shideler, S.E., Munro, C.J., and Taylor, R. (1995) "Urine and Fecal Sample Collection on Filter Paper for Ovarian Hormone Evaluations," *American Journal of Primatology* 37 (4):305–315.

Short, R.V. (1994) "Human Reproduction in an Evolutionary Context," in K.L. Campbell and J.W.Wood (eds.) *Human Reproductive Ecology,* Annals of the New York Academy of Sciences 709:416–425.

Skultans, V. (1988) "Menstrual Symbolism in South Wales," in T.Buckley and A. Gottlieb (eds.) *Blood Magic: The Anthropology of Menstruation,* Berkeley: University of California Press, pp. 137–160.

Small, M.F. (1984) "Aging and Reproductive Success in Female *Macacca mulata*" in M.F.Small (ed.) *Female Primates: Studies by Women Primatologists,* New York: Alan R.Liss.

Smuts, Barbara B. (1987) "Gender, Aggression, and Influence," in B.Smuts, D. Cheney, R.Seyfarth, R.Wrangham, and T.Struhsaker (eds.) *Primate Societies,* Chicago: University of Chicago Press.

Sperling, S. (1991) "Baboons with Briefcases vs. Langurs in Lipstick: Feminism, Functionalism, and Sociobiology in the Evolution of Primate Gender," in M.di Leonardo (ed.) *Gender at the Crossroads of Knowledge: Feminist Anthropology in the Postmodern Era,* Berkeley: University of California Press.

Stavisky, R., Russell, E., Stallings, T., and Smith, E.O. (1995) "Fecal Steroid Analysis of Ovarian Cycles in Free-Ranging Baboons," *American Journal of Primatology* 36 (4): 285–297.

Takahata, Y., Koyama, N., and Suzuki, S. (1995) "Do the Old Aged Females Experience a Long Post-Reproductive Lifespan: The Cases of Japanese Macaques and Chimpanzees," *Primates* 36 (Apr.) 2:169–180.

Tiger, L. and Fowler, H. (eds.) (1978) *Female Hierarchies,* Chicago: Beresford.

Timiras, P. (1974) *Developmental Physiology and Aging,* New York: Macmillan.

Torii, R., Abbot, D.H., and Nigi, H. (1996) "Morphological Changes of the Ovary and Hormonal Changes in the Common Marmoset *(Callithrix jacchus),"* *Primates* 37 (Jan.) 1:49–56.

Townsend, P.K. and McElroy, A. (1992) "Toward an Ecology of Women's Reproductive Health," *Medical Anthropology* 14:9–34.

Treloan, A.E. (1974) "Menarche, Menopause and Intervening Fecundability," *Human Biology* 46 (1):89–107.

Trivers, R. (1972) "Parental Investment and Sexual Selection," in B.Campbell (ed.) *Sexual Selection and the Descent of Man: 1871–1971,* Chicago: Aldine.

Voda, A.M. (1993) "A Journey to the Center of the Cell: Understanding the Physiology and Endocrinology of Menopause," in J.C.Callahan (ed.) *Menopause: A Midlife Passage,* Bloomington: Indiana University Press.

Walker, M.L. (1995) "Menopause in Female Rhesus Monkeys," *American Journal of Primatology* 35 (1):59–71.

Washburn, S.L. and Lancaster, C.S. (1968) "The Evolution of Hunting," in R.B.Lee and I.DeVore (eds.) *Man the Hunter,* Chicago: Aldine.

Watanabe, K., Mori, A., and Kawa, M. (1992) "Characteristic Features of the Reproduction of Koshima Monkeys, *Macaca fuscata fuscata:* A Summary of 34 Years of Observation," *Primates* 33 (Jan.) 1:1–32.

Wilson, E.O. (1975) *Sociobiology: The New Synthesis,* Cambridge, MA: Belknap Press at Harvard.

Wood, J.W. (1989) "Fecundity and Natural Fertility in Humans," *Oxford Review of Reproductive Biology* 11:61–109.

— (1990) "Fertility in Anthropological Populations," *Annual Review of Anthropology* 19: 211–242.

— (1994) "Nutrition and Reproduction: Why Demographers and Physiologists Disagree About a Fundamental Relationship," in K.L.Campbell and J.W.Wood (eds.) *Human Reproductive Ecology: Interactions of Environment, Fertility, and Behavior,* Annals of the New York Academy of Sciences, pp. 416–425.

—, Lai, D., Johnson, P.L., Campbell, K.L., and Maslor, I.A. (1985) "Lactation and Birth Spacing in Highland New Guinea,"*Journal Biosoc. Sci.*17:57–79.

World Health Organization (1981) *Research on the Menopause,* Technical Report Service no. 670, Geneva: WHO.

Worthman, C.M., Jenckins, C.L., Stalling, J.F., and Lai, D. (1993) "Attenuation of Nursing-Related Ovarian Suppression and High Fertility in Well-Nourished, Intensively Breastfeeding Annele Women of Lowland Papua New Guinea," *Journal of Biosoc. Sci.* 25:425–443.

Wright, R. (1994) *The Moral Animal,* New York: Pantheon.

Wynne-Edwards, V.C. (1962) *Animal Dispersion in Relation to Social Behaviour,* New York: Hafner.

Zihlman, A. and Tanner, N. (1978) "Gathering and the Hominid Adaptation," in L. Tiger and H.Fowler (eds.) *Female Hierarchies,* Chicago: Beresford, pp. 163–194.

Chapter Three

The Hierarchy of Nations

The Story—How Things Got to Be This Way

By Sharif M. Abdullah

> *It's all a question of story. We are in trouble just now because we are in-between stories. The Old Story—the account of how the world came to be and how we fit into it—sustained us for a long time. It shaped our emotional attitudes, provided us with life purpose, energized action, consecrated suffering, integrated knowledge, and guided education. We awoke in the morning and knew where we were. We could answer the questions of our children. But now it is no longer functioning properly, and we have not yet learned the New Story.*

—Thomas Berry [23]

Changing our story is the fastest and most effective way to change our world. With a changed story, we can move rapidly to change our toxic relationships with the Earth and each other. Once the story changes, the old paradigm becomes unthinkable.

Introduction to The Story

In order to understand how things got to be the way they are in the human world, let's look at how things got to be the way they were on Rabbit Island.

On Christmas Day, 1776, British explorer Captain Cook arrived on Kerguelen Island, a Connecticut-sized land mass covered with grass in the Indian Ocean.[24] One of the things Cook did while he was there was release a few rabbits. He thought the rabbits would provide fresh meat for any sailors who followed.

The rabbits, in a favorable climate with no natural predators, multiplied. And grew. And flourished. And overpopulated. In a short span of time, the rabbit population exploded into the hundreds of thousands, perhaps millions.

Then, after eating every single blade of grass, they died. They died as they lived, by the hundreds of thousands. The old ones died, the baby bunnies died, the pregnant mothers died. They died because that's how the Web of Life works. Biologists call it "overshoot and dieback." No rabbit was immune.

If you go to the island today, you will see that not one rabbit or one blade of grass exists. Both rabbits and grass were rendered extinct by the rabbits' success. The rabbits were killed by their own story.

Each rabbit had a story that governed its existence and behavior:"Creating a World That Works for Me." According to this story, each rabbit maximized its position, eating as much as it could and producing as many offspring as possible. This formula for "success," in the absence of competing owl and coyote success formulas, was fatal. The rabbits were disastrously successful. Exclusivity is death.

Think about how the rabbits must have felt when their population reached a million and "only" half of their grass was gone. They were in Rabbit Heaven! All the grass you could eat (with no competition), half a million sex partners, and not a coyote in sight! Eat, sleep, and screw all day! The only thing they didn't know was that they were just one generation away from annihilation.

Assume that, at this time, a more-reflective-than-average bunny wrote a book entitled *Creating an Island That Works for All.* In it, he said that if they were to continue to thrive, rabbits everywhere on the island would have to change their *thinking.* No more "maximum food, maximum sex."This strange bunny even went so far as to say that rabbits needed eagles, owls, and coyotes! Without them, the rabbit population would outstrip the generative capacity of the island and all would die. In order for the island to work for rabbits, it had to work for coyotes also. The bunny writer called his concept "inclusivity." He believed that if the rabbits consciously reduced their food intake, consciously restricted their sex habits, and invited in a few owls, eagles, and coyotes, the rabbits and the grass would continue to flourish.

We'll never know whether or not the book bunny was right. We do know, however, that the others were wrong. Dead wrong.

The human population has doubled in my lifetime, and given the current rate of growth, is predicted to double again before I die. We are multiplying like rabbits who have no predators. On a planet with finite resources, our exponential growth makes "overshoot and dieback" our likely destiny. Life can do very well without humans on Earth—or rabbits on a particular island.

Think about this the next time you hear about the stock market's continual rise, the Breaker economy's constant expansion, or the human population's inexorable increase. The Breaker story is as much a recipe for disaster for our planet as the Rabbit story was for Kerguelen Island. Our question is simple: Can we change our paradigm, or will we consume all the grass on this particular island called Earth and die off? Can we change stories in time?

We have failed to take into account the long-run consequences of just doing what we have always done—but better and better.

—Lester Milbrath [25]

What Is a Story?

According to the book *Ishmael*, we enact a story every morning when we get up. As we get out of bed and brush our teeth, we start living our lives according to a story. This enactment continues in our thoughts, words, and deeds throughout the day.

But what *is* a story? According to *Ishmael*, a story is a piece of our culture that explains

- How we got here
- Where we are going
- The interrelationships between ourselves, our environment, and the invisible forces (spirits, ancestors, guides, etc.)[26]

At an early age, we each were given a story to enact. No one sat us down and said, "Mary, I'm now going to tell you the Story of Our Culture." No one gave us a book emblazoned with that title in gold lettering. What happened was that we looked around and saw everyone doing something. They called it

> going to work, catching the bus, catching an antelope, reading a book, reading a palm, conducting a ceremony, conducting a train, eating breakfast, drinking blood, drinking a beer, carrying a gun, tossing rattlesnakes, tossing a salad, killing villagers, making a killing in the market, watching television, watching a sunset, massaging the feet of an elder, visiting the nursing home, making a basket, selling sex, selling stocks and bonds, selling rhino horns, selling military weaponry, stealing a wife, stealing home, stealing a kiss, beating a child, beating a carpet, beating the visiting team, beating a horse, consulting the fortune-teller, consulting a lawyer, consulting the ancestors, consulting the Dow Jones averages, putting on lipstick, putting on cow dung, abstaining from sex, indulging in sex, taking violin lessons, taking drugs, taking a break, driving a car, driving cattle, avoiding the death squads, avoiding taxes, putting on track shoes, putting on high heels, cutting fresh broccoli for a salad, cutting down the rainforest …

We saw these things (or, at least, the ones appropriate to our story) and, without question, we began to imitate those around us. If we saw people eating food they had grown, we did the same. If we saw people eating food purchased from the supermarket, we did the same. If we saw people eating grasshoppers and grubs, we did the same.

A parent doesn't really "teach" his or her child to walk. What the parent does is walk in the presence of the child, modeling the behavior. The child imitates this behavior without regard to whether it is an "improvement" on what it was doing before. What would the child know about improvement? At that stage of its life, conformity to the adult norm is good.

No one tells us, as children, to do this modeling. Enacting the story we see is hard-wired into our systems. According to the research of Jean Piaget and other child psychologists, children don't develop the faculty of abstract reasoning until they are around seven years of age. By that time, most children are fully functioning members of their society. This means you were fully practicing your story well before you developed the capacity to understand it. The story is the only reality you know. You don't question it, you do it. And you are taught to treat every other story as a totally ungrounded fantasy. Excluding other stories is integral to the process.

> I am sitting in the canteen at Sarvodaya headquarters in Sri Lanka, about to eat my first Sri Lankan meal. On either side of me are Westerners; a young guy from England on one side, an even younger American on the other. We're sitting in front of delicious-smelling vegetarian food. There's only one problem: no forks and knives, no chopsticks, nothing.
>
> All around us, everyone else has literally dived in, handfuls of food disappearing from their plates. The other American and I are still staring at our plates, trying to muster the courage to stick our hands into our food. This is not "finger food" like sandwiches or french fries, this is wet, hot, sticky rice and curry dishes.
>
> Leaning over to the American, I whisper, "Are your Mommy tapes running?" He thinks for a second, then bursts into laughter. "Mom is screaming at me right now! 'Get your hands out of your food! Are you some kind of heathen?!' I'm trying to get her to shut up so I can eat!"

"Mommy tapes" are part of our story. They instruct and admonish us, whatever we are doing.

People *always* enact the story given them by their culture, whether the enactment causes benefit or harm to themselves and others. If the story is beneficial and sustainable, people will enact it. If the story is or becomes dysfunctional, they will still enact it, at their peril and the peril of others. People will enact *any* story, including a dysfunctional one, until given a better alternative.

Just as we can't see our own eyes without a mirror, it is difficult to see our own story unless we compare it with stories from outside our culture. However, there is a problem here: our own story tells us to ignore or reject all of the stories of others. We have names for other cultures' stories: tall tales, mythology, fantasy, cultism, old wives' tales, perversion, barbarism. Our own story, of course, is not a story at all—it's "the Truth."

Culture and Story

Conventional wisdom is the dominant consciousness of any culture. It is a culture's most taken-for-granted understandings about the way things are ... and about the way to live. ... It is a culture's social construction of reality and the internalization of that construction within the psyche of the individual. It is thus enculturated consciousness—*that is, consciousness shaped and structured by culture and tradition.*

—Marcus Borg [27]

What's the difference between "culture" and "story"? Culture is what happens. Story is the *explanation* for what happens. It explains what we do, how we got here, what our relationship is to all others, and, most important, where we're going. A story provides the reasons for our actions:

- "We plant our crops this way because our ancestors ..."
- "We pray this way because God spoke to us many years ago ..."
- "I have to sell drugs because the white man ..."
- "I beat up that kid who pushed me because being weak is bad ..."
- "We have to build more nuclear weapons because a strong national defense ..."
- "Don't trust those people, because last time we trusted them ..."
- "We are selling cigarettes to Africa because making money makes America strong ..."
- "Our people are oppressed because an international conspiracy ..."

Such explanations don't have to be logical, good, or true. Provided the behavior they are explaining appears to work, they tend to be accepted without rational analysis. Consider how three groups of cultures explain their eating habits:

Culture	Custom	Rationale
Western	Eating with a fork	"It's cleaner, it's easier. Hands are dirty. Chopsticks are hard to use. Food tastes better."
Asian	Eating with chopsticks	"It's cleaner, it's easier. Hands are dirty. Forks are hard to use. Food tastes better."
Middle Eastern	Eating with the hand	"Its cleaner, it's easier. Forks and chopsticks are dirty—they've been in someone else's mouth. Food tastes better."

These three eating stories are clearly in conflict with each other, the adherents of each believing they are "right" and the others "wrong," if not dirty and disgusting. But as long as everyone is getting fed, there is no compelling need to challenge the stories.

The Tenacity of Story

Once a person has attached himself to a story, asking him to let go of it makes about as much sense as asking him to die. (Actually, the latter may be easier: people are willing to die by the millions to preserve their story.)

> A radio correspondent interviewed a man who was fighting in the former Yugoslavia. The man said: "I will kill and I will gladly be killed to maintain my identity as a Kosovo Albanian. Being a Kosovo Albanian is more important than life itself!"
> The majority of Americans listening to the broadcast were probably wondering what exactly a Kosovo Albanian was.

In our Keeper past, the survival of the narrow group was synonymous with the survival of the individual. Today, it is the survival of the entire planet on which each of us depends. The story we are now defending, the Breaker Story, is a collective myth of destruction.

We need a new story.

Stories That Fit

A Navajo child is given a story to enact. A Manhattan child is given a very different story to enact. Which story is "right"? In reality, neither is right or wrong. The real question is, Which story is appropriate to the world in which those children will in all likelihood live? The Navajo child is given a story that helps her navigate a desert; a Hawaiian child is given a story that helps him navigate an island and the sea; the Manhattan child is given a story that helps her navigate one specific type of urban environment.

> A friend who teaches elementary school in Alaska's Arctic Circle regions related a story to me. "I was giving a geography lesson, pointing out various places on the globe. I asked the children how they would travel from New York to London. Their answer was immediate: 'Dog sled!' I told them that the Atlantic Ocean was not frozen. Again, their answer was immediate: 'Wait for it to freeze, then go by dog sled!' I told them the Atlantic Ocean never freezes solid. There was stunned silence in the room. One boy raised his hand and said, '*Everything* freezes.'
> "I'm not sure I was doing them a favor. In their world, everything does freeze solid. That is a much more important reality to them than what I was teaching."

Each child's upbringing is inappropriate for the others. They each would be ill-equipped for survival in the others' environments. The bunnies on Rabbit Island had a story that was appropriate to a world that contained predators, but completely, fatally inappropriate to a world without predators.

In workshops with contractors, many of them tell stories about the difficulties they faced building government housing for Native Americans on reservations. In the early days, the houses would collapse or go up in smoke in the first few days of occupancy. The Indians were not malicious; they weren't vandals. The houses collapsed from a clash of stories.

The Native American story for "house" is "a place where everyone gathers in the same room" or "a place to build a fire." To accommodate their story, they would remove all of the interior walls (causing the house to collapse) or build a fire in the center of the living room (causing the house to burn down). The Breaker style of housing, based on exclusivity, was wholly incompatible with the Native American story.

There is nothing wrong with the Breaker Story as a story. The problem is that it is the dominant story, trying hard to be the only story. "I am separate," by itself, is not a problem. Thinking objectively is not a problem. The problem arises when "I am separate" becomes the *only* story, because there are vital elements missing from it. Like the rabbits on Rabbit Island, Breakers are not "wrong," they are disastrously inappropriate.

Seven Elements of a Successful Story

What are the elements of a successful story? That depends, of course, on your criteria for success.

The Nazi story, "Creating a World That Works for Aryans," was successful if the criteria for success include the elimination of a significant portion of the population. The industrial story, "We Can Grow Forever," was successful if the criteria include exhaustion of the planet's resources. The slavery story, "Creating a World That Works for Whites," was successful if the criteria for success include exploitation and oppression of other human beings. The scientific determinism story, "We Know Everything," is successful if the criteria for success include suppression of the world of the spirit.

But since these are not our criteria, success must be identified in other ways. Here are seven important elements (you may add others):

To be successful, a new story must be

1. *Inclusive.* The story must have a positive role for every individual and every group. Any story that shames, blames, or ridicules any group is doomed to failure. So are stories that involve mass incarceration or genocide.
2. *Authentic.* Values and actions must be in harmony.
3. *Spiritual.* The story must articulate and demonstrate transcendent values and beliefs. It must include roles for the spirits, ancestors, and other invisible beings, depending on religion or belief system.
4. *Scapegoat-free.* No person or group is made a repository of blame or condemnation.

5. *Sustainable.* The story must pass the test of the seventh generation: will it produce benefits, and cause no harm, to seven generations in the future?
6. *Positive, creative, and adaptive.* The story has to be able to evolve with emerging conditions and events.
7. *Practical, implementable.* The story can be enacted now, without extraordinary innovations (such as contact with space aliens) or materials (such as cheap, safe, inexhaustible fuel).

In the Nazi story, an obvious failure, almost all of these elements were absent. National Socialism was

1. Elitist rather than inclusive.
2. Based on consensual lies rather than authenticity.
3. A travesty of spirituality.
4. Dependent on the existence of a scapegoat.
5. Unsustainable because it was based on the constant expansion of military and political power.
6. Positive, creative, and adaptive—for the elite only.
7. Tragically practical in the short run.

Living Between the Stories

As an entire society, we are between stories. We know the story of the eighteenth, nineteenth, and early twentieth centuries: "Manifest Destiny"—"We must explore and conquer the land, because it is our God-given duty as Americans to extend our borders." We know the story of the mid- to late twentieth century: "Fighting Communism"—"We must pour billions of dollars into armaments and the support of numerous regimes around the world because we have to resist the spread of Communism."

What's our story now? We briefly flirted with the space race as the vertical extension of both the Manifest Destiny and Fighting Communism stories. However, except for a few rocket jockeys, we can't enact a space race story.

Many different stories are now vying to capture the hearts and minds of Americans. They include

Consumption/Success Stories
    "Shop Till You Drop"
    "Lifestyles of the Rich and Famous"
    "Upward Mobility"
    "Martha Stewart Living"
    "Stocks to Watch"
    "Small Is Beautiful" (anticonsumption)

Exploitation/Persecution Stories
    All colonization stories
    Religious persecution (Judaism, Mormonism)
    Ethnic persecution
    Feminism
    Gay/lesbian/transgender rights
    Disability rights
    Animal rights

Liberation Stories
    World War II
    Vietnam War
    Gulf War and anti-Saddam struggle
    Save the Earth

Revolution/Salvation Stories
    People-led revolutions
    Spiritual revolutions
    Cults
    UFOs

Discovery Story
    "The Frontiers of Science"

Distraction Stories
    Alcohol
    Drugs
    Gambling
    Sex
    Entertainment
    Electronic media
    Sports

Image Stories
    Cosmetic surgery
    "No pain, no gain": the gym as second home
    "Dress for Success"
    Anorexia/bulimia
    Piercing/tattooing/scarification

The Three Stories of History

There are three major stories that have shaped or are shaping the behavior of humans on this planet:

The Original Story: "The Keepers"
The Dominant Story: "The Breakers"
The Emerging Story: "The Menders"

Essence of the Stories

We Are Keepers ... We live our lives in harmony with "all our relations." We act out of the belief that the world was not created for any one species. We live here; we don't try to control life. We keep to the ways that work.

We Keepers have been devastated by the Breakers. For thousands of years, the Breakers have killed us, dishonored our ancestors, destroyed our food, ruined our magic, forced us to their ways. The Breakers have been at war with the Earth, and we have suffered for it. The Breakers call us by many names, most of them bad: primitives, savages, natives, aborigines, heathens, pagans, the uncivilized.

Despite this history, we hope that our brothers and sisters who are Breakers will change their ways and come into balance with the Earth, with each other, and with us.

We Are Breakers ... The Earth and everything in it were created for Man; we have the right and the responsibility to place all of it under our control. Because there is not enough for all, the world must be conquered in order for us to exist. We do not live in the Web of Life; we live on top of it. Our story is simple: wildness is bad, human control is good.

We call ourselves by many names, most of them positive or benign: civilizers, settlers, pioneers, missionaries, explorers, industrialists. We will continue to control and dominate all life forms, including humans who are not like us, because control is good.

We Are Menders ... We believe the Earth and our fellow humans need to be healed from the excesses of exclusivity, and we live our daily lives in accordance with this belief. We used to be Breakers, but are consciously turning away from that dead-end path, away from the glitter and allure of the Breaker society. Our goal is to live as a consciously integral part of a living, conscious, and sacred planet, to catalyze a new era, the Mender era.

Our task is simple and profound: to heal the damage caused by the Breakers, those who act as though the Earth and all of her inhabitants were their property. We vow to stop Breaker destruction and begin to restore the balance between the Earth and humanity within this generation.

We Menders are Breakers in recovery. Breaker history is our history. We are not arrogant enough to think that our problems are someone else's fault. We consciously reject all privileges that have come to us at the expense of others' lives, freedom, or comfort.

The Mender story is in harmony with an ancient story, one as old as the Earth itself. We honor the Keepers, who show us the way of wisdom. We honor the Breakers, who show us the way of technology. We heal the damage. We are Menders.

A Synopsis of the Stories

The **Keeper story** is the original story of humans. Keepers are people who live interconnected with their local ecologies and all other beings. They keep the ancient ways of living, perfected over eons of coexistence. Their story is based on a thought, "Living in harmony with all I encounter," and an assumption, "The land is abundant."

Keepers do not have a concept of the Earth as a whole; they are identified with their local ecologies. Within those ecologies, they have, over the course of a million years or more, achieved a dynamic equilibrium with all beings, including human and nonmaterial beings.

Together with their environment, Keepers form a *holobeing*. As a functioning whole, this holobeing repels all invaders.

When Keepers travel to a new ecology, after some period of adjustment, they again arrive at a dynamic equilibrium with the environment.

The ultimate expression of the Keeper story is the village, constructed with local materials and interrelated with the local ecology.

The **Breaker story** is at present the dominant story for humans. Breakers are those of us who act as though everything on and in the Earth were created for us, and that we have the right and responsibility to place it all under our control. The Breaker story is based on a thought, "I am separate," and an assumption, "There is not enough." Breaker behavior is based on control and manipulation of other beings.

Breakers force food to grow in surplus, believing they do not have to be concerned with the ecological consequences of their actions. They force rice to grow in the desert, killing off the beings who live in the desert ecosystems. They prevent other beings from eating the food Breakers grow, destroying beneficial plants, animals, and insects and disrupting forever the local ecological balance. By extending their control over ever greater areas of their environment, Breakers move further out of touch with Nature.

When Breakers travel to another ecology, they completely alter or destroy that ecology in an effort to make it optimal for themselves. All other beings, including other human beings, are either domesticated or eliminated.

The ultimate expression of exclusivity is the city, where Nature is almost totally suppressed. It is worth noting that "civilized" values are those associated with city (Latin, *civitas*) life.

The **Mender story** is the emerging story for humans. Menders are people who are conscious of the global ecology and the interactions of all of the beings who make up that ecology. Menders adapt the values of Keepers to a global reality. The Mender story is based on a thought, "We are One," and an assumption, "There is enough for all."

Menders recognize that humans have become the world's first global species. From the North Pole to Antarctica, there is no local ecology that does not contain humans. Keepers have an ethic that keeps them in harmony with one local ecology. Menders are creating a story that will bring global human behavior back in line with the regenerative capacity of the Web of Life.

Menders dedicate their lives to restoring the balance, integrity, and regenerative capacity of the Web of Life.

Details of the Stories

> *What does it mean to live outside ecosystems? It means that our interests no longer dovetail with those of the natural world around us. ... Inventing agriculture in a very real sense was tantamount to declaring war on local ecosystems.*

—Niles Eldredge [28]

A few thousand years ago, Breakers started us all on a spiral of destruction. In the twinkling of an epochal eye, the Breaker practice of exclusivity has threatened to render the planet virtually uninhabitable and human relations a suicidal, homicidal, demoralized, disenchanted, radioactive tragedy.

Lester Milbrath speaks eloquently about the nature of this change in his book, *Envisioning a Sustainable Society.* He compares the history of our planet to a yearlong movie. If the movie starts in January and ends (at the present) in December, life itself shows up in March. He goes on to state:

> *Compared to most other species, humans have lived on planet earth for a very brief time, (only 11 minutes of our year-long movie). During most of that time humans have lived in harmony with nature; their home was that environment in which they evolved. It is only very recently that our species created an unnatural home for itself as it set out to dominate nature. In that brief period (only two seconds of our year-long movie), we have built a civilization that cannot sustain itself.* [29]

In the short space of ten thousand years (two seconds of Milbrath's movie), Breakers have destroyed, disrupted, and stressed every living system on this planet. (They call this "progress.") Breakers have developed the capacity to end all human life, and most other life as we know it on Earth—no small feat, given the fact that when they started, the most powerful human artifice was a spear.

Even after the drastic reductions in nuclear weapons brought about by treaties, the world's nuclear powers presently have enough destructive capacity to kill thirty-two billion people. There are fewer than six billion on the planet right now. The equivalent of 1.7 tons of TNT exists for every man, woman, and child now living on Earth.[30] This does not take into account our biological and chemical weapons of mass destruction.

We don't have to wait for the Breakers to finally destroy the world to know that they eventually will. We can no longer afford to maintain the fiction that Breaker consciousness is viable. Enough of us know that the ship is going down. Some of us are actively looking for the exits. Some of us are working to change our collective consciousness, our behaviors, and our institutions.

It Ain't All Bad

The Breaker record is not entirely negative, however. In fact, it includes some of humanity's finest achievements.

These words are being written in Havana, Cuba, on the seventh floor of a Fifties-era condominium that faces the glittering blue waters of The Malecon. When I'm done, my laptop computer will be put away and I will eat a delicious lunch. Later this evening, I will take a taxi to a salsa club and listen to some great music. None of this would be possible without the Breaker story.

Without the separating consciousness of Breakers, few of the materially beneficial parts of my life would exist. This consciousness has yielded wonderful results in the fields of health, science, world exploration, commerce, and entertainment. Up until one hundred years ago, the majority of humans lived their entire lives within fifty miles of their birthplace; now, going around the world is not uncommon. Breakers have been able to wipe out polio and smallpox, while controlling malaria and many other diseases that debilitated humans by the millions. They have done this at a very small environmental cost.

The problem is that, like the rabbits on Rabbit Island, Breakers do not know how and when to stop. They splice human genes onto tomato plants to make the tomatoes redder. They have the technology (intelligence about things) to do this, but lack the wisdom (intelligence about relationships) to know *not* to do it.

Parts of Breaker and Keeper thought are essential to the long-range purpose of Earth. Breaker thought allows us to see the world *objectively,* a capacity that can enhance life. Keeper thought allows us to see the world *relationally,* which helps us build our connections with each other. Menders are the blend of these two forms of thought.

Breaker consciousness, which liberated people from local ecologies and brought about an explosion of self-awareness, represented an evolutionary step for humanity; Menders represent the next evolutionary step: bringing human behavior in line with the needs of the Earth.

We are facilitating a fundamental shift from the destructive aspects of Breaker thought. The Breaker mind-set is only a powerful consciousness, a thought. That consciousness can be changed with a different thought.

Menders understand that someone has to repair the damage caused by Breakers, aspects of which will last hundreds of thousands of years. For example, Menders will need to care for the Breakers' nuclear waste dumps. Some of that waste will remain deadly for more than one hundred thousand years. There are 257 tons of plutonium in the world. Only 330 pounds are necessary to kill every human on the planet.[31]

We recognize that living in this world is a sacred act. We behave in ways that heal and restore balance—in our lives, in our communities, in the world. Menders live with wisdom. Menders practice inclusivity. Menders think holistically.

The astronauts gave us our first practical vision of holistic thinking. Although we have known that we live on a round ball since before 1492, it was the space program that gave us the picture of what we really look like as a planet. The Apollo astronauts and Soviet cosmonauts beheld a planet with no lines, no divisions, no right and wrong, no "us" and "other."

This was a startling, paradigm-shifting moment for the astronauts and for those of us on the ground. Until the first images came back to us from space, every globe or map of our planet was seen through Breaker eyes, with borders, political colorings, Cartesian coordinates, and other visual dividers. It was as though the only frogs we had seen were those cut up on the dissection table. The astronauts were the first to see a *living planet.*

The astronauts and cosmonauts gave us a powerful image of what it means to be *homo sapiens holonus,* the thinking human who is part of the whole. In their own words:[32]

When I was the last man to walk on the moon in December, 1972, I stood in the blue darkness and looked in awe at Earth from the lunar surface. What I saw was almost too beautiful to grasp. There was too much logic, too much purpose—it was just too beautiful to have happened by accident. It doesn't matter how you choose to worship God ... God has to exist to have created what I was privileged to see.

—Gene Cernan

[O]nly when I saw [Earth] from space, in all its ineffable beauty and fragility, did I realize that humankind's most urgent task is to cherish and preserve it for future generations.

—Sigmund Jahn

With all the arguments, pro and con, for going to the moon, no one suggested that we should do it to look at Earth. But that may in fact have been the most important reason of all.

—Joseph P. Allen

It isn't important in which sea or lake you observe a slick of pollution, or in the forests of which country a fire breaks out, or on which continent a hurricane arises. You are standing guard over the whole of our Earth.

—Yuri Artyukhin

The first man in space, Yuri Gagarin, made this atheistic statement on his return: "When I was in space, I looked and looked for a God, but did not find him." Perhaps he was looking in the wrong direction.

Menders Are Not Keepers

While we can learn much from the values and wisdom of the Keepers and the way Keepers are interrelated with each other and their local ecosystem, it is safe to say that few of us would trade lifestyles with most Keepers. Just one of many possible stories:

> I was talking with a woman in Uganda, who informed me that she had borne a total of nine children, to watch all but two die within the first five years of life. In her group, they don't even name their children until they are over a year old. Her children died from diseases Breaker science has already cured: diarrhea, stomach worms, and various viruses.

While learning much from this Ugandan mother, I would not trade places with her.

The Keeper story is not adaptable enough to survive the Breakers. Keepers are one with their local ecologies but are not conscious of their oneness; they simply *are.* The lack of consciousness beyond their local ecosystem is their blind spot, which puts them at the mercy of those who have a broader view.

The pioneers of the new society, the Menders, are *conscious* of the global nature of their oneness. Menders seek out opportunities to practice interconnection and interdependence with other beings. At the same time, we are aware of situations where it is advantageous to think and act in an objective fashion. We could be thought of as *tempered* Breakers, or Breakers with a goal of wholeness, healing, and connection.

Keeper, Breaker, and Mender Consciousness Within Each of Us

You can go to the interior of the Amazon basin and visit Keeper communities. You can go to the interior of the jungles of Manhattan Island and visit Breaker communities: tribes of stockbrokers in lower Manhattan, tribes of public housing tenants in upper Manhattan, all living their lives in accordance with the Breaker "I am separate" thought. (It may not be possible to visit Mender communities yet.)

However, without traveling anywhere, you can visit these three states of consciousness within your own heart.

You have a Keeper self that you can honor:

- Your Keeper self needs wildness and reverence for both ecologic and nonmaterial realities.
- Your Keeper self seeks deep harmony with other beings, including other humans.
- Your Keeper self needs to acknowledge that others (beings, ancestors, spirits) are powerful and to trust their power.
- Your Keeper self has no need to manipulate self or others; it experiences satisfaction in community.

You also have a Breaker self that can be honored (but not allowed to dominate):

- Your Breaker self seeks to be defined and honored as an individual.
- Your Breaker self is restless and hungry; it is the source of your urge to explore and grow beyond your boundaries.
- Your Breaker self needs to be in control—of self, others, and the environment.
- Your Breaker self enjoys manipulating its world.

You can acknowledge your Mender self that is now emerging more clearly in your view:

- Your Mender self seeks to transcend the individual self, and desires transcendent experiences.
- Your Mender self is holistic and ecologic, desires peace and sustainability, and thinks in terms of global realities.
- Your Mender self desires to practice compassion—for self, others, and the more-than-human environment.
- Your Mender self celebrates and explores its differences from and similarities to The Other.

As Menders, we acknowledge, then control, minimize, or eliminate Breaker thinking within ourselves. We recognize that we are carriers of the Breaker Disease. We are committed to not continuing the spread of this consciousness and to purposefully catalyzing Mender thinking, in ourselves and others.

The way we control the excesses of Breaker consciousness is to adopt the values of the Keepers and apply them to the Breaker world. The key Keeper values include wisdom, sacredness, and inclusivity with all beings.

Keepers, Breakers, and Menders: Comparisons

	Keeper Consciousness	*Breaker Consciousness*	*Mender Consciousness*
Focus	Life. Keepers see their local environment, including all other beings, as sacred. All beings are part of the Web of Life.	Things. Breakers see their local and distant environments, including all other beings, as property. They treat their environment as a collection of commodities.	Life (primarily). Menders see the total environment, local and global, as sacred, and as "property," to the extent that it benefits the whole.
Highest Priority	Local ecology. No being is more important than another; each has its own unique medicine.	Self. Breakers see "I" as more important than "others."	Global Web of Life.
Characteristic Attitudes	Reverence, honor, and humility before the Web of Life.	Arrogance, dominance.	Compassion.
Relationship to the World	Take what you need with reverence. Ask permission to take it. Use all that you take; leave the rest for others (or later).	Either domesticate or exterminate, control or kill. Take everything, whether needed or not. What is not used is "waste."	Bring life into balance. There is no "waste," only wrong thinking about valuable resources.
Source of Safety	Keepers trust the abundance of the Web of Life.	Safety lies in control.	Safety lies in restoring balance and trust in the Web of Life.
Sustainability	Keepers are sustainable. They have been perfecting their story for one million years or more.	Breakers live on top of the Earth's systems and therefore have no need or desire to be sustainable.	Menders are creating a new story of the sustainability and health of the Web of Life.

The Social Construction of the State

State-Building and State-Destroying as Social Action

By Franke Wilmer

> Without crimes of ethnic cleansing it is impossible to create new states based on national identity, new Serbian state, new Albanian state, new Croatian state, and so on.
>
> —M.Z., Belgrade, 1995

I t was July 1997 when the three of us—my friend Michael, an American I first met in Belgrade when he was working as a translator for the antiwar campaign, Elma, a high school student from Sarajevo who was working as a translator for the "internationals" who now occupied her city, and I—climbed into a cab headed for an interview with the director of the non-governmental organization (NGO) "Žena-Ženema" or "Women to Women." We asked the driver to take us to Hamdija emerlica 25, but the exchange between Michael, Elma, and the cab driver soon heated up until the cab driver was positively irate, furrowing his brow and shaking his hands in dismissive gestures toward us, toward the streets, toward an invisible provocateur. I gave Michael a "what's wrong?" look, to which he replied in a subtle, quiet voice, "Oh, it's nothing really, but he's angry because the names of the streets have been changed and he wasn't sure where 'Hamdija emerlica' is, but when I tried to explain to him where I thought it was he got angry and said "I don't need foreigners telling me how to get around my own city!"

Oddly, there had been much less street-name-changing in Sarajevo than in the Croatian and Serbian capitals of Zagreb and Belgrade. After all, Sarajevo still had a Marsala Tito Boulevard.

I first encountered the street-renaming phenomenon in Belgrade, but for me the larger problem at the time was reading Cyrillic-only street signs. For residents of ex-Yugoslavia, I can imagine how frustrating it must have been when the places where, for fifty years, they had lived, and shopped, and met friends for coffee, suddenly ceased to exist, and in their stead were boulevards and squares named after mostly long-forgotten nineteenth-century nationalists and cultural heroes. (Though in some cases there were interminable debates about whether particular heroes were really Serb, Croat, or Muslim.)

In light of the recent history of fascistic nationalism in Croatia in World War II, however, in the areas of Croatia where Serb majorities lived, the renaming of streets in their hometowns in honor of Croatian nationalists, even long-past historical ones, was perceived as especially foreboding, particularly in conjunction with other policies that seemed overtly or covertly aimed at marginalizing and intimidating the Serb population in Croatia. Even before seceding from Yugoslavia, the Croatian republican government amended its constitution unilaterally to alter the status of Croatian Serbs from "constituent nation" to "national minority." According to Ejub Štitkovac, at a party rally over a year before Croatia seceded from Yugoslavia, Franjo Tudjman declared that: "The NDH [Independent State of Croatia, as the collaborationist regime was known] was not simply a quisling creation and a fascist crime; it was also an expression of the historical aspirations of the Croatian people."[1] To some Serbs, this was tantamount to Holocaust denial. Thus renaming streets and squares throughout Croatia after individuals known for their support of and association with the proNazi Ustaše regime further fueled their fears. Tudjman's "reconciliation" program rested on the premise that the Ustaše and the Croatian army regulars were the unmourned victims of World War II.

The new Croatian "national" flag restored the flag used by the Ustaše, though the new regime claimed it was a symbol of historical continuity with long-standing Croatian aspirations for statehood—the "Thousand Year Old Dream," as it came to be known. The distinguishing feature of the flag was the *sahovnica,* a white-and-red checkerboard insignia, which also began to appear on Croatian national military uniforms. The flag was raised not only on public but also private buildings, shops, cafes, and homes.[2] Serbs serving in the police were fired and replaced with Croats. Mass firings of Croatian Serbs in the public and private sectors followed.[3] These developments, of course, gave tacit permission to the more extreme Croatian nationalists to express openly and even act on anti-Serb prejudices, while Milosevi's government in Belgrade exploited these tensions for its own propagandistic purposes. Serb paramilitaries began to infiltrate mixed or primarily Serbian communities in Croatia. New states were in the making. These developments are described by one of the young émigrés writing to the Open Society Institute:

> A culture that had been "stifled for centuries" was revived in a matter of weeks. Serbia was not alone in its renaissance—people all over Yugoslavia became much more aware of their origins, customs, and religion. ...
>
> What initially seemed to be a cultural appreciation and patriotism developed into a complete misunderstanding and depreciation of other cultures and then into various separatist movements. (J.P., Corvallis, Oregon; Leš 1995:111–112)

Drakuli describes her experience crossing the new "border" between Slovenia and Croatia for the first time:

> There we were, citizens of one country falling apart and two countries-to-be, in front of a border that is not yet a proper border, with passports that are not any good any more. …
>
> Until then, the Slovenian state, the Croatian state, borders, divisions, were somehow unreal. Now, these people with guns in Slovene police uniforms stand between me and Slovenia, a part of the country that used to be mine, too.[4]

Where Do States Comes From?

Americans particularly, but Westerners in general, tend to take the state's existence for granted, albeit within the context of their own romanticized historical narratives and foundational myths about the events and social processes through which it "came into existence." We speak uncritically, casually, and often patriotically, about the "birth" of "our nation." But, as I often tell my students, the United States is not really "orange," Canada is not really "yellow," and Mexico is not really "green." Maps matter. Maps are instruments of political socialization. We internalize an image of the geopolitical reality in which we locate our own experiences, and our identities are bound up with place and place *meaning*. The political entities we call "states" only exist as a set of governing institutions because they are recognized as such by both internal and external agents. Unless those acting authoritatively as agents of the state are willing and able to rely on repressive tactics to maintain power, the existence of the state relies on agreement among most of those living inside its boundaries as well as recognition by agents of other states. In both cases—inside and outside— recognition of some agents is more important than others. *Some* antigovernment activity can be tolerated as long as it remains *marginal*. But it would be quite another story if business, political, and media elites began to defect from their recognition of a state's existence. This is more or less what happened in Yugoslavia. But like most people in Europe and the Americas, whether they live under more or less democratic governments, most of the people in ex-Yugoslavia never expected that their state would cease to exist.

The destruction of Yugoslavia and the apparent ease with which so many of its citizens abandoned their "Yugoslav" civic identity in favor of antagonistic ethnonational identities brings us face to face with the question of state creation: How *do* states, and the identities on which the link between citizen and state rests, come into existence?

Recent criticisms of the organic model of the nation and nation-state, whether from sociological and historical perspectives on group identity and national myths,[5] postmodern and poststructural political analyses,[6] or by inquiring directly into the relationship between narrative and nation,[7] call into question both the basis for social solidarity and the assumption of a normative foundation for the "modern" state. Taken together, critics raise a set of questions crucial to our understanding of both the state and the state system: How do/did states come into existence, and are there important differences in the processes of state creation? What is the basis for solidarity in the state where the citizenry constitute a group? What is the role of identity and what is the role of normative beliefs? Once we denaturalize and demythologize the state, it becomes clear that the state is a set of institutions created through human agency, it is a product of *social processes:* human agents engaged in social relations, the production of meaning, and social acts including speech acts. This is what I mean by the "social construction" of the state; what are the social processes that produce, sustain, and transform the role, functions, and normative basis for the state?

In Chapter 3 I argued that psychoanalytic accounts of the self situated its development within social processes, but what about the state? The state is in a sense an association of selves whose authoritative and allocative acts are structured by institutionalized as well as normative rules about, as Lasswell would say, who gets what, when, where, how, and why. *Where else could the state have come from if not from the minds of men?*[8] And in this case, I do mean men. As Peterson has argued, the modern state has its origins in the political order of the Greeks, an order founded on essentialized sex difference, a privileging of masculine over feminine roles and spheres of action, and a dichotomy between private and public spheres of social life.[9] It is from the public life of the Greeks that Western discourses about the polity as a civic space proceed.

As Michael Ignatieff argues,[10] the narrative of the modern state is often stated in terms of a transition from ethnic to civic identity, but this presumes a preexisting relationship between ethnicity and the state as well as the neutrality of ethnicity with respect to the allocation of values within the state-as-political-community, both of which are highly contestable. Indeed, there is a relationship between ethnicity and the state, but it is much more of a Gramscian relationship of hegemonic ethnic identity, because it is frequently the basis for relations structured by dominance and subjection or more and less privileged (or underprivileged) forms of citizenship. It is precisely because ethnicity is *not* a neutral factor that the justice with which values and goods are allocated by those institutions we collectively call "the state" is so often impaired.

Ethnic Groups, Nations, and States

While I normally disapprove of using dictionary definitions to build academic arguments, it seems useful here because they reflect language practices that represent widely shared meanings within a particular historical setting. Connolly deconstructs the political mythology of "nation" in his essay "The Liberal Image of the State" by critiquing dictionary definitions of "nation." Here he finds that "nation" means "a birth, origin," also a "breed, stock, kind, species, race, tribe," and "race of people" and: The *OED* seconds this, saying that in early European uses race or stock was primary to the idea of nation, while in later usage a people formed through common history takes on more salience.[11]

Although this kind of naturalization of ethnicity as "stock" may seem archaic to more sophisticated thinkers, it was taken seriously enough by the government of Australia in its official treatment of Aboriginal Australians well into the 1960s and 1970s. Aboriginal Australians had difficulties obtaining passports because the Australian government claimed that their Australian nativity could not be verified since their births had often been recorded in "stock books."[12] Australia was not alone. The history of policy toward indigenous peoples in European settler states, as well as the whole of European "colonial science" generally, was rife with the rhetoric of "race" and human "stock" within a schema that cast Europeans as a kind of genetic "crown of creation." In this context, it does not seem such a huge leap to Nazi ideology. In discussing the Western philosophical roots of the modern state, Ernst Cassirir, writing in the mid-1940s, says of the nineteenth century French diplomat and social philosopher Joseph Arthur, Comte de Gobineau, a contemporary of Toqueville whose writings became the basis for twentieth century anti-Semitism:

> One of his firmest convictions was that the white race is the only one that had the will and power to build up a cultural life. This principle became the cornerstone of his theory of the radical diversity of human races. The black and yellow races have no life, no will, no energy of their own. They are nothing but dead stuff in the hands of their masters—the inert mass that has to be moved by the higher races.[13]

European Americans went so far as to claim that Native Americans who had any European blood were by virtue of that blood morally competent to manage title to property responsibly, while their "full-blooded" relatives would have to wait twenty-five years to establish "competency."[14]

Like the *Oxford English Dictionary*, Webster's *International Dictionary*, which probably reflects a more American usage but with an effort to take into account international uses of English, also offers a series of definitions for "nation" that seem grounded in an organic notion of relationship:

1. Kindred; race; lineage.
2. A people connected by supposed ties of blood generally manifested by community of language, religion, and custom, and by a sense of common interest and interrelation; see *people*.
3. Popularly, any group of people having like institutions and customs and a sense of social homogeneity and mutual interest. Most nations are formed of an agglomeration of tribes or peoples either of common ethnic stock or different stocks fused by a long intercourse. A single language or closely related dialects, a common religion, a common tradition or history, and common sense of right and wrong, and a more or less compact territory are typically characteristic, but one or more of the elements may be lacking and yet leave a group that from its community of interest and desire to lead a common life is called a nation.
4. Loosely, the body of inhabitants of a country united under a single independent government; a state.

These definitions begin with the simplest and perhaps most commonly associated attributes related to the idea of *organic relatedness*—"*kinship,* race, lineage"—and culminate with the more modern equation of nation with "state."[15] But the intermediate elaborations emphasize the perceptual—the "supposed ties of blood"—and social dimensions of "nation," perhaps reflecting a more American orientation. The importance of shared history and language are acknowledged in "tradition," "related dialects," and in combination through "long intercourse," pointing to importance of shared meanings, a single, agreed-upon history, and by implication, a tacitly shared worldview. Finally, a normative dimension is indicated both as a social contract in the form of "mutual interest" and "community of interest," and perhaps most important, as a "common sense of right and wrong." The last definition reflects the most recent association of "nation" with the *institutional structure of the state* and its exercise of authority over the people and resources within a territorial space, something ordinarily thought of simply as "country." Surely we do not expect that "countries" can simply cease to exist.

Ideas of "national" and "ethnic" identity do indeed evoke images of kinship, organic relationship, familial loyalties, or, as Donald Horowitz calls it, "a family resemblance."[16] But if the basis of national and ethnic identity is *not* natural, if it does *not* represent common ancestry, then what is it? If the set of markers to which we often make reference as evidence of ethnonational identity—shared history, culture, language, or religion—are not naturally occurring phenomena, how should we think of them? National identities, including ethnic identities, are narrative practices. Some theorists even think of them as metaphoric, though metaphor is itself a narrative practice.[17] They are constituted through "bottom-up" processes: people tell stories of family and regional history; people practice culture and often alter it in the process or, more recently, they "consume" popular culture and by doing so shape its content to some degree; language, of course, contains and transmits culture and structures cognitive development; and both formal and informal religious groups can be influenced to some extent by their practitioners, depending on how hierarchical and flexible the group structure is. But they are also constituted as "top-down" processes, or elite-induced and -manipulated practices, whether in democratic or undemocratic environments.

Let's look at the case of the United States. In order to overcome the ethnic bias of European origins and move toward a more civic-based political culture, the articulation of historical narratives must remain open and contestable. However disturbing and destabilizing "multicultural" discourses are, they have become a persistent as much as contentious feature of civic life in the United States. The production of political culture in the United States is limited only through complex political and legal struggles that engage multiple institutions and actors (the public funding of the arts authorized by Congress, Supreme Court decisions pertaining to the limits of free speech, agents of cultural practice, and direct action by citizens, for instance). Religion remains, for the time being at least, separated from state authority, with multiple institutional and individual actors lined up on both sides of the issue and no lack of religious activists who, arguing that "America has lost its moral foundation" (an argument often made in conjunction with an indictment of multiculturalism), would like to abolish that separation.

The United States, therefore, *aspires* to a civic based identity, though ethnic and religious pluralism seems gripped by perpetual struggles over multiple histories, languages, cultural and religious practices, and right-wing "identity" and "values" groups ever waiting in the wings (and sometimes taking to the streets) to undermine that aspiration. Although the United States was "founded" on the rhetoric of equality, full citizenship was quite exclusive. Because equality originally extended only to a small ruling class of male property owners, it would be difficult to view that ruling class in terms of any kind of pluralism, particularly ethnic pluralism. To the contrary, the norm among early American/ European colonists was the *subjugation* of east Europeans, Asians, Africans, and indigenous peoples. At best, then, what we have in the United States is an ongoing process of *transition* from an *implicitly* ethnic (and/or cultural) basis of political identity to *the ideal* of a civic identity and culture. That transition has been marked by demands—often through direct action and "extraordinary" political action, and sometimes violent—for expanding the basis of inclusion, eradicating traces of second-class citizenship, and emancipating various categories of people subjugated or marginalized on the basis of ethnicity, gender, and/or religious and national identities. American state-building entailed a kind of exclusionary nationalism based on a distinction between "European/Christian/white Americans" and "indigenous/primitive Others of color."[18] Even in the absence of any "ancient hatreds," Euro-Americans managed to kill literally millions of Africans and Native Americans in the course of building their democracy.

Many Western European states are similarly engaged in making a transition from ethnic to civic identities while simultaneously struggling with the process of forging a new "European" civic identity (Weiner 1998). The devolution of authority in Great Britain in response to demands for cultural pluralization, the question of citizenship for Turks and other non-Germans, the persistence of xenophobic political movements and parties in France and, most recently, Austria, all attest to a variety of "ethnic versus civic" identity struggles and adjustments. Meanwhile, the collapse of communism as the ideological basis for states-as-societies has raised a slightly different version of "the identity question" in central and eastern Europe.

These developments, along with violence mobilized around ethnic identities in formerly colonized non-Western states, have given renewed significance to one of the central questions of social theory: *What is the basis for group solidarity within the state?* For no matter how powerfully we imagine that the state is a naturally occurring or "emerging" unit of social order, the creation of real states has been an enormously violent process. The people who live in or "find themselves" living in modern states must confront the consequences of that violence. It is not only the winners who survive to write narratives of political identity, not only the state-makers and their descendants, but a variety of groups, each with its own historical narrative, many who were victimized or exploited by state makers. There are between four and five thousand ethnic groups and fewer than two hundred states. Virtually every state is multiethnic, though some less so than others. Yet every state has an official language and a foundational narrative, however tenuous and unstable it might be. State-making conquers the "Others" within imagined boundaries; assimilates, often brutally, those marginalized as "minorities"; unifies and imposes official languages on speakers of dialects and "nonnative" languages;[19] and excludes particular ethnic groups from citizenship and/or restricts their immigration and emigration. Sometimes states even target specific ethnic/identity groups for forcible relocation. State-making has been violent, both directly and structurally.

Theories of the State

In contrast to realist and neorealist international relations theory, which "takes the sovereign state as a given,"[20] feminist theory, comparative politics, and political theory and philosophy have, in different ways and at different historical moments in the practice of political inquiry, addressed the question of the origins of the state.[21] We have the liberal state, socialist state, welfare state, multiethnic state, totalitarian and authoritarian state, we have states "emerging" from the convergence of historical and social forces, and we have the state-as-polity and the Marxist state withering away. Theorizing the state comes (as it did in the 1960s, as the subject of "political development"), goes (as it did in the 1980s, when theorizing turned to the "states system") and returns (with a rise in poststructuralist, postmodern, and feminist theorizing in the 1990s).

It seems to me that discussions and theories of the state suggest, broadly speaking, five different though not mutually exclusive ways of thinking about the state. One involves an anthropological or sociological relationship between society and state. "Society" precedes the state, so that the state is understood as representing a certain level of societal and organizational complexity, hence it is often thought of as an "evolutionary" model. Gellner summarizes this view:

> Mankind has passed through three fundamental stages in its history: the preagrarian, the agrarian, and the industrial. Hunting and gathering bands were and are too small to allow the kind of political divisions of labor which constitute the state; and so, for them, the question of the state, of a stable specialized order-enforcing institution, does not really arise.[22]

Here, a "prestate" unit of social order, a "society," with perhaps self-evident boundaries, presumably evident also through a shared language as well as shared social norms, reaches a kind of critical evolutionary point of choice: to state-build or not to state-build.[23] Although used primarily by sociologists and some political historians and scientists, an evolutionary model of human society suggests that its roots are in anthropological thinking, even though anthropologists now often acknowledge that their discipline has revealed at least as much about the Western anthropological gaze as about that upon which it gazes.

A second way of thinking about the state also holds that the process of state-building is a function of social complexity, but elaborates and emphasizes the role of *institutions*. Increasing complexity moves social forces in a centralizing direction, producing corporate interests, which in turn create patterns of "behavior," norms, rules, procedures, and decision-making bodies. If this sounds like the basis of regime theory in International Relations, I think it is—an extrapolation from thinking about the state as a particular outcome of political development driven by increasing complexity which both broadens and deepens relationships of social and economic interdependence. According to this view, the state as a set of institutions is a particular response to an evolutionary problem. In a variation on this theme, these institutions can be viewed as the outcome of collaboration and recognition of mutual interests among *elites*, rather than social processes involving collective action in the sense of mobilization by the masses. Again, though employed explicitly or implicitly by nonsociologists, because of its focus on elites and social structures, I tend to think of the state from a sociological perspective.

A third, more overtly political way of thinking about the state views it as the expression of national self-determination. Again, though it draws on and interfaces with anthropological and sociological thinking, the association of statehood with the ability to exercise the fullest capacity for self-determination has the most direct and serious political consequences, particularly as nineteenth-century nationalism gave way to twentieth-century self-determination, notwithstanding the very conflicted and paradoxical relationship between the possible *right of peoples* to self-determination and the *right of states* to sovereignty. The state as an expression of self-determination presumes that the state has an ethnic basis, though a variation on this theme suggests, like the first view, that it is really *societies* that precede states, but that ethnic solidarity is the basis for prestate societies. The idea of *nation* is important here because it does not represent a kind of prestate merging of society with ethnicity. There are currently huge controversies over the international definition of "a people" precisely because that particular unit may, under international law, possess the right of self-determination, though the exercise of that right does not at this point include engaging in any act that violates the sovereignty of an existing state.

Of course the obvious problem here is the discontinuity between the number of ethnic groups and the number of states. It must be possible to exercise the right of self-determination through some means other than by taking, as a group, control of state institutions. The fact (Durkheim would say "social") that there are Chinese people who live in a Chinese state, Japanese people in a Japanese state, Swedes in Sweden, French people in a French state, and so on appeals to our unconscious or at least uncritical assumption that a natural relationship exists between ethnicity and state: ethnic groups, like families, are the basis for societies, and as societies "progressed" they developed into states. This obscures the fact that there are some 55 million people of marginalized ethnic groups in China, and assimilated indigenous Ainu in Japan along with second- and third-generation Koreans denied Japanese citizenship; indigenous Saami have been marginalized in Sweden; and the Frenchness of the French people was achieved (and is still maintained) through a kind of linguistic imperialism,[24] not to mention a very contestable border in the Basque country to the south.

A fourth view of the state has been suggested recently by feminists and various other critical theorists. I alluded to the feminist critique of the state earlier, but it is worth restating here. The state is a "reproduction" of the dominance and subjection socially institutionalized in gender hierarchy, with roots in the Greek *polis*,[25] a defensive response to the "fear of [female] engulfment,"[26] a product of the psychic trauma associated with the realization by the maturing male that control over one's needs is in the hands of one who is "different," and a demonstration of manhood.[27] As in previous cases, there is some overlap between feminist and other views, particularly those emphasizing elite domination, though feminists point out both that hierarchies of dominance may have their roots in gendered hierarchy and that elite structures are, in Western societies anyway and especially under conditions of modernity, dominated by men. Thus in hierarchies of race or class, for example, gender relations within a particular "race" or class will still reflect masculine privileging, both as male dominance and as the privileging of behaviors associated with the socially constructed category of masculinity. Men rule. There is something of each of us in the things we create. The creation of states is a process that both reflects and reproduces gender hierarchy. Therefore the states created by men embody and are understood in terms of "masculine" characteristics and the masculine experience of cognition.

The last perspective on the state follows from discourses on political philosophy within the historical narrative of "Western civilization." It appears sometimes as the image of the modern state as the institutional embodiment of classical liberal ideals, but it could just as well be a Marxist, communitarian, or associationalist state.[28] Here state-building is a humanistic and liberatory project. I include in this category the Marxist variation, for although subverted by the argument that ordinary people could not navigate their own liberation and required an intermediate dictatorship, the modern welfare state in its various shades of social democracy, can, I think, be traced to Marxist influences. The important thing about this perspective is that state-building is understood as a normative project involving the mobilization of *civil society* on the basis of common values and civic, rather than organic, relationship.

Underlying all four perspectives on the foundation of the modern state is an assumption that each attempts to address the basis for legitimacy or, in some cases, social cohesion to the extent that it provides and sustains legitimacy. The first three locate cohesiveness in the realm of organic identity (in the ethnic, rather than Durkheimian, sense), a self-conscious cultural affinity among members of the group, and a shared or at least agreed upon historical narrative, often commingled with the group identity narrative. The fourth—feminist and critical theories of the state—identifies hierarchy, elitism, and patriarchal structures and ideologies not only as the basis for cohesiveness within a race/class/gender-stratified society, but as pitfalls in the progressive development of political institutions legitimized by consent and on the basis of social equity within the framework of the ideal of a liberal polity.[29]

Finally, we have the state as liberator, whether in the form of the liberal state created by the populist revolutions against oppressive, despotic, and arbitrary monarchies of the seventeenth through nineteenth centuries in Western Europe, or in the form of the socialist revolutions in central and eastern Europe, Cuba, and China. In both cases, Marxist and liberal, the *struggle* for liberation provides the normative basis on which postrevolutionary legitimacy rests, and that struggle is mythologized within ideological narratives.

States are, as Giddens and others note, structures of social organization. It is possible as well as useful, I believe, to generalize about social structures to some extent, though we must keep in mind at least two analytical dimensions of distinction: time and complexity. The organization of social life and the structures through which social life is organized vary across time, so they must be historically contextualized, and, if I might add a kind of evolutionary dimension, they will vary in their degree of social complexity. Complexity is indicated by the scope of the organization, that is, the number of individuals whose social life is governed by the organization's norms and rules, and by the breadth and depth of social interaction, that is, the distance between inter-active agents as well as the complexity of their interactions. Thus if we compare the Roman and British empires, the latter would constitute a more complex structure than the former.

The state as a structure of social organization carries out functions that have been carried out by a variety of other social organizations over time, such as the fiefdom, tribe, clan, village, kinship group, and so on. Today, however, as a result of the convergence of a variety of social forces as well as the agency of European political actors, the state is the preeminent structure carrying out or, in Giddens' terminology, "containing" the resources necessary to carry out two kinds of political activities: allocative and authoritative.[30] Any other form of social organization must reckon either with the existence and preeminence of the state, or with agents attempting to construct states in spaces where other forms of organization-tribes, clans, mafias, warlords, and so on—structure social life. Allocative activities involve the distribution of economic opportunities and resources such as jobs, regulating wages, provision of social and welfare services, property rights, access to technology (applied collective/community knowledge, including health care), and so on. Authoritative functions entail regulating social action, mobilizing resources for coercion, and enforcement of allocative rules. In a sense, this combines Laswell's concept of politics as "who gets what, when, where and how," with Easton's idea of politics as the allocation of values.[31] Or almost, for politics is not only about *who gets what* but *who does not get what*. It is, in other words, about allocating *and excluding,* and it is about *mobilizing coercive resources in order to enforce exclusion.* But what is missing, though Easton's emphasis on values nearly gets it, is what Onuf has outlined in his constructivist theory—the *normative* rule on which the basis of allocation, exclusion, and coercion rests. And while we would like to believe that the normative rule on which allocation, inclusion/exclusion, and coercion in modern societies rests is some kind of social contract or citizenship, is it more often, in the end, based on a *perception of sameness,* whether articulated in terms of narratives of organic sameness or narratives of shared historical experience.[32] It is, therefore, identity that secures the social cohesiveness necessary to create and maintain the boundaries of inclusion and exclusion among those who identify themselves as "members" of the social group or "citizens" of the state.

Legitimacy and Social Cohesion

If the state is not "natural" polity or community, then what is the basis for its social cohesiveness, when and where it does exist, and how can cohesiveness be cultivated and, when contested, maintained? As Cohen, Brown, and Organski have shown,[33] most states "came into existence" as a result of violence or by incorporating diverse social groups into a single administrative unit within which a dominant group's identity achieved hegemony. I will limit my remarks, therefore, to the general case of states created through various forms of struggle and conflict, including varying degrees of direct or structural violence. Once such a state "comes into existence," it faces the task of obtaining and maintaining some kind of popular support, even if it is not what Westerners would call a "democratic state." It is, I believe, more a matter of *degree* than *kind* when it comes to the relationship between relying on coercive force (or the threat of it) and relying on consent as the basis for regime legitimacy, for not only direct force counts, but the coercive force of economic survival, and consent is often support given by individuals (even an elite sector of the population, such as religious leaders in South and Central America before Liberation Theology upset the system) in exchange for or in expectation of receiving some kind of personal privilege or benefit, even if only in the form of association with the ruling class or regime.

In explaining civil strife and war or attempting to anticipate states at risk of civil war, we should begin by asking questions about the basis for legitimacy and social cohesion and how cohesion and legitimacy are positioned historically relative to a conflict or potential for conflict. Thus, for example, legitimacy in the United States was weakened during the 1950s and 1960s as social cohesion was stressed as a result of demands for greater inclusion and for ending discrimination and second-class citizenship for blacks and women. The Vietnam War also weakened both social cohesion and legitimacy. While normally the balance between coercion and consent in the United States weighs more heavily on the side of consent, in response to civil unrest arising in connection with both civil rights and antiwar protests, the federal government more than once employed force against those who challenged its legitimacy. The backlash of this period continues to some extent today, as social conservatives continue to chastise various liberation and antiwar movements of the earlier period and claim the need for a "return" to "family values" in order to rebuild the fabric of American society.

Legitimacy in communist countries rested on a combination of coercion and consent, with emphasis on overt and covert coercion. But this does not mean that communist regimes did not also attempt to mobilize consent and, as a consequence, create cohesion. In Poland social cohesiveness was mobilized around both religion and eventually workers' organizations, creating a parallel social structure that undermined the ability of the communist regime to rule with any support other than a minority willing to support the Communist party. In Romania, direct coercion played a larger role than state-sponsored socialization and indoctrination, probably more so than Poland and with less pretense toward consent. In communist states in general, legitimacy would have to rely on intellectuals because social cohesion was based on ideology—the sameness of beliefs—rather than on the sameness of so-called naturalized identities. This was also consistent with Marxist doctrine. Prejudices of ethnicity, class, and gender were supposed to wither away under an enlightened Marxist society, and religion was to become completely irrelevant. What varied among communist countries was the degree to which a particular regime relied on coercion (usually a mixture of direct coercion and state-sponsored socialization) and the degree to which the perception of sameness followed from narrative and ideological abstractions as opposed to organic or concrete naturalized or religious identities.

This emphasis on state-building as an intellectual project, even if it necessitated an interim dictatorship of the "unenlightened masses," profoundly shaped social life in communist societies. Regimes attempted to recruit intellectuals and artists, to censor their cultural production, and, of course, to censor if not fabricate historical narratives consistent with Marxist ideology. Dissidents thus also came to play a critical role in undermining the legitimacy of communist regimes, and Yugoslavia was no different. The historical narrative on which communist Yugoslavia was founded construed "South Slavs" as the relevant kindred identity and a shared struggle against imperialism (Austro-Hungarian and Ottoman) as the basis for creating a liberatory state. Marxist anti-imperialism supplanted earlier forms of anti-imperialism such as Serb, Croat, or Illyrian nationalism. The effort to discredit nationalism, which sometimes took the form of outright government repression, never entirely succeeded, however, and eventually nationalism became an important expression of both demands for reform and outright anticommunist dissidence.

Within this framework, many elements of the breakdown of Yugoslavia and the ability of certain leaders to incite violence becomes much more comprehensible. Alija Izetbegovi's publication of *The Islamic Declaration,* often cited by Serb nationalists to arouse fears of Islamic nationalism in Europe, was more an attempt to articulate Bosnian Muslim dissent from the contradiction of a communist system that claimed to transcend ethnonational identities while at the same time providing unique opportunities for participation on the basis of Serbian, Croatian, Slovenia, Montenegrin, and Macedonian nationalities. The last, failed president of Yugoslavia, Dobrica Ćosić, was a nationalist, a dissident, and a writer. His novel *Vreme srmti,* which tells the story of Serbian "betrayal" and "herosim" during World War I, is said to be one of the two most influential novels in fomenting a climate of toxic nationalism in the 1980s.[34] The 1987 Memorandum of the Serbian Academy of Sciences, often credited with providing the rationale for Serbian hegemonic aspirations and even with starting the war, was influential precisely because it was an intellectual product. Franjo Tudjman was an historian, Radovan Karadži a psychiatrist, his successor, Biljana Plavši a biologist, and so on. The role of intellectuals varied across the various communist states, and I do not mean to oversimplify with generalizations, but in contrast to Western democracies, the party and its ideology functioned as the basis for legitimacy much more than did the constitutions.

Compared to other communist states, the Yugoslav regime relied more on socialization and less on direct coercion, which also meant that Yugoslav intellectuals played a relatively large role in creating and sustaining the legitimacy of the state. Ugreši notes that Yugoslav intellectuals did not have to play the role of dissidents to the extent that their counterparts did in other communist states.[35] Additionally, as a war hero and symbol of pan-Yugoslavism, Tito embodied a naturalized, organic identity, so that when he died, intellectuals began to defect from communism and toward nationalism as the normative basis for solidarity. On a purely rational, intellectual level, the transformation of communist leaders into nationalists (with the exception of Izetbegovi, the secessionist and nationalist leaders of Slovenia, Croatia, Serbia and Macedonia were all former party leaders) and how, when they transformed themselves, the people followed, makes no sense without understanding the legitimating role of intellectuals and the intellectual role of communist leadership. This also explains why Vaclav Havel, a dissident intellectual, was able to lead the Czechs and Slovaks toward a peaceful dissolution, and why the Polish Solidarity movement provided a network for the maintenance of organic identity and later, transition to market democracy.

Both socialist and democratic liberal states attempted to engineer a transition from organic, ethnic conceptions of sameness as the basis for solidarity and cohesiveness to a normative, civic, or ideological basis for reciprocity, sameness, and commensurability among citizens subject to state authority. Communist states may have failed, but that does not mean that liberal states have yet succeeded. Only recently the liberal, democratic, western European state of Austria witnessed the rise to power of a xenophobic nationalist party and leader, to the surprise and outrage of the people and leaders of other EU states. In the process of such a transition, much weight falls on the shoulders of historical narratives, articulating and even mythologizing shared experiences. But why do we assume that democracy is not impaired by the fact that "history is written by the victors"? Why do we seem to be in denial about the distortions of history and their capacity to hinder the democratization of our societies? Why do we assume that the political appropriation of history is unlikely or relatively harmless in our liberal democratic states? I knew from previous research that the construction of indigenous peoples as the backward Other was not as much a thing of the past as more high-minded Western liberals might like to believe. And indigenous people (and other people of color) know that "the victor's history" is neither harmless nor apolitical. Why do marginalized people demand the inclusion of their perspectives, and why do social conservatives so fear this? I have come to believe that an unstable, as contrasted with a "fixed," history, a history inclusive of multiple and conflicting claims, is probably a very good sign in a democracy aspiring to the liberal ideals of social justice.

Balkan Ghosts, Narrative Practices, and Politics

The first breakup of Yugoslavia and subsequent descent into brutal, personal violence rationalized mostly on the basis of imagined ethnic differences occurred during World War II. One-tenth of the population—1,700,000 people—was killed in combat, mass murders, or concentration camps.[36] If we wish to evaluate the broader societal traumatization, then we must also take into account those who killed them, either as members of the collaborationist regime or as fighters for the Serbian nationalist etniks. If we add together the number of people who were either victims or perpetrators, the number of those directly affected is probably doubled, and multiplied again by the number of family members affected. Put differently, something like three million families were directly involved in or tragically affected by the atrocities of a war fueled by both internal and external forces of hatred, even if there was no "natural" basis for it. As the economic and political situation became increasingly unstable after Tito's death, politicians willing to exploit these "open wounds" had little trouble arousing those repressed but not forgotten fears. Drakuli writes poignantly of the interlocking logics of unreconciled grievances, fear, and nationalism:

[N]ow the time has come to count the dead again, to punish and to rehabilitate. This is called "redressing the injustice of the former regime." In the spring of 1990, the monument to the nineteenth-century Croat hero Duke Jelaši, removed by the communist government after World War II and relegated to what was known in the official lingo of the day as the "junkyard of the past," has been returned its original place; Republic Square has been renamed after him. The name of the Square of the Victims of Fascism, where once stood the notorious Ustaše prison, has also been changed. The names of virtually all major streets and squares in the cities throughout Croatia have been changed—even the names of the cities themselves. The symbols, the monuments, the names are being obliterated. ... Thus altered and corrected, the past is in fact erased, annihilated. People live without the past, both collective and individual. This has been the prescribed way of life for the past forty-five years, when it was assumed that history began in 1941 with the war and the revolution.[37]

Mirko Tepavac, former foreign minister in ex-Yugoslavia, finds it miraculous that Tito and his partisan followers, meeting at Jajce in the aftermath of war, managed to establish any basis for peaceful coexistence at all, however coercive, in the aftermath of the war. "[W]ithin two years," he writes, "one could travel safely from one end of Yugoslavia to another, irrespective of nationality, religious beliefs, or language."[38] Pro-Axis war criminals were tried and punished, as well a few political opponents, expressions of nationalism essentially became criminalized, and the slogan of "brotherhood and unity" silenced any open discussion of the horrors of the war. "Terror by remembering is a parallel process to terror by forgetting," writes Dubravka Ugreši, and "Both processes have the function of building a new state, a new truth."[39]

As I formally interviewed and informally chatted with people in the Yugoslav successor states, I was repeatedly struck by their mistrust of history and historians.

M.P. Belgrade 1995

I think it is often the case of history, not only here, being used for political purposes. But it is very clear now, and I agree, it is very difficult because everything has been colored by these very intense emotional issues which were never addressed after World War II. It is very difficult to distinguish between facts and inventions, and we need to learn how to do that. We keep falling into stereotypes of being insufficiently nationally conscious, or of being a traitor, and so history is a battlefield. A lot of my foreign colleagues say "you have to get over the past, you have to look toward the future." But when we try to explain what happened here, that it has some relationship with what happened before—they think this is sort of irrelevant. But this is an extremely complex land geopolitically, and it is not only our choice, but our fate that history has not yet become fully the past here.

R.N., Belgrade, 1995

I don't know if anyone can explain why this is, but so many dimensions of European civilization meet here in such a way that once you touch it, it is just so disruptive and it has been so many times, perhaps like Huntington says.[40] The roots of the religious conflict, relations of central Europe civilization, the division lines between the East and the West, these are things that have been with us, the manipulation by the external powers of the conflict sides, these are all old stories, so obviously the past is a very key dimension in understanding why all this has happened.

And how can you know where you are going until you know where you are coming from? It is overwhelming, that history, once you begin to take it into account, then all other stereotypes and explanations don't hold. So if your intention is not to understand, then you have to ignore history.

When Others take the historical dimension into account then it is always something like "those Balkans people are always fighting" and "ancient hatreds" and so on. But there is something like a posttrauma from these events, and it is passed on from one generation to the next and will continue to do so unless we begin to openly address it.

The question of history, of who gets to decide what constitutes an official or correct version, is not an easy one. How do we not only remember the Holocaust, but remember it *correctly*? And what is the purpose or motivation for remembering? One would think it is in part to draw ethical lessons from the tragedy, the "never again" lesson. But even as Elie Wiesel gave a speech in Washington, D.C., at the dedication of the U.S. Holocaust Memorial Museum in 1992, he reminded his audience of its failure to intervene in Bosnia. All of the people I talked with in ex-Yugoslavia seemed to spend a lot of time thinking about history and the role of history in relation to politics and conflict. Of course, I asked them about the role played by history (see Note on Methodology), but their answers were lengthy and reflective, as if they had been waiting for someone to ask.

M.B., Zagreb, 1997

We were not told the whole truth about World War II, about Bleiburg, and about how most Croats did not support the quisling state. But we were punished as a people for it. I learned later that the symbols used by the Independent State of Croatia were really historical symbols of Croat nationalism long before they were adopted by the Ustaše. So when I display those symbols now, like the flag in my car, it is a *historical* symbol, not a fascist symbol. You know that's how I can tell when I pass other Croats in their cars. They have either the Croatian flag or a rosary, or both, hanging from their rearview mirror.

M.P., Zagreb, 1997

In school of course I learned a lot about World War II, but like everyone else, much more from an ideological and political perspective, not a real historical perspective.

We definitely got a one-sided picture, the picture of the winners, of Partisans, which became the official communist point of view. So communists wrote history from their ideological and political perspective, for their political purposes, and in that case Ustaše, etniks, and others were demonized, stigmatized, and we never had the possibility to experience or to be exposed to the real dimension of that historical tragedy. It was much more a part of the ideological framework of the communist period than a real historical education.

Of course, historical narratives are not only politicized, interpretive acts. They are also the telling of lived experiences. Said one respondent:

S.S., Belgrade, 1995

To speak about how nations or nationalities developed here in Yugoslavia, there is the issue of actually suppressing histories and mythologies. We simply forgot our history as a result of communist education since 1945, which provided us with an internationalist version of history, so to speak. I would add to that the illusion, the official Yugoslav line which the West bought into, that the nationality problem was resolved in Yugoslavia, when in fact it was not resolved. We forgot that it was only relatively recently that there was a fratricidal war here in Yugoslavia, plus another factor—the genocide. The role of genocide in World War II is still very influential among people today, and it is exactly on the territory of Croatia and Bosnia where it occurred that now you have the most intense fighting because, as you know, Bosnia was mainly part of the Ustaše state. Serbs I think suppressed this but never forgot about it. Unlike in Germany, there was not an open discussion about World War II in Yugoslavia since 1945.

The implications of basing state legitimacy on national identity conceived in organic terms were perfectly clear to one very influential philosopher and antiwar activist. He was very angry when I spoke with him; among other, more obvious reasons, he was angry because so many of his graduate students had left the country. This made the prospect for a democratic future even grimmer.

M.Z., Belgrade, 1995

Okay, on my own identity. I am by origin Serb, you know. But I am educated as Yugoslav. In high schools, elementary schools, in the whole of my life I was Yugoslav. And I think that a Yugoslav identity exists. Yugoslav people also exist biologically, in mixed marriages, you know, that would be a biological example of Yugoslav identity, but that is not really the problem. To speak of *biological* Yugoslavs is to take a racist view of identity. The problem is that we were educated as in my generation (I am now 65) not only in Serbian literature, but in Croatian literature, in Slovenian literature, in Macedonian literature. That was our Yugoslav literature. Now people are fighting over whether this or that writer was a Croat or a Serb or a Bosniak. We Yugoslavs don't, for example, have our own philosophy. You know I am philosopher, but I am not interested what nationality, for instance, is Emanuel Kant or Hegel. I was simply educated in philosophy, which is the heritage of humankind. And in that sense I can tell you what my corporeal identity is, but the problem of national identity is the problem of cultural identity, it's not some kind of racism or Nazism which stresses biological identity.

I just came from a symposium in Novi Sad and I had a great dispute with my old friends who were philosophers because now they think that Muslims are "biologically" Serbs. That may be true, but they overlook the fact that the problem of national identity is the problem of *cultural* identity. It is a problem of the historical destiny of some people which existed in Bosnia, and Bosnia was not Serbia during any time of its existence, so those people never lived in Serbia even though they were Serbs. I think that there exists, for example, Bosniak national identity now which was denied at the beginning of this war. Now I think they must have their own identity, but it will depend on the results of this war. Serbs from Pale, these nationalistic Serbs, they leave them only one choice. The Bosniaks had to become nationalistic whether they wanted to or not. But to "cleanse" Bosnia, they are saying "If you are Serb, okay you will stay in our country, if you are not Serbs, if you deny that you are Serbs, then please leave our country. We want to have an ethnically cleansed country." This is insane. This is a move backward, a racist move backward.

D.V., Belgrade, 1995

How did national identity change during the last decade and last several years? Before and during the war? I think that identities have not been changed in the sense that people who are Croats suddenly changed their identity. Most probably thought of themselves as both Croat *and* Yugoslav, both Serb *and* Yugoslav, and it was not a problem for them. Political elites tried to make identity an issue. During the existence of last Yugoslavia, the identity of Yugoslav existed. Period. Probably as the institutions that embodied the Yugoslav state disintegrated, people became frightened, perhaps they could not identify Yugoslavia with something that could solve their problems. There is so little difference between the cultural heritage among Croatian, Serbian, people, especially, they have common language, even common history. The only thing they don't have in common is religion. According to Max Weber, the difference in religion is the main source of the difference among nations in this part of ex-Yugoslavia. But I think that we are now faced with the problem of the identity of Muslims in our country. If your question is how national identity has been changed I must say that the first problem is the appearance of a new question—do we have to neglect the existence of Muslims as special national identity or to affirm it? This was central to the "nationality question" which arose in the sixties and seventies and was never resolved.

I think we must affirm it, must recognize that there exists a type of new national identity which wants to be recognized here. And the main problem is not when we recognize it, but if we neglect those demands for the identity of nations within existing states. Every nation in ex-Yugoslavia wants to have their own state, and this is completely impossible. The right of self-determination was the main ideological model of Serbian nationalists. They say all nations in ex-Yugoslavia had this right of self-determination—Slovenians, Croatians—not only for Serbs, and Serbs must have their own country, a new country in which all Serbs live in a new Greater Serbia. This is completely impossible. Imagine that all Russians want to be in one state!

R.N., Belgrade, 1995

All the nations now aspiring to become states have, in developing their national dreams or aims, recruited various historical myths, so the reconstruction and reinterpretation of history is being done all over the place. You have literally hundreds of books on behalf of each nationality now attempting to prove that either they are the oldest nation in this region, or that they dissociate themselves from the others, that the others come from somewhere else, that their origins are different than they were, that they belong more to Europe and not Balkans, the so-called Europe-Byzantine question. The roots of our existence here are really being reinterpreted, and there are all sorts of preposterous theories coming out. I think it is hard sticking to this kind of mythological legitimation of the national dreams and trying to prove that what they are doing now is actually carrying a continuation of something thousands and thousands of years old. In that sense the machinery of inventing an reconstructing the past is very present, and there are serious problems from the past, and memories and tensions, and mutual ill memories, but also this whole political industry of producing false history.

I think it is often the case of, not only here, [history] being used for political purposes. But it is very clear now, and I agree, it is very difficult because everything has been colored by these very intense emotional issues and it is very difficult to distinguish between facts and inventions and it needs to be, falling into stereotypes of being insufficiently nationally conscious or a traitor, and so history is a battlefield. This is one aspect, and another aspect is that I think (a lot of my foreign colleagues say "you have to get over the past, you have to look toward the future, we are not interested in"—when we try to explain what happened here, that it has some relationship with what happened before—they think this is sort of boring) but this is a very, very complex land, and it is not only our choice, but to some extent, our destiny.

B.J., Belgrade, 1995

Serbs living in one state, it was Yugoslavia, and now they want all Serbs living in one state, but why destroy Yugoslavia? Yugoslavia was where all Serbs lived in one state!

And one of the student émigrés recalls:

> I remember that I had never known my grandfather—he had been hanged by the Ustaše. I remember being told that my family had not been allowed to take him off the gallows for four days because the Ustaše were setting an example for the rest of the village. And I resented the Croats for that.
>
> But at the same time I knew that there was nothing intrinsically evil about the Croats, and nothing inherently altruistic about the Serbs. The Croats' reasons for hating the Serbs seemed reasonable, too. Furthermore, some of my best friends were Croats. I could not resolve the dilemma between love for my own culture and respect for cultures that differed from mine. ... (J.P., Corvallis, Oregon)

In the case of Yugoslavia, the interpretation and reinterpretation of historical "truths" are often regarded as a major factor contributing to the creation of a hostile climate that made war carried out as personal violence almost inevitable. "The terror of remembering," says Ugreši,

> is, of course, also a war strategy of setting up frontiers, establishing differences: we are different from them (Serbs), our history, faith, customs and language are different from theirs. In the war variant this complex (which profoundly penetrates the Croatian collective consciousness) is used like this: we are different from them (Serbs) because we are better, which is proved by our history; we always built, they only destroyed; we are a European, Catholic culture, they are only Orthodox, illiterate barbarians. And so on and so forth.[41]

On the six hundredth anniversary of the Battle of Kosovo, Milosevi evoked the "terror of remembering" in his now infamous 1989 speech in which he grounded Serb nationalism in historical victimization, a move would enable him to contort Serbian aggression in Bosnia and provocation in Croatia into noble and liberatory acts:

> Today, it is difficult to say what is the historical truth about the Battle of Kosovo and what is legend. Today this is no longer important. Oppressed by pain and filled with hope, the people used to remember and to forget as, after all, people in the world do, and it was ashamed of treachery and glorified heroism. Therefore it is difficult to say today whether the Battle of Kosovo was a defeat or a victory for the Serbian people, whether thanks to it we fell into slavery or we survived this slavery. ...
>
> The lack of unity and betrayal in Kosovo will continue to follow the Serbian people like an evil fate through the whole of its history. Even in the last war [World War II], this lack of unity and betrayal led the Serbian people into agony, the consequences of which in the historical and moral sense exceeded fascist aggression. ...
>
> The concessions that many Serbian leaders made at the expense of their people could not be accepted historically and ethnically by any nation in the world, especially because the Serbs have never in the whole of their history conquered and exploited others. Their national and historical being has been liberational through

the whole of history and through two world wars, as it is today. ... Let the memory of Kosovo heroism live forever! Long live Serbia! Long live Yugoslavia! Long live peace and brotherhood among peoples! (From Milosevi's speech on the six hundredth anniversary of the Battle of Kosovo, Gazimestan, June 28, 1989)

The Battle of Kosovo came up in virtually every interview in Serbia because it was widely believed to have become a symbol around which the most intolerant and even racist form of Serbian nationalism was aroused among ordinary people. So powerful is its symbolism that I found Americans quoting Serb propaganda during the NATO intervention in Kosovo in 1999. They told me again and again how "Kosovo is to Serbs like the Alamo is to Americans," one of the official lines coming out of Belgrade at the time.[42]

S.T., Belgrade, 1995

If you asked people on the street what year was the Battle of Kosovo, many people wouldn't know, but the idea of having been conquered by the Turkish empire is what is important in their version of history. The Kosovo played a role in Serb identity for two reasons: (1) to liberate all the Serbs, specifically, and (2) identifying Serbs as liberators vis-à-vis imperial conquest. In the nineteenth century nationalism was important in all of Europe, that was the time of nationalism, not in today's sense, but the nineteenth century was the century of nationalism in a romantic sense. Then between the two wars and after the Second War it was not so important to Serbs, but now they have made it important again. ... It is a revival of Kosovo and revival of nationalism.

D.T., Belgrade, 1995

In the minds of ordinary people, the Battle of Kosovo is a powerful symbol of oppression as told in our history under the Ottomans. The central feature of the story was liberation from the Muslims [Turks] because Kosovo battle was the symbol of this liberation from the Turks. They [the nationalists] repeated this theme all through the nineteenth century very much to create support for [Serbian] uprisings and then finally the Balkan wars. And now they do the same, because after the uprising in Kosovo and the conflict between Albanians and Serbs some intellectuals from the nineteenth century have also been revived as cultural heroes. Serbian national identity has been created by defining itself as a struggle against Muslim—meaning Turkish—domination.

S.T., Belgrade 1995

I have thought about this Kosovo battle. I am not sure that it played some role in the development of national identity because Kosovo was important for identification of Serbs in the nineteenth century but that is not the only fact because we have the same thing in Bulgaria and Macedonia. But it played a greater role in the creation of Serb national identity in the nineteenth century than now because the main goal then was the independence of Serbia, the main interest of Serbs was to liberate Kosovo field and that was important for national identification and for national unity. The main slogan for the Balkan Wars was to liberate Kosovo.

As Milosevi's ranting in Kosovo elevated his influence among the growing number of elite nationalists, some more and some less extreme, Franjo Tudjman the historian had just published his controversial book entitled *Bespuča* (Wilderness), just a year before he was elected as president of Croatia. His revisionist history of Ustaše atrocities gave a figure of 60,000 Serbs and others killed at the compound of camps known as Jasenovac, in contrast with the claim under the postwar communist regime that between 750,000 and 1 million people died there. Many Croats hailed Tudjman for "finally revealing the truth" about the war, relieving them of the collective guilt Tito had manipulated in order to subdue them and any national political or cultural aspirations. His claim not only set off a furious debate in what was still an undivided Yugoslavia (structurally, at least), but provided chilling evidence of how historical narratives as "truths" had structured both identities and interpersonal and intergroup relations in postwar period. The book provoked a campaign to disinter mass graves in order to discredit Tudjman. The crusade was carried out on the ground and in the media, with publically displayed remains and televised funerals. In the process, the heretofore unacknowledged fact of the Bleiburg Massacre of unarmed Croatian refugees also received substantial publicity, and this, in turn, coupled with the implication of collective Croatian guilt for the brutalities of the quisling regime, provoked a significant anti-Yugoslav, anti-Serb backlash in Croatia. Tudjman's book was considered by some as tantamount to hate speech. Croatian and Serbian nationalist narratives became mirror images of victimization and paranoia:

D.C., Korcula, 1997

Of course the Serbs have a fear of so-called Croatian nationalism by the stories given to them by their people who lived through the Second World War. It was not intended to scare them, or to provoke them with talk about what Croats had done to them in the Second World War. In the socialist education system when you talk about history you get the partisan version of history, when you talk about the Croatian situation in the Second World War, you got a very bad picture about the Ustaše and the Croatian nationalists and what they did. Of course the numbers are very interesting, they always played with the numbers. The official line was always to talk about communism as the savior against the Ustaše enemy. But I actually I think that more than that it was just to keep Croats under control. Tito was seen to manipulate the collective guilt of Croats for crimes of Ustaše, and that was also seen [by Croats] as a way of keeping Croats under control. On the other hand, from the Serb perspective, Tito was seen as splitting up Serbs into three different republics and then making autonomous regions in Serbia was a way of controlling Serbs. So each had a paranoia about the other and about the communist system or Tito as the oppressor.

V.D., Belgrade, 1995

The time of Communist totalitarianism as an era in the history of the idea of Yugoslavia, as a Yugoslav state, it was comparatively a very long period in the history, almost fifty years, which is longer than the eleven years of democracy in Serbia before. So you can disregard all the propaganda about this tradition and that tradition, because what they learned under communism lasted longer than any of these other periods when the Serbian state was supposed to have existed as a democracy aspiring to self-determination. And now textbooks have been rewritten, and most of the Stalinists have become nationalists. You have kids here who were twleve or thirteen when Milosevi came to power and now they are seventeen or eighteen. They grew up with one version of things and now they find another. The totalitarian mind has adapted perfectly well to the politics of Milosevi and other, sometimes even more extreme nationalists. I don't believe personally that Milosevi is really a nationalist. He is an opportunist.

J.B., Zagreb, 1997

The Serbs always identify with their own victimization. They tried to manipulate the Croats through a sense of collective guilt for what happened in World War II. Under Tito, with mostly Serbs in the bureaucracy, Croats were disproportionately arrested and imprisoned for crimes against the state. Serb nationalism was expressed as Yugoslav patriotism, since really Yugoslavia was a state where most of the government jobs were taken by Serbs. Croats, on the other hand, were industrious, and preferred not to work in government jobs, but to be educated and more professional. We were punished for expressing any Croat nationalism.

K.V., Belgrade, 1995

Some people are concerned that there will be three Serbian states, and they are concerned about whether they will need a passport to go from, for example Serbian Krajina to Republika Srpska, to Yugoslavia. You know if this was a situation of normal European states it would become quite normal for people to travel without passports as they move from one state to another. It doesn't really matter so much what state you are from. And I say there have been many examples, you know, where people of one nation are not allowed to unite into one state for strategic reasons. Austria is not a part of Germany. But this obsession ... these creatures of myth, the nation, they have a powerful influence on the imagination and, consequently, on our ideas of reality.

D.S., Belgrade, 1995

So okay, there are principles, you know. One is the principle of group identity, a second is the identification with or within the territories or republics, and finally the identity of the man as an individual. You know these are the three principles. And the misalignment of these three was always a problem of Yugoslavia. It began to subside in the twentieth century in this so-called modern Serb state. It has its roots in the nineteenth-century independent Serbia, although it was from Belgrade to Niš, but in this part it was organized administratively in this way, and the political parties were established in the nineteenth century. So some kind of formal political culture existed within Serbia, and some kind of territorial identification. But let us discuss Serbian history. People will talk about Serbian tradition, they talk about heroism, fighting against invaders, but what about five hundred years of Turkish rule, and only occasionally some uprising. It is again very contradictory. So Serbs are some heroic, and some very subservient. People make mythologies about themselves, and about the Others, of course people make mythologies.

S.T., Belgrade 1995

There is not much history of Serbia as an independent state, but the mythology goes to the Middle Ages, the feudal state of Serbia. Then of course, this is where the idea that Kosovo is in Serbia comes from. But it was not until after World War I that Kosovo and Metohija became part of Serbia as a modern state. From some Serbs you get the impression that they had killed all the Turks when they talk of overthrowing their oppressors. ... But Serbs and Croats, Muslims and Croats are essentially the same people. In some sense it is a biblical war between brothers. I mention our case simply because at times it becomes ridiculous. In the case of Yugoslavia, Serbs became, in the eyes of the others, a very big nation, but actually it is a very small nation. Serbia is one of the most megalomaniacal nations in the world. By that I mean this idea that although you are a small nation, you can claim something much larger, which was in fashion at that time. In the eyes of Slovenes or Croats when they talk about Greater Serbia you would think they were talking about the Soviet Union or U.S. or at least Canada or something like that.

S.S., Belgrade, 1995

As a matter of fact my wife is a Serb from Croatia who escaped the genocide there in 1941, her family was killed. People moved back and forth, it is in some sense one nationality, but it is not necessarily homogeneous. There are some differences in traditions, but historically speaking, Montenegrins are in some ways more Serb than I, who come from central Serbia, and still they wouldn't like to be ruled always from Belgrade. If it ever came to some unification or reunification with the Serbs in Bosnia or Croatia, it would have to be some kind of federal state or decentralized state because in spite of how much we try to convince ourselves that being Serb is enough to make us all alike, there are very sharp differences, for instance, between the rural Serbs of Bosnia and the majority of urban Serbs in Belgrade. There has always been a difference between Serbs living in and out of Serbia proper. But speaking about so-called Greater Serbia, it has never been developed as a project. There were some talks historically, but, I think that was at the time of World War I, 1914 to 1915, when there was the possibility that if Serbia and Montenegro became victorious—as they did, later on—they would be able to choose what sort of state to create as a result of their World War I victory, as a result of helping to defeat the crumbling Austro-Hungarian empire. Whether to unite only parts of the southern Slavic areas, primarily Serb majority areas, or to opt for something larger. Today some people think that Serbs made an historical mistake—I don't know, it depends on how you look at that, whether a mistake or not, it certainly was a reflection of Serbian megalomania, self-determination, Versailles, the idea that somehow the Western Allies wanted to get the Balkan parts together, and there were several factors.

Drakuli laments the loss of cosmopolitan identity and the way in which Yugoslav realities collapsed into Manichaean opposites in a political climate of escalating and mutual intolerance:

> Some of my foreign friends from that time cannot understand that being Croat has become my destiny. How can I explain to them that in this war I am defined by my nationality, and by it alone? There is another thing that is even harder to explain—the way the awareness of my nationality, because of my past, came to me in a negative way. I had fought against treating nationality as a main criterion by which to judge human beings; I tried to see the people behind the label; I kept open the possibility of dialogue with my friends and colleagues in Serbia even after all telephone lines and roads had been cut off and one third of Croatia has been occupied and bombed. ...[43]

Conclusion

Perhaps the nation is not entirely imagined. Perhaps there was a time when the boundaries delineating communal life were marked by sharper distinctions in language, physical appearance, and cultural practice, as with many indigenous peoples today, in spite of unrelenting efforts to force their assimilation. But it has been the project of the state to incorporate and expand its control over people and resources. We may even one day come to see imperialism as an historical chapter in the logic of state expansion. In any event, as a consequence of state and imperial expansionism, virtually all states today are to some degree multiethnic, multicultural, and multinational. Their boundaries are more artificial than natural, and their roots lie in violent processes rather than consent. To many of the people living within them, the boundaries of the polity appear contestable. Perhaps we should be surprised that they are not challenged more often. That they are not is probably a result of several factors: the relative openness of some (more or less democratic) states to participation and changes that restructure power; the ability of states to persuade those within their jurisdiction that they can secure basic needs for order, access to economic resources and opportunities, collective decision-making, problem-solving, and so on; and the production of legitimating narratives constructed out of both historical interpretation and a belief that identity and political life are linked—that the inside/outside boundaries between "us" and "others" are real.

Perhaps what we in the Western world call "ethnic" identities today are the remnants of a more organic form of kinship. But modernity, with its capacity for the widespread movement of people and ideas (not to mention guns, germs, and steel), its migrations, conflicts, and logic of domination, has left in its wake many fractured, fragmented, and interpenetrated identities living within the boundaries of a relatively small number of states. We might view the century of conflicts in southeastern Europe, including former Yugoslavia, as postcolonial. "State-making" has been a violent process involving both direct and structural domination, which in turn has led to struggles among groups for and against cultural hegemony. But it is not only a matter of establishing, albeit through violent means, *whose* language will be the official language, *whose* version of history will represent the official history, and *whose* cultural practices and identity constitute the basis for a (mythologized) "national" identity on which the legitimation of the nation-states rests. One identity achieves dominance through state-making by *destroying* (assimilating, marginalizing) "other" cultures, languages, histories, and identities. Yet here we are, as the twenty-first century begins, living in a political world in which thousands of groups who do or might claim nationality on the basis of ethnic, cultural, or religious "sameness" live within a system of fewer than two hundred states.

Historical narratives do not constitute truth, nor can they ever consist of complete knowledge. They attempt to resolve competing truths in accord with struggles over power and interpretation in order to produce legitimating narratives (American history, French history, British history, Irish history, Russian history, and so on). In actuality they can do no more than settle such questions temporarily and in relation to the structure of power underlying complex relationships (including those of domination and subordination) among agents. Historical narratives are a kind of repository for the ongoing project of interpreting collective human experiences. From historical interpretation meanings and identities are constructed; however, neither meanings nor identities are stable and fixed. The stories themselves are less important than either the meanings we assign to them or the way meanings structure power. Only in a democratic environment can multiple histories be told, contested, and become the subject of inclusive civic discourse. But that is not enough. The liberal model of the state as we know it today remains centered on the idea of majority-minority relations, where majority is most often expressed in terms of identity, whether in ethnic, national, or cultural terms or some combination thereof. Perhaps, as both Connolly and Rosenau argue,[44] what we need are decentered identities, where no identity is privileged within a truly pluralistic normative environment.

Chapter Four

The Geographical Exploration of the World

The Ideal of Civilization

Its Origins, Meanings, and Implications

By Brett Bowden

It is never a waste of time to study the history of a word.

Lucien Febvre, *A New Kind of History*

Civilization is a fact like any other—a fact susceptible, like any other, of being studied, described, narrated.

François Guizot, *The History of Civilization in Europe*

"Civilization" Revived

The terms *civilization* and *civilizations* have recently regained some of their lost prominence as tools for describing and explaining how our world works. As will become apparent, the term *civilization* and its plural continue to be interpreted and applied in a variety of manners and different contexts. In response to this revival and as an explanatory tool itself, this study also makes extensive use of the idea of civilization in order to explain certain processes in history and world politics. As will be explained, this includes the idea of civilization as both a process and a destination or state of being; it also includes the ideal of civilization as a comparative benchmark that manifests itself in a "standard of civilization." As the idea of civilization is both a key concept and a broader theme running through the heart of this book, this chapter gives a comprehensive overview of the evolutionary origins and contested meanings of the term *civilization* and its plural.[1] In undertaking this etymological exploration early on, my intention is to lay the foundation upon which the rest of the book is built. It is further intended to illuminate and aid in navigating the key issues addressed in this study.

The first task is to review the circumstances under which the word *civilization*, or its linguistic equivalents, entered into French, English, and German usage. These three languages are the most significant for a number of reasons, not the least of which is the fact that they are the three languages that dominated European diplomacy in the eighteenth and nineteenth centuries, when both the word and ideal of civilization entered into European thought. French was likely the most widely spoken language in Western Europe at the time, while English was the language of the dominant power of the era, and German was used widely because of the vast web of diplomatic relations that linked the various Germanic provinces. Furthermore, French is important because it is the language in which the word *civilization* is first known to have appeared. The next significant development was when *civilization* appeared shortly thereafter in English usage. Whether it was received from the French or came into being independently is unclear, but it carried much the same meanings as it did in French. Perhaps most interesting, though, is the somewhat complicated translation of the word and idea of *civilization* into German, in which *Zivilisation* stands for something quite different and is altogether subordinate or, by some accounts, antithetical to the German concept of *Kultur*.

As seen in following chapters, the Spanish discovery of the New World also played a significant role in shaping the events that led to the birth of the ideal of civilization. However, I think it is fair to say that the Spanish, and the Portuguese, were considered by other European powers to be a declining imperial force by the time of the arrival of the word *civilization*, a time when much of the Americas had already won their independence. That is not to say that French and English second-wave imperialism did not learn many lessons from first-wave Spanish imperialism, two phases of European imperialism that Anthony Pagden describes as "distinct, but [with] interdependent histories."[2] As in German, so too in Dutch and Italian the word *civilization* was confronted by local terms that served a similar purpose, yet did not quite mesh with the ideals of civilization. In the Netherlands the noun *beschaving*, based on the verb *bechaven*, meaning to refine, polish, or civilize, was widely used, while in Italy the word *civilità*, as found in Dante, had long been entrenched in the language.[3] The significance of *civilization* as both a word and an ideal and the key role the three prominent Western European languages played in shaping both have been captured in a rather effusive statement by the French linguist Émile Benveniste: "The whole history of modern thought and the principal intellectual achievements in the western world are connected with the creation and handling of a few dozen essential words which are all the common possession of the western European languages." *Civilization* is one of those words.[4]

For much of the twentieth century, a century in which two World Wars, the Great Depression, and the Holocaust all served to undermine the very *idea* of civilization, it seemed as though it was more the case that it *was* one of those words. Despite this, the middle years of the century did produce a number of comprehensive studies of the rise and fall of major civilizations by noted historians, sociologists, and anthropologists. The 1980s also saw the publication of a major study on the "standard of civilization" in international society,[5] but this too was a largely historical study and by century's end these styles of investigations had become scarce in mainstream fields of inquiry.

A contemporary work that has captured imaginations and helped revive what might loosely be called "civilization studies" as a legitimate or worthwhile field of study is Samuel Huntington's "clash of civilizations" thesis.[6] The airing of this thesis and the post–Cold War international political climate into which it was born, along with the subsequent rise of the threat of fundamentalist terrorism, has generated extensive and ongoing debates that have helped to again popularize the term *civilization(s)*, nowhere more so than in the realm of world politics. Despite being one of the more notable contributors to this revival, Huntington offers only the briefest history and definition of the term, stating that the "idea of civilization was developed by eighteenth-century French thinkers as the opposite of 'barbarism.'" Simply put, "To be civilized was good, to be uncivilized was bad." Huntington acknowledges that out of its origins evolved a distinction between the usage of *civilization* in the singular and "civilizations in the plural," the latter being the concern of his book. But this development is oversimplified to the point that the arrival of the latter merely marks the "renunciation of a civilization defined as an ideal, or rather as the ideal."[7] The study of the plural variant, or "civilizations as fact," however, is not as readily divorced from a concern with "civilization as ideal" as Huntington suggests. As Quentin Skinner notes, it is at once both a descriptive and an evaluative term.[8] Or as Fernand Braudel suggests, the triumph of one over the other "does not spell disaster" for it because they are necessarily tied together in "dialogue."[9] In contrast to Huntington, it is the study of *civilization* that is the greater concern of this book, but, as noted, this concern cannot arbitrarily exclude discussions of *civilizations*, for the two concepts are closely linked. The nature of the dialogue between the singular and the plural begins to reveal itself as soon as one starts to explore the origins of the word *civilization*.

French Origins of Civilisation

The French historian François Guizot's declaration that "civilization is a fact like any other,"[10] susceptible to detailed study, is a little misleading in that it makes the task sound considerably more straightforward than it actually is. Even in Guizot's own use of the term, in fact since its very inception, the word *civilization* has been imbued with a plurality of meanings. Some render it a "fact" amenable to measurement, while others refer to it as a not so readily quantifiable "ideal."

The word *civilisation* has its foundations in the French language, deriving from words such as *civil* (thirteenth century) and *civilité* (fourteenth century), all of which in turn derive from the Latin *civitas*. Prior to the appearance of *civilisation*, words such as *poli* or *polite*, *police* (which broadly meant law and order, including government and administration), *civilizé*, and *civilité* had all been in wide use, but, in Benveniste's view, none of these adequately met the evolving and expanding demands on the language. Upon the appearance of the verb *civiliser* sometime in the sixteenth century, which provided the basis for the noun, the coining of *civilisation* was only a matter of time, for *civilisation* was a neologism whose time had come. As Benveniste states it, "*civilité*, a static term, was no longer sufficient," requiring the coining of a term "which had to be called *civilisation* in order to define together both its direction and continuity."[11] But in its first-known recorded usage, the word *civilisation* held a quite different meaning to that with which it is generally associated today. For some time *civiliser* had been used in jurisprudence to describe the transformation of a criminal matter into a civil one, hence *civilisation* was defined in the Trévoux *Dictionnaire universel* of 1743 as a "Term of jurisprudence. An act of justice or judgement that renders a criminal trial civil. *Civilisation* is accomplished by converting informations (*informations*) into inquests (*enquêtes*) or by other means."[12] But *civilisation*'s life as a term of jurisprudence was a rather brief and sparing one once it was appropriated by thinkers who imbued it with the meanings we associate with it today, meanings which were to catch on quickly and gain wide acceptance in intellectual and popular thought.

Just when the written word *civilisation* first appeared in its more contemporary sense is open to conjecture. Despite his extensive enquiries, the French historian Lucien Febvre admits that he has no accurate idea as to "who was the first to use it or at least to have it printed." But he offers that he has "not been able to find the word *civilisation* used in any French text published prior to the year 1766," when it appeared in a posthumous publication by M. Boulanger titled *Antiquité dévoilée par ses usages*.[13] The passage in which it appeared reads: "When a savage people has become civilized, we must not put an end to the act of *civilisation* by giving it rigid and irrevocable laws; we must make it look upon the legislation given to it as a form of *continuous civilisation*."[14] From this early passage it is evident that *civilisation* is used to represent both an ongoing process and a state of being that is an advance on the condition of "savagery."

Claims to uncertainty aside, Benveniste and Jean Starobinski independently argue that *civilisation* first appeared in written form in its nonjuridical sense ten years earlier than Febvre believed.[15] Dated 1756 but not published until 1757, *civilisation* appears three times (on pages 136, 176, and 237) in Victor de Riquetti, marquis de Mirabeau's (1715–1789) treatise on population, *L'Ami des hommes ou Traité de la population*. Perhaps somewhat curiously, Voltaire makes no use of what one would think would be a highly useful word (*civilization*) in a prominent work of the same year, his *Essay on the Customs and Spirit of Nations*.[16] Reflecting Mirabeau's usage of the term, the 1771 edition of the Trévoux *Dictionnaire universel* included for the first time both the jurisprudential and newer meaning of *civilisation*. The entry reads: "The *ami des hommes* [Mirabeau] *used this word for sociabilité*. See that word. Religion is undeniably the first and most useful brake on humanity; it is the first source of civilization. It preaches to us and continually recalls us to confraternity, to soften our hearts."[17]

Starobinski argues that the authors of the Trévoux *Dictionnaire* chose their example carefully, for Mirabeau's usage of *civilisation* provided a "welcome" contradistinction to the Enlightenment philosophes and encyclopedists' advocacy of reason and the sciences. Rather than singing the praises of reason, virtue, and morality as the successors of religion and the true path to human perfectibility, Mirabeau argued that "religion was 'the principal source' of civilization." Thus, as Starobinski states it, "the word civilization first appeared in a eulogy of religion, which was praised not only as a repressive force (a 'brake') but also as unifying and moderating influence ('confraternity')."[18] For Benveniste, though, "*civilisation* is one of those words which show a new vision of the world," one that is "an optimistic and resolutely nontheological interpretation of its evolution." In this regard, he refers to "the very novelty of the notion and the changes in the traditional concept of man and society that it implies."[19]

Starobinski notes that, once coined, the term *civilisation* was rapidly adopted into common usage because it encapsulated a broad range of terms that were already in use to describe a preexisting concept, one that included notions such as advancements in comfort, increased material possessions and personal luxuries, improved education techniques, "cultivation of the arts and sciences," and the expansion "of commerce and industry."[20] Thus, as *civilisation* became increasingly common in French vocabulary, so too it was defined in greater detail in French dictionaries. This development can be seen in Snetlage's *Nouveau Dictionnaire français contenant de nouvelles créations du peuple français* of 1795, which defined *civilisation* thus: "This word, which was used only in a technical sense to say that a criminal case was made civil, is used to express the action of civilizing or the tendency of a people to polish or rather to correct its mores and customs by bringing into civil society a luminous, active, loving morality abounding in good works. (Every citizen of Europe is today embarked upon this last combat of civilization. Civilization of mores.)"[21] Building on Boulanger's account of *civilisation*, we see in this definition a hint of the notion that the condition of civilization is the preserve of the peoples of Europe (albeit to varying degrees), while its opposites, savagery, barbarism, or the state of nature lay beyond Europe's borders.

As seen in these early appearances of *civilisation*, from the very outset it was a term imbued with a plurality of meanings. Serving as something of a "synthetic" or "unifying concept," *civilisation* was used to describe both a process through which individual human beings and nations became civilized and the cumulative outcome of that process. As Starobinski states, the "crucial point is that the use of the term, *civilization*, to describe both the fundamental process of history and the end result of that process established an antithesis between civilization and a hypothetical primordial state (whether it be called nature, savagery, or barbarism)."[22] Thus, it was used both to describe and to evaluate, or to pass judgment in the very act of describing. In order to explore further the nature of the relationship between the state of civilization and its alternatives (be they antithetical or otherwise), it is helpful to first understand the plurality of meanings attributed to *civilization*.

Apart from the distinction between civilization as process and civilization as the end condition resulting from that process, further distinctions have been drawn between what is characterized as civilization as *fact* and civilization as *value* or *ideal*. In the former sense, it is said to be largely a "descriptive and neutral" term used to identify what are thought to be quantifiable values held in common by a distinct group of peoples, that is, a specific civilization such as that of ancient Greece or contemporary Western civilization. In the latter sense, civilization is a "normative concept on the basis of which it was possible to discriminate the civilized from the uncivilized, the barbarian, and the incompletely civilized."[23] Following a similar line of thought, Febvre notes that the "same word [civilization] is used to designate two different concepts." What is elsewhere described as civilization as "fact" is referred to by Febvre as its "ethnographic" usage.

> In the first case civilization simply refers to all the features that can be observed in the collective life of one human group, embracing their material, intellectual, moral and political life and, there is unfortunately no other word for it, their social life. It has been suggested that this should be called the "ethnographical" conception of civilization. It does not imply any value judgement on the detail or the overall pattern of the facets examined. Neither does it have any bearing on the individual in the group taken separately, or their personal reactions or individual behaviour. It is above all a conception which refers to a group.[24]

But even this definition is more than just descriptive; it too has an (unacknowledged) normative-evaluative component. *Civilization* is not usually used to describe the collective life of just any group, as *culture* sometimes is; rather, it is reserved for collectives that demonstrate a degree of urbanization and organization. This normative assumption is evident in that Febvre's ethnographic markers all relate, either directly or indirectly, to a group's sociopolitical organization.

Immediately following the "ethnographic" account of civilization, Febvre gives a definition of civilization as an ideal or value.

> In the second case, when we are talking about the progress, failures, greatness and weakness of civilization we do have a value judgement in mind. We have the idea that the civilization we are talking about—ours—is itself something great and beautiful; something too which is nobler, more comfortable and better, both morally and materially speaking, than anything outside it— savagery, barbarity or semi-civilization. Finally, we are confident that such civilization, in which we participate, which we propagate, benefit from and popularize, bestows on us all a certain value, prestige, and dignity. For it is a collective asset enjoyed by all civilized societies. It is also an individual privilege which each of us proudly boasts that he possesses. (220)

From these accounts it is evident that the former usage is used to describe distinctive *civilizations* across time and place, while the latter signifies a benchmark or *the civilization*—that is, it represents the *ideal of civilization*—which all other societies or collectives are compared to and measured against. While the former have been the subject of much comparative historical analysis, which in itself is an unavoidably evaluative exercise, it is the conception of civilization as normative ideal that is more the concern herein.

The reason for focusing on the value-laden nature of civilization begins to reveal itself when looking into further accounts of civilization, such as Comte de Volney's, published in 1803 after his travels in the United States in the late 1790s. Reflecting the general principles of social contract theory, but just as importantly for the purposes here, the criteria of requiring a capacity for self-government, Volney wrote: "By *civilisation* we should understand an assembly of the men in a town, that is to say in an enclosure of dwellings equipped with a common defence system to protect themselves from pillage from outside and disorder within. … The assembly implied the concepts of voluntary consent by the members, maintenance of their right to security, personal freedom and property: … thus *civilisation* is nothing other than a social condition for the preservation and protection of persons and property etc."[25]

As becomes increasingly evident, the demand for a nation or people to have the capacity to organize into a cooperative society with a capacity for self-government is central to the ideal of civilization. But the identification of different collectives as civilizations on the basis of their capacity for social cooperation and self-government has really only served to distinguish them from other human collectives. Importantly, I demonstrate in following chapters that it is not just about a people organizing and governing in any fashion that counts. Rather, it is governing in accordance with certain standards—first set by Europe and later by the West more generally—that determines a society's approximation to the idealized "standard of civilization." This factor becomes increasingly apparent when exploring the English language origins and evolution of the word *civilization*.

English Origins of Civilization

According to the *Oxford English Dictionary*, the word *civilization* first appeared in English in 1772, some fifteen years after its initial appearance in a French text. The reference it cites is a passage in James Boswell's *Life of Johnson* that reads: "On Monday, March 23, [1772,] I found him [Dr. Samuel Johnson] busy, preparing a fourth edition of his folio Dictionary. … He would not admit *civilization*, but only *civility*. With great deference to him, I thought *civilization*, from to *civilize*, better in the sense opposed to *barbarity*, than *civility*; as it is better to have a distinct word for each sense, than one word with two senses, which *civility* is, in his way of using it."[26] The entry in Boswell's diary is much in keeping with *civilization*'s French foundations; it also gives a good indication of at least one sense in which the term entered into English usage. But as the context in which Boswell uses it hints at, it appears as though the word had already been in use for some time prior—and indeed it had. The honor of first recorded English usage of *civilization* is in fact thought to go to the Scottish Enlightenment thinker Adam Ferguson, who used *civilization* in his *Essay on the History of Civil Society*, first published in 1767.[27] There is good reason, however, to believe that Ferguson actually used the term some years prior to 1767, as is indicated in a letter of April 12, 1759, from David Hume to Adam Smith in which he makes reference to a "treatise on Refinement" by "our friend Ferguson."[28] If Ferguson also used the word *civilization* in this earlier draft of his *Essay* manuscript, then there is cause to believe that *civilization* was in use in English, albeit rarely, no more than three years after its first recorded use in French.[29] As to whether Ferguson began using *civilization* independently of the French, assuming that he was indeed the first to use and record it, which cannot be guaranteed, or had picked it up from the French remains open to speculation.

While the word *civilization* appears in Ferguson's *Essay* only eight times (on pages 1, 75, 90, 203, 232, 243, 244, and 249), the work itself has been described as "a history of civilization."[30] At its core it is an investigation into the progress of humankind and society from a state of "rudeness" to a "refined" or "polished" state. This theme is established on the very first page of the *Essay*, where Ferguson writes, "Not only the individual advances from infancy to manhood, but the species itself from rudeness to civilization."[31] As Duncan Forbes states it in his introduction to the 1966 edition of the *Essay*, what Ferguson was looking for was a "true criterion of civilization."[32] And as Ferguson clearly states in his later *Principles of Moral and Political Science*, that criterion was some degree of sociopolitical organization. For he writes in the *Principles* that "success of commercial arts … requires a certain order to be preserved by those who practice them, and implies a certain security of the person and property, to which we give the name civilization, although this distinction, both in the nature of the thing, and derivation of the word, belongs rather to the effects of law and political establishment, on the forms of society, than to any state merely of lucrative possession or wealth."[33] From these passages alone, and from the general theme of Ferguson's *Essay* in particular (also from his *Principles*), it is apparent that, like the French, he too uses the term *civilization* to describe both a process and a condition. As becomes evident below, Ferguson's line of thought on the criteria of civilization contains elements that social and political thinkers had been pursuing as early as the ancient Greeks.

As indicated by both Volney's and Ferguson's respective accounts of civilization, it becomes increasingly the case that sociopolitical and legal organization is inherently and inextricably linked to the ideal of civilization. An example of this is John Stuart Mill's essay of 1836 titled "Civilization," which is also an indicator of the general acceptance and widespread use of the term in English around eighty years after it was introduced. At the beginning of his essay, Mill, like others before him, notes that the "word civilization … is a word of double meaning," sometimes standing "for *human improvement* in general, and sometimes for *certain kinds* of improvement in particular."[34] For the purposes of his essay, however, Mill is referring to civilization as ideal condition, or what he calls "civilization in the narrow sense: not that in which it is synonymous with improvement, but that in which it is the direct converse or contrary of rudeness or barbarism." And he is not talking here just about the condition of the individual, but "the best characteristics of Man and Society" (51–52).

The importance of society to the qualification for civilization is expressed in Mill's recipe, in which he lists the "ingredients of civilization." Following Montesquieu to some degree, he states that whereas

> a savage tribe consists of a handful of individuals, wandering or thinly scattered over a vast tract of country: a dense population, therefore, dwelling in fixed habitations, and largely collected together in towns and villages, we term civilized. In savage life there is no commerce, no manufactures, no agriculture, or next to none; a country in the fruits of agriculture, commerce, and manufactures, we call civilized. In savage communities each person shifts for himself; except in war (and even then very imperfectly) we seldom see any joint operations carried on by the union of many; nor

do savages find much pleasure in each other's society. Wherever, therefore, we find human beings acting together for common purposes in large bodies, and enjoying the pleasures of social intercourse, we term them civilized. (52)

The presence, or otherwise, of the institutions of society that facilitate governance in accordance with established (Western) European traditions was widely believed to be a hallmark of the makings of or potential for civilization. Mill was representative of this belief in his assertion that "in savage life there is little or no law, or administration of justice; no systematic employment of the collective strength of society, to protect individuals against injury from one another." Despite the fact that similar institutions performed similar functions in the non-European world, the absence of institutions that resembled those of the "civilized" nations of Europe meant that much of the world beyond its borders was deemed by "civilized" Europe to fall short of meeting Mill's necessary "ingredients of civilization." As Mill stated, "We accordingly call a people civilized, where the arrangements of society, for protecting the persons and property of its members, are sufficiently perfect to maintain peace among them" (52–53).

The requirement of a capacity for sociopolitical organization and the role of society are reaffirmed in Mill's declaration: "There is not a more accurate test of the progress of civilization than the progress of the power of co-operation." For it was widely held that "only civilized beings … can combine," and "none but civilized nations have ever been capable of forming an alliance." Savages, on the other hand, are characterized by "incapacity of organised combination." The reasoning behind this belief was that combination requires compromise: "it is the sacrifice of some portion of individual will, for a common purpose." As such it was thought that "the whole course of advancing civilization is a series of such training" (55–56). But as becomes increasingly evident, there was a prevailing view among the self-declared civilized societies of Europe that savages and barbarians lacked the discipline and predilection for compromise and cooperation among themselves. Rather, savages and barbarians were seen as trapped in a "state of nature" in which "every one trusts his own strength or cunning, and where that fails … is without resource" (52). There were, of course, thinkers like Edmund Burke who recognized the value and achievements of non-European civilizations.[35] But for others like James and J. S. Mill, the only way the "uncivilized" could hope to rise to some degree of civilization—if it was thought possible at all—was under the guiding hand of civilized Europeans who would instill the necessary discipline and training that made society possible.

In essence, for Mill, civilization was marked by "sufficient knowledge of the arts of life," "diffusion of property and intelligence," "sufficient security of property and person," and "power of co-operation" in society so as to "render the progressive increase of wealth and population possible."[36] But the maintenance of civilization did not come cheaply. Adam Smith, for example, argued that an increase in wealth and population was in fact a prerequisite for the discharge of the "first duty of the sovereign" of civilized societies; that of protecting the society from external "violence and injustice." According to Smith, it was "only by means of a standing army … that the civilization of any country can be perpetuated," an exercise that becomes increasingly expensive the larger society grows and the more "society advances in civilization."[37] Smith also maintained that it was "only by means of a well regulated standing army … that a barbarous country can be suddenly and tolerably civilized" (296). In summary, much of British thinking is neatly captured by Herbert Spencer's claim: "We may consider it [civilization] as progress towards that constitution of man and society required for the complete manifestation of every one's individuality."[38]

German Kultur Versus Zivilisation

While the evolution of the word *civilization* ran along roughly parallel lines in French and English thought, in German the term *Zivilisation* stood for something quite different and was altogether subordinate to the concept of *Kultur*. While still useful, *Zivilisation* is a term of "second rank" that deals only with superficialities, such as external appearances. *Kultur*, on the other hand, is a term that is representative of Germany's self-understanding of national pride and sense of achievement—its sense of being. Furthermore, the French and English conceptions of civilization generally refer to political, social, economic, religious, scientific, and or moral issues, while the German term *Kultur* is essentially reserved for expounding intellectual, artistic, and religious facts or values. Moreover, *Kultur* is inclined to include a distinct divide between these more valued concerns on the one side and subordinate political, social, and economic issues on the other.[39]

Some of the reasons behind the distinctions between the French and English concept of civilization and its German counterpart *Kultur* have been set out by Norbert Elias in *The Civilizing Process*. Elias maintains that the differences are attributable to the contrasting roles played by the respective intellectual classes that gave birth to and shaped the meanings of the concepts. In France, the concept of *civilisation*—and French civilization itself—was born at court and in Paris cafés, where it took shape amidst ongoing intellectual exchanges between a politicized and politically engaged French intelligentsia. In contrast, German *Kultur* was generated by a more widely dispersed, less interactive middle-class German intelligentsia that Elias describes as "far removed from political activity, scarcely thinking in political terms and only tentatively in national ones, whose legitimation consists primarily in its intellectual, scientific or artistic *accomplishments*."[40] Given the late development and tenuous unity of the German state, the intellectual middle-class was highly individualized and said to be "floating in the air to some extent," distinctly different from the "closed circle" or "society" that was the French court. The space it occupied was *das rein Geistige* (the purely spiritual), where a preoccupation with scholarship and the development of the mind or intellect (*Bildung*)[41] was both a refuge and source of pride. Politics, commerce, and the economy were peripheral concerns in which there was little scope or prospect for engagement.[42]

Counterpoised to this "floating" intelligentsia was the class equivalent of French intellectuals, an upper-class German courtly aristocracy that produced and accomplished little or nothing in terms of *Kultur*, but which played a significant early role in shaping the national self-image. Elias explains that at the heart of the tensions between middle-class German intellectuals and the courtly aristocracy were "pairs of opposites such as 'depth' and 'superficiality', 'honesty' and 'falsity', 'outward politeness' and 'true virtue' … from which, among other things, the antithesis between *Zivilisation* and *Kultur* grew up" (26–27). Hence, it is also the bedrock on which the antithetical relationship between French *civilisation* and German *Kultur* is based. Given the nature of the intellectual class's relationship with the courtly elite, there were considerable obstacles to the intelligentsia's rise "from being a second-rank class to being the bearer of German national consciousness." Nevertheless, despite the relatively late unification of the German state making this transition even more drawn out, the intelligentsia ultimately rose, albeit conditionally, to an influential class that transformed "the antithesis between *Kultur* and *Zivilisation*" from being a "*primarily social antithesis*" to a "*primarily national one*" (27; emphasis in original). To put it another way, given the changing role and status of the German intelligentsia, the "specific social characteristics" that are its hallmark "gradually become national characteristics" (29–30). And as I shall show, they are characteristics that were incongruous with the ideas and values inherent in the French/English concept of civilization that were thought to be universal, particularly by the French.[43]

In effect, *Kultur* and *civilisation* were said to be squared off against each other as Counter-Enlightenment versus Enlightenment, the "authentic" *Kultur* of Germany versus the "artificial" cosmopolitan *civilisation* of which France was representative.[44] Indeed, Oswald Spengler writes of an "opposition" between the "conceptions of culture-man and civilization-man." He considered that "every Culture has *its own* Civilization" and that "Civilization is the inevitable *destiny* of the Culture." With this in mind, he suggested that "the 'Decline of the West' comprises nothing less than the problem of *Civilization*." Spengler further contended that "civilizations are the most external and artificial states of which a species of developed humanity is capable. They are a conclusion, the thing-become succeeding the thing-becoming, death following life. … *Pure* Civilization, as a historical process, consists in a progressive exhaustion of forms that have become inorganic or dead."[45] As Jeffrey Herf notes, however, while "Spengler juxtaposed German *Kultur* and Western *Zivilisation*," unlike others "he sought to reconcile *Kultur* with twentieth-century German nationalism."[46]

Adam Kuper describes this general oppositional scenario in terms of the forces of civilization engaged in a "struggle to overcome the resistance of traditional cultures, with their superstitions, irrational prejudices, and fearful loyalties to cynical rulers," who in turn saw their "defining enemy" as "rational, scientific universal civilization." He contends that "German intellectuals … were provoked to stand up for national tradition against cosmopolitan civilization; for spiritual values against materialism; for the arts and crafts against science and technology; for individual genius and self-expression against stifling bureaucracy; for the emotions, even for the darkest forces within us, against desiccated reason: in short, for *Kultur* against *Civilization*."[47]

But perhaps this is all a bit of an overstatement, for it does not take into account the many advancements made in Germany in fields of study such as philosophy, the sciences, and technological innovation. A classic case in point is the pioneering work of the naturalist Alexander von Humboldt (1769–1859), a virtual "renaissance man" of science whose five-volume *Cosmos*, among other publications, contributed significantly to the advancement of scientific enquiry.[48] It also fails to explain the perfectionist philosophy of G. W. F. Hegel, whose interpretation of history and its ultimate purpose does not fit with the more pessimistic perspective offered by

Kuper. In fact, during a series of lectures that Hegel gave at the University of Berlin during the winter of 1830–31, he used the terms *Kultur* and *Zivilisation* virtually interchangeably.[49] And Hegel was by no means alone in his thinking; the possibility that *Kultur* and *Zivilisation* were not always directly opposed to one another in the minds of all German intellectuals can also be found in the following passage from Sigmund Freud on what constitutes human culture or civilization:

> Human culture—I mean by that all those respects in which human life has raised itself above animal conditions and in which it differs from the life of the beasts, and I disdain to separate culture and civilization—presents, as is well known, two aspects to the observer. It includes on the one hand all the knowledge and power that men have acquired in order to master the forces of nature and win resources from her for the satisfaction of human needs; and on the other hand it includes all the necessary arrangements whereby men's relations to each other, and in particular the distribution of the attainable riches, may be regulated. The two tendencies of culture are not independent of each other … because the mutual relations of men are profoundly influenced by the measure of instinctual satisfaction that the existing resources make possible.[50]

Nevertheless, there were points of differentiation between *Kultur* and *Zivilisation* in the thought of many intellectuals. In the *Communist Manifesto* Karl Marx and Friedrich Engels effectively prioritize *Kultur* over civilization, arguing that "there is too much civilisation, too much means of subsistence, too much industry, too much commerce."[51] Similar sentiments were later expressed by Thomas Mann, the German Nobel Laureate in Literature of 1929 for whom "culture equals true spirituality, while civilization means mechanization."[52] This line of thinking can also be traced through the respective works of the sociologists Ferdinand Tönnies and Alfred Weber, who saw civilization as little more than the collective practical and technical know-how with which to manage the challenges of nature. *Kultur*, on the other hand, they saw as "a set of normative principles, values and ideals—in a word, the spirit."[53] This particular tension between the two ideals also helps to explain the German historian Wilhelm Mommsen's statement: "It is man's duty today to see that civilization does not destroy culture, nor technology the human being."[54] A further incompatibility arises when recalling that in at least one sense, civilization is said to explicitly relate to an evolutionary process. *Kultur* on the other hand "has a different relation to motion," encapsulating instead the best of the uniquely human endeavors such as the fine arts, literature, painting and poetry, and religious or philosophical thinking—all of which are thought to capture the unique collective identity of a people. Or as Elias further explains it, the "concept of *Kultur* delimits" and "places special stress on national differences and the particular identity of groups," whereas "the concept of civilization plays down the national differences between peoples."[55] It should be noted that while the French/English concept of civilization might play down certain (but not all) differences between the "civilized" peoples of Western Europe in particular, that courtesy is not extended to non-European peoples who were often thought to be "beyond the pale of civilization."

Starobinski insists that the tension between civilization and *Kultur* has been "vehemently express[ed]" by Friedrich Nietzsche, for whom civilization "is nothing but discipline, repression, diminution of the individual; by contrast, culture can go hand in hand with social decadence because it is the fruition of individual energy."[56] The unfathomable depth of this divide is captured in Nietzsche's commentary *Kultur contra Zivilisation* (Culture versus Civilization), as follows: "The high-points of Culture and of Civilization are remote from one another: one should not be misled about the abysmal antagonism between Culture and Civilization. The greatest moment of Culture was always, morally speaking, a time of corruption; and time and again they were epochs of wilfully and forcefully domesticating men like animals (so-called 'Civilization'). These are times of intolerance for the most spirited and hardiest of natures. Civilization is altogether something different than Culture will allow: it is perhaps its inverse."[57]

According to Nietzsche then, not only are civilization and its objectives at odds with the aims and ideals of *Kultur*, but there is an antagonism between them that has the potential to manifest itself in means beyond the realm of theoretical ideology. In the absolute extreme case—in a somewhat overstated manifestation of this antithesis—Kuper asserts that the "First World War was fought behind the rival banners of Western Civilization and German *Kultur*."[58] This is an oversimplification of what was a complex series of events that led to the outbreak of the First World War, but nevertheless, it gives a vivid indication of the extent of the at times irreconcilable differences that are said to exist between the two concepts.

While the forces of civilization might have won the Great War, this has not always been the outcome, for similar arguments to Kuper's have been made in connection with other conflicts in Europe's history. In speaking of a time long before the word *civilization* had come into being, the German historian G. Kuhn characterized the victory of the barbarian hordes of Germany over the armies of Imperial Rome as "the victory of peasants over warriors, of country over town, of culture over civilization."[59] But according to Victor Hugo, even when the "barbarism" of German *Kultur* defeated the "light" that was French civilization; it still lost out because of what it was not. Addressing the French National Assembly in 1871 following defeat in the Franco-Prussian War at the hands of Germany, Hugo proclaimed:

> And while the victorious nation, Germany, the slave horde, will bend its brow beneath its heavy helmet, France, the sublime vanquished nation, will wear the crown of a sovereign people.
>
> And civilization, once again set face to face with barbarism, will seek its way between these two nations, one of which has been the light of Europe, and the other of which will be the night.[60]

The key point here is Hugo's proclamation that, despite its defeat, the French nation was still considered superior to a less than unified Germany precisely because, unlike Germany up to that point, it was, and had long been, a sovereign, centrally and self-governed nation. As reinforced throughout this study, a nation's capacity for sociopolitical organization and self-government, and hence its claims to sovereignty, has a significant bearing on whether it is deemed to meet the requisite "standard of civilization." It also becomes evident in chapter 4 that German critiques of the French/English account of civilization and its claims to universality, as couched in terms of *Kultur*, have much in common with what might be called contemporary "cultural" critiques of cosmopolitanism and its claims to universality. Finally, in regard to the tensions between *Kultur* and civilization, it is an overstatement to say that German intellectuals across the board perceived the aims and objectives of the two ideals as perpetually at odds or antithetical to one another. While the tensions between *Kultur* and civilization are very real, Braudel suggests that perhaps the greater threat to the ideal of civilization is posed by ethnographers and anthropologists working on civilizations rather than the "perfectly defensible persistence of German thinkers."[61]

What Civilization Means and Its Implications

As noted, *civilization* and its plural are interrelated terms and subjects of study that have been examined both independently and with reference to one another. An initial concern with the concept of civilization gave way to detailed studies of civilizations in the nineteenth and twentieth centuries, in large part instigated by the foundation and development of the fields of anthropology and ethnography. Such a shift led to claims that a broader concern with the normative-evaluative aspects of civilization had "lost some of its cachet."[62] The result of this shift was a preoccupation with narrow definitions such as that offered by Émile Durkheim and Marcel Mauss, who state that a "civilization constitutes a kind of moral milieu encompassing a certain number of nations, each national culture being only a particular form of the whole."[63]

One of the leading and most influential exponents of the comparative study of civilizations was the historian Arnold Toynbee. In his *Study of History* and related works, however, he did not completely set aside the ideal of civilization, for he stated that "Civilizations have come and gone, but Civilization (with a big 'C') has succeeded" or endured.[64] Toynbee also sought to articulate a link between "civilizations in the plural and civilization in the singular," noting that the former refers to "particular historical exemplifications of the abstract idea of civilization." This abstract idea of civilization is defined in "spiritual terms" which "equate civilization with a state of society in which there is a minority of the population, however small, that is free from the task, not merely of producing food, but of engaging in any other of the economic activities—e.g. industry and trade—that have to be carried on to keep the life of the society going on the material plane at the civilizational level."[65]

Toynbee's line of argument concerning the organization of society as marked by the specialization of skills, the move toward elite professions, and the effective use of leisure time is one that has long been held in connection with the advancement of civilization (and civilized society). It is found in the work of Thomas Hobbes, for instance, for although his life and work preceded the term *civilization*, Robert Kraynak argues that "the primary theme of Hobbes' studies in civil history is the distinction between barbarism and civilization." Hobbes is said to equate the "*political* characteristics" of "'commonwealths,' 'cities,' or 'polities'" with their "*civilized* qualities," such as "'civil society' or 'civil life,'" to the extent that "he regards civilization as a condition which combined a certain level of political development and a certain manner of living."[66] This is suggested in Hobbes's assertion that the "procuring of the necessities of life ... was impossible, till the erecting of great Commonwealths," which are "the mother of *Peace*, and *Leisure*," which is, in turn, "the mother of *Philosophy*. ... Where first were great and flourishing *Cities*, there was first the study of *Philosophy*."[67] That is to say, "Wherever government is sufficiently strong and well-established to provide peace and leisure, men began to cultivate the finer things in life," the very things that are said to be the outward expression of civilization. In "contrast, savagery or barbarism has been a condition where political authority was developed insufficiently or non-existent." Kraynak concludes that by Hobbes's account, "civilization has been distinguished from barbarism by the power and sufficiency of political authority, the enjoyment of leisure, and the development of philosophy or the arts and sciences."[68] But, it is the first of these hallmarks of civilization, the presence of increasingly complex sociopolitical organization, that, in the first instance at least, is the prerequisite and facilitator of the latter qualities.

Some semblance of this general line of argument has been made time and again throughout history, its influence ebbing and flowing with the times. One of the earliest to do so was Aristotle in the *Politics*, in which he posited that "society [meaning the *polis* or state] ... contains in itself ... the end and perfection of government: first founded that we might live, but continued that we may live happily."[69] On this point, Kraynak argues that for "Aristotle and other classical philosophers the good life is the end or purpose of civilization."[70] While Aristotle's conception of society might differ from contemporary usage, what this is in effect saying is that the realization of the good life is the purpose of government. Furthermore, it is only by living in society with others that this might be achieved, for Aristotle insists, "whosoever is ... unfit for society, must be either inferior or superior to man." He further singles out "the man in Homer, who is reviled for being 'without society, without law, without family,'"[71] for, in effect, the absence of at least the first two of these institutions means he is without civilization. Instead, he is either savage or barbaric, or a god. Such accounts of the relationship between civilization, society, and government fit with Anthony Pagden's claim that the "philosophical history of civilization was, then, a history of progressive complexity and progressive refinement which followed from the free expression of those faculties which men possess only as members of a community."[72]

In a 1940 lecture titled "What 'Civilization' Means," R. G. Collingwood spoke of three elements of civilization: economic civilization, social civilization, and legal civilization. The realm of economic civilization is marked not simply by the pursuit of riches—which might in fact be inimical to economic civilization—but by "the civilized pursuit of wealth." The pursuit of wealth is in turn carried out in two ways: through "civilized exchange" and "civilized production." The former means that exchange is carried out justly and fairly in the absence of domination, such as master-slave relationships (which puts him at odds with Aristotle), in accordance with the principles of *laissez-faire* economics. The latter, "Civilized production is scientific production." It is production that is carried out "intelligently" such that "productive industry [is] controlled by an understanding of natural laws." That is to say, it is a mode of production that employs the practice of "natural science ... wherein, by means of experiment and observation, men find out how to use the forces of nature to the advancement of their own welfare."[73]

The second of Collingwood's three elements of civilization is "social civilization": it is the forum in which humankind's sociability is thought to be satisfied by "the idea of joint action," or what we might call community. It bears the name "civilization" because it is said to have been "civilized" to the point wherein its members refrain from the threat and use of both physical and moral force to induce fellow members to do "what [they] want them to do," instead employing methods of persuasion to win them over. Completing Collingwood's tripartite definition of civilization is the legal component. The final mark of civilization is "a society governed by law," and not so much by criminal law but by civil law in particular, "the law in which claims are adjusted between its members." Furthermore, while military and ecclesiastical law may well have their respective places in such a society, those places are subordinate to the role played by civil law. Moreover, a "society thus governed by civil law is one in which there is no arbitrary power; no executive, however constituted, able to override the law and no judicature able to defy it" (502–11; quote at 510). For Collingwood, then, "Civilization is *something which happens to a community.* ... Civilization is a *process of approximation to an ideal state*" (283; emphasis in original). In essence, what Collingwood is arguing is that civilized society—and thus civilization itself—is guided by and operates according to the principles of the rule of law.

When we combine the collective criteria of Collingwood's tripartite components of civilization—economic civilization, social civilization, and legal civilization—they amount to what I would call sociopolitical civilization, or the capacity of a collective to organize and govern itself under some system of laws or constitution. Not too far removed from Collingwood's concern with the elimination of physical and moral force via "social civilization" are the more recent accounts of civilized society that address issues relating to the historical and ongoing endeavor to manage violence, if only by removing it from the public sphere. Such a concern is extended in Zygmunt Bauman's account of civilization to the more general issue of producing readily governable subjects. The "concept of *civilization*," he argues, "entered learned discourse in the West as the name of a conscious proselytizing crusade waged by men of knowledge and aimed at extirpating the vestiges of wild cultures."[74]

The nature of the "proselytizing crusade" in the name of civilization is one of the central concerns of this book. Its rationale or driving force is not too difficult to determine when one considers Starobinski's assertion that, "taken as a value, civilization constitutes a political and moral norm. It is the criterion against which barbarity, or non-civilization, is judged and condemned."[75] A similar point is made by Pagden, who states that civilization "describes a state, social, political, cultural, aesthetic—even moral and physical—which is held to be the optimum condition for all mankind, and this involves the implicit claim that only the civilized can know what it is to be civilized."[76] Out of this implicit claim and the judgments passed in its name, the notion of the "burden of civilization" was born.

The argument that only the civilized know what it means to be civilized is an important one, for, as Starobinski notes, the "historical moment in which the word *civilization* appears marks the advent of self-reflection, the emergence of a consciousness that thinks it understands the nature of its own activity." More specifically, it marks "the moment that Western civilization becomes aware of itself reflectively, it sees itself as one civilization among others.

Having achieved self-consciousness, civilization immediately discovers civilizations."[77] But as Elias notes, it is not a case of Western civilization being just one among equals, for the very concept of civilization "expresses the self-consciousness of the West. ... It sums up everything in which Western society of the last two or three centuries believes itself superior to earlier societies or 'more primitive' contemporary ones." Elias further explains that in using the term *civilization*, "Western society seeks to describe what constitutes its special character and what it is proud of: the level of *its* technology, the nature of *its* manners, the development of *its* scientific knowledge or view of the world, and much more."[78] Again, it is not too difficult to see how the harbingers of civilization might gravitate toward a (well-meaning) "proselytizing crusade" driven, at least in part, by a deeply held belief in the "burden of civilization." That is not to deny that the same era produced outspoken critics who denounced such a crusade as distinctly uncivilized; apart from Burke, there are the underlying messages of H. G. Wells's *War of the Worlds* and *The Island of Dr. Moreau*[79] and George Orwell's essay "Shooting an Elephant."

The issue is not only the denial of the value and achievements of other civilizations,[80] but the implication that they are in near irreversible decline. From this perspective, their contribution to "big C" Civilization (if any is acknowledged) is seen as largely limited to the past, out of which comes the further implication that if anything of value is to be retrieved, it cannot be done without the assistance of a more civilized tutor. Such thinking is only too evident, for example, in Ferdinand Schiller's mistaken claim that "the peoples of India appear to care very little for history and have never troubled to compile it."[81] Hence, the British took it upon themselves to compile such uneven accounts as that which was prepared by James Mill and published as *The History of British India* in 1817. Despite never having visited India, Mill's *History*, an attack on William Robertson's *Historical Disquisition* of 1791, relayed to European audiences an equally mistaken image of Indian civilization as eternally backward and undeveloped.

Returning to the meaning of civilization, perhaps the best way to summarize it is to follow the lead of Guizot, who claimed not so much to define but rather to describe civilization. For Guizot, "the first fact comprised in the word civilization ... is the fact of progress, of development; it presents at once the idea of a people marching onward, not to change its place, but to change its condition; of a people whose culture is conditioning itself, and ameliorating itself. The idea of progress, of development, appears to me the fundamental idea contained in the word, *civilization*."[82] The progress or development referred to here concerns "the perfecting of civil life, the development of society, properly so called, of the relations of men among themselves." Yet according to Guizot, "instinct" tells us "that the word, civilization, comprehends something more extensive, more complex, something superior to the simple perfection of the social relations, of social power and happiness" (17). That is, *civilization* means something more than just the sociopolitical organization and government of members or citizens of society. This something more is the realm of humankind's general moral progress, that is, "the development of the individual, internal life, the development of man himself, of his faculties, his sentiments, his ideas." As with Aristotle, Hobbes, and others, sociopolitical organization or the government of society is only the first part of the puzzle, for out of this development,

"Letters, sciences, the arts, display all their splendour." Guizot concludes his description of civilization with the declaration: "Wherever mankind beholds these great signs, these signs glorified by human nature, wherever it sees created these treasures of sublime enjoyment, it there recognizes and names civilization." For Guizot, and others, "two facts" are integral elements to the "great fact" that is civilization: "the development of social activity, and that of individual activity; the progress of society and the progress of humanity." Wherever these "two symptoms" are present, "mankind with loud applause proclaims civilization" (18).

Following this proclamation, it was another French historian, Febvre, who stated that the word (and idea of) "*Civilisation* was born at the right time." "Above all," he added, "it was born at a time when, emerging from the entire *Encyclopédie*, the great concept of rational and experimental science was beginning to make itself felt, constituting a whole in its methods and procedures."[83] The air of enthusiasm surrounding the newly born concept of civilization and the general atmosphere it engendered at the time is captured by Febvre in an unidentified citation he quotes from the work of Albert Counson: "Civilisation is inspired by a new philosophy of nature and of man. Its philosophy of nature is evolution. Its philosophy of man is perfectibility."[84]

While this might sound innocuous enough, Starobinski goes to some length in highlighting the dangers associated with this philosophy, in particular, and the deification of civilization, more generally. In a passage worth quoting at some length, he argues that

> because of the connection with the ideas of perfectibility and progress, the word *civilization* denoted more than just a complex process of refinement and mores, social organization, technical progress, and advancing knowledge; it took on a sacred aura, owing to which it could sometimes reinforce traditional religious values and at other times supplant them. The history of the word *civilization* thus leads to this crucial observation: once a notion takes on a sacred authority and thereby acquires the power to mobilize, it quickly stirs up conflict between political groups or rival schools of thought claiming to be its champions and defenders and as such insisting on the exclusive right to propagate the new idea.[85]

Starobinski goes on to highlight some of the consequences of this situation, one of which is his prescient warning that a "term fraught with sacred content demonizes its antonym." He continues:

> Once the word *civilization* ceases to denote a fact subject to judgement and becomes an incontestable value, it enters the verbal arsenal of praise and blame. Evaluating the defects and merits of the civilization is no longer the issue. Civilization itself becomes the crucial criterion: judgement is now made in the name of civilization. One has to take its side, adopt its cause. For those who answer its call it becomes ground for praise. Or, conversely, it can serve as a basis for denunciation: all that is not civilization, all that resists or threatens civilization, is monstrous, absolute evil. As rhetoric heats up it becomes legitimate to ask for the supreme sacrifice in the name of civilization. This means that the service or defence of civilization can

in certain circumstances justify the recourse to violence. Civilization's enemies, the barbarians, if they cannot be educated or converted, must be prevented from doing harm. (29–30; emphasis in original)

This is one of the key issues this book addresses: the sometimes extreme measures that have been and continue to be taken by the "civilized" peoples or states of the world against the "uncivilized" in the name of civilization. As Starobinski notes, in one of the more extreme cases, the consequences of the demands of civilization manifest themselves in a "justification for colonization" (18), as is explored in this book more generally and in part 2 in particular. And as is addressed in part 3, one requires little imagination to recognize how relevant this warning is to the present era, given the foreign policy goals and the general direction that some Western leaders are hotly pursuing in the wake of the global war on terror(ism) and its perceived associates. But before we get to that, Starobinski makes the point that the "word *civilization*, which denotes a process, entered the history of ideas at the same time as the modern sense of the word *progress*. The two words were destined to maintain a most intimate relationship" (4; emphasis in original). It is that topic, the idea of progress and its relation to the ideal of civilization, that I turn to in the following chapter.

Development and Its Discontents

By Philip McMichael and Karuna Morarji

Struggles of the disempowered offer perspective on development claims, and new ways of thinking about social change, approaches that question the development narrative and the market episteme, advocating for the right to represent and realize different ways of living in this world, and transcending the development impasse.

Introduction: The Paradox of Development

"Development" is a concept with a long lineage, deriving from the European experience of urban-industrialization and colonial domination. As such it performs a self-referential function, canonized in classical political economy. It categorizes European endeavors and accomplishments as the touchstone of "modernity": a liberal ideal whereby modern societies are governed by states characterized by political pluralism, universal citizenship, and equal opportunity in the marketplace. Development is the process of achieving this condition via statehood and economic growth. Through colonization, Europe affirmed its development credentials, representing itself as a civilizing force in the non-European world, which force eventually generated independence struggles across Europe's empire. Through decolonization, and the extension of state-hood to the post-colonial world, development came to be seen as the natural, universal destiny of all peoples.[1]

The legacy of this passage from European colonialism to universal development is significant for the social struggles depicted here. Not only was colonialism once considered necessary to the civilizing project, but also colonial subjects were once considered incapable of self-organization. The rupture of the colonial relationship revealed the limiting assumptions of colonial rule, founded on an elemental racism that portrayed subjects as backward, passive, and uncivilized. It took a monumental and historic struggle to unsettle the categories through which Europe perceived the world (in its own image).[2]

Consider the impact on Enlightenment discourse of the late eighteenth century slave revolt in Haiti, a turning point that, for Michel-Rolph Trouillot, revealed the "unthinkable even as it happened." In this revolt the category of "slave" was limiting because European categorical and philosophical discourse could not account for slave self-organization. Trouillot chronicles the silences that forbade Europeans, and slaves, from recognizing the significance of the revolution as it unfolded. Thus, a French colonist in Saint-Domingue wrote to his wife in France, in 1790: "there is no movement among our Negroes. ... They don't even think of it. They are very tranquil and obedient. A revolt among them is impossible." In this way, self-referential discourse simply "othered" the slave: "the more European merchants and mercenaries bought and conquered other men and women, the more European philosophers wrote and talked about Man" (Trouillot, 1995, pp. 72, 75).

Ultimately, Trouillot's point regarding the shock of the Haitian revolution is that the European "contention that enslaved Africans and their descendants could not envision freedom—let alone formulate strategies for gaining and securing such freedom—was based not so much on empirical evidence as on an ontology, an implicit organization of the world and its inhabitants" (p. 73). In other words, systems of domination tend to proclaim their own normalcy, silencing their internal contradictions, and the possibility that the terms of reference can be contested and turned against those who construct these terms. Thus C.L.R. James suggests the Haitian slave revolt was carried out in the liberatory terms of the French Revolution, as the slaves held up a mirror to their French masters, demanding equivalence. In addition, the slave revolt affected the course of the French revolt. The masses supported abolition: "Servants, peasants, workers, the labourers by the day in the fields all over France were filled with a virulent hatred against the 'aristocracy of the skin'. There were so many so moved by the sufferings of the slaves that they had long ceased to drink coffee, thinking of it as drenched with the blood and sweat of men turned into brutes" (in this they anticipated the anti-sweatshop consumer today). And: "The blacks were taking their part in the destruction of European feudalism begun by the French Revolution, and liberty and equality, the slogans of the revolution, meant far more to them than to any Frenchman" (James, 1963, pp. 139, 198).

At the time, while the slaves of Haiti conceived their struggle in (their) terms of liberty and equality, their struggle was not recognized as such, but dismissed by their masters as insurgent resistance. What we can take from this is that the meaning of "social change" is bounded by a set of self-referential categories, reproducing an ontology (a way of being) specific to a political order. Unruliness is regarded as (negative) resistance because of the unthinkability of (positive) self-organization by its subjects. And yet, precisely because colonial ontology underestimated slave revolt as unthinkable, once begun it ignited a long struggle for decolonization. At the point at which empire became too costly, non-European claims for development were given legitimacy as "self-determination," but within an extended European state-system.[3] That which was once unthinkable was now thinkable, within a reformulated power structure.

The struggles documented in this volume perhaps are analogous, in the sense that within the current development frame they represent the unthinkable. Individually and together, their challenge is to reformulate power relations, opening new spaces of social possibility.

The struggles are united by their epistemic critique of development claims in particular settings. These include spatial settings (urban, rural, frontier, interstitial), educational institutions, electoral processes, indigenous territories, and the World Social Forum. The encroachment of market culture on schooling, identity, gender relations, biodiversity, land use, elections, governance, the social contract, and more, presents itself as a moral agenda[4] in a variety of locations—from pasturelands in northern Pakistan through electoral politics in the Nigerian delta to civic education in urban Brazil. Market rule brings an economic calculus to cultural and social relationships, in the name of democratization (individual choice) and market efficiency (individual maximization). These cultural ideals are deeply embedded in the development episteme, which views the market as a vehicle of universal progress. By normalizing market rule, challenges to it appear either "unthinkable" or "negative resistance," and are marginalized by definition. Our ethnographic encounters with these struggles contextualize marginalization, in its intent as well as its impact. They reveal the reductionism of conceptions of normality, opening up future possibilities.

Development and Its Material and Epistemic Exclusions

The reductionism of development discourse and practice is exclusionary. People are not just excluded because they lack the means to participate in the market. They may be excluded because their aspirations and practices do not fit with the market culture, or because the market culture itself consigns them to redundancy. Through the lens of the market calculus they may be excluded, and classified as "undeveloped," "residual," or even "have-nots." The social struggles here contest such classification—not to be academic, but to claim their own definition. These struggles remind us of two things: first, development, particularly in its neoliberal garb, is increasingly exclusionary, and second, there is more than one way to give meaning to social existence. In other words, these are struggles against exclusion, *and* to reclaim multiple meanings of social existence.

Our ethnographic fieldwork has sought to access these other meanings, or claims, as they engage the dominant claims of the market culture. Our concern is with how such engagement challenges the market calculus via an "epistemic critique" of development's failure of imagination (in addition to its failure to deliver). It is also with how people rearticulate meaning and therefore possibility in the struggle against processes of exclusion and disempowerment. That is, their engagement is interactive, and their struggles are effective to the extent that they are able to subvert and appropriate dominant meanings to their own cause. Thus we capture how these struggles generate new formulations of "citizenship," "property," "conservation," "education," "democracy," and "sovereignty," in framing alternative conceptions and practices of development.

More than one in six humans now live in slums, over one billion in a world of jobless growth, or no growth, and in which the link between urbanization and industrialization has been irrevocably undone (Davis, 2006). Symptomatic of a world in which the promise of "development" appears as a receding horizon to its majority, poverty and marginality suggest redundancy. Arguably, it is a modern problem for which there is no modern solution (B. d. S. Santos, 2002, p. 1). Indeed, modern solutions are often the source of the problem, as development continues to generate new inequalities. To the extent that this is so, solutions must come from practices and movements that engage critically with development and its assumptions, and prefigure alternative practices. Thus these struggles challenge the "epistemic privilege" through which powerful institutions and discourses construct particular visions of the world as natural, and as the universal and inevitable path of human progress.

Epistemic privilege is etched into the narrative of development because the terms of human development are power-laden in their origin and their import. Through colonization European elites set the stage for modern capitalist development that has defined a uniform standard and goal institutionalized in the modern state system. Defined as a universal ladder (Sachs, 2005), development is essentially a self-referential metaphor that justifies a particular ordering of the world. While the people at the base of the ladder are presumed to be "developmentally challenged," this definition excludes their self-definition. It assumes their challenge is to develop. But the struggles in this volume suggest that their challenge is *with* development. While they may acknowledge the existence of some kind of "ladder" the meaning they give to it is not necessarily the meaning imparted from those at the top of the "development ladder." Their struggle is precisely to define the terms through which their lives find meaning, and this in turn imparts a different meaning and substantive content to development.

Struggles over meaning or resources raise questions about "development"—questions that focus on both its paradoxical assumptions of equal worth in a diverse world, and its paradoxical outcomes in promoting accumulation of material wealth through inequality and dispossession. At a time when limits to economic growth are becoming apparent in the face of energy, climate, food, and financial crises, these struggles draw attention to new ways of thinking about development from the perspective of its subordinates—approaches that question the consumer ethic and the psychology of self-interest, and, in self-organizing, demand the power of self-representation as a condition of emancipation. This volume has sought to clarify and re-envision development by representing the claims of the disenfranchised.

Clarity comes from recognizing that those who struggle are not necessarily struggling to realize what is valued in the development narrative. Marketplace participation is not always the solution for those with other cultural terms of reference. Survival comes first, and that often implicates protection of life-worlds. Retaining access to resources, most of which are common resources (public lands, forests, pastures, waterways, seeds, knowledges, social networks, public services), is central to survival. It is commonplace for developers (including governments) to proclaim that the route to "inclusion" lies through market mechanisms,[5] ignoring the social resources and resourcefulness of the disenfranchised as foundations for their own life-worlds, however impoverished they seem to those with a development ladder vision of the world. Furthermore, to developers (e.g., governments, banks, corporations, NGOs, the World Bank) the occupation and use of resources in common retards their conversion to private property and inclusion in the marketplace, thereby providing a "development obstacle."[6] But privatizing social resources is precisely the mechanism whereby development can actively undermine durable forms of social reproduction—through sometimes violent processes of imposing a singular and simplifying calculus of market value on complex cultural and ecological relations.

Through the struggles represented here it becomes obvious that people mobilizing against exclusion are not necessarily or simply demanding inclusion, but are questioning familiar binaries with which we work, such as inclusion/exclusion, modern/ backward, and developed/undeveloped. In other words they are questioning how their condition is viewed, and what is considered the appropriate "solution" to their condition. They may not see the world through the same lens, or impart the same meaning to their condition. And as their own lens comes into focus, as this collection allows, it is possible to see the limiting assumptions of the development lens. What is understood as normal (epistemic), they view as problematic.

Thus when peasants mobilize to protect and sustain their life-world, they are not just claiming rights, but also questioning the epistemic assumption that in a modern world they are supposed to disappear.[7] The coincidence of the mass production of slums with an epistemic assumption of peasant obsolescence underscores the limits of "modern solutions." And yet a recent World Bank *World Development Report* argues for more of the same, on the assumption that absorbing peasants into agro-industrial "value chains" will increase their productivity—producing food mostly for export, however, rather than for local food security—deepening fossil fuel dependence, reducing biodiversity, and increasing carbon emissions. The epistemic challenge asserts that smallholders have rights to produce in the modern world, in a sustainable way.[8] But conventional development categories ("economic efficiency," "specialization," and "comparative advantage") legitimize, in this instance, soil mining and the devaluation and displacement of a substantial portion of humanity. These categories belong to an economic calculus. But the people subjected to these terms do not necessarily live by such a calculus. Why should they be held to such an abstract standard, for what purpose, and in whose interest?

These struggles, then, are *diagnostic* insofar as the terms of reference of "development" are held up to examination by those who experience redundancy, in material and epistemic ways. Not only do they lose resources (land, knowledge, networks as peasants), or experience exclusion from social resources (civil and social rights as slum-dwellers), but also they may forfeit a distinctive value calculus forged *in situ*, rather than in an economics textbook. Certainly their calculus is not immune to the objectifying pressures of the global marketplace, but long-standing adaptations draw on values rooted in cultural or ecological attachments. Thus Karuna Morarji's chapter 4 depicts the contradictory epistemic experiences of rural students and their families as they struggle to make sense of the ambiguities of modern education in northern India. Promising individual and social mobility ("progress") through education for a commercialized urban existence, such schooling forecloses the inter-generational securities of agrarian livelihoods, and yet does not guarantee urban employment. The assumed link between education and development (a UN Millennium Development Goal) is not so seamless after all. Insecure villagers from Jaunpur must reconcile the individualizing values of development with the customary collective values and moral codes of the rural culture they are supposed to leave behind. Struggling between two worlds represents what it means to be modern in Jaunpur, underlining the complexity of development as a process across time and space. Across the world, the Afro-Brazilians depicted in Alex Da Costa's chapter 13 struggle to incorporate into municipal education their cultural heritage as a legitimate form of knowledge, complicating the meaning of "inclusion" and recalibrating development assumptions regarding the status of minority cultures.

These struggles do not necessarily reject development ideals or principles (equality, rights, citizenship, education, social contract); rather, they challenge the content of these ideas and suggest different grounds for, or terms of realization of, those ideals. As Hannah Wittman shows in chapter 11, landless workers in Brazil challenge the normalizing association of civilization with urbanization. Instead, they advocate an "agrarian citizenship" that values the social function of smallholding in stabilizing rural populations, providing new opportunities for *favela* inhabitants to resettle the land, and developing agro-ecological methods of food production.

In short, the chapters in this collection describe, with ethnographic detail, social struggles by people *doubly marginalized* by development and its narrowing lens. What is at stake is not just the lives and livelihoods of the people concerned, but development itself, which has become synonymous with a combination of crises (food, environmental, energy, financial, and climate). The single-minded pursuit of an economic calculus in the name of development is marked by violent appropriations and devaluations of material resources, by redundancy of certain categories of people, and by a foreclosure of social visions and possibilities. Yet these dynamics also generate struggles that contest and rework the terms of crisis—struggles incubated within the neoliberal development project[9] but dedicated to transcending its answers by reformulating the questions. New questions bring the unthinkable into play, creating new horizons of possibility, as anticipated in the birth pangs of development during the colonial era.

Development Struggles

Neither a global ethnography concerned to link the "local" to the "global,"[10] nor a conventional analysis of social movements concerned to theorize the political efficacy of mobilization, this collection has addressed a different question: how do social struggles around the world expose the material and epistemic shortcomings of "development"? By questioning the normalizing claims of development, struggles from a variety of settings serve to politicize, and historicize, the current global order. In particular, they uncover the "normative foreclosure" implicit in market rule, namely, the way it reduces culture and development to an economic calculus, erasing history, and rendering alternatives invisible or unthinkable. Thus these struggles potentially alter the conditions of possibility for a paradigm, and world, in crisis.

In this regard, as claimed in chapter 1, the struggles represented here reach beyond the conventions of the "social movement" paradigm: namely, that "development" realizes liberal modernity through statehood and economic growth. Social movements enact (or retard) this process through demands for social justice, democratic representation, equal rights, economic opportunity, and so on. In other words, development is the implicit narrative through which social movements are typically examined. As Della Porta and Tarrow note, although "social movements have often pushed for a conception of 'direct' democracy, the institutions and actors of representative democracy have long structured movements, political opportunities and constraints within the boundaries of institutional politics" (2005, pp. 1–2).

Our struggles, however, work against this grain: they are not constrained or inclined to work to realize the development vision of liberal modernity. Well, all but one, but this is the exception that proves the rule. In Emelie Peine's chapter 9, soy farmers on the Brazilian frontier misconstrue the state as the problem in a market collapse because they have internalized the norm of "market neutrality," which serves agribusiness interests. Their demand for the state to correct the market contradicts their identification as "free market" producers in a global market of highly subsidized U.S. and European farmers. Such self-identification obscures their utter dependence on the real masters of the market, the corporate grain traders, who in turn organize the (neoliberal) state. This seemingly anomalous critical struggle is the proof of the pudding, so to speak, where accommodation by soy farmers affirms the hegemony of the market paradigm, its naturalization of the state as politically neutral, and its appeal to self-gain and the current development ideal.

What distinguishes the other struggles is their reflexivity, in questioning assumptions about their needs or destiny. "Development" implies uniform direction ("stages of growth"), uniform means (market resources), and uniform meanings (self-interest, self-improvement). Instead of simply reforming political structures to manage or regulate development, these struggles refocus on the shortcomings of the development episteme through their own particular experiences. They bear witness to its limitations, not just in material failure, but also in subjective misrepresentations. They self-organize, and, as Gayatri Menon's chapter 10 on pavement dwellers challenging Mumbai's code of citizenship shows, they encroach on and reformulate the terms of their subjection to the development narrative.

In challenging normalized expectations these struggles contest and reveal "that what does not exist is in fact actively produced as non-existent, that is, as a non credible alternative to what exists."[11] That is, they transgress silences that underwrite the *status quo*—thus in Alex Da Costa's chapter 13, Afro-Brazilians assert recognition of their cultural heritage as indispensable to an equitable notion of "civil rights." In doing so, these struggles challenge premature categorical closure, through which existing power relations are normalized. Land markets, for example, may appear as a neutral approach to equitable or efficient distribution of resources, until landless peoples or peasants struggle against land *concentration* for the right to land to make their own contribution to society. The new religious struggles in the

World Social Forum, as depicted in Andreas Hernandez's chapter 14, collapse the religious/ secular dichotomy (and its configuring of power) in order to realize a plural and ecumenical form of spirituality anchored in a collective human ethic. Through self-organization, these critical struggles realize the unthinkable.

Expressing a formative politics of the "margins," generated by the deepening development crisis, these struggles articulate central political questions of our times. Whether women demanding public accountability for the disabling impact of liquor licensing as a government revenue shortcut, peasants invoking food sovereignty, religious subjectivity movements reformulating spiritual experience beyond doctrinal boundaries and individualist faith, or indigenous people making claims for autonomy—such struggles are viewed as anomalies through the self-referential lens of development. Yet these struggles, far from being anomalous, test development norms that presume their protagonists' non-existence. Whether the subjects of these struggles create emancipatory movements or critique social orderings, they point toward alternative, emergent futures of an equitable and sustainable form of development.

Emancipation is not simply about access to resources, but also about the terms of access. Thus, reformulating "citizenship" to include claims of shack-dwellers, peasants, indigenous peoples, and Afro-Brazilians, for example, is a twofold accomplishment. It seeks accommodation of people written out of existence in the development narrative. And in seeking accommodation in their terms it transforms the categories through which we understand modern history. Struggles for indigenous rights and knowledges contest the "monoculture of linear time" presumed by liberal modernity, through which history is presented "as having a unique and known direction" leading to "the Western way of life, its knowledge, its institutions and its social organization" (Agostino, 2008, p. 232). Such struggles reveal the *partial* efficacy and truth of ruling ideas and categories, which serve as a tool of power and dispossession *and* as a tool of struggle and repossession.

Conclusion: The Development Lens in Perspective

While early (Enlightenment) modernity advocated the *desirability* of progress, or human self-improvement, subsequent European state-building and colonial ventures universalized the goal of progress as *inevitable,* spawning "development" as a master concept of the social sciences.[12] Development provided commonsense meanings of social change, consolidated in the era of decolonization. But as master concept, development legitimizes authoritative representations of social change through social scientific knowledge—by which a European self-referential concept has come to frame possibility and how it can unfold. Thus, "[i]f modernity is the figure to which social theory unavoidably refers itself, development is the prime index we use to assess efforts toward modernization," and this ontological construction involves "a public appropriation of societal transformation in the name of development" (Sivaramakrishnan and Agrawal, 2003, pp. 2, 3). As development is naturalized as both process and aspiration, it represents a set of values through which people come to organize their everyday actions.[13]

Yet while development "works" in a sense as a "lodestar" (Wallerstein, 2001), "there is more to the idea of development in its historical context: like other concepts, this one can be seized, turned around from a structure of depoliticization into a claim for entitlements" (Stoler and Cooper, 1997, p. 35). This is our point—struggles problematize the claims and scope of development. To illustrate, the chapters by Alicia Swords and Dia Da Costa highlight struggles in Chiapas, Mexico and West Bengal, India, respectively that transform "private" problems into legitimate subjects of public concern. They reveal how liberal developmentalism limits the domain of rights (and citizenship) to the marketplace, invisibilizing gender exploitation within households and communities. In each case, networks of learning and protest activate community struggles to offset assumptions that the market is the sole appropriate (and neutral) medium of development. In so doing they express the shared goal of this collection: to politicize development, and unsettle its claims to define social change by re-opening possibilities.

Notes

1. For various accounts of this phenomenon, see Escobar (1995), Cowan and Shenton (1996), Rist (1997), Cooper and Packard (1997).
2. Even so, Immanuel Wallerstein notes: "All these categories are now so deep in our subconscious that we can scarcely talk about the world without using them. World-systems analysis argues that the categories that inform our history were historically formed (and for the most part only a century or so ago). It is time that they were re-opened for examination" (1987, p. 322).
3. As Gilbert Rist has noted: "Their right to self-determination had been acquired in exchange for the right to self-definition" (1997, p. 79). See also Saldaña-Portillo (2003).
4. Cf. Corrigan and Sayer's concept of "moral regulation" as central to the process of state formation (1985).
5. Cf. the new industry to develop the two billion at the "bottom of the pyramid" (Prahalad, 2006; Collier, 2007). Julia Elyachar's research (2005) suggests micro-credit "empowerment" exploits and dispossesses cultural resources shared among myriad workshops, owners, and customers in Cairo.
6. Thus Hernando de Soto (1990) pioneered the notion of alleviating urban poverty by converting the "dead" assets of the poor (their shacks) into "live" capital by incorporating shacks "inside the capitalist economy" as loan collateral.
7. Paul Nicholson, representing the international peasant movement, remarks: "To date, in all the global debates on agrarian policy, the peasant movement has been absent: we have not had a voice. The main reason for the very existence of Vía Campesina is to be that voice and to speak out for the creation of a more just society" (quoted in Desmarais, 2002, p. 96).
8. For a critical review of the Bank's Report, see McMichael (2009), and for an elaboration of the epistemic critique embodied in the international peasant movement, see McMichael (2008b).
9. The "neoliberal development project" is a cultural specification of the political-economic restructuring associated with "globalization," and its privatizing neoliberal creed (cf. McMichael, 2008a). The financial crisis notwithstanding, privatization of resources, and displacement of populations, will intensify as energy, food, climate, and security concerns intensify.

10. Cf. Burawoy et al. (2000).

11. Santos, quoted in Agostino (2008, p. 232).

12. For elaboration, see Araghi and McMichael (2006).

13. See, for example, Pigg (1992), Klenk (2004), and Baviskar (2005).

Chapter Five

Progress and Development and the Rise of Poverty and Inequality

Explaining Poverty, Social Exclusion, and Inequality

Toward a Structural Approach

By Gerry Mooney

Overview

- This chapter provides an introduction to structural approaches to poverty and inequality.
- It discusses some of the ways in which structural approaches can be applied.
- It outlines and considers how Marxist class analysis approaches the questions of poverty, wealth, and inequality.
- It is argued that there is a need for 'upstream' analysis to focus on the activities of the rich.

Key concepts:

Inequality; poverty; wealth; structural approaches; social polarisation; class; class analysis; upstream analysis

Introduction

Few would dispute that in the early years of the 21st century much of the thrust of anti-poverty policy in the UK, together with poverty policies developed at a transnational level by the United Nations (UN), the World Bank and other organisations (see Chapter Five, this volume), has at its core a concern to transform people's behaviour—that is, of course, the behaviour of people experiencing poverty, not the rich nor multinational corporations! This both reflects and reproduces the view of 'the poor' as 'other', as beyond 'normal', 'mainstream' society. The ability of powerful groups to generate and present particular representations of people experiencing poverty as, for example, an 'underclass', or as in some way responsible for their own position, is a recurring feature in debates around poverty and its causes and accompanies the growth in poverty and inequality that have characterised the last few decades of the 20th century and early years of the new millennium.

Following from the discussions in Chapters Two and Three, the focus here shifts to the key question of how we should approach the issue of poverty and inequality, why they remain such prevalent features of society today. The main explanations of poverty are distinguishable primarily by whether they offer an individualistic-based analysis or are driven by a more structural understanding of social relations. There are contrasting theories and perspectives within these two broad ways of thinking, but nonetheless the division between individual and structural accounts represents the main fault line that characterises explanations in this field of social scientific study. Arguably, in recent times, at government and policy-making levels, there has been a shift (albeit an uneven and at times tentative one) towards more individualistic and behavioural explanations, for example in many 'underclass' and/or 'cultures' of poverty discourses. In this chapter a structural approach is centred as offering a particularly comprehensive and powerful way of making sense of inequalities in society and of 'social problems' such as poverty.

It is clear from the previous chapters that poverty, wealth and inequality are highly contested areas of study and analysis. That there are multiple and competing definitions, measurements and methodologies surrounding the study of poverty and wealth has long been a feature of social scientific investigations in these fields. Such contestations reflect different political traditions and theoretical controversies, not only about the questions of poverty, wealth and inequality themselves, but of social justice, of equality and, indeed, of how society itself should be organised and structured. Further, and linking directly with the overall themes and concerns of this book, the analysis of poverty and inequality is directly related to and entangled with the study of cross-cutting social divisions and questions of class, gender, ethnicity, 'race' and sexuality. It also connects with other long-term concerns of social policy analysis with the social relations of welfare, *the who gets what and who gets naught* of welfare provision.

Not surprisingly, then, when we begin to turn our attention to the question of how we should analyse and explain such questions, the explanations that are offered immediately bring into focus more fundamental social and political questions. It is therefore impossible to offer a 'balanced' or 'objective' discussion and from the outset this chapter is explicit in favouring, as it does, a structural explanation of poverty and inequality, underpinned by Marxist class analysis.

What is meant by a 'structural' perspective or approach to poverty and inequality? At its most basic structural explanations seek to locate the analysis and explanation of issues from poverty and social exclusion through to inequality, wealth and power in the context of the wider social relations that structure society. Social factors and forces, for instance the organisation of an economy, unemployment, working conditions, educational provision, health, housing, environmental factors and so on, all play significant roles in shaping what the sociologist Max Weber termed 'life chances' (Weber, 1978), the interplay of personal and social factors that shape the opportunities and life that individuals will experience (see also Bendix, 1977, p 2; Hughes et al, 2003, p 107).

Structural approaches are built around the social contexts in which we live and which work to shape our lives in different ways. Most social scientists will argue, many of whom follow Weber's approach, that it is the complex interrelationship between these social contexts and structures and individual agency that shape the lifecourse and the opportunities that may come our way. In the discussion that follows, an introduction to the focus and approach of structural perspectives is outlined and explored.

Introducing Structural Approaches

One-fifth of humanity lives in countries where many people think nothing of spending $2 a day on a cappuccino. Another fifth of humanity survive on less than $1 a day and live in countries where children die for want of a simple anti-mosquito bed net. (UN, 2005, Summary, p 17).

Massive poverty and obscene inequality are such terrible scourges of our times—times in which the world boasts breathtaking advances in science, technology, industry and wealth accumulation—that they have to rank alongside slavery and apartheid as social evils. (Nelson Mandela, quoted in UN, 2005, Summary, p 17)

In the early years of the 21st century we live in a world that is divided and highly unequal as rarely before. In 2005, the 500 richest individuals in the world, the capacity of a large lecture theatre in a UK university today or of an Airbus A380 passenger jet, had a combined income greater than the poorest 416 million people. And 2.5 billion people, around 40% of the world's population, share 5% of global income. By contrast, the richest 10%, the 'super-rich' who live overwhelmingly in the high-income countries, enjoy 54% of the world's income (UN, 2005, Summary, p 18).

On a global scale as well as in UK society, the early years of the 21st century are characterised by massive inequalities in wealth and income, inequalities which have grown enormously since the 1970s. The scale of this inequality is almost beyond comprehension, perhaps not surprisingly as much of it remains hidden from view. How do we understand such inequalities? What issues and questions should be at the core of our explanations? By using the term 'inequality' there is a strong hint as to the direction of our gaze or focus—and to the kinds of explanation that we would wish to offer. Structural approaches of different kinds would share a starting point that there is little that is 'natural' or inevitable about the inequalities that so scar the world today. Instead inequalities are attributed to the unequal social relations between rich and poor. Poverty and wealth, in other words, are related through unequal social and economic relations.

The relationship between poverty and wealth, between rich and poor, is a dynamic one. We can understand that in the 1960s and 1970s in the UK, for instance, the gap between rich and poor narrowed somewhat, although by no means as much as is often argued. We can also find considerable evidence that highlights that since the late 1970s the gulf between rich and poor has increased dramatically (see, for instance, Westergaard, 1995; Walker, 1997). How might a structural approach make sense of this?

Thatcherism and the Strategy of Inequality

The general story of trends in the distribution of income and wealth in postwar Britain is one in which the gradual trend towards a narrowing of inequality between the late 1940s and 1970s is thrown into sharp reverse in the late 1970s (see Chapter Two, this volume, for data on the distribution of personal assets). Between 1979 and 1993 the richest 10% of the population saw their incomes increase on average by around 63% (Novak, 2001, pp 4–5). But this is only part of the story. Seventy percent of the population saw their incomes increase by less than average while for the poorest 10% their incomes actually declined in real terms by 16%. In terms of poverty (measured here as less than 50% of average income; see Chapter Three, this volume, for a critical discussion of the measurement of poverty), the numbers living in poverty increased from 5 million in 1979 to 14 million in 1993/94, from 9% to 25% of the population (Walker, 1997, p 3). Therefore, when we compare the end of the 1970s with the early to mid-1990s, the gap or gulf between rich and poor increased dramatically. This is often referred to by social scientists as 'social polarisation' (see Walker, 1997).

There is considerable evidence to back up the claims made here, but how do we explain this rising inequality? The growth of inequality during the 1980s and 1990s (continuing into the early 2000s) was no accident, no simple unfortunate and unforeseen 'by-product' of longer-term economic change, but for Alan Walker (1990, 1997), part and parcel of what he terms *a strategy of inequality*. Prior to 1979 there was a general political consensus that a key task for government was to address poverty and to try to reduce inequalities. The provision of 'social security', full employment and the expansion of a welfare state were widely (although not universally) supported and reflected to varying degrees in government policy making. All this was to change with the election of the Conservative government in 1979. Instead of a commitment to a broad social democratic agenda, which in any case was under severe threat under the previous Labour administration, Prime Minister Margaret Thatcher and the Conservative government embarked on a radically different policy-making project that prioritised different objectives from those of post-Second World War governments.

In place of a concern to tackle poverty and to reduce inequality, 'Thatcherism' celebrated low taxation, the free market, personal freedoms and responsibilities, reductions in state welfare, denationalisation, privatisation and so on. These are key components of what we have subsequently come to term a 'neoliberal' agenda. As Walker argues, 'rather than seeing inequality as potentially damaging to the social fabric, the Thatcher governments saw it as an engine of enterprise, providing incentives for those at the bottom as well as those at the top' (Walker, 1997, p 5).

During the years of Conservative government, between 1979 and 1997, and thereafter under New Labour, an expansive welfare state was viewed as 'a drain' on the economy, undermining national economic competitiveness but also as contributing to 'welfare dependency' among people experiencing poverty, undermining incentives to work. The idea that an underclass of unemployed, feckless 'poor people', 'scroungers', were only too willing to take advantage of hard-working taxpayers became a recurring theme of the 1980s and 1990s, with echoes of this still evident today in New Labour's oft-repeated references to the problems of 'work-lessness' and the assorted and multiple moral problems created through welfare dependency (see Levitas, 2005). In place of universal benefits there has, as a result, been a shift towards means-tested benefits, more in-work forms of support such as through tax credits and more targeting of benefits towards those most in need. However, it was not only in relation to welfare spending that the government worked to reshape policy. Reducing, tightening and controlling benefits was accompanied by a new tax regime that was highly regressive, with most taxpayers now paying the same basic rate of taxation. Some capital taxes were abolished while in-work taxation increased along with a hike in National Insurance contributions. The overall effect of this was to shift the tax burden from those with high incomes to those with low incomes. Between 1979 and 1989, for instance, £91,000 million was cut from income taxation, 29% of which went to the top 1% of taxpayers with the bottom 50% receiving only 12% of the cuts (Walker, 1990, pp 41–2).

Reforming the 'morally damaging' welfare state, putting responsibility in place of dependency, was only one dimension of Thatcherite social policies, however. There was also a strong commitment to the belief that any form of welfare provision that was non-state generated and managed was necessarily superior to state welfare. This was reflected in a marked shift towards policies that spoke of the role of the family and of community as well as the non- statutory and voluntary sectors in providing welfare. 'Rolling back the state' to enable such sectors to 'flourish' became an important principle of government policy.

Promoting enterprise and attacking 'dependency' were central to this strategy of inequality. State intervention was damaging in that it undermined the former and worked to increase the latter. This represented a sharp break with the policy-making consensus of the post-1945 era, which tended to support the principles of interventionism and egalitarianism. Economic growth, entrepreneurship and enterprise were to replace reducing inequality and tackling poverty as the main objectives of government policy making. By this route, it was argued, in terms that have come to be infamous, that the fruits of economic growth and increasing wealth would 'trickle down' to benefit the rest of society, including among people experiencing poverty who, freed from the constraints of 'dependency' and 'generous' welfare benefits, would feel empowered to take up new jobs that were being created.

There are other dimensions of this strategy of inequality that we are only able to mention in passing here. Rising unemployment in the 1980s, for instance, was also an important element of this strategy, working as it did to reduce wage costs by acting as a brake on wage levels and demands, and this also had the additional effect of eroding the bargaining position of trades unions and their members, which was also under attack from other government policies, and a series of acts which sought to control and reduce the effectiveness of trades unions.

Promoting inequality, therefore, was a central strategy of the Conservatives during the 1980s and 1990s. Inequality and the growth of poverty were viewed as beneficial for society, or at least for the promotion of enterprise and for enhancing economic growth. Walker's (1990) thesis represents an interesting example of a structural approach, with the focus of the analysis on governments, policy making and on the interrelationship between poverty and wealth. In turn, poverty is understood in relation to wider social and economic goals, in particular providing the right conditions for profitability and prosperity and national economic growth and competitiveness. In other ways this strategy of inequality has worked to increase inequalities in other areas of social life, and here again we are reminded of the idea of life chances introduced above.

The Impact of Inequality

What emerges strongly from the discussion thus far is the importance of understanding poverty, wealth and inequalities as social relations. By this we mean that while material resources are central to this, social relations are also economic, political, cultural, geographical, environmental and psychological. Questions of security, insecurity, of risk and uncertainty, vulnerability, harm and well-being, are all fundamentally social and political issues, issues of social justice that go to the heart of what kind of society we would like to live in and how we are going to achieve this. In this regard structural approaches tend to view inequality and poverty not as marginal features of society, some brief aberrations, but long-term social processes and relations that permeate the fabric of society and which are reflected in the way in which society is organised and structured. For Richard Wilkinson, the degree of inequality in the social environment is reflected in society in different ways, including in the levels of trust, involvement in community life, morbidity and mortality, in anti-social behaviour, drug and alcohol addiction, anxiety, stress, depression, insecurity and so on (Wilkinson, 2005, p 23). He argues that 'the quality of social relations in societies is related to the scale of income inequality—how big the gap is between rich and poor' (2005, p 24). In claiming that there is a close relationship between inequality and the quality of social relations, Wilkinson offers a structural approach that seeks to locate the causes of 'social problems', for instance drug addiction or ill-health, as well as problems that are often presented as being more 'personal', such as depression and stress, in the unequal relations and structures of society. This approach begins and ends at the social level, locating individuals and groups in their social contexts and understanding supposedly 'individual' issues as inextricably linked to the organisation and structure of society.

One of the clearest ways of understanding such connections and relations is to focus on the links between inequality and health. Wilkinson shows that ill-health and premature death are linked to levels of inequality in society with the US performing worse than most other industrialised countries in this respect. Life expectancy in the UK also declined during the last two decades of the 20th century when, as we have seen, the income gap between rich and poor was also increasing dramatically.

Wilkinson's approach is outlined here to illustrate how a structural account can offer explanations of issues that are all too often regarded as solely individual-centred. His psychosocial emphasis attributes physiological and psychological illnesses to income levels. The more hierarchical a society, the more people experience insecurity about their position within it as well as fears of 'falling' from a particular social position (see Young, 2007). Inequality matters, therefore, in many different direct and indirect ways and works to shape the myriad of day-to-day interactions and social relations in which we are located.

Poverty and inequality are understood in this approach as social relations, yet Wilkinson tends to underplay the role that material factors play in the generation of ill-health. Inequality is much more than a psychosocial state, however, and for some theorists it can only be understood as a dimension of the exploitative and unequal economic and social relations that characterise contemporary capitalist societies.

Class and Class Analysis: 'An Embarrassing and Unsettling Subject'

Despite the persistence of marked class divisions and structured inequalities across the world today, arguably class has become the social condition that dare not speak its name. The general marginalisation of class in much of the social sciences literature is astonishing. With relatively few exceptions, when class is introduced or mentioned it tends to be as a form of what we might term 'classism', but one of the many discriminations ('-isms') that characterise society. Even where the degree of poverty and deepening inequality is registered, class may be reduced to a descriptive variable, as only one among other equally significant variables in complex systems of stratification, and thereby, in the argument advanced here, minimised as an explanatory concept. As Marxist theorist John Westergaard claimed in 1995, 'class has now been re-declared dead, or dying in all social significance, at a time now when its economic configuration has become even sharper' (Westergaard, 1995, p 114).

Class remains the primary determinant of social life. Intellectually and ideologically, class represented a central point of reference that helped to explain everything from voting patterns and attitudinal differences, political mobilisation, social conflict, to lifestyle and consumption patterns, and even personality traits (see Crompton, 1998; Savage, 2000). Yet, the concept of class no longer occupies centre stage in the analysis of UK society today. Academic, policy and journalistic discourses about modern society have been largely de-classed.

To highlight this eradication of class from the policy lexicon is hardly to make a controversial claim. Class, as Sayer (2005, p 1) put it, has become 'an embarrassing and unsettling subject'. There is something approaching a consensus that class has declined as a significant factor in the routine structuring of social and economic relations in contemporary society. While such claims have been criticised from widely different perspectives (see, for example,

Marshall, 1997; Mooney, 2000; Savage, 2000; Ferguson et al, 2002; Skeggs, 2004; Sayer, 2005), they retain significant potency.

In this part of the chapter the main aim is to highlight some of the different ways in which class analysis offers us a powerful and rich form of structural analysis. It makes no apology for arguing that poverty, wealth and inequality are best analysed and explained from the vantage point of Marxist class analysis that seeks to understand these in relation to the structures and organising principles of capitalist society.

Marxist Explanations of Poverty

Marxism represents the best known of structural explanations of social inequality in capitalist societies. This is not to claim that it is the only structural explanation, but that the entire Marxist tradition is one that readily distinguishes it from all other explanations. In particular, what stands out in Marxist approaches is that the explanation of whatever social issue is taken for investigation always starts from the prioritisation of class and class conflict (see Mooney, 2000). Again constraints of space mean that we are unable to do full justice to the Marxist approach here and instead can only highlight some of the key ways in which Marxists endeavour to analyse and explain poverty and inequality (see also Lavalette, 2006).

As might be expected, the entire thrust of the Marxist approach is to locate the discussion and analysis of poverty within the wider context of class relations and inequalities within capitalist society (see Novak, 1988; Ferguson et al, 2002). In this respect, Marxists make no attempt to isolate people experiencing poverty from the rest of society, but see poverty as part of a relationship of inequality, economically, materially and politically. Thus, poverty is related to inequalities of wealth and income: it cannot be understood outside of the relationship to inequalities of wealth. At the centre of this and underpinning all inequalities is the exploitation and oppressions that are integral to the production of material wealth in capitalist society. For Marxists, the production and accumulation of profit, of wealth, is also simultaneously the production and accumulation of poverty, want and misery. From this position Tony Novak argues that:

> It is the economic and social relationships of capitalist society—the division between a minority who own and control the world's wealth and those who have no choice but to work for them—that is at one and the same time both the root cause of poverty and the motor of capitalist growth and development. ... Poverty thus needs to be understood not just as the end-product of a particular system of distribution—which is how most studies of poverty approach it—but as an essential precondition for the process of production itself. Poverty is not simply about the way that society's resources are distributed, but also about the way these resources are produced. (1995, p 70)

In making such an argument, a Marxist perspective immediately stands out from the other approaches that seek to define, measure and examine people experiencing poverty in isolation from wider society. They also stand apart from the social exclusion approaches (see Chapter

Three) which, while recognising that social exclusion results from wider social processes, ignore the class-based inequalities of capitalist society. Both the social exclusion and Marxist approaches see poverty as a relationship, but they understand and analyse this in very different ways. Through the Marxist approach, poverty is viewed as the product of the normal operations of capitalist society, not an abnormal state of affairs. The threat of poverty is an ever-present fear for many working-class people, although the fact that the overwhelming majority of people experiencing poverty are also working class is something that is generally obscured and overlooked in many accounts. Its study and analysis, therefore, must be located within those very relations by understanding it as a relationship of inequality between a highly powerful and affluent minority and the mass of ordinary workers. Like social exclusion, therefore, Marxist explanations see poverty and inequality as relational, but they offer very different ways of analysing this.

In this respect we need to reflect on the idea of poverty and inequalities as mere 'social problems'. Following the structural approach offered here, poverty and wealth represent very different forms of social problem for people experiencing poverty on the one hand, and for people with high incomes on the other: the task of the latter to maximise income and wealth at the expense of the former; the goal of people experiencing poverty to increase their share of income at the expense of the rich and powerful.

For Marxist theorists, there has been too much concern with counting people experiencing poverty in order to regulate and discipline them and to force them into work (see Jones and Novak, 1999; Gough et al, 2006). This is also accompanied by the recurring representation of people experiencing poverty as a problem to be managed, addressed or, failing that, controlled. Jones and Novak argue that:

> punitive and negative images of the poor are deeply sedimented, historically, within British society. These images reflect not only the periodic reconstruction of the poor as morally degenerate and culpable, but also a more widespread, deep-rooted and long standing antagonism that has characterised social and class relationships in Britain. (Jones and Novak, 1999, p 5)

Therefore we need to be aware that the history of the study of poverty is characterised by a language and approach that has tended to describe 'the poor' often in the most condemning and derogatory of terms. From a concern with the 'dangerous' and disreputable poor in the 19th century (see Mann, 1992; Morris, 1994) through to 'problem families', 'dysfunctional families/ communities' and the 'underclass' and 'socially excluded' of the late 20th and early 21st centuries (Macnicol, 1987; Welshman, 2002; Cook, 2006), how we talk about people experiencing poverty says much about our understanding of the underlying *causes* of poverty and shapes how explanations are then constructed. Labels such as 'underclass', 'hard-to-reach', 'welfare-dependent' (as well as some uses of the notion of 'the socially excluded') are stigmatising and mobilise normative ways of thinking of poverty and inequality that construct 'the poor' and disadvantaged almost as a distinctive group of people living 'on' or 'beyond' the 'margins' of society. In the process this language works to distance 'them' from 'us', the 'mainstream' of society, 'normal', 'hard-working', 'responsible' citizens (see Lister, 2004, chapter 5).

From the 19th century, and reflecting the power of individual-centred explanations, the study and investigation of poverty (and of inequality in general) is highly susceptible to moral condemnation and to blaming people experiencing poverty for their own position. People experiencing poverty are frequently constructed as 'a problem' to be managed and controlled. Poverty itself is often understood and presented as a 'social problem' (although it is not a social problem for everyone). Wealth and the question of 'the rich' are, in stark contrast, rarely viewed in such ways:

> what thoughtful rich people call the problem of poverty, thoughtful poor people call with equal justice a problem of riches. (Tawney, 1913, p 10)

In this oft-quoted comment, social critic and historian Richard H. Tawney immediately draws our attention to the power relations that underpin wider social and political discourses and explanations of, and approaches to, poverty and inequality, throwing into the melting pot that how we approach the study and analysis of poverty and inequality betrays our values and our politics.

So, the othering of many people experiencing poverty is by no means a new development even if it has reached new heights with the Conservatives and New Labour over the past two to three decades. Such othering, however, extends to the ways in which the working class and in particular working- class people experiencing poverty are constructed and represented in many social and political discourses today. Jock Young (2007) makes an important distinction between a conservative form of othering, which attributes negative characteristics to the other, and a liberal form of othering, where the other is deemed to lack the qualities, values and virtues that 'we' hold. In this liberal othering, deficits or a lacking are often seen as a consequence of material and cultural factors that prevent others becoming 'just like us'. Young illustrates some of the many ways in which liberal othering works both to *diminish* others—they are less than us—and to *distance* others from us. As Ruth Lister has shown, this is often central to the many discourses that surround the discussion of poverty and of people experiencing poverty in the contemporary UK. For Young (2007) this binary thinking, 'us' and 'them', permeates public thinking and official discourses and is utilised and extended in constructions of other cultures, countries, nationalities and religions. Young rightly argues that such binary thinking is also evident in social sciences discourses and this might be extended to include the othering of the working class, especially of the white working class.

Haylett (2001) and Skeggs (2005) argue that when the working class features in policy making and in social sciences (as well as in journalistic) commentary, it does so primarily as 'a problem to be solved'. Being working class is often constructed as a 'social condition' in desperate need of remedy. Despite the persistence of marked class divisions and structured inequalities within British society today, there is a recurring identification of that part of the working class suffering most from the effects of long-term economic change and of the strategy of inequality as pathological, as beyond the mainstream, in other words as 'a problem'. Such 'problem' groups occupy a highly precarious relationship in relation to the labour market. The most vulnerable sections of the working class frequently become the focus of overlapping pathologisation processes—in relation to social inclusion policies, in debates around educational attainment, in relation to patterns of ill-health and morbidity, and, most publicly, in the mass media, in relation to questions of criminal justice, especially around urban youth crime.

Such otherings can be understood as part of the wider class antagonisms and hatreds that permeate society today. How we approach the questions of poverty, inequality and wealth reflects such antagonisms. The construction of people experiencing poverty as an underclass or dysfunctional group, as a problem, reflects such antagonisms and works both to produce and reproduce what Jones and Novak (1999, p 73) refer to as the 'abuse of the poor'. As John Macnicol (1987) has forcefully argued, the demonisation of an underclass and of other groups of people experiencing poverty says more about the preoccupations and fears of the rich and powerful and their concerns for a decline in respect for authority and a fragmenting social order. Such discourses carry with them a focus on individual failings or a lacking, sidelining in the process those structural processes that underpin the production and reproduction of poverty and inequality across the world today as in the past. As such they are part and parcel of neoliberalising worldviews that return us time and time again to a focus on the individual (for further detail on individual/behavioural understandings of the causes of poverty, see Alcock, 2006).

Conclusion

This chapter has been primarily concerned to outline some of the key aspects of structural explanations of poverty, wealth and inequality. Structural explanations offer powerful ways of making sense of social issues such as poverty. Against those perspectives, which are largely focused on individual behaviours and 'problem cultures', structural arguments seek to locate the causes of poverty and inequality in the structural organisation of society. These are not approached as some kind of malfunctioning or short-term aberrations in how society is organised. Instead they are made sense of as part of a wider system of oppression, exploitation and inequality that characterises contemporary societies. There is a growing interest among some sections of academic social policy with material inequalities, both at the level of UK society and globally, and how these work to generate and structure disadvantage and poverty. While it is important to maintain a conceptual distinction between poverty and inequality, there is increasing recognition that unless inequality is tackled, then poverty and disadvantage will continue as a pervasive feature of contemporary societies. Inequality matters immensely for our understanding of poverty and social exclusion (see Callinicos, 2000; Jackson and Segal, 2004; Byrne, 2005; Harvey, 2005; Wilkinson, 2005; Orton and Rowlingson, 2007). Through an approach which seeks to centre the unequal social relations of poverty and inequality, we can build a more comprehensive understanding of a wide range of social issues, from ill-health and insecurity through to much more significant concerns with social justice and 'well-being', and to how the wealthy continue to be privileged through economic, social and fiscal policies.

This ties in with growing calls from social policy academics that social policy analysis itself should 'move upstream' (for example, Sinfield, 2004). Sinfield argues that there is an urgent need for social policy researchers to study and explain the underlying structural factors that shape poverty, disadvantage and inequality, an approach which focuses more on the 'root causes' of poverty but which also entails more critical examination of the privileging of the rich through social and economic policies.

Marxism has always offered such an approach. It begins not with poverty, but with the totality of social relations in society, arguing that it is only a totalising explanation that can provide an adequate account of poverty and inequality, relating such issues to questions of class, exploitation and oppression. This has led theorists such as Westergaard (1995) to argue that more emphasis needs to be given to the reproduction of wealth and privilege among the upper class of the rich. Here there is an explicit attack on the preoccupation among politicians, policy makers and in the academy with 'the poor', and we might extend this to include the liberal othering identified by Young.

In many discussions of poverty and of anti-poverty policy, people experiencing poverty exist only as victims or as passive recipients of policies developed by 'us' for 'them'. They are generally denied any sense of 'agency' save attributing to them responsibility for their poverty (see Lister, 2004, pp 124-5). That people experiencing poverty have a 'voice' and can organise to resist attempts to other them as well as to defend the kinds of state services on which they depend has, with some notable exceptions, generally been neglected (cf Piven and Cloward, 1977; Lavalette and Mooney, 2000; Ferguson et al, 2002). As Ruth Lister has argued, there has been a tendency to deny voice and agency to people experiencing poverty, even in some of those structural accounts that dominated UK social policy analysis in the postwar period (Lister, 2004, pp 126-7).

Not all structural approaches are guilty in this respect, however. Let us return to Marxist class theory. This perspective not only recognises and explains that capitalist society is built on and structured around an exploitative set of social relations which work to oppress the overwhelming majority in society, but that working-class people have the capacity, the agency, to resist and to struggle against such exploitations. Poverty and inequality are seen as the inevitable consequence of the exploitative social relations that lie at the heart of capitalist society, not some aberration that can be fully addressed, diluted or managed through social policy alone.

Here is one fruitful way in which we can see that class as structure and class as agency interrelate, and through which the material inequalities that characterise contemporary society can begin to be challenged. What this also reminds us, importantly, is that poverty and inequality are not some naturally occurring or inevitable feature of human society but the product of human relations, that is, of human action and agency. In turn this means that the building of another society is possible in which poverty and inequality are overcome and the pursuit of real social justice becomes the building block of social life.

Summary

- Structural explanations foreground social, economic, political and cultural relations and processes as key factors that generate and reproduce poverty and inequality.
- The idea of a strategy of inequality refers in particular here to the policies and objectives of the Conservative governments during the 1980s and 1990s that sought to increase inequality as a way of disciplining labour, growing the economy and affecting a restructuring of the welfare state.
- Marxist explanations of poverty start from the perspective of exploitative class relations and see poverty and inequality as inevitable features of class society.
- The othering of people experiencing poverty and disadvantaged sections of the working classes has long been central to debates over poverty and its causes.
- People experiencing poverty have generally been denied agency or voice although there is now more recognition that this serves to construct 'the poor' as other.
- 'Upstream analysis' means focusing more on the ways in which the rich are privileged through state policies as well as on the behaviour and activities of the rich.

Questions for Discussion

- What are the basic starting points of structural explanations?
- In what ways might inequalities in wealth and income shape other inequalities in society?
- Why does Marxist theory see poverty, wealth and inequality as part and parcel of the structure of capitalist society?
- In what ways might it be better to relate structure and agency in explanations of poverty and its causes?
- What do you understand by the term 'moving upstream'? What would be the focus of an upstream analysis of poverty, wealth and inequality?

Further Reading

There are many different books, studies and reports which explore different aspects of explaining poverty and some of these have been highlighted by Alcock (see Chapter Three, this volume). Perhaps one of the most accessible overviews is provided by Lister in *Poverty* (2004), while for critical explorations of the idea of social exclusion, Gough *et al's Spaces of social exclusion* (2006), Levitas's *The inclusive society?* (2005) and Byrne's *Social exclusion* (2005) are among the best discussions available. Each seeks to locate poverty in its social and structural contexts. For the relationship between poverty and wealth, see Novak's (1988) *Poverty and the state*, while one of the best all-round accounts, although it is now a little dated, is Scott's *Poverty and wealth* (1994).

For Marxist explanations of equality and inequality, one of the best and most readable accounts is offered by Callinicos in *Equality* (2000). For a Marxist approach to welfare see Ferguson et al's *Rethinking welfare* (2002). Useful general discussions of class are available in Savage's *Class analysis and transformations* (2000) and Sayer's *The moral significance of class* (2005).

References

Alcock, P. (2006) *Understanding poverty* (3rd edn), Basingstoke: Palgrave.

Bendix, R. (1977) *Max Weber: An intellectual portrait*, Berkeley, CA: University of California Press.

Byrne, D. (2005) *Social exclusion* (2nd edn), Maidenhead: Open University Press.

Callinicos, A. (2000) *Equality*, Cambridge: Polity Press.

Cook, D. (2006) *Criminal and social justice*, London: Sage Publications.

Crompton, R. (1998) *Class and stratification* (2nd edn), Cambridge: Polity Press.

Ferguson, I., Lavalette, M. and Mooney, G. (2002) *Rethinking welfare*, London: Sage Publications.

Gough, J., Eisenschitz, A. and McCulloch, A. (2006) *Spaces of social exclusion*, London: Palgrave.

Harvey, D. (2005) *A brief history of neoliberalism*, Oxford: Oxford University Press.

Haylett, C. (2001) 'Illegitimate subjects?: abject whites, neoliberal modernisation, and middle-class multiculturalism', *Society and Space*, vol 19, pp 351–70.

Hughes, J., Sharrock, W. and Martin, P.J. (2003) *Understanding classical sociology: Marx, Weber, Durkheim*, London: Sage Publications.

Jackson, B. and Segal, P. (2004) *Why inequality matters*, London: Catalyst.

Jones, C. and Novak, T. (1999) *Poverty, welfare and the disciplinary state*, London: Routledge.

Lavalette, M. (2006) 'Marxism and welfarism', in M. Lavalette and A. Pratt (eds) *Social policy: Theories, concepts and issues* (3rd edn), London: Sage Publications, pp 46–65.

Lavalette, M. and Mooney, G. (eds) (2000) *Class struggle and social welfare*, London: Routledge.

Levitas, R. (2005) *The inclusive society? Social exclusion and New Labour* (2nd edn), London: Palgrave Macmillan.

Lister, R. (2004) *Poverty*, Cambridge: Polity Press.

Macnicol, J. (1987) 'In pursuit of the underclass', *Journal of Social Policy*, vol 16, no 2, pp 293–318.

Mann, K. (1992) *The making of an English 'underclass'?*, Buckingham: Open University Press.

Marshall, G. (1997) *Repositioning class: Social inequality in industrial societies*, London: Sage Publications.

Mooney, G. (2000) 'Class and social policy', in G. Lewis, S. Gewirtz and J. Clarke (eds) *Rethinking social policy*, London: Sage Publications, pp 156–70.

Morris, L. (1994) *Dangerous classes: The underclass and social citizenship*, London: Routledge. Novak, T. (1988) *Poverty and the state*, Buckingham: Open University Press.

Novak, T. (1995) 'Rethinking poverty', *Critical Social Policy*, vol 44/45, pp 58–74.

Novak, T. (2001) 'What's in a name? Poverty, the underclass and social exclusion', in M. Lavalette and A. Pratt (eds) *Social policy* (2nd edn), London: Sage Publications.

Orton, M. and Rowlingson, K. (2007) 'A problem of riches: towards a new social policy research agenda on the distribution of economic resources', *Journal of Social Policy*, vol 36, no 1, pp 59–77.

Piven, F.F. and Cloward, R.A. (1977) *Poor people's movements: Why they succeed, how they fail*, New York: Pantheon.

Savage, M. (2000) *Class analysis and transformations*, Buckingham: OpenUniversity Press.

Sayer, A. (2005) *The moral significance of class*, Cambridge: Cambridge University Press.

Scott, J. (1994) *Poverty and wealth*, London: Longman.

Sinfield, A. (2004) 'Upstream thinking', *Policy World: Newsletter of the Social Policy Association*, Autumn, no 11 (www.social-policy.com).

Skeggs, B. (2004) *Class, self, culture*, London: Routledge.

Skeggs, B. (2005) 'The making of class and gender though visualising moral subject formation', *Sociology*, vol 39, no 5, pp 965–82.

Tawney, R.H. (1913) 'Poverty as an industrial problem', Inaugural lecture, reproduced in R.H. Tawney, *Memoranda on the problems of poverty*, London: William Morris Press.

UN (United Nations) (2005) *Human development report* (http://hdr.undp.org/).

Walker, A. (1990) 'The strategy of inequality: poverty and income distribution in Britain 1979–89', in I. Taylor (ed) *The social effects of free market policies*, Hemel Hempstead: Harvester Wheatsheaf, pp 29–47.

Walker, A. (1997) 'Introduction: the strategy of inequality', in A. Walker and C. Walker (eds) *Britain divided*, London: CPAG, pp 1–13.

Weber, M. (1978) *Economy and society*, Berkeley, CA: University of California Press.

Welshman, J. (2002) 'The cycle of deprivation and the concept of the underclass', *Benefits*, vol 3, no 1, October, pp 199–205.

Westergaard, J. (1995) *Who get's what?*, Cambridge: Polity Press.

Wilkinson, R.G. (2005) *The impact of inequality*, London: Routledge.

Young, J. (2007) *The exclusive society*, London: Sage Publications.

Toward a Healthier Planet

The Creation of a Democratic Ecosocialist World System

By Hans Baer and Merrill Singer

While global capitalism has resulted in impressive technological innovations, including ones in biomedicine and health care delivery, it is a system fraught with contradictions, including an incessant drive for economic expansion, growing social disparities, undemocratic practices that undermine its claims of equality, militarist and imperialist practices, depletion of natural resources, and environmental degradation (including global warming and associated climatic changes). All of these contradictions entail numerous consequences for people's health and access to health care. The contradictory features of global capitalism are intertwined (e.g., military ventures wreck havoc on the environment and significantly deplete natural resources while promoting global social inequality), and hence it is hard to fully analyze one contradiction separate from the others. Each is so complex in its relationship to health, however, that it requires the kind of detailed single-issue examination presented in this book.

Based on the assessment presented, it is clear that human societies will have to adapt to the reality of global warming in a variety of ways, including technological fixes, reliance upon alternative forms of energy, significant expansion and improvement in mass transit systems, more efficient forms of heating and cooling, the development of buildings and dwelling units that are more energy efficient, the redesign of cities to control their energy demands and heat outputs, restoration of degraded environments, protection of biodiversity, and less reliance upon airplanes as a form of travel. Yet, it is the argument of this book that while these kinds of *reformist reform strategies* will help to limit future greenhouse gas emissions, they are insufficient to reverse global warming if they are implemented within the reigning productivist and consumptionist ethics of global capitalism. Adopting capitalist solutions to the contradictions of capitalism—such as green capitalism and neoliberal approaches—we argue, is a kind of fool's paradise that misdiagnosis both the extent and the ultimate source of the threat facing the ecohealth of the planet and its occupants.

Consequently, we believe it is necessary to adopt *nonreformist reform* transcendent approaches to global warming that move toward the development of a new global system, one committed to social equality, social democracy, and environmental sustainability at local, national, and global levels. In the 19th century, various revolutionaries and reformers, particularly Karl Marx and Frederich Engels, sought to develop alternatives to an increasingly globalizing capitalist world system. Efforts at the national level to create an alternative started out with the Bolshevik Revolution in Russia in 1917 and included subsequent revolutions in other countries, including China in 1949, Vietnam in 1954, Cuba in 1959, Laos in 1975, and Nicaragua and Afghanistan in 1979. Academics and political activists have engaged in considerable discussion and debate in their efforts to determine whether these societies constituted examples of "state socialism" or "actually existing socialism," transitions between capitalism and socialism that needed to undergo democratization, state capitalism, or new class societies. They also have asked why these societies, such as the Soviet Union and China, in different ways failed to transcend the reigning global economic structure and were eventually fully reincorporated into the capitalist world system.

Ultimately, the failure of these societies to develop democratic ecosocialism was related to both internal forces specific to each society (including their initial lower level of technological development) and external forces that created a hostile environment (both economically and politically) which impeded progressive changes and pushed their systems away from democracy toward centralization.

A Vision of Global Democratic Ecosocialism

The collapse of communist regimes created a crisis for people on the left throughout the world. Many progressives had hoped that somehow these societies would undergo changes that would transform them into democratic and environmentally sustainable egalitarian societies. This did not occur. In the aftermath, some politically progressive analysts began advocating shedding the concept of socialism and replacing it with terms such as *radical democracy* and *economic democracy*. While such efforts are understandable given the fate of postrevolutionary or socialist-oriented societies, we believe that it is necessary to come to terms with both the achievements and flaws of these societies and to reformulate the concept of socialism. For example, the tiny country of Cuba, some 90 miles (145 km) offshore from the United States, exhibits health statistics on par with those of highly developed and wealthy societies, exports physicians to various developing countries around the world (particularly those facing crisis situations), and, according to the mainstream World Wildlife Fund, is the only country in the world that meets the criteria of *sustainable development*.

The creation of what we term *democratic ecosocialism*, or what world systems theorists Terry Boswell and Christopher Chase Dunn (2000) term *global democracy*, would entail the following components: 1) an increasing movement toward public ownership of productive forces at local, regional, national, and international levels; 2) the development of an economy oriented toward meeting social needs, such as basic food, clothing, shelter, and health care, and environmental sustainability rather than profit making; 3) a blending of both representative and participatory democratic processes; 4) the eradication of health and social disparities and redistribution of human resources between developed and developing societies and within societies in general; 5) the curtailment of population growth that in larger part would follow from the previously mentioned condition; 6) the conservation of finite resources and the development of renewable energy resources, such as wind, solar, and thermal energy, all of which would counteract the present trend toward rapidly accelerating global warming; 7) the redesign of settlement and transportation systems to cut energy demands and greenhouse gas emissions; and 8) the reduction of wastes through recycling and transcending the reigning culture of consumption.

On a global level, democratic ecosocialism also seeks to address not only the matter of environmental sustainability but also social justice (including environmental justice), both within developed societies, where large numbers of people continue to suffer from poverty, but particularly in developing societies. To achieve these goals, there is no escaping the difficult fact that the majority of people in developed societies will need to scale back their consumption of material goods. In one of his ongoing popular commentaries, Immanuel Wallerstein (2007:1), a principal architect of world systems theory, delineates three powerful obstacles to overcoming global warming: 1) the "interests of producers/entrepreneurs" who function as the purveyors of the constant cycle of production and consumption; 2) the "interests of less wealthy nations," like China and India, that seek to catch up with the core nations, and 3) the "attitudes of you and me," that is ordinary people like the authors and readers of this book who consciously or unconsciously find ourselves embedded in the contradictions of global capitalism wherever we live, including the encultured needs we feel for acquiring "more things." As Wallerstein asserts, mitigation of global warming starts at the individual level, a notion that applies to most people in developed societies, depending on their class status, and the more affluent social classes in developing countries. While poorer regions of the world are in need of economic development—that is, access to basic resources and health care—much of the developed world and parts of the developing world are, in a sense, overdeveloped (although the products of this overdevelopment are not equitably distributed). As Foster argues,

> Sustained economic development over decades ... is ... not the same thing as environmentally sustainable development. ... Any discussion of the global ecological crisis must therefore concentrate on the excesses of the advanced capitalist states, and their impact on the periphery of the world economy. It is here at the heart of the capitalist world system that the problem of unsustainable development arises in its acute form. [Foster 2002:82]

Further, as Loewy observes,

> The countries of the South, where ... [basic material] needs are very far from being satisfied, will need a much higher level of "development"—building railroads, hospitals, sewage systems, and other infrastructures—than the advanced industrial ones. But there is no reason why this cannot be accomplished with a productive system that is environmentally-friendly and based on renewable energies. [Loewy 2006:303]

Democratic ecosocialism rejects a statist, growth-oriented, or productivist ethic and the enshrinement of possession and consumption as pathways to emotional satisfaction and as markers of personal achievement. Instead, it recognizes that we live on an ecologically fragile planet with limited resources and endangered wildlife and plants that must be sustained and renewed for future generations. According to Pepper (1993:234), "the basic socialist principles—egalitarianism, eliminating capitalism and poverty, resource distribution according to need and democratic control of our lives and communities—are also environmental principles." Public ownership of the means of production would blend elements of centralism and decentralism. For example, large-scale operations such as telecommunications or a railway system could be owned and operated by the national government whereas a small-scale operation such as a shoe factory or publishing house could be owned by a local community.

Socialism has the potential to place constraints upon resource depletion and attacks upon biodiversity. As McLaughlin (1990:80–81) maintains, "Socialism provides the conscious political control of those processes of interacting with nature which are left to the unconscious market processes under capitalism." The construction of democratic ecosocialism needs to be based upon a commitment to a long-term sustainable balance between sociocultural systems and the natural environment. As Foster (2005b:9) argues, a *global ecological transformation* requires a socialist transformation. Part and parcel of the transformation to a safer and sustainable way of life is the movement away from the narrow self-interested focus on personal (and familial) wealth that is promoted by global capitalism toward a focus on social responsibility. As Lohmann (2006:339) observes, "no aspect of the discussion on global warming can be disentangled from debates about colonialism, racism, gender, exploitation and the democratic control of technology."

Nonreformist Reforms for Mitigating Global Warming: Pathways to Social Transformation

The types of transformations suggested above require the development of concrete plans and pathways to lead us away from the limited programs of mitigation now being offered by corporate elites, the governments of developed nations, and even some environmentalists as the "solution" to global warming. The Socialist Alliance (2007), an Australian political party, has delineated a 10-Point Climate Action Plan for Australia that could be modified for other countries, both developed and developing countries:

1. "Aim for 60 percent overall emissions reduction, including 95 percent power station reduction by 2020, and 90 percent overall emissions reduction by 2030;
2. Ratify the Kyoto treaty and initiate a further international treaty and mutual assistance program to bring other countries together to meet a global target of 90 percent emissions by 2030;
3. Start the transition to a zero-waste economy, [starting out with a program of energy auditing];
4. Set a minimum 10-star energy efficiency rating for all new buildings;
5. Bring all power industries under public ownership and democratic control;
6. Bring the immense manufacturing potential of the auto industry under public control;
7. Immediately begin constructing wind farms in suitable areas;
8. End industrial farming based on fossil-fuel fertilisers, pesticides and fuels;
9. Stop logging old-growth forests and begin an urgent program of re-forestation and protecting biodiversity to ensure a robust biosystem that can survive the stress of climate change and provide an increased carbon sink; and
10. Make all urban and regional public transport free and upgrade the network to enable all urban residents to use it for all their regular commuting."

While the climate action plan may strike many people as being utopian, like the notion of democracy, it constitutes a vision for an alternative to flawed "business as usual" or existing climate regimes and green capitalism.

While we view the creation of a democratic ecosocialist world order as the ultimate mitigation strategy for addressing global warming, we are not under any illusions that this vision will be implemented any time soon, if ever for that matter, and certainly not without a mass, grassroots and global social movement to promote it. In the meantime, those concerned above the grave threats of global warming and other contradictions of global capitalism need to identify and push for nonreformist reforms. As Pittock (2005:151) observes, "mitigation action taken now will have its most significant effects decades into the future."

Some shorter-term nonreformist reforms might include: lobbying national, regional, and state governments to adopt and implement strong mitigation plans; voluntary personal lifestyle changes, such as relying more on mass transit, cycling, and walking as modes of transportation and traveling more within one's region than over long distances; and supporting progressive social movements that critically challenge the political, economic, and social forces that contribute to global warming and promote narrow solutions for overcoming its dire effects.

Theoretically, a tax on greenhouse gas emissions could also constitute a nonreformist reform. Climate-related regulation and climate-relaxed tax codes already exist in various countries (Lohmann 2006:334). Unfortunately, efforts to impose a carbon tax in the European Union have met with failure because certain member states, such as the United Kingdom, capitulated to the claims of various industries that they would not be able to compete with non-European Union industries (O'Riordan and Jordan 1999:84). Conversely, carbon tax schemes emanating from social movements could incorporate measures to resist capitulation to corporate lobbying, bullying, and nationalist propaganda campaigns.

Various other plans that contain valuable ideas also have been suggested. Ian Angus, the late director of the Centre for Science and Environment in India, for example, recommended the following reforms as key components of a socialist agenda for global warming mitigation:

- Establish and enforce rapid mandatory reductions in CO_2 emissions: real reduction, not phoney trading plans.
- Make the corporations that produce greenhouse gases pay the full cost of cutting emissions.
- End all subsidies to fossil fuel producers.
- Redirect the billions now being spent on wars and debt into public transit, into retrofitting homes and offices for energy efficiency, and into renewable energy projects. [Angus 2007]

Alternately, Firor and Jacobsen (2002) propose an approach to mitigation of global warming that contains a hybrid of the social democratic approach that we discussed in the previous chapter and the democratic ecosocialist approach set forth in this chapter. In contrast to green capitalism advocates, who adhere to the notion that the levels of production must continually grow in order to ensure a robust national economy, Firor and Jacobsen (2002) acknowledge that GDP is an artificial and misleading measure of economic and social well-being in that it does not measure quality of life and environmental sustainability. In line with our discussion above, they argue that there are two needed social revolutions if humans are to flourish on earth: 1) an equity revolution (including in the area of health) across social classes within societies and between societies and 2) an efficiency revolution that would change the relationship between economic activities and the planetary ecosystem. Whereas they argue that "business and industry," which have contributed heavily to environmental degradation, must play a role in saving the environment, we argue that ultimately both activities need to be subsumed within an alternative global political economy.

Finally, Ted Trainer (1989, 1995), an Australian environmental scientist, provides several proposals that might be termed nonreformist reforms in that they could serve as transition points between the present global system and a newer, planet-friendly alternative. Trainer calls for "appropriate development" for both "rich" and "poor" countries. In terms of the former, this would entail an enormous reduction in consumerism (Trainer 1989:196) and essentially reversion to a "zero-growth economy" in which societies "will work hard at reducing the amount of producing and consuming going on" (Trainer 1995:108). In terms of the latter, this would include a focus on local economic self-sufficiency; the utilization of "low, intermediate, and alterative technologies processing locally available resources"; and a commitment to environmental sustainability (Trainer 1989:199–201). Unfortunately, Trainer, who views excessive consumption as the root of global environmental crisis, fails to analyze consumption as an inevitable component of capitalism's insatiable need for ever-expanding economic growth.

Challenging Global Warming at the Grass-Roots Level

Achieving a just, democratic, and environmentally safe world will not be easy, at either the individual or group levels, especially given the fate of earlier efforts to create more equitable and just social systems (e.g., the Soviet Union and the People's Republic of China), but ultimately it is mandatory to mitigate the significant adverse impacts of global warming. The creation of an alternative global social order will require a multifaceted effort drawing upon expertise from many quarters, including not only mainstream political and economic institutions but also progressive social movements. Already there are voices from many quarters bucking the existing global political economy, including the anti-corporate globalization, environmental, labor, indigenous and ethnic rights, peace, and social justice movements. As a result of grass-roots pressure, various city and state governments in developed societies, including the United States and the United Kingdom, have been passing ordinances and implementing programs of greenhouse gas abatement (Bulkeley and Betsill 2003). Indeed, some of these measures may qualify as local nonreformist reforms in that they empower local groups to counteract measures on the part of national governments that capitulate to corporate demands, that undermine mitigation of global warming, and provide these local groups with leverage to mobilize broader national and international campaigns against global warming.

Indeed, an anti-global warming movement has begun to crystallize since the turn of the 21st century, and has built upon warnings about the dangers of global warming emanating over the past two decades from climate scientists, environmental groups, small island states, indigenous groups in the Arctic and South Pacific, other Third World peoples, and some mainstream and even some evangelical churches. Indeed, the antiglobal or climate movement exhibits huge overlaps with the anti-corporate globalization or global justice movement, in that they both struggle against corporate control of the global economy and for environmental sustainability. Agyeman, Doppelt, Lynn, and Hatic (2007:121) assert that the "emerging climate-justice movement shifts the discursive framework of climate change from a scientific-technical debate to one about ethics focused on human rights and justice."

The small island states formed the Alliance of Small Island States (AOSIS) during the Second World Climate Conference in 1992 in Geneva. Most Pacific island nations have ratified the Framework Convention on Climate Change (FCCC). On August 28, 2002, the International Climate Justice Network delineated 26 points in its Bali Principles of Climate Justice (Agyeman, Doppelt, Lynn, and Hatic 2007:122–124). Various bodies from around the world issued a declaration at the Climate Justice Summit in New Delhi on October 26–27, 2002 which included the following words:

> We, representatives of the poor and the marginalized of the world, representing fishworkers, farmers, Indigenous Peoples, Dalits, the poor and the youth, resolve to actively build a movement from the communities that will address the issue of climate change from a human rights, social justice and labour perspective. We affirm

that climate change is a human rights issue. ... We reject the market based principles that guide the current negotiations to solve the climate crisis: Our World is Not for Sale! [Indian Climate Forum 2002:1].

This statement reflects an often overlooked perspective that has been emphasized by various indigenous organizations and spokespersons. For example, the Second International Indigenous Forum on Climate Change, which was held in The Hague, drafted a declaration on November 11–12, 2000, which included the following points:

> Earth is our Mother. ... [It] is not a commodity, but a sacred space. ... Our traditional knowledge on sustainable use, conservation and protection of our territories has allowed us to maintain our ecosystems in equilibrium. ... Our cultures, and the territories under our stewardship, are now the last ecological mechanisms remaining in the struggle against climate devastation. ... Climate change is a reality and is affecting hundreds of millions of our peoples and our territories, resulting in famine, extreme poverty, disease, loss of basic resources in our traditional habitats and provoking involuntary displacements of our peoples as environmental refugees. The causes of climate change are the production and consumption patterns in industrialised countries and are therefore, the primarily responsibilities of these countries. [www.c.3.hu/~bocs/eco-a-/htm, accessed August 6, 2008]

Similarly, the Third International Forum of Indigenous Peoples and Local Communities on Climate Changes, in its declaration in Bonn on July 14–15, 2001, denounced the UNFCCC and the Kyoto Protocol for not recognizing the "existence or the contributions of Indigenous Peoples," noting that

> Indigenous Peoples, as part of the international community, have the right to self-determination over our lives, our territories and our resources. Selfdetermination includes, inter alia, the right to possess, control, and administer our territories. ... The discussions under the UNFCCC and the Kyoto Protocol have totally excluded the indigenous peoples to the extent that neither recognizes the right of indigenous peoples to full and effective participation and to contribute to discussions and debates. [International Indian Treaty Council 2001]

Pointing to the important role of indigenous communities in arctic environments in monitoring climate change, Sheila Watt-Cloutier, president of the Inuit Circumpolar Conference, stated the following in her address before a U.S. Senate Commerce Committee hearing in August 2004: "The Earth is literally melting. ... Protect the Arctic and you will save the planet. Use us as your early-warning system. Use the Inuit story as a vehicle to reconnect us all so that we can understand the people and the planet are one" (quoted in Johansen 2006b). She submitted a petition to the Inter-American Commission on Human Rights on behalf of her people, requesting relief from "violations resulting from global warming caused by acts and omissions of the United States" (quoted in Lynas 2007:84). Native Alaskans, who constitute

17 percent of the state's population, have established a website (www.nativeknowledge.org) to share their experiences with global warming with the world community.

Other opponents of a market approach to addressing global warming have appeared around the world. The Dag Hammarskjoeld Foundation, for example, in collaboration with various civil society groups organized a seminar in South Africa in October 2004 (Lohmann 2006:3). The seminar resulted in the Durban Declaration on Climate Justice, which in turn led to the creation of the Durban Group for Climate Justice. The latter describes itself as "an international network of independent organisations, individuals and peoples' movements who reject the market approach to climate change" and which is "committed to help build a global grassroots movement for climate justice, mobilize communities around the world and pledge our solidarity with people opposing carbon trading on the ground" (www.carbontradewatch. org/durban, accessed September 29, 2007). Other organizations that are part of a growing anti—global warming or climate movement include the Global Justice Ecology Project, the Transnational Institute, and Climate Indymedia (a media activist organization). In April 2001, Redefining Progress, an Oakland, California—based think tank, formed the Environmental Justice and Climate Change (EJCC) initiative, a coalition of 28 environmental justice, climate justice, religious, policy, and advocacy groups (Agyeman, Bulkeley, and Nochur 2007). EJCC released its 10 Principles for Just Climate Change Policies in the U.S. at the 2002 World Summit on Sustainable Development in Johannesburg, South Africa. These principles are: "1) stop cooking the planet; 2) protect and empower vulnerable individuals and communities; 3) ensure just transition for workers and communities; 4) require community participation; 5) global problems need global solutions; 6) the United States must take the lead; 7) stop exploration for fossil fuels; 8) monitor domestic and international carbon markets; 9) use caution in the face of uncertainty; and 10) protect future generations" (Environmental Justice and Climate Initiative n.d.). At the regional and local levels, the climate movement has come to include numerous grass-roots groups, such as the Massachusetts Climate Action Network, the Chesapeake Climate Action Network, the Green House Network, the New England Grassroots Environment Fund, Clean Air-Cool Planet in New England, Grand Canyon Trust, Climate Solutions in the Pacific Northwest, and West Harlem Environmental Action (Agyeman, Bulkeley, and Nochur 2007:141, Finley 2007:39).

The climate movement can now be found worldwide, even in seemingly isolated settings, such as New Zealand. The latter (as well as Tasmania) is sometimes viewed as a place where mainland Australians could potentially retreat if their country becomes too hot and dry. Outsiders often regard New Zealand as either a semi-tropical or temperature paradise, depending upon the location (whether on the North Island or the South Island); a remote place in the South Pacific that, according to some, is the victim of the "tyranny of distance" (i.e., it is geographically quite isolated), and, according to others, is a retreat "far away from the maddening crowd." Despite these perceptions, this country of some 4.2 million people, which is one of the first places on the globe to welcome the new day, is not immune from the contradictions of the global capitalism. New Zealanders (or Kiwis as they are known) have been subjected to two decades of neoliberal policies under both conservative National and social democratic Labour governments. Housing prices are sky-rocketing as affluent Americans are choosing to relocate or establish second homes there. Even in this remote corner of the world, one finds the emergence of the climate movement. Daphne Lawless, a member of Socialist Worker, reports:

> ClimAction, a climate change action coalition, sprang up in Auckland in October 2006. A broad grouping of ecologists, socialists, anarchists, unionists and other activists, ClimAction has already made a name for its feisty and innovative campaigning style. High-profile activities to date include an occupation-cum-carnival in Queen Street and a "call out" when Al Gore swept into town to Sweet-talk the local elite. [Lawless 2006:10]

ClimAction was created only a month before the International Day of Action on Climate Change on November 4, 2006. The organizers made two demands: the creation of a free and frequent public transport system in the Auckland metropolitan area, and the reduction of greenhouse gas emissions by 90 percent by 2030 (Carolan 2006). ClimAction has embarked upon a campaign to spotlight New Zealand's biggest greenhouse gas, namely methane from sheep and cattle farming, which accounts for over half of the country's emissions, as opposed to about a quarter for carbon dioxide.

As the account above suggests, for the most part, the global climate movement is a rather disparate phenomenon that includes not only grass-roots environmental, liberal, and leftist groups, but also religious organizations and even small business organizations. There is always the danger that the climate movement will devolve into a fragmented set of single-issue groups, such as was the case earlier in the anti—nuclear arms movement. Already, as we have seen, the climate movement has splintered into a reformist faction that seeks to work within the parameters of capitalism by relying upon a limited program of carbon trading and other market mechanisms and a radical faction that seeks to transcend capitalism. Green parties around the world appear to have assumed a middleground position between these two polar factions. The climate justice segment of the anti—global warming movement exhibits an authentically progressive impetus. According to Agyeman, Bulkeley, and Nochur,

> Climate justice activists contend that the only way to address the climate crisis is through actual emissions reductions on the part of the developed world. They emphasize the need for participation of vulnerable communities in developing policies that incorporate social and environmental justice concerns, such as equal per capita emissions rights. They also call upon mainstream environmental groups to develop climate justice analyses and to not settle for policies that merely make incremental progess. [Agyeman, Bulkeley, and Nochur 2007:138]

In short, the climate justice movement seeks to identify nonreformist reform strategies for change as it seeks to move step by step toward a broader and enduring social transformation.

An Engaged Anthropology, Global Warming, and the Future of Humanity and the Planet

As researchers committed to understanding life experience, social behavior, and contextual influences on human communities, as well as human biological development, diversity, and health, anthropologists, both at the theoretical and the applied levels, are in a unique position to help assess the human impact of global warming. This impact will be significant but will vary among the diverse peoples traditionally studied within anthropology, such as the Inuit of the Arctic, cattle pastoralists in East Africa, horticultural villagers in the South Pacific and Southeast Asia, and Andean peasants, as well as among peoples that the discipline been more recently studying, such as urbanites in both the developed and developing worlds. There is a critical need for anthropologists to examine in detail ways in which local populations can both adapt to and even circumvent the potentially destructive impact of global warming. Another contribution that anthropologists can make is in the examination of the emergence of an anti—global warming movement and its relationship to other social movements, particularly the social justice, anti-corporate globalization, indigenous and Third World peoples' rights, and environmental movements. No less important is "studying up," namely conducting research on the corporations that most contribute to global warming, their leaders, and their strategies for pushing a productivist program. Beyond research, applied projects involving anthropologists test and disseminate environmentally sound alternative ways of life, settlement patterns, and transportation and other technologies.

The effort to examine and respond to the adverse impacts of global warming on humanity is likely to be most effective as an interdisciplinary effort, one that involves collaboration with climate scientists, physical geographers, environmental studies scholars, and other social scientists, including sociologists, political scientists, and human geographers. Indeed, other social scientists, particularly human geographers, political scientists, and sociologists, already have addressed various aspects of global warming, including adaptations by local populations (Becken 2005, Parish and Funnell 1999, Thompson et al. 2006), international and regional climate change regimes (Liberatore 1994, O'Riordan and Jordan 1999), and corporate and neoconservative stances toward global warming (McCright and Dunlap 2003).

As critical anthropologists, influenced by Wallerstein (1979:ix–xii), we realize that social systems, either local, regional, or global, do not last forever. Global capitalism has been around for some 500 years but we believe that it has so many inherent contradictions that ultimately it must be transcended if humanity and the planet are going to survive in some reasonable fashion. Anthropologists can contribute to a larger effort not only to mitigate the impact of global warming on humanity but also to help devise an alternative global system, one committed to meeting people's basic needs, struggling for social equity and justice, building democracy, and achieving environmental sustainability. As part of this endeavor, it is imperative that anthropologists become politically engaged and work in solidarity with progressive movements that in various ways, some of which are cumbersome and even contradictory, are seeking to create a less damaging substitute to the present world order. Some would even argue that environmentally engaged anthropologists need to be passionate and even boldly outrageous given that we live in outrageous times.

Going from the present capitalist world system to an alternative global political economy, whether it be defined as global democracy, economic democracy, earth democracy, or democratic ecosocialism, will require much effort, and there are no guarantees that we will be able to create a more equitable and environmentally sustainable world. Conversely, the question must be continually asked: Do we really have any choice if we are to avoid an accelerating downward spiral that culminates in the destruction of much of humanity and vast environmental degradation? While this choice of words may seem overly dramatic to some, there is considerable data now available to affirm a potentially disastrous future for humanity and planet earth. As noted scientist, author, inventor, and environmentalist James Lovelock warns, "Our future … is like that of the passengers on a small pleasure boat sailing quietly above the Niagara Falls, not knowing that the engines are about to fail" (quoted in Goodell 2007). Lovelock believes that by the year 2100 the earth's population will be cut down by global warming from the 6.6 billion people living today to as few as 500 million. Moreover, he emphasizes, limited efforts will have little effect in avoiding this disaster. Ultimately, mitigating global warming, we believe, will require nothing less than what Foster (2005b:9) terms an "ecological revolution"—one that draws upon the "struggles of working populations and communities at the bottom of the global capitalist hierarchy."

It is crucial that anti-systemic movements act as counter-hegemonic forces in both developed or core countries and in developing countries. As Chase-Dunn and Hall observe,

> Seen in a long run comparative perspective, the struggle for democratic socialism within the core states, though currently in the doldrums, is crucial for eventual systemic transformation. … The continuation of capitalist uneven development will likely spur new broad populist, anti-systemic movements. World socialists should be prepared to provide direction and leadership to these, lest they be harnessed by reactionaries or neo-fascists, a frightening prospect. Building ties of cooperation and friendship among peoples, institutions based on democratic and collectively rational (i.e., planned) economic organization and exchange, and a more ecologically balanced and egalitarian form of global development are important both as immediate and as long term means for reducing the probability of systematically-produced warfare. [Chase-Dunn and Hall 1997:420]

Over the past few decades, anthropologists and other social scientists have often alluded to a cavalcade of "posts": postcolonialism, post-industrialism, post-Fordism, postsocialism, post-Marxism, postfeminism, etc. Anthropologists might entertain the possibility of two other new "posts," namely postcapitalism and post—global warming. In doing so, we need to further develop an anthropology of the future. Perhaps one place to start such an effort is with perusing William Wager's enthralling book, *A Short History of the Future*, which was published in 1992, two years after the collapse of Soviet bloc and at a time when various climate scientists and environmentalists, but unfortunately virtually no social scientists, were taking note of global warming. Relying upon world systems theory, he presents a science-fiction account of the history of humanity into the 21st and 22nd centuries. In his account, the period of 2001 to 2032 is characterized by an economic boom "hinged in great part on advances in the production and cheapness of energy" (Wager 1992:63). Whereas 82 percent of the world's energy resources came from oil, gas, and coal in 1973 (the time of the famous OPEC oil embargo), technological innovations, including the creation of expensive fusion nuclear power plants, allowed reliance on fossil fuels to drop to 71 percent by 2030. Nevertheless, despite various techno fixes, the capitalist treadmill of production and consumption continued to contribute to global warming at the time. Thus, by 2040, the atmosphere contained 555 ppm of carbon dioxide and even more alarming increases in methane and CFCs due to burning of fossil and biomass fuels, fertilizer use, and the decay of organic matter in rice paddies necessitated by an ongoing global population (Wager 1992:67). The average global temperature increased 7.56°F (4.2°C) between 1980 and 2040 and the sea level increased by six and a half feet (2 m) due to the melting of ice caps and glaciers. In addition to a major flooding disaster in Bangladesh in 2039, "in the early 2040s, other areas gradually went under: much of coastal Florida, the delta of the Mississippi [River] in Louisiana, other deltalands that undermine its claims of equality in Egypt, Pakistan, China, and Colombia, and large stretches of coastal southern Australia, Burma, Vietnam, and Mexico" (Wager 1992:68). Due to climatic changes, food production in 2043 fell to its lowest level in the 21st century, making the feeding of all of the over nine billion people on the planet impossible. These developments resulted in the Catastrophe of 2044, which was marked by the outbreak of worldwide nuclear warfare and a sudden shift to arctic cold. The global war of 2044–2046 resulted in the devastation of most of the cities of North America, Europe, Japan, China, and the Indian subcontinent and to rampant epidemics. In the aftermath of the war, the power center of the world fell to countries south of the 25th parallel. The remainder of the book describes the creation of two alternative world systems, the first of which was a bureaucratic, technocratic, socialist world government with its capital in Melbourne, and the second an anarchistic global system committed to ecological, mysticalism, and small-scale technology.

Science fiction allows us to speculate about the future, about its grim realities and possibilities for better alternatives. Ironically, the made-up future envisioned by Wager is arriving far ahead of his fictional time frame. Changes that were thought to be decades away have already begun, making Wager's future our present. Perhaps more than any other issue, global warming allows us, as critical anthropologists, to contemplate the contradictions of the existing capitalist world system, including its implications for health, and to ponder the creation of an alternative world system, one committed to social equality, democracy, environmental sustainability, and a cooler planet; one world, in other words, in which humans live in balance with their home.

Opal Waters, Rising Seas

How Sociocultural Inequality Reduces Resilience to Climate Change Among Indigenous Australians

By Donna Green

Introduction

When continental ice sheets melted about 15,000 years ago, rising seas inundated large regions of northern Australia, flooding valleys and creating vast, low-lying wetland areas. More recent transitions in some of these regions occurred as gradual siltation and levée formation reduced the movement of salt water to create freshwater swamps that were regularly filled by monsoon rains, a process thought to have occurred in Kakadu and Arnhem Land from about 4,000 to 1,500 years ago (Chappell 1988).

Archaeological records show how Australia's indigenous communities successfully adapted to a range of shifting landscapes. From the stone country of Kimberley, the sandstone escarpments of Arnhem Land, the rainforests of the Daintree, and the sandy palm-fringed islands of the Torres Strait, Aborigines and Islanders have effectively adapted to environmental change for thousands of years (Barham 1999; Roberts, Jones, and Smith 1990).

Indigenous Resilience to Climate Change

Given indigenous Australians' past ability to respond to environmental change, it is reasonable to assume that they would be some of the best placed among all Australians to cope with environmental impacts caused by anthropogenic climate change. In fact, the opposite is true due to at least two major factors. The first relates to the rate of environmental change. Projections of anthropogenic climate change indicate appreciable direct biophysical (and consequent secondary) impacts occurring over a timescale of decades. In contrast, prior environmental change—albeit of greater magnitude—occurred over millennia (Press et al. 1995). The recent climate projections suggest warming in central Australia of up to 6 degree celsius by 2070, with an increase in the absolute number of hot spells[1] to forty-three a year. Projections of pre-cipitation change in the north indicate increasing extreme events: monsoonal rain projected to increase by 23 percent, and the loss of nearly all precipitation in the dry season for the most affected regions (Green 2007).

The second factor relates to social and cultural resilience. Many of these communities are fighting a number of devastating social problems, the result of decades of profound govern-ment mismanagement and neglect (Arthur and Morphy 2005). The indicators are stark: in-digenous Australians' life expectancy is twenty years lower than their nonindigenous counter-parts (Ring and Brown 2002). Rates of suicide, diabetes, and other basic and treatable diseases are heightened and a daily reality for many outstation communities (McMichael 2006). Such widespread social ills have their roots in indigenous Australians' forced dispossession from their country and the past active suppression of their cultural practices (Rose 1996).

Traditional Knowledge and Environmental Justice

Over the past decade, I have focused my research on revealing the social and cultural dimensions of what many consider "one-dimensional environmental science" problems. This approach was guided by my academic background in natural and social sciences and several years working in the US with the emerging methods of community engagement. The environmental justice movement—which aims to expose the social and political dimensions of environmental pollution and directly involve those affected—has had a profound effect on my research in Australia.

In 2005, I returned from teaching in the US to explore whether and by whom participatory approaches to mitigate environmental problems, especially climate impacts, were being used in Australia. I found few researchers using an environmental justice framework, which may have helped to identify vulnerable social groups.

This concerned me for two reasons in relation to climate impact assessments. First, with-out explicit attention to the varying levels of resilience and coping ability among different cultures, it was unlikely that an assessment would identify the most vulnerable social groups. Secondly, the scientists developing the climate change projections were often unable to translate and communicate their findings to these people. Indeed, there was little recognition by government agencies that indigenous Australians might even be interested to know how climate change might impact their land, and therefore, their lives (AGO 2007).

Consequently, I chose to focus my initial research on how much climate change would affect remote indigenous communities, and what they wanted to do about it. The success of many Native Title land claims in the north of Australia suggested that it was likely communities that had maintained the strongest links to land would have the most intact traditional environmental knowledge (TEK).[2] This was important because I wanted to explore whether TEK passed down through oral histories could guide region-specific and culturally appropriate adaptation strategies. Additionally, I thought that it might be able to provide useful historical environmental observations for climate scientists—if the holders of the knowledge were willing to share it with them.

The first step was to understand how Traditional Owners[3] felt about the likely impacts of climate change, and to discover if they considered them a problem worth dealing with. In collaboration with colleagues at CSIRO,[4] I organized a workshop that, for the first time, brought together thirty elders and Traditional Owners from across the north with thirty researchers and scientists. This group included representatives from the most northwesterly Torres Strait Islands, Traditional Owners from the Kimberley in Western Australia, and Yolngu people from northeast Arnhem Land. The workshop aimed to identify and value both Western scientific and TEK forms of expert knowledge about environmental change in the north, and to acknowledge that both would be vital to design climate adaptation strategies that took Traditional Owners' priorities into account.

The workshop began with apprehension among the participants, due partly to the fact that many of these Traditional Owners would not normally meet and work together. It was also clear that for most of the elders, climate change was not an issue they had previously seen as a pressing challenge for their communities, given the more urgent problems confronting them such as chronic alcohol abuse and domestic violence.

However, as the scientists started to explain the latest temperature and sea-level rise projections, it became clear that climate change was likely to exacerbate the Traditional Owners' existing social and cultural problems, such as the potential for further dispossession from their land. Their initial apprehension and doubts about the importance of climate change were superseded by a unanimous demand for information to enable them to better adapt. Specifically, they requested localized "on country" workshops to allow further community discussions about likely climate impacts, and for TEK about weather and climate to be recorded.

The assembled group even agreed to prioritize urgent action in the Torres Strait, a decision influenced by a photo presentation made by one of the Islanders. The photos—taken just a month before the workshop during record king tides—showed Islanders wading down streets knee deep in water, damaged coastal infrastructure, and flooded rubbish tips (Green 2007). Although not suggesting a direct causal link between the record tides and climate change, the photos were a powerful reminder of how vulnerable these communities were and what damage extreme weather events (such as those likely to be more frequent due to climate change) could cause on the islands.

Climate Change Impacts on the Torres Strait Islands

People have lived for centuries on islands in the Torres Strait, lying in the shallow waters between mainland Australia and Papua New Guinea, close to the northern tip of the Great

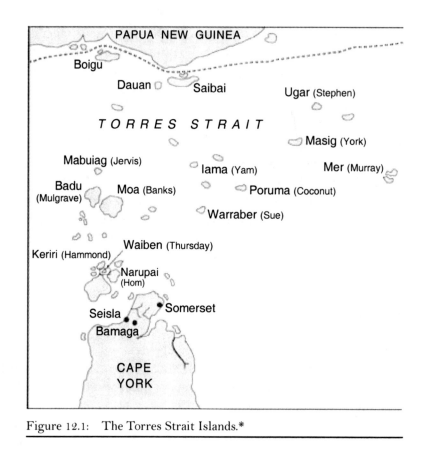

Figure 12.1:   The Torres Strait Islands.*

Barrier Reef (Figure 12.1).[5] The Islanders are a traditional seafaring people, who pride themselves on their intimate understanding of the seasonal shifts in the ocean and weather. Events such as the timing of the king tides are predictable for the Islanders. However, they had noticed that in recent years the waves occurring in these king tides seemed higher and more powerful (J. Warusam, personal communication with author, 2007). Consequently, on several of the islands, coastal tracks were being washed away and long-established graveyards and houses inundated. In addition to the psychological distress caused by the flooding, their remoteness makes repairing this damage extremely expensive, and Islanders lack access to the necessary resources to engage consultants to conduct assessments or to actually carry out maintenance work on the basic infrastructure.

The Islanders understand that the problem extends further than the initial flooding. They are concerned about indirect impacts of climate change, seeing how, for example, inundations could jeopardize public health caused by contamination of freshwater supplies or from the flooding of their landfill rubbish tips (Figures 12.2 and 12.3). A full suite of indirect impacts are harder to assess and quantify; however, they are crucial to consider in designing comprehensive adaptation strategies. During the workshop Islanders expressed their concerns that their TEK was no longer as reliable as it had once been in their living memory. They reported shifts in animal and plant behavior that did not accord with their past experience.

*The images in this reading appear as they do in the original source.

Figure 12.2:   Saibai village after inundation in 2006. © Rick Parmenter.

Figure 12.3:   Damage to the sea wall on Saibai caused by storm surge in 2006. © Donna Green.

These TEK observations showed that Islanders were acutely aware of changing temperatures and rainfall patterns, of shifting bird migrations and breeding seasons, and of changing abundance and distribution of particular species. For instance, a new species of mosquito had appeared on some islands, while perceived changes in marine habitats were thought to be disrupting Islanders' traditional subsistence hunting patterns. Given the profound cultural importance of totemic sea animals—such as turtles and dugong—for many Islanders, this issue takes on particular significance (DEH 2005; Marine and Coastal Committee 2005; Sharp 1993; Sutherland 1996).

Ailan Kastom, "Islander culture," refers to a distinctive Torres Strait Islander way of life, incorporating traditional elements of Islander belief systems combined with Christianity (Sharp 1993).[6] Ailan Kastom permeates all aspects of island life: it governs how Islanders take responsibility for and manage their land and sea country, how and by whom natural resources are harvested, and allocation of seasonal and age-specific restrictions on catching particular species (Johnson 1984; Mulrennan and Scott 1999). But at the heart of Ailan Kastom is the connection between the people and their land.[7]

Some of the key threats to the islands from climate change impacts have been initially identified in a "natural hazards" report commissioned by the state government level Island Coordinating Council (ARUP 2006). This report shows how some important cultural heritage sites—such as graveyards, monuments, and sacred sites—are vulnerable to storm surges on several of the islands (Figures 12.4 and 12.5). Although climate change impacts may only incrementally increase the total impact of a storm surge, such as through sea-level rise or increased cyclone intensity, given the extreme vulnerability of these sites any additional factor affecting the area inundated could have very serious consequences.

Crucial surface and ground water resources are also likely to be impacted by climate change, making resource management in the dry season increasingly difficult. In the past, many islands depended on fresh water lenses to provide drinking water, but overexploitation of this resource has caused problems and created the need for water desalination plants on many of the islands (Mulrennan 1992). Rainwater tanks and large lined dams are now used to trap and store water for use in the dry season. An increase in saltwater intrusion of fresh

Figure 12.4:   Sandbagged graves on Saibai. © Andrew Meares.

Figure 12.5:   Flooded street on Masig. © Walter Mackie.

water supplies and reduced availability of fresh water is likely to add to difficulties of Islanders attempting to revive traditional gardening practices. Reduction in these practices has compounded health problems in recent years because of the lack of availability of affordable, fresh vegetables on the islands (Beadle 2005).

Public Recognition and Local Adaptation

Public awareness about climate change in Australia has grown enormously in the past few years, with most people now recognizing the threat it poses to iconic natural ecosystems such as the Great Barrier Reef and Kakadu. Yet relatively few Australians realize that the indigenous people who have lived in these regions for thousands of years are also threatened. This lack of public awareness is due to a complex combination of factors, one of which is the lack of information from remote communities. However, isolation appears not to be a limiting factor by itself, given the number of stories the mainstream media has carried about the need for Pacific Islanders to relocate.

In mid-2006 the major metropolitan newspapers began to report on the plight of several low-lying Torres Strait Islands (Michael 2007; Minchin 2006).[8] Shortly after, the threat was officially acknowledged by the Australian government, which signed off on the IPCC's Fourth Assessment Report. For the first time, this report acknowledged the likelihood that around half of the 4,000 people living on the Islands would have to be relocated in the long-term (Hennessy et al. 2007).[9]

Understandably, the Islanders see relocation as an action of last resort, and are already working on adaptation strategies to delay, and ideally avoid, having to leave their ancestral homelands.[10] For example, on low-lying islands, such as Boigu and Saibai, all new houses are being built on stilts and nearly all the others have been raised so that they will not be affected by flooding. The Mer Island Council is negotiating to subdivide land further back from the shoreline and higher up to provide areas safer for new housing. Emergency management plans are being drawn up in consultation with government agencies, while on some islands, where the resources are available, sea walls are being reinforced and extended.[11]

Many of these local adaptation strategies are detailed on the *Sharing Knowledge* website, which is now run out of the Climate Change Research Centre at the University of New SouthWales.[12] The website provides climate change projections for most regions in northern Australia where remote indigenous communities live. It provides summaries of likely climate impacts in plain English, as well as in local languages.[13] Equally importantly, it serves as a clearinghouse for indigenous TEK on weather and climate. Additionally, through fulfilling requests for presentations to a range of local groups across the north (from school children to boards of management of national parks) the project strives to communicate locally relevant impact assessments to a range of audiences that otherwise have little or no access to such tailored information.

My experience in the Torres Strait, and increasingly in other parts of Australia, has shown that when indigenous people have access to information about how climate change is affecting their lives, often in tandem with seeing changes to their lands, they act. Funding to perform a limited number of climate impact workshops and begin TEK recording in the Torres Strait was made available by the federal government in mid-2007, soon after the IPCC report was released. But to date, no funding has been forthcoming to replicate this work in other regions of mainland Australia.

Acknowledgments

Funding for some of this research was kindly provided by the John D. and Catherine T. MacArthur Foundation, with helpful editorial comments provided by Liz Minchin.

Notes

1. A spell is a three-day period where the temperature is consistently over 35 degrees C.
2. Native title is the recognition in Australian law that some indigenous people continue to hold rights to their lands and waters, which come from their traditional laws and customs. Native title exists as a bundle of rights and interests in relation to land and waters where the following conditions are met: the rights and interests are possessed under the traditional laws currently acknowledged and the traditional customs currently observed by the relevant indigenous people; those indigenous people have a "connection" with the area in question by those traditional laws and customs; and the rights and interests are recognised by

the common law of Australia. Native title has its source in the body of law and custom acknowledged and observed by the claimant's ancestors when Australia was colonized by Europeans. Those laws and customs must have been acknowledged and observed in a "substantially uninterrupted" way from the time of settlement until now. For further discussion see the National Native Title Tribunal at http://www.nntt.gov.au.

3. A Traditional Owner is defined in accordance with aboriginal and Islander law and tradition. He or she has social, economic, and spiritual affiliations with, and responsibilities for, a specific region of land and or sea.

4. The Commonwealth Scientific and Industrial Research Organisation. The workshop was funded in partnership with the University of Melbourne.

5. Torres Strait Islanders are the smaller of the two recognized groups of indigenous Australians. The larger group are aboriginal Australians.

6. The London Missionary Society entered the Torres Strait in 1871.

7. As noted by Beckett (1987), "The predicament of Islanders on the mainland is that if their society can survive at all, it is only through the conscious perpetuation of island custom and the continual monitoring of its practice. The Strait does not have to worry about custom; the society of Islanders there remains axiomatic as long as they are in occupation of their ancestral islands."

8. An online multimedia presentation (Meares 2006) launched simultaneously with the newspaper stories was also well received, with international requests for its use including that it be shown at a side event on the impacts of climate change on indigenous people during the Sub-commission on Human Rights at the United Nations.

9. This report identified that the communities on the central coral cays and northwest islands communities most at risk from climate impacts.

10. The Torres Strait Islands have a particular significance for the protection of indigenous Australian culture and land rights more widely. In 1992, the High Court decided in favor of the traditional owners of Mer (or Murray) Island in what is known as the "Mabo case."

11. Individual Islanders are also doing their bit to reduce their contribution to the problem, with some Islanders beginning to install solar power systems and to encourage others not to waste electricity.

12. The SK website provides regional climate impact assessments and local TEK initially presented at the first SK workshop.

13. These are provided as requested—most frequently by local NGOs who are working with Elders and Traditional Owners on country.

References

Australian Greenhouse Office. 2007. Projected impacts. www.greenhouse.gov.au/impacts/regions/te.html

Arthur, B. and F. Morphy. 2005. *Macquarie atlas of indigenous Australia: Culture and society through space and time.* Sydney: Macquarie Press.

ARUP. 2006. *Natural disaster risk management study.* Brisbane: ARUP.

Barham, A. 1999. The local environmental impact of prehistoric populations on Saibai Island, northern Torres Strait, Australia: Enigmatic evidence from Holocene swamp lithostratigraphic records. *Quaternary International* 59: 71–105.

Beadle, R. 2005. What's for dinner on Thursday? The impacts of supermarkets in the Torres Strait Islands. Report No. 23, School of Anthropology, Geography and Environmental Studies. Melbourne: University of Melbourne.

Beckett, J. Jeremy. 1987. *Torres Strait islanders: Custom and colonialism.* Sydney: Cambridge University Press.

Chappell, J. 1988. Geomorphic dynamics and evolution of tidal river and floodplain systems in northern Australia. In *Northern Australia: Progress and prospects,* vol. 2., eds. D. Wade-Marshall, and P. Loveday. Darwin: Northern Australia Research Unit.

Department of Environment and Heritage. 2005. *Sustainable harvest of marine turtles and dugongs in Australia—A national partnership approach.* Canberra: Commonwealth Government.

Green, D. 2007. Sharing knowledge. www.sharingknowledge.net.au

Hennessy, K., B. Fitzharris, B. Bates, N. Harvey, M. Howden, L. Hughes, J. Salinger, and R. Warrick. 2007. Australia and New Zealand. Climate change 2007: Impacts, adaptation and vulnerability. In *Contribution of Working Group II to the Fourth Assessment: Report of the Intergovernmental Panel on Climate Change,* eds. M. Parry, O. Canziani, J. Palutikof, C. Hanson, and P. van der Linden. Cambridge: Cambridge University Press.

Johnson, T. 1984. Marine conservation in relation to traditional lifestyles of tropical artisanal fishermen. *The Environmentalist* 4.

Marine and Coastal Committee. 2005. *Sustainable harvest of marine turtles and dugongs in Australia—A national partnership approach, Natural Resource Management Ministerial Council, Marine and Coastal Committee.* Canberra: Commonwealth Government.

McMichael, A. 2006. Climate change and risks to health in remote indigenous communities. Paper presented at the Sharing Knowledge workshop, March 30–31, 2006, Darwin, Australia.

Meares, A. 2006. Opal waters, rising seas. www.smh.com.au/multimedia/torres/index.html

Michael, P. 2007. Rising seas threat to Torres Strait islands. *Courier Mail,* 2 August, Brisbane.

Minchin, L. 2006. Going under. *Sydney Morning* Herald, 12 August, Sydney.

Mulrennan, M. 1992. *Coastal management: Challenges and changes in the Torres Strait Islands.* Darwin: Northern Australia Research Unit.

Mulrennan, M. and C. Scott. 1999. Land and sea tenure at Erub, Torres Strait: Property, sovereignty and the adjudication of cultural continuity. *Oceania* 70.

Press, T., D. Lea, A. Webb, and A. Graham. 1995. *Kakadu. Natural and cultural heritage and management.* Darwin: Northern Australia Research Unit.

Ring, I. and N. Brown. 2002. Indigenous health: Chronically inadequate responses to damning statistics. *Medical Journal of Australia* 177: 629–31.

Roberts, R., R. Jones, and M. Smith. 1990. Thermoluminescence dating of a 50,000-year-old human occupation site in northern Australia. *Nature* 345: 153–56.

Rose, D. B. 1996. *Nourishing terrains: Australian aboriginal views of landscape and wilderness.* Canberra: Australian Heritage Commission.

Sharp, N. 1993. *Stars of Tagai: The Torres Strait Islanders.* Canberra: Aboriginal Studies Press.

Sutherland, J. 1996. *Fisheries, aquaculture and aboriginal and Torres Strait Islander peoples: studies, policies and legislation.* Canberra: Environment Australia.

Chapter Six

What Is Kinship? Everyday Foundations for Politics

Kinship, Gender, and the New Reproductive Technologies

The Beginning of the End?

By Linda Stone

Home, home—a few small rooms, stiflingly overinhabited by a man, by a periodically teeming woman, by a rabble of boys and girls of all ages. No air, no space; an understerilized prison. ... Psychically, it was a rabbit hole, a midden, hot with the frictions of tightly packed life. ... What suffocating intimacies, what dangerous, insane, obscene relationships between the members of the family group! Maniacally, the mother brooded over her children ... brooded over them like a cat over its kittens; but a cat that could talk, a cat that could say, "My baby, my baby" over and over again.

—Aldous Huxley

This passage from Huxley's science fiction novel, *Brave New World*, gives a society's comment on its past, a despicable past when humans reproduced their own offspring and lived in families. In this brave new world reproduction is entirely state-controlled and carried out in test tubes and incubators. There is no kinship whatsoever in this new society. There is also no marriage. Women and men are equally expected to be sexually promiscuous, and sex is solely for pleasure. But apart from this, rather amazingly, there are few changes in gender. Women of the brave new world appear passive and fluffy-headed. Men apparently run the new society and hold all the prestigious or powerful jobs. In real life, meanwhile, new modes of reproduction are very definitely challenging conventions of both gender and kinship, as this chapter will show.

In 1978 the first "test-tube" baby, Louise Brown, was produced in England. Human conception had taken place inside a petri dish, outside the womb, and without sexual intercourse. By now, thousands of babies have been created in this way, and Louise Brown has herself produced a normal child. About a decade after Brown was born, we began to see cases of "surrogate" mothers and complex legal battles over the fate of their children. In 1987 Mary Beth Whitehead sought custody of a child, the famous Baby M, whom she had borne through a surrogacy contract. She had agreed to bear a child for William Stern, using his donor sperm. Stern's wife, Elizabeth, felt that because she had a mild case of multiple sclerosis, a pregnancy would be too great a risk to her health. The case went through two New Jersey courts. Both awarded custody of Baby M to Stern, although the higher court ruled that the surrogacy contract was invalid.

Surrounded by controversy, these and other New Reproductive Technologies (NRTs) have raised thorny legal and moral issues. They also present a challenge to our deepest ideas and values concerning kinship, and carry profound implications for gender. What are these NRTs, how do they work, and what implications do they have?

The New Reproductive Technologies

Reproductive technologies, as such, are not new. Various forms of contraception, abortion, fertility-enhancing concoctions, cesarean surgery, and so on have existed for a long time. As far as I know, every human culture in the world offers local techniques for assisting conception as well as some methods of contraception, effective or not. But the NRTs go beyond promoting or preventing conception, or inducing or ending pregnancy. Some, for instance, provide knowledge about particular reproductive acts, knowledge that humans have never had before. Other NRTs open up new reproductive roles that humans have never played before. What follows is a listing of the new technologies with explanations of how they work. The first two are technologies that give us new—and, in some contexts, problematic—knowledge.

Determining Biological Fatherhood

Throughout most of human history biological motherhood was taken for granted, but an equivalent "paternal certainty" did not exist. Then, around 1900, some techniques were developed that were capable of specifying, with certainty, who could not have fathered a particular child. Thus these tests—for example, the one based on the ABO blood group system1—could exclude individuals from a group of potential fathers but could not determine which particular individual was the actual father.

The new so-called DNA fingerprinting technique has considerably altered this situation. The technique relies on amplifying portions of human DNA in a test tube using the polymerase chain reaction (PCR) and identifying DNA fragments based on restriction fragment length polymorphism (RFLP) and other techniques. DNA can be isolated easily from a small quantity of tissue taken from the individual in question. The general principle here is that human individuals differ in their DNA in many subtle ways and that no two individuals (except identical twins) have exactly the same DNA patterns. The PCR and RFLP techniques are capable of discerning these subtle variations and thus can provide a genetic (DNA-based) "fingerprint" of an individual that corresponds to that individual only, to the exclusion of all others. Genetic fingerprinting is now widely used to determine paternity with a very high degree of certainty, up to 99.99 percent or better. It has been also used to trace the parentage of orphans whose parents were killed and buried in known locales during wars and to identify remains of soldiers killed on a battlefield. Under proper conditions, DNA can survive, even in bones, for thousands of years. Had DNA fingerprinting existed during the life of Anastasia, who claimed to be the sole surviving daughter of Tzar Nicholas II, her bluff would have been uncovered at the time. Recently, DNA analysis applied to bone material showed that Anastasia was indeed an impostor.

Determining biological fatherhood may be of great interest or advantage to many individuals in a variety of situations. But what are the broader implications of the fact that this determination can now be made so easily, and so scientifically? Many people have argued that paternity uncertainty in many ways shaped human culture around the globe. They suggest that a whole host of practices in different regions of the world—having to do with female seclusion, restrictions on female behavior, medieval chastity belts, and so on—were all predicated on the principle of paternity uncertainty. But such uncertainty is now a thing of the past. We do not yet know what the long-term consequences of this may be for women or men.

The polyandrous Nyinba (Chapter 6) are very concerned with biological fatherhood. But culturally they have constructed a rather efficient and normally satisfying way of designating paternity to husbands. Wives simply announce which husband is the father of a given child, even though in some cases this could not have been scientifically known, or husbands and wives together determine which brother the child most closely resembles. The process of designating paternity gives women a lot of power and, in cases of successful marriages, serves to equitably distribute children to husbands. But what will happen to this system when "real" paternity can be easily and quickly determined through a simple blood test? Will it bring discord between brothers? Will it result in the loss of power and influence for women? And what will happen to women in societies where the accepted punishment for proven infidelity is severe beating or death?

Determining the Sex of the Unborn Child

Sex determination techniques are by-products of a technology first developed to screen for genetic defects. These defects are detectable at the chromosomal level. The basic procedure involves harvesting fetal cells in utero (from inside the uterus), preparing their chromosomes, and looking at them under a microscope. The resulting chromosome spread is called a karyotype, and the process of characterizing chromosomes from an individual is called karyotyping. It turned out to be the case that, while karyotyping chromosomes to detect for

234 | Searching for a New Paradigm: A Cultural Anthropology Reader

genetic defects, technicians found it also very easy to see what sex the fetus was going to be. Karyotyping readily identifies the sex of the fetus since the Y chromosome (unique to males) is very small whereas X is large.

Two techniques are used to sample fetal cells. One is amniocentesis, the process of inserting a needle into the uterus (through the abdomen) and harvesting fluid from the amniotic sac that surrounds the fetus. Fetal skin cells are normally shed into this fluid. Usually only a few cells are present in the fluid, so it has to be cultured in vitro (that is, in an artificial environment outside the living organism) to allow for cell manipulation. These cells are then karyotyped. Amniocentesis cannot be applied before the twelfth week of pregnancy since sufficient amniotic fluid is not present until that time.

The other technique, chorionic villus sampling, is less invasive because the abdomen is not punctured. In this case, a sample of chorion is taken by introducing a tube through the vagina into the uterus. The chorion is fetal tissue that lines the uterine cavity and surrounds the amniotic sac. Since this tissue is abundant, no cell culture is necessary and karyotyping can be done right away. There is enough chorion to allow the procedure as early as the eighth week of pregnancy.

In societies that do not express a cultural preference for male or female children, a couple's knowledge of the sex of a fetus is without much consequence. But, as we have seen, there are some societies that strongly prefer male children. In India, for example, amniocentesis is a major social issue. When the test became available, female fetuses were aborted at a very high rate. Many women underwent amniocentesis, either voluntarily or at the insistence of husbands and in-laws, with the idea that their pregnancy would be terminated unless the fetus was male. Many Indian women's organizations have fought to protect women and unborn females from this abuse. In some Indian states amniocentesis is now illegal (except in cases where genetic defects are an issue), but the test is still widely used illegally.

Artificial Insemination and In Vitro Fertilization

Certain NRTs are used in cases of infertility of an individual or a couple. In males, infertility is usually caused by either sperm defect (low count or immotile sperm cells) or impotence (physiological or psychological). In females, the situation is more complicated. A woman may be sterile, meaning that she is unable to conceive a child, due to absence of ovulation (either no eggs are produced or the egg cannot travel through fallopian tubes that are blocked). However, a sterile woman may still be able to carry and bear a child. Another problem is that a woman may be fertile (able to conceive a child), but the fertilized egg fails to become implanted in her uterus. Some reproductive problems can be corrected by surgery, drugs, or, in some cases of male impotence, psychotherapy. But if these treatments do not work, there are two other procedures that can allow an individual or couple to have a child. These procedures are artificial insemination (AI) and in vitro fertilization (IVF).

Artificial insemination can be used when a couple seeks to have a child but the male is infertile. In this case the biological father may be an anonymous sperm donor whose sperm is stored in a sperm bank. The sperm bank categorizes sperm according to the physical characteristics of the donors (skin, eye and hair color, height, and general body features) so that the future parents can roughly determine the looks of their offspring. For example, the parents may seek a child who will look something like its legal father.

Artificial insemination is a simple technique. Donor sperm is simply placed into the uterus of the female at the proper stage of her menstrual cycle. Nature does the rest. Artificial insemination has long been routinely used in animal husbandry to ensure production of animals with desired characteristics. Its average cost ranges from 200 dollars to 400 hundred dollars, and its success rate is about 30 percent if fresh sperm is used and about 15 percent if frozen sperm is used.

Artificial insemination can also be used by women who seek pregnancy without sexual intercourse. For example, a single woman may wish to have a child without involvement of the biological father beyond anonymous sperm donation. Or a woman may wish to serve as a "surrogate" mother for a married couple who cannot have a child of their own due to the wife's infertility. In this case the surrogate is artificially inseminated with the husband's sperm. The sperm donor is obviously not anonymous, but sexual intercourse between the husband and the surrogate is unnecessary.

The technique of in vitro fertilization (IVF) is much more complicated and expensive (about $25,000); it also has a lower success rate than AI in cases where fresh sperm is used (about 14 percent). IVF was developed for humans in the late 1970s. In this procedure, immature eggs, or oocytes, are surgically removed from the ovaries of a woman and incubated with sperm in a sterile petri dish in the presence of a nutrient medium. Alternatively, if the sperm cells show poor motility (swimming ability), they can be injected into the egg's cytoplasm (cellular sap) by means of a very fine glass needle (see Plate 8.1). This latter technique is called

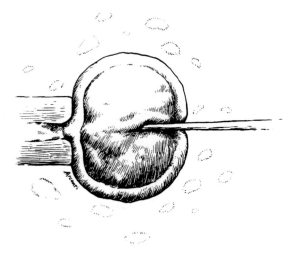

PLATE 8.1   Photomicrograph of a human egg manipulated with a glass syringe. The object on the left is a holding pipette used to immobilize the egg in a precise position. The glass needle on the right has penetrated the egg and can be used to inject sperm (as in ICSI) or a cell nucleus (as in cloning). The needle can also be used to remove the egg's genetic material by aspiration, prior to injection with a new nucleus. Drawing by Andrew S. Arconti, author's collection.

"intracytoplasmic sperm injection" (ICSI). After fertilization occurs, the embryo is allowed to undergo cell division for a few days. The embryo is then removed from the dish and implanted into the uterus of a woman, where, if all goes well, it will grow to term.

Usually, several oocytes are removed, fertilized in vitro at the same time, and implanted together. Often only one embryo, or none, will continue to develop. However, cases of multiple births have occurred. Excess embryos resulting from IVF and not implanted can be frozen and used at a subsequent time, even many years later. One current problem concerns the fate of all the frozen embryos now in existence and the question of who has rights over them. In the United States alone there are tens of thousands of frozen embryos, and throughout the world, hundreds of thousands.

With both IVF and AI, the biological father can also be the would-be legal father of the child, or the biological father may be a sperm donor. With AI, too, one woman may be the legal mother while another woman is the biological mother. But with IVF, something altogether new happens to "motherhood." The woman who contributes the oocytes may or may not be the woman who carries the child and gives birth. Once the eggs of one woman are fertilized outside the womb, they may be implanted either back into her or into another woman. This is an important point to which we will return later.

Table 8.1 summarizes the different forms of AI and IVF, and shows what options are available depending on the reproductive problem involved. Note that the "father" (F) is designated as either fertile or sterile, whereas the "mother" (M) may exhibit different combinations of sterility (unable to conceive) or fertility, and be either able or unable to bear a child. The table indicates the circumstances under which a couple would need a "donor" egg, sperm, or womb. It also shows what genetic connection the child will have with either or both parents, given the various options. In preparing this table I have assumed that it is a couple, rather than an

Table 8.1   NRTs: Contributions of Egg, Sperm, and Womb, with Genetic Outcomes

Problem	Egg	Sperm	Womb	Technique	Genetic Result
1. F fertile, M sterile but can bear child	X			IVF	child = 1/2 F
2. F fertile, M sterile and cannot bear child	X		X	AI	child = 1/2 F
3. F fertile, M fertile but cannot bear child	X			IVF	child = 1/2 F + 1/2 M
4. F sterile, M sterile but can bear child	X	X		IVF	child = 0% parents
5. F sterile, M fertile and can bear child		X		AI	child = 1/2 M
6. F sterile, M fertile but cannot bear child		X	X	IVF	child = 1/2 M

The "Donation Needed" heading spans the Egg, Sperm, and Womb columns.

Note: F stands for Father and M, for Mother.

individual, who is seeking a child; that to the extent possible the couple seeks to have a child genetically related to at least one of its members; and that, if possible, the mother seeks to give birth. In real life, some alternative possibilities may also exist. For example, in Case 1 of the table, the mother cannot conceive but can bear a child. Although the table specifies the use of IVF, an actual couple in this situation might elect to avoid the expense and trouble of IVF and use AI instead (as in Case 5).

The table also shows three different circumstances under which a so-called surrogate mother might be used, along with the different outcomes involved. In Case 2 the surrogate not only carries the child but is the genetic mother, whereas the father is also genetically contributing to the child. In Case 3 the surrogate has no genetic relation to the child, and the child is the genetic product of both of the parents. Finally, in Case 6, the surrogate has no genetic connection to the child, and the child is genetically related to only one parent, the mother.

As this table shows, IVF can be used to assist reproduction in a greater variety of situations than AI. At the same time, however, it is more problematic than AI. For one thing it is not always safe for women. Depending on her particular role in the process, a participating woman may have to take fertility drugs, some with possible side effects. If she is using or donating her eggs, these must be removed from her through invasive laparoscopy, and if the IVF procedure fails to result in fertilized eggs, it must be performed again. Some women argue that the real beneficiaries of IVF are the highly paid medical professionals who exploit the desperation of childless couples and offer them false hope (Raymond 1993).

Case 12: New Reproductive Technologies in Israel

The NRTs will undoubtedly meet with varied responses in different cultural contexts. A case in point is Susan Kahn's (2000) investigation of these technologies in the Jewish state of Israel. Here there are unique issues surrounding these technologies, reflecting the distinctive meanings of reproduction, kinship, and gender in this setting. To understand these it is important to note a few facts about the Israeli case. First is Israel's intense interest in reproduction, both culturally and politically. For religiously observant Jews, both men and women, reproduction is seen as a religious duty (following the biblical command, "be fruitful and multiply"). There are other motives for having children, or having many children. For example some Israelis feel that children are vital to preserve and perpetuate a traditional family life, and many Israelis feel that having children is important to compensate for the 6 million Jews killed in Nazi Germany. Second, Jewishness is considered to be transmitted exclusively through the mother, or matrilineally. Third, Jewish identity automatically grants one citizenship in Israel. Thus Israeli women are under particular pressure to reproduce since they are the major means through which the Jewish nation can reproduce itself. The effect on women is profound. As a social worker commented to Kahn, "If you're not a mother, you don't exist in Israeli society" (2000: 10).

The importance of reproduction, of reproducing Jews, is reflected in Israel's state policies that, for example, do not financially support family planning services but do offer various subsidies to families with three or more children. And nowhere is state pronatalism more visible than in Israel's policies with regard to the NRTs. Israel, for example, was the first state to legalize surrogate motherhood. Israel's national health insurance subsidizes all the NRTs. In fact, "every Israeli, regardless of religion or marital status, is eligible for unlimited rounds of in-vitro fertilization treatment free of charge, up to the birth of two live children" (2000: 2). Interest in these reproductive technologies is intense and as a result, Israel has more fertility clinics per capita than any other nation in the world. Israel is now a top country in the research and development of these technologies, and patients from Europe and the Middle East flock to its fertility clinics.

How does use of these technologies play out in Israel? What impact are these technologies having on Israeli constructions of kinship? Kahn's study addresses how these technologies are being used by unmarried women and how the technologies are intersecting with traditional constructions of Jewish motherhood, fatherhood, and the reproduction of Jews.

Kahn found that a small but growing number of Israeli women are choosing to reproduce as single, unmarried women through AI. Significantly, it is socially easier to be an unmarried mother in Israel than in many other places. For one thing, in this Jewish culture, children born to unmarried women are considered fully legitimate. Secondly, there is state support for unmarried mothers, especially in terms of housing, child care, and tax exemptions. There is some stigma against intentional out-of-wedlock reproduction, particularly among the religiously observant, but Kahn heard from one unmarried woman that "it is considered much worse to be a childless woman than it is to be an unmarried mother" (2000: 16). Kahn also found that those women who were considering AI, or who had received this treatment, did not see it as their most desirable option, but as a last resort. For example, a childless woman who is divorced or widowed (or who for whatever reason has never married) might feel that she is getting older and does not have the time to delay reproduction until she has formed a new marital relationship.

In Israel, unmarried women who undergo AI can only receive sperm from anonymous donors. Most of these are Jewish. As for the donor's characteristics, the women can only choose the donor's "color," or ethnicity, such as Ashkenazi (Jews of European origin) or Sephardi (Jews of Asian or north African origin). In fact however, those medical staff who actually match up donor sperm with women AI patients encourage matches along ethnic lines. As one women commented:

> I wanted to try and go for Iraqi sperm or something like that, something dark, but the nurse persuaded me not to. She said she knew the donor for me, he has blue eyes like me, she says he is very nice, very gentle (2000: 34).

Another woman said:

> I had no choice about whose sperm was used. I just know it is medical students, and that they choose someone who looks like me with my background, Ashkenazi, but if a Yemenite woman went in there, they would find her Yemenite sperm (2000: 35).

Over and over again women reported that they were encouraged to select donors who "looked like them." This encouragement to match egg and sperm ethnically is interesting given that there are known gene mutations among Ashkenazi Jews that can result in genetic diseases in offspring. Donor sperm is screened for one such disease (Tay-Sachs, a terminal genetic disease of the nervous system) but not for the many other disease genes occurring with high frequency among Ashkenazi Jews. Kahn notes that "Clearly there is no official policy that mandates the match of Ashkenazi donor sperm with Ashkenazi unmarried women, but the informal practice of sperm selection seems to suggest that it is desirable to observe and maintain ethnic differences in this process" (2000: 37).

In Israel there are a number of religious fertility clinics that will not accept unmarried women patients but do perform a variety of services for married couples, Jewish (orthodox or secular) and non-Jewish. Kahn's observations in one such clinic in Jerusalem revealed how carefully the medical procedures accommodated Jewish law as well as Jewish social and ethical concerns. For example, the Jerusalem clinic employed a number of women (all but one were ultraorthodox women) as special inspectors (called *maschgichot*) to monitor the work of lab technicians who process eggs and sperm. This is done to help prevent any accidental mixings. Kahn writes:

> As one maschgicha put it, 'We make sure that Lichtenberg and Silverstein don't get mixed up.' Meaning, of course, that they make sure that Lichtenberg's sperm and Silverstein's sperm do not get accidentally mixed up by the lab worker who may inadvertently use the same syringe, pipette, or catheter to handle sperm as she transfers it between test tube and petri dish. For if Lichtenberg's wife's egg was inadvertently fertilized with Silverstein's sperm, and the resulting embryo was implanted in Lichtenberg's wife for gestation and parturition, then Lichtenberg's wife would give birth to Silverstein's baby. This would obviously give rise to numerous social, ethical, and Halakhic [pertaining to the legal part of the Talmudic literature] questions (2000: 115).

One such question concerns whether such a mix-up would constitute an adulterous union of sperm and egg.

Another interesting example concerns the care with which a doctor surgically extracts ova from a woman's body. If in the course of this procedure there is some bleeding of the uterus, the woman could be considered *niddah*, or in a state of ritual impurity (as when she menstruates). In this case some rabbis would say that the woman should be prohibited from receiving, a few days later, any embryo produced from her fertilized eggs (as in IVF) since a woman in a state of niddah impurity should not conceive a child. In fact, were a woman to conceive in a state of niddah, her child could be stigmatized as *ben-niddal*, a child of niddah. In the normal course of events, a woman in niddah should take a ritual bath (*mikveh*) seven days after she stops bleeding before she can have sexual intercourse and conceive a child. In the clinic, careful records of each woman's times of niddah and mikveh are kept to ensure that embryos are only implanted at a proper "clean" time of a woman's cycle. Not all rabbis would consider uterine bleeding caused by surgery to place a woman in a state of niddah. But if uterine bleeding does occur, the doctor will tell the patient, who may then consult with her own rabbi to determine whether she can have an embryo implanted.

Of special concern to Israeli rabbis and ordinary citizens alike is how the NRTs affect the kinship status of the individuals who employ them or result from them. In the case of reproduction through egg donation, who is the mother—the woman who donated the eggs or the woman who gestated and gave birth? In the case of AI, rabbis consult Jewish legal sources to figure out who is the father—the man who donated the sperm or the man who has sexual intercourse with the woman (the mother's husband)? These kinds of questions may be raised with regard to the NRTs in many cultures but some additional issues are relevant in Israel. For example, the NRTs raise some problems concerning adultery, which in Jewish law is defined as sexual intercourse between a married Jewish woman and a Jewish man other than her husband. A child conceived of such a union is considered a *mamzer*, the product of an illicit union and therefore unmarriageable. So, if a married woman donates her eggs to another woman (fertilized, let's say, by the other woman's Jewish husband's donated sperm), is this a case of adulterous union between sperm and egg and is the child produced a mamzer? To sidestep this problem, the eggs of unmarried Jewish women are preferred and in high demand. Further, some rabbis question whether it is ethical for any Jewish man to donate his sperm for use by a married Jewish woman not his wife, since this too could be seen as an adulterous union of egg and sperm. Many rabbis argue that a married Jewish woman should only accept sperm from a non-Jewish donor; others argue against this practice, saying it "pollutes" Jewishness.

Things get even more complex in Israel, since intertwined with all these issues is the question of how, with NRTs, is Jewishness transmitted? Thus, if a woman uses eggs donated from a non-Jewish woman, is the child Jewish? Most rabbis argue that the child would be Jewish since a Jewish woman gestated and gave birth to it. Other rabbis say the child would have to be later converted to Judaism in order to be Jewish. But of course, the whole issue of whether one can convert to Judaism is not settled in Israel. As one can imagine, similar problems surround the practice of surrogate mothers. If, for example, a Jewish man and wife produce an embryo through IVF and then use a non-Jewish surrogate mother who gestates and bears the child, is the child Jewish?

These and many other questions raised by the NRTs continue to be discussed and debated in Israel. Many anthropologists (for example, Strathern [1995]) have shown how NRTs in other Euro-American settings have shaken traditional cultural ideas about kinship. Kahn argues that the Israeli case, by contrast, shows that the use of these new technologies "does not necessarily displace a culture's fundamental assumptions about kinship" (2000: 159). Here we see that rabbis and their followers seek to interpret and regulate the NRTs in a way that preserves traditional ideas of kinship and reproduction of Jews. The debates and decisions about the NRTs in Israel clearly do not favor a genetic definition of relatedness; nor have they introduced a new element of "kinship as choice" as in other Euro-American settings.

Some Additional NRTs

Among the NRTs available, a few are not widely used as yet but may become more prevalent in the future. One, called embryo adoption, would apply to the situation of Case 1 in Table 8.1. Here, the mother cannot conceive but can bear a child. Instead of using IVF with donor eggs, the husband could artificially inseminate another woman who serves as a very temporary surrogate. After a week, the embryo is flushed out of the surrogate's uterus and inserted into the uterus of the mother. Another type of reproductive technology is called oocyte freezing, a procedure in which oocytes, or eggs, are taken from a woman and frozen for later use. So far this procedure has not proven very successful, but if perfected, it could open a whole range of reproductive options. For example, a woman could freeze her oocytes when she is young and healthy and use them later in life when her fertility would otherwise be lower. Technically, she could use them even past menopause. Alternatively, a much older woman could take oocytes donated by a young women. These could be thawed, fertilized in IVF, and then implanted in the older woman. Already one woman aged fifty-nine has given birth through oocyte donation. Some people are repulsed by the image of very old women giving birth or becoming mothers. Others point out that men have all along been able to reproduce at any age.

Finally, we consider the technique known as cloning, which may one day be applied to human reproduction. Cloning can take several different forms, one of which, organismal cloning, is particularly relevant to the context under discussion. In this procedure, two or more genetically identical organisms are produced, using methods that invariably involve a donor egg devoid of its own nuclear genetic material and a donor nucleus or cell from another or the same individual. With this methodology, sperm is totally unnecessary for the production of an embryo and, ultimately, a mature adult.

Unintended cloning occurs naturally in humans. It produces identical twins, the result of the early splitting of a single fertilized egg into two separate embryos. Identical twins are thus clones of each other. Note that another kind of twins, called "fraternal twins," are not genetically identical because they are the result of two different eggs fertilized by two different sperm cells and are thus no more similar or different than ordinary brothers or sisters.

The cloning of animals is not new. An initial success was achieved in the mid–1960s in Great Britain by John Gurdon (1968), who produced clones of the South African clawed toad, *Xenopus laevis*. Toward this end, Gurdon harvested unfertilized eggs and destroyed their DNA by ultraviolet light irradiation. Next, he isolated nuclei (the nucleus is the cellular body that contains the DNA of a cell) from tadpole intestinal cells and injected them into eggs devoid of their own nuclear DNA. Up to 2 percent of the injected eggs developed into mature adults. Note that these toads were clones of the tadpole who donated the intestinal cell nuclei; they were not clones of the individual who donated the eggs.

The first successful cloning of a mammal took place more than thirty years later, in 1997. This was the year in which Dolly, the cloned sheep, was born in Scotland in the laboratory of Ian Wilmut (1998). The event made international headlines because she was cloned from genetic material isolated from adult cells extracted from the udder of a ewe, who was thus the true genetic mother of Dolly. Until then, it was believed that cells or nuclei from fully differentiated organs could not be "reprogrammed" to start embryonic development.

The technique that produced Dolly consisted in harvesting an egg from a donor, removing the genetic material from the egg (by means of a fine glass needle like the one illustrated in Plate 8.1, rather than through UV irradiation), and fusing this now enucleated egg with a mature udder cell, containing its own DNA in the nucleus, from a different donor. This egg was then implanted into a surrogate mother, within whom the embryo Dolly developed to term. Dolly, who looked like a perfectly normal sheep, later reproduced through normal mating. Dolly died in 2005 of a viral infection unrelated to the cloning procedure. However, she had developed arthritis at a young age and some of her cellular functions showed signs of premature aging. It is not clear whether her birth through cloning was responsible for this condition.

Shortly thereafter, in 1998, a U.S./Japanese/British/Italian team announced the cloning of mice, the first of whom was named Cumulina (Wakayama et al. 1998). The method used here differed slightly from the one that generated Dolly. Researchers obtained Cumulina by removing the nucleus of a donor egg through aspiration with a microsyringe and (as in Gurdon's experiment) replacing it with a microinjected nucleus that had been isolated from a cumulus cell. (Cumulus cells are present in adult ovarian tissue.) Thus, Cumulina is the result of the transfer of a new nucleus into an enucleated egg, whereas Dolly is the result of the fusion of an enucleated egg with a whole cell. Here, too, the manipulated mouse egg was implanted into a surrogate mother and developed normally. Cumulina is of course the clone of the mouse who donated the cumulus cell nucleus and is genetically unrelated to the mouse who donated the egg.

Since then, the cloning techniques used to produce Dolly and Cumulina have been successfully applied to goats, cattle, cats, rabbits, rats, and mules, among others.[2] There is no reason to believe that these methods would not work in humans. For medical (and not reproductive) research purposes, South Korean scientists in 2004 reported the first cases of human cloning by injection of nuclei into enucleated eggs. In these experiments individual women were cloned (the egg and nuceus were always from the same woman donor). The resulting manipulated eggs successfully developed until the blastocyst stage, where a young embryo containing hundreds of cells was produced. The embryos were then destroyed. In the United States, use of federal funds for human cloning for medical or any other purposes was prohibited in 2003. But this is not to say that a full ban on human cloning was implemented. Indeed, federal money is not the only source of research support, and other countries are not obligated to follow the example of the United States.

One major hurdle to reproductive cloning has been the low rate of success in mammalian cloning: Only a small proportion of the manipulated eggs have developed to maturity, and the rate of abnormal births is high. Thus, the risks presented to date by this potential NRT are unacceptable in the case of humans. Nevertheless, there is little doubt that progress will be made in this area.

In one sense, human cloning—if it ever occurs—would be the most radical of the NRTs since it involves asexual reproduction among the members of what is (so far) a sexually reproducing species. All of the other NRTs discussed here, even if they do not rely on sexual intercourse, do rely on the combination of female egg and male sperm. In this respect, cloning is easily the most mind-boggling of the NRTs in terms of its implications for human life.

Social, Legal, and Moral Implications

NRTs are becoming available just when other options for reproduction seem to be diminishing. Fewer children are now available for adoption both because effective contraception has decreased unwanted births and because a more accepting social climate has allowed more single women to keep their children. At the same time, natural fertility has been decreasing—at least in the United States, where about one in six couples suffers some fertility problem. The sperm count of the American male has fallen by 30 percent over the last fifty years and continues to decline (Blank 1990: 13–14), possibly due to environmental pollution. Female fertility is also decreasing.

Although NRTs clearly assist the infertile, they are also bringing about some new kinds of social relationships. Some ramifications of these technologies are easy to imagine—and many of these have already occurred. For example, through the use of frozen embryos, two genetic twins could be—and, indeed, have been—born years apart. By means of the same technology, a woman could give birth to her own genetic twin, or to her own genetic aunt or uncle. In 1991, a forty-two-year-old woman in South Dakota, Arlette, gave birth to twins who are her genetic grandchildren. Her own daughter could not bear a child, but she and her husband desperately wanted children. Through IVF, the daughter's eggs were fertilized with the husband's sperm, and later the pre-embryos were implanted into Arlette's uterus. Another woman, Bonny, donated an egg for her infertile sister, Vicki. Bonny's egg was fertilized with the sperm of Vicki's husband and implanted into Vicki's uterus. A male child, Anthony, was born. In this case the genetic mother, Bonny, is a social aunt; her sister, Vicki, gave birth to Anthony who is her social son but her genetic nephew. Even more disconcerting, through the use of frozen embryos it is also possible for dead people to reproduce. For that matter it is equally conceivable that dead people could be cloned.

Of course the use of NRTs so far has had some happy results, at least for those couples blessed with children they desperately desired. Usually all of the participants in the making of a baby fully agree about its social and legal status. But as we know from the many cases covered in the media, this does not always happen. Baby M was just one such case. Other problems have emerged with the use of frozen embryos. In a famous case of 1989, Davis v. Davis, a Tennessee couple attempted IVF because Mrs. Davis was able to conceive but could not bear a child. Nine eggs were fertilized. Two were implanted, unsuccessfully, in Mrs. Davis's uterus, and the remaining seven were frozen for a later try. But then the couple divorced. They went to court over the fate of these embryos. Mrs. Davis wanted to have them implanted, but Mr. Davis wanted them destroyed. He argued that he had a right not to be a father. In the end, Mrs. Davis remarried and requested that the embryos be donated to some other infertile couple. Thus the case was resolved; but it opened the difficult question: Who should have rights over frozen embryos? Or, for that matter, should frozen embryos have any rights, protected by the law?

In another interesting case, this one from Australia, a woman's eggs were fertilized in IVF by an anonymous donor. One of these was unsuccessfully implanted in the woman and the other two were frozen. This woman and her husband then died in a plane crash. It turned out that the couple left a sizable fortune. Should the embryos have rights of inheritance? This was a question that troubled the couple's adult children. Even more pressing, morally speaking, are the larger questions of whether frozen embryos should have rights to be born, or who should decide if, when, and under what circumstances human embryos are to be donated to medical research. Should frozen embryos even be produced in the first place? Certainly, embryo freezing is a useful NRT for infertile couples; and in the case of IVF, a woman is spared repeated laparoscopies through the option of freezing the extra embryos produced the first time. But is embryo freezing a form of irresponsible reproduction? What kind of society, with what views of human life, are we constructing? How should we even think about frozen embryos? Sarah Franklyn (1995: 337) argues that the frozen embryo straddles the boundary between science and nature, giving it an ambivalent status such that its identity and meaning will be contested:

> The embryo is a cyborg entity; its coming into being is both organic and technological. Though it is fully human (for what else can it be?) it is born of science, inhabits the timeless ice land of liquid-nitrogen storage tanks. ... At once potential research material (scientific object), quasi-citizen (it has legal rights) and potential person (human subject), the embryo has a cyborg liminality in its contested location between science and nature.

Moral and legal difficulties also surround the practice of surrogacy, particularly "contract" or "commercial" surrogacy. This form of surrogacy, though permitted in the United States, is illegal in most countries that have laws regulating the NRTs (Blank 1990: 157). Some people have severely censured surrogates, calling them "baby sellers." Others have merely wondered what sort of woman would contract to carry a baby for another woman or couple. Surrogates typically receive a fee of about $10,000 for their service. Yet most surrogates insist that they do it not for the money but because they're genuinely motivated to provide a child to an infertile couple. Apparently some women also enjoy the experience of pregnancy and seek to experience it again after they have had all the children they want for themselves. Helena Ragoné's (1994) study of surrogate motherhood in America shows how the surrogate role gives women confidence and a sense of self-importance and worth. These women, she says, are adding meaning to their lives by going beyond the confines of their own domestic situations or their unrewarding jobs to do something vital for others.

Other studies have shown that surrogates are usually not poor women in desperate need of cash but, rather, working-class women. According to Ragoné's (1994: 54) study, the personal income of unmarried surrogates ranged from $16,000 to $24,000, and the average household income of married surrogates was $38,000. Still, in the context of surrogacy the issue of social class and economic inequality is easily raised. The couple seeking a surrogate is generally wealthy, at least wealthy enough to be able to afford a surrogate plus the other expenses ($25,000 or more) that they will pay to doctors and a fertility clinic. But surrogates, though not poor, are not of this privileged social class. They may feel rewarded by the attention, care, gifts, and positive social treatment they receive from the couples they are assisting (Ragoné 1994: 64–66). Is this all well and good, or is contract surrogacy enmeshed in a new type of class exploitation?

In a discussion of surrogacy, Sarah Boone (1994) invokes both racial and class inequality by drawing some disturbing cultural parallels between contemporary surrogate motherhood and the position of black women slaves in an earlier America. Boone describes black slave women as "bottom women" in the gender and racial hierarchy of earlier American society, a hierarchy that placed white males on top, followed by white females and black males. One measure of the "bottom" status of black slave women was wide sexual access to them, for in their position in slave society white male slaveholders could easily exploit them sexually. In addition, black women were themselves considered property and had no legal rights to their children. Meanwhile, "the white woman as top woman became the physically delicate asexual mother/wife, subordinate helpmate" (Boone 1994: 355). Boone asks whether the surrogate mother is another kind of "bottom woman," one whose status is measured not by sexual access to her but by reproductive access to her body: After all, "CCM [commercialized contract motherhood] allows men and privileged women to purchase or rent the gestational capacities of other women in order to produce a genetic heir" (Boone 1994: 358).

A new "top woman" thus emerges here too, but she is still a wife and the member of a privileged class. Yet this is a "top woman" with a new twist: "Now a career woman in her own right but naturally drawn to motherhood, she is fully appropriate for the more refined roles of genetic contributor and rearer of children," whereas the "bottom woman" surrogate is given "the 'unrefined' work of gestation and childbearing for men and more privileged women who are incapable or unwilling to do this work" (Boone 1994: 358). We may argue that, unlike slave women, surrogates choose their "work" and, as we have seen, are not poor or disadvantaged persons. Still, Boone's observations suggest that surrogacy occurs not in a vacuum but in a sociocultural context where it is inseparable from issues of gender and social inequality.

Moral concerns and debates rage on over the NRTs. But it is on kinship and gender that these new technologies may yet have their greatest impact.

Kinship and Gender

We have already seen how the use of frozen embryos confounds some conventional notions of kinship relation. Is the woman who gives birth to her genetic uncle his niece or his mother? What happens to our kinship system when the boundaries of our core concepts of "kin," set long ago by our ancestors and taken for granted for so many centuries, are blurred? Even more jolting, perhaps, is the fragmentation of motherhood that results from the technological ability to separate conception from birth and eggs from wombs. Robert Snowden and his colleagues (1983: 34) claim that, with the advent of NRTs, we now need a total of ten different terms to cover the concepts of "mother" and "father." The terms they propose are as follows:

1. Genetic mother
2. Carrying mother

3. Nurturing mother
4. Complete mother
5. Genetic/carrying mother
6. Genetic/nurturing mother
7. Carrying/nurturing mother
8. Genetic father
9. Nurturing father
10. Complete father

The first three terms cover the distinct stages of conception, gestation, and care for a child. These three aspects of motherhood can be carried out by one, two, or three different women. If one woman does all three, she is the "complete" mother. Note that a child could conceivably have five different persons as "parents" in this system (1–3 as mothers and 8 and 9 as fathers), even without including stepparents (Blank 1990: 10). But it is really only motherhood that has fragmented as a result of the NRTs, since we have long been accustomed to the idea that a child can have one man as its "genetic" or "biological" father and another as its "nurturing" (or perhaps a better word here might be "legal") father. Similarly, we are familiar with the idea that "legal" or "nurturing" mothers can be different from "natural" or "biological" mothers. What is new is the division of biological motherhood into two parts: conception and gestation.

In comparison to our society, a people like the Nuer (Case 2) would perhaps have had different conceptual problems with kinship in relation to the NRTs. For them, legal rights to children were held by fathers (and their patrilineal kin groups), not by mothers. Also, these rights were clearly established by cattle payments, not by concerns with biological fatherhood. Recall that Nuer culture constructed kinship such that children belonged to fathers, defined as the men who paid bridewealth for the mothers.

In the United States, however, ideas about kinship have been based on cultural notions of biology (Schneider 1968). Americans have strongly defined "real" parenthood as biologically based. And they have taken for granted that this way of thinking about kinship is in line with "science." But now science itself has thrown a wrench into the American system of kinship by showing that unitary "natural" motherhood is actually divisible. In the courts and in our own minds we thus face the challenge of reconstructing motherhood and, hence, reconstructing kinship. Will we need to devise a nonbiologically based definition of the mater as the Nuer have done for the pater? Marilyn Strathern (1995) discusses how the NRTs challenge Euro-American notions of "nature" itself as well as fundamental ideas about what constitutes personal "identity." Many other studies have discussed the implications for kinship of the NRTs, especially in European and American culture (see Edwards et al. 1999; Franklin and Ragoné 1998).

We do not know what the future may bring. But what seems to be happening at present is that those involved with the NRTs are not discarding the old cultural ideas about kinship but, on the contrary, are making every effort to preserve the notions of "real" biological parenthood. Toward this end, they are reinterpreting the NRTs and their tricky implications so as to reconcile them with these core cultural notions of biological parenthood and the resulting family ideal. This process has played out in two very interesting contexts.

One context concerns lesbian couples. Those seeking to have children and to become a family in the conventional sense have of course benefited from the NRTs. At a minimum, one member of the couple may become impregnated with donor sperm. Corinne Hayden's (1995) study shows that some American lesbian couples with children are constructing something truly new in kinship: double motherhood. They are raising their children to perceive that they have two mothers. One way to support this perception is to have the children call both of them "mother." Another way is to hyphenate the comothers' names to form the children's surname. In short, these couples seek to raise their children in an environment of parental equality—a process that, in their view, constitutes a true challenge and alternative to the conventional husband-dominant household of the broader United States society. Of course, the creation of equal, dual motherhood is confounded by the fact that only one woman can be the biological mother. Even if the lesbian partners themselves perceive their motherhood to be equal, the surrounding society, and courts of law, may not.

In trying to create new forms of kinship and family, lesbian couples are not so much rejecting biology as a basis for kinship as making use of the NRTs to bring their situation into line with biologically based kinship. For example, they may strive for a more equitable double motherhood by getting pregnant by the same donor. In this way, each partner becomes a mother, their children are born genetically related to one another, and they all more closely resemble a family in the conventional sense. Another possibility is for one woman to be artificially inseminated using the sperm of the other woman's brother. Each woman would then have some genetic relation, as well as a conventional kinship relation, to the child. Even more creative is what Hayden (1995: 55) refers to as the "obvious and 'perfect' option for lesbian families: one woman could contribute the genetic material, and her partner could become the gestational/birth mother." Thus even the idea that homosexual unions are "inherently nonprocreative" (Hayden 1995: 56) is challenged, now that a woman can give birth to the genetic child of her female partner. Going a step further, a lesbian couple could combine the last two options: One woman could contribute an egg to be fertilized by the brother (or, for that matter, son) of her lesbian partner, after which the egg would be implanted in her partner.

The other context in which efforts are being made to reconcile the NRTs with core cultural notions, especially American ideas about kinship, concerns surrogate motherhood. As Ragoné (1994: 109) concluded from her study of surrogate mothers in the United States, "Programs, surrogates and couples highlight those aspects of surrogacy that are most consistent with American kinship ideology, deemphasizing those aspects that are not congruent with this ideology. Thus, although the means of achieving relatedness may have changed, the rigorous emphasis on the family and on the biogenetic basis of American kinship remains essentially unchanged." One way in which surrogates and their couples maintain this emphasis is to downplay the relationship between the husband and the surrogate in cases where the surrogate has been impregnated with the husband's sperm. Indeed, since the surrogate is carrying the husband's (and her) child, there are disturbing parallels with adultery. In some surrogate programs the relationship that is given priority and becomes strong is that between the surrogate and the wife. This arrangement is obviously more comfortable for the surrogate; it also allows the wife to feel that she is participating in the process of creating the child. In addition, the wife, or the adoptive mother, in such cases may emphasize her role in the creation of the child as one of intention, choice, and love: "One adoptive mother ... described it as conception in the heart, that is, the belief that in the final analysis it was her desire to have a child that brought the surrogate arrangement into being and therefore produced a child" (Ragoné 1994: 126).

The NRTs have spurred debates among women in general and feminists in particular over how these technologies are affecting women and relations between the sexes. Some feminists approve of the NRTs precisely because they fragment motherhood and in many ways distance women from "nature" and "natural" reproduction. Their argument is that women have been trapped by their reproductive roles, that their lower status has been due all along to their entrenchment in reproduction and motherhood. According to this view, the NRTs not only expand reproductive choices for individual women and men but can help to liberate women from the inferior status that their biological roles have given them. Other feminists have argued that the legal use of NRTs supports women's right to control their own bodies. They also approve of contract surrogacy because it allows a surrogate to use her body as she wishes for her own economic benefit.

Yet another argument is that the NRTs are potentially good for women but need to be subjected to proper controls and approached with caution (Purdy 1994). Thus, for example, regulations should be implemented to ensure that surrogate mothers retain control of their pregnancies and, by extension, that contracting fathers not be given rights to say how a surrogate should behave while pregnant, to decide whether she should have a cesarean, to sue her for miscarriage, and so on. With such controls in place, according to this argument, contract pregnancy can considerably benefit infertile women or women with high-risk pregnancies. As for accusations of "baby selling" by surrogate mothers, those taking this position raise an important question: Why are there no parallel objections against the payments made to men who donate their sperm? Laura Purdy (1994: 316) also questions the view that "women can be respected for altruistic and socially useful actions only when they receive no monetary compensation, whereas men—physicians, scientists, politicians—can be both honored and well paid."

Perhaps the strongest feminist criticism of the NRTs has come from Janice Raymond (1993). In her book, *Women As Wombs*, Raymond describes the NRTs as a form of "violence against women": Since a male-dominant "medical fundamentalism" defines both the problem (infertility) and the cure (the NRTs), application of the new techniques entails "appropriation of the female body by male scientific experts" (1993: xx). Raymond argues directly against the position that NRTs liberate women by freeing them from their previous reproductive roles. On the contrary, she says, the fragmentation of motherhood, the conceptual wedge that the NRTs place between a woman and a fetus, results in the loss of women's control over reproduction. When the fetus is seen as so separable from a woman, the fetus itself becomes the focus of attention and, in the process, male rights over reproduction are increased: "Reproductive technologies and contracts augment the rights of fetuses and would-be fathers while challenging the one right that women have historically retained some vestige of— mother-right" (Raymond 1993: xi).

Raymond notes that in the case of Baby M, even though William Stern and Mary Beth Whitehead were equally the genetic parents and Whitehead was also the birth mother, Stern was continually referred to in the media as "the father" whereas Whitehead was always "the surrogate." The courts also awarded custody to Stern. About this situation Raymond (1993: 34) writes: "A woman who gestates the fetus, experiences a nine-month pregnancy, and gives birth to the child is rendered a 'substitute' mother. On the other hand, popping sperm into a jar is 'real' fatherhood, legally equivalent, if not superior, to the contribution of egg, gestation, labor, and birth that is part of any woman's pregnancy."

Of course, one could retort that the genetic/birth mother in the Baby M case did sign a surrogacy contract, thus bringing about the whole trouble in the first place. But Raymond's point is that the NRTs are changing our society's perceptions of motherhood and fatherhood, conceptually and legally, and that women may be losing out in the process. Legally speaking, what Raymond (1993: 30) calls "ejaculatory fatherhood" does appear to be gaining ground—in part, perhaps, because ideas about biological fatherhood have not been fundamentally changed by the NRTs whereas ideas about motherhood most definitely have been. In the American biogenetic ideology of kinship, fatherhood is still simple, but motherhood is no longer so.

And what of future reproductive technologies? Human cloning may be a long way off, but it opens up particularly intriguing scenarios with respect to kinship and gender. For example, a woman could donate an egg that, after enucleation, could be injected with the nucleus of one of her own cells. The treated egg could then be implanted into her womb and carried to full term. This woman's baby would of course be a female and the exact clone of the donor woman. In addition, the baby would have no biological father. Yet the woman who donated her egg and cell nucleus would be a true biological mother, since no surrogate would be involved. Further, the donor woman and her clone would be like identical twins whose births were separated in time by one or more generations. In that sense, a woman could be the sole genetic and biological parent of her own, younger twin sister who is at the same time her daughter. Similarly, male clones would have no genetic mother, only a father who was the donor of the nucleus. (In this case, of course, a surrogate mother would be necessary to carry the embryo to term.) Indeed, a world without men, but not without women, can be theoretically imagined, were cloning to one day replace ordinary human reproduction.

Continuities

In this book we have examined a variety of ways in which kinship and gender are culturally constructed and interrelated. This analysis has involved us in discussions of sexuality and reproduction, and of the interests of many people and groups in exercising control over women's reproductive capacities. We have seen cases, specifically among the Nuer and the Nyinba, in which female sexuality is largely unrestricted but cultural rules allocate a woman's children to her legal husband or husbands and their kinship groups. And among the matrilineal Nayar, female sexuality is unrestrained (except for sexual intercourse before the tali-tying ceremony and at any time with a lower-class man), but children are allocated to a woman's own kinship corporation under the leadership of her senior matrilineal kinsmen. In all three societies, female sexuality and female fertility are separate social concerns.

We have also seen cases in which a woman's sexuality is, or was, ideally restricted to one man, her husband: Examples include the Nepalese Brahmans, the ancient Romans, and Europeans in Europe and North America. In these societies, a woman's "inappropriate" sexual behavior (premarital sex or adultery) could result in devaluation of her person, dishonor to her family, and, among the Nepalese Brahmans, devaluation of the woman's future fertility. The Nayar, sharing some of the Hindu caste ideas related to female purity and pollution, also showed this connection between female sexuality and fertility, inasmuch as sex with a lower-caste man would expel a woman and her future children from her caste and kin group. In all of these Eurasian cases we have seen that the concern with female sexual "purity" is interwoven with concerns over property and its transmission, as well as with the maintenance of class and caste divisions; in other words, they are bound up with larger issues of socioeconomic inequality.

Many of the cases discussed in this book have dealt with male-led kin groups seeking control over women's reproduction. We have also seen a few cases where a woman's reproduction was not of much concern to larger groups of kin. Among the Navajo, for instance, although a woman reproduces for her own and her husband's matriclans, clan continuity is not a strong concern. Navajo culture venerates women for their reproductive powers, but it does not punish women for childlessness. Another group, the early Christians in Europe, valued celibacy over reproduction and held that sexuality was equally unspiritual for women and men. As noted, one historian argues that early Christian women found in Christianity a welcome liberation from both marriage and reproduction.

By and large, white, middle-class Euro-American women have not had to contend with the interests of kin groups in their reproduction, nor have they been under pressure to reproduce for anyone but themselves and their partners. Furthermore, over the centuries, restrictions on their sexuality have relaxed. Yet, paradoxically, these Euro-American women have expressed problems and tensions of their own in the process of trying to reconcile their sexuality, fertility, and personhood in a meaningful and satisfying way.

With the emergence of the NRTs, we cannot fail to ask ourselves who we will become, as women, as men, as persons, and as kin. But this is not a new question. All human groups throughout history have continually constructed kinship and gender, seeking meaning and identity within these cultural constructions. And along the way, the constructions themselves have been contested between men and women, young and old, powerful and powerless. Now, as we face the development of new (and newer) reproductive technologies, the struggle continues. In this way, perhaps the NRTs are not taking us into a brave new world so much as dealing out new cards in an older dynamic human game of self, kin, and gender definition.

Notes

1. All humans are phenotypically either A, B, AB, or O. The A phenotype corresponds to an I^AI^A or I^AI^O genotype; the B phenotype corresponds to an I^BI^B or I^BI^O genotype; the AB phenotype is always I^AI^B; and the O phenotype is always I^OI^O. Let us assume that a child belongs to the A blood group and that its mother is in the O group. This means that the mother is I^OI^O and the child is either I^AI^A or I^AI^O. We know that this child could not possibly have inherited the I^A gene from the mother and, therefore, that the I^A gene had to have come from the father. Let us assume that a particular man is thought to be the father and that the mother is suing him for child support. The ABO blood test is performed and the man is found to belong to the B group. In other words, the man's genotype is I^BI^B or I^BI^O, meaning that he could not have contributed the I^A gene; by extension, he could not possibly be the father, and he is *excluded*. But even if the suspected man turns out to belong to the A group (making it possible for him to have contributed an I^A gene), he is not proven to be the biological father. Indeed, since the whole human population is subdivided into only four blood groups, hundreds of millions of men can be found in each category. But obviously not all A-type men should be suspected, as it would be impossible for the mother to have had sexual intercourse with hundreds of millions of men from all over the planet.

2. Embryo splitting is another example of cloning now routinely used in cattle and potentially applicable to humans. In this technique, a young embryo composed of two, four, or eight cells is disaggregated, and each component cell is forced in vitro to originate a new embryo. The two, four, or eight embryos are of course clones of one another, since they all came from the same original embryo. The embryos are then reimplanted into several surrogate mothers and develop into identical twins, quadruplets, or octuplets, each individual being born to a different surrogate mother. (Note, however, that multiple births are usually not possible in cattle.) In this case, the clones are not identical to either the mother or the father; rather, as noted, they are clones of one another, just like human identical twins.

Suggested Further Reading

Ragoné, Helena. 1994. *Surrogate Motherhood: Conception in the Heart.* Boulder, Colo.: Westview. One of the first in-depth studies of surrogate motherhood, how it affects individuals' lives, and its impact on kinship construction in the United States.

Franklin, Sarah. *Embodied Progress: A Cultural Account of Assisted Conception.* London: Routledge. Explores assisted conception, especially IVF, in Britain, with discussion of implications for cultural constructions of kinship and procreation.

Suggested Classroom Videos

That's a Family! 2000. Produced by Debra Chasnoff, Ariella J. Ben-Dov, and Fawn Yacker. Women's Educational Media, San Francisco, Calif. Thirty-five minutes. This film is designed for elementary school children, but it works well for adults too and is a pleasure to watch. In the film children themselves describe their own nontraditional families in the United States.

These include families of adoption, mixed ethnic families, and families with gay and lesbian parents.

Making Babies. 1999. Produced by Dough Hamilton and Sarah Spinks. *Frontline* co-production with Cam Bay Productions. Sixty minutes. This film explores a wide range of NRTs. It raises issues about the changing nature of the family and the commercialization of reproduction.

References

Blank, Robert H. 1990. *Regulating Reproduction.* New York: Columbia University Press.

Boone, Sarah S. 1994. Slavery and Contract Motherhood: A "Racialized" Objection to the Autonomy Argument. In Helen Bequaert Holmes, ed., *Issues in Reproductive Technology*, pp. 349–366. New York: New York University Press.

Edwards, Jeanette, Sarah Franklin, Eric Hirsch, Frances Price, and Marilyn Strathern. 1999. *Technologies of Procreation: Kinship in the Age of Assisted Conception*, second ed. London: Routledge.

Franklin, Sarah, and Helena Ragoné, eds. 1998. *Reproducing Reproduction: Kinship, Power and Technological Innovation.* Philadelphia: University of Pennsylvania Press.

Franklyn, Sarah. 1995. Postmodern Procreation: A Cultural Account of Assisted Reproduction. In Faye D. Ginsburg and Rayna Rapp, eds., *Conceiving the New World Order: The Global Politics of Reproduction*, pp. 323–345. Berkeley: University of California Press.

Gurdon, J. B. 1968. Transplanted Nuclei and Cell Differentiation. *Scientific American* 219: 24–35.

Hayden, Corinne P. 1995. Gender, Genetics, and Generation: Reformulating Biology in Lesbian Kinship. *Cultural Anthropology* 10(1): 41–63.

Huxley, Aldous. 1946 [orig. 1932]. *Brave New World.* New York: Bantam Books.

Kahn, Susan Martha. 2000. *Reproducing Jews: A Cultural Account of Assisted Conception in Israel.* Durham, N.C.: Duke University Press.

Purdy, Laura M. 1994. Another Look at Contract Pregnancy. In Helen Bequaert Holmes, ed., *Issues in Reproductive Technology*, pp. 303–320. New York: New York University Press.

Ragoné, Helena. 1994. *Surrogate Motherhood: Conception in the Heart.* Boulder, Colo.: Westview Press.

Raymond, Janice G. 1993. *Women As Wombs: Reproductive Technologies and the Battle over Women's Freedom.* San Francisco: Harper San Francisco.

Schneider, David M. 1968. *American Kinship: A Cultural Account.* Englewood Cliffs, N.J.: Prentice-Hall.

Snowden, Robert, G. D. Mitchell, and E. M. Snowden. 1983. *Artificial Reproduction.* London: Allen and Unwin.

Strathern, Marilyn. 1995. Displacing Knowledge: Technology and the Consequences for Kinship. In Faye D. Ginsburg and Rayna Rapp, eds., *Conceiving the New World Order: The Global Politics of Reproduction*, pp. 346–363. Berkeley: University of California Press.

Wakayama, T., A. C. F. Perry, M. Zuccotti, K. R. Johnson, and R. Yanagimachi. 1998. Full-Term Development of Mice from Enucleated Oocytes Injected with Cumulus Cell Nuclei. *Nature* 394: 369–374.

Wilmut, Ian. 1998. Cloning for Medicine. *Scientific American* 279: 58–63.

Feminists or "Postfeminists"

Young Women's Attitudes Toward Feminism and Gender Relations

By Pamela Aronson

In contrast to popular presumptions and prior research on women of the "postfeminist" generation, this study found an appreciation for recent historical changes in women's opportunities, and an awareness of persisting inequalities and discrimination. The findings reveal support for feminist goals, coupled with ambiguity about the concept of feminism. Although some of the women could be categorized along a continuum of feminist identification, half were "fence-sitters" or were unable to articulate a position. There were variations in perspectives among those with different life experiences, as well as by racial and class background.

Keywords

feminism; postfeminism; young women; identity; gender relations

A late 1990s cover of *Time* magazine with the caption "Is feminism dead?" featured photos of prominent feminist activists, including one of the flighty television lawyer character. Ally McBeal (Bellafante 1998). Such media pronouncements of the "death" of feminism rest on widespread presumptions that young women do not appreciate

AUTHOR'S NOTE: This research was supported by a National Research Service Award from the National Institute of Mental Health (Training Program in Identity, Self, Role, and Mental Health—PHST 32 MH 14588), the National Institute of Mental Health (MH 42843, Jeylan T. Mortimer, principal investigator), the Personal Narratives Award from the Center for Advanced Feminist Studies, University of Minnesota, and a Graduate School Block Grant Stipend Award from the Department of Sociology, University of Minnesota. The author would like to thank a number of people who provided comments and suggestions on earlier versions of this article: Ronald Aronson, Christine Bose, Donna Eder, Debbie Engelen-Eigles, Amy Kaler, Barbara Laslett, Jame McLeod, Jeylan T. Mortimer, Irene Padavic, Katie See, Beth Schneider, and Kim Simmons, as well as the social psychology seminar members at Indiana University and several anonymous reviewers.

Pamela Aronson, "Feminists or 'Postfeminists': Young Women's Attitudes toward Feminism and Gender Relations," *Gender and Society*, vol.17, no.6, pp. 903–922. Copyright © 2003 by Sage Publications. Reprinted with permission.

gains made by the women's movement, are not concerned about discrimination, and do not support feminism. These suppositions have rarely been tested.

How do young women view their own opportunities and obstacles, particularly when compared to those faced by women of their mothers' generation? How do they perceive and experience gender discrimination? How do they identify themselves with respect to feminism, and how can we make sense of their seemingly contradictory perspectives? Finally, what are the impacts of racial and class background and life experience on attitudes toward feminism? Although prior studies have considered aspects of these questions, my research examines them through interviews with a diverse sample. This diversity reveals the importance not only of race and class, but also life experience, in the development of attitudes toward feminism. Furthermore, by not imposing a set definition of feminism but letting it emerge from the interviewees themselves, my study reveals great ambiguity in the meanings of feminism today and suggests that we need to rethink some of the assumptions about young women's identities.

Literature Review: Growing Up in the Shadow of the Women's Movement[1]

Since the mid-1980s, 30 to 40 percent of women have called themselves feminists, and by 1990, nearly 80 percent favored efforts to "strengthen and change women's status in society" (Marx Ferree and Hess 1995, 88). Although the media often question why so few women call themselves feminists. Marx Ferree and Hess (1995) pointed out that the number of women who do so represents the same percentage of people who label themselves as Republicans or Democrats. Addressing the same concerns, Gurin (1985, 1987) distinguished between four components of gender consciousness: identification (recognizing women's shared interests), discontent (recognizing women's lack of power), assessment of legitimacy (seeing gender disparities as illegitimate), and collective orientation (believing in collective action). Although women historically have become more critical of men's claims to power, women's gender consciousness has been weaker than the group consciousness of African Americans, the working class, and the elderly. At the same time, women, especially employed women, are often conscious of women's structural disadvantage in the labor market (Gurin 1985). However, an average woman may have somewhat vague understandings of political labels such as "feminism," as activists and political elites are generally more consistent and coherent in their positions (Converse 1964; Unger 1989).

In the early 1980s, the media began to label women in their teens and twenties as the "postfeminist" generation[2] (Bellafante 1998; Bolotin 1982; Whittier 1995). Twenty years later, the term continues to be applied to young women, who are thought to benefit from the women's movement through expanded access to employment and education and new family arrangements but at the same time do not push for further political change. Postfeminism has been the subject of considerable debate, since its usage connotes the "death" of feminism and because the equality it assumes is largely a myth (Coppock, Haydon, and Richter 1995; Overhotser 1986; Rosenfelt and Stacey 1987; Whittier 1995). The term has been used by researchers to reflect the current cycle and stage of the women's movement (Taylor 1989; Taylor and Rupp 1993; Whittier 1995). Indeed, Rossi (1982) has written of a cyclical generational pattern in the women's movement, with each feminist wave separated by roughly fifty years, or two generations. "Quiet periods" (Rossi 1982, 9) see diminished political action, but continued progress in private arenas, such as education and employment. Because movement stages greatly influence how women identify with the movement (Taylor 1989; Taylor and Rupp 1993; Whittier 1995), women's individual attitudes toward feminism are likely to vary.

The second-wave women's movement has simultaneously experienced great successes and backlash. Successes include the maintenance of movement organizations (Marx Ferree and Yancey Martin 1995; Whittier 1995), as well as a "broadly institutionalized and effective interest group," with an institutional base in academia, particularly women's studies programs (Brenner 1996, 24). Backlash is evident in a decline in grassroots mobilization and negative public discourse by antifeminist organizations and media figures (Faludi 1991; Marx Ferree and Hess 1995: Schneider 1988).

Scholars have found that young women tend to be depoliticized and individualistic and that few identify as feminists (Rupp 1988; Stacey 1987)—they typically focus on individual solutions (Budgeon and Currie 1995) and express feminist ideas without labeling them as such (Henderson-King and Stewart 1994; Morgan 1995; Percy and Kremer 1995; Renzetti 1987; Rupp 1988; Stacey 1987: Weis 1990). Many of these apolitical women assume that discrimination will not happen to them (Sigel 1996). The lack of grassroots mobilization results in no framework for understanding individual experiences in politicized terms (Aronson 2000: Taylor 1996) and limits "postfeminists" to viewing gender disparities as illegitimate, rather than in collective terms or in terms of women's shared interests (Gurin 1985, 1987). Their attitudes are also influenced by the media, which have supported the antifeminist backlash (Faludi 1991; Marx Ferree and Hess 1995) and have implied that "no further feminist action is needed" (Schneider 1988, 11).

This generally negative picture of contemporary feminist consciousness is occasionally countered by researchers who have been discovering a "third wave." They point to more than one micro cohort within the postfeminist generation, noting that women who came of age in the 1990s more frequently support feminist goals and are more politically active to achieve these goals (e.g., abortion rights activism) than women who came of age in the 1980s (Whittier 1995). From activists who seek to represent a diversity of young women's experiences (Walker 1995), to the Riot Grrrl movement in music (Rosenberg and Garofalo 1998; Wald 1998), third-wave feminism is said to explicitly embrace hybridity, contradiction, and multiple identities (particularly "connections between racial, sexual and gender identities" (Heywood and Drake 1997, 7, 8, 15). However, this new emphasis is questioned by scholars arguing that African American and Chicana feminists have focused historically, and continue to focus, on organizing not only in terms of gender but also along racial lines (Hurtado 1998; Springer 2002). In addition, the third wave is sometimes perceived as nonactivist in nature (Heywood and Drake 1997).

Although not explicitly defining themselves as feminists, other women are said to have the "potential for feminist critique" (Weis 1990, 179). Stacey (1991, 262) argued that young women have "semiconsciously incorporated feminist principles into their gender and kinship expectations and practices." This approach includes "taking for granted" many recent gains: women's work opportunities, combining work with family, sexual autonomy and freedom, and male participation in domestic work and child rearing (Stacey 1991, 1987). This "simultaneous incorporation, revision and depoliticization" (Stacey 1987, 8) of feminism indicates that worldviews include more feminist principles while being less explicitly feminist.

The negative as well as the positive prognosis of these studies should be taken with a grain of salt. They tend to operate with uniform definitions of feminism, ignore generational differences, and/or study groups that are too homogeneous to provide conclusions about the full diversity of today's young women. My study seeks to correct each of these limitations and hopes to provide insights that are more nuanced, complex, and attentive to diversity.

Some research has assumed that when women are asked their views of feminism, they react to a common, uncontested definition. For example, Renzetti (1987) asked college women to respond to an attitudinal inventory survey and found that about a quarter agreed with the statement "I consider myself to be a feminist." Similarly, Boxer's (1997) survey found that three-quarters of women of all ages agreed that the status of women has improved in the past twenty-five years, although only about a third considered themselves to be feminists. By requiring women to define themselves as either for or against feminism, these studies are not likely to tap into the highly complex and contested meanings of feminism today and the ways these diverse meanings influence people's reactions to the term itself. In contrast, my study did not impose a uniform definition of feminism when probing or interpreting interviewees' attitudes but instead left this term for the women themselves to define. In so doing, I did not assume that feminism's meaning is commonly understood or agreed upon.

Research that has recognized feminism's multiple meanings has either focused on a broad age span of women or has centered on homogenous groups of young women. Focusing on more than one cohort, Taylor's (1996) study (with women aged 18 to 43 who were active in the postpartum depression movement) found that feminist identification can be classified on a continuum: Some women call themselves feminists, others reject the label "feminist" but support its principles, while some reject feminism altogether. In her study of women of all ages,[3] Sigel (1996, 113) observed that feminism was often characterized by ambivalence: Women felt that the movement had been positive but that it may have "gone too far" and negatively affected relations with men. The women in Sigel's study called themselves feminists, endorsed feminist goals but rejected the label, or were uncertain about their positions. Neither of these studies explored the potential generational differences in these attitudes. However, a generation has common experiences that structure its worldview (Mannheim 1952). A political generation—persons coming of age in a particular historical period—shares a similar consciousness (Schneider 1988, 6). Despite such a "a common interpretative framework" (Whittier 1995, 16), an individual's place within the social structure and the extent to which she or he is aware and involved in politics can influence her or his belief systems (Converse 1964).

Studies based on homogenous samples may obscure important differences in feminist orientations. For example, Renzetti (1987) surveyed college students at a predominately white, Catholic university—a very privileged sample. Similarly, Stacey's (1987) insights about "postfeminist consciousness" are based on her interviews with two "kinship networks." Kamen (1991), a journalist, reports a similar continuum of identification as Taylor (1996) described, yet she did not examine the perspectives of women with diverse backgrounds and life experiences.

In fact, no prior studies examine differences in the attitudes of young women with diverse life experiences. We might expect, however, that varying life experiences or class backgrounds will lead to divergent ideas about feminism. Women of some backgrounds have greater supports for the development of feminist identities than others, especially those who have taken women's studies courses in college and have thus been exposed to the institutional legitimization of feminist ideas. Other women are limited to conceptions of feminism advanced by their family and friends and institutions such as the media. These life paths can be tied to class differences. Many middle-class feminist issues, such as the "glass ceiling" and alienation from the housewife role, are far from the daily struggle to make ends meet that is faced by working-class women. Even feminist activists develop different feminist identities as a result of their social class backgrounds (Reger 2002).

In addition, women of different racial and ethnic backgrounds may develop varying views of feminism and gender relations. Women of color have argued that the women's movement has put white, middle-class concerns at its center and ignored the ideas of women of color (Hill Collins 1991). Historically, women of color have not been "full participants in white feminist organizations," despite these organizations' claims that their concerns are universal to all women (Hill Collins 1991, 7). For women of color, racial identities might also be more salient and politicized than gender identities, constituting barriers to the development of feminist identification (Hunter and Sellers 1998). At the same time, prior studies suggest that African Americans are more likely than whites are to support feminist positions, to have egalitarian gender role attitudes, and to engage in collective action (Hunter and Sellers 1998).

This article explores young women's attitudes toward feminism in relation to differences in background and life experience. In contrast to prior research, I recognize the ambivalent and sometimes contradictory orientations of the women who have grown up in the shadow of the women's movement. While prior research has given some attention to the contexts within which feminist attitudes develop (Sigel 1996; Stacey 1987; Taylor 1996; Whittier 1995), many studies have not directly considered women's perceptions of some key goals of feminist organizing, such as advancing women's opportunities, and the obstacles and discrimination that feminism addresses. To discern the context of young women's attitudes toward gender relations, I begin my analysis with an examination of perceptions of women's opportunities, obstacles, and discrimination. I continue the analysis by considering young women's attitudes toward feminism and the impact of race, class, and life experience on these attitudes. Taken together, this article reveals support for feminist goals and complexity in attitudes toward the term *feminism*.

Method

This study is based on in-depth interviews with members of a panel study of young people, the Youth Development Study, an ongoing longitudinal study of adolescent development and the transition to adulthood (Jeylan Mortimer is the principal investigator). The larger survey sample ($N = 1,000$) was randomly chosen from a list of enrolled ninth-grade students in St. Paul, Minnesota. Respondents completed surveys annually, with the first year (ninth grade) in 1988. Of the original 1,000 panel members who took part in the first year of data collection, the Youth Development Study retained 77.5 percent through 1995, the last year of the survey before my interview study.

For my in-depth interviews, I followed Glaser and Strauss's (1967) suggestions for theoretical sampling and interviewed women with varying trajectories of life experience and background, as reported in surveys during the four years following high school (1991 to 1995). I focused on differences in education, parenthood, and careers and interviewed nearly equal proportions of women in each group. Obviously, these categories of experience are not mutually exclusive. However, the groups were defined as nonoverlapping categories for this reason. A "school" group had attended a four-year college or university for at least eight months annually in three of the four years following high school. A "parent" group had become mothers by the eighth year of the study and could also be engaged in school and/or work. A "labor force" group did not have an extensive school trajectory, nor had they become mothers. Instead, they typically worked full-time or moved between postsecondary school and work after high school.

By mail, the Youth Development Study invited 138 women to be interviewed; 42 consented by returning a postcard indicating their interest. Interviews took place in 1996 and 1997. Of the 448 Youth Development Study women who responded in the eighth year of the larger study (1995), I interviewed 9.4 percent. The women were aged twenty-three or twenty-four at the time of my interviews. Among them, 33 percent were women of color (11.9 percent African American, 9.5 percent Asian American, 9.5 percent biracial and multiracial, and 2.4 percent Latina). Their socioeconomic backgrounds included 31 percent from working-class families, 48 percent from the middle class, and 21 percent from upper-middle-class back-grounds.[4] At the time of the interviews, two-thirds of the women were working full-time (28), 3 were working part-time, 7 were in school full-time (and not working), and 4 were out of the labor force for other reasons (2 were caring for their young children, 1 was not working as a result of a severe disability, and 1 was in prison). Slightly more than one-third had completed a bachelor's degree.

Half of the interviewees were involved in committed relationships: 10 were married, 3 were engaged, 8 were in exclusive relationships, and 1 was divorced and involved in a new relation-ship. Although none of the women directly labeled themselves as lesbians, 2 suggested this possibility. One woman was questioning her sexuality, although she had never had an intimate relationship. The other (who had been in prison since she was a teenager) suggested that her intimate relationships had been with women, although she was looking forward to having a relationship with a man. Although it would be interesting to examine whether young lesbian and bisexual women would report different perceptions of feminism than heterosexual young women, this issue cannot be adequately addressed with my sample.

One-third (14) of the interviewees had become mothers by the time of the interviews. Ten of these women were single parents, while 4 of them were married. However, nearly all had previously been single parents; only 1 woman was married prior to becoming a parent.

Interviews were conducted face to face, in a place chosen by each participant, and were tape-recorded and transcribed. They ranged from 45 minutes to 3 hours long, although most lasted 1½ hours. The interviews were "structured conversations" (Taylor and Rupp 1991, 126) and allowed space for participants to bring up issues they found to be important. After each interview, I wrote field notes, including the main themes, my reflections, and emerging research questions. A qualitative data analysis program (QSR NUD*IST 1996) facilitated the identification and organization of emergent themes.

The interview guide covered a range of themes related to education, work, family, and feminism (Aronson 1998, 1999). The study relied on grounded theory (Glaser and Strauss 1967). This inductive approach served my purpose well as I left open the possibility of multiple meanings of feminism. In the analysis that follows, using pseudonyms for my respondents, I examine several key issues that emerged during the interviews. First, to provide a context for attitudes toward feminism, I consider two themes about women's treatment by society:

perceptions of opportunities and obstacles, and experiences with gender discrimination. I then explicate the five approaches to feminist identification that came out of my analysis of the interviews.

Perceptions of Opportunities and Obstacles

My interviews revealed a general optimism about women's expanded opportunities, coupled with a realization that older women have struggled to create these new opportunities. At the same time, most (35 out of 42) of the interviewees were quite aware that gender-based obstacles still remained. These perspectives were shared by women of all racial and class backgrounds and life experiences.

Chapter Seven

Truth as Culturally Constructed Realities

Is Postmodernism Just Modernism in Drag?

By Michael Eric Dyson

This interview, conducted by the gifted poet, scholar, and church pianist Jonathan Smith when he was a graduate student, is one of the best I have participated in. Smith's questions are razor-sharp and knowing, smart without being smug, brilliant without being ostentatious. I had great fun in probing the complex dimensions of black culture and in exploring the modern and postmodern implications of black identity. We discuss music, literature, basketball, religion, literary and cultural theory, sexuality, slavery, boxing, masculinity, politics, television, civil rights and race, and a great deal more. It is a tribute to Smith's preparedness that the interview went so well. One can feel the electricity of the lived, dialogic moment, as his enthusiasm for the subjects we discuss contagiously passes to me, allowing me to catch fire and blaze through our exchanges. If I had to point to a single piece of writing that best expresses my ideas about black culture and identity, this would be the one.

The first thing I'd like to ask is: Who is Michael Eric Dyson? And I want you to take the liberty of answering this in a manner that is not strictly auto-biographical. One reason I ask this is because your book jacket begins describing you as "welfare father, ordained Baptist minister, Princeton Ph.D." Then in your chapter on the black public intellectual, you give yourself the shameless self-promotion award.

One of the reasons I take postmodernism so seriously, even as I refuse to make a fetish of its insights, is a notion that has been championed by its theorists, especially in cultural and literary studies: an evolving, fluid identity. What I take from the postmodern conception of identity is captured in the terms beautifully phrased in black Christian circles, namely, "I don't have to be what I once was." That Christian conception of the evolution of character highlights the variability and flexibility of human identity, even if such a view clashes profoundly with postmodern arguments against a fixed human nature on which many Christian conceptions of identity rest. But for black Christians—who are arguably situated deep inside modernism with its impulse to dynamism and disruption, as well as its unyielding quest for the new—and secular postmodernists alike, identity is a process, a continual play of existential choices over a field of unfolding possibility. The self today can be radically different from the self of yesterday.

Taking that seriously, Mike Dyson is an experiment in identity, a testament to a process of evolving self-awareness; some of the elements of my self are surely in conflict, while other fragments of my self are made coherent because they've been sewn together by the threads of history, culture, race, and memory. Who I was, say, ten years ago, was a scholar in the making, and eight or ten years before that, I was a welfare father, a hustler on Detroit's streets, a divorcing husband, a young man who was trying to figure out what to do with his life. I was twenty-one, and I hadn't gone to college or prepared myself academically to take up my vocation. So, who I am is constantly implicated in the themes I take up in my work. What does it mean to be young, black, and male in this country? What are the racial and economic forces that shape black life? How can we achieve racial justice and equality? What does it mean to be an intellectual in a world that prizes image more than substance? How should we treat the vulnerable and the destitute? How can we bridge the psychic and social gulfs between the generations? How can we speak about God in a world where religion has been hijacked by fundamentalists and fascists? How do we untangle the vicious knots of patriarchy, sexism, and misogyny in our nation? How do we affirm and protect gay, lesbian, bisexual, and transgendered people in our communities? All these questions, and many more, play out in my intellectual and political pursuits.

Who I am, then, in many senses, is a bridge builder, a bridge figure. I want to span the streets and the academy, and the sacred and the secular. I also want to bridge traditions and the transformations of those traditions, including religious belief, intellectual engagement, scholarly investigation, racial solidarity, class struggle, resistance to economic oppression, and feminist insurgence. Of course, the parts of my identity that might obviously be in tension, say the academic and the activist, suffer pressure in both directions: the academy is suspicious of the streets, and vice versa. The tension is one of proximity and distance. To the academy, there is the threat of proximity to the chaotic, propulsive, unregulated, sometimes uncivil passions of the world beyond the university. To the denizens of the streets—including its natural constituency of grassroots activists, conspiracy managers, and on-the-ground, indigenous, concrete intellectuals—there is the fear that academics will remain aloof, indifferent to their suffering, and intellectually unavailable to supply strategies to resist their oppression. I want to do the best I can to answer the threat of proximity, not by less but by more interaction between academics and activists, hoping to prove that the interactions benefit the university.

And I want to help heal fears of distance by bringing the resources of intelligence and compassion to bear on the hurts of the socially vulnerable. It is that desire to bridge gulfs that unifies my disparate selves, making me much more sympathetic to the prophetic mystic Howard Thurman, who once prayed to God, "make me unanimous in myself."

I'll ask you then this question. Baldwin in *Giovanni's Room* says: "Perhaps home is not a place but an irrevocable condition." In *South to a Very Old Place*, Albert Murray begins with this thought: "But then, going back home has probably always had as much if not more to do with people as with landmarks and place names and locations on maps and mileage charts anyway. Not that home is not a place, for even in its most abstract implications it is precisely the very oldest place in the world. But even so, it is somewhere you are likely to find yourself remembering your way back to far more often than it is ever possible to go by conventional transportation." Given that, in that context, where do you feel most at home?

Yes. Yes. Good question, man. Well, as both of these writers make clear, home is about the geography of imagination. For me, it's also about the architecture of identity through aspiration and yearning, since home is carved from hope and memory. It is both forward-looking and backward leaning. And that means that home is not simply a place forever anchored by concrete foundations. It is not simply a fixed point with tangible coordinates in space and time. Home is a metaphysical possibility that seeds the ground of experience and infuses our finite encounters in local spaces with meaning. That's why Burt Bacharach's writing partner, Hal David, could pen a lyric that makes the philosophical argument that "a house is not a home," distinguishing the two by the quality of relations that turn the former into the latter. Like identity, home, to a large degree, is composed of an evolving awareness about how you can decrease the discomfort you have in the world as a result of your roots. That's why our foreparents spoke of "a house not made with hands," as it says in 1 Corinthians, casting biblical language in their own religious accents. And they suggested that this world "ain't no friend to grace," since it was alienated from God's purpose. For a people who were often homeless—rootless and adrift in a sea of chattel slavery, and later, exploitative sharecropping—home assumed a high priority. That's why many of our foreparents hoped for a day when they could, in the words of one slave, "read my title clear." Home had intense metaphoric value for our foreparents in another way: as the imagined space of unlimited access to God in heaven, a place they hoped to go after they died, signified in songwriter Charles Tindley's familiar refrain in black Christian circles, "I'll make it home, someday."

Of course, there are dangers to the notion of home in black life as well, especially when it comes to elevating one's imagined geography of spirit, one's own sense of home, as the sole source of authentic blackness. After all, roots are meant to nourish, not strangle, us. I'm thinking in particular of the vicious debates raging in many black communities about what is really black, how we define it, and how the spaces of black identity are linked increasingly to a narrow slice of black turf—the ghetto. Our kids are literally dying over a profound misunderstanding about our culture that links authenticity to geography, that makes one believe that if she is black, she must pledge ultimate allegiance to the ghetto as the sole black home of the black subject. The exclusive identification of the ghetto as the authentic black home is wholly destructive.

Out of this grows the "keep it real" trope that punishes any departure from a lethally limited vision of black life, one that trades on stereotype and separation anxiety, since there is a great fear of being severed from the fertile ground of the true black self. But to subscribe to these beliefs is to be woefully misled. Sure, the beauty of the impulse to authenticity is altogether understandable: to protect a black identity that has been assaulted by white supremacy through the assertion of a uniquely guarded and qualified black self, rooted in a similarly protected view of the authentic black home. Plus, too many blacks who "made it" have surely forgotten "where they came from." But the legitimate critique of blacks besieged by what may be termed *Aframnesia*—the almost systematic obliteration of the dangerous memory of black suffering and racial solidarity, a gesture that is usually rewarded by white elites—is different from imposing rigid views on black life of how and where blackness erupts or emerges. Thus we end up with vicious mythologies and punishing pieties: for instance, one cannot be gay and be authentically black in some circles, which means there's no home, no place of grace in many black communities for black homosexuals. Or the black male assault on black female interests is justified as the necessary subordination of gender to race in the quest for liberation. Or the only real black is in the ghetto, a ghetto that in the social imagination of its romantic advocates rarely looks like the complex, complicated, contradictory place it is. As a former resident of the ghetto, I wholeheartedly concur with the notion that we can neither forget its people nor neglect its social redemption through strategic action. Further, I think it's beautiful for folk who have survived the ghetto, who've gotten out, to carry the blessed image of its edifying dimensions in their hearts and imaginations, and to pledge to never leave the ghetto even as they travel millions of miles beyond its geographical boundaries. That means that they'll never betray the wisdom, genius, and hope that floods the ghetto in ways that those outside its bounds rarely understand. It is, after all, a portable proposition, a mobile metaphor. But we must not seize on the most limited view possible of ghetto life and sanctify it as the be-all and end-all of black existence. That leads to kids killing each other in the name of an authentic ghetto masculinity that is little more than pathological self-hatred. The black ghetto working class, the working poor, and the permanently poor have always been more complex, and more resilient, than they have ever been given credit for. We've got to avoid the trap of existential puniness and racial infantilism and see our way to a robustly mature vision that shatters the paradigm of the authentic black self and, by extension, the acceptable black home.

Given that analysis, I feel most at home in the intersection of all the energies provoked by my different roles, as preacher, teacher, public intellectual, political activist, agent provocateur, and paid pest. In one sense, I couldn't rest all of my energy in one place doing one thing; the ability to do them all gives me the vocational patience to do any of them. And I feel a sense of transgression, a sense of irreverence (and to my mind, those are good qualities) in fulfilling all these roles that gives me, oddly enough, a feeling of being at home, because I feel I'm being truest to myself when I vigorously, and critically, engage my various communities of interest or, as the anthropologists say, my multiple kinship groups. For instance, I love to preach, and whenever I get the chance, I'm in a pulpit on Sunday morning "telling the story," as black ministers elegantly phrase preaching the gospel. For all of its problems and limitations, the black pulpit, at its best, is still the freest, most powerful, most radically autonomous place on earth for black people to encourage each other in the job of critical self-reflection and the collective struggle for liberation. I think theologian Robert McAfee Brown put it best when he said the church is like Noah's ark: if it wasn't for the storm on the outside, we couldn't stand the stink on the inside.

But the stink in the black church is surely foul. There are still a lot of negative beliefs about gender and sexual orientation, and even class, that need to be addressed. There are big pockets of staunchly conservative sentiment that, I think, have to be opposed. I try not to avoid these subjects as I preach, and sometimes what I say goes over like a brick cloud! Still, I try to seduce people into seeing things differently, as I make arguments about why the opposition to gay and lesbian folk, for instance, reeks of the same biblical literalism that smashed the hopes of black slaves when white slave masters deployed it. But I try to win the folk over first, by preaching "in the tradition," so to speak, warming them up first before I lower the boom. When I was a young preacher and pastor, one of my members told me you "gain more by honey than vinegar." So I give honey before I give vinegar. I invite the folk to the progressive theological, ideological, and spiritual terrain I want them to occupy, but I try to issue that invitation in ways that won't immediately alienate them. And once they're there, they're a captive audience.

One gains his bona fides by preaching well, evoking "amens" by articulately referencing the black religious tradition, and this can be done with little fear of surrendering the politics I favor. The rhetorical forms are themselves neutral, so to speak, and thus the political uses to which they're put is something that's strictly TBD: to be determined by the rhetor, the prophet, the priest, the speaker, or the pastor. Then when I've got them where I want them, rhetorically speaking, in a velvet verbal vice, I squeeze hard, using the good feeling and theological credit I've gained from preaching well to assault the beliefs that are problematic, from homophobia, sexism, patriarchy, ageism, racism, and classism to environmental inequities. And sometimes, they're giving assent against their wills, shouting amen to ideas that they may not have otherwise supported without being pushed or prodded—or seduced. They might even muse to themselves, "Well, he's got a point," or "I disagree, but I'll at least think about it." But as much as I love the black church, and see it as my home, it's too narrow to be my only home. That's why I claim the classroom, the lectern, and the academy as my home as well, a place I love immensely, but the inbred snobbishness and well-worn elitism of elements of this home mean that I can't rest my entire self there either. I'm involved in both mainstream and radical politics, but elements of the latter are hostile to the spiritual traditions I cherish, which means my home in such circles is not one that accommodates my entire being. So I float among all of these stations of identification, so to speak. My home, while certainly not carved from a process of elimination—cutting away features I find unattractive, offensive, or burdensome in each "home"—is certainly the product of a stance of critical appreciation that allows me to derive benefit, pleasure, and sustenance from each space.

So I conceive of home as a moveable feast of identity that I'm constantly feeding on. Because of the many communities in which I'm involved, I'm constantly rethinking who I am. In a way, I'm also constantly trying to get back home to Detroit, perhaps in a more spiritual than physical manner, since I go back fairly frequently to preach and visit my mother and brothers. There's an elusive state of contentment that you nostalgically associate with home even when it was a turbulent and trying place. Detroit was, in many ways, such a place far me, but it also provided so much joy and fulfillment, and it gave me a sense of the appropriate things to grasp hold of in life, beyond the material blessings one might seek. It was a great beginning, and as I heard Toni Morrison once say, beginnings are important because they must do so much more than start. While starting is crucial, beginnings also propel us along paths of influence whose real impact we may not be able to detect for years and years to come. That's certainly the case with me.

Detroit has become for me a metaphor of the complex convergence of fate and human volition. It's a symbol for me of how destiny is at best partly determined by living one's life in a meaningful, coherent fashion. That's most acutely obvious to me in grappling with my brother's imprisonment and my quest for improvement in every sphere of my life, including my professional life, my spiritual infrastructure, and my moral landscape. Home is a complicated place for me now, which is why nostalgia is inevitable, pleasurable, even desirable—and quite problematic, perhaps dangerous at points. Nostalgia, of course, is crucial to the project of black identity, largely as a defensive move against the brutal memories of suffering we endured at the hands of those outside our communities, and from within. Nostalgia, at least in that light, is an attempt to exercise sovereignty over memory, to force it into redemptive channels away from the tributaries of trauma that flood the collective black psyche. It is the attempt to rescue ethical agency and hence manage and control the perception of suffering—from the fateful forces of racial terror. One of the most bruising racial terrors is to have the dominant culture determine what memories are most important to the dominated minority.

In that case, nostalgia is an attempt to take back the political utility of memory. After all, if you remember a horrible experience as something from which you can squeeze some good, then you've refused the hegemonic power the prerogative to define your fate. By remembering the same event with different accents, with different social purposes, through different eyes, one gives memory a racial and moral usefulness that can challenge dominant culture. I suspect that's at stake when black folk wax nostalgic about segregation and the sort of relatively self-determining culture we were able to carve out of Jim Crow apartheid. You hear it as black folk say, "When we were forced to live together under segregation, we had more unity, we lived in the same neighborhoods, we helped each other more, economically and spiritually, and we did not depend on white patronage but promoted black self-reliance. Now under desegregation we've lost the power we had. Our colleges have suffered a brain drain to elite white schools. Our black businesses that catered to black needs suffered when we were able to buy white. And our neighborhoods were turned over to the poor and destitute when 'white flight' was mimicked by 'black track' to the suburbs."

The downside of such nostalgia is that it fails to explicitly engage the radical inequality of such segregated arrangements. It also tends to exaggerate the moral differences between generations, especially as the rose-colored tint of the black past is not used to cast an eye on the present or the future, for that matter. The net result is that one's own generation is made golden, while those following are seen as tarnished by the surrender to urges, forces, and seductions that were heroically resisted in the past. Hence jazz was great and hip-hop is awful. People believe that even though earlier black generations thought jazz was terrible and preferred religious music. But there were problems there too, since many blacks felt that religious music too easily compromised its purity by integrating elements from secular blues. And it goes on and on. Then too, we've got to be careful not to ultimately justify or legitimate the oppression by nostalgically recalling its good effects. Nostalgic blacks end up reinforcing what may be termed subversive empathy from the dominant culture, which, after all, provided the conditions under which our race and culture could thrive under segregation, even if those conditions were harmful and oppressive.

Subversive empathy is similar, I suppose, to anthropologist Renato Rosaldo's notion of imperialist nostalgia, where hegemonic culture destroys an indigenous minority tradition and then has the gall to weep with those folk over the destruction of their culture. In subversive empathy, the dominant culture empathizes with our need to restore the conditions of our relative prospering under Jim Crow. While not explicitly invoking a return to the racist past, it nevertheless puts forth arguments and supports practices that have the same effect. That's why black folk have to be especially cautious about supporting Bill Bennett's partnership with C. Delores Tucker in combating hard-core hip-hop. They appeal to a golden age: nostalgic belief about the black family that is turned viciously against us in Bennett's conservative cosmology. For that matter, we ought to be careful about uncritically celebrating Bill Clinton's nostalgic appeal to black America to return to a bygone moral era. In a speech before a black religious audience in Memphis, Tennessee, Clinton invoked Martin Luther King Jr.'s memory to chide black America about pockets of immorality in our communities and pathological family structure, ignoring the harmful social impact of many of his policies on the black family. He sounds like a friend, and in many ways he is, but he is also a foe to our best political interests. His political beliefs, in many ways, are emblematic of subversive empathy.

If the impulse to nostalgia is not disciplined, it can be used to fashion moral judgments out of fantasies of the past that downplay our failures and project them more vehemently on someone, or something, else. A huge example is how older blacks nostalgically recall their idyllic lives in comparison to the ills of modern youth, assaulting their relative moral failures while extolling their own virtues.

But to sum it all up, I suppose home conjures for me that Frankie Beverly anthem, "Joy and Pain." But it remains the quintessential space of possibility, of hope, of unending yearning and unfulfilled expectation.

I guess I'd like to hear you talk about that notion in relation to this generation you belong to, "the betweeners"—very late baby boomers and very early generation x or hip-hop. This also, in the academy, seems to stand right at that modern-postmodern divide. When I hear you talk about your relationship to home, I hear an important question about history and home, time and home. I'm the minister of music at my church, so you

know that when I show up with the dread thing going on and I play for the senior choir, there is this odd sense of dissonance and I feel completely at home there even though there are some looking at me as if to say "What's wrong with that brother?" But there's this odd sort of thing that goes on because where you are is always where you feel most at home. I imagine that that's what happens to you when you're in the pulpit: that it's the most natural home, but when you walk out into the classroom there is no rupture. But given our notions of race and culture and some of our stereotypes, it seems as if people would expect there to be a rupture, but there isn't.

No, no. In that sense it's seamless for me, moving from one rhetorical situation to another, from the pulpit as the axis of convergence of history, spirituality, and morality, to the classroom, where there are other axes of convergence, including inquiry, skepticism, and excavation. The orbits of these rhetorical universes might be seen to be in collision with one another. But skillful black rhetoricians, speakers, teachers, intellectuals, and orators can, by virtue of an enchanted imagination, speak worlds of discourse into existence that cross disciplinary fault lines, that move among genres, and that navigate through discursive minefields, such as the question of what constitutes "real knowledge." At its base, black culture has always been about migration and mobility. Its members, in one way or another, have been about the business of adapting ourselves to foreign spaces and creating home in the midst of them. We've constantly raised the question of Psalm 147, "How can we sing Zion's songs in a strange land?" To borrow more biblical imagery, the book of Acts contains that famous passage about Paul and his mates being shipwrecked and making it to shore "on broken pieces." Black people have always been able to take the fragments and shards of our lives, the pieces of our existence broken by oppression, and rework them into a pattern of purposeful existence. That's not simply about fragmentation as a trope of black existence in the postmodern moment. It's also about the black modernist quest for a stable identity in the midst of flux and upheaval, often articulated, ironically enough, through a premodern religious worldview.

Thus the premodern black biblical universe accommodates black modernist pursuits in postmodern conditions. "Making it in on broken pieces" has long been a rhetorical staple in the grassroots theodicies—in both the Weberian, sociological sense and in theological terms—that shape the preaching of figures from C. L. Franklin, Aretha Franklin's father, to Jesse Jackson. Add to that the fragments of European cultural influences and African cultural retentions that shape black life, and the unavoidability of black folk negotiating between disparate vocabularies, indeed, different worlds, should be dramatically apparent. I think that Levis-Strauss's notion of bricolage, of taking what's at hand, what's left over, so to speak, in the construction of culture to shape one's survival and identity, is a crucial concept as well in coming to terms with this black gift to move in and through a variety of rhetorics and discourses. In that sense, then, our identities have always been fabricated out of the content of our surroundings. Forced migration and permanent exile will make one into a sophisticated cultural polyglot and sometimes into a cosmopolitan citizen. Home was often a compromise of contexts: wherever we found ourselves, we made that home or at least we transported our home there. Home was not something we could leave and come to again, so home often had to travel with us, across turbulent waters, into hostile countries, and within resistive communities.

That's not to deny the reality of fixed points of domestic reference in time and space, and in body and memory. But the reality is that black people had to have multiple notions of home, and often multiple homes, which is why there's a thin line between coerced migration and homelessness. You've got to remember that home is a noun, verb, adjective, and adverb, and it is both a means and an end. So the lack of a sense of rupture grows from the seamless interweaving of multiple meanings articulated through a variety of rhetorical situations, whether it's preaching, teaching, writing, and so on. In my case, I can't deny that at some points all the communities I'm involved in may experience tension and conflict because I don't feel a radical rupture in moving from one vocabulary to another. But as Gerald Graff argues, we've got to teach the conflicts, and by extension we've got to illustrate the tensions. For me, that means we've got to mix rhetorical styles in edifying fashion. So when I get up in the classroom, for instance, and I really get going, talking about Foucault and Derrida, perhaps, and about Judith Butler, and about Stuart Hall and his distinction between preferred meanings versus negotiated meanings and oppositional meanings, my intellectual excitement translates to my verbal style and energizes my peculiar semantic trace. And my Baptist roots begin to nourish my oratorical engagement, and before I know it, I'm preaching postmodernism.

So here you have a professor with a staccato rhythm and a tuneful cadence who's invested in the articulation of postmodern conceptualizations of identity and power. I'm baptizing my lecture in the rhetorical waters of my religious tradition. There is no rupture, no discontinuity, nothing but seamless negotiations between diverse styles of intellectual and rhetorical engagement. There may be problems for interlocutors who believe that an etiquette of articulation should prevail, one that polices style and dictates proprietary usage. But I ain't with that, so there's no problem for me. The irony is that even in this so-called postmodernist moment, which ostensibly celebrates pastiche, fragmentation, collage, difference, irreverent fusions, and the like, black style remains problematic. When black identity marks postmodernity with its embodied articulation, there's a rupture going on in the midst of the rupturing context itself. It involves the problem that has confronted us in premodernity, modernity, and postmodernity: race, and more specifically, the issue of blackness and its unwieldy complement of transgressing expressions.

Yes. There seems always to be this move to delegitimize, to make it …

Literally illegal.

I remember my first semester as an undergraduate at Princeton. So, to my mind, this white guy says to me, How are you ever going to go home again? Aren't you afraid that these people won't understand?

Yes, would have to unbirth you …

There's some rupture. I've thought about this black Ivy League tradition that we seem to silence. Although we celebrate these people, we silence the fact that they were educated in and present at these institutions at the same time as the Eliots, Stevenses, Santayanas, and Jameses. Inhabiting the same physical space.

That's exactly right. And that's why postmodernity is so crucial, at least in theory: it helps us uncover and claim the useful legacies of modernism that were submerged in its racial silences. Of course, it could be that postmodernism is really modernism in drag. As you said, when you think of modernism, you think of Eliot and Stevens. And as you noted, you think of Santayana and James too, and we could add Royce, just to keep the Harvard modernists in line. And we could add Joyce, Pound, Frost, Crane, and a host of others. Gender got a strong foothold in the modernist canon in a way that race was never quite able to do, with figures like Marianne Moore, Virginia Woolf, Rebecca West, and Djuna Barnes. But at the same time, W.E.B. Du Bois is right in the middle of modernism, along with Countee Cullen, Langston Hughes, Zora Neale Hurston, Dorothy West, Richard Wright, Chester Himes, Ralph Ellison, James Baldwin, and many, many more. They were all thinking, writing, imagining, and populating black universes, even as many of them insisted that it was impossible to limn the American experience without viewing the nation through the eyes of blacks who were more American than African, as Ellison contended, or as they emphasized the universal moral impulse that echoes through black demands for dignity and humanity, as Baldwin argued.

The black modernists were attempting to breathe freely beyond the claustrophobic boundaries of race, trying to refigure black identity and, by extension, American identity. Yet they're always seen in these boxed, fixed, localized categories, when indeed they're trying to help us reimagine the project of America: "I, too, sing America," as Hughes sang, ringing a change, varying a theme, signifying upon and harkening metaphorically back to Walt Whitman's "I sing the body electric." Hughes and the great black modernists inserted black America into the mainstream flow and thereby proved that America must bend itself to our tune, song, riff, beat, meter, prose, rhythm, and the like in order to be truly, fully, wholly itself. For instance, Duke Ellington and Louis Armstrong swung in the mainstream and then swung the mainstream to a black rhythm, and through their music, helped America grasp the self-enlarging principle of subordinating color to culture and craft. Hughes was aggressively insinuating himself, and black folk, into the American stream of consciousness, into the American song—much like King would later do with the American dream—and thus proving that our meters hypnotically swayed the nation to our virtuosic, vernacular voices. Hughes locates the context of the development of his identity in those physical spaces in his American "home" where he is expelled to feed his growing self-awareness on the leftovers of racial exclusion.

But he flips the script. He grows strong on the negative diet of marginality that he turns into a wholesome meal of aesthetic and moral combat against white supremacy, especially its failure to recognize black beauty of every sort. So Hughes in his poem talks about being sent to the kitchen to eat, "When company comes." But he eats well, grows strong, and pledges that when company comes again, he'll be at the table and that no one will dare scold him for his presence and send him to the kitchen, because, "They'll see how beautiful I am / And be ashamed—." And then he ends by declaring, "I, too, am America." So there's a significant shift from singing America to being America, from performance to enactment. And the company, to extend my reading of modernism through Hughes's poem, is Wallace Stevens, T.S. Eliot, Hart Crane, James Joyce, Marianne Moore, and so on, grand figures whose large egos dominate the psychic rooms and intellectual tables of American modernism. At the same time, the black subject, the black ego, the black self, is shunted to the kitchen.

So what Langston Hughes does is articulate the fixed space of his own modernist identity—the kitchen, metaphorically speaking—as the locus classicus of American identity, because when you're in the kitchen, the smell of the food wafts beyond its borders. When you're in the kitchen cooking—and Hughes was cooking, really he was smoking, burning, or whatever term one might conjure from the culinary arts as a symbol of black vernacular for achieving broad excellence—the smells will pull people in to ask, "Hmm, where's that smell coming from? What's cooking in the kitchen?" If you had to be somewhere away from the dining room or living room, it was crucial to be exiled to the kitchen. This is what black folk knew, especially as they served as domestics, butlers, and cooks. Black moderns turned their limited, localized spaces into rhetorical, musical, aesthetic, political, or spiritual kitchens that emitted pleasing smells and seductive scents, so that people who picked up on them were immediately, irresistibly drawn to them. That's the language ...

To pick up on that, even if they don't come to the kitchen, the kitchen has to come to them. They are sitting at the table waiting for the kitchen to come to them. The kitchen produces that which they consume for nourishment.

There you go, man. Metaphor is power.

I'd like to push a little away from that now and turn to something that seemed to resonate in an earlier comment you made about black rhetoricians and the premodernist Christian tradition as it relates to black resistance. The notion of speaking things that are not as though they were ... this is not a space of acquiescence, but of resistance.

Oh, exactly right. That's very important and I'll just say something briefly about it. Too often, we read the history of black resistance, and the speech or action that supported it, through a distorted lens. Either black folk were for or against oppression, either they cooperated or resisted, and we can tell all of this in dramatically demonstrable fashion. Well, it's not quite that simple. Life has put black folk in complex, often compromising positions, especially during slavery, post-Reconstruction, and Jim Crow. Many folk were not able to outwardly resist, not simply for fear of reprisal but because to do so would have undermined their long-term plans of survival and liberation. Black folk en masse had to survive, even under conditions of harsh oppression, so that they could produce black folk who could liberate us. Their survival tactics had to be hidden, concealed to the larger white world, masked to the oppressor. These networks of hidden meanings and concealed articulations were the predicate of black survival through a signifying, symbolic culture. For instance, many of the sorrow songs of the slaves contained dual meanings. While the white masses found the songs entertaining, the slaves simultaneously signaled each other about plans for emancipation. In effect, they were, as the title of the book aptly summarizes it, *Puttin' on ol Massa*. The patterned quilts that slaves made contained crucial directions to black slaves seeking to ride the Underground Railroad to freedom. In a sense, they evoked the principle that later underlay Edgar Allen Poe's famous short story, "Purloined Letter," since the stolen missive was hidden in plain sight.

The very act of imagination was critical to strategies of resistance and proved dangerous to the hegemonic white world order. That's why the white world was so intent on controlling the black imagination, as far as such a thing was possible, by restricting its enabling mechanisms, particularly those rooted in literacy. Reading and writing were outlawed, and even earlier in slavery, blacks were divided from other blacks from the same tribe during the "seasoning" process so they couldn't effectively communicate. If blacks learned to read and write, they might grow restless with their degraded status, gaining a false and subversive sense of equality with whites. Of course, Frederick Douglass perhaps confirmed the worst fears of the white overclass when he reported in his autobiography that knowledge "unfits a child" for slavery. And if slaves spoke to each other without strict supervision, they might hatch plans to escape, so their speech and social organization were regularly policed.

But black slaves were able to carve out free spaces of intimate contact and communication that promoted racial solidarity and forms of resistance that eluded the master's ear and eye. Still, dominant whites rightly viewed the black imagination as a wedge between slaves and their oppression. The act of imagining a world of liberty was threatening. I think in this regard of a humorous statement that Muhammad Ali made about an opponent when he said, "If Sonny Liston dreams he can beat me, he better wake up and apologize." That's a brilliant gloss on the function of imagination and dreaming in black combat, and in the struggle for self-assertion and mastery of one's opponent. The attempt to regulate the black imagination is the attempt to restrict acts of black self-reinvention through dreaming of a different world where justice and freedom prevailed. That's why black folk were full of dangerous dreaming, insurrectionist imagining, and resistive revisions. The act of conceiving of an alternative world, a racial utopia, was a gesture of radical resistance that interrupted the totalizing force of white supremacy.

And a question of values, which we'll return to later. I want to push you in the direction here of talking about black bodies. Black male bodies, black women's bodies. One of the things that enters my mind here is the notion of the black masculine journey. To my mind, Morrison's *Song of Solomon* ranks right up there with Ellison's *Invisible Man* as a benchmark text for black masculinity. It's the condition our condition is in ...

Right, it's rough all over.

To me, this statement has to do with black male bodies in everything from the Million Man March to Dennis Rodman.

Oh, no question. It's almost a cliché to say by now, but black masculinity is one of the most insightful and complex texts of American identity. For instance, millions want to, as the commercial slogan says, "Be like Mike." They're in awe of Michael Jordan, asking themselves what it is like to inhabit that pigment, that physiology, that 6'6" body whose ligaments, whose alignment of muscles determine the semblance of flight that folk around the globe vicariously identity with. Michael Jordan's head, clean shaven with those two ears poking out, at once conjures E.T.—the extraterrestrial—a sports spectacle, an incredible genius that we can scarcely imagine while also signifying the globe—round and smooth. And what can be written on its surfaces is always something that can be erased and rewritten. At the same time, that black masculine head is a signifier of the power of the black phallus. In an interesting, perhaps even subversive fashion, Michael Jordan's physical and aesthetic genius can be symbolized as a massive phallus whose seminal meanings explode on American culture, fertilizing a range of barren cultural landscapes with creative expression.

His body is a contradictory text of black masculinity. Jordan is at once embraced and fed upon as a Michael Jordan burger at McDonald's. He's being eaten by the masses, consumed, symbolically speaking. So the closest they may be able to get to Mike, besides watching him and emulating his moves on the court in their neighborhood playgrounds, sports gyms, or health clubs, is to purchase a symbolic portion of his body and consume it in market culture. It's a kind of secular Eucharist, where, at least in Protestant theology, the sacramental elements of Christ's body and blood are substituted by wafer and wine, or in Catholic theology, these elements are transubstantiated into the actual body and blood of Christ. Jordan's body is symbolically transmuted, through the material conditions of the political economy of consumption, into an edible commodity.

Or think of the symbolic and contested body of another prominent and complicated black man, the late rapper Tupac Shakur. Tupac's dead but still signifying body has the potential to become one of the first black candidates for cultural survival. I don't mean survival in the sense that he remains a vital cultural influence, like Martin Luther King Jr. I mean cultural presence beyond death through the articulation of a mythological body that defies mortality through urban legend, such as what has happened with James Dean, John F. Kennedy, Marilyn Monroe, and Elvis Presley. Particularly in the case of Elvis, there's a literal quality to his mythological persistence, since tabloid magazines claim to spot him, or JFK, on an island somewhere avoiding their fans, the media, and especially their "past" lives. I've often wondered why no one ever saw Sam Cooke, for instance, or Otis Redding, Dinah Washington, or Donny Hathaway. Tupac may be the first black figure to ascend to such heights—or depending on how one views this cultural phenomenon, to the depths—of pop memorialization.

I must confess I'm an addict, although I hope a critical one, of tabloids like the *National Enquirer* and *Star Magazine,* although since the same company that owns the *Enquirer* purchased *Star,* they often recycle the same information. Without overinterpreting or rationalizing their appeal, I think, at their best—and I place best in scare quotes—these tabloids offer counterhegemonic narratives to prevailing cultural truths. Besides that, they allow ordinary people to sound as if they're speaking the King's English to the Queen's taste. Instead of presenting an "informant" as saying, "I got afraid when I thought about that stuff later on," they sound more formal, more literate, and might be quoted as saying, "It startled me as I pondered it later."

But in the tabloids, Elvis is spotted in California somewhere, Elvis is in some secluded villa in Italy, Marilyn has joined J FK in what only appears to be a posthumous romp on the Riviera, while black icons remain sequestered in their unsexy, earthbound mortality. I think that Tupac may be the first black icon to join the pantheon of the posthumously alive, people who symbolically defeat their own death through episodic appearances in the mythological landscape. Folk are now saying that Tupac is not dead, but alive somewhere in Cuba, perhaps enjoying a stogie with Fidel. There are Web sites and chat rooms all over the Internet dedicated to debating whether Tupac is dead or is hanging out on some Caribbean retreat to escape the cruel demands of fame. His cultural survival says a great deal about how black masculinity can come to signify contested social and political meanings that erupt in popular culture.

When I think about contemporary black masculinity, I can't help reflecting on another intriguing, contradictory, infuriatingly complex figure: Dennis Rodman. In fact, he's helping redraw the boundaries of black masculinity in the most archetypically black masculine sport there is, basketball. Basketball has arguably replaced baseball as the paradigmatic expression of the highly mythologized American identity, since sport is a crucial means by which America regenerates its collective soul and reconceives its democratic ideals, to borrow Emersonian language. Basketball also has elements of spontaneity; individual genius articulated against the background of group success; and the coalescence of independent creative gestures in a collective expression of athletic aspiration. In a sense, basketball provides a canvas on which American identity can be constantly redrawn. The cultural frameworks of American identity, especially American masculinity, are being symbolically renegotiated in black masculine achievement in basketball.

Dennis Rodman has the sublime audacity to challenge the codes of masculinity at the heart of black masculine culture in the most visible art form, besides hiphop culture, available to black men. He transgresses against heterosexist versions of machismo that dominate black sport. For instance, he wears fingernail polish and he occasionally cross-dresses in advertisements and public relations stunts, wearing a wedding gown in its white purity against that 6'9" brown body that "the Worm," as he's nicknamed, inhabits. Even his nickname signifies; it suggests the burrowing of an earth-bound insect into the hidden spaces of the soil, deep beneath the surface of things. And it's not as if Rodman were a marginal figure. He's acknowledged as the most gifted rebounder in the N BA today, and one of the greatest of all time. His specialty is unavoidably representative. He's constantly grabbing the ball off the backboard, taking shots that are left over from the failed attempt to score, enhancing the ability of the team to win. His genius on the court is, in précis, a symbolic articulation of black masculine identity; it is a major trope of black masculinity, since black men are constantly "on the rebound," and "rebounding" from some devastating ordeal. Black men are continually taking missed shots off the glass, off the backboard, and feeding them in outlet or bounce passes to some high-flying teammate who is able to score on the opposition. Ordinary and iconic black men are constantly helping American society to rebound from one catastrophe or another and to successfully overcome the opposition in scoring serious points, serious arguments, serious goals.

This is precisely why you are reviled in some circles. This reading of Dennis Rodman, with which I agree wholeheartedly. Consider me now as the organist who plays those chords behind the sermon. Dennis Rodman is terribly fascinating. I laughed uproariously to see him show up with arched eyebrows and fingernail polish in the championship series on the day after wearing a boa to his book signing. And here he is performing the dirtiest, roughest, most "masculine" aspects of the game for his team.

He's inscribing those aspects in the text of black masculinity—because 80 percent of the players in the N BA now are black, so we have to talk about it as a black man's game. Dennis Rodman's relationship to basketball is similar to disco's relationship to American music, and especially black pop music. The black gay aesthetic informed the construction of the post-R&B era before the rise of hip-hop culture. It was widely reviled, although it is now being reexcavated in popular culture for archetypal images of American identity. Disco focused on the rhythm as opposed to the substance of the words; it highlighted the rhythmic capacity of the voice against the lyrical content of what was being articulated. Disco culture was about a kind of rapturous and transgressive move against the sexual segregation of gay and lesbian bodies in social space. It was about the freedom and ecstasy of dance where clubs became sanctuaries for the secular worship of the deities of disco: rhythm, carnival, play, movement, and sexualized funk, elements that helped its adherents choreograph an aural erotopia. Those streaming, swirling globe lights that fixed on the dance floor assured that artifice was taken as the ultimate reality. I guess you could say in a sense that Sylvester got a hold of Baudrillard. The way that disco prefigures and precipitates a postmodern American sensibility often gets erased. Disco was dissed because its black gay aesthetic vogued against what was in vogue, and therefore its sexual transgression was the subtext, or what they call in philosophy the suppressed premise, of the logic of an ostensibly "straight" black pop musical culture.

Dennis Rodman's effect is comparable. He's the suppressed premise of the logic of black masculinity's prominence in basketball. So he helps to construct the public face of black masculinity along with Connie Hawkins, George Gervin, Earl "the Pearl" Monroe, Walt "Clyde" Frazier, Julius "Dr. J" Erving, Earvin "Magic" Johnson, Charles Barkley, and Michael Jordan. Through Dennis Rodman's body of work, the homoerotic moment within sport, and especially within black masculine athleticism, surfaces: Patting one another on the behind to say "good game" or "good play," hugging and kissing one another, falling into each other's sweating arms to boost camaraderie, and so on. This is a sexualized choreography of suppressed black desire and the way it is portrayed from the gridiron to the hardwood floor, pun intended! Dennis Rodman's figure invites us to see that homoeroticism has a lot to do, ironically enough, with the seminal production of black masculine athletic identities. The homoerotic and gay sensibility, contrary to popular perception, doesn't stop—and certainly in his case may even fuel—great athletic and masculine achievement. My God! The brother is an outlaw in what was formerly an outlaw and, racially speaking at least, outlawed sport.

There was a time, remember, when blacks weren't allowed to play professional basketball. When they were relatively early in their tenure in the NBA, in the early 1970s, *Ebony* magazine did an annual article that featured every black player on every team, something unimaginable today. And don't forget that the New York Knickerbockers during this time were called by racist fans the New York "Niggerbockers" because of the presence of Frazier, Monroe, Willis Reed, Dick "Fall Back Baby" Barnett, and Henry Bibby. Rodman's homoeroticized black athletic body is "outlaw(ed)" in several simultaneously signifying fashions, so to speak. The outlaw and the rebel, with apologies to Eric Hobsbawm, are countercultural figures whose lives embody the hidden and contradictory ethical aspirations of the masses, or at least some of them, even if the masses are not altogether aware of, or don't consciously identify with, the ideals the outlaw or rebel embodies. So Dennis Rodman is performing a kind of above ground "dream work" for the collective sexual unconscious of black masculinity. What Dennis Rodman's example shows is that even as black masculine culture overtly represses sexual difference and attempts to conceal or mystify homoerotic elements and behavior, it often depends on that very homoerotic dimension for athletic entertainment.

This homophobic dimension would seem to explain why most groups distance themselves from Rodman. Black people explain his absurdities by pointing to his time in Oklahoma. White people can point to his black urban ghetto origins. He thus seems to be an unusual signifier who can be whatever you need him to be. In other words, there are no false statements you can make about Dennis Rodman.

He's a successor next to Michael Jackson, in that sense. Not only is what you say about Dennis Rodman true, but what you say about Dennis Rodman is what you say about yourself. Even as you try to read Dennis Rodman, you're reading yourself. There's a relationship between ethnography and epiphany, between selfrevelation and the excavation of the other.

To talk for a moment of this modern/postmodern divide about which you spoke earlier, could you talk for a moment of how your intellectual development has been affected by television and cyberspace. When I look back over Walter Benjamin's "Art in the Age of Mechanical Reproduction," I think to myself how differently he might have perceived things in the face of television.

I think immediately of what legendary singer and spoken word artist Gil Scott-Heron famously said, "The Revolution Will Not Be Televised." Well, in many ways, it has been televised, except the revolution about which he spoke has been replaced by the revolution of the medium itself. It's like Marshall McLuhan meets Barney Fife. I'm a child of television, even though my mother tells me that early on when I was mad at my family because I wanted to read a lot, I'd say, "Y'all don't read enough, you watch too much TV." I think it's God's joke on me that part of my life as a cultural critic is to be an analyst of television. Television has very deeply influenced my understanding of pop culture and my intellectual development in the sense that I take it as another very powerful text that we have to read, that we have to interpret, that we have to consume. I think that my self-understanding certainly has been to a degree both shaped by and articulated against the images, ideas, and ideologies on television, as they enable an on sight—and that's deliberately ambiguous for me, both s-i-g-h-t and s-i-t-e—negotiation of black identity. The evolution of television, along with the evolution and influence of film, sport, and music, has coincided with the evolution of the popular conception of black people in this country.

Besides its effect on my intellectual development and the professional pleasure it has provided me in reading its various texts, television has also extended an outlet to me to advocate social change, analyze culture, and argue about ideas. I know that's not the sense you meant by your question, but it leads me to reflect on another reason I'm drawn to TV, I think it's a legitimate medium through which to educate the public and to disrupt, subvert, and transgress against hegemonic forces. First of all, I talk so fast, which is both a good and bad thing for television. I can get a great deal in during a five-minute span on a news or talk show, and even more when I've got more time. On the other hand, I know I should slow down sometimes, but sometimes I'm really suspicious of slowing down. I sometimes prefer the machine-gun approach, given the often coarse and certainly fast-paced nature of television time and rhetoric. So, on occasion, the staccato, rapid-fire rhetorical style I have is usefully unfettered on television. I want my style to shatter that airtight medium. I want it to put a dent in television because it's an incredibly pedagogical medium.

As intellectuals, we ought to get used to the fact that television is a medium that affects people's identities and perceptions of reality, sometimes for the good. There have been studies carried out that show that people trust their local newspeople more than they trust their clergy people. People still look to conventional news broadcasts on TV to get their information, even more than from written journalism or from the alternative press. So I want to bring my alternative, non-traditional, perhaps even subversive viewpoint to bear on and within this most hegemonic of mediums.

In some ways, television has proved to have ideological flexibility, especially when radicals pop up on rare occasions. At least there's the potential to shatter dominant ideological modes, if even for a brief moment. We should definitely take advantage of television's episodic fluidity. I don't see television in a snobbish way. I've been on *Oprah* to talk about black oppression, black masculinity, and female identity. I've gone on CNN to talk about race, white supremacy, and electoral politics. I want to seize television as a pedagogical tool to help liberate or transform folk, or at least contest what Stuart Hall calls the preferred meanings of the dominant culture, juxtaposing them to what he terms the negotiated meanings, as I acknowledge the prevailing ideological framework while arguing for alternative structures of thought and oppositional practices. I want to use television to challenge our culture's common sense, in the way Gramsci meant it, and to help educate and occasionally uplift those who pay attention.

That does fit within the ways that I wanted to hear you talk about the medium. This also points me back to your notion of this betweener generation—people in their late thirties and very early forties. People just a few years older than the betweeners remember television in its early, formative stages, when televisions weren't ubiquitous. They remember Uncle Milty, and TV was still a novelty. But, for me, when I wake up to memory it's there and it's unremarkable. It's on and it's unremarkable. One of my earliest TV memories, at three, almost four years old, is seeing Jack Ruby shoot Lee Harvey Oswald. That's

a vivid scene I remember seeing—sitting on my mother's bed—that scene. That's one of those moments I've somehow written into my mind as an early moment. That and also realizing, somewhere around my thirtieth birthday, that from as far back as I could remember until my thirteenth birthday that the news started every day with the body count from Vietnam. That's pretty deep—to realize that there is a generation of us, eight years old in 1968, old enough to be aware of the assassinations, of the riot in Chicago, of moon landings, of Detroit and Newark, of all the stuff happening around you, seeing it come at you and nobody talks to you about it. So, in 1987 and 1988 I carried around a grudge because *People, Time,* and *Newsweek* did "summer of love" and "summer of discontent" retrospectives. So, they talked to (all) the people who were adult participants in '67 and '68. Then they talked to people who were twenty years old in '87 and '88. And I thought: "you did it again!" In 1968 no one said anything about this to me. Here, again, in 1998 you ask everybody but me.

You're so right. You've brought up here what is not my first memory of television, but it is my most important one. That is when I saw the newscaster interrupt the regular program to announce that MARTIN LUTHER KING JR. had been shot in Memphis, Tennessee. That is the most powerful moment of the television bonding with me, and of me bonding with the TV. I identified, almost beyond volition or consciousness, with the television as a medium, as an apparatus, that brought me an ideologically contested moment in black rhetoric. That is, MARTIN LUTHER KING JR. speaking his last speech. They flashed an image of him as he said what would immediately become some of his most famous words, "I may not get there with you, but I want you to know tonight that we as a people will get to the Promised Land." That was a very profound and electrifying episode that shaped my life forever. I asked my mother, "Which one is he? Which one is he?" I remember distinctly, and I don't know why they showed it, Dr. King at some point reeling back on his foot. I immediately felt his power; his words were like containers brimming with the pathos of black life. Later, the newsman broke faith again with the printed program by saying, "MARTIN LUTHER KING JR. has just died at thirty-nine in Memphis, Tennessee."

And now, here I am thirty-eight, and you're thirty-seven, so we're basically the same age and almost the age at which King died. King's death was stunning to me. I had never heard of Martin Luther King Jr. before that point, and when he died in 1968—I was nine years old—it changed my life. Television literally changed my life because, after his death, I began to watch all the programs about Dr. King. I began to go to the library to read all the books I could about him that were available. I then ordered, through a telephone number I got off of the television, speeches that were available on records. I had my little record player back then, when vinyl was the medium of choice and analog was the order of the day. Then, through television, I ordered the commemorative book on Martin Luther King Jr. So, television was a very powerful medium that fused with my evolving self-consciousness as a young black person. The 1967 riots in Detroit also made me pay attention to television. It brought me scenes of social ignomiy and racial deterioration right before my eyes, and made me realize that what I could see from my front porch in the streets—as people scurried up and down the pavement with money stashed in their big fros, televisions on their backs, and carrying all kinds of ill-gotten gains and goods—was refracted through the prism of a medium that made it larger than life.

Thinking back on the brothers and sisters in the streets, I'm reminded of the old joke Dick Gregory told about black people being stopped in the riots. These people were carrying a couch when the police stopped them. Dick Gregory said that when these people were stopped, they said, "Goddamn! A black psychiatrist can't even make house calls anymore!" And what else is it that they say? In a riot black people destroy everything but libraries and bookstores. Lord have mercy! Anyway, the reality is that the riots and the death of Martin Luther King Jr. point to how social catastrophe and transformation is either covered or concealed on television. These events spring from deeply embedded social processes of resolving or reinforcing conflict that are not usually explored in great depth on television, save in the rare in-depth documentary.

The contested and conflicted meanings of race in the 1960s were frequently papered over and smoothed out, resulting in the McDonaldization of Martin Luther King Jr. in a McLuhan universe where the medium was the message. It's important to me that the medium through which Dr. King was articulated for me was a televisual apparatus—since I never met him in the flesh. And the message I got from him was about social change. My early identification with TV grew from the fact that it had the radical potential to transform, not merely to anesthetize, to open up and not merely to constrain, to shatter and not merely to constitute, social reality. I saw it as an imaginative apparatus through which, ideologically, we could resist and challenge dominant racial and cultural narratives. Now, I didn't know all of this back then, but I felt a connection to King that transcended time and place and allowed me to identify with this figure whose life just revolutionized my consciousness. So, there's no question that television changed my life.

The next week in Sunday school I remember that our teacher asked us about that. That, I'm sure, was one of the very few times an adult asked about our response to current events. If I remember correctly, it was a Wednesday or Thursday evening when King was assassinated. That was when *Batman* came on. That was probably why I was hanging out in front of the tube— waiting for *Batman*.

Aww, man! Batman and Robin, brother! My boys Adam West and Burt Ward! And there was Bruce Lee as Cato on the *Green Hornet,* and I don't remember the cat who played the Green Hornet that Cato drove around in the Hornet's Lincoln Continental.

I remember that on the Sunday following my Sunday school teacher asking us how the assassination made us feel—probably the only time anyone asked us. One girl in the class said she was glad King died because some show she wanted to watch had been interrupted. There was some TV show she wanted to see, but the news preempted all that. That seems, again, to be one of the interesting ways television plays out in our culture. And occasionally I'm one of those people—I'd rather watch some sitcom than

the Republican convention. I can catch what I need to later on CNN or C-SPAN. I don't have to sit there and watch it all unfold live.

These news programs are part of the option glut that television now presents. Our nation, indeed our world, has been deeply affected by the CNNing of American discourse where all information, or at least the information that is deemed worth knowing, is immediately available. Therefore, there's little psychic space for reflection, little intellectual or emotional space in which to recover what we learn or reconstitute the ideas we absorb. We have little time to figure out the meaning of what we learn. As Derrida taught us, understanding is not simply about what something means but how it signifies. However, you can't even figure that out unless you have some space, some remove, from hugely influential events. I'm not embracing the myth of news objectivity, since I think the best we can hope for is fairness, which includes placing our biases right out in the open. I'm thinking here of the need to recover the fragments of events, and to experience them as fully as possible through interpreting and articulating them.

What the immediacy of communications technology has done is to make us believe that because we've perceived something, that because we've got the raw data through our senses, we've thoroughly experienced it. But we don't know what we know until we begin to think critically about what it means, and until we intervene with a conscious, deliberate intent to classify, to categorize, and to filter our experiences. It takes much more than empirical access to information to create understanding. Without interpretation and analysis, experience remains mute and inarticulate beneath the sheer fact of its existence. The phenomenological weight of immediacy results in a distorted capacity for interpretation and analysis.

As you mention the idea of space, there is a glut of options and information such that if you know that you need space to reflect, interpret, and reinterpret, you don't have time before the next fragment hits you. This is a totally unplanned but nice little segue. There was a Jay Wright symposium here at which Harold Bloom was a speaker. Jay Wright said this in a 1983 interview: "These last two terms, explication and interpretation, should call attention to one of my basic assumptions: that naked perception (just seeing something), is misprision in the highest degree. Every perception requires explication and interpretation. Exploration means just that. A simple report of experience, if you could make such a thing, isn't good enough." Although he's talking about the art of poetry, this seems to apply to this sort of experience of information. One of the things that Harold Bloom lamented at this conference was the absence of learnedness, although he put Jay Wright on this wonderful pedestal as a learned poet in the tradition of Dante and Milton. Somehow, it occurred to me that there's something about this peculiar postmodern information glut that makes "learnedness" impossible. Bloom mentioned that earlier in his career, although it wasn't often, he would hear people referred to as a "learned" scholar.

In the light of our postmodern option glut, erudition becomes nearly obsolete and impossible to attain, at least according to a specific understanding of the concept. You can't master the discursive tongues that have proliferated via the media in our own time. In some senses, I lament the loss of such erudition because I'm a nontraditional traditionalist at that level, reared on *The Harvard Classics,* TV, and Motown. I saw no disjuncture between *Two Years Before the Mast* by Richard Dana, and William "Smokey" Robinson's "My Girl" sung by the Temptations. Although I understand and even empathize with elements of Bloom's lament, I've got disagreements with him and other critics over canon formation and related literary issues, because I think there are multiple canons and multiple forms of literacy that we ought to respect. The intellectual and rhetorical integrity of these traditions ought to be acknowledged, and not in a condescending, compensatory fashion designed to make sure that "the other" is represented, except such inclusion is usually a procedural and not a substantive engagement with a given work. We've got to take the revelations about America that "minority" authors offer as seriously as we do conventional heroes of literature. We have much to learn from black writers' engagement, for instance, with what Baraka termed "vicious modernism."

On the other hand, I think that there's a need to historicize our conceptions of erudition, too. We should constantly be reevaluating what we mean by learnedness and erudition, since those qualities were never absolutely divorced from the priorities and prisms of the dominant culture. The learned and erudite were not simply revered for their knowledge, but they reflected a hierarchy of privilege that provided some the opportunity to acquire such a status while foreclosing the possibility to others in an a priori fashion. Ironically enough, even though the possibility of a particular kind of erudition may be quickly vanishing with the proliferation of information systems, it may offer a relatively more democratic conception of literacy that invites us to acknowledge a wider range of people as legitimate bearers of "learning."

In the past, the erudite person could only be a white male whose prodigious learning was acknowledged by his peers and intellectual progeny. Now, at least, we've widened the view of what counts as erudite and learned, and in many ways that's a very good thing.

Interview by Jonathan Smith
St. Louis, Missouri, 1996

People as Symbol Makers and Users

Language and the Creation of Social Reality

By Kent L. Sandstrom, Daniel D. Martin, and Gary Alan Fine

"This probably sounds strange," Bill announced, "but for me AIDS has been more of a blessing than a curse. Of course, there are days when I don't feel like that—days when my face breaks out in a terrible rash, my legs ache for hours, and I can hardly get out of bed. But, overall, I'd have to say that living with AIDS has been a beneficial and even spiritual experience for me. It's really changed me! For example, it's helped me to see what's truly important in life and what isn't. And it's given me a stronger sense of freedom—freedom to accept my limits and enjoy life. I don't worry so much about pleasing other people anymore. I do more of the things that I really want to do. Like I go outside with my dog for a couple of hours and just sit out in the grass with him, and I don't worry about it because that's something I enjoy doing—it's relaxing and life giving. And no one expects me to explain why I took the time to do that. So, I feel freed up from normal pressures and expectations. I guess that's been one of the 'blessings' of AIDS. Another blessing is that it's led me to appreciate the opportunities that each day brings. ... I've learned, you know, to feel grateful for each day really—for the sun, the trees, everything. And that gives me a more intense experience of life. There's times when it even comes off as feeling high—like a high from drugs or something like that, except it's not from that. It's just from being so immersed in life—there's a high in that for me!"[1]

How could anyone define the "reality" of AIDS like Bill does? How could he see and experience a potentially life-threatening illness as a blessing and source of freedom? These questions cannot be answered adequately by theories that emphasize reinforcement histories, reward exchanges, cognitive schemas, or the strategies of impression management. To explain Bill's experience of AIDS, one must recognize the symbolic aspects of human behavior. More specifically, one must appreciate how Bill's experience is shaped by the meanings that he gives to this illness. These meanings are not intrinsic to AIDS or the physical symptoms it evokes. Rather, they are conferred on the illness through the social processes of interpretation, communication, and interaction. In the following discussion, we elaborate on this point by focusing on how people give meaning to realities such as AIDS. In doing so, we highlight the symbolic nature of human experience and action.

Creating and Transforming Reality

All human behavior consists of, or is dependent upon, the use of symbols. Human behavior is symbolic behavior; symbolic behavior is human behavior. The symbol is the universe of humanity.

–Leslie A. White, *The Science of Culture*

Compared with other animals, we find ourselves in a unique situation as human beings. We do not live directly in a state of nature, nor do we see "reality" nakedly. As the philosopher Suzanne Langer observed, human perception consists of the continuous creation and recreation of images and symbols.[2] Our only means of taking in the world of objects and people around us is through continually re-creating them. In other words, we convert our experiences into images and symbols. Our brains do not simply record or relay what is going on "outside" or "inside" of us. Instead, when processing information or sensations, our brains act like giant, symbolic transformers, changing virtually everything that passes through them into a stream of symbols.[3]

According to Langer, this tendency for our brains to act like symbolic transformers is a crucial feature of our experience as human beings. It allows us to have a "constructive" rather than passive relationship to our environment. We do not simply react to things that exist in the world around us. Nor do we see these things "in the raw." Instead, we transform and interpret them through a symbolizing process.[4] Thus, as we participate in the process of **perception**—the process of making sense of stimuli in our environment—we rely on our capacity to create and use symbols. Through this capacity we transform the stimuli that bombard us, such as a cluster of stars on a clear night, into a coherent and meaningful pattern—in this case, a pattern we call the Big Dipper.

Sensation

Throughout our lives we are barraged by a flood of sensory experiences. We swim in a sea of sensation. Consider this very moment. Your attention is (we hope) focused on this book and the words you are reading in this sentence. But pause for a moment and think of all the other things you are experiencing. For instance, what else are you seeing besides this page and sentence? Are you seeing what's above, below, and to the sides of the page? Are you periodically glancing up to see what else is around you? Are you being affected by anything besides visual images? For instance, are you hearing any noises or smelling any odors? Do you feel any pressures on your body, such as the touch of your fingers on the book, your back on a chair, your elbows on a table, or your feet on the floor? After briefly paying attention to what's going on around you, you can recognize that you are being bombarded with stimuli.

If we remained at the level of sensation, we would soon be overwhelmed. Our world would lack continuity or coherence. Life would be a booming, buzzing confusion of lights, sounds, smells, colors, and movements. We would bounce from one experience to another with little if any direction or purpose. We would not be able to organize our sensory experiences into broader patterns or configurations. Our perceptions, then, are not merely a matter of sensation; they also involve interpretation.[5] Our senses provide us with the raw data to arrive at meaning.

As commonly recognized, we rely on five major senses as we interact with and gather information from our environment: sight, hearing, taste, smell, and touch. When any of these senses are stimulated, as when the receptors in our ears respond to sound waves emitted by a roaring engine, they transmit a message to the brain, which processes this input. Each sense can be aroused by external stimuli, as when we are moved by a beautiful sunset, refreshed by a cool breeze or, less pleasantly, repulsed by the smell of manure. Our senses can also be aroused by stimuli that come from sources within us, as when we feel a pang of hunger, a flash of pain, or a surge of sexual desire.

Most important, we do not react passively to our environment. We actively seek out stimuli through our bodily senses. For instance, we move our head, eyes, hands, and body to explore the sensations of light, sound, and contact that surround us.[6] In this process, we extract information about our sensations and select what is relevant. We turn toward or away from shades of light. We turn toward or away from various noises, such as a whispering voice or an exploding firecracker. We sniff for pleasant odors and hold our nose at unpleasant odors in the air around us. We feel physical objects, enjoying their texture, evaluating how we can use them, and gauging their potential dangers. Our senses, then, do not merely receive stimuli; they actively seek out stimuli until they achieve a clearer understanding of their nature.[7]

Conceptualization and Categorization

We understand our sensory experiences through grouping them into units, categories, or concepts, based on their similarities. We thereby engage in the process of *conceptualization*.

That is, we experience the world in terms of **concepts**—regularized ways of thinking about real or imagined objects and events. These concepts enable us to picture "things" in our world, to describe or represent these things to ourselves and one another, and to grasp their meaning.[8] We use concepts because we are "cognitive misers" and we want to find relatively simple ways to deal with the stimuli picked up by our senses. By sorting these stimuli into related and manageable units and giving them labels, we recode their contents into summary categories—categories such as *red, tall, dark, beer, roommate, professor,* and *dorm room.* By using these and other categories, we simplify and generalize the world—we chunk and cluster its elements into meaningful concepts. For example, we look into the sky and register a collection of light waves striking our retinas as "blue"; we bite into a candy bar and interpret thousands of transmissions from our taste buds as "sweet"; we walk up to a person in a store and recode the range of sensations she emits into "friendly looking clerk." Through condensing and transforming our perceptions into these categories, we simplify the abundance of stimuli and information available to us. We organize our experiences.

At the same time, we bring order, continuity, and predictability into our perceptual world. Through plugging various stimuli into categories, we can link our present sensations to past sets of experience and perceptual organization. We can identify an object or event as the same object or event despite the fact that it changes during each moment and from various perspectives. For example, we can recognize an event that shifts back and forth from one person lecturing to several people exchanging ideas as a "social psychology course." We can also treat a number of objects that differ in a few ways, such as cars, vans, and trucks, as essentially similar "vehicles." Through this ability to categorize objects, we can reduce the anxiety we would feel in an otherwise disordered and ambiguous world of stimuli.

Conceptualization allows us to sort and organize stimuli in a meaningful and orderly way. Through this process we actively attune ourselves to certain stimuli while ignoring others. We lump or group stimuli together and then respond to these groups as if they were objects. The key point is that we do not respond to the world "as it is." It does not have an inherent meaning. Instead, as human beings we actively slice up the world and organize it into concepts—plants and animals, fruits and vegetables, cities and villages—that allow us to give it meaning and see it as orderly. Although this is an intricate process, it seems fairly simple because many of the concepts we rely on are supplied by the groups to which we belong. We learn these concepts as we learn the language and culture of our society.

Symbols, Signs, and Meanings

Human experience takes on distinctive characteristics because people respond not only to signs but also to symbols. A **sign** is directly connected to an object or event and calls forth a fixed or habitual response. Its meaning is associated with its physical form and can be grasped through the senses. For instance, dark clouds are a sign of rain, and smoke is a sign of fire. Both animals and people can make sense of and respond to these signs. Symbols, however, are a uniquely human phenomenon. Roughly speaking, symbols are something that people create and use to stand for something else. A powerful example is a flag. People use a colored rectangle of cloth to stand for a nation and its guiding principles. This cloth evokes passionate sentiments—pride, loyalty, patriotism, and, for some, disgust or animosity. Another example of a symbol is a hug. In our society a hug is widely regarded as a symbol of affection; thus, the willingness of one person to hug another is seen as an expression of his or her caring for that person. Among the various sets of symbols, the most important are linguistic symbols, those combinations of spoken sounds or written marks that are used for all meanings. A **symbol,** then, is any object, gesture, or word that becomes an abstract representation of something else. Whatever it represents constitutes its meaning.

In most cases, the association between a symbol and the meanings it represents is arbitrary. The meanings designated by a symbol have no intrinsic relationship to the object it describes; the meanings are generally a matter of convention. Therefore, the meaning of a symbol cannot be discerned by examining the nature of the symbol itself. Think, for example, of the word *rose*. There is nothing inherent in this combination of four letters that would necessitate or even suggest it as a representation for a particular plant. The word has no color, smell, or thorns. Nor does it have anything in its spoken or printed form that would lead one to automatically think of the flower it describes. We conjure up an image of a velvety and sweet-smelling flower when hearing the word "rose" only because we have learned to make this association since childhood. We could just as easily have learned to call a rose "by any other name." Of course, if we had been born in a non-English-speaking country, such as Romania, a rose would not be a rose to us—it would be a *trandafir*.

The Importance of Symbols

Our ability to use symbols has several important implications for our experience and activity. First, because symbols are abstractions, their use allows us to transcend our immediate environments and to have experiences that are not rooted in the here and now. We do not simply respond to the stimuli that arouse our senses in our current situation. We interpret these stimuli and respond to them in terms of our images of the past, present, and future, as well as our images of what is good, right, or important. In essence, we respond to stimuli of our own creation—that is, stimuli provided by the shadowy world of symbols. Thus we act within and toward a world that we have a major part in creating, a world that is inherently abstract rather than concrete, a world of symbols that in some senses is imaginary.[9]

To understand this point, think of the abstract concepts that guide people's outlooks and actions, such as equality, justice, freedom, love, and honesty. At bottom, these are humanly created symbols. They do not exist "in nature" or have a material reality. But most of us tend to respond to them as if they are representations of essential truths about the world that should guide our actions.

Even in situations that have a physical character, such as sporting events, people are guided by and respond to symbolic realities. For example, athletes know that coaches stress the concepts of hustle, sportsmanship, and teamwork. These concepts are real only in terms of the representations that players and coaches make of them. Coaches presume that they can gauge "hustle" through observing the behavior and demeanor of their players. If a player displays a high level of effort, he or she is hustling. "Sportsmanship" is behavior that accords with certain moral standards of fair play and thoughtfulness. When a player behaves "properly" in an instance when improper behavior is possible, we have witnessed sportsmanship. If his or her team, having just lost a hard-fought game, graciously congratulate their opponents, they are seen as demonstrating sportsmanship. Likewise, "teamwork" is not the act of a single player but depends on the relationship among players. A single action doesn't demonstrate teamwork, but two or more coordinated actions (such as a throw, a catch, and a tag) do. Hustle, sportsmanship, and teamwork are not objective behaviors but rather depend on symbolic interpretations within the context of a sports event.

In addition to allowing us to transcend our immediate environment, symbols allow us to remember, imagine, plan, and have vicarious experiences.[10] Whenever we remember things, imagine things, or make plans to do things, we rely on and manipulate symbols. We also use symbols to have vicarious experiences. These experiences allow us to learn about the world and understand others' experiences through observation; we do not have to experience everything ourselves in order to understand it. This ability is important not only for our individual and collective survival but also for another distinctive human characteristic: the transmission of culture.

Symbols provide the mechanism by which we create and acquire **culture**, or the ways of thinking, feeling, and acting that characterize a person's society. Interactionists believe that it is through a process of communication, or symbolic interaction, that we learn, create, and pass on culture. The boundaries of the spread of culture are linked to the boundaries of effective communication.[11] This point is important in that groups develop their own symbol systems, which come to exemplify how people are expected to think, feel, and behave. Every group develops its own **idioculture**, or system of shared knowledge, beliefs, sentiments, and behaviors that serves as a frame of reference and basis of interaction for group members.[12] Nicknames serve as a case in point. Often they characterize members of the group to each other and demonstrate that the individuals truly belong. Further, these nicknames are frequently connected to a particular group itself. In Gary Alan Fine's research on Little League baseball, many of the players had team nicknames that reflected their position on the team. One boy, for instance, was called "Maniac," both a linguistic play on his last name and an indicator that he often threw the ball wildly. The next year this same boy became the starting third baseman, his throwing skills improved, and his teammates started calling him "Main Eye."

Finally, the most crucial implication of symbols is that they provide us with templates for categorizing our experiences and placing them within a larger frame of reference. Without symbols, we cannot give meaningful form to what is happening around us, and our understandings of the world have a hit-or-miss quality. We combine and cluster symbols to form concepts that we use to sort our sensory experiences into orderly social categories. These categories often take the form of *names*—names that have shared meanings for the members of a culture. Through using these names, we come to "know" the world around us.

Naming 'Reality' and Creating Meaningful Objects

As Anselm Strauss has observed, people act toward objects in light of the names they give to these objects.[13] Naming is an integral part of human cognition. In naming an object, we classify and give meaning to it, thereby evaluating it and calling forth action toward it. The name organizes our perceptions and serves as a basis for our subsequent behavior; that is, it intervenes between the "stimulus" provided by the object and our "response" to it. In other words, we respond to the name that we give to the object and not to the essence of the object itself.

Take the example of a green, 2½" × 6" rectangular piece of paper with Andrew Jackson's picture on it. Call it "money" or, more specifically, a "twenty-dollar bill." Based on this name, you immediately know how to act toward it. You know that you can use it at a store or business to purchase goods or services, such as groceries, clothing, or a haircut. And you know this because you have learned the meaning that the name "money" calls forth in our society. This meaning is not inherent to green, 2½" × 6" rectangular pieces of paper, as demonstrated by the fact that it is also granted to silver and copper circular-shaped pieces of metal. Instead, it emerges out of a shared agreement about what the objects we call "money" represent and how we should act toward them.

As another example of how we respond to things based on the names we give them, imagine a situation that involves you interacting with an unnamed person. It's late at night and you're walking across campus on your own. After you walk through a passageway between two buildings, you suddenly hear footsteps about 50 feet behind you. Feeling somewhat nervous, you glance backward and see a large male figure in the shadows. You pick up your pace. The man behind you matches your speed and even starts to gain on you. You tentatively name (or categorize) this man as a potential "mugger" or "rapist," and panic wells up within you. In turn, as he draws steadily closer to you, you prepare to run, yell, or defend yourself. Just as you're about to take defensive action, the man behind you calls out your name and says, "Hey, I've been trying to catch up with you since you walked between those buildings back there! I was going to yell 'wait up,' but I wasn't sure it was you until now. Anyway, I was wondering if you'd like to walk back to the dorm together." As you hear these words, you quickly recognize that it is one of your friends who has been walking behind you. In that moment he is transformed from "mugger" or "rapist" into "thoughtful friend." Your response to him shifts accordingly. Your feelings of anxiety dissipate and you feel relaxed and reassured. You respond warmly rather than with a scream or a punch.

What these examples illustrate is that we formulate lines of action within and through the symbolic processes of naming and categorization. We use these processes to give meanings to things around us and to our actions as well as those of others. In other words, when we engage in the processes of naming and categorization, we transform things, events, and actions into **social objects**, or objects that have shared meaning. These objects call out a common mode of response in us.

According to interactionists, meaning is a socially created phenomenon. As such, it has three key features. First, it is extrinsic; that is, it is not a quality innate to particular objects but is conferred on those objects "from the outside" based on how they are named and their intended use. Second, the meaning of objects is not fixed but varies with time, culture, situation, and the people acting toward them. For example, a bank is a different social object to student loan-seekers, to its managers and employees, and to potential bank robbers. Each acts differently toward the bank, and, consequently, to each it is a different object with a different meaning. This point leads us to the third important feature of meaning: It emerges and gets transformed through our communication with others as we learn from them how to define the meaning of an object and as we offer our own meaningful view of that object. Think, for instance, of how we learn the meaning of an upright middle finger in our culture. We observe the anger or upset feelings that others convey when they raise this finger or have it displayed toward them. In turn, we quickly learn that raising one's middle finger toward others, or "flipping them off," is not a kind gesture, nor is it meant to tell them to look up in the air. Instead, we learn that this is a lewd and hostile gesture that conveys feelings of anger and tells others that we wish them harm (ironically, through engaging in sexual activity). Most important, what this example demonstrates is that meaning emerges and becomes established through the process of social interaction. The establishment of meaning through this process is essential because human action requires symbolization. Without meaning, we do not know how to act toward the "things" around us—including others and ourselves. To name "things" is not only to know them but also to know how to respond to them. The names, or symbolic categories, we attribute to things represent knowledge, communication, and action.

Box 2-1

The Power of Names: North Dakota and Palmetto Bugs

In the following excerpt, Dave Barry, a humorist writer, offers a comical and obviously exaggerated illustration of how names (and the meanings they reflect) powerfully influence our perceptions and actions.

* * *

North Dakota is talking about changing its name. I frankly didn't know you could do that. I thought states' names were decreed by the Bible or something. In fact, as a child I believed that when Columbus arrived in North America, the states' names were actually, physically written on the continent, in gigantic letters, the way they were on maps. I still think this would be a good idea, because if an airplane's navigational system failed, the pilot should just look out the window and see exactly where the plane was. ("OK, there's a huge 'W' down there, so we're over Wyoming. Or, Wisconsin.")

But apparently states can change their names, and some North Dakotans want to change "North Dakota." Specifically, they don't like the word "North," which connotes a certain northness.

In the words of North Dakota's former governor, Ed Schafer: "People have such an instant thing about how North Dakota is cold and snowy and flat."

We should heed the words of the former governor, and not just because the letters in "Ed Schafer" can be rearranged to spell "Shed Farce." The truth is when we think about North Dakota, which is not often, we picture it having the same year-round climate as Uranus.

... That's how powerful a name can be.

I'll give you another example. I live in Florida, where we have BIG cockroaches.

Q.: How big are they?

A.: They are so big that, when they back up, they are required by federal law to emit warning beeps.

These cockroaches could harm Florida's image. But we Floridians solved that problem by giving them a new name, "palmetto bugs," which makes them sound cute and harmless. So when a guest walks into a Florida kitchen and screams at the sight of an insect the size of Charles Barkley, we say: "Don't worry! It's just a palmetto bug!" And then we and our guest have a hearty laugh, because we know there's nothing to worry about, as long as we do not make any sudden moves toward the palmetto bug's sandwich.

So changing names is a sound idea, an idea based on the scientific principle that underlies the field of marketing, which is: People are stupid. Marketing experts know that if you call something by a different name, PEOPLE WILL BELIEVE IT'S A DIFFERENT THING. That's how "undertakers" became "funeral directors." That's how "trailers" became "manufactured housing." That's how "We're putting you on hold for the next decade" became "Your call is important to us."

And that's why some North Dakotans want to give their state a new name, a name that will give the state a more positive, inviting, and forward-looking image. That name is: "Palmetto Bug."

No, seriously, they want to drop the "North" and call the state, simply, "Dakota." I think this change is brilliant, and could also work for other states with image problems. New Jersey, for example, should call itself, simply, "New."

Be advised that "Dakota" is not the first shrewd marketing concept thought up by North Dakotans. Are you familiar with Grand Forks, ND? No? It's located just west of East Grand Forks, MN. According to a letter I received from a Grand Forks resident who asked to remain nameless ("I have to live here," he wrote), these cities decided they needed to improve their image, and the result was—get ready—"The Grand Cities."

The Grand Cities, needless to say, have a website (grandcities.net), where you can read sentences about The Grand Cities written in Marketing Speak. ... Here's an actual quote: "It's the intersection of earth and sky. It's a glimpse of what lies ahead. It's hope, anticipation, and curiosity reaching out to you in mysterious ways. Timeless. Endless. Always enriching your soul. Here, where the earth meets the sky, the Grand Cities of Grand Forks, North Dakota, and East Grand Forks, Minnesota."

Doesn't that just make you want to cancel your trip to Paris or Rome and head for the Grand Cities? As a resident of Florida ("Where the earth meets the water, and forms mud") I am definitely planning to go to Dakota. I want to know what they're smoking up there.

Source: Dave Berry, "North Dakota Wants Its Place in the Sun," *Waterloo-Cedar Falls Courier*, August 12, 2001, p. C1. Reprinted by permission of Tribune Media Services.

Language, Naming, and the Construction of Reality

Given the emphasis that interactionists place on symbols and the process of communication, they accord a special place to language. Language is the key medium through which people share meanings and construct "reality." As noted in Chapter 1, **language** is a system of symbols that members of a culture use for representation and communication. Hence, language is the source of the symbols we use to give meanings to objects, events, or people and to convey these meanings to ourselves and others.

Language serves as the foundation for the development of the most important kind of symbols: words. Words have a unique and almost magical quality—they not only have meaning on their own but also when joined with others. In addition, words serve as the basis for other symbols.[14] While people often use other modes of communication, such as gestures, facial expressions, and postures, these expressions become meaningful to us through words. For instance, in our culture a red light at an intersection means "Stop!"; a side-to-side turning of the head means "No!"; a waved hand toward an arriving friend means "Hi!"; and a police siren means "Pull over to the side of the road!"

Words facilitate our ability to communicate and share meanings. To understand this fact, try the following exercise. Approach several friends and tell them something about yourself without using any spoken or written words. Try to let them know what you are going to do this weekend. If this task seems too difficult, try letting them know what day it is. Obviously, without using words you face a challenging task. That is part of the amusement of the game of charades. Even if you are adept at using nonverbal gestures, you could probably communicate much more easily and accurately with your friends through relying on spoken or written words.

Overall, words are important because they offer shared names or categories through which we give meanings to our experiences and share these meanings. Words have their fullest impact and significance in relationship to other words within a language. As a part of the structure of language, words frame our conceptions and understandings of the world and guide our actions toward it.

Although words facilitate our ability to communicate and act, they do not necessarily make it easy for us to interact with others. The words we use are often ambiguous, and they may lead us to experience gaps or difficulties in our conversations with others. As an example, consider the following exchanges between a mother and her teenage daughter:

Daughter: Mom, can I take the car for a while to see my friends?

Mother: Okay, but don't be out too late—it's a school night and I need to use the car sometime to go to the grocery store.

Daughter: Okay, that's no problem. I'll see you later.

The daughter returns four hours later, at 10:30 p.m.

Daughter: Hi, Mom, I just wanted to let you know I'm home and the car is back.

Mother: [Angrily] Where the heck have you been? I told you not to be out too late!

Daughter: [Defensively] I wasn't out late—its only 10:30! I don't go to bed until midnight!

Mother: But it's a school night; you should be in earlier than that!

Daughter: Well, you didn't tell me a time. You just said that I shouldn't be out too late. 10:30 is not late!

Mother: Well, I did tell you that I needed the car sometime tonight to go grocery shopping.

Daughter: Yeah, and I brought it back for you. You can go shopping now. The grocery store is open until midnight.

Mother: It's too late for me to go grocery shopping now! It's 10:30 and I'm tired.

Daughter: Well, I don't see how that's my fault.

Mother: Oh, go to your room! I don't know why you can't listen to me better!

As this dialogue illustrates, the words we use do not always have a straightforward meaning, nor are they always interpreted in the way we intend them. Instead of leading to shared understanding and effective interaction, a number of the words we use, such as "a while," "later," and "sometime," have imprecise meanings and can lead to misinterpretations that result in frustrating or ineffective interaction. Thus, even when we use the same words as others, we do not necessarily "speak the same language" (and interact smoothly with them), as most parents and teenagers can attest.

In addition to containing abstract and arbitrary symbols known as "words," human languages have another essential feature: grammar, or syntax. Syntax is a set of rules for combining symbols to produce more extended meaning. Syntax allows us to indicate who is talking or acting, when something happened, to ask a question, to disagree, to speak about things that haven't happened yet or could never happen, to construct alternative visions of what might happen if we do this or do that. In other words, syntax enables us to use symbols to *think*, and to communicate thoughts to others.

The Necessity of Language

What would have happen to us as children if we were not exposed to an existing language? Would we invent a language of our own? As far as researchers can tell, the answer is no. This

Box 2-2

Language, Ethnomethods, and the Construction of Reality

As illustrated thus far in this chapter, people construct reality and "order," albeit tenuous and fleeting at times, through their everyday talk and interactions. The social psychological perspective that most closely examines how people use talk to construct and sustain a sense of order is called **ethnomethodology**. This perspective was created and developed by Harold Garfinkel and his students.[1] It highlights the strategies, or "ethnomethods," that people use to make sense of their everyday life and interactions, focusing on the structure and consequences of their talk as it occurs naturally in a variety of contexts. A prime example of how people use talk and "ethnomethods" to construct order is provided in Harvey Sacks' study of a psychiatric hospital. While recording conversations from an emergency hotline at the hospital, Sacks observed key differences in the sequence and structure of worker-caller conversations, noting that these differences were accompanied by hidden but evident procedural rules. Consider the differences in openings from the following two emergency calls, differences that Sacks found repeatedly as he studied hundreds of calls:

(Call 1) Worker: Hello

Caller: Hello

(Call 2) Worker: This is Mr. Smith may I help you?

Caller: Yes, this is Mr. Brown[2]

While both exchanges are brief and seem to offer little information, they reveal deep procedural codes for interaction. As Sacks explained: "We can say there's a procedural rule ... that a person who speaks first in a telephone conversation can choose their form of address and thereby choose the other's. ...[3] That is, through presenting ourselves in certain ways in conversations, we can control how others present themselves. Sacks reveals two ethnomethods common among emergency hotline workers. First, hotline workers can control a caller's disclosure of personal information by first disclosing their own names, thereby invoking the norm of reciprocity. Second, even when callers refuse to yield their names or other personal information, the workers may exercise control by asking the question "Why not?" This question compels callers to construct an "account" or explanation for why they won't reveal important personal information—an account that the workers can in turn question. By asking for and offering "accounts," people negotiate the meaning of a situation and, through their ongoing talk, construct a sense of order. (We will discuss this process in greater detail in Chapter Five when examining how people coordinate their actions and negotiate order in everyday life.)

The Etcetera Principle

In analyzing the construction of order through everyday talk, ethnomethodologists also emphasize the **etcetera principle**, which is another hidden interactional rule. This principle first of all specifies that conversational partners should try to achieve shared understandings. It also specifies that in order to minimize misunderstandings, ruptures, or disjunctures in a conversation, partners can ignore parts of it that they misunderstand if these parts are deemed unimportant. Thus, we may lack full understanding of our conversational partner's meanings, definitions, and points of reference, but we often "play along" or act "as if" we truly understand, thereby keeping the conversation going. This principle is illustrated when we use the phrase "you know" in a sentence. This phrase serves as a conversational bridge that glosses over misunderstandings and gaps in knowledge that arise when we talk with others. Note, for example, the use of the phrase "you know" by Julia, in the following interview excerpt from a television program in Cincinnati. Julia's teenage son, Ron, was the victim of a high school shooting in that city.

> Television host: So how do you cope with this tragedy?

> Julia: ... What I do now is go talk to mothers that go through the same thing [I do] when their son or daughter has been murdered. ... That's how I deal with my healin' today. I still have my moments ... you *know*, when I want to get high, want to drink, you *know*, take some valium so I won't have to think about Ron's death. ... But I reached a point ... I just went down on my knees and I looked up, you *know*, and I just told the Lord that I was tired of being burdened down, drug down and I started going back to church and I just started being around positive people, you *know*, like coming to the support sessions with positive people with positive things on their mind.[4] (Emphasis added.)

Julia uses the phrase "you know" as she explains her experience of first using drugs to cope with grief and then turning to religion. This phrase implies that both the television host and the viewing audience with whom she is engaged share enough background knowledge so that she does not have to elaborate fully on the experiences related to the traumatic death of her child. But how many members in the television studio or viewing audience actually share such experiences? National statistics suggest proportionately few. Yet, as a conversational bridge, the words "you know" allow the television interview to proceed relatively smoothly despite the fact that the audience and host may understand little of what Julia is actually feeling and talking about. Indeed, if Julia would have elaborated on the emotional pain she has experienced, the audience would have heard about the many times she contemplated suicide as well as the variety of drugs she used to "medicate the pain." But this is glossed over. What results through Julia's use of "you know" (and the etcetera principle) is a communication that gets a general point across, creates a sense of logical sequence in her experience, and spares her from revealing other details that might disturb the audience and discredit her in their eyes.

Indexical Expressions

Ethnomethodologists use the term "indexicality" to refer to the degree to which the meanings of a word, term, or phrase are embedded in a given social context or circumstance. An **indexical expression** is a word or phrase whose meaning can only be interpreted and understood according to the context in which it is used.[5] Consider, for instance, the following statement: "Hey girls, the drinks are at my place right across the street. Come on over!" Imagine that the person talking is a soccer coach directing her team of 8 year olds who are awaiting refreshments after a strenuous practice. Notice how that meaning changes if the context is not a soccer field but a corporate office and the person speaking is a female manager addressing her employees. The phrase "girls" as it is applied to people out on the soccer field is an expression that simply communicates the gender of the participants and their stage in the life course. In the context of the corporate office, the same statement would not convey age but it certainly would convey gender. It might also reveal a special kind of bond among the female workers, even if a more critical analysis might suggest that they were "infantilizing" themselves. However, this meaning would change radically if the office manager talking to female staff were male instead of female. In this case, the expression "Hey girls, the drinks are at my place, right across the street. Come on over!" might be interpreted as lecherous or sexist behavior. Moreover, the word "drinks" as it is used within the adult context of the corporate office would represent alcoholic beverages rather than a beverage appropriate for an 8 year old.

Now imagine that the same statement is made by a gay man who walks into a gay bar where his male friends are seated. How would it be interpreted? In her ethnography of straight and gay bars in San Francisco, Sherri Cavan observed that where "mock sexual behavior," nicknames, coarse language, and recurrent jokes are a part of the bar's culture, they are "transformed into a game with special rules that are expected to be known and respected. ..."[6] Thus, within the context of a gay bar, the phrase "Hey girls" as it is directed from one gay patron to another is likely to be a playful expression as well as an assertion of a common identity that stands in opposition to heterosexual, masculinist culture.

What these examples reveal is that the full meaning of any comment or expression can only be derived from the context, relationships, and circumstances in which it is used. Of course, it is difficult to conceive of any words that are not indexical expressions. Even the meaning of the word "you" is contingent upon the circumstances and context in which it is used. If your professor declares in class, "I want you to read all of Chapter Two before we meet again," she is most likely referring to the "collective you"– that is, your entire class, not you personally.

1. Harold Garfinkel, Studies in *Ethnomethodology* (Englewood Cliffs, NJ: Prentice Hall, 1967). See also Harold Garfinkel, *Ethnomethodology's Program: Working Out Durkheim's Aphorism* (Lanham, MD: Rowman and Littlefield, 2002).
2. Harvey Sacks, *Lectures on Conversation*, Volume I (Cambridge, MA: Blackwell, 1992), p. 4.
3. Ibid.
4. For a more extensive analysis of parental loss and the management of blame, see Daniel D. Martin, "Acute Loss and the Social Construction of Blame," *Illness, Crisis and Loss* 13, 2005, pp. 149–167.
5. See Harold Garfinkel, (Note I), pp. 6–11.
6. Sherri Cavan, "The Home Territory Bar." in G. Jacons, ed., *The Participant Observer: Encounters With Social Reality* (New York: George Braziller, 1970), p. 186.

is a fascinating question for social psychologists and philosophers, because it is linked to the question of what it means to be human. It is a challenging question to answer, however, because it is difficult, if not impossible, to take care of an infant's physical needs without also interacting with it in some land of language. There are, of course, accounts of "wild children," children who have for unusual reasons lived to late childhood without being spoken to. These children are reported to be lacking in many human qualities and, unless taught a language, cannot take care of their own needs for food or shelter. (See, for example, Susan Curtiss' book entitled *Genie: A Psycholinguistic Study of a Modern-Day "Wild Child."*[15])

Some evidence about the importance of language comes from studies of otherwise normal children who are born deaf and have not been exposed to a language with a visual basis, such as one of the sign languages. These children also seem to have difficulties with what we think of as basic human activities, such as thinking, learning, or forming relationships with other people. By contrast, deaf children who do learn a sign language do not have such difficulties.[16]

The impact of language on a deaf child's cognitions and behaviors is poignantly illustrated in the story of Helen Keller, a well-known American who lived in the early twentieth century. She was both blind and deaf as the result of a severe illness that she suffered when she was less than 2 years old, before she had learned to talk. Ms. Keller began to learn language at the age of 7, after her parents hired a teacher who was trained to work with deaf children. Ms. Keller eventually graduated from college and became a writer, lecturer, and advocate for the rights of persons with disabilities. In the following excerpt from her autobiography, she describes the intense feelings she experienced when learning language and, in turn, acquiring the power to name things:

> The most important day I remember in all my life is the one on which my teacher, Anne Mansfield Sullivan, came to me. I am filled with wonder when I consider the immeasurable contrast between the two lives which it connects. It was the third of March, 1887, three months before I was seven years old.
>
> The morning after my teacher came she led me into her room and gave me a doll. When I had played with it a little while, Miss Sullivan slowly spelled into my hand the word "d-o-l-l". I was at once interested in this finger play and tried to imitate it. When I finally succeeded in making the letters correctly I was flushed with childish pleasure and pride. Running downstairs to my mother I held up my hand and made the letters for doll. I did not know that I was spelling a word or even that words existed; I was simply making my fingers go in monkeylike imitation. In the days that followed I learned to spell in this uncomprehending way a great many words, among them *pin, hat, cup,* and a few verbs like *sit, stand,* and *walk.* But my teacher had been with me several weeks before I understood that everything has a name.
>
> One day, while I was playing with my new doll, Miss Sullivan put my big rag doll into my lap also, spelled "d-o-l-l" and tried to make me understand that "d-o-l-l" applied to both. I became impatient with her repeated attempts and, seizing the new doll, I dashed it upon the floor. I was keenly delighted when I felt the fragments of the broken doll at my feet. Neither sorrow nor regret followed my passionate outburst. I had not loved the doll; in the still, dark world in which I lived there was no strong sentiment or tenderness. I felt my teacher sweep the fragments to one side of the hearth, and I had a sense of satisfaction that the cause of my discomfort was removed. She brought me my hat, and I knew I was going out into the warm sunshine. This thought, if a wordless sensation may be called a thought, made me hop and skip with pleasure.
>
> We walked down the path to the well-house, attracted by the fragrance of the honeysuckle with which it was covered. Someone was drawing water and my teacher

placed my hand under the spout. As the cool stream gushed over one hand she spelled into the other the word water, first slowly, then rapidly. I stood still, my whole attention fixed upon the motions of her fingers. Suddenly I felt a misty consciousness as of something forgotten—a thrill of returning thought; and somehow the mystery of language was revealed to me. I knew then that "w-a-t-e-r" meant the wonderful cool something that was flowing over my hand. That living word awakened my soul, gave it light, hope, joy, set it free! There were barriers still, it is true, but barriers that could in time be swept away.

I left the well-house eager to learn, everything had a name, and each name gave birth to a new thought. As we returned to the house every object I touched seemed to quiver with life. That was because I saw everything with a strange, new sight that had come to me. On entering the door I remembered the doll I had broken. I felt my way to the hearth and picked up the pieces. I tried vainly to put them together. Then my eyes filled with tears; for I realized what I had done and for the first time I felt repentance and sorrow.

I learned a great many new words that day. I do not remember what they all were; but I do know that *mother, father, sister, teacher,* were among them—words that were to make the world blossom for me. It would have been difficult to find a happier child than I was as I lay in my crib at the close of the eventful day and lived over the joys it had brought me, and for the first time longed for a new day to come.[17]

As Helen Keller's story reveals, our genetically acquired capacity to learn a symbolic language can only be activated through its use in interaction with other humans. Moreover, we rely on language to realize our full human capacities for thinking, acting, and forming relationships with others.

Language, Naming, and Our Constructions of Others

For the most part, we do not first see and then define, we define first and then see.

—Walter Lippmann

To illustrate how language structures our perceptions of the world, let's look at how people think of and act toward one another. In general, we make sense of each other in roughly the same way we make sense of other social objects: We pick up sensory "data," sort and organize these data through naming or applying categories to them, and use these categories to interpret each other's meaning. We thereby engage in the process of **social cognition.**

Social cognition takes place whenever we come into contact with others. During our encounters, we actively seek and gather information about each other. This information is vital if we are to engage in effective interaction. Without having information about one another, a person cannot determine the other's "meaning" and thus will not know how to act toward him or her. The result is embarrassing, awkward, or alienating interaction. Think of what happens when someone stops to chat with you and, try as you might, you just can't remember who she is. Until you can name and place this person, you'll feel uncomfortable talking with her. You might act as if you know her, but you'll feel uncertain about what to say and how to behave. Without knowing her identity, you won't know how best to relate to her.

Processing information about others: Forming impressions through stereotypes. As we interact with others, particularly those we know little about, we quickly form an impression, or overall mental picture, of them. We do so by considering and piecing together a number of highly perceptible cues and clues we glean from their appearance and behavior. The meanings that we give to these cues or clues may be modified as we evaluate them in terms of other information we acquire about an individual. In most cases, we develop a more or less coherent impression of others by making inferences based on their social and physical attributes, apparent character traits, and verbal and nonverbal expressions.

In developing an impression of others, we often "fill in the gaps." We do so by drawing on prototypes. A **prototype** is a mental image, or schema, that we use to represent a typical set of features that exemplify an object or person. For instance, the idea of a church calls up the prototype of a building with a sanctuary, cross, organ, and pews. We draw on a variety of such prototypes in our experiences and interactions with others. They offer us a fuzzy and schematic guide for assessing people.[18] One example is the prototype "extrovert." When labeling someone as extroverted, we assume that person to be outgoing, boisterous, friendly, and loud, even if some of these traits are not evident. This example shows how we fill in the gaps about a person's characteristics and behavior in a way that goes beyond the information we can gather at the immediate moment. Apparently, we make such inferences spontaneously so that we can make sense of the information we gather about other people. We also store these inferences in our memories.

One important form of prototype is the stereotype. A **stereotype** is a mental image that attributes a common set of characteristics to all members of a particular group or social category. In popular thinking, stereotypes are understood as hostile and inaccurate attitudes that rigid people hold toward members of "minority" groups. This characterization is, however, overly narrow. Stereotypes are not necessarily negative or false beliefs. Nor are they necessarily directed toward members of oppressed groups or held only by rigid people. All of us rely on stereotypes to some degree in our everyday lives. They are an outgrowth of our inclination to simplify the world through naming it, or putting it into summary categories.

In coining the word *stereotype*, Walter Lippmann, an influential journalist and political commentator, defined it as an oversimplified picture of the world. Lippman observed that the world is characterized by "so much subtlety, so much variety, so many permutations and combinations ... we have to construct it on a simpler model before we can manage with it."[19] Stereotypes provide us with these models. They enable us to avoid the strain involved in evaluating every reaction of every person we interact with, moment by moment, as we participate in social encounters. Drawing on stereotypes, we group individuals into categories based on some characteristics, such as their age, gender, or job status, while simultaneously disregarding other characteristics. Doing so enables us to make rapid decisions based on minimal information about others. Stereotypes, then, allow us to assess others quickly, to anticipate their actions, and to plan our own actions accordingly.

Of course, even though stereotypes offer the advantages of convenience and efficiency, they have significant drawbacks. One major drawback is their unreliability. Because stereotypes are generalizations, they distort, overlook, or disregard potentially significant information about others. When we use a stereotype, we are prone to exaggerate or neglect important details about a person and thus to operate on the basis of false or misleading assumptions. We may subsequently make the mistake of assuming that a person has characteristics that, in fact, he or she does not possess, or we may fail to see the actual characteristics that a person possesses. In addition, we may subtly "push" the person into acting in ways that reflect our expectations rather than their attributes.[20]

In summary, stereotypes are useful and necessary human tools, but they can be blunt and sometimes harmful. While they enable us to deal with the ambiguous "realities" of the others we encounter, they can also lead us to overlook a person's important features. Stereotypes can therefore blind and constrain as well as guide and enable us. Nevertheless, given our tendency to carve up the world into simple and distinct categories, stereotypes remain part of our everyday thinking and action. By allowing us to group information into identifiable categories, they make impression formation and information processing more efficient. Our lives would be incredibly chaotic if we couldn't categorize people quickly in terms of their attributes. In the following section, we consider the salience of stereotypes in the process through which we interpret the prominent attributes of others, form impressions of them, and assign them social identities.

Forming impressions of character traits. As Solomon Asch revealed in landmark studies conducted more than 50 years ago, people form distinct impressions of one another within a short period of time. Asch illustrated how we use small amounts of information about others to make stereotypical inferences about their implicit personality traits. We do this based on our assumptions that people have basic traits that form consistent patterns. For example, we assume that an "industrious" person is also likely to be "skillful" and "intelligent" while a "lazy" person is not apt to have these traits, at least to the same degree.[21]

In addition to making inferences about the consistency of traits, we tend to organize traits in particular ways. We regard some traits as more influential and salient than others; these central traits serve to inform our overall perceptions of a person, influencing the meaning or connotation of the other traits we see him or her possessing. For instance, compare the description of a person as "warm and determined" to that of "cold and determined." Does the connotation of the trait "determined" change from one description to the other?

Asch discovered that changing "warm" to "cold" in a list of traits about a person drastically altered other people's perceptions of that person. Changing other traits on the list had much less effect. Based on this finding, Asch identified a person's perceived level of warmth as a central **organizing trait**[22]—a trait that has the greatest impact on the overall impression we form of him or her. In a related vein, he also concluded that different types of information about a person's character traits have different effects on the formation and organization of impressions.

In the years since Asch conducted his research, other cognitive social psychologists have further investigated the importance of various traits in the impression formation process. They have discovered that the centrality of a trait depends on the nature of the judgment we are making. "Warmth" is central when we assess another person's sociability, but "bluntness" becomes the most salient trait when we consider another person's honesty.[23] Most important, through their studies Asch and other cognitive social psychologists have demonstrated how the character traits we infer about others not only shape our impressions of them but also influence the social identities we attribute to them.

When assigning others a social identity, we name and place them as a social object. Thus, a **social identity** is a mental category we use to locate a person in relation to others, highlighting how he or she is similar to and different from these others. It can consist of a single characteristic, such as being a female, an environmentalist, or a Republican, or it can consist of a cluster of traits and statuses, such as being a tall, outgoing, African-American man who is a Democrat. We assign a social identity to others based on the information we glean from their appearance, actions, and social context.

While appreciating the insights that cognitive psychologists have offered into the identity attribution process, symbolic interactionists critique them for unduly emphasizing the importance of character traits in this process. As people gather information about and assign identities to others, they focus their attention on a number of other features, including social statuses, physical attributes, moods and emotions, and patterns of speech. In addition, individuals negotiate and alter the identities they attribute to others as they communicate with them. People rarely if ever give meaning to others through considering a list of static traits, except when asked to do so in a social psychology experiment. Instead, they give meaning to others through actively gathering information about them through an ongoing and ever-evolving process of interaction.

In the following discussion we highlight how people gather and make use of information about others' social attributes as they come into their presence. We also consider how this information-gathering process is influenced by prevailing stereotypes about gender, age, ethnicity, and physical appearances.

Identifying others based on social statuses. In our everyday interactions, we are influenced by cultural beliefs about what we can expect from people with particular attributes. We acquire these beliefs through a variety of social sources, including parents, relatives, friends, and the mass media. These sources teach us what it means to be young or old, male or female, Christian or Muslim, white or nonwhite. They also teach us, directly or indirectly, how to act toward people who occupy these statuses. We do not enter into interactions with others free of biases. We bring along a set of cultural preconceptions (or stereotypes) about how people with particular attributes are likely to act and how we in turn should act toward them.

Some attributes, such as gender, age, and ethnicity, are particularly likely to activate stereotypical beliefs. For many people, these characteristics override any other features. For instance, when a woman becomes a minister, others often put her gender ahead of her profession. They relate to her first as a woman and second as a minister. In such a case, gender becomes a *master status*—a status that powerfully affects how others define and interact with an individual.

The information provided by master statuses such as gender, ethnicity, and age is so often taken for granted that we can easily overlook its impact on our interactions. We become more aware of its significance when we are confronted by situations where it is not available. This was nicely highlighted some years back by the androgynous character Pat on NBC's *Saturday Night Live.* As the other characters humorously demonstrated in their interactions with Pat, life becomes complicated when we do not know someone else's gender. We cannot give that person a clear-cut meaning and, consequently, do not know how to relate to him or her. We feel confused, uncomfortable, and perhaps even annoyed.

Identifying others based on gender. As noted above, gender is a key status we take into account as we develop impressions of others and gauge their meaning for us. Once we know a person's gender, we often make a number of inferences about how he or she is likely to think, feel, and act. While these inferences have changed somewhat over the past few decades in the United States, some patterns of belief have persisted. In general, Americans tend to perceive men and women in terms of a number of stereotypical beliefs about gender-related character traits, role behaviors, physical characteristics, and work roles. Deaux and Lewis illustrated these stereotypes when asking people to give descriptions of a hypothetical woman and a hypothetical man.[24] The participants assumed that women possessed character traits such as being nurturing, gentle, and cooperative; physical characteristics such as being graceful, dainty, and soft-spoken; and jobs such as being an elementary school teacher or secretary. On the other hand, men were assumed to have character traits such as being confident, unemotional, and competitive; physical characteristics such as being strong, tall, and broad-shouldered; and work roles such as being a police officer or an automobile mechanic.

More recent studies also document how people form distinctively different impressions of others based on their gender.[25] These studies demonstrate that, despite the important changes provoked by the women's movement, gender images continue to shape our perceptions of and relationships to others in our everyday interactions. Although many strongly believe in the equality of men and women, we are still influenced by underlying stereotypes that encourage us to think of men and women in terms of disparate and unequal categories. Because of the influences of these stereotypes, we give different meanings to very similar actions and expressions presented to us by men and women. This process of attributing different meanings and identities to men and women imposes restrictive limits on both genders, but it has particularly burdensome consequences for women in our society.

Identifying others based on age and ethnicity. In addition to considering how gender stereotypes influence our perceptions of and relationships with others, social psychologists have focused attention on the related impact of age and ethnicity. Like gender, these two social characteristics are "priority attributes," or attributes that we take into account in almost all situations as we make decisions about the kinds of people others are, the kinds of actions they are most likely to engage in, and the beliefs and attitudes they are most likely to hold. We use people's age and ethnicity as important templates in deciding how we might act appropriately in our contacts with them.

Age is clearly a prominent characteristic that guides our images of others. In our society we place people into a variety of age-related categories, such as baby, child, teenager, adult, and senior citizen. These categories call forth different social expectations. When encountering children, we expect them to be active, playful, happy, and carefree. When interacting with adolescents, we expect them to be moody, reserved, rebellious, and independent. When coming into contact with elderly people, we expect them to be sickly, depressed, senile, and slow moving or, on the more positive side, to be serene, wise, and nurturing. Regardless of which stereotypes we adopt, we define and form impressions of others in terms of the generalized expectations activated by their perceived age.

We also form stereotypical impressions and expectations of others based on their ethnic status. Ethnic stereotypes are the most widely researched form of stereotype, probably because they have limiting and harmful effects on our social appraisals and relationships. In comparison to gender- and age-based stereotypes, ethnic stereotypes vary more dramatically across cultures and historical periods. Recent research indicates that ethnic stereotypes have changed substantially in the United States during the past 60 years. In this process of change, a number of negative stereotypes have become less pervasive. Regrettably, however, some negative ethnic stereotypes have persisted and continue to have a strong influence on American life. For example, studies conducted during the past two decades reveal that many whites tend to regard African Americans as relatively unintelligent, unpatriotic, and unmotivated;[26] Asian Americans as intelligent but methodical and passive; and Native Americans as lazy, passive, drunken, and immoral.[27]

In addition to revealing the persistence of negative stereotypes, social psychologists have uncovered the emergence of a more subtle form of prejudice toward ethnic groups, particularly African Americans. Some have described this viewpoint as "modern racism" or "symbolic racism."[28] Those who hold this type of prejudice stress the value of equal opportunity and often regard themselves as fervently antiracist. However, they believe that African Americans now have equal opportunities and only fail to succeed because they lack motivation, individualism, and deferred gratification.[29] They also believe that African Americans stay in low-paid positions because they do not work hard enough to succeed or have come to believe that others are prejudiced against them. Finally, they frequently view African Americans as overly demanding and militant and as seeking to implement policies of reverse discrimination or quotas.

In sum, although ethnic stereotypes have changed significantly over the past few decades, they cannot help but have a powerful influence on the judgments we make about others. When a person becomes identified as Jewish, Hispanic, Irish, Native American, or Asian American, he or she is presumed to have a certain set of characteristics. Even when we consciously reject ethnic stereotypes, they often continue to affect our interpretations of others on a semiconscious level.[30] They encourage us to see certain aspects of others' behavior or appearances and to disregard others as we interact with them. Unfortunately, these attitudes pose major difficulties for the millions of Americans who are the targets of such stereotypes.

They become understood in terms of relatively rigid categories and expectations that can significantly constrain their opportunities for self-expression, educational and occupational achievement, and rewarding interethnic relationships.

Identifying others based on physical appearance. Along with the attributes of gender, age, and ethnicity, a person's overall physical appearance—including facial features, mannerisms, hygiene, hairstyle, height, weight, and body type—becomes relevant in virtually all of his or her interactions. These aspects of self give others cues about what to expect and serve as a basis for character judgments. In this sense, an individual's physical appearance serves as an important symbol. It represents "who the person is" and communicates this to others.

Box 2-3

Person Perception on the Streets: The Impact of Age, Race, and Gender

While conducting ethnographic research on the streets of Philadelphia, Elijah Anderson noticed that public perceptions of "strangers" varied quite dramatically. Some of the factors that shaped these perceptions included the people's clothing, jewelry, companions, demeanor, and physical movements. The most important factors, however, were the age, race, and gender of strangers, as Anderson highlights when describing who is most likely to be seen as threatening or dangerous on the streets:

> If a stranger cannot pass inspection and be assessed as "safe" (either by identity or by purpose), the image of predator may arise, and fellow pedestrians may try to maintain a distance consistent with that image. … In the street environment, it seems, children readily pass inspection, white women and white men do so more slowly, black women, black men, and black male teenagers most slowly of all. The master status assigned to black males undermines their ability to be taken for granted as law-abiding and civil participants in public places: Young black males, particularly those who don the urban uniform (sneakers, athletic suits, gold chains, "gangster caps," sunglasses, and [cell phones]), may be taken as the embodiment of the predator. In this uniform, which suggests to many the "dangerous underclass," these young men are presumed to be troublemakers or criminals. Thus, in the local milieu, the identity of predator is usually "given" to the young black male and made to stick until he demonstrates otherwise, something not easy to do in circumstances that work to cut off communication, (p. 167)

Anderson points out that even when young black men act in ways that refute or disavow the image of predator, this does little to change public perceptions or public relationships between blacks and whites on the streets. "Common racist stereotypes persist, and black men who successfully make such disavowals are often seen not as the norm but as the exception–as 'different from the rest'–thereby confirming the status of the rest" (p. 168).

Source: Elijah Anderson, *Street Wise: Race, Class, and Change in an Urban Community* (Chicago: University of Chicago Press, 1991).

Of course, the symbol provided by our appearance (or its specific components) must be interpreted by others. The meaning of our thinness, fatness, tallness, shortness, hair length, or earrings depends on our cultural, historical, and situational contexts.

Our awareness of how our physical appearance serves as a symbol to others is demonstrated in our careful preparations to present ourselves in public. Before going into many social situations, we spend a lot of time considering our physical readiness for it. Most of us, for instance, thoughtfully prepare for interactions with others by making sure our hair is combed, our face is clean, our clothes are appropriately casual or formal, our breath is fresh, our shirt or blouse is buttoned, and so on.[31] Of course, the degree to which we are concerned about these matters is a function of the specific situation in which we find ourselves.

In general, we regard physical appearances as valid bases for making inferences about the essential character traits and moral qualities of others. For better or worse, we examine physical attributes to discern whether others are friendly, serious, diligent, lazy, confident, nervous, intelligent, dull, good, evil, and so on.

In making "identifications" of others, we pay particular attention to their facial characteristics and expressions. As Georg Simmel observed, the face serves as a window to the self.[32] We see it as something that reveals people's inner nature and life experiences. In essence, we believe that people's experiences and ways of being become "crystallized into permanent features" on their faces. In addition, we regard others' faces as the most crucial medium through which to gauge their current feelings and attitudes. Through reading their facial expressions, we assess how they feel at the moment and how they are likely to act toward us. In turn, we identify them as happy, sad, angry, afraid, bored, kindhearted, or the like.

In this process of attributing traits and identities to others, we also use their faces, in combination with their bodies, as the basis for evaluating their physical attractiveness. If we deem them to be attractive, we assume that they possess a host of other desirable traits and qualities. For example, we tend to think they are more intelligent, personable, and likable than other people and that they have better sex lives, happier marriages, higher social status, and better mental health. In essence, we make inferences about their identities based on the notion that "what is beautiful is good." Social psychologists refer to this as the **halo effect,** or the tendency to believe attractive people have more socially desirable qualities than their less attractive counterparts do.

Along with considering the physical attractiveness of others, we form impressions of them in terms of their body type. In a study conducted in the 1960s, Wells and Siegel analyzed the qualities attributed to people having different body types.[33] They showed silhouette drawings of three separate body types to the participants in their study: *ectomorphs,* individuals whose body type is tall and thin; *mesomorphs,* those whose body type is more muscular and athletic; and *endomorphs,* those whose body type tends toward roundness, softness, or fatness. Participants rated each of the types on a set of two dozen characteristics, such as sociable and withdrawn. Their answers revealed stereotypical responses to body builds. The participants rated ectomorphs as tense, anxious, serious, cautious, and detached. They saw mesomorphs as active, enthusiastic, adventurous, assertive, and competitive. And they regarded endomorphs as relaxed, sluggish, warm, forgiving, and cooperative.

Finally, in evaluating the physical appearance of others, we make assessments based on the clothing that they wear. Their clothes operate as a kind of "social skin" that conveys important information about their statuses and characteristics. As Gregory Stone insightfully observed, we rely on people's clothing to discern many of their attributes, including their age, gender, ethnicity, social class, job, moods, feelings, attitudes, and political beliefs.[34] Clothes thus set the stage for us as we evaluate, identify, and interact with others. Through assessing their style of dress, we appraise their value, appreciate their moods, anticipate their attitudes (or behavioral tendencies), and assign them an identity. We thereby determine their meaning for us as we interact with them. Of course, those whose clothing is being assessed don't play a passive role in this process. They use their clothes as a prop to actively manipulate the impressions that we form of them and the identities that we attribute to them. These dynamics are discussed further in Chapter Four, when we consider how people manage impressions and present selves to others.

Identifying others through discourse. Although the appearance of others clearly affects how we think of them and, in many respects, shapes the nature of our interactions with them, it often fails to give us some of the details we want to uncover. For instance, we cannot gain full knowledge of such important aspects of others' identities as their occupation, social class, educational background, religious beliefs, political affiliations, or even ethnicity through observing their appearance alone.[35] We have to rely on their discourse, or verbal communications, to gather this information.

As Karp and Yoels have pointed out, many of our everyday conversations with others are designed to elicit comments from them that will give us insight into their identities. As we interact with them, we ask questions and share remarks that reveal our interest in placing them as social objects. We might ask, "What do you do?" to find out their occupation and education level. Or we might ask, "What does your spouse do?" to discover their marital status. Or, if we know them fairly well, we might ask, "What's up?" to detect the identity they are putting forward in their current situation. If they say, "I'm going to start studying now," you think of them as students. If, on the other hand, they say, "Hey, sit down and have a beer with me—I just bought a 12-pack and I'm going to get wasted," you regard them as partiers. In either case, you use their discourse to determine what identity to assign them and, correspondingly, what actions to adopt toward them.

As we respond to the discourse and implicit identity claims of others, we listen not only to the contents of their remarks but also to the tone, style, and patterns of their speech. In this process, we make inferences about their social characteristics, along with their attitudes and moods, and consider whether these factors contradict the claims they make through their appearance. When contradictions or inconsistencies arise, we question the authenticity of the image the person is presenting.

Overall, then, we rely on the processes of both discourse and appearance as we form impressions and attribute identities to others. Each process informs and potentially contrasts with the other. Put simply, we compare what people say and how they say it to how they appear during their interactions with us. Doing so enables us to carefully evaluate the identity claims they are making and to decide whether to honor them.

Making sense of complex configurations of identity. As suggested in the preceding discussion, our interactions with others are often nuanced and complicated. In making sense of others, we rarely think of them in terms of one isolated characteristic, such as age. Instead, we see them in terms of a complex configuration of identities. For example, rather than categorizing people only in terms of their age, we identify them as young, rich, ambitious, African American, and female, or as old, middle-class, hardworking, Hispanic, and male, or as some other cluster of attributes. Thus, in making assessments of others, we consider the meaning and implications of the combination of attributes they possess. We do not respond to one attribute at a time. Instead, we perceive and respond to people in terms of the impressions and interpretations we have formed of their particular combination of attributes taken as a whole.

Social psychologists have conducted much research on how we process and integrate the information we receive about the complex configuration of attributes that others present to us. In this research they have discovered that we use different **schemas** to interpret specific attributes, such as gender, when they are combined with certain other attributes. For instance, some white students think differently about the attribute of female when it is connected with African American. While these students describe "women in general" as intelligent, materialistic, sensitive, attractive, and sophisticated, they describe African-American women as loud, talkative, aggressive, intelligent, and straightforward.[36] They also group African-American women into subtypes such as "threatening" and "welfare mothers" that they do not use when describing women in general.

In addition to examining how gender and ethnicity become combined in the perceptual process, researchers have found that the schemas used to interpret these attributes are superseded at times by schemas that emphasize the linkages of occupation, role behaviors, physical characteristics, and character traits.

Overall, social psychological research indicates that we try to fit together people's social, physical, and character attributes into a unified and coherent impression. We seek to organize them into a meaningful whole. We often do so by reevaluating and redefining attributes depending on whether we associate them (and their possessor) with a favorable or an unfavorable group. Thus, the long hours worked by a person associated with an ingroup illustrate his or her devotion, while the same number of hours worked by a person belonging to an outgroup reveal his or her compulsiveness and inability to relax.

The peculiar dynamics of person perception. In discussing the process of person perception, we have highlighted how it is influenced by the linguistic categories we draw on as we come into contact with others. We have focused special attention on the schemas and stereotypes activated by "priority attributes" such as gender, age, and ethnicity. In so doing, we have drawn on a number of insights and concepts developed by cognitive social psychologists. These researchers recognize the importance of the social and symbolic aspects of human perception. Above all, they have highlighted how we perceive and act toward others on the basis of the impressions or images we form of them. These images are derived from stereotypes and schemas and thus are always somewhat incomplete and inaccurate. Yet they are all we have to guide us. We must act toward others based on our images of them and not in terms of who they might "really" be beyond these images. In this process, we confer attributes upon them that fit with our images of them and then respond to them as if they possess these attributes. Doing so enables us to engage in meaningful interaction with them.

In revealing these dynamics, cognitive social psychologists have helped us to see some of the central conceptual processes and social categories we bring to bear as we perceive others. Unfortunately, however, they have also overlooked some key factors, such as how people's perceptions of others are influenced by the nature and dynamics of their interactions with them. From a symbolic interactionist perspective, the analyses offered by cognitive social psychologists fall short in two important respects. First, they imply that the people (or groups) who are the targets of perception play a rather passive role in conveying information about themselves. Clearly this is not the case. Individuals (and groups) actively try to manipulate the information others receive about them. They conceal certain facts about themselves while advertising others in their efforts to shape our appraisals and impressions of them. Moreover, when interacting with other people who have different relationships with them, they adjust their strategies of information control, hiding some details they previously emphasized and accentuating others that had been previously concealed. As a result, a particular individual is a somewhat different object (with different meanings) to different observers. These observers' interpretations of the person are derived from their relationship with him or her. What is "true" about the individual from the perspective of a person in one relationship with him or her may be highly inaccurate from the perspective of another person in a quite different relationship with him or her.[37] Pragmatically speaking, then, the "reality" of the individual is not inherent to his or her characteristics and behaviors but rather emerges out of the nature of his or her interactions with others. (These themes are discussed in further detail in Chapters Four and Six).

A second and related shortcoming of the analyses provided by cognitive social psychologists is their neglect of how particular types of social interactions and situations influence people's interpretations of the information presented by others. Within a given interaction, individuals direct their attention to selective features of others' appearances and actions based on how they define the specific situation. They consequently gather different information about a person and interpret that information differently depending on whether they define the situation as a party, a funeral, a job interview, a date, a business deal, an experiment, or something else. In some of these situations, a person's priority attributes, such as gender or ethnicity, may have little if any bearing on how he or she is perceived, but in others they may have a central impact.

Language, Naming, and the Construction of 'Inner' Reality: Emotional Experience

As symbol-reliant creatures, human beings interpret and define the "reality" not only of their natural and social worlds but also of their internal world. They have to make sense of what happens "inside" their bodies in the same way that they make sense of what happens "outside" of them—by translating the sensations they experience into linguistic categories, or names. Ironically, then, people do not even have a direct and unmediated experience of their "insides." Instead, they must rely on symbols and *social* processes, particularly the processes of interpretation and interaction, to understand and meaningfully respond to their internal experiences. To illustrate this, we focus on how people define and respond to their emotional experiences.

Most people think of emotions as instinctive or spontaneous reactions they experience as they go through life. In many respects, they see emotions as being similar to reflexes such as sneezing; that is, emotions are "naturally" triggered by certain stimuli and have to be released in specific behaviors. For instance, when you get cut off in traffic, you "naturally" feel angry and curse the inconsiderate driver. Or, when you get a thoughtful gift from a family member, you "naturally" feel grateful and express this through a kiss or a hug. According to this commonsense view, emotions are internal, irrational, and almost automatic bodily reactions that lead individuals to act in particular ways. Because these reactions are not rational, people presumably have little ability to control or manage them.

For years many students of human emotion adopted a similar view. In turn, they focused their research on discovering the biological bases of emotion and on detecting how particular emotions served as the underlying sources of specific behaviors. This research gave little consideration to the social dimensions of emotions. In recent decades, sociologists, led largely by the analyses of symbolic interactionists, began to challenge this approach. They emphasized how emotions, like other meaningful human experiences, are profoundly social in their origins, nature, and expression. Through their analyses these sociologists illustrated how emotions cannot be understood simply as individual physiological reactions to specific stimuli. Instead, they must be seen as embedded in and arising out of social behavior, processes, and relationships.[38]

In analyzing emotion, symbolic interactionists emphasize how it is a nuanced *form of action* that involves a complex combination of experiences and processes that operate at various levels.[39] On one level, emotion involves biological processes; it includes physiological sensations and bodily experiences. We feel things "in our gut or heart" as we respond to specific situations. In some circumstances, we literally quake with fear, shake with rage, or feel overwhelmed by grief or excitement. Even when we feel less intense emotions, we often experience noticeable bodily changes, including an accelerated heartbeat, increased blood pressure and perspiration, and a rush of blood to the face. Yet, although our emotions have these biological aspects and implications, it is important to emphasize that they are ultimately grounded in and mediated through social rather than physiological realities.

According to symbolic interactionists, emotions arise and are expressed through an interactive process characterized by three phases.[40] In the first phase, a specific stimulus or situation is interpreted or defined. As we have stressed repeatedly in this chapter, people do not simply react to stimuli; they interpret them in light of their situation and then formulate a response, which often includes an emotion. Consider a scenario that unfolds in the hallway outside one of your classrooms. One young man, Dave, greets another man, Marcus, and then punches him sharply on the upper arm, inducing a sensation of pain. What does this mean? It depends on how Marcus defines the situation and the meaning of the punch. If Marcus sees Dave as a rival who is trying to initiate a fight, he will likely define the punch as an act of hostility. On the other hand, if Marcus sees Dave as a friend who is playfully jousting with him, he may define the punch as an act of affection.

As Marcus defines the "stimulus" of the punch, he moves into the second phase of the interactional process surrounding emotional experience. During this phase, he experiences an internal response to the defined situation. This response includes both physiological and symbolic processes. Physiologically, Marcus may be experiencing a fairly unpleasant sensation of pain, along with an increase in his heart rate and blood pressure. But, if he defines Dave's punch as an act of friendship, he will respond to these bodily sensations very differently than if he defines it as an act of hostility. This is where the symbolic processes fit. Through his social experiences, Marcus has learned how to name (or define) and appropriately respond to particular bodily sensations in the context of given situations. In this case, let's assume that Marcus is part of a friendship group that practices a greeting consisting of a sharp punch to the shoulder. Through his interactions with others in the group, Marcus has learned to define the pain that he currently experiences in his shoulder as a sign of the caring and camaraderie that members of the group feel for one another.

During the third and final phase of the social process involved in emotional experience, Marcus communicates his emotional response to Dave's punch by drawing on conventionalized symbols, including words, gestures, and facial expressions. Assuming that he defines it as an act of friendship, he might convey that he feels caring and connection toward Dave by laughing loudly about the punch and then returning the gesture. In doing so, Marcus has used his thoughts, or cognitions, to suppress and transform the pain he initially felt into an expression that communicates the emotion of caring. He is thereby engaging in a nuanced process of emotion management that may or may not entail a genuine expression of his feelings about Dave or his punch. Marcus may choose to act "as if" he defines the punch as an act of friendship and "as if" he cares about Dave when he actually feels annoyed by both the punch and Dave. In this event, Marcus mimics the feeling expected of him without truly feeling it. On the other hand, he may choose to suppress his feelings of pain and to consciously call forth feelings of caring toward Dave, which he then expresses in laughter and the return of the ritual punch. When making this choice, he actually works on his feelings to evoke an emotional response that fits the expectations of the situation.

In presenting this scenario, we have tried to highlight how emotions are generated, defined, and expressed through a social process. Implicitly, we have also touched on some major assumptions of a symbolic interactionist approach to emotion. For the sake of clarity, let us briefly state these five assumptions:

First, emotions originate in and arise out of our participation in social life.[41] Our experience of feelings such as anger, joy, frustration, and satisfaction are tied to our social behavior, positions, and interactions. When we engage in behavior and interactions that allow us to successfully realize our goals in a situation, such as making connection with a friend or earning a good grade in a course, we are likely to feel happiness or satisfaction. On the other hand, when we engage in behavior and interactions that block our attainment of desired goals, we are likely to feel anger or frustration.

Second, the emotions we feel as a consequence of our action and interaction are embodied—that is, they are connected to physiological processes and reactions that take place in our bodies. However, these processes and reactions must be interpreted in terms of symbols and social categories. In other words, they must be named. Feelings such as "joy" and "anger" are not only experienced as bodily sensations but are also named and thus socially defined, both by those experiencing them and those who observe this experience. In fact, while we can have the physiological sensations linked to a particular emotion, such as anger, we will not experience these sensations as the feeling of anger until we name them as such.[42] The process of naming allows us to organize and give the meaning of anger to particular sensations, such as an increased heartbeat and adrenaline flow. It also allows us to see ourselves as "angry" and to act upon ourselves in light of that definition, reflecting on and deciding how or whether to express that feeling in a given situation.

Third, as implied above, our emotions are self-feelings; they are experiences that refer to and have implications for self.[43] We link emotions to the self, saying "I am mad," "I am happy," "I am sad," "I am nervous," "I am in love," or "I am bored." As Norman Denzin has suggested, our emotions arise out of and reflect our self-interactions as well as our interactions with others.[44] In the process of experiencing emotion, we engage in acts and judgments directed toward the self. Doing so involves imagining ourselves in the eyes of others and responding to the self as a social object. Through this reflexive process we define ourselves as feeling a certain way—whether angry, sad, joyous, or passionate.

Fourth, while emotions involve the self, they are identified, shaped, and expressed in accord with the social definitions and expectations provided by the groups to which we belong. As a result, *emotions are social objects* that we manipulate and act toward much like other social objects. We can manage, express, and use emotions in various ways to realize our goals for self and to negotiate meaningful interactions with others. In this process, we are often guided by the "feeling rules" that predominate in our social groups.[45] Through our interactions with others in these groups we learn an unwritten set of expectations about what emotions are appropriate to feel in given situations and how we ought to express or display them. For instance, we learn that we are supposed to feel happy at weddings and that we should express this feeling by smiling during the ceremony and by engaging in rowdier behavior afterward, such as throwing rice at the bride and groom and "celebrating" at the reception. We also learn to suppress or hide less positive feelings that might arise during the wedding, such as jealousy, anger, sadness, or worries about the likely success of the marriage.

Fifth, and perhaps most important, as we learn how to manage various emotions in light of feeling rules, we develop the ability proactively to shape and control our bodily sensations and emotional experiences. We do not simply react to situations based on physiological processes that take place within us. Instead, we learn how to interpret these processes and translate them into emotional experiences and actions that fit with the demands of specific situations. We also learn to formulate emotional acts in ways that involve both suppressing and calling forth various feelings. In turn, we use our emotions not merely to shape our actions to meet the expectations of others but also to influence and direct the responses of others. For instance, we express sympathy toward a classmate who has done poorly on an exam not only because doing so is expected of us but because we want to encourage him or her to see us as a "nice" person and to treat us thoughtfully. Emotions, then, become a crucial part of the processes of communication, role taking, and self-presentation. They serve as a vital channel of communication through which we convey how we are defining others, ourselves, and our situation, and also how we try to shape others' responses to us, themselves, and this situation. Thus, the process of constructing and negotiating meaning is not simply cognitive; it is also emotional. We define reality through the processes of both thinking and feeling. Our cognitions do not simply shape our emotional responses; rather, our thoughts and emotions work hand in hand, mutually influencing each other.

Summary

- As human beings, we do not passively perceive or respond to the world "as it is." Instead, we actively and selectively transform a world of ambiguous stimuli into images and concepts, thereby giving it meaning and order. Although this is a nuanced and complex process, it seems fairly unproblematic to us because many of the concepts we rely on are ready-made and supplied to us by the groups to which we belong. We learn these concepts as we learn the language and culture of our society. These concepts are known as symbols.

- What makes us distinctive as human beings is our ability to use and create symbols. This capacity enables us to transcend the bonds of our immediate environment. Unlike other animals, we do not simply respond to our experiences in the here and now. Instead, we build up our actions in terms of our images of the past, present, and future as well as our images of what is good, right, or important. In essence, we act and live in a world of our own creation—a world that is inherently abstract rather than concrete, a world of symbols that, in some senses, is imaginary.

- In addition to enabling us to transcend and transform our environment, symbols allow us to think, fantasize, remember, make plans, and create and pass along culture. Perhaps most important, symbols enable us to "name" the objects, events, and people we encounter in our world and, in so doing, to transform them into *social objects*. Through the naming process, then, we define the "reality" of the objects of our daily experience and know how to act toward them.

- In defining the "reality" of others, we engage in the same types of processes we use to define the reality of other social objects. We gather information through our senses, we sort and organize this information into categories or names, and we utilize these categories to interpret each other's meaning. In this process of person perception, we often rely on categories known as *stereotypes*. Stereotypes are mental images that attribute a common set of characteristics to members of a particular group or social category. They enable us to simplify the reality of others and to make fast decisions about them based on a small amount of information. Through drawing on stereotypes, we can assess others quickly, assign them social identities, anticipate their actions, and plan our own responses to these actions.

- The stereotypes we use to interpret and respond to others are often activated by the "priority attributes" people possess, such as their age, gender, and ethnicity. However, stereotypes can also be called forth by other attributes or information that people present, such as their physical attractiveness, clothing, or style of discourse. Regardless of when, why, and how stereotypes are activated, we often pay a price for the efficiency and direction that we derive from using them. Stereotypes can lead us to distort, exaggerate, or overlook important information about others and, correspondingly, to respond to them on the basis of misleading or faulty assumptions. Stereotypes can also prompt us to "see" or call forth attributes and actions in others that fit our preconceived expectations.

- In general, we rarely define another person only in terms of a specific, isolated attribute. Instead, we respond to that individual in terms of his or her complex configuration of identities. Typically, we seek to organize this configuration into a coherent and meaningful whole—we form an overall impression of the person. We often do so by reevaluating and redefining his or her attributes depending on whether we associate him or her with a favorable group or an unfavorable group.

- We make sense of our "inner worlds" through the same processes of "naming" and symbolic interaction that we use to give meaning to the natural and social worlds. This phenomenon is revealed in how we define and respond to our emotional experiences. We identify and express our emotions through a three-phase interactional process that involves us in (1) interpreting a specific stimulus or situation in a particular way; (2) experiencing an internal response to that interpreted stimulus or situation; and (3) formulating and conveying an emotional response by means of conventionalized symbols, including words, gestures, and facial expressions.

- While our emotions have a physiological component and seem to originate inside our bodies, they are rooted in our social acts and interactions. They are also shaped by the social definitions and feeling norms provided by the groups to which we belong. Our emotions, then, are social objects and socially constructed actions rather than biological states or reactions. In light of this, we manipulate and shape their meanings in the same manner that we manipulate and shape the meanings of other social objects and acts. Most important, we actively manage and control our emotions as we engage in social acts and interactions. We also use them to communicate meanings to others, thereby influencing or directing how others respond to us.

Glossary of Key Terms

Central Organizing Trait A character trait that has the greatest impact on the overall impression we form of another individual. According to research on the person perception process, the perceived "warmth" of another is a central organizing trait.

Concepts Regularized ways of thinking about real or imagined events and objects. A concept enables us to picture a "thing" in our world or to describe or represent things to ourselves and one another and to grasp their meaning.

Culture The ways of thinking, feeling, and acting that characterize a society or group. These ways of thinking, feeling, and acting are learned, transmitted, sustained, and transformed through our interaction and communication with one another.

Etcetera Principle A rule specifying that, in attempting to reach an understanding or agreement, conversational partners may disregard parts of a communication of which they do not have full knowledge, and pretend that they do, as long as those portions are deemed unimportant.

Ethnomethod A conversational strategy used by people to make sense of everyday life and construct a sense of order.

Halo Effect The tendency to believe that people with one positive trait are likely to have other positive traits.

Idioculture A system of shared knowledge, beliefs, feelings, and behaviors that serves as a frame of reference and basis of interaction for members of a particular group.

Indexical Expression A word or phrase whose meaning can only be interpreted and understood—"indexed"—according to the context in which it is used.

Language A system of symbols shared by members of a culture and used for the purposes of communication and representation. These symbols have standardized meanings and catalog events, objects, and relations in the world.

Perception The process of drawing meaning from the stimuli that reach our senses. Perception is an active process by which we gather and interpret information about our external and internal environments.

Prototype A mental image, or schema, we use to represent a typical set of features that exemplify an object or person.

Schema A set of beliefs or preconceptions that organizes the information we gather about a specific object, person, or concept. Schemas allow us to simplify reality by interpreting specific instances in light of general categories.

Sign An object or event to which a fixed or unchanging response is made. Its meaning is associated or identified with its physical form.

Social Cognition Sorting and organizing data by naming or applying social categories to them, thereby giving them meaning.

Social Identity A mental category that locates us in relation to others, highlighting how we are similar to and different from these others. A social identity can consist of a single characteristic or it can consist of a cluster of traits and statuses.

Social Object An object that we give meaning to through our interaction with one another. An object becomes a social object when we name it and act toward it in terms of that name.

Stereotype A mental image that attributes a common set of characteristics to members of a particular group.

Symbol An object, gesture, or word that we use to represent, or take the place of, something else.

Questions for Reflection or Assignment

1. Form two or more groups in class, each having an equal number of members. Next, have the groups compete with one another in doing the following task without *speaking a single word*. The task: Group members should inform one another of the month and date they were born and then arrange themselves in chronological order—that is, from the earliest birthday in January to the last birthday in December. The first team to do so successfully "wins" the contest. After participating in the contest, analyze what happened. How did people in your group communicate what they needed to with one another? Did they use symbols? If so, what kinds of symbols did they use? What characteristics do these symbols have? Do they have the same characteristics and consequences as verbal symbols? What are the key consequences of symbols?

2. Go on a 15- to 30-minute walk in a "nature center" or a wooded area. Try to see and hear as much as you can as you proceed on your walk. Stop and carefully examine the plants, trees, birds, animals, and insects that are in your vicinity. How many can you name? How many do you not have names for? Which are you more likely to notice? Would you agree with the statement that "people see things that they have words for"? Why or why not?

3. Do the names we give to certain people or situations make a difference? For instance, does it matter whether we call a person "crippled," "handicapped," or "disabled"? Does it matter if we call someone an "AIDS victim," an "AIDS patient," or "a person living with AIDS"? Or does it matter if we call an adult female a "girl," a "lady," or a "woman"? Explain and offer support for your answer.

4. Analyze the speech of a local or national politician. What kind of language and symbols does he or she use when speaking? What does this language emphasize? What does it conceal? How does it frame the "issues" that the speaker addresses? Is language an important aspect of exercising power? How and why?

5. It has been said that "in the animal kingdom, the rule is to eat or be eaten," whereas "in the human kingdom, the rule is to define or be defined." Do you agree with this maxim? Why or why not?

6. Interview someone with a chronic pain condition and ask the person to talk about the pain that he or she feels. What words does the person use to describe the pain? Does the person have difficulty putting the pain into words? If so, why would this be the case?

Overall, what meanings does the pain have for him or her? What emotions does it evoke? How are these meanings and emotions influenced by the person's social interactions and social statuses, such as the person's gender, ethnicity, or class?

7. Think back to a group that you belonged to in the past, especially in your childhood. What unique terms or "special language" did this group use? Did members of the group call one another by nicknames? If so, what were some of these nicknames? What purposes did they serve for the group and its members?

Suggested Readings for Further Study

Burke, Kenneth, *On Symbols and Society* (Chicago: University of Chicago Press, 1989).

Chayko, Mary, "From Cave Paintings to Chat Rooms: The Sociomental Foundation of Connectedness," pp. 7–37 in *Connecting* (Albany, NY: SUNY Press).

Edelman, Murray, *Political Language: Words That Succeed and Policies That Fail* (New York: Academic Press, 1977).

Lakoff, George, *Women, Fire, and Dangerous Things* (Chicago: University of Chicago Press, 1987).

Larch, Doug, *Father Gander Nursery Rhymes* (Santa Barbara, CA: Advocacy Press, 1985).

Pinker, Stephen, *The Language Instinct: How the Mind Creates Language* (New York: Harper Perennial, 1994).

Sacks, Oliver, *Seeing Voices* (Berkeley: University of California Press, 1989).

Zerubavel, Eviatar, *Social Mindscapes: An Invitation to Cognitive Sociology* (Cambridge, MA: Harvard University Press, 1997).

Endnotes

1. This quote is taken from an interview conducted by the first author, Kent Sandstrom, when studying the lived experience of men with HIV/AIDS. For further discussion of the themes highlighted in this interview, see Kent L. Sandstrom, "Preserving a Vital and Valued Self in the Face of AIDS," *Sociological Inquiry* 68(3), 1998, pp. 354–371.

2. Suzanne Langer, *Philosophy in a New Key* (New York: Mentor Books, 1948).

3. Ibid., p. 46.

4. For a related and more detailed discussion, see Anselm Strauss, *Continual Permutations of Action* (New York: Aldine de Gruyter, 1993), pp. 140–160.

5. James W. Vander Zanden, *Social Psychology*, 3rd ed. (New York: Random House, 1984), p. 36.

6. Ibid.

7. Ibid., p. 38.

8. Alfred R. Lindesmith, Anselm L. Strauss, and Norman K. Denzin, *Social Psychology*, 7th ed. (Englewood Cliffs, NJ: Prentice-Hall, 1993), P. 55.

9. John P. Hewitt, *Self and Society*, 6th ed. (Boston: Allyn and Bacon, 1994), p. 35.

10. Jodi O'Brien and Peter Kollock, *The Production of Reality*, 2nd ed. (Thousand Oaks, CA: Pine Forge Press, 1997), p. 55.

11. Tamotsu Shibutani, "Reference Groups as Perspectives," *American Journal of Sociology* 60, 1955, pp. 962–965.

12. Gary Alan Fine, *With the Boys: Little League Baseball and Preadolescent Culture* (Chicago: University of Chicago Press, 1987), p. 125.

13. Anselm L. Strauss, *Mirrors and Masks* (San Francisco: Sociology Press, 1959).

14. Joel Charon, *Symbolic Interactionism: An Introduction, an Interpretation, an Integration*, 4th ed. (Englewood Cliffs, NJ: Prentice-Hall, 1992), p. 46.

15. Susan Curtiss, *Genie: A Psycho linguistic Study of a Modern-Day "Wild Child"* (New York: Academic Press, 1977). See also Kingsley Davis' classic article, "Final Note on a Case of Extreme Isolation," *American Journal of Sociology* 52(5), 1947, pp. 432–437.

16. Oliver Sacks, *Seeing Voices: A Journey Into the World of the Deaf* (Berkeley and Los Angeles: University of California Press, 1989).

17. Helen Keller, *The Story of My Life* (New York: Doubleday, 1917).

18. James W. Vander Zanden, *Social Psychology*, 2nd ed. (New York: Random House), p. 43.

19. Walter Lippmann, *Public Opinion* (New York: Harcourt, 1922), p. 16.

20. Mark Snyder, "When Beliefs Create Reality: The Self-Fulfilling Impact of First Impressions on Social Interaction," in A. Pines and C. Maslach, eds., *Experiencing Social Psychology* (New York: Alfred Knopf, 1977), pp. 189–192.

21. Solomon Asch, "Forming Impressions of Personality," *Journal of Abnormal and Social Psychology* 41, 1946, pp. 258–290; and Solomon Asch, *Social Psychology* (Englewood Cliffs, NJ: Prentice-Hall, 1952).

22. Ibid.

23. J. Wishner, "Reanalysis of 'Impressions of Personality,'" *Psychological Review 67*, 1960, pp. 96–112.

24. Kay Deaux and Laurie Lewis, "Structure of Gender Stereotypes: Interrelationships Among Components and Gender Label," *Journal of Personality and Social Psychology* 46, 1984, pp. 991–1004.

25. See Sandra L. Bern, *The Lenses of Gender* (New Haven, CT: Yale University Press, 1993); B. J. Skrypnek and Mark Snyder, "On the Self-Perpetuating Nature of Stereotypes About Men and Women," *Journal of Experimental Social Psychology* 18, 1992, pp. 247–305; and Naomi Wolf, *The Beauty Myth* (New York: William Morrow, 1991).

26. Jeannye Thornton and David Whitman with Dorian Freidman, "Whites' Myths About Blacks," *U.S. News and World Report*, November 9, 1992, pp. 41–44.

27. James Wiggins, Beverly Wiggins, and James Vander Zanden, *Social Psychology*, 5th ed. (New York: McGraw Hill, 1995), p. 183.

28. M. B. Brewer and R. M. Kramer, "The Psychology of Intergroup Attitudes and Behavior," *Annual Review of Psychology* 37, 1984, pp. 515–521.

29. J. R. Kluegel and E. R. Smith, *Belief About Inequality: Americans' Views of What Is and What Ought to Be* (New York: Aldine de Gruyter, 1986).

30. Judith A. Howard, *Gendered Selves, Gendered Situations* (Thousand Oaks, CA: Sage, 1997), p. 78.

31. David Karp and William Yoels, *Sociology and Everyday Life* (Itasca, IL: F. E. Peacock, 1986).

32. Georg Simmel, "Sociology of the Senses: Visual Interaction," in Robert E. Park and Ernest W. Burgess, eds., *Introduction to the Science of Society* (Chicago: University of Chicago Press, 1924).

33. W. Wells and B. Siegel, "Stereotyped Soma-types," *Psychological Reports* 8, 1961, pp. 77–78.

34. Gregory P. Stone, "Appearance and the Self: A Slightly Revised Version," in Dennis Brissett and Charles Edgley, eds., *Life as Theater: A Dramaturgical Sourcebook,* 2nd ed. (Chicago: Aldine Press, 1990), pp. 141–162.

35. David Karp and William Yoels, *Sociology and Everyday Life* (Note 30), p. 78.

36. Rose Weitz and Leonard Gordon, "Images of Black Women Among Anglo College Students," *Sex Roles* 28, 1993, pp. 19–34.

37. George McCall and J. L. Simmons, *Identities and Interactions* (New York: The Free Press, 1966), pp. 119–120.

38. See Steven L. Gordon, "The Sociology of Sentiments and Emotion," in Morris Rosenberg and Ralph Turner, eds., *Social Psychology: Sociological Perspectives* (New York: Basic Books, 1981), pp. 562–592; Arlie R. Hochschild, "Emotion Work, Feeling Rules, and Social Structure," *American Journal of Sociology* 87, 1979, pp. 551–575; Trudy Mills and Sherryl Kleinman, "Emotions, Reflexivity, and Action: An Interactionist Analysis," *Social Forces* 66, 1988, pp. 1009–1027; and Susan Shott, "Emotion and Social Life: A Symbolic Interactionist Analysis," *American Journal of Sociology* 84, 1979, pp. 1317–1334.

39. Alfred R. Lindesmith, Anselm L. Strauss, and Norman K. Denzin, *Social Psychology* (Note 8), p. 98.

40. Ibid., p. 100.

41. John P. Hewitt, *Self and Society,* 7th ed. (Boston: Allyn and Bacon, 1997).

42. Ibid.

43. Norman K. Denzin, *On Understanding Emotion* (San Francisco: Jossey-Bass, 1983).

44. Norman K. Denzin, "A Note on Emotionality, Self, and Interaction," *American Journal of Sociology* 89(2), 1983, pp. 402–409.

45. Arlie R. Hochschild, "Emotion Work, Feeling Rules, and Social Structure," (Note 37).

Learning Privilege

Lessons of Power and Identity in Affluent Schooling

By Adam Howard

"Why are we learning about those people?" Jonas, one of my seventh-grade students, asked me during a discussion about homelessness. "This isn't about social issues. Those people are just bad business people," he insisted. "We're discussing it because homelessness is a big problem in our country and even in our city. It's an important issue for us to be aware of instead of just ignoring it," I responded.

Jonas replied, "Yeah, but it's because they don't spend their money right and don't get jobs to get them out of their situation."

Another boy sitting across from Jonas added, "It's a problem because they just don't want to work so they can live in a house. They're too lazy to get a job."

"I think it's because they don't make the good decisions in life and it's gotten them where they're at," another boy told us.

"Why do you think they don't make the right decisions?" I asked. "What makes people not make good decisions?"

"I think Jonas said it. They're bad business people," one of the boys replied. Fortunately, the bell rang, because I did not know how to respond to their comments at the time. It was one of those moments as a teacher when I couldn't come up with the right response or the perfect question to challenge students' thinking. I was speechless.

During my first year of teaching at an elite private school, I met with ten seventh-grade boys for forty-five minutes two days a week to cover a broad range of issues—everything from puberty to larger societal concerns. It was a designated time for them to feel safe (no girls around) to discuss personal and societal issues openly. On this particular day, I started our discussion by asking them if they had ever seen a homeless person in our city. At first, all of them declared that they had not. Although our city did not have a large homeless population, a visible number of people lived on our downtown streets. To probe further, I asked them if they had attended sporting or other events downtown. Finally, one advisee said that he had seen two homeless men sitting outside the entrance of a sporting event asking for money. "I wasn't about to give them money and nobody else was going to either, because they were drinking and would have just spent it on getting drunk," he reported. After he gave this example, most of the boys said that they also had seen a homeless person at some point in their lives. I discovered that the reason they hadn't remembered coming across a homeless person at the beginning of our conversation was because they ignored them. We continued to talk about homelessness in a very general sense until Jonas questioned the value of "learning about those people."

Later that same year, with another group of students, a discussion of the welfare system emerged from an assigned reading in my sophomore English class. The majority of the students in the class argued that the system did not work, that their parents should not be forced to "support" the poor through their taxes, and that those who were receiving government assistance should just get a job. For the sake of exploring the issue further and sharing my own beliefs, I proposed an opposing argument to them that supported the welfare system: "Some people are forced to rely on government support to survive. They are put in situations where they don't see alternative options for providing for their families. Their circumstances in life are very different than what we take for granted," I argued. My response provoked a debate that eventually spread to the various issues relating to poverty.

The importance of this class discussion for me was in learning my students' perceptions of poor people. One of my students commented, "Our parents have worked hard for what we have. We shouldn't be forced to give it to people who don't do anything." Another student intensely argued, "Those people just want a free ride and want everything handed to them without working for it." The central point of their argument was that since their parents had worked hard, they deserved their wealth and were not obligated to share it with the poor. In their perspectives, wealth meant working hard and poverty meant laziness. The discussion concluded with a student pointing out, "Besides, we don't have to worry about them. Don't you know that's the reason why we have woods around our neighborhood? It blocks the view so we don't have to see them." Again, the students posed the question, "Why are we discussing those people?"

While teaching at this school I frequently found myself lost for words when trying to respond to my students' assumptions of others and the world around them. Their beliefs often represented a view in opposition to what I held to be true. My beliefs and thinking had been powerfully influenced by my upbringing in poverty. I was too unfamiliar with this world of privilege and abundance to teach my students lessons about others and themselves different from the ones they had been taught by most of the adults in their lives. Frustrated, I began to explore my burning questions about this unfamiliar world I had entered.

A Critical Interpretative Study of Privilege

These questions eventually led me to begin a six-year research project at four elite high schools. I began this project by conducting a small-scale ethnographic study at McLean Academy, a private high school located in a suburb of a large Northeastern city. My research at McLean explored questions I'd had before I began teaching affluent students. What were the everyday experiences of students? What were their prevailing ways of knowing and doing? What were the different styles and substances of classes? What were the qualities of school life? These were some of the questions that guided my inquiry. During this study, I made half-day visits to the school every week for two months. During my visits, I observed classes, assemblies, sporting events, and all-school gatherings; conducted interviews with three teachers and the headmaster; and gathered classroom documents (e.g., assignments, examinations) and school publications (e.g., brochures, catalogues, school newspapers). This study gave me a better sense of the social and cultural particularities of school life at a privileged private school.

My experiences teaching the affluent led me to additional and more specific questions about privilege and the advantages of elite schooling. By this point, I was familiar enough with affluent schooling both as a teacher and as a researcher to form critical questions about privilege itself and the processes and structures that reinforced and regenerated it. I extended the scope of the research that I began at McLean to explore questions about the structures, routines, understandings, and practices that influenced the educational experiences of affluent students and what students learned about their place in the world, their relationships with others, and who they were from these experiences. My interest in understanding the processes involved in reinforcing and regenerating privilege as an identity led me to a critical interpretative approach (Brantlinger, 1993, 2003), which drew from the interpretative (e.g., Gilligan, Brown, & Rogers, 1989; Mehan, 1992) and critical ethnography (Anderson & Irvine, 1993; Carspecken & Apple, 1992) traditions. Mehan (1992) claims that interpretative studies can take a closer examination of the processes by which social stratification is generated and, therefore, as Brantlinger (2003) explains, "offers a means to understand the complexities[,] ... conflicted views" (p. 29), and, I would add, experiences of a dominant class. Interpretative studies do not always follow a critical perspective; however, in my approach, I applied critical theoretical positions (e.g., Apple, 1996, 1999; Arnowitz, 1980, 1992; Giroux, 1981, 1992; McLaren, 1989) to interpret participants' understandings and actions. Similar to Brantlinger (2003), I used a critical genre to situate affluent schooling and privilege in the larger context of "unequal power relationships among people" and "the nature of power differentials" (p. 29) in American schooling.

From 1997 to 2001, I conducted studies at two private high schools located in a midsize Midwestern city, Parker Day School and Bredvik School, and at a public school located in a small, affluent town in the Midwest, Oakley High School. During these studies, I observed primarily one teacher's class at each of the three schools. I observed each class approximately thirty times during a school year. I also observed other classes, assemblies, sporting events, and faculty meetings. Additionally, I conducted three interviews with the teacher whom I primarily observed and two students in the teacher's class (one male and one female), who were selected from the students who agreed to participate in the study. I also conducted an interview with the senior administrator at each school. In total, I conducted approximately forty hours of interviews with administrators, teachers, and students at each of the three schools. Finally, as I did in my research at McLean, I collected classroom and school artifacts to gather additional facts about school policies and classroom practices.

The Everyday Nature of Privilege

Contradictions often arise in what schools *say* they want their students to learn and what they actually *teach* them. Students learn both intended and (purportedly) unintended lessons that are often in conflict. In part, this conflict results from the myriad factors that influence student learning such as social contexts, organizational structures, institutional rules, curriculum, community influences, norms, values, and educational and occupational aspirations. These factors often give shape and life to the unintentional lessons, even when educators and parents *say* and *claim* they want their children/students to learn other lessons. Frequently, these unintentional lessons end up being the ones that are the most consequential for students' lives. Because these lessons often reflect and are parallel with the norms of society, they are experienced as the way things are or perhaps should be even when these norms support oppressive conditions (Kumashiro, 2002). The everyday nature of these lessons allows them to remain hidden as they pervade students' educational experiences and reinforce powerful messages to students about who they are, how they should live and relate to others, what is important in life, and what the future holds for them. The impact on students' lives is far reaching, influencing how they think about others and how they view and feel about themselves.

Just as the term *hidden agenda* conjures up something covert, deceitful, and undisclosed, the hidden nature of unintentional lessons "suggests intentional acts to obscure or conceal—a conscious duplicity that may not always be present" (Gair & Mullins, 2001, p. 23). However, because these lessons often are framed as "normal" and everyday, they are not usually hard to detect. In most cases, they are taught in plain sight and repetitively. The contradiction of something open being hidden not only legitimizes these lessons but masks the cultural processes behind them. By way of analogy, this allows the "white elephant in the room" to remain unrecognized, disguised, and not talked about. The commonsense nature of these lessons functions as a barrier to exposing the meanings and purposes embedded in them, which often reinforce domination. As Apple (1995) explains, what gets defined as common sense may appear to be just the way things are, but they are actually social constructs that function to "confirm and reinforce ... structurally generated relations of domination" (p. 12). Their commonsense appearance, as Kumashiro (2002) elaborates, "not only socializes us to accept oppressive conditions [and I would add, cultural processes of domination] as 'normal' and the way things are, but also to make these conditions [and processes] normative and the ways things ought to be" (p. 82). These norms function to suppress alternative versions of what ought to be.

Within the context of affluent schooling, these "unintentional" lessons play an important role in normalizing and hiding in plain view the cultural processes that reinforce and regenerate privilege. They have an everyday presence that keeps them both known and unknown to insiders of these school communities, which validates and supports the cultural processes that they reinforce and regenerate. The unknown, even when it is partially known, cannot be combated. Protected by lessons that make these cultural processes seem how things ought to be, privilege is perpetuated, regenerated, and re-created (Wildman, 1996). These hidden lessons of privilege, therefore, must be brought to an overt level and made less unknown in order to expose the concealed and sophisticated processes involved in the cultural production of privilege. In the next section, I summarize the findings of the research project to surface these lessons that reinforce and regenerate privilege.

Lessons of Privilege

All four schools of this research project are as different as they are similar. Their communities hold different political orientations (conservative/liberal), different forms of social status (old money/nouveau riche), and different types of relationships with their local communities (detached/connected). Oakley is a public institution, while the other three are independent schools. Each school has its own distinctive mission statement, customs, set of rules, requirements and policies, and ideals. Most teachers, students, and parents at these four schools would argue that my list of differences is just a starting point. The four school communities take great pride in their distinctive qualities. Even though there are differences, these communities take similar norms for granted as natural and legitimate. These norms reflect core values—academic excellence, ambition, trust, service, and tradition—that are expressed in a variety of ways and contexts (e.g., in their ideals, missions, and standards; in and outside classrooms; in their school culture; in curriculum) and guide ways of knowing and doing that both create high standards for their educational programs and reinforce privilege.

On one hand, these values reveal their excellence. They promote student success, trust within the community, choices, the importance of service, and the value of connecting the past to the present to give certainty of the future. The schools are places where excellence is the order of the day and students and educators are really good at being good. Of course, their abundance of resources also contributes to their excellent qualities, but all that is good at these four schools does not entirely result from their affluence. The confluence of motivated, dedicated, and hardworking educators and students significantly contributes to the "goodness" (Lawrence-Lightfoot, 1983) found at these schools. However, on the other hand, and often not as apparent to outsiders, the values by which the schools define their excellence also encourage win-at-all-costs attitudes, unhealthy levels of stress, deception, materialism, competition, white ways of knowing and doing, selfishness, and greed. Their values validate "unintentional" lessons that teach students that:

- There's only one right way of knowing and doing.
- Success comes from being superior to others.
- Do whatever it takes to win.
- Fulfillment is gained by accumulating.
- Others are too different from us to relate to.

These lessons and the values behind them embrace particular norms, perspectives, dispositions, ways of knowing and doing, and ideologies that reinforce and regenerate privilege.

There's only one right way of knowing and doing. In pursuing academic success, students at these schools describe what they do at school and what it takes for them to gain academic success as playing a game. Attempting to win the favor of their teachers, participating in the right amount of service and academic and athletic activities, and playing to win are some of the rules of this game. Most students at the four schools abide by these rules and are really good players at the school game. They are hardworking and talented, get good grades and top scores on college entrance exams, and are involved in numerous athletic, service, and other extracurricular activities. They have spent most of their years of schooling learning how to play this game the right way to achieve academic success. This right way is mutually constituted, whereby students both shape and are shaped by the rules of this game (Grenfell & James, 1998). It is within and through the dialectic between the game and the players that hierarchies of power are played out and students' relative positionings are determined.

Like most other African American students at the four schools, Janora, a Bredvik student, believes that she is on the "losing team" in the school game. As she explains, "It sure is a game all right, but we're the underdogs. ... [The whites] are on the team that wins all the time." She goes on to explain that the "right way" of playing the school game reflects a "white way" of knowing and doing. She explains, "Everything runs the way that white people do things," and African American students must "act white" in order to be successful (or even "survive") in the school game. An African-American parent at Bredvik similarly points out that white values and ideals dominate the culture of her son's school. Another parent at Parker adds that these values and ideals are often in conflict with those of African Americans. Most of the African American parents who participated in this study believe that their children's schools respect only white ways of knowing and doing and, by so doing, place their children at a disadvantage. African American students remain at a decided disadvantage in a game where the rules are controlled by whites.

Not only are the rules of the game not as fair for students of color as for white students, but they also send powerful messages to all students that white cultural understandings are superior to other cultural groups' ways of knowing and doing. White notions determine the standard for academic success, and this standard encourages narrow-mindedness by providing little room for respecting and learning other ways of knowing and doing. Students keep too occupied with following the "right way" to build the capacity to imagine other ways. The power of this certain way regulates identities, knowledge, and practices. It is through this "right way" of identifying, knowing, and doing that the social transmission of privilege is itself legitimized (Lamont & Lareau, 1988). This version of how things ought to be establishes a set of class-based dispositions, perceptions, and appreciations that reinforce and regenerate privilege.

Success comes from being superior to others. A McLean teacher's statement, "Competition is not a dirty word," represents the general attitude at the four schools in this study. To varying degrees, the schools promote a competitive culture within and outside the classroom context to prepare their students for the "harsh realties and demands of the world outside school" and "to give them the skills necessary to have a competitive edge in life." Outside the classroom, all the schools except for Oakley require students to participate in their athletic programs in order to hone their competitive attitudes and skills. Instead of a requirement, Oakley strongly encourages participation in sports "to give students a more appropriate venue to be competitive than the classroom." Similar to the other schools, Oakley's athletic program is a site for students to strengthen their competitive character.

Students carry their competitive attitudes that are valued and reinforced on playing fields with them into the classroom context. In fact, all but Oakley have designed their overall educational program in ways that encourage students to use skills and attitudes in the classroom that they have learned and developed on playing fields in order to gain higher levels of academic success. Most of the students in this study do act in similar ways in the classroom as they do on playing fields. They are playing to win and do what it takes to achieve academic success. Although Oakley students are less competitive in the classroom than students at the other three schools, the increased focus in recent years on gaining admission to selective colleges has spurred competitive attitudes in order to stand out among others. At all four schools, the college-oriented desires and expectations of students and their families provide further encouragement for competition. Students and their families are competing for the college prize.

The competitive environments at these four schools promote individual student achievement over the value of cooperation and group success. Students are taught that academic success is gained by being better than others, or as I heard numerous times over the course of my research, "standing out above the rest." Although all four schools claim to promote a strong sense of community and emphasize the value of community in their mission statements and school publications, their competitive environments disrupt connection, making closeness among students and educators impossible (hooks, 2003). Their emphasis on competition precludes collaboration, which limits the opportunities for students to learn what it means to build and sustain meaningful relationships with others. In an environment where competition is the order of the day, there is little room for arousing collective concern for anything other than self-interests.

Do whatever it takes to win. Most students in this study explain that they are playing the game of school to win and will do what it takes to gain academic success. In their pursuits of academic success, they regularly act in ways to prove that they are "the fittest," such as putting other students down to make themselves look better, dominating class discussions to get the attention of their teachers, getting on the good side of the adults in their lives, and, at times, cheating on assignments. Often these strategies successfully give them the advantage in the game. Although I observed students cheating only a few times over the course of my research, several students in these studies, except those at Oakley, claim that cheating is a common practice at their schools. Even at Oakley, Kevin, a student, explains that cheating is acceptable "when teachers put too much or unfair amount of pressure on [students]." Similar to what I heard from several students at the four schools, Kevin believes that cheating is "a survival thing" and "something that you're forced to do." Students believe that cheating is justified in a competitive environment.

Similar to what Pope (2001) found in her study of five students "doing school," behaviors such as cheating, however, contradict "the very traits and values many parents, students, and community members expect schools to instill" (p. 150). By encouraging (and, more importantly, rewarding) success over others, the four schools involved in this research project, some more than others, promote win-at-all-costs behaviors and attitudes. Students learn to value winning above all else, even if this means acting in ways that go against other values that the adults in their lives have attempted to instill in them. Instead of fostering traits such as cooperation and honesty, the schools' competitive environments promote the opposite and provide little room to uphold more important and meaningful values than winning.

Fulfillment is gained by accumulating. Parents in these studies place a tremendous amount of pressure on their children to achieve the level of academic success necessary to gain admission to highly selective colleges. They claim that the reason for this pressure is to make sure their children have fulfilling lives. They describe fulfillment as a sense of happiness and accomplishment, and believe that "going to a good college will make this [fulfillment] more possible. It sets them on the right path," as a Parker parent explains. Parents are acutely aware that a degree from a highly selective college often leads to careers providing wealth and power, which allows their children to maintain their class advantages. Parents believe that their children will feel fulfilled in life if they achieve a level of success that allows them to keep "the comforts of life that they're accustomed to," as a Bredvik mother explains.

Only a few parents mention the cachet associated with their children attending highly selective colleges. A mother at Parker admits, "Every parent wants to be able to tell others that their child goes to Harvard or Yale or colleges like those. … If your child goes to a top-notch college, then you know you're a good parent. You've done your job as a parent." Consistent with what Brantlinger (2003) found in her study of affluent mothers, most of the parents' "self-definitions extended to and incorporated their offsprings' success," and a source of parents' "positive identity was attributing their children's achievement to their child rearing" (p. 40). Some teachers at the four schools, however, argue that the primary source of parents' college-oriented desires and expectations for their children is associated more with status than their feelings about themselves as parents. A Bredvik teacher claims that "[parents] want the status that comes along with their kids going to good schools like they want other things that represent status. I'm not saying it's completely the same as a fancy car, but it's close. If your kid gets into Harvard, then it's like everything else in their lives that shows how successful they are." Symbolic markers of both parents' sense of self and class privilege are figured prominently in parents' ambitious aspirations for their children. Their understandings of what it means to be fulfilled in life are constructed around these markers.

Students feel an intense pressure to achieve the goals that their parents have set for them. The majority of students at these schools believe that their "parents are the biggest factor in what [they] do to get into a good college," as a student at Bredvik explains. A student at Oakley elaborates, "It's never been really an option not to go to college. My parents have been talking about going to college since I was in kindergarten. I've always been told that's what I have to do after high school to be successful later on." These two students' sentiments reverberated throughout my conversations with other students. In striving to meet the expectations of their parents, they do what they have to do to get good grades and high test scores, and they participate in the right number of activities to secure admission to selective colleges. Their schools mediate their parents' expectations by making their "primary responsibility ... to get their students into top colleges," as a teacher at Parker explains. The four schools provide the institutional culture, the college counseling, and the college preparatory programs necessary for students to gain entrance into high-status colleges. Everything about all four schools conveys that all students will continue on to college, and most likely to "good" colleges.

The interaction of family and institutional influences places students at these schools on the ambitious track toward gaining admission to high-status colleges and acquiring the educational credentials necessary to secure and maintain their class privilege. They keep jam-packed schedules that often begin early in the morning (earlier than most adults begin their workdays) and end late at night. After school hours, they are involved in sports, service projects, committee meetings, homework, and for a very few, paid job responsibilities. They study, read, and complete what their teachers assign to get high grades and select courses based on college requirements. They spend most of their time inside and outside school doing what they have to do, or what they think they have to do, to win the college prize, not because they find what they do necessarily engaging. Although not all of what students do is entirely motivated by "transcript packing" (Peshkin, 2001), they are "always thinking about how [what they do] will benefit [them] in getting into college," as Nicole, a Parker student, explains. The ever-present reality in their choices, activities, and schoolwork is how what they do helps them fulfill their and their parents' college-oriented desires and expectations. Being engaged in what they do takes a back seat to their drive to accumulate the credentials necessary to keep them on the "right path" to a selective college and, as their parents claim, to fulfillment in their lives. They have learned to associate fulfillment with accumulation.

Others are too different from us to relate. One of the striking qualities that all four schools share is their exclusive nature. They promote and emphasize their distinctive, exclusive, and superior qualities to set them apart from others. They are closed off from others and, in various forms, are gated communities. The incredible beauty and abundance of the campuses of McLean and Parker, for example, are a far cry from their surrounding communities. Both schools sit on top of hills detached from their neighbors. Quite the opposite, Oakley and Bredvik share a close relationship with their local communities, but these communities are themselves exclusive. Like McLean and Parker, they are isolated from communities different from themselves.

Oakley is the only school in this study for which this isolation goes against the school's ideals and values. In fact, school officials at the three private schools work hard at promoting their elite status; they want others to know that they are above the rest. They promote their exclusivity, in part, because they are private and have to "sell their school to families. We have the job of convincing them that they're getting their money's worth," as Parker's admission counselor explains. As a public school, Oakley has a similar form of pressure that comes from the need to demonstrate educational excellence to local citizens for financial support; they have to "sell their school" to their community. Similar to the private schools, Oakley's officials work hard at making sure that people, both within and outside their community, know that they stand above other schools, even though this attitude runs counter to the school's liberal character. The pressure to secure financial support overrides their liberal ideals. In various ways, all four schools promote their differences from, and pit themselves against, others in expressing their excellence. They regulate "others" to a lesser status to justify and legitimate and thus protect their interests. The class segregation of their school communities is a deliberate choice to maintain their superiority over those perceived as other.

All four schools do emphasize, however, the importance of their students going outside the "bubble" of their privileged environments to be involved in service. Even though the schools place a value on service (and all but Bredvik even require their students to do service), their service projects and activities operate by the "charity model," which allows their students to "give back"—that is, help those who are less fortunate—without promoting social transformation. In fact, the goals of the charitable model of service reinforce privileged ways of knowing and doing by embracing certain unpleasant assumptions about people, especially those different from the service providers. One basic assumption is that any community would function better if only it would act like the service provider. Another assumption is that there are no connections between those who provide service and those who receive service, that they are more different than they are similar. This assumes that their lived experiences, hopes, dreams, and aspirations are so profoundly different that difficulties can be resolved only by finding the one right answer. In this context, service is mainly about the nature of the activity and the work of the service provider. Students are not provided the necessary conditions to step outside their privileged positions to learn from others in the population at large in order to understand and appreciate different ways of knowing and doing. The charity model of service provides little room for students to develop meaningful, mutual, and respectful relationships with individuals outside their closed communities. Even though they are physically stepping outside their "bubble" and crossing lines in social interactions through these service activities, they are not provided the types of experience that allow them to become sensitive to the nature and needs of other social classes and other cultural groups (Brantlinger, 2003). Students continue to be isolated from "others."

Instructional Settings That Interrupt Privilege

For the most part, these five lessons are not "officially" taught as part of the formal curriculum at the four schools. Instead, they are part of the hidden curriculum; that is, "the norms, values, and belief systems embedded in the curriculum, the school, and classroom life, imparted to students through daily routine, curricular content, and social relationships" (Margolis, Soldatenko, Acker, & Gair, 2001, p. 6). There is an extensive body of literature on the hidden curriculum. Phillip Jackson (1968) is generally recognized as the originator of the term *hidden curriculum*. In his observations of public elementary classrooms, Jackson identified aspects of classroom life that were inherent in the social relations of schoolings. He found that particular values, dispositions, and behavioral expectations led to rewards for students and shaped their learning experiences. Furthermore, he found that these features of school life had little to do with the stated educational goals but were essential for success in school.

Since then, several scholars (e.g., Anyon, 1980; Apple, 1982, 1993; Giroux, 1983) have explored the complex ways that the hidden curriculum powerfully influences the educational experiences of students and transmits important lessons to them about particular ways of knowing and doing that correspond to their social class. For example, Jean Aynon's (1980) study of five elementary schools in contrasting social class settings documented how the hidden curriculum works in ways to perpetuate social class stratification of the larger society. School experience of the students at the five schools differed qualitatively by social class. Anyon found class distinctions not only in the physical, cultural, and interpersonal characteristics of each school, but also in the nature of instruction and schoolwork. These differences, as she explained, "not only may contribute to the development in the children in each social class of certain types of economically significant relationships and not others, but would thereby help to *reproduce* this system of relations in society" (p. 90). Anyon argued that classroom practices have theoretical meaning and social consequences that contribute to the reproduction of unequal social relations.

Consistent with this body of research, the lessons that are a part of the hidden curriculum of the four schools hide in plain view the cultural processes that reinforce and regenerate privilege. These lessons send powerful messages to students about their place in the world, who they are and should be, and their relations with those outside of their world. Unacknowledged, these lessons often teach students unintended knowledge, values, dispositions, and beliefs. In fact, most of these lessons are in direct contradiction to the schools' stated goals, which aim to teach students high moral character, integrity, respect for others, and responsible participation in the world. These lessons instead prepare students to lead their lives guided by distinctive ways of knowing and doing that overshadow these more positive, productive goals. They contribute to establishing the taken-for-granted sets of ideas for how things ought to be and the frame of reference for what is considered common sense that function to reinforce and regenerate the cultural meanings students use to construct their identities. As conduits for learning privilege and power, these lessons assist students in constructing privilege as a central component of their identities.

Identities, however, are neither constant nor stable. They are constantly shaped and reshaped by the complex interactions of everyday realities and lived experiences. As students mediate their sense of self-understanding, they can be offered the necessary cultural tools and resources that can interrupt privilege. Students can be taught alternative lessons about themselves, their place in the world, and their relations with others; lessons not only that are more aligned with (purportedly) intended goals for student learning, but that also offer alternatives to privileged ways of knowing and doing. Over the course of my research, I observed only a few moments when instructional settings offered students the necessary tools and resources to interrupt privilege. These moments challenged the everyday, commonsense nature of the lessons that reinforce and regenerate privilege. These instructional settings, often created by the adults in students' lives but sometimes facilitated by the students themselves, shared particular qualities in imagining beyond the taken-for-grantedness of privilege.

One of these qualities was honesty. Students were provided opportunities in their pursuits of academic success to learn ways to deal with, and work through, failure in healthy ways. Students were provided safe spaces to make mistakes and then learn from them. During these moments, the adults in students' lives served as important models by being honest about what they knew and didn't know, honest about moments in their lives when they wished they had made different decisions, and honest about moments when they "messed up." These role models were upholding natural human qualities in their work with students or in their roles as parents. They provided their students/ children opportunities to learn from these quali-ties—even the imperfect ones. By so doing, these adults taught students important lessons about dealing with failure.

These instructional settings also encouraged openness by expanding the scope of what was considered "the real fudge," to use the words of Ms. Perry at Parker, or in other words, what knowledge was acknowledged as legitimate (Apple, 1999). Curricula, however, are not simply a collection of facts; they tell a story, from which students learn some important (often unintended) lessons. These lessons emerge from what is and what is not included in curricula. As Kumashiro (2002) points out, "What educators do *not* do is as instructive as what they do" (p. 82). When instructional settings encouraged openness, teachers included different, conflicting stories in their curricular choices. They offered their students opportunities to learn from others outside their own cultural group and to learn that there was not just one way of seeing things, or even two or three—there were multiple perspectives on every issue and every story. During these moments, teachers encouraged students to open their minds to others' points of view and to the complexity of the world and the many perspectives involved (Nieto, 2002).

These instructional settings also engaged students in what they were doing and learning. When a student at Parker spent her free time during the school day painting, a group of aspiring writers at Bredvik published a zine of their creative work once a month, another Bredvik student shared her poetry regularly on open mike nights at a local coffee shop, and an Oakley student devoted hours a day on his computer designing a virtual reality game, they were not thinking about how these activities would help them get into a good college. They also were not focused on accumulating. Instead, they were doing what they loved and were passionately committed to doing their best. In these moments, students stepped outside materialistic ways of knowing and doing to find a more meaningful purpose for their activities and pursuits. Even though these moments of engaged learning and doing occurred mostly outside the classroom context, there were a few occasions when students during class discus-sions and activities struggled for understanding, wanted to learn and work with others, and found fulfillment in what they were doing. These moments allowed students to establish a more intimate connection with their learning (hooks, 1994).

These instructional settings encouraged collaboration and emphasized the value of community. Over the course of my research, I witnessed moments when students worked together on their train ride to school, in the hallways, at lunchtime while grabbing a bite to eat, and on campus during their breaks. In these moments students were going against the competitive nature of their schools in order to learn from each other. Rather than trying to outdo each other, they were engaging with each other in meaningful ways that recognized the value of cooperative learning. Students in these instructional settings learned how to work with others. While doing so, they were building their capacity to imagine someone else's point of view, what Kohn (1992) calls "perspective taking," and learning what it took to establish and maintain supportive, healthy, and positive relationships with others.

Finally, these instructional settings encouraged students to develop the habits of heart and mind necessary for working toward critical awareness. In these settings, a few teachers at Parker and Oakley, for example, used such practices as journal writing, reading, writing, reflection, research, analysis, and observation to develop their students' awareness of the world around them and to urge students to live more meaningfully and justly. These teachers taught students to see through versions of truth that teach people to accept unfairness so that their students were able to envision, define, and identity ways they could work toward a more humane society. In this process, an encounter was created between students and their capacity to imagine beyond privileged ways of knowing and doing. Students were encouraged to make decisions to live their lives as if the lives of others truly mattered. Students were provided opportunities to develop an awareness of the world around them and to learn what it meant to live more meaningfully and justly.

These characteristics do not translate into easy prescriptions for interrupting privilege. They do not serve as easy, quick, or certain alternatives to the ways that privilege is perpetuated, re-created, and regenerated in schools. Moreover, there are other characteristics that could be added. My purpose has been not to be exhaustive but to illuminate the primary ways that educators, students, and parents at the four schools worked toward interrupting privilege. Their efforts serve as examples of the possibilities for redefining, reenvisioning, and reimagining how things ought to be.

A Broader Agenda

Interrupting the cultural production of privilege requires intentional efforts on the part of educators to confront and transform lessons students learn about their place in the world and their relations with others. By creating instructional settings—in and outside of the classroom context—that interrupt privilege, we can be more certain about what lessons we are actually teaching students about themselves and others. We can begin imagining ways to work toward "the process through which students learn to critically appropriate knowledge existing outside their immediate experience in order to broaden their understanding of themselves, the world, and the possibilities for transforming the taken-for-granted assumptions about the way we live" (McLaren, 1989, p. 186). By working toward this transformation, we can imagine the possibilities for changing the everyday practices and routines that miscommunicate the ways we want (or, at least, what we say and claim we want) our students to live their lives (Howard & EnglandKennedy, 2006).

We can, however, only imagine and work toward interrupting the cultural processes that reinforce and regenerate stratified structures in schooling. The effects of macroeconomic policies (see Anyon, 2005) and the social class divisions of the larger society overshadow efforts toward *disrupting,* rather than *interrupting,* these cultural processes in schools that perpetuate unequal relations. The United States not only is the most highly stratified society in the industrialized world but does less to limit the extent of inequality than any other industrialized democratic country. Class distinctions operate in virtually all aspects of American life. In the United States, democracy has become more of an economic metaphor than a political concept/ideal (Darder, 2002). It should not be surprising, therefore, that stratified schooling remains durable even with all the efforts over the years toward making American schooling more equal. Replete with uneven access and outcomes, schools continue to reflect the divisions of the larger society (Nieto, 2005). The efforts toward transforming stratified school structures will remain uncertain until democratic ideals are reflected and realized in the larger society. Working toward transforming stratified school structures and outcomes requires us to extend our efforts and attention beyond educational institutions. We must, in the end, develop a larger scope for our equality-seeking work.

However, comprehensive analyses of the reproductive nature of affluent schooling can elaborate and extend our understandings of the ways privileging systems are produced and reproduced. We can develop the necessary cultural script to extend beyond commodified notions that divert attention from, and protect, the concealed and sophisticated processes involved in the cultural production of privilege. By mapping out and exposing the contours of privilege, we can engage in the type of complicated conversation that is needed for understanding how the success of some relates to the failure of many. If social justice is at least one of the aims of scholarship and inquiry (Purpel, 1999), then we must work to unravel the cultural processes that reinforce and regenerate privilege. We must cast our scholarly gaze upward even when this means looking critically at ourselves and unmasking our own complicity with oppression and privilege. We can then hopefully develop a vision for American schooling that has yet to be imagined from the perspectives of our current theoretical frameworks.

Discussion Questions

1. Why do contradictions exist in elite schools? Do these contradictions exist in other types of schools (for example, schools with a majority of poor students)?
2. Why are some lessons that students learn in schools unintentional? Why are these unintentional lessons the most consequential for what students are learning in school?

3. What social, political, and economic forces keep the United States a highly stratified society? What ways do educational institutions help maintain this stratification of the larger society?
4. What other qualities could be added to the author's list in creating the types of instructional settings that teach students lessons about living justly and meaningfully?

References

Anderson, G. L., & Irvine, P. (1993). Informing critical literacy with ethnography. In C. Lankshear & P. McLaren (Eds.), *Critical literacy: Politics, praxis, and the postmodern* (pp. 81–104). Albany: State University of New York Press.

Anyon, J. (1980). Social class and the hidden curriculum of work. *Journal of Education, 162,* 67–92.

Anyon, J. (2005). What "counts" as educational policy? Notes toward a new paradigm. *Harvard Educational Review, 75,* 65–88.

Apple, M. (Ed.). (1982). *Cultural and economic reproduction in education: Essays on class, ideology and the state.* London: Routledge & Kegan Paul.

Apple, M. (1993). *Official knowledge: Democratic education in a conservative age.* New York: Routledge.

Apple, M. (1995). *Education and power* (2nd ed.). New York: Routledge.

Apple, M. (1996). *Cultural politics and education.* New York: Teachers College Press.

Apple, M. (1999). *Power, meaning and identity.* New York: Peter Lang.

Arnowitz, S. (1980). Science and ideology. *Current Perspectives in Social Theory, 1,* 75–101.

Arnowitz, S. (1992). *The politics of identity: Class, culture, social movements.* New York: Routledge.

Brantlinger, E. (1993). *The politics of social class in secondary schools: Views of affluent and impoverished youth.* New York: Teachers College Press.

Brantlinger, E. (2003). *Dividing classes: How the middle class negotiates and rationalizes school advantage.* New York: Routledge Falmer.

Carspecken, P. F., & Apple, M. (1992). Critical qualitative research: Theory, methodology, and practice. In M. LeCompte, W. Millroy, & J. Preissle (Eds.), *The handbook of qualitative research in education* (pp. 507–553). San Diego, CA: Academic Press.

Darder, A. (2002). *Reinventing Paulo Freire: A pedagogy of love.* Boulder, CO: Westview Press.

Gair, M., & Mullins, G. (2001). Hiding in plain sight. In E. Margolis (Ed.), *The hidden curriculum in higher education* (pp. 21–41). New York: Routledge.

Gilligan, C., Brown, L. M., & Rogers, A. G. (1989). Psyche embedded: A place for body, relationships, and culture in personality theory. In A. Rubin, R. Zucker, R. Emmons, & S. Frank (Eds.), *Studying persons and lives* (pp. 86–147). New York: Springer.

Giroux, H. (1981). *Ideology, culture, and the process of schooling.* Philadelphia: Temple University Press.

Giroux, H. (1983). Theories of reproduction and resistance in the new sociology of education: A critical analysis. *Harvard Educational Review, 53,* 257–293.

Giroux, H. (1992). *Border crossings: Cultural workers and the politics of education*. New York: Routledge, Chapman & Hall.

Grenfell, M., & James, D. (1998). *Bourdieu and education: Acts of practical inquiry*. London: Palmer.

hooks, b. (1994). *Teaching to transgress: Education as the practice of freedom*. New York: Routledge.

hooks, b. (2003). *Teaching community: A pedagogy of hope*. New York: Routledge.

Howard, A., & England Kennedy, E. (2006). Breaking the silence: Power, conflict, and contested frames within an affluent high school. *Anthropology and Education Quarterly, 37*, 347–365.

Jackson, P. W. (1968). *Life in classrooms*. New York: Holt, Rinehart, and Winston.

Kumashiro, K. K. (2002). Against repetition: Addressing resistance to anti-oppressive change in the practices of learning, teaching, supervising, and researching. *Harvard Educational Review, 72*, 67–92.

Lamont, M., & Lareau, A. (1988). Cultural capital: Allusions, gaps and glissandos in recent theoretical developments. *Sociological Theory, 6*, 153–168.

Lawrence-Lightfoot, S. (1983). *The good high school: Portraits of character and culture*. New York: Basic Books.

Margolis, E., Soldatenko, M., Acker, S., & Gair, M. (2001). Peekaboo: Hiding and outing the curriculum. In E. Margolis (Ed.), *The hidden curriculum in higher education* (pp. 1–19). New York: Routledge.

McLaren, P. (1989). *Life in schools: An introduction to critical pedagogy in the foundations of education*. New York: Longman.

Mehan, H. (1992). Understanding inequality in schools: The contribution of interpretive studies. *Sociology of Education, 65*, 1–21.

Nieto, S. (2002). *Language, culture, and teaching: Critical perspectives for a new century*. Mahwah, NJ: Lawrence Erlbaum.

Peshkin, A. (2001). *Permissible advantage? The moral consequences of elite schooling*. Mahwah, NJ: Lawrence Erlbaum Associates.

Pope, D. C. (2001). *"Doing school": How we are creating a generation of stressed out, materialistic, and miseducated students*. New Haven, CT: Yale University Press.

Purpel, D. (1999). *Moral outrage in education*. New York: Peter Lang.

Wildman, S. M. (1996). *Privilege revealed: How invisible preferences undermine America*. New York: New York University Press.

Chapter Eight

Childhood and Social Hierarchy—Social and Cultural Constructions of Power

Childhood

By Marcia Mikulak

S ince the Industrial Revolution, most Western societies have come to consider childhood as a time of innocence rooted in biological processes that gradually progress
from infancy, childhood, and adolescence into adulthood. In this concept, all youth
are defined as minors who are dependent upon adult guidance and supervision; accordingly,
youth are denied legal rights and responsibilities until they reach the age that legally defines
adulthood. Progressive social scientists view childhood as a concept dependent upon social,
economic, religious, and political environments. Rather than see childhood as a time of
nonparticipation and dependence, social constructionists see childhood as an expression of
society and its values, roles, and institutions. In this sense, childhood is conceptualized as an
active state of participation in the reproduction of culture. Indeed, constructionist views of
childhood state that childhood is not a universal condition of life, as is biological immaturity,
but rather a pattern of meaning that is dependent on specific sets of social norms unique to
specific cultural settings.

Childhood can be characterized as the interplay and conflict of and between institutions,
individuation, and individualization. Childhood is positioned within this triangulation, revealing how institutions such as day care and kindergarten are rooted in women's labor issues,
creating a pull between the pedagogical needs of children versus the economic needs of adults.
Individuation is the process by which individuals become differentiated from one another
in society. This process identifies childhood as the target for the attention of the state and
produces institutions and care providers who delimit the individuality of children. Therefore,

a basic tension exists between individual development and collective needs, between the real needs of children and the economic and political needs of adults. Hence, childhood is kept within specific boundaries defined by institutions administered by adults. Therefore, children can be seen to be at the beginning of the process of individualization, long ago achieved by men and only recently achieved by women.

It has been suggested that childhood constitutes a social class, in that children are exploited in relation to adults, who determine and define the needs of childhood according to adult terms. This forces us to place the analysis of childhood in a political-economic frame and shows how children are actually buried in the ongoing division of labor within the adult world.

Childhood Reflects Structures of Power and Domination

The Industrial Revolution in 19th-century Europe resulted in major transformations in economic and social relations. These transformations resulted in the concentration and penetration of capital, which generated two distinct classes: bourgeoisie and proletariat. With this transformation, we see the separation of childhood as distinct from adulthood. Children were differentially affected by industrialization according to class and family relations. Innocence, purity, protection, and guidance define the children of the bourgeois class, while children of the proletariat were considered to be miniature adults who constituted a reserve pool of labor power in early and middle industrial capitalism. Children of the upper classes received private education that trained them for positions of leadership and power, while children of the working class were often put to work alongside adults in factories and sweatshops in industrial Europe.

Economics

A key step in redefining childhood beginning in the mid-1800s was the removal of children from the public sphere. The state, religious, and civil societies each had particular interests in redefining childhood and in removing children from their exposure to the adult world. Growing industrialism demanded an unimpeded free labor market, where child labor was plentiful and cheap. However, toward the end of the 1800s, new reformist attitudes about the detrimental effects of child labor were forming. Protestant Christians and social reformers' concerns about the physical and emotional hazards of child labor helped to initiate the welfare movement and led to debates about the desirability and feasibility of controlling the child labor market.

Childhood Changes Culturally

Conceptualizing childhood in diverging cultural settings requires an anthropological perspective that sees children and childhood as windows into societies. Unfortunately, anthropologists have not taken childhood and children seriously enough, focusing instead on adult society as the locus of interest and change. Currently, there is a growing movement in social science to view children as active agents who construct meanings and symbolic forms that contribute to the ever-changing nature of their cultures. Not only are children contributing to the complex nature of cultural reproduction, they are accurately reflecting the unique nature of their specific culture.

Margaret Mead's Coming of Age in Samoa (1928) explored the theoretical premise that childhoods are defined by cultural norms rather than by universal notions of childhood as a separate and distinct phase of life. The term youth culture was introduced in the 1920s by Talcott Parsons, who defined the life worlds of children as structured by age and sex roles. Such a definition marginalized and deindividualized children. The work of Whiting and Edwards, during the 1950s to late 1970s, in diverse cultural settings, developed methodologies to explore what they exemplified as cross-societal similarities and differences in children. Their attempts at producing a comprehensive theory about childhood development, cognition, and social learning processes were informative and groundbreaking. Their work linked childhood developmental theories to cultural differences, demonstrating that children's capacities are influenced as much by culture as by biology. By the 1980s, social research had moved into predominately urban studies, where youth groups and gangs were conceptualized and defined by American sociologists as deviants rebelling against social norms. Current authors such as Qvortrup, Vered Amit-Talai, Wulff, and Sharon Stephens are recasting global research on childhood by defining children as viable, cogent, and articulate actors in their own right. Such research has spawned strident debates concerning the legal rights of children versus the legal rights of parents.

Managing the Social Space of Childhood

Reform of child labor laws required that the needs of poor families, reformers, and capitalists be balanced. In this equation, public education became a means by which children could be removed from the public sphere and handed over to the administrative processes of the state. Statistics from the late-19th-century censuses reveal the effectiveness of the reformers: In England, by 1911, only 18% of boys and 10% of girls between the ages of 10 and 14 were in the labor market, compared with 37% and 20%, respectively, in 1851. Economically, children moved from being an asset for capitalist production to constituting a huge consumer market and a substantial object of adults' labor in the form of education, child care, welfare, and juvenile court systems. Although reformers and bureaucrats could claim a successful moral victory in the removal of child labor from the work force, in reality, children had been made superfluous by machinery and the requirement that industrial work be preserved for adult male and female laborers. In this respect, culture is not only perpetuated by children, but changed by it. The late-modern constructions of childhood acknowledge that children are placed and positioned by society. The places that are appropriate for children to inhabit have widened, and children are now seen as targets of media and marketing campaigns, though children as individuals and as a class have few legal rights.

The definitions of childhood as a state of innocence and purity follow long historical cycles of economic change that correspond to the development of capitalism as it spread within the world system. Immanuel Wallerstein's world systems theory describes historical economic relations in terms of exchanges between the core, semiperiphery, and periphery states. The evaluation the role of children in the world system has led to an agreement by many social scientists that childhood is historically and culturally relative. Recent anthropological political economy theory demonstrates how relations between nation-states and the development of capitalism affect growing child poverty. In addition, these relations determine the role of children economically, socially, and educationally throughout the world, affecting policy development at both the state and federal levels, particularly in the areas of child poverty and child development. Social scientists should turn their attention to a generational system of domination analogous to the gendered oppression that has captured the attention of feminist scholars for the last several decades. If successful, this agenda will advance the legal status of childhood globally, freeing future generations to participate as viable actors within political, economic, and legal realms within their unique cultures.

Recent research on street children around the world demonstrates that childhood is a social construction dependent on geographical, economic, ethnic, and cultural patterns. Patricia Márquez, in *The Street Is My Home* (1999), explored how street youth in Caracas, Venezuela, are brought together because of economic scarcity and social violence, by describing the ways in which these youth are able to gain financial resources and material wealth through the creation of meaningful experiences and relationships in their lives. Tobais Hecht, in *At Home in the Street* (1998), portrayed street children in Recife as socially significant themselves, acting as both a part of and a reflection of the concerns of adults. He found that Recife's street children took pride in working and earning an income.

Social reality may be seen as a process of constructing one's social world through the skillful actions of everyday life. Alongside the development of the constructionist view of race, gender, and ethnicity, childhood is simultaneously viewed as dependent on location. Historically, theoretical views of childhood have profoundly affected how children are positioned socially, politically, economically, medically, and legally. Due to the recognition of the ways in which both popular and academic views of childhood have impacted children, recent social science research now seeks to redefine childhood as a time of agency and self-directed learning and participation in society, while developing new theoretical paradigms that view children as subjects worthy in their own right, not just in their social status as defined by adults.

Further Readings

1. Amit-Talai, V., & Wulff, H. (Eds.). (1995). *Youth cultures: A cross-cultural perspective.* New York: Routledge.

2. Blanc, S. C. (1994). *Urban children in distress: Global predicaments and innovative strategies.* Grey, Switzerland: Gordon & Breach.

3. James, A., & Prout, A. (1997). *Constructing and reconstructing childhood: Contemporary issues in the sociological study of childhood.* London: Falmer Press.

4. Mickelson, A. R. (2000). *Children on the streets of the Americas.* New York: Routledge

5. Qvortrup, J., Bardy, M., Sgritta, G., & Wintersberger, H. (Eds.). (1994). *Childhood matters: Social theory, practice, and politics.* Brookfield, VT: Avebury.

6. Rogers, R., Rogers, S., & Wendy, S. (1992). *Stories of childhood: Shifting agendas of child concern.* Toronto, Canada: University of Toronto Press.

7. Scheper-Hughes, N., & Carolyn S. (Eds.). (1998). *Small wars: The cultural politics of childhood.* Berkeley: University of California Press.

8. Stephens, S. (1995). *Children and the politics of culture.* Princeton, NJ: Princeton University Press.

Social Constructions of Childhoods

Historical Framework

By Marcia Mikulak

The idea of childish innocence resulted in two kinds of attitude and behavior towards childhood: firstly, safeguarding it against pollution by life, and particularly by the sexuality tolerated if not approved of among adults; and secondly, strengthening it by developing character and reason. We may see a contradiction here, for on the one hand childhood is preserved and on the other hand it is made older than its years; but the contradiction exists only for us of the twentieth century. The association of childhood with primitivism and irrationalism or prelogicism characterizes our contemporary concept of childhood. (Ariès 1962:119)

This chapter will compare and contract post-industrial Western European conceptions of childhood as a time of innocence and separateness with the constructionist theoretical view, which describes children as active and viable social agents who construct knowledge of themselves and the world. The constructionist theory, also known as the constructivist theory, dramatically changes the ways in which child learning, and hence child abilities, are viewed by placing the child's own efforts to learn and understand experiences at the center of knowledge acquisition (Prawat 1992:354–395). I discuss how these two opposing theoretical notions of childhood continue to affect the ways in which street children are viewed. I draw upon the theoretical work of Philippe Ariès, who identified childhood as a distinct phase of life that is socially constructed and dependent on race, place, politics, religion, and other cultural factors. In addition, I discuss recent literature on constructionist theory. Finally, I argue that imported constructions of the innocence and purity of childhood affect the development of NGO programs and the kinds of services that are deemed important or necessary for street children.

In keeping with post-industrial Western European conceptions, most middle- and upper-class Brazilians view childhood as a time of innocence and protection. Because Brazilian street children view themselves as independent, knowledgeable, and necessary economic social actors, they do not fit into the upper-class definition of normal childhood. Therefore, they tend to be ignored, marginalized, and/or branded as delinquents.

Puritan writers during the Reformation had portrayed childhood as a state of original sin, where the child was born of evil, prone to sin, without moral knowledge, but with the potential and capacity to learn goodness. Hobbes (1588–1679) ascribed similar qualities to human nature at large. Locke (1632–1704), on the other hand, viewed the infant as a "tabula rasa," and as such, subject to influence more by nurture than by nature. A century later, Rousseau, in *Emile* (1762), championed a more humanistic developmentalism, putting his faith in child-centered education and socialization based on developing Enlightenment notions of childhood (James and Prout 1990).

The industrial revolution in nineteenth-century Western Europe culminated in the concentration and penetration of capital, which generated two distinct classes: bourgeoisie and proletariat. Among the major transformations in economic and social relations that ensued was a redefinition of childhood. For the bourgeoisie, childhood came to be understood as distinct from adulthood in more than a biological sense: it was a special time of innocence and purity requiring a degree of protection and guidance. In contrast, children of the proletariat did not often enjoy the same specialness and protection; most often they were viewed as miniature adult workers, a reserve labor pool. Philippe Ariès discusses how the concentration and penetration of capital impacted childhood in *Centuries of Childhood: A Social History of Family Life*. Ariès states that, "Henceforth it was recognized that the child was not ready for life, and that he had to be subjected to a special treatment, a sort of quarantine, before he was allowed to join the adult" (Ariès 1962:412). Hence, children of the proletariat and the middle and upper classes were removed from the adult world.

The industrial revolution also spawned a variety of theoretical definitions of childhood. Social reformers in the 1840s and 1850s warned that the children of the poor were wild animals inhabiting the streets of growing urban centers and endangering the future of society. In keeping with their conception of the evolutionary stages of mankind, anthropologists such as Sir John Lubbock, J. F. MacLennan, and E. B. Tylor defined childhood as a state of savagery regardless of class or geography (Stocking 1968:126). Christian missionaries viewed all primitive societies as proof of degeneration, while polygenists viewed them as evolving from inferior branches of the human race. Civilization, by contrast, embodied the bourgeois virtues developed in the Victorian era (James and Prout 1990; Ariès 1962). This historical reiteration is necessary here because it is linked to the recasting of childhood as a time of innocence and ignorance. After abolition in Brazil, freed African slaves constituted the majority of Brazil's poor and destitute. In Brazil, negative stereotyping of street children as degenerate savages has been linked to the innocence and ignorance of childhood as well as with the ongoing stereotypes of Afro-Brazilians as lower on the evolutionary scale. Such stereotypes produce a socially sanctioned discourse that describes street children as dangerous and immoral (Burdick 1998; Twine 1998; Skidmore 1995; Jahoda 1999; Reichmann 1999).

Street children in this research identified themselves using a variety of terms that included *moreno* (brown to dark brown), *preto* (black), *pardo* (brown), *mulato* (brown), *mulatinho* (little brown person), and Afro-Brazilian (Brazilians of African descent).[1] I have chosen to use the term Afro-Brazilian because it was commonly used by the street children I knew who were consciously using the term to increase awareness of their racial links to Africa. Many times I was asked to talk about the black movement in America, and as I talked about the civil rights movement and affirmative action, street children were amazed and excited by my stories. It is my hope that by using the term Afro-Brazilian in reference to street children, this research will aid Brazil's burgeoning racial equality movement.

Ariès states that moralists, administrators, and churches in Western Europe successfully removed children from the everyday world of adults.

> Family and school together removed the child from adult society. The school shut up a childhood, which had hitherto been free within an increasingly severe disciplinary system, which culminated in the eighteenth and nineteenth centuries in the total claustration of the boarding school. The solicitude of family, church, moralists and administrators deprived the child of the freedom he had hitherto enjoyed among adults. (Ariès 1962:413)

Schooling in Western European industrial countries successfully removed poor children from the streets while significantly improving their life possibilities. It is important to divert here and state that in the case of Brazil, street children (initially freed slave children and poor children of mixed blood) have not had their life possibilities significantly improved. Indeed they were "freed" from slavery and forced to work in order to survive. Today, street children (as with their freed slave counterparts) must work in the streets, while struggling to learn in an educational system with a high degree of inequality and an extremely high dropout rate for poor children and youth. The public educational system in Brazil is notoriously dismal. For example, in 1998 sixty-seven percent of poor children dropped out of school before completing eight years of fundamental education (Ferreira 2000). A comprehensive assessment of Brazil's current educational system can be found in *Opportunity Foregone: Education in Brazil* (Birdsall and Shabot 1996). Schooling among non-whites (people of darker skin colors) in both rural and urban settings is significantly lower in Brazil, having on average only seventy percent of the schooling of their white counterparts. In general, the educational gap between poor youth and privileged youth is staggering: the median level of education for privileged youth is almost three times higher than that for poor youth (Kerstenetzky 2001). Hence, placing Brazilian street children in schools has not successfully removed them from the streets, nor has it significantly improved their life possibilities.

The colonial project to civilize the world's primitive people through Christianity and capitalism also manifested itself in Europe's major cities, London in particular. The doctrine of the utility of poverty called for the masses to work cheaply for the benefit of the privileged. In this sense, the poor were put to work in the informal labor market, often performing hard and arduous physical labor. In the same sense, child idleness (specifically for the children of the poor) was thought to be a great danger to society. As defined by the English Poor Laws of the 1800s, children of the poor were not cared for as a matter of charity (Fyfe 1989; Standing 1982). Rather, they were required to work for their upkeep. Research in archival records by historian Hugh Cunningham found that "The Poor Laws provided the legal and administrative framework within which the lives of the poor [and their children] could be monitored and controlled" (Cunningham 1991:29). Such notions about the colonial project also transferred to Brazil's poor as slavery ended and the push for industrialization began in earnest.

By the 1860s, the bourgeois class had come to worship childhood. According to Cunningham, childhood in this conception

> became the repository of good feelings and happy memories which could help the adult to live through the stickier patches of later life ... it was both a place of refuge for those wearied by life's struggles and a source of renewal which would enable the adult to carry on. In effect, that is, childhood was a substitute for religion. (1991:151–52)

In the latter part of the century public schooling served to prolong childhood. Schools of the bourgeoisie became walled gardens where, "… within their bounds the Peter Pan fantasy came near to being a reality" (Cunningham 1991:154).

The proletarian childhood experience was decidedly different. In pre-capitalist modes of production, the extended family worked together as a productive unit. Under capitalism, the average proletarian nuclear family was principally supported by its adult male wage earner. Women and children generally entered the labor market in order to generate supplementary wages, but because their contributions were considered secondary, they constituted a class of even lower-paid, super-exploited workers (Elson 1982; Diamond and Dilorio 1978). Karl Marx observed that while industrial capital paid the patriarchal head of households a "family wage" barely sufficient for survival, penetration of capital into all sectors of production forced lower wages and higher prices, leaving poor families no recourse but to send every member of the family to work, thereby further stratifying power relationships between state and individuals, men and women, and adults and children (Marx 1977:353–359). Similar processes occurred in Brazil, where poor families, especially freed slaves and their children, were forced to put every member to work as early as possible in order to ensure survival (Beiber 1994; Conrad 1984; Degeler 1986; Del Priore 1991).

As capitalism advanced and populations became concentrated in urban areas, poor children became more visible. Their presence was seen as a social problem to be solved by public policy and the benevolent efforts of religious and charitable societies. Such institutional control of children sought to provide the "right" environment for children in the eighteenth and nineteenth centuries. For the upper classes, notions of innocence and the need for guidance provided the motivation for childhood education. By contrast, schooling for the proletariat represented a deliberate movement to tighten control over the next generation of laborers. Industrial schools and reformatories flourished in mid-nineteenth-century England (May 1973:7–29). As the social construction of childhood innocence spread into Brazil during the early twentieth century, politicians, church organizations, and judicial sectors began making plans to develop policies that would define children on the streets as delinquent (Rizzini 1994).

During the eighteenth century, civil society, the church, and the state each had particular interests in redefining childhood and protecting children from the adverse effects of exposure to the adult world. Although the tendency in the early years of the industrial revolution had been to put the children of the poor to work, reformers called for the modification of child labor, insisting that children's work be tailored to their strength and capacity. Concern for the proper environment for children was expressed in sentimental arguments about religious and moral values. The religious and social reform forces feared that the working child was not being exposed to environments that would mold and form good character. Working (i.e., corrupted) children were seen as a potential threat to society. On the other hand, growing industrialism demanded an unimpeded cheap labor market (Cunningham 1991). The concerns about physical and moral hazards of child labor inevitably clashed with industry's demands and led to wide-ranging debates about the desirability and feasibility of controlling the child labor market.[2]

Labor reform focused on two kinds of "evil" thought to be particularly harmful to children: physical and moral. The bodies of working children suffered from long work hours in overheated and polluted mills. They were also often physically punished. From the perspective of the reformers, children lacked education and religious training, and they suffered from their immersion in the adult world. Together, these two concerns implied that the continuity of society was in danger, evidenced by the growing number of the working poor in urban centers. Religious leaders pleaded for the removal of children from the adult world in order to protect them from exposure to adult ways, mainly vulgar language and explicit sexual play. In the liberal imagination, poverty and crime were inextricably linked and youth were seen as powerless victims caught in a culture of poverty, vulgarity, and amorality.

The new conception of childhood as a time that ought to be characterized by innocence and guidance collided with the presence of poor children laboring in industrial settings. Historian Hugh Cunningham states, "If children in all ranks of society were perceived to be essentially the same, then the road was indeed open for an attack not only on child labor in the cotton mills, but on child labor of any kind" (Cunningham 1991:69). Historically, child labor had been protected by the practice of apprenticeship, but Cunningham points out that by the second decade of the nineteenth century, apprenticeship practices were seen as exploitative of children as well as "… an unjustified interference with the free operation of the market …" (1991:71), where increases in free labor were used in preference to apprenticed labor. It was recognized that child labor laws were a way to protect against a particular type of inhuman exploitation, as well as a way to remove children from the adult world of the streets.

While the first part of the nineteenth century in England witnessed a rise in concern for black slaves and for "white child slaves," many privileged liberals who had campaigned for the former were blinded by their economic interests to rights of the latter. Researchers take a dim view of reformers and state that only when the market was glutted with cheap child labor did the battle for reform begin in earnest with the Child Labor and Education Acts of 1847 (Cunningham 1991; Brick-Panter and Smith 2000; Austin and Willard 1998).

Administrative and Institutional Control of Children

In England, the Factory and Education Acts of 1802 banned children under fourteen from factory employment. In 1851, thirty-seven percent of boys and twenty percent of girls between the ages of ten and fourteen were in the labor market. By 1911, those numbers had dropped to eighteen percent and ten percent, respectively (Cunningham 1991:166). Although reformers and bureaucrats could claim a successful moral victory in the removal of child labor from the workforce, in reality children had been made superfluous by machinery and because (like foreign sweatshops today) they threatened the interests of adult male laborers.

The removal of children from the urban workforce transformed the nature of childhood in Europe. Within the family, children's economic contributions may have been curtailed, but their value in emotional and psychological gratification to their parents generally rose. From the capitalist industry's standpoint, if they had lost a source of cheap labor, at least they had gained an enormous potential consumer market. Children were also a substantial new source of labor for adults in educational and juvenile justice systems, in that an entire system of government jobs came into being, requiring education, training, and hiring of scores of adults (Postman 1982; Zelizer 1985). This new construction of children as being economically useless but emotionally priceless was imported into Brazil and had grave implications for poor working children of color.

As the understanding of childhood as a protected, almost sacred province gained in popularity, so did the focus on the child's education, discipline, and potential pathologies. R. Stainton Rogers states that Freud, the "father" of developmental psychology and personality theory, expressed a vision of the

> diverse tensions in his culture (e.g. the savage child over the innocent child, the impulsive over the rational, the hidden face over the public face) and set others in perpetual tension (the biological and the social, the act and the wish, the real and the fantasy), molding the whole into a powerful mythology. (Stainton Rogers 1992:89)

Freud sexualized the child and defined a potpourri of undirected human drives that children, unless restrained, would unleash upon society (Stainton Rogers 1992). What is significant here is that only by external intervention could the individual be saved, through psychotherapy for the upper classes and social work (government social workers) for the lower classes. Such outward intervention resulted in a plethora of new professionals: psychologists, social workers, child protection agents, delinquency courts, and more.

Jean Piaget (1896–1980) is credited with "uncovering" the developmental processes of children through a model deeply embedded in the social values of his time, namely the progress from childhood (the primitive) to adulthood (modern enlightenment). His conception was similar to Freud's in that both saw adulthood as the *goal* of childhood; the inferiority of the child's operational (logical) functions yields to the superior command of the adult mind. Buck-Morss points out that "The abstract formalism of Piaget's cognitive structures reflects the abstract formalism of the social structure," thereby reflecting the social constructions that defined twentieth-century Western European behavioral sciences (Raskin, Bernstein, and Buck-Morss 1987; Watson 1928; Inhelder 1958).

B. F. Skinner's and J. B. Watson's behaviorism brought renewed attention to the nature vs. nurture debate (Stainton Rogers 1992; Morss 1990; Ozmon and Craver 1990). In their conception, children are products of their environment; their behavior can be correlated with their social, physical, and psychological history. Watson went so far as to assert that he could produce any kind of adult human being by controlling his or her environment (Watson 1928; Skinner 1974). In short, Watson and Skinner believed children could be trained to become model citizens. Their ideas had wide-ranging impact on social and educational policy throughout the western world, and sometimes fed the ambitions of totalitarian regimes. Stainton Rogers argues that

> Behavior modification has taken on not a utopian cast, but a distinctly social control orientation in which "clients" often turn out to be the already oppressed and disadvantaged inmates of total environments. (Stainton Rogers 1992:100)

As Brazil entered the twentieth century, the influence of Western European and American theories of psychology, medicine, education, and justice were responsible for the creation of court systems dealing with a new species of child: the juvenile delinquent. Prior to the creation of the Minors' Court in 1923, that classification had not formally existed. Brazilian sociologists developed quasi-scientific tests to 'diagnose' children who demonstrated 'abnormal' or 'deviant' behaviors. In most cases, the subjects of such testing were lower-class youths whose greatest deviation from the norm was in their living conditions, not necessarily their psychological or intellectual makeup. Afonso Louzada, in *O Problema da Criança: A Ação Social do Juízo de Menores* (The Problem of the Child: The Social Action of the Judgment of Minors) states that,

> ... one observes the growing importance ascribed to psychological, physical, social, and economic causes in explaining deviant behavior by minors. Moral causes, such as "bad habits," "loose morals," and "weakening of family authority" began to coexist with other causes, such as "physical and psychological disturbances," "hereditary factors," "urban overcrowding," "industrialization," and "impoverishment." (Louzada 1940:18)

Today, even with the ratification of the Statute for Children and Adolescents, street children continue to be profiled according to social, economic, and racial attributes. In the following section I discuss the constructionist view of childhood and its theoretical implications on the study of children.

Constructionist View of Childhood

Childhood is not a universal condition of life. Humans, indeed most species, experience biological immaturity. But childhood is a uniquely human experience. It is the manner in which we understand and articulate the physical reality of biological immaturity. Viewed in this light, the "child" becomes a metaphor—a pattern of meaning—and childhood can be conceived of as socially specific sets of ideas, attitudes, and practices. Unlike gender or race, childhood is a temporary and temporal classification. But like race and gender, it acts as a set of power relationships revolving around different axes. Notions of "childhood" map implicit ideological (and moral) assumptions in the conceptualization of what it "is 'to be a child' as well as what it 'ought' to be." (Woodson 1999:4)

History

If the nineteenth century gave birth to the notion of the innocence of childhood in Western Europe, the twentieth century can be said to have consigned and confined childhood within legal, medical, and educational institutions, isolating children from the everyday work world of adults. As technology advanced in the twentieth century, television became a common household item. Children from around the world were brought into the homes of all social classes in the US and Europe. Advertisements and programs presented by international organizations such as United Nations Children's Fund (UNICEF) and the World Health Organization (WHO) projected images of children living in conditions that utterly contradicted what the modern West (post-industrial Western Europeans) wanted to envision as the province of childhood. As James and Prout state,

> The consequences of famine, war, and poverty for children threw the very idea of childhood into stark relief. The "world's children" united "our" children and "their" children only to reveal the vast differences between them. (James et al. 1998:1)

Children in tattered clothes with distressed or blank expressions began to stare from magazine covers and television screens. Agencies such as child protection and legal services grew in response to the recognition that childhood was a vulnerable and potentially devastating time. Public attention was drawn to child poverty and the physical, psychological, and sexual abuse of children, not only in third world countries, but also within the presumed protection of the developed West. The unpleasant images of children in distress heightened the tension between the idealized visions of childhood born of the West's affluence and the stark realities of an uncomfortable percentage of the world's poor children in industrializing countries.

Social Science Literature on the Constructionist View of Childhood

My theoretical approach has been informed and influenced by various social scientists active in the formation of the social constructionist view of childhood. The constructionist view defines children as viable and cogent social agents. I discuss the significance of this new theoretical approach to childhood by reviewing the social science literature on the social constructionist view as it currently stands within the field of anthropology. Next, I illustrate and discuss how street children view themselves in accordance with the constructionist view. I conclude with a brief discussion of how conflicting views of childhood have kept society polarized about street children, and how these views impede the creation of NGOs, which are most often conceptualized, funded, and administered by middle- and upper-class elites who use Western constructions of childhood to create programs for street children. Frequently, such programs are ineffective in meeting the real-life needs of the children they seek to serve because they are based on notions of childhood that conflict with the social constructions that define childhood as it is experienced by poor children of color in Brazil.

During the 1970s and 80s, a growing body of literature about the dominant discourse on childhood grew from a need to redefine the ways in which childhood had been idealized, discussed, studied, and written about. During the 1990s social science and historical studies attempted to address the tension between the reality of childhood and the idealized constructions of it. Psychological literature criticized previous theories of child development and children's needs (Richards1974; Richards and Light 1986). Martin Woodhead unpacked the vocabulary used to rationalize the efforts of social welfare workers, teachers, policy-makers, and parents. Woodhead states that:

> ... by systematically analyzing the concept of "need," I hope to show that this seemingly innocuous and benign five-letter word [child] conceals in practice a complex of latent assumptions and judgments about children. Once revealed, these tell us as much about the cultural location and personal values of the user as about the nature of childhood. (Woodhead 1990:39)

Philippe Ariès introduced a historical perspective of the construction of childhood as an invention (meaning a social construction in anthropological terms) (Ariès 1962), while other authors debated traditional social science theories about children and socialization (MacKay 1973).

Such scholarly debates eventually led to the development of a still-emerging paradigm concerning childhood and children's social relationships. This new paradigm views "... children as worthy of study in their own right, and not just in respect to their social construction by adults" (James and Prout 1998:4). The constructionist view of childhood also informs the various disciplines of child psychology by going directly to children in order to gather data about their lives. The emergent paradigm redefines children as active social agents instead of passive subjects. In addition, the new paradigm assumes that concepts of childhood (who children are, what they do, what they are capable of saying and understanding, and how they are socially positioned) are dependent on culture, race, gender, and ethnicity rather than only on biological maturity.

Anne Solberg has written about the changing nature of Norwegian childhood by using empirical studies of changing roles of children within the family as she investigated their contributions to household management and division of labor within the home (Solberg 1987). Solberg's work is an example of identifying and recasting the abilities of children. In her work, Solberg does not draw upon biological or developmental models to inform her on the abilities that children possess, but rather she draws upon actual real-life experiences and events in the lives of her informants in her research. In this case, her informants are children.

In relationship to street children, there has been a significant amount of attention given to the social practice of removing them from the street. Some social scientists have developed and supported practices that remove children from the streets by building on the work of Roberto da Matta, who produced the seminal work on the symbology of street-versus-home in Brazilian society (da Matta 1985; Rizzini 1994; Impelizieri 1995). On the other hand, several social scientists have studied the way in which the street is viewed as a place of transition in order to move from one location to another and not as a place to live, sleep, and eat. Finally, other social scientists such as Benno Glauser, Judith Ennew, Nancy Scheper-Hughes, and Sharon Stephens have written about poor children in developing countries and the social constructions that define their childhood in terms of their inclusion in the adult world (Glauser 1997; Ennew 1994b; Ennew 1990; Scheper-Hughes 1989; Stephens 1995). Ennew states that "One of the clearest cross-cultural findings in the 'Childhood as a Social Phenomenon' project is that, in developed countries, children inhabit spaces within an adult constructed world" (1994a). Ennew has linked the intense organization of children's temporal experience (day care, nursery school, pre-school, school, extra-curricular activities) to industrialization, where all time is commodified and conscripted, especially children's time. According to Ennew "free time" is related to idleness, which has no economic value. The idea of children governing their own time while they work in adult spaces and on public streets is viewed as posing a serious threat to society's interests. Ennew concludes her argument by stating that

> the purposelessness of "doing nothing" threatens collective representations: For this reason there exists a whole range of benevolent institutions precisely to give young people something to do. Thus, curiously, what little knowledge we have of what children do when they take control of their own time returns us to the economy. (Ennew 1994:142)

Irma Rizzini has researched and written about the impact of Western notions of behavioral sciences on the development of the concept of the "minor" in the Brazilian court system. Children who were removed from the streets were frequently administered psychological and intelligence tests resulting in diagnoses that described them in negative stereotypes (Rizzini 1994:83–101). Today, despite the replacement of the Minors' Code with the Statute for Children and Adolescents, street children continue to be stigmatized, stereotyped, and incarcerated simply for having been on the street.

Constructionist Theoretical Implications for the Reconstruction of Childhood

During the 1980s, conferences headed by Judith Ennew and Jans Qvortrup on the sociology and ethnography of childhood were held in Cambridge, UK; Canada; Europe; and Zimbabwe, Africa. These conferences have stimulated the emergence of a new paradigm in the constructionist theory of childhood. Some of the predominant characteristics of the emerging paradigm are 1) childhood is a social construction dependent on the criteria of culture, race, gender, and ethnicity, which form structural and cultural components in each location; 2) it is biological immaturity, not "childhood" that is a universal feature of all human groups; and 3) idealized social constructions of childhood that stress the innocence of children by removing them from the adult world are common to the middle and upper classes, while children of the poor are often stereotyped and stigmatized because they do not fit middle/upper-class notions of childhood. The new paradigm pays attention to the absence of children from official statistics and social accounting methods and recognizes how this absence marginalizes children and removes them from everyday agency. The new paradigm recognizes that in western cultures, children have become economically worthless, yet emotionally priceless (Postman 1982; Zelizer 1985). The villainization of childhood labor is thus a consequence of the construction of childhood innocence. In the following section, I will discuss the ways in which Brazilian street children view themselves and compare these views with the constructionist theory of childhood.

How Street Children View Themselves

How Brazilian street children view themselves can be linked to the statistical data about them. Studies indicate that 83.5 percent of all street children live with their families (50 percent with both parents, 33.5 percent with one parent, usually the mother). Fewer than 10 percent of street children have severed all ties to their families (Rizzini 1986a; Oliveira 1989). These studies show that street children often work more than 40 hours a week on the street and that their labor provides on average 30 percent of their families' incomes. My own research in Curvelo found that street children contribute on average between 20 and 60 percent of family income.

My investigation supports the constructionist view. For example I found that street children saw themselves as important people, and that their ability to work and earn money is an integral part of their sense of self-worth. One street youth told me that his dream "... is to have a good home for my mother and my father, and to work and to study ... so that they won't need to keep working like they are. [I want] to have money to pay them too." Street children commonly told me that working and earning an income made them responsible people who were far from worthless. For them, working, paying bills, participating in household work and sibling care, and going to school were the accepted norm.

Working on the street, however, interferes with successful completion of education. Brazil's public primary school dropout rate is alarming. Seventeen percent of Brazilians over seven years of age are illiterate. Ayesha Vawda, in a report for The World Bank on the failure of Brazilian public education, wrote that,

> in 1990, the average schooling for the adult population was only 4 years, approximately the same as El Salvador, Guatemala and Nicaragua, countries with less than half the income level of Brazil. Brazil's low educational attainment rates are directly related to high repetition in primary education, particularly in the early grades. Each year over 50 percent of students in the first grade of primary school repeat, the highest first grade failure rate in Latin America. The average Brazilian student currently spends 7.7 years in primary school, longer than for any other Latin American country. Yet during those 7.7 years, the average student does not even complete the fourth grade. According to a 1993 report, sixty-three percent of children drop out of primary school before completing it. One of the main reasons for such high dropout and repetition rates is the need for children to contribute to family income by working either for wages or on family enterprises. Currently, about seven million children work in Brazil. (Vawda 1997)

Recent literature about the ways in which street children view themselves most frequently takes a constructionist view, focusing on the actual voices of street children as they talk about themselves and their lives. Patricia Márquez in *The Street Is My Home* explores how street youth in Caracas are brought together because of economic scarcity and social violence. She describes the ways in which street youth are able to gain financial resources and material wealth by creating meaningful experiences and relationships in their lives while describing the types of risks they face daily on the streets (Márquez 1999:2). Tobias Hecht, in *At Home in the Street*, wonders why there are so few street children in Recife, in the Northeast of Brazil. Hecht views street children in Recife as "socially significant protagonists while also bringing into focus the adult debates in which they are enmeshed" (Hecht 1998:4–6). Hecht's findings about the pride Recife's street children take in working and earning an income conform with my own in Curvelo. Both of us found that street children's status within their family is enhanced in proportion to their successful economic enterprises on the street. Judith Ennew (1994) found that street children develop supportive networks and coping strategies by developing meaningful relationships with friends outside of the traditional adult supervision of the home (Ennew 1994a). Sharon Stephens similarly noted in *Children and the Politics of Culture* that street children "develop their own social organizations, relatively stable attachments to territories, and support networks linked to the sharing of food and goods" (1995:12). Stephens links the negative stereotypes of street children to Mary Douglas' work *Purity and*

Danger, where dirt is conceived as "matter out of place." Mary Douglas defined "dirt" as a form of matter out of place in this way:

> For us dirt is a kind of compendium category for all events which blur, smudge, contradict, or otherwise confuse accepted classifications. The underlying feeling is that a system of values which is habitually expressed in a given arrangement of things has been violated. (Douglas 1975:50–51)

In this sense then, I came to see that street youth blurred the boundaries between the social classes and their related constructions of childhood.

Street children, argues Stephens, are people out of place in that they defy the social consensus on what constitutes "normal" childhood (1995:12). Stephens suggests that as childhood is being redefined by children themselves and by the social, political, racial, and economic factors of their respective societies, childhood itself is being recast as dangerous. She calls on researchers

> to develop more powerful understandings of the role of the child in the structure of modernity, the historical processes by which these once localized Western constructions have been exported around the world, and the global political, economic, and cultural transformations that are currently rendering children so dangerous … the challenge is to grasp the specificity of childhood and children's experiences in different world regions, national frameworks, and social contexts … . (1995:14)

Her call for an investigation into the contextual ways in which childhood is constructed is also a call for reassessing children in general by empowering them with social agency.

Taking a constructionist approach to childhood, I agree with Wacquant (1992:9), who asserts that social reality is a "contingent ongoing accomplishment of competent social actors who continually construct their social world via the organized artful practice of everyday life." In addition, alongside the development of the constructionist view of childhood, race, gender, and ethnicity simultaneously have come to be viewed as social constructions dependent on location. Everyday life in this sense includes consideration of the actual social, political, and economic conditions faced by street and working children from impoverished backgrounds. In addition, race, gender, and ethnicity are constructed in tandem with social, political, economic, and historical practices. Hence, I have taken street children as my main informants. Their own descriptions of daily life on the streets, in the NGOs, in schools, and in their homes form the body of my qualitative data.

NGOs

The conflicting constructions of childhood discussed above create difficulties in the creation of effective programs for street children in Brazil. NGOs are most often created, funded, and administered by people from the middle and upper classes who view childhood in their own class as a time of freedom from responsibility. Conversely, street children view themselves as viable social actors and as "acting adults." During the early 1990s, many NGOs, particularly in Brazil's large metropolises, attempted to offer programs directly on the streets where children worked and/or lived. In this sense, these NGOs at least acknowledged street children as living outside the social consensus of what constituted a "normal" childhood. Attempts were made to create moving classrooms in order to teach literacy and basic computational skills, while offering popular cultural activities such as *capoeira* (an Afro-Brazilian martial art) and street theater.

Other NGOs opened centers where street children came to receive food, blankets, medication, and some educational assistance. At the end of the day, these children returned to the streets. NGO attempts to encourage children off the streets and either back to their families or into various residential institutions have been largely unsuccessful. Factors involved in the lack of success in these programs include extreme family violence, alcoholism, and sexual abuse, not to mention economic stress. When street children have been asked what they most value in the NGO programs they participate in, they most often cite job training, leisure, respect of NGO staffers who take the time to interact and talk to them, and nutritious meals (Impelizieri 1995). My data on street children in Curvelo concur with these observations.

The theoretical views of childhood discussed in this chapter affect how street children are perceived by the public at large and by the NGOs that seek to service them. More recent views of childhood, as a time of agency and self-directed learning and participation in society, may assist in the development of more effective programs for street children. In the next chapter, I discuss the historical background of Brazil's political economy and address how slavery, racism, social class, and educational and economic inequality act in tandem to limit the life possibilities of street and working children in the city of Curvelo.

Endnotes

[1]The term Afro-Brazilian is used throughout this dissertation to denote street children of various degrees of darker skin color. I have chosen to align myself with contemporary Afro-Brazilians, the street children in my sample, and with social scientists who declare that race and racism play a key role in Brazil's historical economic and social inequality. Rebecca Reichmann points out that the color line, as perceived in Brazil, is one of the greatest areas of contention that continues to divide those "... who believe that Brazil is a racial democracy from those who perceive discrimination based on color" (Reichmann 1999:7). Reichmann points out that color (skin color) in Brazil is THE dominant category for social classification of individuals, while one's racial or biological ancestry are underemphasized by elites (Reichmann 1999:7). Such a fluid color line is a product of miscegenation that describes skin colors from darkest to lightest. Hence, the darker the skin color, the more stigmatized the individual. Throughout its history, Brazil has adopted several national discourses on race. During the late 1800s. abolitionists embraced the notion of miscegenation and the mixture and fusing of races. During the 1920s, scientific notions about race that validated racism were embraced and the official doctrine became one of "whitening" through encouraging immigration of European immigrants and prohibiting immigration of darker-skinned races. Brazilian anthropologist Gilberto Freyer, in later decades, developed the notion that Brazil's

racial democracy was developing a "meta-race" that would in the end unify the Brazilian people into a new racial identity (Reichmann 1999:8). During the 1950s, UNESCO sponsored a series of studies on race in Brazil. Anthropologist Marvin Harris participated in the UNESCO study and found that the plethora of terms used to define color in Brazil was in actuality linguistic markers that avoided the identification of a person's skin color. Since Brazil has never legally enforced racial segregation policies, civil rights movements based on the color of a person's skin have never occurred. Indeed, dark-skinned people at times do move vertically upward in social status dependent on their income. Hence, the term "money whitens" is a common expression in Brazil. The wealthier a person becomes, the whiter they become; however, The 2000 Global Justice Center reported that "Of the 146 million inhabitants [of Brazil] in the 1991 Census, approximately 51% declared themselves to be white and 5% black, whereas 42% considered themselves brown. If we consider that most people designated as 'brown' have black African blood, Brazil's black population ranks second only to that of Nigeria." Brazilians of color (*preto, pardo, moreno*) do not proportionally share in Brazil's wealth. The 2000 Global Justice Center report stated that "According to the 1990 Census, whites earned 2.12 times the average salary for *pardos* (browns) and 2.41 times more than *pretos* (blacks). That same census indicated that while 18.9 percent of whites had eleven or more years of schooling, only 6.0 percent of blacks (*pretos*) had reached this level" (http://www.global.org.br/english/annual_report_documents/annual_report_inequality.htm). In 1995, one of Brazil's leading survey organizations, the *Datafolha* found that 89% of respondents to a survey on racial discrimination in Brazil stated that whites were prejudiced against blacks (*Sabia como É a Escala. Folha de São Paulo.* June 25, 1995). In 1999, The United Nations Development Program ranked Brazil 74th among 174 nations based on income per capita, literacy, and education level. This ranking places Brazil in the mid-range for development. However, if only the black population were counted and analyzed, it would put Brazil 108th among 174 nations. If the white population alone were counted and analyzed, it would put Brazil in 49th place among 174 nations. This analysis would place the Afro-Brazilian population lower than such African nations as Algeria and South Africa (Federation of Agencies for Social Assistance and Education *Justiça Global*, Human Rights in Brazil. *Federação de Órgãos para Assistência Social e Educativa*, or FASE*)*.

In this dissertation, racism in Brazil is based on current research data by Brazilian researchers whose social inequality indexes are cited here. In addition, racism, as defined here, is based on my fieldwork with street children who experienced frequent discrimination based on the color of their skin as well as their poverty. It was their stories about racism that informed this research.

References

Ariès, Philippe. *Centuries of Childhood: A Social History of Family Life.* New York, 119, 413.

Austin, Joe and Willard, Michael Nevin (Eds.). *Generations of Youth: Youth Cultures and History in Twentieth-Century America.* New York: New York University Press, 1998.

Beiber, Judy. *Power, Patronage, and Political Violence: State Building on a Brazilian Frontier*, 1999, 1822–1889.

Birdsall, Nancy and Sabot, Richard. *Opportunity Foregone: Education in Brazil. Inter-American Development Fund.* Washington, D.C. Inter-American Development Bank. Baltimore: Johns Hopkins University Press, 1996, 7–44, 124.

Brick-Panter and Smith, M. T. *Abandoned Children*. Cambridge, UK: Cambridge University Press, 2000.

Burdick, John. *Blessed Anastácia: Women, Race, and Popular Culture in Brazil*. New York: Routledge, 1998.

Conrad, Robert Edgar. *Children of God's Fire: A Documentary History of Black Slavery in Brazil*. University Park, PA: The Pennsylvania State University Press, 1984, 100, 341–350.

Cunningham, Hugh. *The Children of the Poor: Representations of Childhood Since the Seventeenth Century*. Oxford: Blackwell, 1991, 29, 69, 71, 151–152, 154, 166.

Da Matta, Richard. *A casa e a rua: espaço, cidadania, mulher e morte no Brasil*. São Paulo: Brasiliense, 1985.

Degeler, Carl. *Neither Black nor White: Slavery and Race Relations in Brazil and the United States*. Madison, WI: The University of Wisconsin Press, 1986. Quote from Azevedo as a footnote citing Nogueira and Bastide, from *Relações raciais*.

Del Priore, Mary (org.); Laura de Mello e Souza [et al.]. "O Abandono de Crianças Negras No Rio de Janeiro." In *Historia da Criança no Brasil*, Mary del Priore, Ed. 1991. São Paulo: Editora Contexto: CEDHAL, 1978, 67, 70.

Diamond, Timothy, J. and Dilorio, Judith, A. *The Status of Children Under Advanced Capitalism: A Critical Perspective*, 1978. Circulated by the Red Feather Institute for Advanced Studies in Sociology as part of The Transforming Sociology Series. Sent to me by author.

Douglas, Mary. *Purity and Danger: An Analysis of the Concepts of Pollution and Taboo*. New York: Routledge, 1975, 50–51.

Elson, Diane. "The Differentiation of Children's Labour in the Capitalist Labour Market." *Development and Change*, 1982, 13:419–497.

Ennew, Judith. "Parentless Friends: A Cross-Cultural Examination of Networks Among Street Children and Street Youth." In *Social Networks and Social Support in Childhood and Adolescence*. Ed. by Frank Nestmann and Klaus Hurrelmann. Berlin: Walter de Gruyter, 1994a, 409–426.

Ennew, Judith. "Time for Children or Time for Adults?" In *Childhood Matters: Social Theory, Practice, and Politics*. Qvortrup et al., Aldership: Avebury, 1994b.

Ennew, Judith. *The Iconography of Street Children*. Paper presented at Department of Social Anthropology, University of Oslo, 1990, 142.

Fyfe, Alec. *Child Labour*. Cambridge, UK: Polity Press, 1989.

Glauser, Benno. "Street Children: Deconstructing a Construct," in James, A. and Prout, A. (Eds), *Constructing and Reconstructing Childhood*. London: Falmer Press, 1997.

Hecht, Tobias. *At Home in the Street: Street Children of Northeast Brazil*. Cambridge, UK: Cambridge University Press, 1998, 4–6.

Impelizieri, Flávia. "Street Children and NGOs in Rio: A Follow-Up Study on Non-Governmental Projects." Rio Janeiro: *AMAIS Livaria e Editora: IUPERJ*, 1995, 37–38, 69–73, 101–103, 115.

Inhelder, Bärbel and Piaget, Jean. *De la logique de l'enfant à logique de l'adolescent*. [English: *The Growth of Logical Thinking*] [translated by Anne Parsons and Stanley Milgram]. New York: Basic Books, 1958.

Jahoda, Gustav. *Images of Savages: Ancient Roots of Modern Prejudice in Western Culture*. London: Routledge, 1999.

James, A., Prout, A., et al. *Theorizing Childhood*. New York: Teachers College Press, 1998, 4, 14.

James, A. and Prout, A. *Constructing and Reconstructing Childhood: Contemporary Issues in the Sociological Study of Childhood*. London: The Falmer Press.

Kerstenetzky, Celia Lessa. "The Violence of Inequality." *Instituto Brasilero de Análises Sociais e Econômicas (IBASE)*, (Brazilian Institute for Social and Economic Analysis). *Instituto del Tercer Mundo—Control Ciudadano: Uma rede ONG de monitoreo y vigilancia de los compromisos realizados por los gobiernos en la Cumbre Mundial de Desarrollo Social y la IV Conferéncia Mundial sobre la Mujer*, 2001. <observatorio@ibase.org.br>.

Louzada, Afonso. *O Problema da Criança: A Ação Social do Juizo de Menores*. Rio de Janeiro: Imprensa Nacional, 1940, 18.

MacKay, R. "Conceptions of Children and Models of Socialization," in Dreitzsel, H. P., (Ed.) *Childhood and Socialization*. London: Collier-Macmillan, 1973.

Márquez, Patricia. *The Street Is My Home: Youth and Violence in Caracas*. Stanford, CA: Stanford University Press, 1999, 2.

Marx, Karl. *Das Kapital*. Volume One. New York: Vintage Books, 1977, 353–359.

May, Margaret. "Innocence and Experience: The Evolution of the Concept of Juvenile Delinquency in the Mid-Nineteenth Century." *Victorian Studies*, XVII, 1973, (1):7–29.

Morss, John, R. *The Biologising of Childhood: Developmental Psychology and the Darwin Myth*. Hove, UK: Lawrence Erlbaum, 1990.

Oliveira, Cleide de Fátima Galiza. *Se essa rua fosse minha: um estudo sobre a trajetória vive dos meninos de rua do Recife*. Recife, UNICEF, 1989.

Ozmon, Howard and Craver, Samuel. *Philosophical Foundations of Education*. New York: Macmillan, 1990.

Postman, Neil. *The Disappearance of Childhood*. New York: Delacorte Press, 1982.

Prawat, R. S. "Teachers' Beliefs About Teaching and Learning: A Constructivist Perspective." *American Journal of Education*, 1992, 100(3):354–394. ERIC Journal No. EJ448049.

Raskin, Marcus G.; Bernstein, Herbert J.; and Buck-Morss, Susan. *New Ways of Knowing: The Sciences, Society, and Reconstructive Knowledge*. Totowa, NJ: Rowman and Littlefield, 1987.

Reichmann, Rebecca. *Race in Contemporary Brazil: From Indifference to Inequality*. University Park, PA: The Pennsylvania State University Press, 1999, 234–249.

Richards, M. (Ed). *The Integration of a Child into a Social World*. Cambridge, UK: Cambridge University Press, 1974.

Richards, M. and Light, P. (Eds). *Children of Social Worlds*. Cambridge, UK: Polity Press, 1986.

Rizzini, Irma. "In Praise of Science, or the Concept of 'Minors' in Legal Practice." In *Children in Brazil Today: A Challenge for the Third Millennium*. Rio de Janeiro: Editora Universitária Santa Úrsula, 1994, 83–101, 179.

Scheper-Hughes, N. (Ed.). *Child Survival: Anthropological Perspectives on the Treatment and Maltreatment of Children*. Dordrecht, Holland: Reidel, 1989.

Skidmore, Thomas. "Fact and Myth: Discovering a Racial Problem in Brazil." In Calvin Goldscheider, Ed., *Population, Ethnicity, and Nation-Building*. Boulder: Westview Press, 1995, 91–117.

Skinner, B. F. *About Behaviorism*. New York: Knopf, distributed by Random House, 1974.

Solberg, Anne. "The Working Life of Children." Report no. 15, Trondheim: Norwegian Center of Child Research, 1987.

Stainton Rogers, R. and Stainton Rogers, W. *Stories of Childhood: Shifting Agendas of Child Concern.* Toronto: University of Toronto Press, 1992, 89, 100.

Standing, G. "State Policy and Child Labour: Accommodation versus Legitimization." *Development and Change*, 1982, 13(4).

Stephens, Sharon. *Children and the Politics of Culture.* Princeton: Princeton University Press, 1995, 12, 14.

Stocking, George, W. Jr. *Race, Culture, and Evolution: Essays in the History of Anthropology.* Chicago: University of Chicago Press, 1968, 126.

Twine, France Winddance. *Racism in a Racial Democracy: The Maintenance of White Supremacy in Brazil.* New Brunswick: Rutgers University Press, 1998.

Vawda, Ayesha. "Human Development, Network Educational Development." 1997 December 1. <http://www.fordham.edu/economics/mcleod/Brazil-Bolsa-Escola.pdf> (accessed 9-7-13).

Watson, John B. *Psychological Care of Infant and Child.* New York: Norton, 1928.

Woodhead, Martin. "Psychology and the Cultural Construction of Children's Needs." In *Constructing and Reconstructing Childhood* by A. James and A. Prout (Eds). London: Falmer Press, 1990, 39.

Woodson, Stephani. 2000 "Exploring the Cultural Topography of Childhood: Television Performing the 'Child' to Children." In *Bad Subjects: Political Education for Everyday Life*, Issue #47, December 1999, 14–17. <http://eserver.org/bs> accessed on 9-8-13.

Zelizer, Viviana A. Rotman. *Pricing the Priceless Child: The Changing Social Value of Children.* New York: Basic Books, 1985.

Curricular History and Social Control

The Creation of Ideological Hegemony in Education

By Michael Apple

E ducation is not a neutral enterprise. By the very nature of the institution, the educator is involved, whether he or she knows it or not, in a political act. I first argued this point a few years ago, and I believe it even more strongly now. In the last analysis, educators cannot fully separate teir educational activity from the institutional arrangements and forms of consciousness that dominate advanced industrial economies like our own. My work has focused on better understanding the relationship between education and economic structure and the linkages between knowledge and power, and how our educational system works in a hegemonic system, a system of domination and cultural control that is complicit in creating and maintaining social inequality.

One of the ways schools are used for hegemonic purposes is in their teaching of cultural and economic values and dispositions that are supposedly "shared by all," while at the same time "guaranteeing" that only a specified number of students are selected for higher levels of education because of their "ability" to contribute to the maximization of the production of the technical knowledge also needed by the economy. This is not a recent phenomenon; it has a long history in American education. In this essay I shall examine in how it came about historically through the school's response to ideological and economic conflicts among classes at a time of rapid change from an economy based on agricultural capital to one rooted in industrial capital in the beginnings of this century. As we shall see, schools were not necessarily built to enhance or preserve the cultural capital of classes or communities other than the most powerful segments of the population. The *hegemonic role of the intellectual,* of the professional educator, in this development is quite clear.

Toward a Sense of the Present as History

Imagine yourself as living in one of the larger ghettos of an American city. Another community member comes up to you and says, "You know, schools work." You look at him somewhat incredulously. After all, your children are doing relatively poorly on intelligence and achievement tests. Most of the community's young go on to lower paying jobs than their white counterparts. Many are rather disheartened about their futures. The school has increasing violence and vandalism. The curriculum seems out of touch with the reality

You lay this all out for him, explaining each of these issues and trying to show him that he is either just plain wrong or one of the least perceptive people you have seen in a long time. Then he says, "I agree with all you have told me. All these things you have just mentioned occur, not only here but throughout the United States in communities where people live who are poor, politically and culturally disenfranchised, or oppressed." Yet he begins documenting an important set of facts. Carefully, yet somehow passionately, he shows that these "community" schools are doing what they were in fact historically built to do. They were not built to give you control; quite the opposite is the case. As he talks, it slowly begins to make sense to you. A few more pieces of a larger picture begin to come together. What if he is correct? What if schools and the curriculum within them evolved in such a way that the interests of my community were to be subsumed under the interests of more powerful people? What if existing social and economic arrangements *require* that some people are relatively poor and unskilled and others are not? Then you begin to get a tacit understanding of how schools may help to maintain this set of institutional arrangements. You begin to agree, but you add something important he forgot to verbalize. You say, "Yes, schools work … for them."And you both nod.

Now this little vignette was meant to be more than simply an exercise in imagining. Rather, it was meant to reiterate points that lie at the heart of this book: both that schools have a history and that they are linked through their everyday practices to other powerful institutions in ways that are often hidden and complex. This history and these linkages need to be understood if we are to know the real possibilities for our own action on schools in that hypothetical community.

The curriculum field has played a major part in this history of the relationship between school and community. Because of this, it can also serve as an excellent exemplar for an analysis of the linkages schools have had with other institutions. By focusing on some of the past moments of the curriculum field here, I hope to show that the conclusions of the people in the imaginary story we started out with are not that imaginary at all. They provide, unfortunately, quite an accurate description of the hopes, plans, and conservative vision of community of a significant portion of a group of educators who had a large impact on how and what knowledge was chosen for, and ultimately got into, schools.

In order to illuminate these things, there are a number of questions we need to ask here. What did "community" mean for the educators and intellectuals who had the strongest influence on the early curriculum field? What social and ideological interests guided their work? These questions are critically important for a number of reasons. As has been repeatedly argued here, the knowledge that got into schools in the past and gets into schools now is not random. It is selected and organized around sets of principles and values that come from somewhere, that represent particular views of normality and deviance, of good and bad, and of what "good people act like." Thus, if we are to understand why the knowledge of only certain groups has been primarily represented in schools, we need to see the social interests which often guided curriculum selection and organization.

As I shall demonstrate here, the social and economic interests that served as the foundation upon which the most influential curriculum workers acted were not neutral; nor were they random. They embodied commitments to specific economic structures and educational policies, which, when put into practice, contributed to inequality. The educational and cultural policies, and the vision of how communities should operate and who should have power in them, served as mechanisms of social control. These mechanisms did little to increase the relative economic or cultural efficacy of these groups of people who still have little power today. But before examining the roots the curriculum field has in the soil of social control, let us look briefly at the general perspective which underpins this essay's critical analysis.

Power and Culture

Social and economic control occurs in schools not merely in the forms of discipline schools have or in the dispositions they teach—the rules and routines to keep order, the hidden curriculum that reinforces norms of work, obedience, punctuality, and so on. Control is exercised as well through the forms of meaning the school distributes. That is, the "formal corpus of school knowledge" can become a form of social and economic control.[1]

Schools do not only control people; they also help control meaning. Since they preserve and distribute what is perceived to be "legitimate knowledge"—the knowledge that "we all must have," schools confer cultural legitimacy on the knowledge of specific groups.[2] But this is not all, for the ability of a group to make its knowledge into "knowledge for all" is related to that group's power in the larger political and economic arena. Power and culture, then, need to be seen, not as static entities with no connection to each other, but as attributes of existing economic relations in a society. They are dialectically interwoven so that economic power and control is interconnected with cultural power and control. This very sense of the connectedness between knowledge or cultural control and economic power once again serves as the basis for our historical analysis here.

Two things have been central to this approach, so far. First, it sees schools as caught up in a nexus of other institutions—political, economic, and cultural—that are basically unequal. That is, schools exist through their relations to other more powerful institutions, institutions that are combined in such a way as to generate structural inequalities of power and access to resources. Second, these inequalities are reinforced and reproduced by schools (though not by them alone, of course). Through their curricular, pedagogical, and evaluative activities in day-to-day life in classrooms, schools play a significant role in preserving if not generating these inequalities. Along with other mechanisms for cultural preservation and distribution, schools contribute to what has elsewhere been called the *cultural reproduction of class relations* in advanced industrial societies.[2]

These two central concerns—the problem of schools being caught in a powerful set of institutions and the role of the school in reproducing inequalities—mean that one interprets schools in a different way than is usually done by educators. Rather than interpreting them as "the great engines of democracy" (though there is an element of truth in that), one looks at schools as institutions which are not necessarily or always progressive forces. They may perform economic and cultural functions and embody ideological rules that both preserve and enhance an existing set of structural relations. These relations operate at a fundamental level to help some groups and serve as a barrier to others.

This is not to imply that all school people are racist (though some may in fact be) or that they are part of a conscious conspiracy to "keep the lower classes in their place." In fact, many of the arguments for "community" and about curriculum put forth by some of the early educators, curriculum workers, and intellectuals whom I shall examine were based on the best liberal intentions of "helping people." Rather the argument being presented here is that "naturally" generated out of many of educators' commonsense assumptions and practices about teaching and learning, normal and abnormal behavior, important and unimportant knowledge, and so forth are conditions and forms of interaction that have latent functions. And these latent functions include some things that many educators are not usually aware of.

As has been pointed out elsewhere, for example, one important tacit function of schooling seems to be the teaching of different dispositions and values to different school populations. If a set of students is seen as being prospective members of a professional and managerial class of people, then their schools and curriculum seem to be organized around flexibility, choice, inquiry, etc. If, on the other hand, students' probable destinations are seen as that of semiskilled or unskilled workers, the school experience tends to stress punctuality, neatness, habit formation, and so on. These expectations are reinforced by the kinds of curricula and tests schools give and by the labels affixed to different kinds of students.[3] Thus, the formal and informal knowledge that is taught in schools, the evaluative procedures, and so forth, need to be looked at connectedly or we shall miss much of their real significance. For these everyday school practices are linked to economic, social, and ideological structures outside of the school buildings. These linkages need to be uncovered both today and in the past. It will be just this past that will concern us here.

Urbanization and the Historical Function of Schooling

Any serious attempt at understanding whose knowledge gets into schools must be, by its very nature, historical. It must begin by seeing current arguments about curriculum, pedagogy, and institutional control as outgrowths of specific historical conditions, as arguments that were and are generated by the role schools have played in our social order. Thus, if we can begin to comprehend the economic and ideological purposes schools have served in the past, then we can also begin to see the reasons why progressive social movements which aim at certain kinds of school reforms—such as community participation and control of institutions—are often less successful than their proponents would like them to be.

To make this clear, I shall briefly focus on some historical purposes of urban schooling (the model from which most public schooling was generated), on what its "community" role was seen to be and how it functioned. Then I shall turn to a more extensive historical examination of the part of schooling that dealt with the knowledge students would "receive" in schools—the curriculum field.

It is easy to forget the roots of schools in cities in the U.S., but revisiting these roots might help explain why many working class, Black, Latino, and other communities find little of their own culture and language in schools. Recent investigations of the growth of education in the urban centers of the East are quite helpful in this regard. In New York City in the 1850s, for example, when the public school system became increasingly solidified, schools were seen as institutions that could preserve the cultural hegemony of an embattled "native" population. Education was the way in which the community life, values, norms, and economic advantages of the powerful were to be protected. Schools could be the great engines of a moral crusade to make the children of the immigrants and the Blacks like "us." Thus, for many people who were important in the growth of schooling as we know it, cultural differences were not at all legitimate. Instead, these differences were seen as the tip of an iceberg made up of waters containing mostly impurities and immorality. The urban historian Carl Kaestle catches this attitude exceptionally well when he quotes from a New York State Assembly report that warned, "Like the vast Atlantic, we must decompose and cleanse the impurities which rush into our midst, or like the inland lake, we shall receive their poison into our whole national system."[4]

This moral mission of the school had a major impact on the kinds of curricular selections made and on general school policy as you can well imagine. But this was not all. The crusade to eliminate diversity was heightened by another set of factors. The scale of city problems increased as the population increased. Something had to be done about the rapid growth in the numbers upon numbers of "different" children to be acculturated. The answer was bureaucratization—the seemingly commonsensical consolidation of schools and standardization of procedures and curriculum, both of which would promote economy and efficiency. Thus, the emphases on acculturation and standardization, issues community members still confront today, were intimately intertwined. In essence, "the bureaucratic ethic and the moral mission of the schoolmen arose from the same problem—the rapid expansion and diversification of the population—and they tended toward the same result—a vigorously conformist system."[5]

This moral mission with its emphasis on cultural conformity was not simply found in New York; nor was it limited to the early and middle parts of the nineteenth century. The moral values became increasingly coupled with economic ideologies and purposes as the country expanded its industrial base. Schools in New York, Massachusetts, and elsewhere, were looked at more and more as a set of institutions that would "produce" people who would have the traditional values of community life (a life that may never really have existed in this ideal form) and, as well, the norms and dispositions required of industrious, thrifty, and efficient workers for this industrial base. Not just in 1850, but even more between 1870–1920, the school was pronounced as the fundamental institution that would solve the problems of the city, the impoverishment and moral decay of the masses, and, increasingly, would adjust individuals to their respective places in an industrial economy.[6] Thus, at the base of schooling was a set of concerns which, when put together, embodied a conservative ideology. "We" must preserve "our" community by teaching the immigrants our values and adjusting them to existing economic roles.

This account gives us a general picture of the ideological climate of the times, particularly in the urban areas of the East, when the curriculum field began to define itself. It was a climate that pervaded the perceptions of more than just the public at large. It also affected many articulate intellectuals and educators, even those whose own roots were outside of the urban centers. As we shall see, neither the members of the rising intelligentsia nor the early members of the curriculum field were immune from these perceptions. Both the school's role in the moral crusade or in economic adjustment and stratification were things with which they felt more comfortable than not. In fact, the notion of immunity is something of an inaccurate one. A large portion of the early leaders of the movement to make curriculum selection and determination into a field of professional specialization wholeheartedly embraced both the moral crusade and the ethic of economic adjustment as overt functions of schooling. They saw the standardized procedures for selecting and organizing school knowledge as contributing to both of these purposes.

Social Homogeneity and the Problem of Community

The formative members of the curriculum field, as well as most of the early leaders in sociology, psychology, and education, were by birth and upbringing members of a native and rural middle class, Protestant in religion, and Anglo-Saxon in descent. In defining the nature, boundaries and interests of their fields of study, these intellectual leaders, along with other social scientists, reflected and spoke to the concerns of the middle class. Specifically, they reflected what they believed was the declining power and influence of the middle class in the wake of America's transition in the late nineteenth and early twentieth centuries from a rural, agrarian society to an urban, industrialized one. They defined the issues in a particular way, as a problem of the *loss* of community.

The period during which these future leaders came to maturity, 1865 to 1900, was a time of doubt and fear for the small farmers, merchants, and professionals who made up the nation's middle class. They felt their social order, which they viewed as being rooted in the small rural town with its deep, face to face personal relationships, was endangered. They were afraid of the emerging dominance of a new economic unit, the corporation. They also felt that a new economic and social class of great wealth and power, composed of the owners of these corporations and their financial backers, would threaten the economic security and political influence of the small town, thus harming its economic base in agriculture and small-scale manufacturing. But the growth of a corporate economy also was tied to the growth of urban centers. The cities were increasingly being populated by immigrants from eastern and southern Europe and Blacks from the rural South. These diverse people were seen as a threat to a homogeneous American culture, a culture centered in the small town and rooted in beliefs and attitudes of the middle class. The "community" that the English and Protestant forebearers of this class had "carved from a wilderness" seemed to be crumbling before an expanding urban and industrial society.

Of these two concerns, the early spokespeople of the new social sciences focused most of their attention on the problem of immigration. They suspected that these immigrants, who seemed to have a higher birthrate than the native population, would soon outnumber the "native well bred population." Increasing numbers of immigrants, with their urban enclaves and different political, cultural, and religious traditions, were a threat to a homogeneous culture. This unitary culture was not only the source of America's stability and a key to progress, but was synonymous for these members of the intelligentsia with the idea of democracy itself.[7]

At first these intellectuals talked of the issue of community in terms of a threat to the existence of the rural town, which, to early social scientists, assumed almost mystical proportions as the guarantor of social order and stability. The small town, its politics, its religion, its values, came to be seen, as the sociologist Robert Nisbet puts it, as the very essence of the American community.[8] Later and more importantly, the members of this new group of intellectuals (who in actuality owed the emergence of their professions and the opportunities it offered them to both urbanization and industrialization) took a different tack in defining the problem of community, one that did not require them to defend the small town as a physical entity.[9] Instead, they took what they thought constituted the basis of the small town's ability to provide for stability, its like-mindedness in beliefs, values, and standards of behavior, and idealized this feature of small town life as the basis of the order necessary for an emerging urban and industrialized society. For these intellectuals the notion of community became synonymous with the idea of homogeneity and cultural consensus. If their upbringing in the rural town taught these individuals anything, it taught them that order and progress were dependent on the degree to which beliefs and behavior were common and shared. Applying this view to the increasingly urban society in which they lived, they argued for the maintenance of a unitary culture (what they meant by a sense of community) rooted in the values, beliefs, and behavior of the middle class. When it seemed to them that cultural homogeneity was dissolving, because of urbanization, industrialization, and immigration, and that their sense of community was being eclipsed, they acted by "striking out at whatever enemies their view of the world allowed them to see."[10]

Social Control and the Problem of Community

In the name of cultural conformity, these early social scientists "struck out" with a particular passion at the Eastern and Southern European immigrant. Adopting for the most part an hereditarian perspective, they viewed the immigrants and workers as being inferior to the native population. Given the high birthrate, they were concerned that these immigrants would come to threaten the existence of the more economically advantaged classes with what Ross called "race suicide."[11] More immediately, however, these immigrants were perceived as a threat to the existence of democracy itself. Charles A. Ellwood, another early American sociologist, argued that genetically immigrants did not seem to have "the capacity for self government and free institutions which the peoples of Northern and Western Europe have shown."[12]

To deal with this supposed threat, the intellectuals joined the growing movement during the late nineteenth and early twentieth centuries for immigration restriction.[13] However, to insure cultural homogeneity in the face of the immigration that had already occurred, they saw a need for a second line of defense. In essence, they perceived that the imposition of meaning could be an instrument of social control. The immigrant could be increasingly acculturated into middle class values, beliefs and standards of behavior. One such instrument was the school. The formative leaders of the curriculum would use the curriculum to serve the cause of community. The *curriculum* could restore what was being lost

The Curriculum Field and the Problem of Community

The most influential early members of the curriculum field seemed for the most part to share these views about the declining position of the middle class and the threat posed by immigrants and other diverse peoples. Ross L. Finney, not only an early curriculum theorist but one of the first educational sociologists, like earlier social scientists and educators viewed the middle class as being threatened from above by a class of corporate capitalists and from below by an immigrant working class, who were entering the population in growing numbers to meet the demands of industrialization for a cheap labor supply. Writing in the post World War I period, he reflected the national paranoia known as the Red Scare. He argued that the Eastern and Southern European immigrants, whom he believed had carried with them to America a Bolshevik ideology, would attempt to overthrow the nation and with it the middle class in a revolution similar to the Russian Revolution of 1917.[14]

In making his defense of the middle class, Finney bemoaned the loss of community. He spoke longingly of what he viewed as a more serene time in the history of the nation, a time when industrialization had not taken the ownership of the nation's wealth out of the hands of those who had produced it and in the process had created conflicting economic and social classes and interests.[15]

Finney's solution to this problem was familiar. The nation must instill the immigrants with specific values and standards of behavior. The immigrant working class had to hold the same firm commitments to their work which he attributed to people from his own class. It was this commitment, he believed, that would reduce their potential revolutionary threat by making them happy performing the "humbler" economic functions that he saw as the future lot of the mass of the American population in an industrialized society.[16] Along with the other intellectuals of his day, he argued that "if a democratic people's conduct is to be dependable and harmonious, they must think and feel alike."[17]

Other major curriculum workers had a similar commitment to like-mindedness. Charles C. Peters, who like Finney was both an influential curriculum theorist and educational sociologist, viewed the immigrants as a threat to American civilization until they came "to think about, and act on, political, social, economic, sanitary, and other matters in the approved American way."[18] Just as importantly, Edward L. Thorndike, who did more than any other individual to articulate the behavioristic psychology that has dominated the curriculum field since its earliest times, viewed Blacks in the same way as these other educators viewed the immigrant. He not only doubted their ability to adjust to democratic institutions, but he saw them as an undesirable element within the population of most American cities.[19] But how were we to cope with these undesirable elements? Since the people were already here, how could we make them to be like us? How could we restore community?

Just as in earlier periods, these individuals looked to the schools. The school curriculum could create the valuative consensus that was the goal of their economic and social policies. Finney in this respect argued that "a far wiser propaganda for the workers is one that will ally and amalgamate them with the middle class. And such an alliance and amalgamation should be forced upon the lower classes, whether their agitators like it or not by compulsory attendance laws that make high school graduation practically universal."[20]

Curriculum Differentiation and the Problem of Community

The central feature of the view of curriculum construction that dominated the thinking of these early educators, and in fact still dominates the thinking of contemporary curriculum theorists, was that the curriculum needed to be differentiated to prepare individuals of differing intelligence and ability for a variety of different but specific adult life functions.[21] This is a critical point. These varying adult functions were seen to involve *unequal* social responsibilities yielding unequal social power and privilege. These educators believed that individuals of high intelligence were more moral, more dedicated to their work, and more willing to apply their talents to the benefit of the larger society than were the majority of the population. As a consequence Thorndike and others argued that the views of these individuals were of more social import than those of the majority. Therefore, these individuals deserved a position of social and political preeminence.[22]

This view of the unequal distribution of responsibility and power was reflected when they talked about how curriculum differentiation would fulfill two social purposes—education for leadership and education for what they called "followership." Those of high intelligence were to be educated to lead the nation by being taught to understand the needs of the society. They would also learn to define appropriate beliefs and standards of behavior to meet those needs. The mass of the population was to be taught to accept these beliefs and standards whether or not they understood them or agreed with them.[23] As Finney argued, "instead of trying to teach dullards to think for themselves, the intellectual leaders must think for them, and drill the results, memoriter, into their synapses."[24] In this way, curriculum differentiation based on "intelligence" would create cultural homogeneity and thereby stability within American society.[25]

Ethnicity, Intelligence, and Community

As we just saw, in defining the function of the curriculum many of the most influential members of the field, although they seemed to fear and dislike the immigrants, increasingly talked of the issue of maintaining community as a problem of widespread low intelligence within the population. But there is evidence to suggest that this redefinition was not indicative of a change from the viewpoint they shared with the earlier leaders in the social sciences. When Thorndike identified those within American society whom he believed possessed greater natural capacity and high intelligence, he pointed to the businessman, scientist, and lawyer.[26] These were occupations that during his day were almost totally monopolized by members of the native, middle class. The highly intelligent, hence, were to be predominantly found within this class and not the lower ones. The unintelligent masses were the elements of diversity within the population, primarily the eastern and southern European immigrant and to a lesser degree the Black population. Thus, what was originally seen by American intellectuals as a cultural problem of ethnic and class differences was redefined in the seemingly neutral language of science as a problem of differences in intelligence, as a problem in differing "abilities" to contribute to the maximization and control of "expert" moral and technical knowledge, in this way divesting the problem of its economic and social content. Social control, hence, became covered by the language of science, something that continues to this day.[27] By controlling and differentiating school curricula, so could people and classes be controlled and differentiated as well.

But why did they do this? The formative theorists of the curriculum field, despite their identification with the middle class, increasingly viewed industrialization and the emergence of the corporation with favor. They were particularly enamored of the seeming efficiency and productivity of industrial processes and thus incorporated into their conception of curriculum construction the principles of scientific management that were thought to be responsible for it.[28] But beyond this faith in corporate procedures, they were committed to its hierarchical mode of organization as *a model for society itself.* We can see this most clearly in Finney's vision for American society:[28]

> This conception of leadership and followship—leads us again to the notion of a graduated hierarchy of intelligence and enlightenment. ... At the apex of such a system must be the experts, who are pushing forward research in highly specialized sectors of the front. Behind them are such men and women as the colleges should produce, who are familiar with the findings of the experts and are able to relate part with part. By these relatively independent leaders of thought, progressive change and constant readjustment will be provided for. Back of these are the high school graduates, who are somewhat familiar with the vocabulary of those above them, have some feeling of acquaintance with the various fields, and a respect for expert

knowledge. Finally, there are the duller masses, who mouth the catchwords of those
in front of them, imagine that they understand, and follow by imitation.

Notice that this view of social organization does not attempt to eliminate all diversity
but rather to control it by narrowing its scope and channeling it toward areas that do not
seem to threaten the imperatives of social stability, the production of "expert knowledge," and
economic growth. Industrialists, for example, from the 1880s to the early 1920s, the period
in which these formative theorists grew to maturity and carried on their work, resisted the
growing national movement for immigration restriction. Instead they attempted to diminish
the immigrants' supposed threat to American society by instilling them with middle-class
attitudes, beliefs, and standards of behavior. At the same time, they employed their seeming
"willingness" to work for low wages to meet the demands of industrialization for a cheap
source of labor.[29] Here, the formative members of the curriculum field, unlike some of the early
social scientists, seemed to share this view held by the industrialists. They may have believed
that, given the growing nativistic sentiments of the post First World War period, they would
be more successful in promoting the integration of diverse elements of the population into a
hierarchically organized society if they conceptualized that diversity in terms of intelligence
and not ethnicity. In the context of the time, they no doubt believed that American society
was more willing to deal with diversity in intelligence than diversity in ethnicity or race.[30] But
they undoubtedly felt secure in their belief that a "real" community could be built through
education, one with "natural" leaders and "natural" followers, and one in which people like
"us" could define what "they" should be like.

But this does not explain all of it. To this must be added the role of "science" as once
again providing the "ultimately right principles" about which there must be consensus. As the
scientific justification of stratification increased, as it became more systematic, it provided the
ideal solution to the ideological problem of justifying one's power over other competing and
ultimately threatening groups. And it provided it in two ways: giving an "adequate" definition
of these individuals' situation and in serving the interests of these classes in the competition
over economic and cultural capital. By treating science as a form of technology, as a neutral
method that could be applied to the economic and cultural dilemmas these people faced
in their attempt to recreate and create hegemony, the role (the scope and function) of their
ideological vision is obvious.

For these "reformers" were faced with an interesting dilemma. Generally speaking, with
the breakdown of a once accepted economic and moral order—caused in part by rapid industrialization, the shift from the accumulation of agricultural to industrial capital, the growth
of technology, immigration, the perceived disintegration of community life, the increasing
"need" to divide and control labor to increase profits, and so on—bonds of affiliation became
shaky. The meanings that provided ties among people had to be reconstituted, often on a new
foundation. The language form of science and technology provided these ties in a number
of ways for educators by giving a whole new range of meanings around which they could
affiliate.[31] First, it offered a mode of description that seemed more powerful than previous
ways of talking about educational events and policy, a way of describing both the relationship

between schools and the problems of society and for describing what went on or should occur in and out of schools. Third, and quite important, the language of science and technology held forth the promise of better control, giving educators a greater ease of prediction and manipulation. It would help us in our goal to get different students from point A to point B quickly and efficiently (though whether the ends and means of getting from A to B were themselves ethically and economically "just" is one of the critical questions that was not adequately raised by these people), thereby going a long way toward creating the categories and procedures that have maintained the abstract individual, the unconnected educator and student, to this day.

Conclusion

It is this commitment to maintaining a sense of community, one based on cultural homogeneity and valuative consensus, that has been and remains one of the primary, though tacit, legacies of the curriculum field. It is a function that is embedded in the historic reliance of the field on procedures and techniques borrowed from corporate enterprises. As we shall see in Chapter 6, oddly (though perhaps not, given what we have seen of the field's past) this reliance remains as strong today (with the dominance within the field of things, for example, like systems management procedures) as it did almost sixty years ago when the leaders of the field turned to the scientific management movement for direction in articulating the nature of curriculum construction. Since the historic tendency of this commitment is to build "community" (and curricula) that reflects the values of those with economic and cultural power, it is a commitment that may pose the same threat to contemporary workers, women, Blacks, Latinos, and American Indians as it did to early twentieth century Blacks and immigrants from Eastern and Southern Europe. Given the tendency of many curriculum theorists since the earliest days of the field to articulate their rather conservative commitments in the scientific and seemingly neutral language of intelligence and ability, it is also a threat that historically has remained unrecognized. Only by seeing how the curriculum field often served the rather conservative interests of homogeneity and social control, can we begin to see how it functions today. We may still find, unfortunately, that the rhetoric of science and neutrality covers more than it reveals. At the very least, though it may be unfortunate, we should not expect the curriculum field to totally overthrow its past. After all, as in our imaginary vignette at the beginning of this analysis, schools do work … for "them." In education, as in the unequal distribution of economic goods and services, "them" that has, gets.[32] If we are indeed serious about making our institutions responsive to communities in ways they are not now, the first step is in recognizing the historical connections between groups that have had power and the culture that is preserved and distributed by our schools. This recognition may do something else. It may cause us to ask similar questions today.

Discussion Questions

1. Return to the vignette presented at the beginning of the essay and answer the question posed there: For whom do schools really work?
2. How are the philosophies of the early curriculum leaders represented in the contemporary public school experience?
3. How does the contemporary educational system work to create and reinforce a certain notion of "community"?

Notes

1. Pierre Bourdieu,"Intellectual Field and Creative Project,"in Michael F. D. Young, ed., *Knowledge and Control* (London: Collier-Macmillan, 1971), pp. 161–88.
2. Basil Bernstein, *Class, Codes, and Control, Volume 3: Towards a Theory of Educational Transmissions* (2nd ed.: London: Routledge and & Kegan Paul, 1977.) See also, Samuel Bowles and Herbert Gintis, *Schooling in Capitalist America* (New York: Basic Books, 1976).
3. Cf. chapter 7 in Michael W. Apple, *Ideology and Curriculum*, 3rd ed. (New York: Routledge, 2004) and Michael W. Apple, "Power and School Knowledge," *The Review of Education* III (January/ February 1977). See also, James E. Rosenbaum, *Making Inequality: The Hidden Curriculum of High School Tracking* (New York: John Wiley, 1976) and Herbert Gintis and Samuel Bowles, "The Contradictions of Liberal Educational Reform," *Work, Technology, and Education,* Walter Feinberg and Henry Rosemont, Jr., eds. (Urbana: University of Illinois Press, 1975), pp. 92–141.
4. Carl E. Kaestle, *The Evaluation of an Urban School System* (Cambridge, Mass.: Harvard University Press, 1973), p. 141.
5. Ibid., p. 161.
6. Marvin Lazerson, *Origins of the Urban School* (Cambridge, Mass.: Harvard University Press, 1971), p. xv. See also, Elizabeth Vallance, "Hiding the Hidden Curriculum" *Curriculum Theory Network, IV* (Fall, 1973/1974), 5–21.
7. These fears about industrialization and urbanization had important implications for the development of the curriculum field as well as for the social sciences generally. See Barry M. Franklin, "The Curriculum Field and the Problem of Social Control, 19181938: A Study in Critical Theory" (unpublished Ph.D. dissertation, University of Wisconsin, 1974). For a similar analysis of the development of the field of educational sociology, see Philip Wexler, *The Sociology of Education: Beyond Equality* (Indianapolis: Bobbs Merrill, 1976).
8. Robert A. Nisbet, *The Quest for Community* (New York: Oxford University Press, 1967), p. 54.
9. Robert H. Wiebe, *The Search for Order:* New York: Hill & Wang, 1967), chapter 5.
10. Ibid, p. 44.
11. Edward A. Ross, *Foundations of Sociology*, 5th ed. (New York: Macmillan, 1919), pp. Charles A. Ellwood, *Sociology and Modern Social Problems* (New York: American Book Co., 1913) p. 220.
12. Ibid, pp. 217–21,
13. Edward A. Ross, *Principles of Sociology* (New York: Century, 1920), pp. 36–37.

14. Ross L. Finney, *Causes and Cures for the Social Unrest: An Appeal to the Middle Class* (New York: Macmillan, 1922), pp. 167–72.

15. Ibid., p. 43.

16. Ross L. Finney, *A Sociological Philosophy of Education* (New York: Macmillan, 1928), pp. 382–83.

17. Ibid., p. 428.

18. Charles C. Peters, *Foundations of Educational Sociology* (New York: Macmillan, 1928), p. 25.

19. Thorndike seemingly accepted the views of the American anthropologist R. H. Lowie that "the Negroes evince an inveterate proclivity for at least the forms of monarchical government." See Edward L. Thorndike, *Your City* (New York: Harcourt Brace, 1939), pp. 77–80.

20. Finney, *Causes and Cures for the Social Unrest,* op. cit., p. 180.

21. Bobbitt, *How to Make A Curriculum,* op. cit., pp. 41–2, 61–2; Edward L. Thorndike, *Individuality* (Boston: Houghton Mifflin 1911), p. 51; Edward L. Thorndike, *Education: A First Book* (New York: Macmillan, 1912), pp. 137–319; David Snedden, *Sociological Determination of Objectives in Education* (Philadelphia: Lippincott, 1921), p. 251; Peters, *Foundations of Educational Sociology,* op. cit., p. vii.

22. Finney, *A Sociological Philosophy of Education,* op. cit., pp. 388–9; Thorndike, *Human Nature and the Social Order,* op. cit., pp. 77–9; 792–4; 800802; Edward L. Thorndike, "A Sociologist's View of Education," *The Bookman,* XXXV (November, 1906), pp. 290–1; Edward L. Thorndike, *Selected Writings from a Connectionist's Psychology* (New York: Appleton-Century-Crofts, 1949), pp. 338–9.

23. Finney, *A Sociological Philosophy of Education,* op. cit., pp. 386, 389; Edward L. Thorndike, "How May We Improve the Selection, Training, and Life Work of Leaders," *How Should a Democratic People Provide for the Selection and Training of Leaders in the Various Walks of Life* (New York: Teachers College Press, 1938), p. 41; Walter H. Drost, *David Snedden and Education for Social Efficiency* (Madison: University of Wisconsin Press, 1967), pp. 165, 197.

24. Finney, *A Sociological Philosophy of Education,* op. cit., p. 395.

25. Ibid., pp. 397–8.

26. Thorndike, *Human Nature and the Social Order,* op. cit., pp. 86–7, 783–5, 963.

27. For an examination of this tendency in social thought see Trent Schroyer, "Toward a Critical Theory for Advanced Industrial Society," *Recent Sociology* No. 2, Hans Peter Dreitzel, ed. (New York: Macmillan, 1970), p. 212. For the appropriateness of this view for interpreting American education see Walter Feinberg, *Reason and Rhetoric* (New York: John Wiley, 1975), p. 40.

28. Finney, *A Sociological Philosophy of Education,* op. cit.

29. John Higham, *Strangers in the Land* (New Brunswick: Rutgers University Press, 1955), pp. 51, 187, 257, 303–10, chapter 9.

30. Higham argues that in the decade of the 1920s, the period in which curriculum emerged as a field of study and in which the educators I am considering did their most important work, American nativist sentiments turned away from attempts at assimilation through Americanization programs and instead turned to support of immigration restriction. It was in 1924 that the Johnson-Reed Act was passed which firmly established the "national origins principle," with the restrictions it applied to Eastern and Southern European peoples, into American law. See Higham, *Strangers in the Land,* op. cit., Chapter II.

31. Dwayne Huebner, "The Tasks of the Curricular Theorist," *Curriculum Theorizing: The Reconceptualists,* William Pinar, ed. (Berkeley: McCutchan, 1975), p. 256.

32. For further explication of this relationship, see Michael W. Apple and Philip Wexler, "Cultural Capital and Educational Transmissions," *Educational Theory,* XXVIII (Winter, 1978).

Chapter Nine

Violence and Society and Violence and Culture

The Texas–Mexico Border Wall and Ndé Memory

Confronting Genocide and State Criminality, Beyond the Guise of "Impunity"

By Margo Tamez

The imagination of genocide begins with a body count. Numbers are crucial in determining whether or not a group was killed "in whole or in part" to justify the term genocide. Yet this visceral reaction is only the beginning. . . . genocide does not end when the killing stops, but . . . it may echo in efforts at social mourning, repair, and reconciliation. Finally, genocide does not occur in a vacuum, but is embedded in an ambivalent international community that is quick to condemn mass killings but slow to mobilize into action.

—Antonius C. G. M. Robben. "Epilogue: The Imagination of Genocide"

Introduction: Shi Ndé—I Am of/from the People

Ha'shi? Shi Kónitsąąhįį dá'ááš̨ gokíyaa, gòłgà' Gònìcéi. I am Ndé from there, our homeland, along the Big Water, also known as the Rio Bravo/Rio Grande. I was born from Gochish (Lightning People), Gònìcéindé (Big Water People), Suma Ndé (Red Mud Painted People), Cúelcahén (Tall Grass People), and Cìš̨įhíindé (Black Rock People). In this chapter, I use "Ndé Lipan Apache" and "Lipan Apache" interchangeably. Since the mid- to late eighteenth century, Ndé have interrelated in kinship, marriage, reciprocity, ceremony, governance, cosmology, justice, and land-based knowledge systems with Tlaxcaltecas, Nahuas, Coahuilas, Kickapoo, Jumano Apaches, and Mescalero Apaches. Interexchange and alliance building through inclusive kinship relations—rural to urban—are persistent features of Ndé forms of cultural resilience and adaptation, responses to ongoing threats to indigenous worldviews and rights.

I situate the Texas-Mexico border wall within Ndé oral history and narratives of genocide, colonization, carceral containment systems, and land-based struggles as an act of reclaiming the Ndé homeland, Kónitsą́ąhįį gokíyaa. This chapter challenges the state's normative sovereignty and the uncritical acceptance of zones of impunity, such as the U.S. "constitution-free zone" identified by the American Civil Liberties Union.[1]

It is time for a radical rethinking of indigenous anticolonial movements along and traversing U.S. borders as a key nexus where indigenous revolutionary consciousness, resistances to state violence, and reclamations of indigenous rights are reshaping the governance of lands, territories, and communities. On and across the Texas-Mexico border, Ndé people's memories of genocide point to sites where indigenous knowledge challenges Texas, the United States, and the Texas-Mexico border wall as constructions of "the state of exception, and the state of siege."[2]

Situating the border wall within the Ndé genocide and social memory of the prison offers a counterhistory of indigenous narrative memory locked up in bodies, photographs, earth, and containment. This witnessing shatters the normative conception of European American history as predetermined, compartmentalized periods where indigenous peoples in the Texas-Mexico border region are merely shadows, dehumanized and dismembered figures.

I build upon Achille Mbembe's analysis of necropolitics, and indigenize it to Ndé constructions of history wherein the wall is an architecture of necropower. Necropolitics creates a "new form of sovereignty [which] is no longer the body as such, but the dead body of the 'civilian.'"[3] Necropower—wielded by the United States, Texas, corporations, and a group of elite local actors—accumulates, consolidates, and reinscribes colonial and patriarchal power both horizontally and vertically, through exploitation, bribery, manipulation, coercion, blacklisting, and threats of extreme exclusion.

I will focus on the narratives and analyses of indigenous peoples in resistance to death, what Mbembe refers to as "war machines," where "severing power imagines itself and is deployed in the interest of maximum destruction of persons and the creation of deathscapes, new and unique forms of social existence in which vast populations are subjected to conditions of life conferring upon them the status of living dead."[4] The border wall is one of these war machines.

Indigenous confrontations with settler colonialism defy the official public memory, which normalizes the Texas deathscape, the killing fields, the prisons, the internment camps, the mega-ranches, monoculture cotton and citrus fields, and oilfields. Ndé views, within enclosed and supervised spaces, continually narrate against forgetting the truth of what was witnessed, that "colonial occupation itself was a matter of seizing, delimiting, and asserting control over a physical geographical area—of writing on the ground a new set of social and spatial reiations."[5]

The Ndé extended kin—who ground resistance to the border wall in a community-based, antistate alliance—bear indigenous witness in defense of a worldview connected to responsibilities and accountability. This framework demands from them a confrontation against capitalist and patriarchal normality, atrocity, gender violence, and settlers' ritual coloniality. Ndé are actors in a resurging revolutionary consciousness across the region; Ndé popular constructions (denouncements, posters, artwork, song, poetry, film) demonstrate the resilience and persistence of more than four centuries of forging alliances with Tlaxcaltecas, Nahuas, Coahuilas, Purepechas, Mescaleros, Jumanos, Kickapoos, and urban Xicanos—*all* Mexico border region indigenous peoples in extended kinships impacted by the wall. Drawing from the taproots of this history, Ndé have galvanized a multiplural indigenous reality, challenging identities imposed by state and oligarchic wardens upon indigenous peoples: "Mexicans," "Latinos," "illegals," "foreigners."

Privileging the testimonies of elders, women, and chiefly peoples, I illustrate the importance of Ndé's inherent relationship to a homeland not bounded by borders, nor based in biological "Native" authenticity, ethnicity, or race. Rather, it is bound up in a worldview of kinship, remembrance, and the recovery of mother tongues, first foods and water governance, and gender complementarity in self-governance. Demanding an interrogation of state criminality relative to the border wall has been at the front of indigenous women's call for shared participation in decision making, critical ethics, and revitalizing indigenous protocols and principles based in respect and regard for elders and indigenous knowledge systems. As witnessed in the creation of women-led lawsuits against the government, indigenous women's concepts of self-governance—founded in reclaiming and recovering matrilineal, matrilocal, and matrifocal knowledge systems—critique the patriarchal violence aligned with coloniality. Ndé elders', women's, extended families' and chiefly peoples' knowledge systems, in conversation with

Figure 1. Eloisa García Tamez (Gochish ndédeeshch'ił Ndé, Lightning Clan), El Calaboz Ranchería, 2009. Photo by Jeff Gaines Wilson.

Figure 2. Elizabeth García (Nahua-Mexica), El Cabooz Rancheria, 2009. Photo from the collection of Eloisa García Tamez.

each other, have historically been a resource shaping indigenous peoples' analyses and interrogations of genocide and state crimes.

Since 2006, I have been working alongside Ndé people in the recovery of memories, stories, and documents for the express purpose of supporting self-determination and rights recovery. Here, I provide remembered and recovered Ndé clan and kinship knowledges from Kónitsąąhįį dá'ą́ą́šį̧ gokíyaa—the Ndé customary territory encompassing over 6.5 million acres in the Texas-Mexico binational region. These are fragments from a much larger project by, with, for, and alongside indigenous peoples, involving mapping and digitizing Ndé experiences prior to and after genocide and state criminality.[6]

From the Ndé methods approach, the U.S. border wall and its attendant capitalist, development, and destructive intent are situated within Ndé memory and story.[7] This perspective centers indigenous agency prior to and enduring *beyond* the wall. I borrow Patrick Wolfe's statement on settler colonialism, which is useful for understanding the European American occupation of indigenous time, place, and space. Thus, decolonizing the construct of European American history is understanding the indigenous viewpoint: "invasion is structure not an event."[8]

For generations, indigenous decolonialist challenges and defenses were enacted through ritualized remembering, memorializing, and returning. Reclaiming indigeneity as a positive—as a struggle to protect indigenous self-governance in a multi-gender value system and within a constellation of gendered worldviews of Kónitsąąhįį dá'ą́ą́šį̧ gokíyaa—is central to rethinking indigenous peoples' genocidal trauma, and its reoccurrences. Recovering is inevitably interwoven with remembering and reenvisioning ourselves as the landowners of our customary lands, and with breaking the chains of anthropological objectification. It is within the indigenous conception of temporal, spiritual, psychic, and physical continuums of endurance and adaptation that confrontations, refusal, dissidence, and resistance to replacement and elimination get enacted.

War Respatialized, Containment Remembered, and Americanization as Deathscape

To experience the community lands in the current period is to be subjected to peering through the narrow gaps between heavy, thick, steel bars. Eloisa García Tamez and elders, women, youth, and workers from Brownsville, El Calaboz, El Ranchito, La Encantada, La Paloma, Las Milpas, Los Indios, and Las Rusias—a whole kinship and ecological knowledge system—are experiencing life radically reduced, as people are prevented access to movement on their own lands, cemeteries, cornfields, and the pathways between residences. Concerted efforts to challenge the impunity of U.S. deathscapes and U.S. sovereign immunity in one of the poorest counties in the United States, Cameron County, rather than being addressed through "aid," are instead answered with war:

> i.e.: a technology-saturated "roof" of militarized airspace,
> is a resistance against the enclosure, surrounded
> by satellites, space debris plummeting to Earth
> zapped
> by NASA Space Engineers in Florida
> night Sky is no longer shell in blue-black corn mosaic,
> but steel-colored ceiling
> spotted with stadium lights positioned arbitrarily,
> where Border Patrol agents stalk indigenous women
> refusing sentence in shadows of wall
> aiming cell phones at agents
> government purchased soldiers of war
> and the colonized perform ritual control
> community wardens,
> harvested for payroll and benefits,
> under cover uniform surveilling an Elder rebel refuser
> infrared radar, watch towers, drones, and cyber fusion centers
> pieces of colonizer's status,
> mimicking master's crackdowns, spearheading individual roles
>   in his "Virtual Border Neighborhood Watch Program,"
> "border radio interoperability,"
> "Texas Data Exchange" programs,
> yanked to the Elder's scent by "K-9 units."[9]

"This is an occupation" and "We're in the open-air prison now" were two frequently repeated statements made by Ndé elders, women, youth, and men after October 20, 2009, when the United States condemned community lands with armed force. Elders had refused the government's taking of the lands through other methods. From their views, sovereignty, steel, concrete, transnational corporations, the rhetoric of "terrorism" and "aliens," U.S. Army Corps bulldozers, low-wage labor, and dispossession all symbolized the history of American white supremacy, brutality, and expropriation in the region. The wall currently bifurcates community lands. This leaves elders, women, men, children, and workers cut off from family-held and individually held lands, which have a complex legal history bound up in Spanish crown title ("land grants"), treaties (also known as "constructive mechanisms"), and Aboriginal title (indigenous proprietary title predating and still existing *beneath* European American fee simple and scrip). From indigenous views, crown title, Aboriginal title, and treaties are not extinguishable by the United States.[10]

"Americanizing" Texas was contingent upon the death, or violent removal, or subjugation of surviving indigenous peoples. Texas deathscapes were birthed through the giveaway of so-called free lands through a "head right" system, "allowing anyone residing in the state prior to March 1, 1836, to receive 4,605 acres free."[11] This was only one of numerous illegal measures in the Anglicization of Texas, and it has been followed by many waves of destruction.

Figure 3. The border wall in the middle of residential and subsistence pasture areas, El Calaboz Ranchería, Cameron County, Texas, 2011. Photo by Margo Tamez.

Between 1845 and 1860, roughly six hundred thousand people had settled in Texas and were growing cotton. This came about through heavily militarized zones containing indigenous resistance, "cleansings," and the establishment of U.S. military bases across Texas.

In 1938, Ndé captive of war Augustina Zuazua challenged the American anthropologist Harry Hoijer. She deflected his attempts to enclose her narrative histories within the prison camp of the American military anthropological gaze. She would not be corralled into his notebook, in which he chronicled the "tribes" of the U.S. Southwest and peoples of "the past": "ni'ąą sháhanát'ahí biyaayá kónitsąą gokíyaa kįgołgah. 'akaa konitsąą gokiyaaná. 'áshį nóóshch'eshį naagókáh (Over there the east to it the Lipan their country [was] Many Houses. Right there the Lipan [was] their country, it is said. And to this way they went across)."[12] Confronting Hoijer with a more profound reality—"konitsąą gokiyaaná"—this Ndé elder simultaneously challenged Americans as fraud sovereigns."

Indigenous memory structures perceptions of enclosure and taking. Ndé survivors of killing fields remember the 1873 Remolino massacre; the subsequent abduction of Ndé massacre-survivor children by U.S. Army employees and their internment in U.S. industrial boarding schools; and the erasure of Ndé children's and massacre survivors' indigenous cultural and political identity by Mexico, Texas, and the United States at the beginning of the twentieth century. Ndé remember the 1873-1930 forced separation of Ndé peoples into Mexico, California, New Mexico, and Texas; the 1903 death marches from Mexico to New Mexico; the subsequent escapes, diasporas, seclusions, isolations, starvations, and undergrounding of identity; the 1915-1916 Cameron County killing fields; the 1916 "blueprint" by South Texas oligarchic, white, ranching elites to construct concentration camps in Cameron County; and the 1919 executions of indigenous rebel leaders in El Ranchito and El Calaboz. And they remember the 1938 El Calaboz women's rebel movement against the state's and corporations' land and water grabs; the 1954 El Calaboz antisegregation rebel movement; and the backlash by elites, who continue to target lands and peoples along the Texas-Mexico border with low-intensity conflict measures into the post-nafta terrorizing present.[13]

In 2009, many witnesses along the last seventy miles of the border wall saw firsthand how the United States cleared and excavated the earth through their residential places. The bulldozing destroyed mature biodiversity in a riparian zone known worldwide as one of the last diverse regions in the hemisphere. Digging eight to ten feet into the earth, the government filled deep trenches with cement, making a footer for the wall. Thousands of cubic feet of earth were dumped to the side. It was only a matter of time before the ancestral presence surfaced: shards and other objects accumulated from intense human activity over generations (undoubtedly deemed "trash," "waste," "dirt," or perhaps even "nothing" by the U.S. bulldozer operators). These occupied spaces, these walls, penetrate women's and elders' intimate living spaces, culturally significant sacred lands, and traditional subsistence areas.[14]

These clearances offer an eerie, troubling view of Ndé-settler and Ndé-state relationships, past and present. After many years of drought, the rains of June 2011 exposed objects emerging out of the large, eroding heaps created by the wall construction. On dose study, I soon realized that these artifact fragments belonged to our ancestor generations, who lived here and experienced a bare existence, persecution, excessive discrimination, and killing fields in

Figure 4. Materials rescued from earthen heaps, EI Calaboz Ranchería, 2011. Photo by Margo Tamez.

the 1875-1919 period (documented extensively in my dissertation). Well aware that my every move by the wall was under constant surveillance by drive-by U.S. agents and by agents flying above me in helicopters and drones, I gathered what I could. I shared this information with elders, our traditional medicine people, and our community legal partners.

I struggle to articulate what confronts the Ndé elders and community members at this moment. We see what faces us inside the many heaps of earth along the wall in the lower Rio Grande valley. What will the fragments of daily life of our ancestors who suffered during former U.S. occupations say? We are confronted by the narrative continuum which will not be silenced. Chief Daniel Castro Romero Jr. stated, "When this happened, before, the Anglos came in many waves, and the ancestors had to leave our northern homeland, rather than face harm and destruction by white settlers and the armies. We are here because they protected the women, elders, and children. It wasn't just the U.S. Army, but many branches of armies, like roving gangs, professional killers, Rangers, and killers that some people just hired privately . . . [who were] wanting the lands cleared."[15]

Impunity and Tyrannical Governance

The material, structural, and legal containments and enclosures which maintain indigenous peoples like the Ndé in a political limbo in Texas and along the Texas-Mexico border region can be seen in Ndé confrontations of the so-called impunity of state sovereignty. The guise of impunity is a tactical move to avoid discovery, evidence, unmasking. State criminality and the fiction of legal impunity mask a troubling concept—sovereign immunity. Denise Gilman, a legal scholar who spearheaded the University of Texas School of Law's human rights investigation into the Texas-Mexico border wall, has challenged sovereign immunity as a legal "bluff," or, put another way, a fiction. Gilman argues:

> International human rights law seeks to protect individuals against abuse by governments. The United States system, through the operation of broad sovereign immunity doctrines, instead protects the government against individuals who lay claim to redress for abuses they have suffered. . . . while it is theoretically possible to overcome governmental immunity to many cases by suing individual officials, qualified immunity also constitutes a major impediment for victims seeking to obtain a remedy for violations of their rights. The gap between right and remedy is real and severe.[16]

Indeed, this "gap" has had serious consequences for those historically constructed as racialized Others ("Apaches," "Mexicans," "illegals," border wall "refusers"). For example, Esequiel Hernández was a Jumano-Apache youth, labeled "Mexican," "Hispanic," and "ethnic Mexican," who was murdered upriver from El Calaboz in May 1997. Hernández's death is often considered a sign of the modern U.S. militarization of the U.S.-Mexico border. Esequiel, a teenage goat herder, was murdered by a U.S. Marine under the direct orders of Joint Task Force 6, which authorized an operation in Esequiel's home village. The reality of snipers burrowed near the intimate living spaces of families, in a remote West Texas border community, and that the U.S. Border Patrol was aware of this operation, was a flashpoint for movement among people who were familiar with U.S. methods in Nicaragua, El Salvador, Honduras, and Guatemala. The naturalization of low-intensity conflict and militarization in a remote community on the Texas border became a subject of great debate, concern, and activism among many people. But, after years of struggling to open up new inquiries, community voices have been muted by government rhetoric about sovereign immunity and by the palpable fear of community members whose lives are at risk for challenging the state and exposing a conspiracy. There has been a monetary payoff to the loved ones of the deceased. Case closed.[17]

Esequiel Hernández's death is also part of a longer history of killing fields. The massacre of Remolino, which occurred on the Texas-Mexico border, is forever etched in the social memory of Ndé and related indigenous peoples with whom they share a territory—and with whom they share historical trauma and experiences of US. and Texas criminality. On May 18, 1873, U.S. colonel Ranald S. Mackenzie led four hundred soldiers to destroy Lipan Apache peoples in the customary land near Remolino, Coahuila, Mexico. The exact number of survivors is still unknown due to the level of undergrounding which occurred to protect the ones who escaped. Today, in the process of recovering indigenous community histories in the shadow of the border wall, it is being revealed that many Lipans dispersed to South Texas, Coahuila, and Tamaulipas, while many were driven into hiding and absorbed as "Mexican American" laborers. Some were captured and taken into U.S. prisons and internment camps ("reservations").

Some captured children were separated from their parents and contracted out to U.S. white families for domestic labor, while others were forced into the Carlisle Indian Industrial School.[18]

In 1915-1919, in Cameron County on the Texas-Mexico border, it is conservatively estimated that over five thousand people were destroyed (dismembered, mutilated, lynched, burned, shot, hacked, dragged) in waves of white violence directed against indigenous peoples and rebel leaders. The boom days of industrial agriculture, including cotton and citrus farming, ushered in industrial-scale removals and the overthrow of the indigenous primary governing institution—the extended family.[19]

In 1919 at La Encantada and El Caloboz on the Texas-Mexico border, a group of Anglo males entered the rancherías, located the men in traditional jacals (huts, wikiups), and murdered them. This was a massacre of all-male victims by all-male killers. The executed men were all family heads, brothers, and cousins of the Esparza (de Moctezuma) family, from a large extended kinship network of rancherías in crown land grants on both sides of the Rio Grande. One survivor, Nicolás Villarreal Esparza, escaped with a bullet wound to his leg. However, he was later found hanging from a tree.

Reimagining Texas: Critical Indigenous Genocide

Customary Ndé lands have been bifurcated by what Chief Daniel Castro Romero Jr. refers to as "a line of death," evoking the still grim reality that for Ndé, the Texas border was established through and by the structures and institutions of race and ethnicity, and Ndé have been persecuted by Mexico, Texas, and the United States.[20] According to Eloisa García Tamez, her father, José Emilio Cavazos García, described the border as "a *political* line, *not* a cultural line." Following in his footsteps, Tamez learned to challenge the line and confront those who demanded that she assimilate to the regulations and management of the state's fictive histories of the "Native."[21]

One lesson of the border wall—which indigenous rights defenders are learning daily—is that American genocide returns, comes back for more, and forces indigenous peoples along the border to live a bare existence. Our elders are forced to witness the desecration of our sacred grounds, the memory of our ancestors, and our culture, and to deal with the brutal process involved in being forced to exhume fragments from the current genocide (the wall) and the heaps of earth where a whole new confrontation is beginning.

I have been struck by my discovery of these excavation heaps and their contents, the ongoing disregard for elder rights defenders, and the troubling adaptations to the wall in the Texas-Mexico region. I am against forgetting. Yet, I am confronted by silences among some people *along the wall*. Exhuming the loss of their everyday intimate physical spaces, silence spreads like illness; people adapt to the treadmill; outrage is repressed.

The aim of this chapter has been to enact indigenous rights by speaking with, for, and alongside indigenous peoples against what Mbembe calls the "permanent spatial arrangement that remains continually outside the normal state law."[22] The Ndé prison camp, the internment

Figure 5. El Caláboz Gathering on Knowledge, Lands, Territories, and Human Rights, June 24–26, 2011. Elder Richard Gonzalez (right), Chief Daniel Castro Romero Jr. (left), and soundman Gino DiStefano (center) discuss impacts of the border wall on Ndé peoples. Photo by Erik Tamez Hrabovsky.

configuration normalized, was firmly challenged between 2007 and 2009 by Eloisa García Tamez et al. But why was she the *only* indigenous person along the entire U.S.-Mexico border to take up formal legal actions of defiance against the United States? This question, relative to Native American co-optation along the wall, deserves sustained engagement. Ndé challenges to the state's use of sovereignty to dispossess and to contain engage in what Speed and Reyes call "a more direct confrontation with the logic of the State, and a more direct engagement with the law as an aspect of it, [which] is not only desirable, but necessary."[23] Ndé resilience and revolutionary consciousness, before and after the border wall, demand new analytical tools engaging indigenous peoples' self-determination and autonomy movements.

In this chapter, I focused on three interlocking concepts: indigenized situating of the border wall within Ndé oral history, genocide and criminality in settler South Texas, and normalization of carceral containment in South Texas's industrial-scape. Elevated here as protest and as a denouncement against the state, the "generalized instrumentalization of human existence and the material destruction of human bodies and populations" are occurring in Texas as a legacy, where the wall works to "uphol[d] the work of death" in the lives of indigenous peoples along the Texas-Mexico border.[24] The Ndé community's demands, as articulated by the elders, are these: the dismantling of the wall, the return of all lands, an official apology from the Obama government, and a truth commission to call for the trial of George W. Bush and Michael Chertoff for mass human rights violations.[25]

The prison complex of South Texas, open-air containment warehouses designed in parallel with the extermination of Ndé and the industrialization of cattle production and slaughter, was always designed for the industrialization of death on a mass scale. Refuting Ndé defiance against the wall, based in indigeneity and our inherent rights to land and territories, the state masks the fictive basis of its claim to sovereignty—the doctrine of "discovery," the European legal rationale giving Europeans so-called rights to steal lands from indigenous peoples. The wall, as a carceral architecture of containment, produces slow deaths and deaths nationalized as nothing more than taking life from nonsubjects. However, Ndé and related peoples in the impacted communities have been existing in a space beyond, where genocide and bureaucracy are performed by wage-earning functionaries and high-paid technocrats in Washington, D.C., Austin, and Mexico City, deploying decisions by cell phones. This has no currency, no legitimacy, in indigenous collective consensus building, and is a denial that the indigenous Other on the Texas-Mexico border is recuperating memory, reclaiming a community social memory, and counternarrating the carceral worldview.[26]

A product of force, the wall has catalyzed the excavation and eruption of repressed memories, artifacts, and the flashpoints of killing fields and carceral systems incising indigenous peoples' shadowy existence in Texas for two centuries. I propose an ongoing engagement with Texas indigenous killing fields, and the creation of transformative legal genealogies and cartographies of indigenous memory. These will reveal the rupture points where we must confront how, by whom, and from whom lands were taken, most recently by U.S. DHS agents between August 2007 and October 2009. We are confronted by the suffering of deeply harmed and managed peoples still residing in and defending marginalized colonias, ranchitos, rancherías, and barrios along the Texas-Mexico border.

Ndé memory ruptures the projects of the deathscape and the prison. To the Ndé, working in alliances to confront the violent cartographies unfolding along the wall links Texas to the hemisphere and to global resistances. National discourses targeting indigenous and multiply raced and minoritized peoples as foreign Others have engendered a solidarity movement of counter-occupations foregrounding peace and consensus to address indigenous peoples' principles and protocols in the new, emerging Indigecas in the Americas. A direct confrontation of the state's brutality and negation of indigenous peoples on the Texas-Mexico border will make this the birthplace for transformative redress and restitution in Kónitsąąhįį gokíyaa, Lipan country.

Notes

Special thanks to Eloisa García Tamez and Chief Daniel Castro Romero Jr. for interviews, oral history transmission, photographs, genealogies, letters, court records, land studies, historical, anthropological, and archaeological cultural analyses, and critical reflections. A special thanks to the readers who offered invaluable feedback. The author acknowledges and bears responsibility for any errors or omissions.

1. American Civil Liberties Union, "Are You Living in a Constitution Free Zone?"

2. Mbembe, "Necropolitics," 16.

3. Hoeller and Mbembe, "Interview with Achille Mbembe."

4. Ibid.

5. Mbembe, "Necropolitics," 25.

6. See Tamez, "Nádasi'né' nde."

7. Due to limitations of space, it is not possible to provide here the full relevant history, context, and policy analysis of the U.S. border wall and its impacts on indigenous peoples. For analysis related to the Texas-Mexico border wall, see Gilman et al., "Obstructing Human Rights"; Gilman, "Seeking Breaches in the Wall; Miller, "How Property Rights Are Affected by the Texas-Mexico Border Fence"; Sancho, "Environmental Concerns Created by Current United States Border Policy"; Eagle Woman, "The Eagle and the Condor of the Western Hemisphere."

8. Wolfe, *Settler Colonialism and the Transformation of Anthropology*, 163.

9. Tamez, "Decolonize U.S. Brdr Prznz: #4."

10. On Aboriginal title, see Langton, "Ancient Jurisdictions."

11. Anderson, *Conquest of Texas*, 213.

12. Hoijer, "History and Customs of the Lipan, as told by Augustina Zuazua," 25. Augustina Zuazua, a Gònìcéindé, or "Lipan" woman, was a U.S. war prisoner, who along with "nineteen Lipan Apaches" was forcibly removed from Mexico to a U.S. internment camp ("reservation") in 1903 or 1905. See also Webster, "Lipan Apache Placenames of Augustina Zuazua."

13. Eloisa García Tamez and Daniel Castro Romero Jr., interviews with author. See also Tamez, "Nádasi'né' nde," 507.

14. Tamez, "Report."

15. Daniel Castro Romero Jr., interview with author, December 15, 2008.

16. Gilman, "Calling the United States' Bluff," 5.

17. See Nevins, "Death as a Way of Life"; Serafino, "Congressional Research Service Report 98-767"; WikiLeaks, document release, October l5, 2011.

18. Daniel Castro Romero Jr., oral history, June 25, 2011, El Calaboz Ranchería.

19. See Tamez, "Nádasi'né' nde."

20. Daniel Castro Romero Jr., interview with author, June 26, 2011.

21. José: Emilio Cavazos García, oral history spoken to Eloisa García Tamez; transmitted to the author in history lessons.

22. Mbembe, "Necropolitics."

23. Speed and Reyes, "In Our Own Defense."

24. Mbembe, "Necropolitics," 14.

25. Tamez, "Mandate."

26. Ibid., 23.

Bibliography

American Civil Liberties Union. "Are You Living in a Constitution Free Zone?" Last modified December 15, 2006. http://www.aclu.org.national-security_technology-and-liberty/are-you-living-constitution-free-zone.

Anderson, Gary Clayton. *The Conquest of Texas: Ethnic Cleansing in the Promised Land, 1820–1875.* Norman: University of Oklahoma Press, 2005.

Eagle Woman, Angelique. "The Eagle and the Condor of the Western Hemisphere.: Application of International Indigenous Principles to Halt the United States Border Wall." *Idaho Law Review* 45, no. 3 (2009): 1–18.

Gilman, Denise. "Calling the United States' Bluff: How Sovereign Immunity Undermines the United States' Claim to an Effective Domestic Human Rights System." Bepress Legal series, paper no. 1528 (2006).

———. "Seeking Breaches in the Wall: An International Human Rights Law Challenge to the Texas-Mexico Border Wall." *Texas International Law Journal* 46 (2011): 257–93.

Gilman, Denise, et al. "Obstructing Human Rights: The Texas-Mexico Border Wall." Working Group Briefing Papers on Human Rights Impact, University of Texas, School of Law. Last modified June 2008. http://www.utexas.edu/law/centers/humanrights/borderwall/analysis/briefing-papers.html.

Hoeller, Christian, and Achille Mbembe. "Interview with Achille Mbembe." [n.d.]. http://www.utexas.edu/conferences/africa/ads/1528.html.

Hoijer, Harry. "The History and Customs of the Lipan, as Told by Augustina Zuazua." *Linguistics* 161, no. 7 (1975): 5–37.

Langton, Marcia. "Ancient Jurisdictions: Aboriginal Polities and Sovereignty." Keynote address at the Indigenous Governance Conference, Canberra, Australia, April 3–5, 2002.

Mbembe, Achille. "Necropolitics." *Public Culture* 15, no. 1 (2003): 11–40.

Miller, Nicole. "How Property Rights Are Affected by the Texas-Mexico Border Fence: A Failure Due to Insufficient Procedure." *Texas International Law Journal* 45 (2010): 631–54.

Nevins, Joseph. "Death as a Way of Life: Ezequial [*sic*] Hernández Jr. and the Making of the U.S.-Mexico Borderlands." *Znet*, July 26, 2008. http://www.zcommunications.org/death-as-a-way-of-life-esequial-hern-ndez-jr-and-the-making-of-the-u-s-mexico-borderlands-by-joseph-nevins.

Robben, Antonius C. G. M. "Epilogue: The Imagination of Genocide." In *Genocide: Truth, Memory, and Representation,* edited by Alexander Laban Hinton and Kevin Lewis O'Neill, 317–32. Durham, N.C.: Duke University Press, 2009.

Sancho, Andrea C. "Environmental Concerns Created by Current United States Border Policy: Challenging the Extreme Waiver Authority Granted to the Secretary of the Department of Homeland Security under the Real ID Act of 2005." *Southeastern Environmental Law Journal* 16 (2008): 421–56.

Serafino, Nina M. "Congressional Research Service Report 98–767, U.S. Military Participation in Southwest Border Drug Control: Questions and Answers." Washington, D.C.: Foreign Affairs and National Defense Division, September 14, 1998.

Speed, Shannon, and Alvaro Reyes. "In Our Own Defense: Rights and Resistance in Chiapas." *Political and Legal Anthropology Review* 5, no. 1 (2002): 60–89.

Tamez, Margo. "Decolonize U.S. Brdr Prznz: #4." From *Indigenous Brdr Narratives after the Wall, Indigifem,* October 26, 2011. http://indigifem.blogspot.com/2011/10/decolonize-us-brdr-prznz-4-series-from.html.

————. "Nádasi'né' nde' isdzáné begoz'aahi' shimaa shini' gokal Gowa goshjaa ha'áná'idiłí texas-nakaiyé godesdzog" [Returning Lipan Apache Women's Laws, Lands, and Strength in El Calaboz Ranchería, Texas-Mexico Border]. PhD diss., Washington State University, 2010.

————. "Report: Ndé Principles & Protocols from El Calaboz Ranchería after the Wall: Indigenous Peoples, Knowledge, Land, Territories & Human Rights." (Forthcoming).

Tamez, Margo, ed. "Mandate from the EI Calaboz Summer 2011 Gathering on Indigenous Peoples, Knowledge, Lands, Territories and Human Rights, June 24–26, 2011." (Forthcoming.)

Webster, Anthony K. "Lipan Apache Placenames of Augustina Zuazua: Some Structural and Discursive Features." *Names* 55, no. 2 (2007): 103–22.

WikiLeaks. Document release, October 25, 2011. http://stuff.mit.edu/afs/sipb/contrib/wikileaks-crs/wikileaks-crs-reports/98-767.pdf.

Wolfe, Patrick. *Settler Colonialism and the Transformation of Anthropology: The Politics and Poetics of an Ethnographic Event.* London: Cassell, 1999.

An Illustrative Supergenocide

The Holocaust

By David Hamburg

Nature and Scope of the Disaster

The Holocaust was an immense crime against humanity and is the quintessential genocide. It sought the annihilation of the entire Jewish population of Europe. It was the deliberate policy decision of a powerful state that mobilized all of its resources to destroy an entire people. They were killed not for what they had done but for the simple fact of their existence. Gypsies, Russians, Poles, and other eastern European peoples, and even ethnic Germans deemed physically or mentally defective were also victims of Nazi racial ideology. Nazi military, police officials, and guards practiced highly organized brutality on a previously unknown scale. Why were Jews worked to death on senseless, unproductive tasks when the Reich had an acute labor shortage? Why were skilled Jewish armament workers killed despite pressing military needs of the Wehrmacht? Why did the Nazis insist they were fighting an omnipotent Jewish power even as their mass murder of Jews revealed their enemy's powerlessness? Professor Robert Wistrich thoughtfully addressed these questions in 2001, drawing on decades of research on the Holocaust.[1]

The Nazis' millenarian worldview saw Jews as the source of all evils—especially internationalism, pacifism, democracy, and Marxism. They were declared responsible for Christianity, the Enlightenment, and Freemasonry. They were identified with urban civilization's fragmentation, rationalism, and moral laxity. They were said to stand behind the "rootless cosmopolitanism" of international capital and the threat of world revolution. Hitler's racist ideology and personal obsession insisted that the redemption of "Aryan" humanity depended on a Final Solution of the Jewish question. World War II was at once a war for territory and a battle against the Jewish minority throughout Europe.[2]

War made the Holocaust possible, though there were terrible prewar precursors. The grand scheme of degradation was published in 1924 in Hitler's *Mein Kampf*—years before he came to power—hence vivid warning.

The Holocaust required more than ideology to be implemented. It was also the product of the most technologically developed society in Europe, with a highly organized bureaucracy. The streamlined, industrialized mass killings carried out in death camps such as Auschwitz-Birkenau and Treblinka went beyond previous genocides in world history. But millions of Jews were also killed in more primitive ways in Russia, eastern Europe, and the Balkans. The Einsatzgruppen and police hunted down Jews and executed them in pit killings in forests, ravines, and trenches. Russian, Poles, Serbs, and Ukrainians also perished in the same manner. Three million Soviet prisoners of war died in German captivity.

Germany before 1933 was a state based on the rule of law, where despite long-standing prejudice, Jews had achieved remarkable economic success, were integrated into society, enjoyed intellectual and scientific accomplishment, and helped shape its modern culture. Hitler's rise to power would not have been possible without the humiliating German defeat in World War I, embodied in the Treaty of Versailles; the economic crises of the postwar Weimar Republic; and fear of Communist revolution. Anti-Semitism, even though central to Hitler and the Nazi leadership, was not the Nazi's main vote getter. But when Hitler came to power, racist anti-Semitism became the official state ideology of the Third Reich, reinforced by incessant, virulent propaganda and anti-Jewish laws.

The receptiveness of Germans and other Europeans to the demonization of Jews owed much to an older tradition of Christian anti-Judaism. Nazism, though it intended ultimately to uproot Christianity, built on age-old Christian prejudice against Jews.

Though Germans were the Holocaust's driving force, they found many willing collaborators among Lithuanians, Latvians, Ukrainians, Hungarians, Romanians, Croats, and others. Austrians (who had been annexed to the Reich in 1938) formed a disproportionate number of the Schutzstaffel (SS) killers, death camp commandants, and personnel involved in the Final Solution. Even official France collaborated, not in killing, but in deportation and in passing anti-Jewish legislation.

The Holocaust was a Europe-wide event that could not have happened unless millions of Europeans had wished to see an end to the age-old Jewish presence in their midst. This consensus was especially strong in the countries of east central Europe, where most Jews lived and kept their own cultural distinctiveness. But anti-Semitism was growing in western Europe and the United States, tied to hardships caused by the Great Depression, fear of immigrants, politically stimulated xenophobia, and the influence of fascist ideas.

This hostility is seen in the reluctance of British and U.S. policymakers to try to rescue European Jews from the Holocaust. Hitler inferred from these responses that he could continue his expansionism without risk and that the West would not interfere with his increasingly radical anti-Jewish measures. Plundering Jewish assets was an integral part of early

Nazi policy and made Nazism attractive to many non-Jews. By 1939 it was clear that wartime conditions would greatly facilitate ethnic cleansing of Jews, Gypsies, and German "defectives."

All the resources of the modern German state were at the disposal of the SS in the death camps for the purpose of racial murder. Raul Hilberg observed that the machinery of destruction was German society organized as a whole.[3] Trains to the death camps would not have run without the indirect involvement of tens of thousands of Germans. Mass destruction utilized a highly bureaucratized, methodical society, modern in its systematic division of responsibilities and routinizing of operations.

Throughout his career Hitler pursued a policy of deliberate incitement against Jews while he left the execution of his policy to subordinates, depending on the long history of European anti-Semitism as a solid underpinning for mass murder. There is no reasonable way to blur the decisive role of Hitler and his close associates in initiating, centralizing, and unifying the multitude of regional actions.

The Holocaust was unprecedented in the hideous scale of the suffering inflicted on the victims and the depravity of their tormentors. Sadism and torture were common and were carried out with enthusiasm.[4] For the SS, to torture and destroy was a proof of maturity and superiority.

Primo Levi emphasized how the camp system sought to maximize the degradation of its victims by making them participate in their own victimization. Perhaps the most demonic of the Nazi crimes was giving their victims the filthiest part of their work: running the crematoriums, extracting corpses from the gas chambers, and pulling the gold teeth from the jaws of victims.[5]

Hitler admired Stalin. Before they started their own program of concentration camps, the Nazis studied closely how the Soviets had destroyed millions of people through forced labor in the gulags. The result was not total imitation; no industrialized killing process occurred in the Gulags. But Margarete Buber-Newmann, a survivor of both, observed that it was not easy to say which was less humane—immediate death in a gas chamber or a slow death from hunger.[6]

Stalin did not set out deliberately to murder the gulag population, because he needed them as slave labor to modernize Russia. He used Soviet camps to eliminate political enemies, and millions died there, but the camps were oriented to the production of wealth and the industrialization of a backward country. Mining of gold and other minerals and felling of timber for export were integral parts of the gulags. Thus, the two most destructive dictators of the twentieth century provided variations on the theme of mass murder.

Yehuda Bauer specified distinctive features of the Holocaust:

- People were killed merely for being born with grandparents of a certain lineage— Jewish.
- The killing was international in scope.
- The Nazi ideology bore no relation to reality.
- Although the Nazis did not invent the concentration camp, they used it to subject its inmates to a new level of humiliation.
- The Nazis left nothing positive behind them—only death camps and mass murder.[7]

How, then, can we explain the Nazis? There are many contributing factors. Bauer argued that a pseudointellectual elite took control in Germany, not because they had popular support for a murderous ideology but because they promised to lead the public out of the catastrophe in which Germany found itself after World War I into a "wonderful utopia." "The determining factor [of Nazi success] was that the layer of intellectuals—the academicians, the teachers, the students, the bureaucrats, the doctors, the lawyers, the churchmen, the engineers—joined the Nazi Party because it promised them a future and a status."[8] By identifying these intellectuals, professionals, and civil servants with the regime and publicizing their consensus for Nazi rule, the new government could convince the public that genocide was an unavoidable step toward achieving this utopia and enlist their services in carrying it out.

The churches, despite the gospel of love they preached and the Messiah they worshiped, remained silent about—if they did not collaborate in—the slaughter of his people by baptized murderers.

The Holocaust is remembered throughout the world as a universal symbol of evil because it represents the most extreme form of genocide, because it contains elements that are unprecedented, and because its victims, the Jews, had been significant contributors to modern civilization since the beginning of history.[9]

Missed Opportunities for Prevention

Ironically, the very fact that all of the democracies were sickened by the destruction caused by World War I and fearful of a recurrence made them ill-equipped to prevent it. Strong, popular pacifist movements arose that would later make vigorous diplomatic and military stances against aggression difficult. The European countries could not develop effective strategies of cooperation that might prevent genocidal behavior and war. And the League of Nations, which represented the first tentative effort in history to create a worldwide institution for international cooperation, was a much weaker body than today's UN even at its inception, before it became evident that the United States would not be a member. Nothing remotely comparable to the European Union existed. World War I may have chastened the nations of Europe and made them dread further armed conflict, but it had not taught them to stop viewing each other with reciprocal suspicion and feelings of rivalry (and, in the case of Germany, desire for revenge on all sides).

The bitter recollections of war and the greedy self-interested squabbles at the peace negotiations after it ended were two major reasons why the world's two leading democracies, Britain and the United States, returned to isolationism and disengagement from continental European affairs during the 1920s. Then came the devastating worldwide depression. Germany, already strapped with payment of reparations, was hit especially hard, but economic collapse also severely exacerbated existing internal class divisions throughout the West and turned the focus of almost all governments to domestic affairs during the early 1930s.

Western leaders were aware from the start of Hitler's worldview. *Mein Kampf*, published in 1924, vividly outlined Hitler's plan for a racially cleansed Europe under German domination.

The dangers that German fascism and Hitler presented were quickly laid bare by a number of thoughtful statesmen and writers in the established democracies—notably, but not only, Winston Churchill. By and large these clear early warnings were dismissed in London, Paris, and Washington, where government leaders took it for granted that sober businessmen, the military, and other powerful interests in German society would eventually moderate Hitler's excesses. Throughout the West a lack of concern about what was happening in Germany pervaded governments, the media, and the general public.

In the beginning, Hitler's lawless rule even won a degree of sympathy. A number of foreign observers agreed with the majority of Germans that the weak and fractious Weimar Republic had met a predictable, even desirable end. Western conservatives were inclined to excuse—and in some instances, even admire—the style of fascism promoted by Hitler in Germany and Mussolini in Italy. Since the 1920s Western statesmen had been concerned that Germany might turn sharply toward the left (a concern that did not extend so far that they helped the weak Weimar Republic out of its dire economic situation). Hitler's Third Reich not only promised a stable Germany; his rabid antagonism to communism also made Nazi power seem a welcome bulwark against Marxist expansion in Eastern Europe.[10] Furthermore, throughout the West the targets of German aggression attracted painfully little sympathy—European Jews, long objects of widespread prejudice; Gypsies, universally vilified; Socialists and Communists, whom many feared far more than they feared the Nazis; and the vulnerable countries of eastern Europe, most of them unstable, fragile former territories of defunct empires, distant and politically insignificant. Even after Germany was finally acknowledged as a dangerous threat, many "leaders" still hoped that someone else, perhaps the USSR, perhaps decent and sensible Germans, would take the initiative and responsibility for checking Nazi ambitions.[11]

Today, historians such as R.A.C. Parker argue that had the West adopted the firm policies of deterrence advocated by Winston Churchill, World War II might well have been avoided.[12] But in the early 1930s, when determined, concerted preventive action could have had a real effect, other matters seemed more urgent than a ranting man with a comical moustache, who was, after all, restoring order and stability to his failing country. Serious political and economic action was not taken until the only response left was military action of unprecedented force—the catastrophe of World War II.

Narrow and short-term conceptions of national interest reinforced the West's failure to appreciate the true extent of the danger. The 1930s were a dangerous time. As on the eve of World War I, the distribution of international power and colonial wealth established in the nineteenth century was being challenged by ambitious nations. Germany, Italy, the USSR, and Japan—who had modernized or unified only after Britain and France had already built their colonial empires—all felt that as latecomers they were being unfairly denied their proper high status in the world order. Britain and France continued their efforts to preserve or improve their own global position. They did not recognize in Adolf Hitler a man who was more than willing to use massive violence not only to persecute his "internal enemies" but also to change forcefully the existing international order in his favor. What was needed was strong multilateral cooperation to mount a credible deterrence to his aggression. Just at that time, however, a retreat into isolation, in Europe but especially in the United States, had weakened international efforts at cooperation and opened the way for Hitler's bold, ruthless strokes. This isolationism further incapacitated the already feeble League of Nations, the one organization that might have been used to mobilize an effective, united opposition to Hitler.[13] No nation was willing to stand up to Hitler alone, and the West had abandoned its commitment to international cooperation and its avowed sense of responsibility for weaker nations. Nations large and small lacked the capacity and tools for effective preventive action.

Recent historians emphasize the powerful impact internal matters had on English and French policy in the 1930s (matters still important to this day in every country). The effects of the Great Depression and concerns about safeguarding their empires shaped the responses of those two nations to fascist aggression. Any benefit they imagined they might gain from checking Hitler, Mussolini, and Hirohito was balanced against fears of placing further burdens on their economy at home and their capacity to preserve their colonial possessions overseas.[14]

Most nations took it as a given truth that Britain's level of industrial development was based on its colonial dominions and that successful competition would require an empire of equal size.[15] And as victors of World War I, both England and France had considerably increased their already vast holdings (in large part at the expense of Germany). This was in fact a mixed blessing; reduced resources made this new property difficult to maintain. The great empires were further threatened by the growth of the Communist International (Comintern), which was eager, along with other leftist groups, to support colonial struggles for independence.[16] Nevertheless, the belief that a far-reaching empire was a requirement for lasting economic prosperity made its substantial cost acceptable.

World War I had created a general repugnance toward war. The victors of the war, however, saw no inconsistency in their peace-loving position and a very harsh interpretation of the Treaty of Versailles (1919), which imposed heavy economic reparations on Germany, stripped it of territory, and required it to accept primary responsibility for the war. The severe conditions and punitive implementation of this treaty undercut the authority of the fragile Weimar democracy and added to Germany's sense of grievance—a feeling that Hitler cultivated and manipulated by blaming others, especially Jews, for Germany's defeat.

Furthermore, the partnership of the former Allies did not remain solid. Each was suspicious of the other's imperial designs, particularly in the Middle East.[17] Support for international cooperation was declining outside Europe as well. The United States was not eager to continue its involvement in European affairs. Congress, with strong popular backing, defeated President Wilson in his struggle to make the United States a member of the League of Nations. Throughout the interwar period, many Americans felt they had been tricked into entering World War I by greedy Wall Street bankers, arms merchants, and wily Europeans. U.S. reluctance to maintain a positive involvement in continental affairs had a major influence on events in the 1930s.

In the east the Soviet Union's size and ideology made it a potential threat to western and central Europe. When Hitler's regime replaced the weak Weimar Republic, many in the West approved because of Nazism's clearly expressed opposition to communism and its promise to restore stability.

World War I had transformed the political map of eastern Europe. Austria-Hungary had disappeared, for the most part replaced by small, unstable states. A new, enlarged Poland was cobbled out of the former Hapsburg and Romanov empires. Most profound were the social effects of a war in which the human costs had been so terribly high. People spoke of a "lost generation" of young men. Displaced populations had been scattered across Europe. The global depression at the beginning of the 1930s was the finishing shock to the old international order.

Technological advances in communication, such as radio and film, allowed leaders to organize large-scale discontent and created genuine mass politics. Fascists and militaristic nationalists used the new technology to exploit popular dissatisfaction and gain tight control, as with Mussolini in Italy and the military junta in Japan.[18]

It was in Germany that these global changes had their most profound consequences. Soon after World War I, disenchantment and impatience with the powers of Europe led the United States to dun the British and French for prompt repayment of their war loans. This was a terrifying time of hyperinflation throughout Europe, and Germany was its greatest victim. The figures seem incredible today: at the height of the inflation, prices rose to 14,000 times their prewar level in Austria, to 23,000 times in Hungary, to 2,500,000 times in Poland, but to a billion times in Germany.[19] A German who sat down for an hour in a restaurant nursing a 5,000-marks cup of coffee would find it cost 8,000 marks when his check came.[20] Nevertheless, England and France responded to the U.S. demands by turning on Germany—already bitter, restive, and economically desperate—with their own demand for prompt payment of its reparations.

The great historian Gordon Craig has beautifully expressed the meaning of the demise of the Weimar Republic:

> While totalitarian regimes were consolidating their power in Russia and in Italy, an experiment was being conducted in Germany to determine whether a democratic republic could be made to work in that country. After 15 years of trial and crisis it failed, and the ultimate consequences of that failure were the Second World War and the death of millions of men, women and children. If some benevolent spirit had granted the peoples of Germany and neighboring European states even a fragmentary glimpse of what lay in store for them in the 1940s, it is impossible to believe that they would not have made every possible sacrifice to maintain the Weimar Republic against its enemies. But that kind of foresight is not given in this world, and the German Republic always lacked friends and supporters when it needed them most.[21]

The ill-designed parliamentary democracy of Weimar, based on a series of postwar compromises, was an object of scorn both at home and abroad and had gained few supporters by the beginning of the 1930s. Burdened with all of Germany's disastrous political and economic troubles following the war, the Weimar constitution became the target of nationalists bitter about Germany's diminished position in the world. To them Weimar symbolized all that was bad about Western liberal democracy, in a period when democracy was not nearly as widely accepted as it is today. The republic, dominated by the Social Democrats, was unable to reassert German strength in the world. Much of the German public had tired of its ineffective politics, exacerbated by the large number of constantly squabbling parties that made it impossible even to begin to deal effectively with such catastrophes as dizzying postwar inflation, and then depression, with epidemic unemployment. By the beginning of the 1930s, the government appeared unable even to maintain civil order, as paramilitary groups attached to parties from both the left and the right fought in the streets. To observers both in Germany and abroad, Communist revolution seemed imminent.[22]

In this context, as the eminent historian Fritz Stern noted, National Socialism promised prosperity after deprivation, strength after national humiliation, and stability after disorder. It attracted support from many elements of German society—workers, the middle class, aristocrats, students, members of the intelligentsia, adherents to a number of religious denominations, and many capitalists.

It was Germany's and the world's bad fortune that an adept and ruthless manipulator such as Adolf Hitler appeared to dramatize and exacerbate traditional racial and religious prejudices. His cynical identification with Christianity at the beginning of his career in piously Catholic Bavaria, an identification he also used to fuel anti-Semitism, is typical of his technique. In his early speeches Hitler often cited Christ's driving the Jewish "enemies of all mankind" from the temple. Like the Germans, he pointed out, Jesus had lived under a corrupt and incompetent government, contaminated by Jewish materialism. He portrayed Christ as a Siegfried-like warrior hero who preached an anti-Jewish and intensely nationalistic faith. From 1922 on, Hitler made impassioned speeches that claimed Jesus, when he drove the moneylenders out of the temple, was a trailblazer of the Nazi program against Jewish world domination, and Hitler promised that the Nazis would fulfill the task that Christ had begun—but could not accomplish—against his archenemy, the Jew.[23]

Hitler learned from the failure of Otto von Bismarck's Kulturkampf to avoid alienating the Catholic Church, even after his influence spread outside Bavaria. Protestants who tried to exclude Catholics from the Nazi Party were ousted or accused of national betrayal and working for Jewish interests. Hitler considered war between Christian denominations as a dangerous diversion from the "Jewish peril." This was a shrewd strategy in Catholic Bavaria, the cradle of the Nazi movement from 1919 to 1925, where he made use of longstanding anti-Jewish religious traditions as well as the popular equation of Jews and Communists. The fervent nationalism that many German Christians adopted after 1914 made a significant proportion of them enthusiastic supporters of Nazism.

The Catholic Church in Germany was less susceptible to the Nazis than Protestant denominations—as an institution it did not encourage strong nationalism. But negotiations with the Vatican had a successful result: like many Catholics in Europe, Pius XI found grounds for agreement with anti-Communist authoritarian regimes, and in July 1933 his concordat with the Third Reich gave international legitimacy to the Nazi regime and restricted the Church to its religious, educational, and pastoral functions. Civic institutions, from local choirs to women's groups to athletic clubs, were simply declared Nazi organizations and given Nazi leaders.

In the 1932 elections, the Nazis received 37 percent of all votes cast—a significant victory given Germany's divided politics.[24] The Nazis won power legally—but not absolute control.

Once in power, they fed German nationalism with pomp and spectacle that produced a superficial image of renewed national power.[25] They improved the economic circumstances of many people. They brought order to the streets, and the repressive means they used seemed acceptable at first, even welcome. An end to the fear of Communist revolution was an agreeable development for many both in Germany and in the international community.

The underside of the dictatorship soon appeared. In February 1933 a fire in the Reichstag became the excuse for an emergency decree that swept away the liberties guaranteed by the Weimar Constitution. Protections of speech and assembly and against unwarranted search and confiscation of property vanished.[26] Labor unions and opposing political parties were banned. The SS and the Sturmabteilung (SA) were given overriding police powers, and their offices became sites of state-sponsored torture and harsh intimidation. Concentration camps for dissidents were established. Jews became targets of an official program that aroused a virulent strain of traditional anti-Semitism.[27]

These activities were apparent to the German public and to any interested observer, but few chose to resist them. Some wishfully thought the regime would eventually be satisfied, that its latest power grab would become its last, and that it might be brought under control by other, more sober elements of German society. Others accepted to some extent the Nazi's specious justification that Germany's crisis situation made drastic action necessary, conveniently ignoring that the crisis had been deliberately and skillfully manipulated, exacerbated, and sustained by Nazi propaganda and brutality.

The excesses of the Nazi regime during its first years in power should have alerted leaders of the international community to action, but with few exceptions, they did not yet make the connection between lawless domestic violence and international aggression. Many in influential positions still believed that a revision of the Versailles Treaty would be enough to satisfy Hitler and continued to ignore striking evidence to the contrary, from *Mein Kampf* in 1924 to Hitler's increasingly aggressive, hateful public statements and actions over the years, before and during his accession to government leadership. Opportunities for prevention of war and genocide in these years were wasted.

An especially valuable issue in Hitler's search for popular support was the Versailles Treaty. His assaults on the settlement as grossly unfair to Germany found a sympathetic hearing. Many Germans, not only the nationalists, bitterly resented the slights of the treaty, and a number were willing to support an aggressive foreign policy to reverse them. And many outside observers in Europe and the United States considered the German objections legitimate and were willing to regard Hitler's violent rhetoric as pardonable political hyperbole. But Hitler's intentions went far beyond correcting the wrongs of an unjust treaty and restoring Germany's 1914 boundaries. In *Mein Kampf* he stated clearly that Germany must remove the Slavic threat by expanding eastward, bringing under German control a fertile land well situated to increase its security in Europe. For a short while after he took power, Hitler softened his talk about expansion so as not to awaken alarm while Germany was still weak, just as he later occasionally moderated his tone to lull his opponents into inaction and leave Germany unimpeded. Gordon Craig noted that although the Nazi regime occasionally assumed a more responsible public face, Hitler's foreign policy ambitions remained consistent and well known.[28] Hitler's vision, like the kaiser's before him, demanded massive violence on a global scale.[29] And this was apparent to anyone who cared to pay attention.

Hitler saw total control at home as essential to his preparation for war abroad. Directly after taking power he had banned all other political parties and organizations. He arranged with the Vatican to dissolve the powerful Catholic Center Party. He imprisoned Marxists and leftists. Hitler even turned on his own Sturmabteilung, the brown-shirted goons who had supported the party during its rise to power with bloody violence in the streets.

Hitler began to see Ernst Rohm, the leader of the SA, as a threat to his position. In June of 1934, in a spate of bloodletting that left 300 persons dead, Hitler liquidated the organization's leadership and took the opportunity to kill a number of other opponents of the Nazi regime. He quickly dissolved the SA in order to ensure the loyalty of the army, which had also felt threatened by the SA's strength. The Night of the Long Knives was a warning that even Hitler's longtime followers were not safe if they could threaten his authority.[30]

Once Hitler had consolidated power, he could begin to strengthen the German military, repudiate international commitments made by his Weimar predecessors, and test international resistance to his ambitions preparatory to pursuing them. Not all authoritarian governments plan expansionist wars; but as the Nazi experience illustrates, leaders who have brutally silenced public dissent in their own land have a free hand to carry out bloody policies in others; and those who conduct massive human rights abuse at home are likely to be harsh in their international relations.

Hitler and Europe, 1933–1936: Fatal Missed Opportunities for Prevention

In his classic monograph, *Germany, 1866–1945,* Gordon Craig clarified missed opportunities to prevent World War II. On the failure of the Allies to respond quickly and forcefully to Hitler's progress in the early 1930s, he wrote:

> The first *assessments by the Western governments* of Hitler's likely course in foreign policy were characterized by an *extraordinary amount of wishful thinking.* Despite the clear evidence provided by events inside Germany that the country's new rulers were contemptuous of law and morality and the standards of common decency in the treatment of those who disagreed with them, politicians in London and Paris showed no alarm about what this might portend for Germany's future behavior as a member of the international community.[31] (Emphasis added.)

Not everyone was fooled or indifferent. Already in 1933 the English and French ambassadors in Berlin had clearly and correctly assessed Hitler's threat to world peace in reports to their governments. The British ambassador mentioned the construction of concentration camps and cautioned that the aims of German policy were to "bring Germany to a point of preparation [for war], a jumping-off point from which she can reach solid ground before her adversaries can interfere." He added, "There is a mad dog abroad once more and we must resolutely combine either to ensure its destruction or at least its confinement until the disease has run its course."[32] Both the French and English diplomats urged their governments to refer to *Mein Kampf* for an understanding of Hitler's plans, and both recognized that the brutality occurring within Germany could expand its borders if Hitler were not stopped and stopped quickly.[33]

Some other influential members of the English government accurately identified Nazi intentions. In 1933, Sir Duncan Sandys predicted the remilitarization of the Rhineland. Sir Robert Vansittart, permanent undersecretary for foreign affairs for much of the 1930s, warned that only international cooperation would prevent Germany's speedy takeover of Austria and eventual move against Poland.[34] Their warnings were pushed aside.[35]

The failure of early awareness to generate an effective response is all the more tragic in light of the fact that Hitler, in his first years of power, was well aware of his real vulnerability. The purge of his SA leadership showed that he did not consider his control secure. Early that same year, plans for unification with Austria—which included the murder of its chancellor—created international protest and were eventually checked by Fascist Italy. Concerted international action at an early stage might well have restrained or even removed Hitler from power.[36]

The opposite occurred: a weak response emboldened him. As Ian Kershaw pointed out in his excellent biography, Hitler began a series of Saturday Surprises, boastful revelations that enhanced his menace. One week he disclosed that Germany had a new air force; the next that he was increasing his army fivefold, in defiance of the Versailles Treaty. This troubled his own military leadership, not because they disagreed with his objectives but because they thought (here as elsewhere) that the rashness of his methods might endanger Germany. Their concern, like that of the German public at large, turned into enthusiastic support when his risky actions met with no resistance.[37] This was a critical turning point. If a vanquished Germany could thumb its nose at the whole postwar network of treaties with impunity, Hitler's path to war and genocide was open in all its destructive potential.

The British were willing to give Germany wide latitude in areas that did not seem to conflict with essential British interests, and given their growing disengagement from the continent, they considered very few matters essential.[38] British leaders did not make a consistent and responsible attempt to educate the public about the extent of the emerging threat. Although two leading newspapers, the *London Times* and *Manchester Guardian*, both warned against permitting German repudiation of the Versailles Treaty, many British wishfully hoped that concessions would bring good relations with Germany.

The French felt betrayed and increasingly insecure. International cooperation was nowhere to be found, especially between the two most powerful democracies in Europe—despite the manifestly critical nature of the danger. The strength of the democracies was wasted. In 1935 the Western democracies had unchallenged strategic superiority over Germany on land, at sea, and in the air. German moves toward rearmament were not as significant a threat to peace as the West's reaction to them. It was timid diplomacy and the lack of international cooperation that encouraged Hitler to attempt the remilitarization of the Rhineland. He recognized that Germany was not yet strong enough to overcome military opposition, but he was convinced that a well-executed bluff could work. His assessment was correct. France, with by far the most powerful army in Europe, was nonetheless badly divided.[39] Nor was it confident about British support. In 1936 France found itself unsettled at home, without a sure ally abroad, and facing another war with Germany over the Rhineland.

Resolute military and diplomatic resistance would almost certainly have succeeded. Hitler's recklessness generated real anxiety and restiveness in his military leaders. If the French Army had resolutely resisted, the German forces would have had a humiliating defeat that might well have led to a military coup against Hitler. Hitler himself admitted later that the two days after German forces entered the Rhineland were the most anxious period of his life. He is reported to have remarked that if the French had defended the Rhineland, the Germans would have had to retreat with their tails between their legs.[40]

Even though a few French leaders contended that German boldness was a bluff, the French government and military succumbed to fear and indecision. A panicked French intelligence estimate inflated the 3,000 soldiers that Germany actually sent to the Rhineland into 295,000 men available for the operation. And France balanced these exaggerated estimates of Germany's strength against a serious underassessment of its own. Germany was just recovering from compulsory demilitarization, but French statesmen were very apprehensive, since they expected a Rhineland confrontation to expand into a larger war.

These inflated misgivings became excuses for inaction at a time when a single French division probably would have repelled the Germans.[41] French hesitation is considered a primary reason the Germans felt confident to move into the Rhineland. But poor judgment on the part of the international community deserves much blame. France had been left alone to oppose a resurgent Germany.

The Coming of War

World War II was a preventable war in the opinion of Winston Churchill, who made the theme of his history, *The Gathering Storm*, "How the English-speaking peoples through their unwisdom, carelessness, and good nature allowed the wicked to rearm." He held that German rearmament should have been forbidden from the start, that Britain and France should have joined against Germany when it moved into the Rhineland. He was right. After 1936, stopping Hitler became increasingly more difficult and costly. The relative military strength of the democratic powers declined as Germany relentlessly continued rearmament (a rearmament that involved developing state-of-the-art weaponry rather than relying on old military stock).

The period from 1935 to 1936 marks a decisive point on the road to cataclysmic war and genocide. With the move into the Rhineland, Hitler had abolished the constraints imposed on German military and industrial power after World War I. His foreign successes increased his support at home and German prestige abroad, convincing initially skeptical Italy and

Japan to join the German camp, beginning in November 1936 with the Anti-Comintern Pact directed against the Soviet Union. At the same time, Hitler's successful disregard of Versailles led smaller nations to question the credibility of Britain and France, whose inaction planted seeds of doubt about their assurances of support to less powerful neighbors. In 1936, Belgium annulled a 1920 agreement for defense cooperation with France.

These triumphs emboldened Hitler to begin implementation of the vision he had elaborated in *Mein Kampf.* His plans began with the annexation of Austria and Czechoslovakia, followed by movement into eastern Europe to acquire an empire with the "living space" and natural resources necessary to make Germany a dominant world power.[42]

At the same time France and Britain remained almost exclusively concerned about preserving their own empires. The appeasement policy associated with Neville Chamberlain, who came to power in 1937, was really a continuation of the old national principle to prevent the rising powers, Germany and Japan, from encroaching on British imperial possessions.[43] What Germany did on the continent was not important unless its actions challenged what were seen as important British interests.

In 1938, Hitler solidified his power over German foreign and military policy. He took control of the German armed forces by replacing the old army high command with the Oberkommando der Wehrmacht, of which he became head.[44] Then he named as head of the Foreign Ministry an ambitious nonentity, Joachim von Ribbentrop, who was happy to approve any policy Hitler adopted.[45]

At this time, the democracies needed military strength and political determination, but both Britain and France were late to recognize the need to face a rearmed Germany. They were more worried that preparation for a confrontation in Europe would reduce resources available to defend their overseas possessions and weaken domestic economic recovery by increased military spending. Appeasement was an expression of *wishful thinking.*[46] British and French policy rested on a wishful appraisal of the Nazi threat and an unwillingness to face it. In principle, they might have avoided the draining expense of a military buildup by seeking an alliance with the United States, the Soviet Union—or both—to halt the growing Nazi danger.

The Soviet Union was a willing candidate for alliance. Its ideology, if not its leadership style, was totally antagonistic to Germany's, and Nazi rhetoric, rearmament, and ambitions for eastern expansion had made the USSR increasingly nervous. In 1935 it signed a mutual assistance pact with the French, who took care to stop short of a military alliance, and in 1936 it sponsored the Popular Front against fascism, acknowledging the need of temporary collaboration with capitalist regimes to oppose the greater danger posed by Hitler and his allies. But fear of communism was as powerful in Paris and London as fear of Nazism.[47]

Both Chamberlain and his predecessor, Stanley Baldwin, feared that Franco-Soviet cooperation might draw France into a war that would end by leaving much of Europe under Communist threat. And German expansion into eastern Europe might be valuable in containing the Soviets. Given these concerns, the British and French never seriously considered a close alliance with the Soviets.

The other major power that might have helped to constrain Hitler was the United States. President Franklin Delano Roosevelt had internationalist sympathies and considered Hitler a madman and a threat to world peace. But his urgent campaign for domestic reform left him little opportunity to promote an unpopular foreign policy in the face of entrenched isolationist interests.[48] His situation forced him into exploratory moves to discover what foreign policy actions the U.S. public would accept.[49]

In October 1937 in Chicago, a stronghold of isolationist sentiment, Roosevelt delivered his famous Quarantine Speech, which warned that treaty violations were creating "international anarchy" that would end in a conflict the United States could not escape and must act to prevent.

> An epidemic of world lawlessness is spreading. … When an epidemic of physical disease starts to spread, the community approves and joins in a quarantine of the patients in order to protect the health of the community against the spread of the disease. … War is a contagion, whether it be declared or undeclared. It can engulf states and peoples remote from the original scene of hostilities.[50]

But Roosevelt realized that the political climate would not allow him to follow his dramatic words with immediate action.[51] His politically essential delay had international consequences. It convinced Chamberlain that U.S. isolationism was so powerful that the United States could not be "depended upon for help if [Britain] should get into trouble." He concluded, "it is always best and safest to count on *nothing* from the Americans except words."[52] England became even more committed to a policy based on appeasement.

Hitler gobbled up Austria in March 1938 and was again gratified by the absence of opposition. Japan's expansion, which had led to armed conflict with Nationalist China in 1937, threatened British, French, and U.S. interests in Asia and made them reluctant to expend resources against Hitler that might leave their Pacific territories victims to the Japanese, despite growing recognition that Hitler had to be stopped. Even Chamberlain was forced to note in the spring of 1938 that force was the only argument Germany understood.[53]

Upon digesting Austria—but just barely—the Nazi regime turned its eyes toward the Germans in Czechoslovakia's Sudetenland. Throughout the spring and summer, Czechoslovakia continued to reject German demands. Britain and France were both anxious that long-standing French agreements with the Czechs might drag France into a conflict, and both Britain and France began mobilization in September. War was only averted by Mussolini's call for a conference to resolve the dispute. Hitler actually wanted war but consented to a meeting in Munich. Only Germany, Italy, France, and Britain sat at the negotiation table. Czechoslovakia, Russia, and other interested eastern European countries in the region from Poland to Hungary were not invited to participate. Four major powers made globally momentous decisions on the basis of their own selfish interests and fears.[54] Fear of German military strength persuaded the British and French to accept the severing of the Sudetenland from Czechoslovakia.

Chamberlain's boast of "peace in our time" gave relief to people across Europe. Even Roosevelt sent him a two-word cable, "Good man."[55] In Britain, "God bless you, Mr. Chamberlain" was the title of a popular song. Appeasement appeared to have spared Europe another major conflict. But the Munich Agreement made war inevitable. In March, German forces devoured all that remained of Czechoslovakia, weakened by losing valuable factories and mines in the Sudetenland. Only then did the British begin full military discussions with the French general staff and offer guarantees to Poland.[56] But it was too late for Allied policies to have any effect other than inciting further German aggression. As for the United States, President Roosevelt could make only a few diplomatic efforts to check growing Nazi power. They were contemptuously dismissed by Hitler, who felt that the U.S. president's hands remained tied by U.S. isolationism.

In the summer of 1939, the British and French finally attempted to form an alliance with the Soviet Union against Germany. They were again too late. Anger at not being invited to participate in the Munich Conference, mistrust of the Western powers (which included fear of abandonment that would leave the USSR to battle Germany alone), and ambitions in eastern Europe led Stalin to sign a nonaggression pact with Nazi Germany on August 23.[57] This agreement made the German takeover of Poland possible.

But France and Britain had at last resolved to take firm action. When Germany invaded Poland on September 1, 1939, World War II began. The opportunity to halt German expansion by peaceful means had passed, and only total war could stop Nazi aggression. In the end, Hitler would be thoroughly defeated and discredited, but only at incredible cost, a cost that included the most extensive genocide the world has yet seen. As in other genocides, the context of war made it easier for the killers to implement their genocidal preferences.

The Allies missed their last opportunity for the peaceful prevention of World War II when they did not stop Hitler's Rhineland occupation in 1936. Joseph Goebbels, Hitler's close confidant and minister of propaganda, clearly realized that well-timed, early international preventive action would have stopped the Nazis. Goebbels sneered at Europe's indecisive response: if *he* had been the French premier in 1933, he would have seen that the strategy already spelled out in *Mein Kampf* clearly revealed Hitler as a danger—and would have marched against him. At that time, he admitted, the Allies could have won easily. Instead they let Germany become better armed than the rest of Europe—and only then did they start the war.[58]

Because of fearful hesitation, wishful thinking, faulty appraisal of danger, multiple prejudices, and lack of international cooperation during that crucial period, Europe—and the world—had to pay an inconceivable amount in lives, resources, and human suffering.

What Can the 1930s Tell the Twenty-first Century About Prevention of Genocide?

Do World War II and the Holocaust offer us clues on how to deal with ruthless, aggressively ambitious dictators and their power over obedient and enthusiastic followers? The second half of the twentieth century and the first decade of the twenty-first mainly indicate a tragic record of failure. But this book notes significant exceptions and learning processes.

The global context today is different from that of the 1930s. We have seen the end of colonialism and the fall of fascism and communism. International organizations such as the European Union, the United Nations, and the North Atlantic Treaty Organization (NATO) have been created that offer possibilities for cooperation far beyond anything available in the 1930s. Nevertheless the lessons of the 1930s are not limited to that period, and we must study them together with the lessons of the Cold War and the bloody 1990s. In a previous book I outlined some general principles that deserve serious consideration today.[59] These were foreshadowed in the introductory chapter of this book but deserve fuller consideration here, given their central relevance to the tragedy of the Holocaust and the crucial lessons to be learned from it.

1. Egregious human rights violations within a country are associated with a high risk of mass violence—they create internal polarization that may lead to civil war, and when they strengthen an ambitious despot's power over his subjects through control of the police and military, can serve as a precursor to external aggression.
2. Intolerance, prejudice, and ethnocentrism, especially when characterized by hypernationalistic or other fanatical orientations that insist on sharp dichotomies (us or them, for or against, true believer or infidel), can spread like infectious diseases throughout populations and across national boundaries. Once released, they are hard to contain.
3. Preventing deadly conflict—even genocide—hinges on the competence and the will of the international community to take early warnings seriously. Executing this task requires alert identification and a judiciously hardheaded case-by-case assessment of potentially spreading dangers—such as abuses of human rights, incitement to hatred and violence, or military build-up—in their first phases. Wishful thinking here can lead to catastrophic missteps. It encourages widespread denial, avoidance of serious problems, and delay in facing them. When necessity finally forces leaders to cope with such problems later, the costs and risks are inevitably much greater.
4. A major challenge is learning to make accurate appraisals of hyperaggressive leaders. When they offer reassurances, it is tempting to believe that the danger is under control. Since the means they use to seize and hold power tend to attract or create calculating, opportunistic, deceitful, intimidating, suspicious, and grandiose personalities, a realistic appraisal of such leaders must include consideration of their earlier behavior in a variety of situations and their most powerful associates.
5. Dictators and demagogues readily exploit the bitter frustrations and fears that their prospective followers experience during times of severe economic and social hardship and convert them to aggressive behavior. By fanning hatred they can consolidate support among their chosen in-group. Long-standing tensions among ethnic, religious, or other groups provide a fault line that ruthlessly opportunistic leaders may widen by identifying an out-group as a threat to the nation that must be eradicated and stirring up fears of in-group survival.

6. The human species is susceptible to genocide; the historical record makes this abundantly clear. The constraints against it are not powerful, especially when there is an autocrat or dictator in control and the culture has established prejudicial stereotypes to provide a convenient target. This is particularly dangerous since the international community is usually so reluctant to undertake concerted action.

7. Circumstances of extreme turbulence such as war, revolution, a failed state, or economic freefall are conducive to mass expulsion or genocide in the context of highly inflammatory leadership and authoritarian social structures.

8. The absence of clear opposition is conducive to the escalation of hatred and violence. Either internal or external opposition, preferably both, can be helpful. There can be a constructive interplay between opposition to a violent regime within a country and beyond its borders. For outsiders, it should be a powerful warning when the leadership is intransigent and uses terror against such opposition.

9. The best opportunity to prevent genocide is through international cooperative action to overthrow, or at least powerfully constrain, a genocidal regime—if possible, on the basis of strong warning information well before the genocide is under way.

10. Fear induced by a terroristic aggressor can readily lead to an overestimate of his strength or the difficulties in confronting the problem. This in turn is conducive to appeasement that whets the appetite of the aggressor.

11. Alternative approaches and policies beyond appeasement are almost always available. It is crucial to consider them seriously, not to avoid them on the basis of ideological preference, personal rigidity, or wishful thinking. There are usually more ways to block a genocide-prone leader than initially meet the eye, especially if the problem is recognized early and dealt with in a resolute way.

12. Careful preparation for serious danger is helpful, especially since it is so difficult to improvise under severe stress. Having institutionalized structures, criteria for intervention, problem-solving procedures, an array of tools and strategies—all this contributes to rational assessment, sound contingency planning, and effective responses.

13. Leadership is crucial. This involves the vision to recognize real dangers and the courage to address them, not impulsively, but thoughtfully. It requires the ability to transcend wishful thinking. It can be greatly enhanced by building genocide-relevant professional competence in the small advisory group and the institutional setting in which leaders make decisions—so that they can get the best available information, analyze it carefully, weigh their options, and reach conclusions for the general well-being. Moreover, authentic leaders must have the capacity to build constituencies for prevention through a base of public information and skill in forming political coalitions.

14. The multiple failures of cooperation in the face of grave danger during the 1930s, even among major democracies, point vividly to the need for international cooperation—pooling strengths, sharing burdens, dividing labor as necessary to cope with serious dangers.

15. Since dictatorial and/or failed states are so dangerous in their predispositions to mass violence, it is vitally important to build competent, democratic states. To do so, the

international community will have to produce intellectual, technical, financial, and moral resources to aid democratically inclined leaders and peoples all over the world. Such aid, often multilateral in origin, may have to be sustained over many years as capacity is built within the country or region for coping with its own problems.

16. The painful lessons of U.S. isolationism and unilateralism in the 1920s and 1930s are even more salient now in the maximally interdependent and super-armed world that is emerging.

17. Many of these considerations apply not only to genocide but also to interstate warfare and to intrastate violence, which have recently been so prevalent and intense.

In any event, preventing deadly conflict well before genocide occurs is essential.

Coda: What We Learn

Such conditions can occur again. The seductive justifications for hideous atrocities can be provided as they were by Hitler. Indeed, advanced communications can spread them more efficiently and vividly today than ever before, and the killing power of worldwide weaponry has moved beyond prior experience.

The events of the 1930s show that World War II was a conflict that was *preventable* even with the limited tools available at the time. This was strongly emphasized by Winston Churchill. Too often our view of history assumes that conflagrations are preordained. The purpose of this chapter has been to highlight those moments when preventive action could have been taken and to identify some of the factors that precluded action. One central obstacle to prevention was the narrow, shortsighted definitions of national interest, which undermined the high degree of international cooperation that was necessary to block Hitler's path to genocide and war.

As in the 1930s, we are today living through a period of profound change in our economic, social, cultural, and technological life. As in the 1930s, the international arena is not bounded by the global confrontation of two superpowers. Although the world does not now face a threat identical to that of Hitler's Germany, we have seen many incidents in recent decades of mass violence in various places and various forms. Today Islamic extremist leaders in the Middle East and the Persian Gulf are, in a sense, echoing Hitler's promise of a triumphant to-morrow—in their case an apocalyptic promise based more on resentment and perceived slight than on hope of a bright future for a populace in even more difficult circumstances than were the Germans of the Weimar Republic. The inadequacy of the response by the international community in these situations bears a disturbing similarity to the events of the 1930s. But, unlike the 1930s, we now have numerous international institutions, legal norms, economic measures, technological capabilities, and diplomatic practices that have been painstakingly built up since the catastrophe of World War II. If these resources are cultivated and exercised effectively, they can serve as *vital tools to prevent violent conflict and, above all, to prevent genocide.* This is the essential content of the present book.

One remarkable—indeed, almost incredible—aspect of the German story is what happened after World War II and the Holocaust. Today, Germany is a thriving democracy, a force for human rights, intergroup respect, and peaceful resolution of conflicts in Europe and elsewhere. This is not the place to describe the transformation, but it must be noted as an *authentic basis for hope.*

In the second half of the twentieth century, West Germany (to some extent under the tutelage of the United States) set about building democratic institutions, educating its children for peace, facing honestly up to its past, paying reparations to Israel, and giving real meaning to the term "never again." It is interesting that East Germany, under Soviet control, made none of these changes and moved slowly and ambivalently in this direction after German unification. It is a kind of experiment in nature: the democratic part of Germany overcoming its past and creating a far better future; the dictatorial part of Germany doing nothing of the sort until freedom came with the end of the Cold War. Altogether, the dramatic contrast of post-Holocaust with pre and Holocaust Germany is a powerful testimonial to the influence of social conditions on human behavior. If in Germany, why not elsewhere?

The Sociology and Anthropology of Genocide

By Adam Jones

Introduction

The disciplines of sociology and anthropology are distinguished by the types of societies they study. Anthropologists have carried out work on the non-industrialized "Third World" or Global South, while sociologists have focused on social patterns and processes within the industrialized "First World" or Global North.[1] Anthropology also possesses a distinctive methodology: fieldwork. Nonetheless, the disciplines are linked by a common concern with societal and cultural processes, and it is appropriate to consider them together.

Sociology and anthropology also shared a reluctance, until fairly recently, to engage with genocide and state terror. "Many sociologists," stated Irving Louis Horowitz in the late 1980s, "exhibit a studied embarrassment about these issues, a feeling that intellectual issues posed in such a manner are melodramatic and unfit for scientific discourse."[2] Nancy Scheper-Hughes similarly described "the traditional role of the anthropologist as neutral, dispassionate, cool and rational, [an] objective observer of the human condition"; anthropologists traditionally maintained a "proud, even haughty distance from political engagement."[3]

Fortunately, Horowitz's evaluation is now obsolete, thanks to a host of sociologists who have contributed seminally to genocide studies. They include Kurt Jonassohn, Helen Fein, Zygmunt Bauman, Michael Mann, and Daniel Feierstein. Anthropological studies came later, but recent years have seen the first anthologies on anthropology and genocide, as well as groundbreaking works by Alexander Laban Hinton, Victoria Sanford, and Christopher Taylor, among others.[4]

In examining sociological perspectives, this chapter focuses on three key themes:

(1) the sociology of modernity, which has attracted considerable interest from genocide scholars in the wake of Zygmunt Bauman's *Modernity and the Holocaust*;

(2) the sociology of "ethnicity" and ethnic conflict; and (3) the role of "middleman" or "market-dominant" minorities. It then addresses anthropological framings of genocide, focusing also on the work of forensic anthropologists.

Sociological Perspectives

The Sociology of Modernity

Is genocide a modern phenomenon?[5] At first glance, the question seems banal. We saw in Chapter 1 that the destruction of peoples on the basis of group identity extends back to early history, and probably to prehistory. Yet we also know that in recent centuries, and especially during the past hundred years, the prevalence of genocide has taken a quantitative leap. The central issue is: Has that leap also been *qualitative*? Is there something about modernity that has become *definitional* to genocide?

In one of the most discussed works on the Jewish Holocaust, *Modernity and the Holocaust*, sociologist Zygmunt Bauman delivered a resounding "yes" to this question. "Modern civilization was not the Holocaust's *sufficient* condition; it was, however, most certainly its *necessary* condition. Without it, the Holocaust would be unthinkable."[6] Bauman's argument revolved around four core features of modernity: nationalism; "scientific" racism; technological complexity; and bureaucratic rationalization. Modern nationalism divided the world "fully and exhaustively ... into national domains," leaving "no space ... for internationalism" and designating "each scrap of the no-man's-land ... [as] a standing invitation to aggression." In such a world, European Jews—with their international and cosmopolitan identity—could be construed as alien. They "defied the very truth on which all nations, old and new alike, rested their claims; the ascribed character of nationhood, heredity and naturalness of national entities ... . *The world tightly packed with nations and nation-states abhorred the non-national void. Jews were in such a void: they were such a void.*"[7]

This existential unease towards the Jew was combined with scientific racism, which Bauman depicted as a modern phenomenon,[8] overlaying traditional intercommunal antipathies with a veneer of scientific and medical rationality. This brought with it an impetus to total extermination of the racial Other: "The only adequate solution to problems posited by the racist world-view is a total and uncompromising isolation of the pathogenic and infectious race—the source of disease and contamination—through its complete spatial separation or physical destruction."[9]

How could such a totalizing project be implemented? For Bauman, the advent of modern technology and bureaucratic rationality was essential. The mass death that the Nazis developed and inflicted relied on products of the Industrial Revolution. Railway transport, gas chambers, Zyklon B cyanide crystals administered by men in gas masks—all were essentially modern inventions and had to be managed by a bureaucracy of death. The great German theorist of modern bureaucracy, Max Weber, emphasized "its peculiar, 'impersonal' character," which "mean[s] that the mechanism ... is easily made to work for anybody who knows how to gain control over it." Weber also argued that "the bureaucratization of all [social] domination very strongly furthers the development of 'rational matter-of-factness' and the personality type of the professional expert," distinguished by his or her cool amorality and devotion to efficiency. Moreover, bureaucracy cultivates secrecy: "the concept of the 'official secret' is the specific invention of the bureaucracy."[10]

The processing of millions of "subhumans" for anonymous death was unthinkable in the absence of such a culture, according to Bauman:

> By its nature, this is a daunting task, unthinkable unless in conjunction with the availability of huge resources, means of their mobilization and planned distribution, skills of splitting the overall task into a great number of partial and specialized functions and skills to co-ordinate their performance. In short, the task is inconceivable without modern bureaucracy.[11]

Moreover, this "splitting [of] the overall task" into isolated and fragmented units of time, space, and work created a vital psychological distance between the victims and those participating in their annihilation. No individual—except, by reputation, the distant and semi-mythical *Führer* figure—exercised overall authority or bore overall responsibility. One did not commit mass murder *per se*. Rather, one operated a railroad switch, or dropped a few cyanide crystals into a shaft: "a cool, objective operation ... mechanically mediated ... a deed performed at a distance, one whose effects the perpetrator did not see," in Wolfgang Sofsky's words.[12] Much the same set of values, procedures, and behaviors characterized the nuclear mentality, with its potential for rationally administered omnicide (Chapter 2).[13]

Figure 11.1 Are the technologies, ideologies, and state capacities of modernity inextricably linked to genocide? Some argue that the connection is so intimate that we should find another word for the mass killings of pre-modern ages. Even those who take a longer view, like this author, acknowledge distinctive features of genocide in the modern age. Pictured: a canister of Zyklon B, the chemical pesticide which the Nazis developed to murder Jews and others in the gas chambers.

Source: Michael Hanke/Wikimedia Commons.

More recently, historian Mark Levene, in his magisterial work *Genocide in the Age of the Nation State*, has argued that "the problem of genocide lies in the very nature of modernity."[14] This, together with the subtitle of his second volume (*The Rise of the West and the Coming of Genocide*), suggests that genocide is *essentially* modern and inextricably linked to the West's imperial expansion from the fifteenth century on (see Chapters 2 and 3): "the crystallization of the phenomenon we call 'genocide'—as opposed to other categories of mass murder—could only be really achieved in the context of an emerging, global, interlocking system of nation-states which finally came to its *fullest* fruition in the twentieth century."[15] While this was "accompanied by no overarching political agenda for the annihilation of foreign peoples," for Levene, it established "a broader cultural discourse in which such annihilation was considered perfectly acceptable." The bureaucratic features which Bauman emphasized resurfaced in Levene's contention that "we normatively name people as members of given tribes, nations, races, religions" because of "modernity's facility for reducing and simplifying complex phenomena—humans included—'into a more manageable and schematized form,'" while failing or refusing "to imagine human beings as potentially possessing multi-layered identities and loyalties."[16]

Two main criticisms of this modernity-of-genocide thesis may be advanced. First, the supposed dividing line between historical and modern genocide seems more stylistic than substantive. It is simply not the case that "the Holocaust left behind and put to shame all its alleged pre-modern equivalents, exposing them as primitive, wasteful and ineffective by comparison," as Bauman contended.[17] Rather, the clear conviction of the founder of genocide studies, Raphael Lemkin, was that "genocide is not an exceptional phenomenon, but ... occurs in intergroup relations with a certain regularity like homicide takes place between individuals."[18] Lemkin's own historical analysis of genocide encompassed millennia. The UN Genocide Convention that resulted from Lemkin's lobbying efforts likewise recognized in its preamble "that *at all periods of history* genocide has inflicted great losses on humanity" (emphasis added). Levene, for his part, is far too good a historian to ignore the continuities, so he hedges his bets at points—referring to "our phenomenon, *at least in its modern and contemporary manifestations*"; "genocide—*or at least a modern variant of it*"; "any *broad historical examination* of the phenomenon ..."[19]

To explore the distinctively "modern" features of modern and contemporary genocides is a worthwhile inquiry, and both Bauman and Levene have made foundational contributions to the field. But precisely the same line of inquiry could be launched into the human institution most intimately allied with genocide—war. While we could note all manner of modern expansions and deadly innovations, we would not, I think, suggest that war thereby is *essentially* a modern creation.[20] So, too, with genocide. As Alex Alvarez argued, "What modernity has done is reshape genocide into a more efficient and rational endeavor capable of killing on an industrial scale. The modern age has not created genocide; rather it has altered its nature, application, and efficiency."[21]

Another criticism of the modernity-of-genocide thesis may be summarized in one word: Rwanda (see Chapter 9). There, around one million people were hunted, corraled, and exterminated in *twelve weeks*—a rate of killing exceeding by a wide margin that of the "modern"

Nazi holocaust. Yet the genocide was not only more modern in chronological terms; it was carried out by men and women armed with little more than guns and traditional agricultural implements.[22] It involved no appreciable role for scientific or technical experts. And *the killing was conducted up close, often face-to-face, publicly,* with no resort to the physical and psychological distancing strategies and official secrecy supposedly necessary for "modern" mass slaughter.[23] One can argue that the Rwandan holocaust depended on a complex administrative apparatus; a racist ideology tinged with pseudo-science; and the industrial mass production of machetes, hoes, firearms, and grenades. But are these inherently "modern"? Bureaucracy is ancient, as various Chinese dynasties remind us.[24] One suspects that the ideology of hate developed by Hutu Power would have been just as functional without its vaguely modernist overtones.[25] With regard to Rwanda's technology of death, the basic implements of guns, machetes, and explosives all pre-date the Industrial Revolution.

Ethnicity and Ethnic Conflict

> Loe, this is the payment you shall get, if you be one of them they terme, without.
>
> Thomas Merton, 1637

Few concepts are as amorphous and yet important as ethnicity. On one hand, ethnic identifications seem so fluid and mutable as to lack almost any "objective" character. On the other hand, ethnicity is arguably the dominant ideological impetus to conflict and genocide worldwide.

Three historical phenomena account for the prominence of ethnicity in today's "global society." The first is nationalism, touched on in Chapter 2. As medieval Europe moved away from a quilt of overlapping sovereignties and towards the formation of modern states, it first fell under the sway of strong, centralizing monarchs. With the onset of the democratic age via the American and French Revolutions, sovereignty was held increasingly to reside in "the people." But *which* people? How defined? The popular thrust gave rise in the nineteenth century to modern ethnic nationalism, as Western rulers and their populations sought an ideology to unify the new realms. The result was what Benedict Anderson called "imagined communities": geographically disparate but mutually identified agglomerations defining themselves as "French," "German," "British," "Italian," and so on.[26] The core idea was that the "imagined community" required a particular political form, the "nation-state," to achieve true realization.

On what basis were these communities imagined? It is worth pausing briefly to consider the bases or foundations of ethnicity, as they have been listed by a prominent scholar of the subject. Anthony Smith cited six foundations of ethnic identity: "1. a collective proper name, 2. a myth of common ancestry, 3. shared historical memories, 4. one or more differentiating elements of common culture, 5. an association with a specific 'homeland,' 6. a sense of solidarity for significant sectors of the population."[27]

While a refined concept of ethnicity is often considered to be a Western invention, this is open to challenge. Han Chinese, for example, had a well-developed ethnic sensibility well before the West's rise to dominance.[28] So too, clearly, did the peoples of the ancient Middle East, whose ethnic rivalries and extermination strategies were quite well-advanced, if the relevant religious texts are granted credence. (Even if the genocides mentioned in Chapter 1 were fantasies, the fact that people felt drawn to fantasize them speaks to ethnoreligious distinctions and divisions as sharp as any in modern times.) Indeed, it could be argued that ethnicity is at least latent in all societies, independent of Western penetration and influence. Other social units—notably extended family, clan, and tribe—evince many of the same solidaristic bonds as ethnicity; they may be considered proto-ethnic groupings. Like ethnic groups, moreover, these identifications are meaningless without an Other to define against oneself. There are no in-groups without out-groups, with what anthropologist Fredrik Barth has called "boundary maintenance mechanisms" serving to demarcate the two.[29]

When a dominant ethnic collectivity is established as the basis of a "nation-state," a quandary arises in dealing with the out-groups—"ethnic minorities"—that also find themselves within the boundaries of that state. Such minorities exist everywhere; even supposedly unified or organic nation-states (Japan is the most commonly cited example) have them. This often carries explosive consequences for intercommunal violence, including genocide, as we have had numerous opportunities to witness in these pages.

The second historical factor is the spread of Western imperialism and colonialism around the world (Chapter 2), which shaped the present-day configuration of nationalisms in important ways. Most obviously, it spurred the idea of ethnic nationalism (though some nationalisms, and a wide range of ethnic *identifications*, clearly existed independently of it). Despite the best efforts of colonizers to preserve those they subjugated from such dangerous influences, ethnic-nationalist ideologies were gradually absorbed and integrated into the anti-colonial movements that arose from the mid-nineteenth through mid-twentieth centuries. In addition, following the time-honored strategy of divide and rule, aimed at *preventing* nationalism, the colonialists typically gathered a host of clans, tribes, and long-established "national" entities into a single territorial and administrative unit. A glance at the ethnic composition of countries such as Nigeria, Congo, and Indonesia suffices to remind one of the enormous diversity of peoples that comprised the deliberately *un*imaginable "communities" of colonialism.

The nationalist leaders who sprang to prominence in the colonized world in the 1920s and 1930s were thus confronted with the crushing challenge of either forging a genuine sense of national community among diverse peoples, or negotiating a peaceful and viable fragmentation of the colonial unit. For the most part, they chose to maintain the colonial boundaries. In some cases, this produced viable multiethnic states (see Chapter 16), but in many instances it did not. Sometimes the managed breakup of multiethnic entities led to massive violence (India, Palestine); in states where the leadership chose to preserve an artificial unity, time-bombs were set for the future (Nigeria, Indonesia, Yugoslavia). The ethnic violence associated with the collapse of the Soviet empire in 1991 is a recent example of this trend.

A final historical conjuncture, often overlooked, is *globalization*. Although globalizing trends can be traced back many centuries, they have reached a new stage of complex interconnectedness at the turn of the millennium. One advantage of ethnic identifications is that they offer a strong sense of psychological rootedness amidst change and upheaval. Given the rapid transformations associated with globalization, where is a stable sense of "we," and therefore of "me," to be found? The anthropologist Clifford Geertz has argued that

> during the disorienting process of modernization ... unintegrated citizens, looking for an anchor in a sea of changes, will grab hold of an increasingly anachronistic ethnic identity, which bursts onto the scene and then recedes as the process of structural differentiation moves toward a reintegrated society.[30]

One can question, though, whether such ethnic resurgence is a transitory phenomenon. As globalization is accompanied by intense nationalist sentiment in many parts of the world, the "transition" seems to be taking rather longer than expected. Part of the misunderstanding may lie in a tendency to believe that ethnic identifications are not primordial but fictional—created and manipulated by self-interested elites to mobilize their followers. (This line of argument has been bolstered by recent "postmodern" orientations in the humanities and social sciences.)

There *is* an important sense in which ethnic identifications are "imagined" or "mythical."[31] As I will show below, they are also subject to endless manipulations by elite figures and violence specialists. Ethnic identifications are protean in the sense that all of the six "bases" that Anthony Smith identifies for ethnicity can be altered, though not always at will or completely. One can change one's territorial base and recast one's primary ethnic identification, as generations of immigrants to the ethnic "melting-pot" of the United States have done (while often maintaining a secondary attachment to the previous identification). Ancestral myths can be revised, reinterpreted, or abandoned. Historical memory, language, culinary taste, forms of artistic expression—all are highly mutable.

Over time, however, ethnic identifications often achieve intergenerational stability. They assume a practical force in individual and group psychology, societal structure, and political behavior that is impossible to ignore, least of all by those seeking to understand and confront genocide and other mass violence.[32] In *Becoming Evil*, James Waller presented evidence from psychology, sociology, and anthropology to show that these identifications originate deep in human social behavior: "Knowing who is kin, knowing who is in our social group, has a deep importance to species like ours." Moreover, "We have an evolved capacity to see our group as superior to all others and even to be reluctant to recognize members of other groups as deserving of equal respect." Members of a cannibal tribe in Irian Jaya, Indonesia, convey this pointedly: they define themselves as "the human beings," and all others as "the edible ones."[33]

Ethnic Conflict and Violence "Specialists"

Some defining work on the sociology of mass violence pointed to the role of individual and organizational actors in provoking and channeling violent outbreaks. Donald L. Horowitz, for example, stressed the importance of

> organizations, often tied to ethnically based political parties, [that] reflect and rein-force interethnic hostility through propaganda, ritual, and force. They run the gamut from civilian to proto-military organizations, operating under varying degrees of secrecy and with varying degrees of coherence and military training. Their raison d'être is the alleged danger from the ethnic enemy.[34]

For his part, Paul R. Brass emphasized the role of violence "specialists" operating within "institutionalized ... systems" of violence generation:

> The kinds of violence that are committed in ethnic, communal, and racial "riots" are, I believe, undertaken mostly by "specialists," who are ready to be called out on such occasions, who profit from it, and whose activities profit others who may or may not be actually paying for the violence carried out. In fact, in many countries at different times in their histories, there have been regions or cities and towns which have developed what I call "institutionalized riot systems," in which known actors specialize in the conversion of incidents between members of different communities into ethnic riots. The activities of these specialists are usually required for a riot to spread from the initial incident of provocation.[35]

The significance of this category of actors to the fomenting and implementing of genocide should be recognized.[36] Note some of the "specialists" that Brass identifies: "criminal elements and members of youth gangs," "local militant group leaders," "politicians, businessmen, religious leaders," "college and university professors," "pamphleteers and journalists ... deliberately spreading rumors and scurrilous propaganda," "hooligans" (ranging from Nazi thugs to modern soccer hoodlums), "communal political elites."[37] Add to this list the violence specialists cited by Charles Tilly in his study of *The Politics of Collective Violence*: "Pirates, privateers, paramilitaries, bandits, mercenaries, mafiosi, militias, posses, guerrilla forces, vigilante groups, company police, and bodyguards."[38] Beyond the essential (and universally acknowledged) role of state officials and security force commanders, what we have here is a veritable who's-who of the leading *agents provocateurs* of genocide, its foot-soldiers, and its ideological defenders.

"Middleman Minorities"

The Greeks and Armenian merchants have been the leeches in this part of the world sucking the life blood out of the country for centuries.

Admiral Mark L. Bristol, US High Commissioner to Turkey, 1922

Perhaps no collectivities are as vulnerable to hatred and large-scale killing as those "characterized as possessing an excess of enterprise, ambition, energy, arrogance, and achievement by those who believe themselves lacking such traits."[39] Such minorities are not necessarily immigrants or descendants of immigrants, but often they are, and this foreignness is a key factor in their targeting. Worldwide, reflecting both centuries-old patterns and more recent globalizing trends, populations have arrived or been introduced from outside the established society. Lacking access to land, as well as the network of social relations that dominant groups can utilize, such groups normally settle in the cities or towns—often in neighborhoods or zones that quickly acquire a minority tinge. Even when they are brought in by a colonial power as indentured laborers (as with the Indians whom the British imported to Uganda, South Africa, Fiji, and elsewhere), there is a strong tendency for such groups to establish themselves in commercial trades.

Occupying an inherently vulnerable minority position, these sectors historically have been attractive to colonial powers as local allies and intermediaries. Such alliances allowed colonizers to "divide and rule," with the aid of a minority that was (1) less anchored to the territory and dominant culture in question, and therefore less prone to push for autonomy or national independence; and (2) heavily dependent on colonial favor, and therefore more likely to be loyal to the colonizers. Colonial favor often translated into greater educational opportunities and positions in lower and middle sectors of the bureaucracy. However, even in the absence of such colonial backing, and in the face of strong opposition from the dominant society, such groups almost universally emphasize education as a means of moving beyond their marginal position and attaining prosperity. They typically display strong bonds of ethnic, cultural, and material solidarity among their members, and they may have the advantage of access to capital and trading relationships through remaining ties with their (or their ancestors') countries of origin.

A frequent result is that these minorities establish a high degree of prominence, sometimes even outright dominance, in key sectors of the national economy. Well-known examples include Jews, whom Amy Chua refers to as "the quintessential market-dominant minority,"[40] and the Chinese of Southeast Asia. East Indians achieved a similar position in many East African economies, while Lebanese traders came to dominate the vital diamond trade in West Africa. The Dutch, British, and Portuguese-descended Whites of southern Africa may also be cited, along with the White "pigmentocrats" who enjoy elite status in heavily indigenous countries of Latin America. The potential for conflict, including for the violent or genocidal targeting of middleman minorities,[41] is apparent, though far from inevitable.[42] Through their common and preferential ties to colonial authorities, these minorities were easily depicted as agents of the alien dominator, opponents of national liberation and self-determination, and cancers in the body politic. Even today, their frequently extensive international ties and "cosmopolitan" outlook may grate on the majority's nationalist sentiments. Moreover, their previous relationship with a colonial power has often translated into a quest for alliances with authoritarian regimes in the post-colonial era. Elite Chinese businessmen in the Philippines and Indonesia, for example, were among the most enthusiastic and visible backers of the Marcos and Suharto dictatorships. When authoritarian rule collapsed, the mass hostility, resentment, and humiliation could be vented under democratic guise—a pattern that Chua has described well:

> In countries with a market-dominant minority and a poor "indigenous" majority, the forces of democratization and marketization directly collide. As markets enrich the market-dominant minority, democratization increases the political voice and power of the frustrated majority. The competition for votes fosters the emergence of demagogues who scapegoat the resented minority, demanding an end to humiliation, and insisting that the nation's wealth be reclaimed by its "true owners." Thus as America toasted the spread of global elections through the 1990s, vengeful ethnic slogans proliferated: "Zimbabwe for Zimbabweans," "Indonesia for Indonesians," "Uzbekistan for Uzbeks," "Kenya for Kenyans," "Ethiopia for Ethiopians," "Yids [Jews] out of Russia," "Hutu Power," "Serbia for Serbs," and so on. ... As popular hatred of the rich "outsiders" mounts, the result is an ethnically charged political pressure cooker in which some form of backlash is almost unavoidable.

Among the strategies of backlash, the "most ferocious kind ... is ethnic cleansing and other forms of majority-supported ethnic violence," up to and including genocide.[43] Rwanda in 1994 is the best example of democratization helping to spawn genocide against a relatively prosperous minority. However, if we remove the democratic element from the equation, we can also add to the list the two other "canonical" genocides of the twentieth century. The relative wealth, industriousness, and educational attainment of the Armenian minority, even under conditions of discrimination and repression in the Ottoman lands, made them an easy target for the fanatical nationalism of the Young Turks (Chapter 4). Similar hatred or at least distaste towards Jews in Germany and other European countries contributed to popular support for the Holocaust against them (Chapter 6). Note that all three of these genocides featured massive looting and plundering along with mass murder (see the discussion of genocide and greed in Chapter 10). Genocide offers an unprecedented opportunity to "redress" an economic imbalance by seizing the wealth and property of the victims, and to inflict on them the kind of humiliation that the majority population may have experienced.

Anthropological Perspectives

A confession: I have long been envious of anthropologists. Political scientists like myself are commanded to maintain a detached, "objective" view of their subject. Our research stratagems are usually confined to the library and the office, with only occasional forays into the outside world. Anthropologists, by contrast, are allowed and encouraged to get their hands dirty. The defining method of anthropology—fieldwork—commands them to wade into the thick of their subject matter, and get to know the people they study. They may "emerge from the field exhausted," but they carry with them "a material of extraordinary richness and depth."[44] Reading anthropological case studies, one sees and hears the subjects, smells the air, tastes the food.

Anthropology "calls for an understanding of different societies as they appear *from the inside*,"[45] where anthropologists are seen as inevitable and integral participants in the cross-cultural encounter. They are expected to describe the impact of the experience on their own subjectivity. Assisting with the forensic excavation of mass graves in Guatemala, Victoria Sanford reported: "I'm not vomiting, I haven't fainted, what a beautiful valley, everything is greener than green, those are real bones, my god 200 people were massacred here, their relatives are watching."[46] It would be hard to describe such an experience as enjoyable. But it is certainly *revelatory*, both to author and reader, in a way that more detached analyses rarely are.

Consider the approach adopted in another recent and impressive work on the anthropology of genocidal conflict: Ivana Macek's *Sarajevo Under Siege: Anthropology in Wartime* (2009). In April 1992, Bosnian Serb forces closed a ring around the cosmopolitan city of Sarajevo, beginning a siege that lasted for nearly four years (see pp. 320–22). Macek—a Croat scholar from Zagreb whose anthropological research had previously focused on Africa—found herself drawn not to "aggressive Croatian nationalism," but to the besieged multiethnic population of Sarajevo, which was "being hit hardest by a nationalistic war." She decided "to let individuals' lived experiences of violence stand at the center of research and from that point to trace the effects of war on society and culture." In so doing, she consciously took "a poet's approach to fieldwork, as well as to writing." In contrast to the emotional disengagement and bloodless prose of most social-science writing, Macek proclaimed the anthropologist's right to adopt "a disciplined subjectivity [which] becomes not a flaw or obstacle but a crucial element for creating meaningful knowledge."

For six months over the period of the siege, during several visits, Macek shared the struggle and toil of Sarajevans, "employ[ing] all of my faculties ... in order to manage from day to day, as well as record what they and I were undergoing." She emerged with a unique perspective: both insider/participant and rigorous scholarly observer. She documented the "deep sense of shame and humiliation" that always lurked, as people desperately clawed the means of subsistence from their austere and dangerous environment. But she also documented the strategies of coping and resistance: from the "fantastically inventive solutions to wartime shortages"; to the "magical thinking and small private magic routines" which people adopted as a "'childish' solution to an objectively unbearable situation"; to the gallows humor that citizens indulged in ("What is the difference between Sarajevo and Auschwitz? There is no gas in Sarajevo"). Perhaps surprisingly, and inspiringly, an outpouring of creative talent occurred as a reaction to life under siege, resulting in "an amazingly active artistic life": as one Sarajevan told her, "arts became the fount of the lifeforce. It gave back life to people, gave birth anew to optimism and strength, and gave meaning in a time when it looked as if life had lost all meaning." But Macek also witnessed expressions of "the emotional numbness and irrationality that followed an excess of pain": "People I saw who simply stood in open places during the shelling as if nothing was going on ..."

Perhaps most poignantly, Macek captured the slow erosion of the cosmopolitan and interethnic identity that the overarching designation of "Sarajevan" had long sponsored and permitted. Increasingly, Sarajevans grew

> divided along ethnonational lines into Muslims, Serbs, and Croats. Ethnoreligious identities became politicized and grew more salient in everyday life ... . Family members, friends, colleagues, and neighbors were judged by new, wartime standards, as people almost invariably tried to understand whether or not others' actions were influenced by their national identity ... . Sarajevans started to "remember" the ethnoreligious traditions that most of them had lost during the secularization of society following the Second World War.[47]

The result of Macek's investigations was a portrait of a community under siege, with acts of genocide and urbicide underway (and resisted), with identities and memories summoned and reshaped. It provided further evidence that, in historian Anton WeissWendt's assessment, it is anthropologists who "have made probably the most valuable contribution to genocide studies in ... recent years."[48] However, this emergence of an anthropological critique in genocide studies required, and derived from, a broader shift in the discipline's focus: "a theoretical and ethnographic move away from studying small, relatively stable communities toward looking at those under siege, in flux, and victimized by state violence or insurgency movements."[49] The declaration issued in *Anthropology Today* in 1993, "Anthropologists Against Ethnic Violence," stated that "we must not shirk the responsibility of disputing the claims of demagogues and warning of the dangers of ethnic violence."[50]

The declaration, and the broader paradigm shift it represented, also reflected a conviction that anthropology had been deeply compromised, in the past, by its alliances with European imperialism and Nazism.[51] Most nineteenth-century anthropologists took for granted European dominance over subject peoples. Their schema of classification tended to revolve around hierarchies of humanity: they sifted and categorized the peoples of the world in a way that bolstered the European claim to supremacy. Modern "scientific" racism was one result. Even the most liberal anthropologists of the pre-First World War period, such as Franz Boas, viewed the disappearance of many primitive civilizations as preordained; "salvage ethnography" was developed in an attempt to describe as much of these civilizations as possible before nature took its supposedly inevitable course.[52]

Perhaps neither before nor since have anthropologists played such a prominent role in state policy as during the Nazi era (Chapter 6). Gretchen Schafft noted that "German and, to a lesser extent, Austrian anthropologists were involved in the Holocaust as perpetrators, from its beginning to its conclusion ... Never had their discipline been so well respected and received. Never had practitioners been so busy ... while the price for not cooperating was 'internal exile,' joblessness, or incarceration."[53] Prominent anthropologists such as Eugen Fischer, Adolf Würth, and Sophie Ehrhardt flocked to lend a scientific gloss to the Nazis' preposterous racial theories about Jews, Roma, and Slavs; many of these "scholars" continued their work into the postwar period.[54]

However, contradictorily and simultaneously, anthropology was emerging as the most pluralistic and *least* ethnocentric of the social sciences. Under the influence of the discipline's leading figures—Franz Boas, the revolutionary ethnographer Bronislaw Malinowski, the Englishman A.R. Radcliffe-Brown, and the American Margaret Mead—a methodology was developed that encouraged nonjudgmental involvement in the lives and cultures of one's subjects. Hierarchies of "development" were undermined by anthropologists' nuanced study of "primitive" societies that proved to be extraordinarily complex and sophisticated. And the supposedly scientific basis for racial hierarchy was powerfully challenged by work such as that of Boas, who "researched the change in head shape across only one American generation," thereby "demonstrat[ing] to the world how race, language, and culture are causally unlinked."[55] Anthropologists played a notable and little-known role in drafting the Universal Declaration of Human Rights, cautioning the UN Commission devoted to the task against "ethnocentrism, the assumption of the superiority of one's own cultural values."[56] With the great wave of decolonization after the Second World War, it was anthropologists above all who went "into the field" to grapple with, and in a sense validate, diverse "Third World" societies.

Anthropology's guiding ideal of cultural relativism requires that the practitioner "suspend one's judgement and preconceptions as much as possible, in order to better understand another's worldview." In studying genocidal processes, the relativist approach emphasizes "local understandings and cultural dynamics that both structure and motivate genocide," and examines them in their broader cultural context. Rather than "simply dismissing *génocidaires* as 'irrational' and 'savage,'" the approach "demands that we understand them and their perspective regardless of what we think of perpetrators."[57]

Arguably, though, cultural relativism has its limits. At some point, if one is to confront atrocities, one must adopt a universalist stand (i.e., that atrocities are always criminal, and cannot be excused by culture). Nancy Scheper-Hughes, among others, has criticized cultural relativism as "moral relativism" that is "no longer appropriate to the world in which we live." If anthropology "is to be worth anything at all, it must be ethically grounded."[58] Alexander Hinton likewise suggests that relativism "played a key role in inhibiting anthropologists from studying genocide," together with other forms of "political violence in complex state societies."[59]

Partly because of relativist influences, and partly because of its preference for "studying small, relatively stable communities,"[60] anthropology's engagement with genocide came relatively late. Only recently has a "school" begun to coalesce, developing a rich body of literature, particularly on terror and genocide in Latin America, Africa, and Southeast Asia. Deploying fieldwork-based ethnography (literally, "writing about ethnic groups"), these researchers have amassed and analyzed a wealth of individual testimonies about the atrocities. In Victoria Sanford's estimation, this "is among the greatest contributions anthropology can make to understanding social problems—the presentation of testimonies, life histories, and ethnographies of violence."[61] Together with the reports of human rights organizations and truth commissions (see Chapter 15), these provide important evidence, for present and future generations, of the nature and scale of atrocity.

Anthropologists go further still, to analyze how atrocity is ritualized within cultures, and how when collectively "performed," it serves to bolster communal identity and solidarity. A wide range of commentators have noted, for example, the atmosphere of festive cruelty that regularly pervades genocidal frenzies. Where the killing and celebrations of it are not tightly circumscribed, limited to a core genocidal cadre, they often assume a carnival-like flavor. In a North American context, one can recall the party atmosphere that prevailed among the all-white spectators at the lynching of two black men in Indiana (p. 485), or the Colorado militia perpetrators of the Sand Creek Massacre of Cheyenne (p. 115), who "put their accomplishments on public display, a deliriously received victory parade through Denver providing the opportunity for them to bedeck their horses, uniforms and other accoutrements with the various bodily parts—mostly female genitalia—that they had garnered as trophies."[62] In both cases, the performance and ritual celebration of genocidal acts helped to fortify white tribal solidarities, constructed against a threatening tide of "savage" Indians or "depraved" black males. Where these subaltern identifications are not fantastical but actual, one sees not only a similar ritual quality to acts of vengeance against (real) oppressors, whether localized or generalized, but the incorporation of *fantasies* of vengeance into cultural rituals and performances located along a continuum of subaltern genocide. My own exploration of this theme in *Genocides by the Oppressed* was strongly influenced by anthropological inquiries into ritual performances of retributive victory and atrocity.[63]

Questions of genocide and memory, explored further in Chapter 14, are also informed and interpreted by anthropological researchers: how coping strategies are adopted in the aftermath of mass atrocity;[64] how atrocities may become literally "part of the landscape" for communities, attached to familiar objects, irrupting to the forefront of consciousness at unexpected moments:

> [The] living memory of terror can reinvoke the physical and psychological pain of past acts of violence in unexpected moments. A tree, for example, is not just a tree. A river, not just a river. At a given moment, a tree is a reminder of the baby whose head was smashed against a tree by a soldier. The tree, and the memory of the baby it invokes, in turn reinvoke a chain of memories of terror, including witnessing the murder of a husband or brother who was tied to another tree and beaten to death— perhaps on the same day or perhaps years later.[65]

Culturally specific practices of terror are especially well suited to anthropological investigation. In his study of the Rwandan genocide, *Sacrifice as Terror*, Christopher Taylor showed how cultural dynamics, rituals, and symbolism may help to explain the particular course that the holocaust took. His analysis demonstrated—in Alexander Hinton's summary—that anthropological methods "explain why the violence was perpetrated in certain ways—for example, the severing of Achilles tendons, genital mutilation, breast oblation, the construction of roadblocks that served as execution sites, bodies being stuffed into latrines." The violence "was deeply symbolic," representing cultural beliefs about expulsion and excretion, obstruction and flow.[66] For example, Taylor pointed out the symbolism of the Nyabarongo River as a route by which murdered Tutsis were to be "removed from Rwanda and retransported to their presumed land of origin," thereby purifying the nation of its internal "'foreign' minority." Figure 9.1 on p. 354 shows the grim results. In Taylor's interpretation,

> Rwanda's rivers became part of the genocide by acting as the body politic's organs of elimination, in a sense "excreting" its hated internal other. It is not much of a leap to infer that Tutsi were thought of as excrement by their persecutors. Other evidence of this is apparent in the fact that many Tutsi were stuffed into latrines after their deaths.[67]

Figure 11.2 Nancy Scheper-Hughes's concept of the "genocidal continuum" focuses attention on "everyday acts of violence that make participation ... in genocidal acts possible," especially strategies of social marginalization, anathematization, and exclusion. A homeless African American man sits on a bench in New York City, 2005.

Source: Colin Gregory Palmer/ Wikimedia Commons.

An intimate familiarity with day-to-day cultural praxis allows anthropologists to draw connections between "exceptional" outbursts of atrocity, such as genocide, and more quotidian forms and structures of violence. The leading theorist in this regard is Nancy Scheper-Hughes, whose classic study of a Brazilian village, *Death without Weeping*, explored the desensitization of women-as-mothers to the deaths of their infant children amidst pervasive scarcity.[68] This extended even to complicity in their offspring's deaths through the deliberate withholding of food and care, with the resulting mortality viewed as divinely ordained. Subsequently, Scheper-Hughes outlined a *genocidal continuum*, composed of a multitude of "small wars and invisible genocides" conducted in the normative social spaces of public schools, clinics, emergency rooms, hospital wards, nursing homes, court rooms, prisons, detention centers, and public morgues. The continuum refers to the human capacity to reduce others to nonpersons, to monsters, or to things that give structure, meaning, and rationale to everyday practices of violence. It is essential that we recognize in our species (and in ourselves) *a genocidal capacity* and that we exercise a defensive hypervigilance, a hypersensitivity to the less dramatic, *permitted*, everyday acts of violence that make participation (under other conditions) in genocidal acts possible, perhaps more easy than we would like to know. I would include all

Figure 11.3 Isabel Reveco, a Chilean forensic anthropologist, examines the skull of a Kurdish victim of Saddam Hussein's Anfal Campaign against Iraqi Kurds (see p. 178). She is "helped by the father of two young men who were executed at Koreme," one of the major Anfal genocide sites. Saddam Hussein was tried and condemned to death for genocide against the Kurds, among other crimes; he was hanged on December 30, 2006. The evidence amassed and sifted by forensic anthropologists has been vital to sustaining charges of genocide and crimes against humanity in this and other prosecutions.

Source: Mercedes Doretti/Equipo Argentino de Antropología Forense (EAAF).

expressions of social exclusion, dehumanization, depersonalization, pseudo-speciation, and reification that normalize atrocious behavior and violence toward others.[69]

She noted, for instance, that Brazilian "street children" experience attacks by police "that are genocidal in their social and political sentiments." The children "are often described as 'dirty vermin' so that unofficial policies of 'street cleaning,' 'trash removal,' 'fly swatting,' and 'pest removal' are invoked in garnering broad-based public support for their extermination." Through such practices and rhetoric, genocide becomes "socially incremental," something that is "experienced by perpetrators, collaborators, bystanders—and even by victims themselves—as expected, routine, even justified."[70] There seems a clear connection between such everyday rhetoric and the propaganda discourse of full-scale genocide, in which Native American children were referred to as "nits [who] make lice," Jews as "vermin," and Rwandan Tutsis as "cockroaches."

In closing this brief account of anthropological framings and insights, it is worth considering the role of *forensic anthropologists*. Bridging the natural and social sciences, they "have worked with health professionals, lawyers, photographers, and nongovernmental organizations to analyze physical remains and gather evidence with which to prosecute perpetrators."[71] Their core activities consist of the "search for, recovery, and preservation of physical evidence at the outdoor scene" of crimes and mass atrocities. They document how evidence relates to its "depositional environment," and use the data collected to reconstruct the events surrounding the deaths of the exhumed victims.[72]

In recent years, forensic anthropologists have become the most visible face of anthropology in genocide investigation and adjudication. Among the pioneers of the field is Clyde Snow, a US specialist who in the 1990s oversaw the exhumations at the Balkan massacre sites of Vukovar and Srebrenica. These excavations form the basis of an inevitably gruesome but illuminating book of photographs and text, *The Graves* (see Further Study). As Snow described his task:

> When [societies] choose to pursue justice, we forensic anthropologists can put the tools of a rapidly developing science at the disposal of the survivors. We can determine a murder victim's age, sex and race from the size and shape of certain bones. We can extract DNA from some skeletons and match it with samples from the victims' relatives. Marks on the bones can reveal signs of old diseases and injuries reflected in the victims' medical histories, as well as more sinister evidence: bullet holes, cut marks from knives, or fracture patterns produced by blunt instruments. Taken together, such clues can tell us who victims were and how they died—clues crucial to bringing the killers to justice.[73]

Snow's earliest digs were conducted in Argentina during the 1980s, where he helped to train the Argentine Forensic Anthropology Team (Equipo Argentino de Antropología Forense, EAAF) that exhumed victims of the "Dirty War" (see Figure 11.3). "Ample forensic evidence" underpinned the report of the Argentine truth commission, *Nunca Más* (Never Again), and the prosecutions of former *junta* leaders.[74] The team went on to conduct exhumations in

El Salvador, at the site of the military massacre of some 700 civilians at El Mozote.[75] With assistance from the American Association for the Advancement of Science (AAAS), Snow subsequently trained members of the Guatemalan Forensic Anthropology Team.[76] The team's investigations were equally vital to the truth commission report that labeled the military regime's campaign against Mayan Indians in the Guatemalan highlands as genocidal (see Box 3a), and assigned responsibility for more than 90 percent of the atrocities of the "civil war" to the government and the paramilitary forces it mobilized.[77]

Snow has conducted excavations at atrocity sites as geographically disparate as Ethiopia, Iraq, and the Philippines. His comment on the nature of his investigations summarizes the work of the conscientious anthropologists—and many others—who have informed our understanding of individual genocides: "You do the work in the daytime and cry at night."[78]

Further Study

Zygmunt Bauman, *Modernity and the Holocaust*. Ithaca, NY: Cornell University Press, 2000. Influential sociological interpretation of the Jewish Holocaust.

Pierre L. van den Berghe, ed., *State Violence and Ethnicity*. Niwot, CO: University Press of Colorado, 1990. One of the best sociological works on genocide and state terror.

Paul R. Brass, ed., *Riots and Pogroms*. New York: New York University Press, 1996. Vigorous edited volume on the dynamics of ethnic violence.

Amy Chua, *World on Fire: How Exporting Free Market Democracy Breeds Ethnic Hatred and Global Instability*. New York: Anchor, 2004. Provocative overview of "market-dominant minorities."

Daniel Feierstein, *El genocidio como práctica social: Entre el nazismo y la experiencia argentina* [Genocide as a Social Practice: Between Nazism and the Argentine Experience]. Buenos Aires: Fondo de Cultura Económica, 2007. Sophisticated comparison of the sociology of Nazism with Argentina's culture of terror under military rule.

Helen Fein, *Genocide: A Sociological Perspective*. London: Sage, 1993. Short, influential treatise.

H.H. Gerth and C. Wright Mills, eds, *From Max Weber: Essays in Sociology*. New York: Oxford University Press, 1954. Writings of the great German theorist of authority, modernity, and bureaucracy.

Alexander Laban Hinton, ed., *Annihilating Difference: The Anthropology of Genocide*. Berkeley, CA: University of California Press, 2002. A groundbreaking anthology; see also *Genocide: An Anthropological Reader*; *Genocide: Truth, Memory, and Representation* (ed. with Kevin Lewis O'Neill).

Donald L. Horowitz, *The Deadly Ethnic Riot*. Berkeley, CA: University of California Press, 2001. Massive, eye-opening treatise on ethnic violence.

Irving Louis Horowitz, *Taking Lives: Genocide and State Power* (4th edn). New Brunswick, NJ: Transaction Publishers, 1997. Rambling sociological account.

Victoria Sanford, *Buried Secrets: Truth and Human Rights in Guatemala*. New York: Palgrave Macmillan, 2003. Sanford worked alongside the Guatemalan forensic anthropology team.

Gretchen E. Schafft, *From Racism to Genocide: Anthropology in the Third Reich*. Urbana, IL: University of Illinois Press, 2004. Explores anthropologists' complicity in Nazi social engineering.

James C. Scott, *Seeing Like A State: How Certain Schemes to Improve the Human Condition Have Failed*. New Haven, CT: Yale University Press, 1998. Fascinating study of "high-modernist" social planning, relevant to studies of state terror and totalitarian systems.

Jeffrey A. Sluka, ed., *Death Squad: The Anthropology of State Terror*. Philadelphia, PA: University of Pennsylvania Press, 2000. Another important anthology. Anthony D. Smith, *National Identity*. London: Penguin, 1991. Fine primer on the ethnic and cultural roots of nationalism.

Wolfgang Sofsky, *The Order of Terror: The Concentration Camp*, trans. William Templer. Princeton, NJ: Princeton University Press, 1999. Essential book on the camps.

Eric Stover and Gilles Peress, *The Graves: Srebrenica and Vukovar*. Zurich: Scalo Publishers, 1998. Images and text of forensic excavations in Bosnia and Croatia.

Christopher C. Taylor, *Sacrifice as Terror: The Rwandan Genocide of 1994*. Oxford: Berg, 1999. Anthropological insights into the Rwandan holocaust.

Sarah E. Wagner, *To Know Where He Lies: DNA Technology and the Search for Srebrenica's Missing*. Berkeley, CA: University of California Press, 2008. Moving anthropological study of the exhumation of victims of the 1995 Srebrenica massacre, and continuing attempts to identify the dead.

Notes

1. See Thomas Hylland Eriksen, *Small Places, Large Issues: An Introduction to Social and Cultural Anthropology* (London: Pluto Press, 2001), p. 29.

2. Horowitz quoted in Helen Fein, *Genocide: A Sociological Perspective* (London: Sage, 1993), p. 6.

3. Nancy Scheper-Hughes, "The Primacy of the Ethical: Propositions for a Militant Anthropology," *Current Anthropology*, 36: 3 (1995), pp. 410, 414.

4. See Alexander Laban Hinton, ed., *Annihilating Difference: The Anthropology of Genocide* (Berkeley, CA: University of California Press, 2002); Alexander Laban Hinton, ed., *Genocide: An Anthropological Reader* (London: Blackwell, 2002); Nancy Scheper-Hughes and Philippe Bourgois, eds, *Violence in War and Peace: An Anthology* (London: Blackwell, 2004); Jeffrey A. Sluka, ed., *Death Squad: The Anthropology of State Terror* (Philadelphia, PA: University of Pennsylvania Press, 1999).

5. "Modernity," as Hinton notes, "is notoriously difficult to define," but "can perhaps best be described as a set of interrelated processes, some of which began to develop as early as the fifteenth century, characterizing the emergence of 'modern society.' Politically, modernity involves the rise of secular forms of government, symbolized by the French Revolution and culminating in the modern nation-state. Economically, modernity refers to capitalist expansion and its derivatives—monetarized exchange, the accumulation of capital, extensive private property, the search for new markets, commodification, and industrialization. Socially, modernity entails the replacement of 'traditional' loyalties (to lord, master, priest, king, patriarch, kin, and local community) with 'modern' ones (to secular authority, leader, 'humanity,' class, gender, race, and ethnicity). Culturally, modernity encompasses the movement from a predominantly religious to an emphatically secular and materialist worldview characterized by new ways of thinking about and understanding human behavior." Hinton, "The Dark Side of Modernity: Toward an Anthropology of Genocide," in Hinton,

ed., *Annihilating Difference*, pp. 7–8. For an ambitious anthology, see Stuart Hall *et al.*, eds, *Modernity: An Introduction to Modern Societies* (Malden, MA: Blackwell, 1996).

6. Zygmunt Bauman, *Modernity and the Holocaust* (Ithaca, NY: Cornell University Press, 2000), p. 13.

7. Ibid., pp. 53, 55; emphasis in original.

8. "As a conception of the world, and even more importantly as an effective instrument of political practice, racism is unthinkable without the advancement of modern science, modern technology and modern forms of state power. As such, racism is strictly a modern product. Modernity made racism possible." Ibid., p. 61.

9. Ibid., p. 76.

10. Max Weber, "Bureaucracy," in H.H. Gerth and C. Wright Mills, eds, *From Max Weber: Essays in Sociology* (New York: Oxford University Press, 1954), pp. 229, 233, 240. Lester R. Kurtz notes that bureaucracy evinces a tendency "to promote formal rather than substantive rationality, that is, the kind of thinking that emphasizes efficiency rather than moral or contextual considerations." Quoted in Robert Jay Lifton and Eric Markusen, *The Genocidal Mentality: Nazi Holocaust and Nuclear Threat* (New York: Basic Books, 1990), p. 180.

11. Bauman, *Modernity and the Holocaust*, p. 76.

12. Wolfgang Sofsky, *The Order of Terror: The Concentration Camp* (Princeton, NJ: Princeton University Press, 1999), p. 264. "Modern terror has no need of big criminals. For its purposes, the small-time tormentor suffices: the conscientious bookkeeper, the mediocre official, the zealous doctor, the young, slightly anxious female factory worker" (p. 278).

13. The classic study is Markusen and Kopf, *The Genocidal Mentality*.

14. Mark Levene, *Genocide in the Age of the Nation State, Vol. 1: The Meaning of Genocide* (London: I.B. Tauris, 2005), p. 10.

15. Ibid., p. 144. See also the emphatic formulation that "the specificity of genocide cannot be divorced from the very modern framework within which it occurs" (p. 155).

16. Levene, *Genocide in the Age of the Nation State, Vol. 1*, pp. 12–13, quoting Alexander Hinton.

17. Bauman, *Modernity and the Holocaust*, p. 89.

18. Lemkin, letter of July 22, 1948, quoted in John Docker, "Are Settler-Colonies Inherently Genocidal?," in A. Dirk Moses, ed., *Empire, Colony, Genocide: Conquest, Occupation, and Subaltern Resistance in World History* (New York: Berghahn Books, 2008), p. 87.

19. Levene, *Genocide in the Age of the Nation State, Vol. 1*, pp. 20, 130, 145. Emphases added.

20. Likewise with racism: though Levene correctly points to a modern scientific or pseudo-scientific discourse, he also acknowledges that "differentiating people on the basis of gradations of skin colour, and other physical attributes, as a tool whereby a dominant group legitimizes its social control over other groups is very old in history. It is certainly not exclusive to Europeans. One only has to look at the caste system in India to note its longevity and invidiousness." Levene, *Genocide in the Age of the Nation State, Vol. 2*, p. 189.

21. Alex Alvarez, *Governments, Citizens, and Genocide: A Comparative and Interdisciplinary Approach* (Bloomington, IN: Indiana University Press, 2001), p. 2.

22. Michael Mann similarly notes that in the Nazi genocide against the Jews, "foreign collaborators, Romanian and Croatian fascists, used primitive techniques to almost as devastating effect" as high-tech gas chambers. Mann, *The Dark Side of Democracy: Explaining Ethnic Cleansing* (Cambridge: Cambridge University Press, 2005), p. 241.

23. "As for the supposedly desensitizing effects of bureaucratic distancing, the brutal face-to-face murder of the Tutsis by tens of thousands of ordinary Hutus, many of them poor farmers, utterly disproves that thesis." Marie Fleming, "Genocide and the Body Politic in the Time of Modernity," in Robert Gellately and Ben Kiernan, eds, *The Specter of Genocide: Mass Murder in Historical Perspective* (Cambridge: Cambridge University Press, 2003), p. 103.

24. Levene likewise acknowledges "the military-bureaucratic power and organizing outreach of *pre-modern* states" (his emphasis). Levene, *Genocide in the Age of the Nation State, Vol. 1*, p. 148.

25. For a contrary view, defining the core features of the Rwandan holocaust as "manifestations of the modern world," see Robert Melson, "Modern Genocide in Rwanda: Ideology, Revolution, War, and Mass Murder in an African State," ch. 15 in Gellately and Kiernan, eds, *The Specter of Genocide.*

26. Benedict Anderson, *Imagined Communities: Reflections on the Origins and Spread of Nationalism* (London: Verso, 1991).

27. Anthony D. Smith, *National Identity* (London: Penguin, 1991), p. 21.

28. I am grateful to Benjamin Madley for this insight.

29. Barth cited in Andrew Bell-Fialkoff, *Ethnic Cleansing* (New York: St. Martin's Griffin, 1999), p. 73. As Alexander Hinton notes, "It is one of the most vexing problems of our time that imagined sociopolitical identities are so often forged out of hatred toward contrasting others." Hinton, *Why Did They Kill? Cambodia in the Shadow of Genocide* (Berkeley, CA: University of California Press, 2005), p. 220. For a famous reading of the phenomenon, examining the constitutive impact of the "Orient" upon the "West," see Edward Said, *Orientalism* (New York: Vintage Books, 1979).

30. Geertz quoted in Ray Taras and Rajat Ganguly, *Understanding Ethnic Conflict: The International Dimension* (New York: Longman, 1998), p. 14.

31. See John R. Bowen, "The Myth of Global Ethnic Conflict," ch. 15 in Hinton, ed., *Genocide: An Anthropological Reader*, pp. 334–43.

32. Nancy Scheper-Hughes wrote sardonically: "'Race,' 'ethnicity,' 'tribe,' 'culture,' and 'identity' were dutifully deconstructed and de-essentialized in Anthropology 101, where they were taught as historically invented and fictive concepts. Meanwhile ... South African Xhosas and Zulus (manipulated by a government-orchestrated 'third force') daily slaughtered each other in and around worker hostels in the name of 'tribe,' 'ethnicity,' and 'culture.'" Scheper-Hughes, "The Primacy of the Ethical", p. 415.

33. James Waller, *Becoming Evil: How Ordinary People Commit Genocide and Mass Killing* (Oxford: Oxford University Press, 2002), pp. 153–54. He also points out (pp. 241–42) that in social–psychological experiments, "complete strangers arbitrarily assigned to groups, having no interaction or conflict with one another, and not competing against another group behaved as if those who shared their meaningless label were their dearest friends or closest relatives," and would rapidly come into conflict with those defined differently, but equally meaninglessly.

34. Donald L. Horowitz, *The Deadly Ethnic Riot* (Berkeley, CA: University of California Press, 2001), p. 243.

35. Paul R. Brass, "Introduction," in Brass, ed., *Riots and Pogroms* (Washington Square, NY: New York University Press, 1996), p. 12.

36. Horowitz makes explicit the link between ethnic rioting and genocide: "The deadly ethnic riot embodies physical destruction combined with degradation and the implicit threat of genocide. ... The random, brutal killing of targets based merely on their ascriptive identity has ... a proto-genocidal quality about it; it is an augury of extermination." Horowitz, *The Deadly Ethnic Riot*, pp. 432, 459.

37. Brass, "Introduction," pp. 12–13.

38. According to Charles Tilly, these actors "operate in a middle ground between (on one side) the full authorization of a national army and (on the other) the private employment of violence by parents, lovers, or feuding clans." Tilly, *The Politics of Collective Violence* (Cambridge: Cambridge University Press, 2003), p. 19.

39. Horowitz, *The Deadly Ethnic Riot*, p. 187. See also Walter P. Zenner, "Middleman Minorities and Genocide," in Isidor Wallimann and Michael N. Dobkowski, eds, *Genocide and the Modern Age: Etiology and Case Studies of Mass Death* (Westport, CT: Syracuse University Press, 2000), pp. 253–81. Groundbreaking genocide scholar Leo Kuper refers to these as "hostage groups"; that is, "hostages to the fortunes of the dominant group." Kuper, "The Genocidal State: An Overview," in Pierre L. van den Berghe, ed., *State Violence and Ethnicity* (Niwot, CO: University Press of Colorado, 1990), p. 44. See also the discussion in Kuper's *The Prevention of Genocide* (New Haven, CT: Yale University Press, 1985), p. 201.

40. Amy Chua, *World on Fire: How Exporting Free Market Democracy Breeds Ethnic Hatred and Global Instability* (New York: Anchor, 2004), p. 79.

41. Genocidal massacres may also be cited, such as the centuries of pogroms against European Jews, Indian uprisings against Whites in Upper Peru and Yucatán (Chapter 1), and the Hindu slaughter of Sikhs in India in 1984. Short of genocide or genocidal massacre, the strategy most commonly adopted against market-dominant minorities is mass expulsion. Idi Amin's banishing of Indians from Uganda in 1972 is an example; another is the "Boat People" expelled from Vietnam following the nationalist victory of 1975, aimed at "the elimination of ethnic Chinese and bourgeois Vietnamese from Vietnamese society." Richard L. Rubinstein, *The Age of Triage: Fear and Hope in an Overcrowded World* (Boston, MA: Beacon Press, 1983), p. 176. This was also, of course, the dominant Nazi policy towards German Jews between 1933 and 1938 (Chapter 6).

42. Horowitz, for example, argues that "in comparative perspective," the targeting of "unusually prosperous or advantaged ethnic groups ... is only a minor factor in target selection [for deadly ethnic rioting], operative under certain, specific conditions of riot leadership. Quite often, prosperous minorities are not targeted even during the most brutal riots." Horowitz, *The Deadly Ethnic Riot*, p. 5.

43. Chua, *World on Fire*, pp. 124–25.

44. Eriksen, *Small Places, Large Issues*, p. 27.

45. Ibid., p. 7.

46. Victoria Sanford, *Buried Secrets: Truth and Human Rights in Guatemala* (New York: Palgrave Macmillan, 2003), p. 31.

47. Ivana Macek, *Sarajevo Under Siege: Anthropology in Wartime* (Philadelphia, PA: University of Pennsylvania Press, 2009). The quotes in these passages are drawn from pp. x, 4, 8, 11, 12, 31, 48–49, 53, 54–55, 62, 123, 161.

48. Anton Weiss-Wendt, "Problems in Comparative Genocide Scholarship," in Dan Stone, ed., *The Historiography of Genocide* (London: Palgrave Macmillan, 2008), pp. 42–70.

49. Alexander Laban Hinton, "The Dark Side of Modernity: Toward an Anthropology of Genocide," in Hinton, ed., *Annihilating Difference*, p. 2.

50. Declaration quoted in Macek, *Life Under Siege*, p. 28.

51. "The work of anthropology, in its earliest instances of practice, composed a necessary first step that gave substance and justification to theories of 'natural' hierarchy that would eventually be employed to rationalize racism, colonialism, slavery, ethnic purifications and, ultimately, genocide projects." Wendy C. Hamblet,

"The Crisis of Meanings: Could the Cure be the Cause of Genocide?," *Journal of Genocide Research*, 5: 2 (2003), p. 243.

52. See also the discussion of Patrick Brantlinger's *Dark Vanishings* in Chapter 3.

53. Gretchen E. Schafft, "Scientific Racism in Service of the Reich: German Anthropologists in the Nazi Era," in Hinton, ed., *Annihilating Difference*, pp. 117, 131. See also Schafft's full-length book, *From Racism to Genocide: Anthropology in the Third Reich* (Urbana, IL: University of Illinois Press, 2004).

54. See Sybil Milton, "Holocaust: The Gypsies," ch. 6 in Samuel Totten *et al.*, eds, *Century of Genocide: Eyewitness Accounts and Critical Views* (New York: Garland Publishing, 1997). According to the Web Hyperdictionary, "physical anthropology" is "the scientific study of the physical characteristics, variability, and evolution of the human organism." See http://searchbox.hyperdictionary.com/dictionary/physical+anthropology.

55. Paul A. Erickson and Liam D. Murphy, *A History of Anthropological Theory* (Toronto, ON: Broadview Press, 2003), p. 76.

56. Geoffrey Robertson, *Crimes Against Humanity: The Struggle for Global Justice* (New York: The New Press, 2000), pp. 31–32. An anthropologist, W.G. Sumner, first used the term "ethnocentrism" in 1906, defining it as "the technical name for [a] view of things in which one's own group is the center of everything, and all others are scaled and rated with reference to it … . Each group nourishes its own pride and vanity, boasts itself superior, exalts its own divinities, and looks with contempt on outsiders." Quoted in Waller, *Becoming Evil*, p. 154.

57. Alexander Hinton, personal communication, July 24, 2005.

58. Scheper-Hughes, "The Primacy of the Ethical," p. 410.

59. Hinton, "The Dark Side of Modernity," in Hinton, ed., *Annihilating Difference*, p. 2.

60. Ibid.

61. Sanford, Buried Secrets, p. 210. In anthropological parlance, individual testimonies constitute the "emic" level of analysis, academic interpretations the "etic" level. See Eriksen, *Small Places, Large Issues*, p. 36.

62. Mark Levene, *Genocide in the Age of the Nation State, Vol. 2: The Rise of the West and the Coming of Genocide* (London: I.B. Tauris, 2005), p. 94.

63. Adam Jones, "'When the Rabbit's Got the Gun': Subaltern Genocide and the Genocidal Continuum," in Nicholas A. Robins and Adam Jones, eds, *Genocides by the Oppressed: Subaltern Genocide in Theory and Practice* (Bloomington, IN: Indiana University Press, 2009), pp. 185–207; see especially pp. 187–88.

64. See, e.g., Antonius Robben, "How Traumatized Societies Remember: The Aftermath of Argentina's Dirty War," *Cultural Critique*, 59 (Winter 2005), pp. 120–64.

65. Sanford, *Buried Secrets*, p. 143.

66. Hinton, "The Dark Side of Modernity," p. 19. Hinton argues that symbolism "mediate[s] all our understandings of the world, including a world of genocide" (personal communication, July 24, 2005). Jacques Sémelin also points to "the ways in which bodies are taken over, twisted, cut into pieces" as constituting "wholly cultural acts, through which the perpetrator expresses something of his own identity." Sémelin, *Purify and Destroy: The Political Uses of Massacre and Genocide* (New York: Columbia University Press, 2007), p. 301.

67. Christopher C. Taylor, *Sacrifice as Terror: The Rwandan Genocide of 1994* (Oxford: Berg, 1998), p. 130. The phenomenon has its counterpart in other genocides; as early as 1940, the English novelist and essayist H.G. Wells pointed to "the victims smothered in latrines" in Nazi concentration camps, exemplifying "the cloacal side of Hitlerism." Quoted in Robertson, *Crimes Against Humanity*, p. 23. For another fascinating study of violent ritual and symbolism, see Antonius Robben, "State Terror in the Netherworld: Disappearance and

Reburial in Argentina," in Robben, ed., *Death, Mourning, and Burial: A Cross-Cultural Reader* (London: Blackwell, 2005), which explored the symbolic violation of "disappearance" in a culture that ascribes great significance to the physical corpse and rituals of burial.

68. Nancy Scheper-Hughes, *Death without Weeping: The Violence of Everyday Life in Brazil* (Berkeley, CA: University of California Press, 1993).

69. Nancy Scheper-Hughes, "Coming to Our Senses: Anthropology and Genocide," in Hinton, ed., *Annihilating Difference*, p. 369. See also Scheper-Hughes, "The Genocidal Continuum: Peace-time Crimes," ch. 2 in Jeannette Marie Mageo, ed., *Power and the Self* (Cambridge: Cambridge University Press, 2002), pp. 29–47.

70. Scheper-Hughes, "Coming to Our Senses," pp. 372–73.

71. Hinton, "The Dark Side of Modernity," p. 33.

72. D.C. Dirkmaat and J.M. Adovasio, "The Role of Archaeology in the Recovery and Interpretation of Human Remains from an Outdoor Forensic Setting," in William D. Haglund and Marcella H. Sorg, eds, *Forensic Taphonomy: The Postmortem Fate of Human Remains* (New York: CRC Press, 1997), p. 58.

73. Clyde Snow, "Murder Most Foul," *The Sciences* (May/June 1995), p. 16.

74. Ibid., p. 20.

75. See Leigh Binford, *The El Mozote Massacre: Anthropology and Human Rights* (Tucson, AZ: University of Arizona Press, 1996); Mark Danner, *The Massacre at El Mozote: A Parable of the Cold War* (New York: Vintage, 1994).

76. "Originally a five-member group, the Guatemalan Forensic Anthropology Foundation now employs more than 60 people and has carried out more than 200 exhumations." Victoria Sanford, personal communication, June 15, 2005.

77. The activities of the Guatemalan forensic team are movingly described by Victoria Sanford in her book *Buried Secrets*, centering on exhumations in the Mayan village of Acul.

78. See the "Clyde Snow Information Page" at http://www.ajweberman.com/cs.htm.

CPSIA information can be obtained
at www.ICGtesting.com
Printed in the USA
LVOW09s2131090118
562423LV00001B/5/P

9 781609 273989